MANAGEMENT

SKILLS AND APPLICATION

MANAGEMENT

SKILLS AND APPLICATION

EIGHTH EDITION

Leslie W. Rue, Ph.D.

Professor Emeritus of Management
Robinson College of Business
Georgia State University

Lloyd L. Byars, Ph.D.

Professor of Management
DuPree College of Management
Georgia Institute of Technology

Boston   Burr Ridge, IL   Dubuque, IA   Madison, WI   New York   San Francisco   St. Louis
Bangkok   Bogotá   Caracas   Lisbon   London   Madrid
Mexico City   Milan   New Delhi   Seoul   Singapore   Sydney   Taipei   Toronto

McGraw-Hill Higher Education

A Division of The McGraw-Hill Companies

Management: Skills and Application

Copyright © 2000, 1997, 1995, 1992, 1989, 1986, 1983, 1980, 1977 by The McGraw-Hill Companies, Inc. All rights reserved. Printed in the United States of America. Except as permitted under the United States Copyright Act of 1976, no part of this publication may be reproduced or distributed in any form or by any means, or stored in a data base or retrieval system, without the prior written permission of the publisher.

This book is printed on acid-free paper.

international   1 2 3 4 5 6 7 8 9 0 QPD/QPD 9 0 9 8 7 6 5 4 3 2 1 0 9
domestic   2 3 4 5 6 7 8 9 0 QPD/QPD 9 0 9 8 7 6 5 4 3 2 1 0 9

ISBN 0-07-228885-X

Vice president/Editor-in-chief: *Michael W. Junior*
Publisher: *Craig S. Beytien*
Sponsoring editor: *John Biernat*
Marketing manager: *Ellen Cleary*
Senior project manager: *Denise Santor-Mitzit*
Senior production supervisor: *Heather D. Burbridge*
Designer: *Jennifer McQueen Hollingsworth*
Cover image © C.S.C./Naomi/Photonica
Supplement Coordinator: *Rose Range*
Compositor: *Carlisle Communications, Ltd.*
Typeface: *10/12 Berling*
Printer: *Quebecor Printing Book Group/Dubuque*

Library of Congress Cataloging–in–Publication Data

Rue, Leslie W.
    Management : skills and application / Leslie W. Rue, Lloyd L.
Byars. —9th ed.
        p.   cm.
    ISBN 0-07-228885-X
    1. Management.   I. Byars, Lloyd L.   II. Brooks, John R., 1945-
    III. Title
HD31.R797   2000
658—dc21   99-26770

International Edition
Copyright © 2000. Exclusive rights by The McGraw-Hill Companies, Inc. for manufacture and export. This book cannot be re-exported from the country to which it is consigned by McGraw-Hill. The International Edition is not available in North America.

When ordering the title, use ISBN 0-07-116983-0

http://www.mhhe.com

Preface

Since this book's inception nine editions ago, the field of management has evolved and changed in ways that could not have been anticipated. Through each revision we have attempted to keep pace with the times and adapt to these changes. In the fifth edition, for example, we introduced a skill-building approach that remains one of the book's hallmarks. In subsequent editions we have continued to add content and pedagogy that address shifts in the field of management. And always, we have worked to create a book that prepares students for a future in business. This edition continues that tradition.

Relying on the suggestions of other professors, reviewers, students, and our own thoughts, we have attempted to retain the strongest parts of the previous editions and strengthen the weaker parts. As a result of the extensive input received, we have updated and revised some material, added new material, and eliminated some material. The effect of this work can be summarized by examining this edition more closely:

NEW TO THIS EDITION OF THE BOOK

- Separate chapters on **Leadership (Chapter 16)** and **Motivation (Chapter 15)** have been created. As the field continues to focus more on these related but distinct topics we have increased coverage of both areas and separated them into two chapters in this revision.
- The chapter on **Information Systems for Managers (Chapter 5)** has been thoroughly revised. In response to the impact of information technology on today's organizations, this chapter has been totally revamped, reorganized, expanded, and moved closer to the front of the text.
- **Internet references** have been added to the text. With increasing speed, the internet has become an important reference for both students and instructors. For that reason, we have added references to URLs for key companies mentioned in the text.
- An additional experiential exercise entitled **"Skill-Building Exercise"** and **Case Incident** have been added to the end of each chapter. To enhance the skill-building approach mentioned earlier, we have added another exercise and another case incident for the student at the end of each chapter. There are now two of each of these from which to choose.

STRUCTURE OF THE CHAPTERS

The text's pedagogy has been revisited and revised as necessary to give readers the best tools to apply and understand the material presented. Look for these features in each chapter:

- Learning Objectives—chapter-opening guidelines for students to use as they read. This list of key objectives provides the reader a roadmap for venturing into the text.
- Chapter Previews—real-life, up-to-date vignettes that illustrate one or more of the major points covered in the respective chapters. Preview analysis

questions are presented at the end of each chapter to help the student related the chapter material to the preview vignette.

- Management Illustrations—brief, chapter-related corporate examples found in boxes throughout the chapters. These illustrations present more than 50 examples of concepts contained in the text, and more than 75% of them are new to this edition.

- Corporate/Organization References—more than 200 references to actual corporations and organizations. We are extremely proud of these references that best serve to bridge the gap between theory and practice. Look for them in the text itself, chapter previews, and management illustrations.

- Margin Glossary—key terms defined where mentioned in the text. This feature is especially helpful to students reviewing chapter material for study and/or testing.

- Review Questions—these questions, at the end of each chapter, tie directly back to the learning objectives. By tying the chapter concepts together from beginning to end, students can evaluate their understanding of key constructs and ideas.

- Skill-Building Questions—end-of-chapter questions designed to promote critical thinking. These questions ask students to get to a deeper level of understanding by applying, comparing, contrasting, evaluating, and illustrating ideas presented in the chapter.

- Skill-Building Exercises—end-of-chapter tools for students and instructors. These exercises can be assigned on the spot in class or as homework.

- Case Incidents—end-of-chapter short cases for students. These incidents present lifelike situations requiring management decisions related to the material covered in the respective chapters. As with the skill-building exercises, these can be assigned in class or as homework.

THE TEACHING PACKAGE

A variety of support materials helps the instructor in teaching this dynamic field of management. These key items available with the ninth edition of the text are described below:

- Lecture Resource Manual and Test Bank
  The Lecture Resource Manual and Test Bank is the instructor's tool box for enhancing student learning. The manual contains brief chapter overviews; lecture outlines that include topical headings; definitional highlights; coordination points for key terms, review questions, and learning objectives: suggested answers to in-text questions; and transparency masters. The popular "Barriers to Student Understanding" feature addresses areas that are most often stumbling blocks for students. In this section, a series of suggestions guide the instructor in preparing for difficulties, covering easily misunderstood concepts, and aiding the student learning experience through directed discussion. The Test Bank section of the Lecture Resource Manual includes true-false, multiple choice, and essay questions is tied to the chapter learning objectives and classified according to the level of difficulty.

- Brownstone Testing Software
  This computerized testing software is available for users of both PCs and Macintosh computers. It provides instructors with simple ways to write tests that can be administered on paper, over a campus network, or over the Internet.
- Power Point presentation software contains tables and graphs from the text as well as extra material.
- Videos are available from the Irwin/McGraw-Hill Video Library. Contact your local sales representative for more information about these videos.

ACKNOWLEDGMENTS

We thank the Irwin/McGraw-Hill sales staff is the best in the industry and we thank them for their continued efforts on our behalf. Our thanks, also, to the members of the Irwin/McGraw-Hill in-house staff who have provided their support throughout this revision.

We have relied on the assistance so many people throughout this book's history. As we come now to the ninth edition we wish to thank all of those who have been involved with this project and to make special mention of those involved in the most recent reviewing and marketing research processes:

Lawrence P. Brown, University of Maryland

Bernard Elliott Budish, Fairleigh Dickinson University

Frank Butros, Central Michigan University

Joseph Byers, Community College of Allegheny county

Julie Campbell, Adams State College

Joseph J. Dobson, Western Illinois University

Edwin A. Giermak, College of DuPage

Joseph Gray, Nassau Community College

John Groetsch, Allegheny County Community College

James A. Guyor, St. Clair County Community College

Jack Heinsius, Modesto Junior College

Richard P. Herden, University of Louisville

Nancy B. Higgins, Montgomery College

Rebecca J. Murchak, ICM School of Business

Lucy Newton, Berry College

Janet Overdorf, SUNY College at Buffalo

Richard Randall, Nassau Community College

Eugune Richman, University of Nevada–Las Vegas

Pamela B. Riegle, Ball State University

Joseph C. Santora, Essex Community College

Thomas E. Schillar, Pierce College

Richard J. Stanish, Tulsa Junior College

Gary Wagenheim, Purdue University

Kenneth L. Westby, University of North Dakota

Ron Weston, Contra Costa College

We are indebted to our families, friends, colleagues, and students for the numerous comments, ideas, and support that they have provided. A special thanks goes to our assistant, Charmelle Todd, for her work on this revision.

In our continuing efforts to improve this text, we earnestly solicit your feedback.

Leslie W. Rue
Lloyd L. Byars

About the Authors

Leslie W. Rue is professor emeritus of management and former holder of the Carl R. Zwerner chair of Family Owned Enterprises in the Robinson College of Business at Georgia State University. He received his Bachelor of Industrial Engineering (with honor) and his Master of Industrial Engineering from Georgia Institute of Technology. He received his Ph.D. in Management from Georgia State University.

Prior to joining Georgia State University, Dr. Rue was on the faculty of the School of Business, Indiana University at Bloomington, Indiana. He has worked as a data processing project officer for the U.S. Army Management Systems Support Agency, in the Pentagon, and as an industrial engineer for Delta Airlines. In addition, Dr. Rue has worked as a consultant and trainer to numerous private and public organizations in the areas of planning, organizing, and strategy.

Dr. Rue is the author of over 50 published articles, cases, and papers that have appeared in academic and practitioner journals. In addition to this book, he has coauthored numerous other textbooks in the field of management. Several of these books have gone into multiple editions.

Dr. Rue has just celebrated his 31st wedding anniversary. He has two daughters and a son. His hobbies include the restoration of antique furniture and antique wooden speedboats.

Lloyd L. Byars received his Ph.D. from Georgia State University. He also received a Bachelor of Electrical Engineering and a Master of Science in Industrial Management from Georgia Tech. He has taught at Georgia State University, Clark Atlanta University and is currently professor of management, DuPree College of Management at the Georgia Institute of Technology.

Dr. Byars has published articles in leading professional journals and is also the author of four textbooks which are used in colleges and universities. He has served on the editorial review board of the *Journal of Systems Management* and the *Journal of Management Case Studies.*

Dr. Byars has worked as a trainer and consultant to many organizations, including: Duke Power Company, Georgia Kraft Company, Kraft, Inc., South Carolina Electric and Gas Company, the University of Florida—Medical School, the Department of the Army, and the U.S. Social Security Administration. Dr. Byars also serves as a labor arbitrator, certified by both the Federal Mediation and Conciliation Service and the American Arbitration Association. He has arbitrated cases in the United States, Europe, Central America, and the Caribbean.

Dr. Byars has been married to Linda S. Byars for 29 years. They have two daughters and a son.

Contents in Brief

Contents

༺

SECTION II   CONTEMPORARY ISSUES   *85*

SECTION IV   ORGANIZING AND STAFFING SKILLS   *183*

Chapter 10   Organizing Work   *184*

Chapter 11   Organization Structure   *202*

SECTION V   DIRECTING SKILLS   *287*

Chapter 15   Motivation   *288*

Chapter 16   Leadership   *308*

Section

I

FOUNDATIONS

1

Introduction to Management

LEARNING OBJECTIVES

After studying this chapter, you should be able to:

1. Define management.

2. Describe the levels of management.

3. Discuss the functions of management.

4. Explain the roles of a manager.

5. Describe the skills required to perform the work of management.

6. Explain how principles of management are developed.

7. Define entrepreneur.

8. Define small business.

9. Outline three requirements for encouraging entrepreneurship in medium-size and large businesses.

10. Discuss the increasing role of women and minorities in management.

11. Define the "glass ceiling" facing women and minorities.

Microsoft's wealth and power seem to grow and grow. By any account Microsoft's founder, Bill Gates, is one of the richest people in America. His stock in the computer software giant was estimated to be worth $584 billion in 1998.

In his book *The Road Ahead*, Bill Gates recently gave a new and bold view of the future: He forecasts that the information highway (the I-way) will bring sweeping changes to how we educate and amuse ourselves. The impact of the changes will mean more working from home, less commuting, a squeeze on inefficient intermediaries, an in-home shopping revolution, and perhaps the advent of the "virtual corporation."

To get there with the most marketing muscle, Gates demands that his colleagues be remarkably well informed, logical, vocal, and thick-skinned. When Gates meets with his development teams, the meeting is more like a graduate seminar where challenge and criticism are not only encouraged but demanded. According to Gates, "My goal is to prove that a successful corporation can renew itself and stay in the forefront."

Sources: Adapted from Alan Deutschman, "Bill Gates' Next Challenge," *Fortune*, December 28, 1992, pp. 31–41; Christopher Power, "American Power Performer," *Business Week*, July 10, 1995, p. 63; Geoff Lewis, "Heavy Fog on the I-Way," *Business Week*, December 4, 1995, pp. 13–16.

Management Illustration 1.1
Land of the Giants

Today's merger mania differs from the 1980s roller coaster ride into buy-and-sell adventure. The overriding goal in the 1990s is market dominance. Alliances, joint ventures, hostile bids, and corporate raiders are still among the buzzwords. However, the marketplace and an eye toward challenges brought on by the exploding information technology revolution appear to be the spark that has set off a conflagration of mergers and acquisitions that would have been thought impossible only a decade ago. Acquisitions totaled more than $270 billion in 1995.

As the following table shows, six key areas seemed to be the most popular as the race to the year 2000 gathered steam. The trend toward diversification and the management skills necessary to manage in this ever-changing environment are truly dynamic.

Sources: Michael Oneal, "The Unlikely Mogul," *Business Week*, December 11, 1995, p. 91; Michael Oneal, "Disney's Kingdom," *Business Week*, August 14, 1995, p. 31; Michael J. Mandel, "Land of the Giants," *Business Week*, September 11, 1995, pp. 34–35. For more articles on management in the year 2000, visit *Business Week* online at: www.businessweek.com.

Change Industries	Big Players
Entertainment: Vertical integration may yield clout in the new age of information technology.	Disney + ABC ($19.3 billion in revenues); Time Warner + Turner Broadcasting ($20.5 billion in revenues)
Financial services: Focus on cost reduction and economies of scale.	Chemical Bank + Chase ($10 billion merger); First Union + First Fidelity Bancorp ($5.4 acquisition)
Utilities: Slow growth in domestic consumption and the continuing deregulation environment are causing increased activity in this usually stable area.	PECO bids $3.8 billion for PP&L; Union Electric + Cipsco ($1.2 billion merger)
Health care: Drug companies, HMOs are all looking to reduce costs and expand market share.	Upjohn + Pharmacia ($6 billion merger)
Consumer goods: The global marketplace and the need to always expand shelf space are constant pressures to expand and diversify.	Kimberly-Clark + Scott Paper ($7 billion buyout)
Transportation: Deregulation, deregulation, deregulation are the three magic words that all mean vast change in this industry.	Union Pacific + Southern Pacific ($5.4 billion buyout) Burlington Northern + Santa Fe Pacific ($4 billion buyout)

Some businesses grow to be extremely large and profitable, while others go bankrupt. Some businesses diversify into many new activities, while others stick to their core activities. Management Illustration 1.1 highlights some of the many changes that have occurred at Disney, ABC, Time Warner, Turner Broadcasting, Chemical Bank, Upjohn, Kimberly-Clark, and other corporations.

In the decades to come, the rising rate of environmental, social, and technological change, the increasing internationalization of business, the growing scarcity and cost of natural resources, and the increasing sensitivity to diversity in the workplace will make the environment of business even more complex and subject to change. Making decisions about future business activities in this dynamic environment is the job of management. More specifically, **management** is a form of work that involves coordinating an organization's resources—land, labor, and capital—to accomplish organizational objectives.[1]

management A form of work that involves coordinating an organization's resources—land, labor, and capital—toward accomplishing organizational objectives.

Management concepts apply equally to public, private, not-for-profit, religious organizations, large corporations, and small entrepreneurial firms. Management principles are as useful to a local restaurant, a small office supplies firm, or a college football team as they are to giant corporations such as Coca-Cola or Ford Motor Company. Basic management principles also apply to a university, the Mayo Clinic, the Baptist Church, Kiwanis International, the U.S. Department of Defense, the Ford Foundation, and the National Association for the Advancement of Colored People.

THE MANAGEMENT HIERARCHY

All but the smallest organizations need several managers to coordinate the organization's resources. The management staff generally consists of three different levels or types of managers. **Top or senior management** usually includes the chairperson of the board, the chief executive officer (CEO), the chief operating officer (COO), and the senior vice presidents. This level of management establishes the objectives of the business, formulates the actions necessary to achieve them, and allocates the resources of the business to achieve the objectives. **Middle management** normally consists of people with job titles such as production superintendent, auditing manager, and sales manager. Middle management is responsible for implementing and achieving organizational objectives. Middle management also develops departmental objectives and actions for achieving organizational objectives. The final level of management is **supervisory management.** Job titles of supervisory managers include foreman, crew leader, office manager, and head nurse. The supervisor manages the operative employees who physically produce the organization's goods and services.

top or senior management   Establishes the objectives of the business, formulates the actions necessary to achieve them, and allocates the resources of the business to achieve the objectives.

middle management   Responsible for implementing and achieving organizational objectives; also responsible for developing departmental objectives and actions.

supervisory management   Manages operative employees; generally considered the first or lowest level of management.

These three levels of management form a pyramid or management hierarchy as shown in Figure 1.1. Within the management hierarchy are a number of supervisors, a smaller number of middle managers, and only a few at the very top. In addition, job titles for managers within the hierarchy vary from organization to organization and from industry to industry.

FIGURE 1.1   The Management Pyramid or Hierarchy

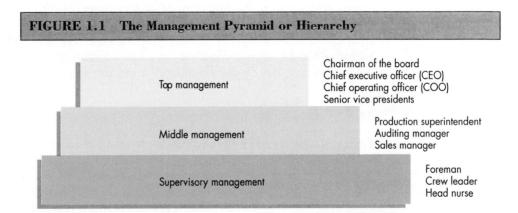

APPROACHES TO ANALYZING MANAGEMENT

Several approaches have been used to analyze the job of management. One common approach examines management by categorizing the functions (work) managers perform. A second approach looks at the roles managers perform. A third approach analyzes the skills required of managers. Each of these categories is discussed next.

Management Functions

Managers engage in certain basic activities. These activities are often grouped into conceptual categories called the *functions of management*. These functions are as follows:

planning Deciding what objectives to pursue during a future period and what to do to achieve those objectives.

organizing Grouping activities, assigning activities, and providing the authority necessary to carry out the activities.

staffing Determining human resource needs and recruiting, selecting, training, and developing human resources.

leading Directing and channeling human behavior toward the accomplishment of objectives.

controlling Measuring performance against objectives, determining the causes of deviations, and taking corrective action where necessary.

1. *Planning.* deciding what objectives to pursue during a future period and what to do to achieve those objectives.
2. *Organizing.* grouping activities, assigning activities, and providing the authority necessary to carry out the activities.
3. *Staffing.* determining human resource needs and recruiting, selecting, training, and developing human resources.
4. *Leading.* directing and channeling human behavior toward the accomplishment of objectives.
5. *Controlling.* measuring performance against objectives, determining the causes of deviations, and taking corrective action where necessary.

The functions of management are merely categories for classifying knowledge about management. Because management functions overlap, it is difficult to classify them purely as planning, organizing, staffing, leading, or controlling. Figure 1.2 classifies several managerial activities based on the different functions of management. This does not imply that managers perform each activity sequentially for each function. In fact, the functions of management are interdependent and inseparable. For example, organizing is difficult without a plan. Similarly, good employees obtained through staffing are unlikely to continue to work well in a poorly planned, poorly organized work environment.

In addition, as Figure 1.3 indicates, each level of management tends to place a different emphasis on the functions of management. Furthermore, the degree of responsibility a manager has in each function depends on his or her position in the management hierarchy. For example, top management is responsible for long-range planning for the overall organization, while supervisory management is responsible for short-range, day-to-day planning of a specific work group.

Management Roles

Henry Mintzberg has proposed another method of examining what managers do by introducing the concept of managerial roles.[2] A **role** is an organized set of behaviors that belong to an identifiable job.[3] But remember that the delineation of managerial working roles is essentially a categorizing process, just as it is with the managerial functions.

role An organized set of behaviors that belong to an identifiable job.

FIGURE 1.2   Functions of Management

Planning

1. Perform self-audit—determine the present status of the organization.
2. Survey the environment.
3. Set objectives.
4. Forecast the future situation.
5. State actions and resource needs.
6. Evaluate proposed actions.
7. Revise and adjust the plan in light of control results and changing conditions.
8. Communicate throughout the planning process.

Organizing

1. Identify and define work to be performed.
2. Break work into duties.
3. Group duties into positions.
4. Define position requirements.
5. Group positions into manageable and properly related units.
6. Assign work to be performed, accountability, and extent of authority.
7. Revise and adjust the organizational structure in light of control results and changing conditions.
8. Communicate throughout the organizing process.

Staffing

1. Determine human resource needs.
2. Recruit potential employees
3. Select from the recruits.
4. Train and develop the human resources.
5. Revise and adjust the quantity and quality of the human resources in light of control results and changing conditions.
6. Communicate throughout the staffing process.

Leading

1. Communicate and explain objectives to subordinates.
2. Assign performance standards.
3. Coach and guide subordinates to meet performance standards.
4. Reward subordinates based on performance.
5. Praise and censure fairly.
6. Provide a motivating environment by communicating the changing situation and its requirements.
7. Revise and adjust the methods of leadership in light of control results and changing conditions.
8. Communicate throughout the leadership process.

Controlling

1. Establish standards.
2. Monitor results and compare to standards.
3. Correct deviations.
4. Revise and adjust control methods in light of control results and changing conditions.
5. Communicate throughout the control process.

Mintzberg identifies 10 managerial roles, which he divides into three major groups: interpersonal roles, informational roles, and decisional roles. Figures 1.4 and 1.5 illustrate and define these managerial roles. The manager's position is the starting point for defining a manager's roles. Formal authority gives the position status. Authority and status together generate certain interpersonal roles for a manager. The interpersonal roles, in turn, determine the informational roles of the manager. Finally, access to information, authority, and status place the manager at a central point in the organizational decision-making process.

Mintzberg further suggests that the management level and the types of work the manager directs significantly influence the variety of roles the manager must assume.[4]

FIGURE 1.3   Relative Amount of Emphasis Placed on Each Function of Management

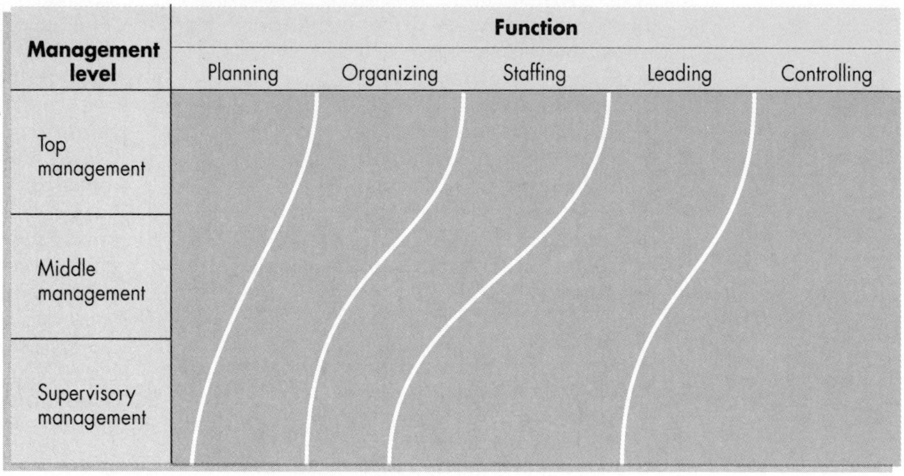

Management level	Function				
	Planning	Organizing	Staffing	Leading	Controlling
Top management					
Middle management					
Supervisory management					

FIGURE 1.4   Roles of a Manager

Source: Henry Mintzberg, *The Nature of Managerial Work* (New York: Harper & Row, 1973), p. 59.

FIGURE 1.5   Definitions of Managerial Roles

Interpersonal

1. Figurehead: Manager represents the organizational unit in all matters of formality.
2. Liaison: Manager interacts with peers and other people outside the organizational unit to gain information and favors.
3. Leader: Manager provides guidance and motivation to the work group and defines the atmosphere of the workplace.

Informational

1. Monitor: Manager serves as a receiver and collector of information.
2. Disseminator: Manager transmits special information within the organization.
3. Spokesperson: Manager disseminates the organization's information into its environment.

Decisional

1. Entrepreneur: Manager initiates change.
2. Disturbance handler: Manager must assume this role when the organization is threatened, such as when conflicts arise between subordinates, a subordinate departs suddenly, or an important customer is lost.
3. Resource allocator: Manager decides where the organization will expend its resources.
4. Manager assumes this role when the organization is in major, nonroutine negotiations with other organizations or individuals.

Source: Adapted from Henry Mintzberg, *The Nature of Managerial Work* (New York: Harper & Row, 1972), pp. 54–99.

For example, managers at lower levels of the organization spend more time in the disturbance handler and negotiator roles and less time in the figurehead role. On the other hand, the chief executive of an organization concentrates more on the roles of figurehead, liaison, spokesperson, and negotiator.[5]

Management Skills

A third approach to examining the management process categorizes the skills required to perform the work. Three basic skills have been identified:

conceptual skills   Involve understanding the relationship of the parts of a business to one another and to the business as a whole. Decision making, planning, and organizing are specific managerial activities that require conceptual skills.
human relations skills   Involve understanding people and being able to work well with them.
technical skills   Involve being able to perform the mechanics of a particular job.

1. **Conceptual skills** involve understanding the relationship of the parts of a business to one another and to the business as a whole. Decision making, planning, and organizing are specific managerial activities that require conceptual skills.
2. **Human relations skills** involve understanding people and being able to work well with them.
3. **Technical skills** involve being able to perform the mechanics of a particular job.

Figure 1.6 shows the mix of skills used at different levels of management. In practice, management skills are so closely interrelated that it is difficult to determine where one begins and another ends. However, it is generally agreed that supervisory management needs more technical skills than managers at higher levels. Human relations skills are essential to effective management at all levels. Finally, conceptual skills become increasingly important as a person moves up the managerial hierarchy.

All three approaches to examining the management process look at the process from a different perspective, and all have their merits. But in the final analysis, a

FIGURE 1.6   Mix of Skills Used at Different Levels of Management

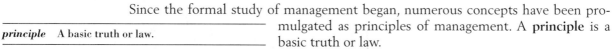

Management level	Skill		
	Conceptual	Human relations	Technical
Top management			
Middle management			
Supervisory management			

successful manager must (1) understand the work to be performed (the management functions); (2) understand the organized set of behaviors to be performed (the management roles); and (3) master the skills involved in performing the job (the management skills). Thus, these approaches to analyzing management are not mutually exclusive; they are necessary and complementary approaches.

PRINCIPLES OF MANAGEMENT

Since the formal study of management began, numerous concepts have been promulgated as principles of management. A **principle** is a basic truth or law.

principle   A basic truth or law.

Numerous laws or principles exist in the physical sciences. Examples include the law of gravity, Ohm's law, and the law of action and reaction. These laws were developed through a careful research process involving controlled experimentation. In this process, the researcher sets up an experiment in which control can be maintained on many of the input variables. For instance, in a chemical experiment, the researcher may control input variables such as temperature, humidity, and pressure to determine the effect of change in one of these variables on a chemical. By varying one of the input factors and measuring the corresponding change in the other factors, the researcher can establish a relationship between the changes and the chemical.

After the experiment has been repeated many times with identical results, the initial ideas (called *hypotheses* in scientific terminology) of the researchers are converted into laws or principles. Furthermore, after a hypothesis has been accepted as law, the law can be used to develop other laws.

Unfortunately, one major problem in developing principles of management is that it is very difficult to conduct a controlled experiment in a management environment. Cost and the inability to place absolute controls on one of the primary inputs, people, make controlled experimentation difficult. Given the inability to use the time-tested method of scientific experimentation to develop laws, the remaining logical alternative is to use observation and deduction. This is the method by which most principles of management have been developed. However, a word of caution is appropriate. Management principles are much more subject to change and interpretation than are the laws of the physical sciences. Thus, management principles must be viewed as guides to action and not laws to be followed. In summary, management principles should be followed except where a deviation can be justified on the basis of sound logic. The abilities to change and adapt are skills the creative manager needs to survive in times of unrest and uncertainty.

ENTREPRENEURSHIP AND MANAGEMENT

A basic distinction is often made between a manager and an entrepreneur. An **entrepreneur** conceives the idea of what product or service to produce, starts the organization, and builds it to the point where additional people are needed. At this time, the entrepreneur can either make the transition to professional manager or hire a professional manager. A **professional manager** performs the basic management functions for the ongoing organization. However, an entrepreneur who is not a professional manager must perform many, if not all, of the basic management functions in starting and building the organization.

entrepreneur   An individual who conceives the idea of what product or service to produce, starts the organization, and builds it to the point where additional people are needed.

professional manager   An individual who performs the basic management functions for the ongoing organization.

Studies indicate that basic trait and personality differences exist between typical entrepreneurs and professional managers.

A study conducted by the Gallup Organization for *The Wall Street Journal* found that entrepreneurs as a group were less distinguished students, more likely to have been expelled from school, and less likely to have been student leaders or fraternity members than were big-business leaders. Entrepreneurs ran businesses at an earlier age but had been fired more frequently and had jumped from job to job before starting their own businesses.[6] In fact, Microsoft's founder and chairman, Bill Gates, was a Harvard dropout.

In addition, not all entrepreneurs are young. *Inc.* magazine's 1995 Entrepreneur of the Year was 68-year-old Allen Breed, who works 14-hour days at Breed Technologies, Inc., where his development of and research into automotive air bags earned his company $401 million in sales in 1995. Like Bill Gates, Breed has a visionary CEO philosophy: select the right people, let them do their own work, and terminate them quickly if they turn out not to be the right people.[7]

In the late 1980s through 1995, women were starting new businesses at about twice the rate men were. However, women still own only a small share of U.S. businesses. According to a 1991 report from the National Foundation for Women Business Owners, the number of female-controlled businesses has recently grown 9.1 percent, besting the overall U.S. growth rate of 8.6 percent. From 1991 to 1994, the most significant changes occurred in the finance and real estate industries (up 21 percent) and in transportation (up 18 percent).[8] Management Illustration 1.2 describes one of America's hot new female entrepreneurs, Barbara Samson.

Scope and Importance of Small Business

Entrepreneurs start businesses that sometimes grow into major firms. For example, Bill Gates (described in the Preview to this chapter) and Paul Allen founded Microsoft in 1975. However, 80 to 90 percent of new businesses are started with the intention of staying small.[9] A **small business** is a company that is independently owned and operated and is not dominant in its field. Because the size of a business can be measured in terms of employment, assets, or sales, it is difficult to define

small business   A company that is independently owned and operated and is not dominant in its field; generally has fewer than 100 employees.

Management Illustration 1.2
Woman with a Mission

Barbara Samson, a 24-year-old graduate of the University of Florida with a telecommunications degree, does not take no for an answer; she takes it as a challenge. Thus did a young novice launch a highly successful telephone company in Tampa, Florida. Intermedia Communications of Florida sells long-distance service to business customers. Samson had heard numerous complaints about how expensive and unreliable businesses found it to connect to their long-distance carriers through the local phone companies. Solution: Build a network to bypass the local phone lines and give customers a cheaper alternative.

Though most entrepreneurial endeavors are capital intensive, Samson began with $50,000 and a $450,000 loan. This was not much considering the task before her: compete with the Baby Bells. By the time the first fiber-optic line was laid, venture capitalists had raised an additional $18 million. According to Samson, "We had to prove ourselves every step of the way." Her philosophy is to sell service first, then lay cable. The strategy seems to be working. Among her first and top customers are General Mills, Florida state government offices in Tallahassee, and Merrill Lynch. From her company's small beginnings in 1989, revenues soon mushroomed; 1995 revenues reached $42 million.

Intermedia Communications, Inc. is now the largest competitive-access provider in the Southeast, with 480 miles of fiber-optic cable. In Florida its network connects 350 buildings in five major cities. It recently acquired fiber networks in Cincinnati; Raleigh/Durham; Huntsville, Alabama; and St. Louis. With its hard-charging spirit, Intermedia has won business away from AT&T, BellSouth, GTE, and others. Hard work, dreams, and a youthful, entrepreneurial spirit sometimes do pay off!

Source: Adapted from Toddi Gutner Black, "Women with a Mission," *Forbes*, September 25, 1995, pp. 172, 174. For more information about Intermedia Communications, Inc., visit their Web site at: www.intermedia.com.

a small business. Nevertheless, the Small Business Administration uses a detailed employment breakdown to define a continuum of business activity as follows: under 20 employees, very small; 20 to 99, small; 100 to 499, medium-size; and over 500, large.[10] Under this definition, small businesses make up over 98 percent of America's companies. They account for nearly half of the nation's gross national product and are a key source of new jobs.[11]

Entrepreneurship or Intrapreneurship in Large and Medium-Size Businesses

Developing the entrepreneurial traits of innovation and willingness to take risks is increasingly being emphasized among managers and employees in large and medium-size organizations. A National Science Foundation study illustrated the need for innovation and risk taking in larger organizations. It found that small organizations produced about 4 times as many innovations per research and development dollar as medium-size organizations and about 24 times as many as large organizations.[12]

Yet many large organizations, such as 3M, General Electric, and Bristol Myers, have enviable records of innovation. They have done this by encouraging entrepreneurship (or, as it is sometimes called in large organizations, *intrapreneurship*) among their people. In a study of America's "excellent companies," Thomas Peters and Robert Waterman, Jr., identified several characteristics essential for the devel-

FIGURE 1.7	Critical Elements in Intrapreneurial Environments
The presence of explicit goals:	These goals need to be mutually agreed upon by employees and management so that specific steps are achieved.
A system of feedback and positive reinforcement:	This feedback is necessary for potential inventors, creators, or intrapreneurs to realize there is acceptance and reward.
An emphasis on individual responsibility:	Confidence, trust, and accountability are key features in the success of any innovative program.
Rewards based on results:	*A reward system that enhances and encourages others to risk and to achieve must be established.*

Source: Donald F. Kuratkv, Jeffrey S. Hornsby, Douglas W. Nattzinger, and Ray V. Montagno, "Implement Entrepreneurial Thinking in Established Organizations," *SAM Advanced Management Journal*, Winter 1993, p. 30.

opment of an entrepreneurial spirit within large organizations.[13] First, businesses must develop a system that supports and encourages people to develop new products and services. Next, organizations that want to encourage entrepreneurship must tolerate failures. Failures are to be expected when innovation is encouraged. Persistence in the face of failure and encouragement by management after a failure are key elements in developing entrepreneurship. Finally, effective communication systems encourage entrepreneurship. The absence of barriers to communication is essential. Figure 1.7 summarizes critical elements in developing intrapreneurial environments. Peters also believes that for entrepreneurship to really work, it must be sustained and nurtured within the firm. Peters asserts, "I'm convinced, after watching and working in organizations for three decades, that there are five constants that mark success sustainers: decentralization, empowerment, a passion for product, great systems, and paranoia."[14] Entrepreneurs not only strive to make it and then make it better. They also strive to disrupt the status quo and change the environment in which we live and work.

THE INCREASING ROLE OF WOMEN AND MINORITIES IN MANAGEMENT

As you will see in the chapters to come, one of the primary themes of this text is the ever-changing and expanding role of women and minorities in the management structure of the modern corporation. White males still run corporate America, but as the workforce becomes more diverse, women and minorities are slowly gaining. These gains, their causes and effects, the structural changes they have brought about, and the long-term outlook will be closely examined in the chapters that follow.

One of the most significant issues facing women and minorities in management is the glass ceiling. The **glass ceiling** refers to a level within the managerial hierarchy beyond which very few women and minorities advance.[15] During the 1990s business, government, and interest groups placed much emphasis on this issue, and recent studies show improvement in this area. According to an annual survey by Catalyst, a research organization in New York City, for the first time more than one-half of the Fortune 500 companies have at least one woman on their boards of directors.[16]

glass ceiling   Refers to a level within the managerial hierarchy beyond which very few women and minorities advance.

ORGANIZATION OF THIS BOOK

This book is divided into six sections:

- Section I: Foundations
- Section II: Contemporary Issues
- Section III: Planning Skills
- Section IV: Organizing and Staffing Skills
- Section V: Directing Skills
- Section VI: Controlling Skills

Section I provides an overview of the management process. Chapter 1 defines management and describes the functions and skills of management. Chapter 2 presents a historical view of management. Chapter 3 describes the importance of communication skills in management. Chapter 4 focuses on the decision-making skills required in management.

Section II analyzes contemporary issues in management. Chapter 5 examines the roles that information systems for managers play in today's organizations. Chapter 6 focuses on ethics and social responsibility, and Chapter 7 describes the increasing internationalization of business.

Section III focuses on planning skills in management. Chapter 8 describes the planning process, including its objectives, strategy issues, and the principles of strategic management. Chapter 9 focuses on applying planning skills to the operations processes of the organization.

Section IV analyzes the organizing and staffing skills of management. Chapters 10 and 11 describe organization principles and the development of organizational structures. Chapter 12 discusses the role of formal and informal work groups in businesses. Chapter 13 describes the staffing process. Chapter 14 describes the process of training and developing employees and managers.

Section V analyzes the directing skills of management. Chapters 15 and 16 examine motivation in business and the importance of leadership in improving organizational performance. Chapter 17 describes approaches to managing conflict and stress. Chapter 18 focuses on managing change, culture, and diversity.

Section VI explores the controlling skills of management. Chapter 19 describes the controlling function of management. Chapter 20 discusses appraising and rewarding performance as a method of control and direction. Chapter 21 describes the application of managerial control in the operations processes.

Summary

1. *Define Management.* Management is a form of work that involves coordinating an organization's resources—land, labor, and capital—to accomplish organizational objectives.

2. *Describe the Levels of Management.* Three levels of management exist. Top management establishes the goals of the organization and the actions necessary to achieve them. Middle management develops departmental goals and actions necessary to achieve organizational objectives. Supervisors manage operative employees.

3. *Discuss the Functions of Management.* The functions of management are

- Planning: deciding what objectives to pursue during a future period and what to do to achieve those objectives.

- Organizing: grouping activities, assigning activities, and providing the authority necessary to carry out the activities.

- Staffing: determining human resource needs and recruiting, selecting, training, and developing human resources.

- Leading: directing and channeling human behavior toward the accomplishment of objectives.
- Controlling: measuring performance against objectives, determining causes of deviations, and taking corrective action where necessary.

4.   *Explain the Roles of a Manager.* The roles of a manager fall into three major categories: interpersonal, informational, and decisional. Formal authority and status together generate certain interpersonal roles. The interpersonal roles, in turn, determine the informational roles of the manager. Finally, access to information, authority, and status place the manager at a central point in the organizational decision-making process.

5.   *Describe the Skills Required to Perform the Work of Management.* The three skills required in management are

- Conceptual skills: involve understanding the relationship of the parts of a business to one another and to the business as a whole. Decision making, planning, and organizing are separate managerial activities that require conceptual skills.
- Human relations skills: involve understanding people and being able to work well with them.
- Technical skills: involve being able to perform the mechanics of a particular job.

6.   *Explain How Principles of Management Are Developed.* Typically, principles are developed through a controlled experiment process. However, management principles are developed through observation and deduction.

7.   *Define Entrepreneur.* An entrepreneur conceives the idea of what product or service to produce, starts the organization, and builds it to the point where additional people are needed.

8.   *Define Small Business.* A small business is a company that is independently owned and operated and is not dominant in its field. As a rule, small businesses have fewer than 100 employees.

9.   *Outline Three Requirements for Encouraging Entrepreneurship in Medium-Size and Large Businesses.* Organizations must develop a system that supports and encourages people to champion their new ideas or products; they must tolerate failures; and they must have effective communication systems.

10.   *Discuss the Increasing Role of Women and Minorities in Management.* The number of women in the civilian labor force has grown faster than the growth rate of the total number of people employed. Women and minorities have also had a higher percentage growth rate than the overall growth rate of employment in managerial and professional jobs.

11.   *Define the "Glass Ceiling" Facing Women and Minorities.* The glass ceiling refers to a level within the managerial hierarchy beyond which very few women and minorities advance.

Preview Analysis

1.   What types of management skills do you believe have helped Bill Gates establish Microsoft as the world's number one software company? Explain.

2.   What changes does Bill Gates forecast in his book *The Road Ahead?* Which of these changes do you believe will have the greatest impact on business? What other changes do you think the 21st century will bring?

3.   What do you think of the demands Bill Gates places on employees and his approach to managing employees? Would you want to work for Microsoft? Why or why not?

Review Questions

1.   What is management?
2.   Describe the levels of management.
3.   Name and describe the basic management functions.
4.   Define the basic skills required in management.
5.   How are principles of management developed?
6.   Distinguish between a professional manager and an entrepreneur.
7.   What is a small business?
8.   What are three essential characteristics for developing an entrepreneurial spirit in larger corporations?
9.   Explain how the composition of the managerial work force is changing in terms of gender and race.
10.   Define glass ceiling and give examples of how it affects women and minorities.

Skill-Building Questions

1. Management has often been described as a universal process, meaning the basics of management are transferable and applicable in almost any environment. Do you believe a good manager in a bank could be equally effective in a college or university? Explain your reasoning.

2. How does one decide who is and who is not a manager in a given organization? For example, is the operator of a one-person business, such as a corner grocery store, a manager? Explain.

3. Do you think management can be learned through books and study or only through experience?

4. Discuss the following statement: "All entrepreneurs are managers, but not all managers are entrepreneurs."

5. Explain how you would deal with the difficulties and challenges of the "glass ceiling."

SKILL-BUILDING EXERCISE 1.1

Success of a Business

Have each student go to the library and bring back to class an actual example of an entrepreneurial business and a small business. Possible sources of information include *Venture, Inc., Business Week,* or The *Wall Street Journal.*

Each student should then prepare a five-minute report on the following:

a. History of the organization.

b. Main product of the organization.

c. Reasons for success.

d. Role of management.

SKILL-BUILDING EXERCISE 1.2

Are You an Entrepreneur?

In recent years, entrepreneurs, or folks who do things their own way, have become a highly analyzed species, but often the data uncovered have been so voluminous as to confuse rather than clarify.

Among the most confused, perhaps, are thousands of would-be entrepreneurs whose friends tell them they aren't equipped with the qualities for success.

Recognizing this, Northwestern Mutual Life Insurance Co., which considers its own agents to be entrepreneurial, wondered what it is that makes a good entrepreneur. And so it commissioned a test.

Professor John Braun, a psychologist at the University of Bridgeport, is the author of this somewhat revealing—if not entirely scientific—quiz that aims to clarify your understanding.

- Significantly high numbers of entrepreneurs are children of first-generation Americans. If your parents were immigrants, add one to your score. If not, subtract one.

- As a rule, successful entrepreneurs weren't top achievers in school. If you were a top student, deduct four. If not, add four points.

- Entrepreneurs weren't especially enthusiastic about group activities in school. If you enjoyed such activities, subtract one. If not, add it.

- As youngsters, entrepreneurs often preferred to be alone. Did you prefer aloneness? If so, add one. Otherwise, subtract it.

- Those who started childhood enterprises, such as lemonade stands, or who ran for elected office at school can add two because enterprise is easily traced to an early age. Those who weren't enterprising must subtract two.

- Stubbornness as a child seems to translate into determination to do things one's own way. If you were stubborn enough to learn the hard way, add one. Otherwise, subtract it.

- Caution may involve unwillingness to take risks. Were you a cautious child? If so, drop four points. Otherwise, add them.

- If you were more daring than your playmates, add four.

- If the opinions of others matter a lot to you, subtract one. Add one otherwise.

- Weariness with daily routine is sometimes a motivating factor in starting a business. If this would be a factor in your desire to go out on your own, add two points. Otherwise, deduct them.

- If you enjoy work, are you willing to work overnight? Yes, add two. No, deduct six.

- Add four more if you would be willing to work as long as it takes with little or no sleep to finish a job. No deductions if you wouldn't.

- Entrepreneurs generally enjoy their activity so much they move from one project to another without stopping. When you complete a project successfully, do you immediately begin another? Yes, plus two. No, minus two.

- Would you be willing to spend your savings to start a business? If so, add two, and deduct that many if you aren't.

- Add two more if you'd be willing to borrow from others to supplement your own funds. If not, you lose two points.

- If you failed, would you immediately work to start again? Yes gives you four, no takes that many away.

- Subtract another point if failure would make you look for a good-paying job.

- Do you believe entrepreneurs are risky? Yes, minus two. No, plus two.

- Add a point if you write out long-term and short-term goals. Otherwise, subtract one.

- You win two points if you think you have more knowledge and experience with cash flow than most people. You lose them if you don't.

- If you're easily bored, add two. Deduct two points if you aren't.

- If you're an optimist, add two. If you're a pessimist, erase two.

Scoring:

If you score 35 or more, you have everything going for you. Between 15 and 35 suggests you have background, skills, and talent to succeed. Zero to 15 indicates you ought to be successful with application and skill development.

Zero to minus 15 doesn't rule you out, but it indicates you would have to work extra hard to overcome a lack of built-in advantages and skills. And if you score worse than minus 15, your talents probably lie elsewhere.

Source: Northwestern Mutual Life Insurance Company. Used with permission.

SKILL BUILDING EXERCISE 1.3

Required Attributes of a Manager

The following ads were taken from the Want Ads section of a newspaper. All company names and locations have been disguised.

A. Choose the job that is most attractive to you.

B. Your instructor will form you into groups with other students that selected the same job as you. Your group should then develop a list of required and desirable skills for the job.

C. Each group should be prepared to present and defend their list before the class.

CORPORATE MANAGER
CONSOLIDATIONS AND BUDGETS

Challenging career opportunity with moderate-size international machinery manufacturer with primary manufacturing locations overseas. Report to V.P.-Finance. Responsible for monthly consolidations, analysis, and financial reports. Prepare annual consolidated budgets and periodically monitor performance.

5 years' relevant experience in similar environment, familiarity with foreign exchange transactions preferred. Must be intelligent, self-disciplined, high-energy professional. We offer competitive compensation and benefits package. For prompt, totally confidential consideration please forward full resume including earnings history to: Vice President, Employee Relations.

A&B MODERN MACHINERY CO., INC.

An Equal Opportunity Employer M/F/HC

MANAGER SYSTEMS DEVELOPMENT

American Health Care Plans, which operates a number of HMOs across the country is seeking an experienced professional who can take a leadership role in the development of state-of-the-art claims processing systems. This position will report to the VP of MIS, and will involve extensive interaction with claims operational personnel as well as the programmer analysts who are implementing the new systems.

The ideal candidate will have a management, accounting, or computer science degree with a strong emphasis on information systems. The candidate's background should include at least five years in systems development and operational management in an insurance environment. Health insurance, experience and advanced degree are pluses.

We are looking for a very special person, who will bring intelligence, leadership, and creativity to the position. The selected candidate must also be able to take on expanding responsibilities as the company grows. We offer a competitive compensation package and a full range of benefits.

Qualified persons respond by sending resume and salary requirements to our Personnel Director.

American Health Care Plans

An Equal Opportunity Employer

Human Resource Manager

Jackson & Brown's Professional Products Division, the world leader in the development, manufacture, and sale of contact lenses, currently seeks a Human Resource Manager. Responsibilities will include managing personnel policies, practices, and procedures in the area of employee relations, training, organizational development, recruitment, and compensation.

The successful candidate will have a bachelor's degree, preferably in a business related field and 5 years' experience as a generalist in Human Resources. 1-2 years must be in a supervisory capacity. This highly visible position will report directly to the Vice President of Human Resources, Professional Products Division.

For immediate reply, send your resume to: Ms. Jane L. Doe, Professional Products Division.

Jackson & Brown

An Equal Opportunity Employer

VICE PRESIDENT OF MARKETING

... Office Automation Systems

Established Midwest manufacturer has an outstanding career opportunity available for an experienced, marketing professional.

You will be responsible for developing marketing plans and overseeing subsequent activities. Specific duties include:

- Market Analysis
- Product/Pricing Strategy
- Field Sales Support
- Advertising & Promotion
- Revenue Reporting and Projection

This is a prestigious opportunity to work in an industry-leading corporation, international in scope, to assure that our present and future products meet customers requirements and increase our market share. Career growth potential is exceptional. Benefits and salary are executive level. To apply, rush an outline of your qualification to the address below. All responses will be kept in inviolable secrecy. We are proud to be an equal opportunity employer.

CASE INCIDENT 1.1

The Expansion of Blue Streak

Arthur Benton started the Blue Streak Delivery Company five years ago. Blue Streak initially provided commercial delivery services for all packages within the city of Unionville (population 1 million).

Art started with himself, one clerk, and one driver. Within three years, Blue Streak had grown to the point of requiring 4 clerks and 16 drivers. It was then that Art decided to expand and provide statewide service. He figured this would initially require the addition of two new offices, one located at Logantown (population 500,000) in the southern part of the state and one at Thomas City (population 250,000) in the northern part of the state. Each office was staffed with a manager, two clerks, and four drivers. Because both Logantown and Thomas City were within 150 miles of Unionville, Art was able to visit each office at least once a week and personally coordinate the operations in addition to providing general management assistance. The statewide delivery system met with immediate success and reported a healthy profit for the first year.

The next year, Art decided to expand and include two neighboring states. Art set up two offices in each of the two neighboring states. However, operations never seemed to go smoothly in the neighboring states. Schedules were constantly being fouled up, deliveries were lost, and customer complaints multiplied. After nine months,

Art changed office managers in all four out-of-state offices. Things still did not improve. Convinced that he was the only one capable of straightening out the out-of-state offices, Art began visiting them once every two weeks. This schedule required Art to spend at least half of his time on the road traveling between offices.

After four months of this activity, Art began to be very tired of the constant travel; operations in the two neighboring states still had not improved. In fact, on each trip Art found himself spending all his time putting out fires that should have been handled by the office managers.

Art decided to have a one-day meeting that all of his office managers would attend to discuss problems and come up with some answers. At the meeting, several issues were raised. First, all of the managers thought Art's visits were too frequent. Second, most the managers did not seem to know exactly what Art expected them to do. Finally, each of the managers believed they should have the authority to make changes in their office procedures without checking with Art before making the change.

Questions

1. What suggestions would you offer to Art to improve his operation?

2. What management skills must Art master if he is to resolve his problems and continue to grow?

CASE INCIDENT 1.2

Wadsworth Company

Last year, Donna Carroll was appointed supervisor of the small parts subassembly department of Wadsworth Company. The department employed 28 people. Donna had wanted the promotion and thought her 15 years of experience in various jobs at the company qualified her for the job.

Donna decided to have two group leaders report to her. She appointed Evelyn Castalos and Bill Degger to these new positions. She made it clear, however, that they retained their present operative jobs and were expected to contribute to the direct productive efforts. Evelyn is ambitious and a highly productive employee. Bill is a steady, reliable employee.

Work assignment decisions were to be made by Evelyn. She took on this responsibility with great enthusiasm and drew up work-scheduling plans covering a period of one month. She believed productivity could be increased by 8 percent due primarily to work assignment improvements. She went regularly from workplace to workplace,

checking the finished volume of work at each station. Bill assumed, at the suggestion and support of Donna, the task of training new employees or retraining present employees on new work coming into the department.

Donna spent most of her time preparing and reading reports. She made certain to be friendly with most of the other supervisors. She talked with them frequently and helped them fill out forms and reports required by their jobs. She also frequently circulated among the employees of her department, exchanging friendly remarks. However, when an employee asked a question concerning work, Donna referred the person to either Evelyn or Bill.

Some of the employees complained among themselves that the work assignments were unfair. They contended that "favorites" of Evelyn got all the easy jobs and, although the present volume of work had increased, no extra help was being hired. Several times the employees talked with Donna about this, but Donna referred them to Evelyn each time. Likewise, many of the employees complained about Bill's performance. They based their opinions on the apparent lack of knowledge and skill the new employees had after receiving training from Bill.

Questions

1. Do you think the duties Evelyn and Bill are handling should have been delegated by Donna?

2. What difficulties do you see for Evelyn and Bill in being both group leaders and operative employees?

3. Do you consider Evelyn and Bill to be managers? Why or why not?

Notes and Additional Readings

[1] Throughout this book, the terms *objectives* and *goals* will be used interchangeably.

[2] Henry Mintzberg, "The Manager's Job: Folklore and Fact," *Harvard Business Review,* July–August 1975, pp. 49–61.

[3] T. R. Sarlin and V. L. Allen, "Role Theory," in *The Handbook of Social Psychology,* 2nd ed., vol. 1, ed. G. Lindzey and E. Aronson (Reading, MA: Addison-Wesley, 1968), pp. 488–567.

[4] Henry Mintzberg, *The Nature of Managerial Work* (New York: Harper & Row, 1972), pp. 54–99.

[5] For more information on the roles of managers, see John P. Kotter, *The General Managers* (New York: The Free Press, 1982).

[6] Ellen Graham, "The Entrepreneurial Mystique," *The Wall Street Journal,* May 20, 1985, sec. 3, p. 1.

[7] Anne Murphy, "Entrepreneur of the Year," *Inc.,* December 1995, pp. 43–44.

[8] "Where Women are Making Great Strides," *Business Week,* May 8, 1995, p. 8.

[9] "Matters of Fact," an interview with David Burch, *Inc.,* April 1985, p. 32.

[10] *The State of Small Business: A Report of the President* (Washington, DC: U.S. Government Printing Office, 1989), p. 18.

[11] Ibid., pp. 1, 27. For additional information, see Genevieve Soter Capowski, "Be Your Own Boss? Millions of Women Get Down to Business," *Management Review,* March 1992, pp. 24–30.

[12] Lucien Rhodes and Cathryn Jakobson, "Small Companies: America's Hope for the 1980s," *Inc.,* April 1981, p. 44.

[13] See Thomas J. Peters and Robert H. Waterman, Jr., *In Search of Excellence* (New York: Harper & Row, 1982), pp. 202–9.

[14] Thomas J. Peters, "Still Leadership," *Forbes ASAP,* October 9, 1995, p. 184.

[15] See Barbara Kalish, "Women at Work: Dismantling the Glass Ceiling," *Management Review,* March 1992, p. 64. Also see Sue Mize, "Shattering the Glass Ceiling," *Training & Development Journal,* January 1992, pp. 60–62.

[16] "More Women at Board Meeting," *Working Mother,* July 1995, p. 16.

2

The Management Movement

LEARNING OBJECTIVES

After studying this chapter, you should be able to:

1. Explain why management did not emerge as a recognized discipline until the 20th century.

2. Describe the three facets of the U.S. Industrial Revolution.

3. Discuss the role the captains of industry played in the development of modern organizations.

4. Define scientific management and outline the role Frederick W. Taylor and his contemporaries played in its development.

5. Summarize Henri Fayol's contributions to modern management.

6. Discuss the human relations thrust in management, with emphasis on the role of the Hawthorne experiments.

7. Define the management process period, the management theory jungle, the systems approach, and the contingency approach.

8. Summarize the major points made in Theory Z.

9. Summarize the eight characteristics of excellent companies identified by Peters and Waterman.

10. Explain why the international aspects of management are currently being emphasized.

11. Discuss some predictions as to how managers might manage in the 21st century.

One of the greatest management challenges of the 20th century was the Manhattan Project, that vast endeavor to produce the atomic bomb. Whatever one thinks of the final result of the project, the accomplishment of harnessing and focusing a huge number of talented, temperamental, single-minded scientists and engineers represents a marvel of leadership. Other great historical tasks such as building the great pyramids of Egypt and South America, the digging of the Panama Canal, and placing a person on the Moon were no less complicated. All great tasks have been completed because of great leaders and pioneers of management thought.

According to Bill Walsh, one great example was the Manhattan Project's General Leslie Groves. He was known for his willingness to let ideas succeed or fail on their merit rather than on his own managerial instincts. He recognized that there was rarely a single best way to accomplish a task. In other words, in an almost Darwinian situation, if the manager will let ideas compete fairly the fittest idea will usually survive.

The great contributors to management thought described in this chapter all had unique ideas, went against the established thoughts of their day, learned from their peers, were never willing to accept defeat, and persevered when criticized. Their gift to contemporary business managers is the set of tools with which to mold and create the ideas and success of the future. Our responsibility is to use the tools wisely.

Source: Adapted from Bill Walsh, "Managing the Monster," *Forbes*, October 9, 1995, p. 17.

A knowledge of the history of any discipline is necessary to understanding where the discipline is and where it is going. Management is no exception. For example, how often have you read a news story covering a particular incident and formed an opinion only to change it when you understood the events leading up to the incident? Many of today's managerial problems began during the early management movement. Understanding the historical evolution of these problems helps the modern manager cope with them. It also helps today's managers develop a feel for why the managerial approaches that worked in earlier times do not necessarily work today. The challenge to present and future managers is not to memorize historical names and dates; it is to develop a feel for why and how things happened and to apply this knowledge to the practice of management.

Some forms of management have existed since the beginning of time. Ever since one human tried to direct another, management thought has been developing. In his book *The Evolution of Management Thought*, Daniel Wren indicates that professional management, organization principles, and merit pay based on ability were discussed as early as 1750 BC.[1] However, the development of management thought as we know it is a relatively modern concept. The age of industrialization in the 19th century and the subsequent emergence of large corporate organizations called for new approaches to management. The environment that led up to and surrounded the emergence of management thought is the subject of this chapter.

U.S. INDUSTRIAL REVOLUTION

As the name suggests, the U.S. Industrial Revolution encompassed the period when the United States began to shift from an almost totally agrarian society to an industrialized society. The year 1860 is generally thought of as the start of the Industrial Revolution in this country.

Daniel Wren has described the Industrial Revolution in America as having three facets: power, transportation, and communication.[2] Many new inventions, such as the steam engine, allowed industries to expand and locate in areas that at one time were devoid of factories and other signs of progress. Industry was no longer dependent on water and horses for its power.

Transportation moved through periods of industrial and commercial traffic on canals, railroads, and eventually efficient road systems. However, progress always brings its own set of unique problems. Communication lines were extended, decisions had to be made within a rapidly changing framework, scheduling difficulties arose, and new markets developed. All of these changes required new management skills.

Communication by way of the telegraph, telephone, and radio changed the way U.S. organizations functioned. Speed and efficiency dramatically increased. The trend away from an agrarian society forced many behavioral changes on the workers of the land. Schedules, work tasks, workloads, compensation, and safety were hotly debated issues well into the 20th century.

CAPTAINS OF INDUSTRY

Once industrialization began, it continued at a rapid pace. By the end of the 19th century, the economy had shifted from a mainly agrarian one to an economy heavily involved with manufactured goods and industrial markets.[3]

During the last quarter of the 19th century, American business was dominated and shaped by captains of industry. These captains of industry included John D. Rockefeller (oil), James B. Duke (tobacco), Andrew Carnegie (steel), and Cornelius

Vanderbilt (steamships and railroads). In contrast to the laissez-faire attitudes of previous generations, these individuals often pursued profit and self-interest above all else. While their methods have been questioned, they did obtain results. Under these individuals, giant companies were formed through mergers in both the consumer and producer goods industries. They created new forms of organizations and introduced new methods of marketing. For the first time, nationwide distributing and marketing organizations were formed. The birth of the corporate giant also altered the business decision-making environment.

For the empire building and methods of the captains of industry, previous management approaches no longer applied. Government began to regulate business. In 1890, the Sherman Antitrust Act, which sought to check corporate practices "in restraint of trade," was passed.

By 1890, previous management methods were no longer applicable to U.S. industry. No longer could managers make on-the-spot decisions and maintain records in their heads. Corporations had become large scale, with national markets. Communication and transportation had expanded and spurred great industrial growth. Technological innovations contributed to industrial growth: The invention of the internal combustion engine and the use of electricity as a power source greatly speeded industrial development at the close of the 19th century.

However, despite what seemed to be an ideal climate for prosperity and productivity, wages were low.[4] Production methods were crude, and worker training was almost nonexistent. There were no methods or standards for measuring work. Work had not been studied to determine the most desirable way to complete a task. The psychological and physical aspects of a job such as boredom, monotony, and fatigue were not studied or even considered in the design of most jobs.

At this point in the development of management, the engineering profession made significant contributions. Engineers designed, built, installed, and made operative the production systems. It was only natural, then, for them to study the methods used in operating these systems.

SCIENTIFIC MANAGEMENT AND FREDERICK W. TAYLOR

The development of specialized tasks and of departments within organizations had come with the rapid industrial growth and the creation of big business. One person no longer performed every task but specialized in performing only a few tasks. This created a need to coordinate, integrate, and systematize the work flow. The time spent on each item could be significant if a company was producing several thousand items. Increased production plus the new need for integrating and systematizing the work flow led engineers to begin studying work flows and job content.

The spark generally credited with igniting the interest of engineers in general business problems was a paper presented in 1886 by Henry Towne, president of the Yale and Towne Manufacturing Company, to the American Society of Mechanical Engineers. Towne stressed that engineers should be concerned with the financial and profit orientations of the business as well as their traditional technical responsibilities.[5] A young mechanical engineer named Frederick Winslow Taylor was seated in the audience. Towne's talk sparked an idea in Taylor's mind for studying problems at Midvale Steel Company. During his years at Midvale Steel Company, Taylor worked with and observed production workers at all levels. It did not take him long to figure out that many workers put forth less than 100 percent effort. Taylor referred to this tendency to restrict output as **soldiering.** Because soldiering conflicted with Taylor's

soldiering Describes the actions of employees who intentionally restrict output.

Quaker-Puritan background, it was hard for him to understand and accept. He decided to find out why workers soldiered.

Taylor quickly saw that workers had little or no reason to produce more; most wage systems of that time were based on attendance and position. Piece-rate systems had been tried before but generally failed because of poor use and weak standards. Taylor believed a piece-rate system would work if the workers believed the standard had been fairly set and management would stick to that standard. Taylor wanted to use scientific and empirical methods rather than tradition and custom for setting work standards. Taylor's efforts became the true beginning of scientific management.

Taylor first formally presented his views to the Society of Mechanical Engineers in 1895.[6] His views were expanded in book form in 1903 and again in 1911.[7] **Scientific management,** as developed by Taylor, was based on four main principles:

---

scientific management   Philosophy of Frederick W. Taylor that sought to increase productivity and make the work easier by scientifically studying work methods and establishing standards.

---

1. The development of a scientific method of designing jobs to replace the old rule-of-thumb methods. This involved gathering, classifying, and tabulating data to arrive at the "one best way" to perform a task or a series of tasks.

2. The scientific selection and progressive teaching and development of employees. Taylor saw the value of matching the job to the worker. He also emphasized the need to study worker strengths and weaknesses and to provide training to improve employee performance.

3. The bringing together of scientifically selected employees and scientifically developed methods for designing jobs. Taylor believed that new and scientific methods of job design should not merely be put before an employee; they should also be fully explained by management. He believed employees would show little resistance to changes in methods if they understood the reasons for the changes and saw a chance for greater earnings for themselves.

4. A division of work resulting in an interdependence between management and workers. Taylor believed if they were truly dependent on each other, cooperation would naturally follow.[8]

For both management and employees, scientific management brought a new attitude toward their respective duties and toward each other.[9] It was a new philosophy about the use of human effort. It emphasized maximum output with minimum effort through the elimination of waste and inefficiency at the operative level of the organization.[10] A methodological approach was used to study job tasks. This approach included research and experimentation methods (scientific methods). Standards were set in the areas of personnel, working conditions, equipment, output, and procedures. The managers planned the work; the employees performed it. The result was closer cooperation between managers and employees.

The scientific study of work also emphasized specialization and division of labor. Thus, the need for an organizational framework became more and more apparent. The concepts of line and staff emerged. In an effort to motivate employees, wage incentives were developed in most scientific management programs. Once standards were set, managers began to monitor actual performance and compare it with the standards. Thus began the managerial function of control.

Scientific management is a philosophy about the relationship between people and work, not a technique or an efficiency device. Taylor's ideas and scientific management were based on a concern not only for the proper design of the job but also for the worker. This aspect has often been misunderstood. Taylor and scientific management were (and still are) attacked as being inhumane and aimed only at increasing output. In this regard, scientific management and Taylor were the targets of a congressional investigation in 1912.[11] The key to Taylor's thinking was that he saw scientific management as benefiting management and employees equally: Management could achieve more work in a given amount of time; the employee could produce more—and hence earn more—with little or no additional effort. In summary, Taylor and other scientific management pioneers believed employees could be motivated by economic rewards, provided those rewards were related to individual performance. Management Illustration 2.1 provides some interesting personal history on Taylor.

OTHER SCIENTIFIC MANAGEMENT PIONEERS

Several disciples and colleagues of Taylor helped to promote scientific management. Carl Barth was often called the most orthodox of Taylor's followers. He worked with Taylor at Bethlehem Steel and followed him as a consultant when Taylor left Bethlehem. Barth did not alter or add to scientific management to any significant degree; rather, he worked to popularize Taylor's ideas.

Morris Cooke worked directly with Taylor on several occasions. Cooke's major contribution was the application of scientific management to educational and municipal organizations. Cooke worked hard to bring management and labor together through scientific management. His thesis was that labor was as responsible for production as management was. Cooke believed increased production would improve the position of both.[12] Thus, Cooke broadened the scope of scientific management and helped gain the support of organized labor.

Henry Lawrence Gantt worked with Taylor at both Midvale Steel and Bethlehem Steel. Gantt is best known for his work in production control and his invention of the Gantt chart, which is still in use today. The Gantt chart graphically depicts both expected and completed production. (Gantt charts are discussed in Chapter 8.) Gantt was also one of the first management pioneers to state publicly the social responsibility of management and business. He believed the community would attempt to take over business if the business system neglected its social responsibilities.[13]

Frank and Lillian Gilbreth were important to the early management movement both as a husband-and-wife team and as individuals. The Gilbreths, inspired by Taylor and scientific research, were among the first to use motion picture films to study hand and body movements to eliminate wasted motion. Frank Gilbreth's major area of interest was the study of motions and work methods. Lillian Gilbreth's primary field was psychology. Following Frank's untimely death in 1924 (he was in his mid-50s), Lillian continued their work for almost 50 years until her death in 1972. During this time, Lillian's work emphasized concern for the worker, and she showed how scientific management should foster rather than stifle employees. Because of her many achievements (see Figure 2.1), Lillian Gilbreth became known as the "First Lady of Management." By combining motion study and psychology, the Gilbreths contributed greatly to research in the areas of fatigue, monotony, micromotion study, and morale.

FAYOL'S THEORY OF MANAGEMENT

Henri Fayol, a Frenchman, was the first to issue a complete statement on a theory of general management. Though popular in Europe in the early 1900s, the theory did not really gain acceptance in America until the late 1940s. Today Fayol's greatest

Management Illustration 2.1
The Man Who Changed Work Forever

Frederick Winslow Taylor was born in Germantown, Pennsylvania, in 1856 of Quaker-Puritan stock. From his boyhood Taylor had sought to improve everything he saw. Other kids viewed him as weird, since he seemed more interested in laying out the ball field correctly than in playing the game.

His parents wanted him to be a lawyer like his father and hence enrolled him at Phillips Exeter Academy to prepare for Harvard. Though Taylor passed the Harvard exams with honors, his poor health and eyesight forced him to take up an apprenticeship as a pattern-maker and machinist with the Enterprise Hydraulic works at Philadelphia in 1874. At the end of his apprenticeship period, Taylor joined Midvale Steel as a common laborer and rose to machinist, to gang boss of the machinists, to foreman of the shop, to master mechanic in charge of repairs and maintenance throughout the plant, and to chief engineer in the short span of six years.

After a three-year stint as general manager at Manufacturing Investment Company, Taylor set up practice as a consulting engineer for management. It was as a consultant to Bethlehem Steel Company that Taylor made his greatest contribution to management with his time and motion studies. Employees willing to follow Taylor's "one best way" of doing a job found that their productivity soared and that they could double or even triple their old pay. As the pace of work accelerated, some employees rebelled and complaints against Taylor by organized labor even landed him in front of a Senate investigatory panel in 1912.

The world of management was indeed poorer when Taylor died of pneumonia a day after his 59th birthday. The epitaph on his grave in Philadelphia reads "Frederick W. Taylor, Father of Scientific Management" and rightly so.

Source: Daniel A. Wren, *The Evolution of Management Thought* (New York: Ronald Press, 1972) and Alan Farnham, "The Man Who Changed Work Forever," *Fortune*, July 21, 1997, p. 114. For more information about Bethlehem Steel Co. please visit their Web site at: www.bethsteel.com. You can read more about Frederick Winslow Taylor by visiting the Taylor Archive Web site at www.lib.stevens-tech.edu.

FIGURE 2.1   Lillian M. Gilbreth: First Lady of Management

- First female member of the Society of Industrial Engineers (1921).
- First female member of the American Society of Mechanical Engineers.
- First female selected to attend the National Academy of Engineering.
- First woman to receive the degree of Honorary Master of Engineering (University of Michigan).
- First female professor of management at an engineering school (Purdue University, 1935).
- First female professor of management at Newark College of Engineering.
- First and only female recipient of the Gilbreth Medal (1931).
- First female awarded the Gantt Gold Medal.
- First and only recipient of the CIOS Gold Medal.
- Received over 20 honorary degrees and served five U.S. presidents as an adviser.

Source: Daniel A. Wren, *Evolution of Management Thought*, 4th ed. (New York: John Wiley & Sons, 1994), p. 143.

contribution is considered to be his theory of management principles and elements. Fayol identified the following 14 "principles of management":

1. Division of work: concept of specialization of work.
2. Authority: formal (positional) authority versus personal authority.
3. Discipline: based on obedience and respect.
4. Unity of command: each employee should receive orders from only one superior.
5. Unity of direction: one boss and one plan for a group of activities having the same objective.
6. Subordination of individual interests to the general interest: a plea to abolish the tendency to place individual interest ahead of the group interest.
7. Remuneration: the mode of payment of wages was dependent on many factors.
8. Centralization: the degree of centralization desired depended on the situation and the formal communication channels.
9. Scalar chain (line of authority): shows the routing of the line of authority and formal communication channels.
10. Order: ensured a place for everything.
11. Equity: resulted from kindness and justice.
12. Stability of tenured personnel: called for orderly personnel planning.
13. Initiative: called for individual zeal and energy in all efforts.
14. Esprit de corps: stressed the building of harmony and unity within the organization.

Fayol developed his list of principles from the practices he had used most often in his own work. He used them as general guidelines for effective management, but stressed flexibility in their application to allow for different and changing circumstances.

Fayol's real contribution, however, was not the 14 principles themselves (many of which were the products of the early factory system) but his formal recognition and synthesis of these principles. In presenting his "principles of management," Fayol was probably the first to outline what today are called the *functions of management*. In essence, he identified planning, organizing, commanding, coordinating, and controlling as elements of management. He most heavily emphasized planning and organizing because he viewed these elements as essential to the other functions.

The works of Taylor and Fayol are essentially complementary. Both believed proper management of personnel and other resources is the key to organizational success. Both used a scientific approach to management. The major difference is in their orientation. Taylor stressed the management of operative work, whereas Fayol emphasized the management of organization.

PERIOD OF SOLIDIFICATION

The 1920s and most of the 1930s were a **period of solidification** and popularization of management as a discipline. The acceptance of management as a respectable discipline was gained through several avenues. Universities and colleges began to teach management; by 1925, most schools of engineering were offering classes in management.[14] Professional societies began to take an interest in

period of solidification   A period in the 1920s and 1930s in which management became recognized as a discipline.

FIGURE 2.2   Significant Events Contributing to the Solidification of Management

- First conference on "Scientific Management," October 1911.
- First doctoral dissertation on subject of scientific management by H. R. Drury at Columbia University, 1915.
- Founding of professional management societies: Society to Promote the Science of Management, 1912; Society of Industrial Engineers, 1917; American Management Association, 1923; Society for Advancement of Management, 1936.
- First meeting of management teachers, December 1924.

---

management. Much of the management pioneers' work was presented through the American Society of Mechanical Engineers. After the turn of the century, many other professional societies began to promote management. By the mid-1930s, management was truly a recognized discipline. Figure 2.2 summarizes the major events leading to this recognition.

THE HUMAN RELATIONS THRUST

The Great Depression of 1929–32 saw unemployment in excess of 25 percent. Afterward, unions sought and gained major advantages for the working class. In this period, known as the Golden Age of Unionism, legislatures and courts actively supported organized labor and the worker. The general climate tended to emphasize understanding employees and their needs (as opposed to focusing on the methods used to conduct work). Figure 2.3 summarizes several of the most important pro-union laws passed during the 1920s and 1930s. A major research project, known as the Hawthorne studies, is generally recognized as igniting the interest of business in the human element of the workplace.[15]

The Hawthorne Studies

The **Hawthorne studies** began in 1924 when the National Research Council of the National Academy of Sciences began a project to define the relationship between

hawthorne studies   Series of experiments conducted in 1924 at the Hawthorne plant of Western Electric in Cicero, Illinois; production increased in relationship to psychological and social conditions rather than to the environment.

physical working conditions and worker productivity. The Hawthorne plant of Western Electric in Cicero, Illinois, was the study site. First, the researchers lowered the level of lighting, expecting productivity to decrease. To their astonishment, productivity increased. Over the next several months, the researchers repeated the experiment by testing many different levels of lighting and other variables. Regardless of the level of light, output was found to increase.

Baffled by the results, in early 1927 the researchers called in a team of psychologists from Harvard University led by Elton Mayo. Over the next five years, hundreds of experiments were run involving thousands of employees. In these experiments, the researchers altered such variables as wage payments, rest periods, and length of workday. The results were similar to those obtained in the illumination experiments: Production increased, but with no obvious relationship to the environment. After much analysis, the researchers concluded that other factors besides the physical en-

FIGURE 2.3   Significant Pro-Union Legislation during the 1920s and 1930s

Railway Labor Act of 1926	Gave railway workers the right to form unions and engage in collective bargaining; established a corresponding obligation for employers to recognize and collectively bargain with the union.
Norris–La Guardia Act of 1932	Severely restricted the use of injunctions to limit union activity.
National Labor Relations Act of 1935 (Wagner Act)	Resulted in full, enforceable rights of employees to join unions and to engage in collective bargaining with their employer, who was legally obligated to do so.
Fair Labor Standards Act of 1938	Established minimum wages and required that time-and-a-half be paid for hours worked over 40 in one week.

vironment affected worker productivity. They found that employees reacted to the psychological and social conditions at work, such as informal group pressures, individual recognition, and participation in decision making.

The researchers also discovered that the attention shown to the employees by the experimenters positively biased their productivity. This phenomenon has since become known as the "Hawthorne effect." Yet another finding was the significance of effective supervision to both productivity and employee morale. While the methods used and the conclusions reached by the Hawthorne researchers have been questioned, they did generate great interest in the human problems in the workplace and focused attention on the human factor.[16] Management Illustration 2.2 describes the specific phases of the Hawthorne studies.

EARLY CHAMPIONS OF HUMAN RELATIONS

Mary Parker Follett was not a businesswoman in the sense that she managed her own business. However, through her writings and lectures, she had a great impact on many business and government leaders. While concerned with many aspects of the management process, her basic theory was that the fundamental problem of any organization is to build and maintain dynamic yet harmonious human relations within the organization.[17] In 1938, Chester Barnard, president of New Jersey Bell Telephone for many years, published a book that combined a thorough knowledge of organizational theory and sociology.[18] Barnard viewed the organization as a social structure and stressed the psychosocial aspects of organizations. Effectively integrating traditional management and the behavioral sciences, Barnard's work had a great impact on managers and teachers of management.

THE PROFESSIONAL MANAGER

The career manager, or professional manager, did not exist until the 1930s. Until this time, managers were placed into one of three categories: owner-managers, captains of industry, or financial managers. The owner-managers dominated until after the Civil War. The captains of industry controlled organizations from the 1880s through the turn of the century. The financial managers operated in much the same ways the captains of industry did, except that they often did not own the enterprises they

Management Illustration 2.2
The Hawthorne Studies

The Hawthorne studies were comprised of four major categories of experiments. The illumination experiments took place before the Harvard researchers were involved. In these experiments, the level of illumination was altered in one test group, and the resulting outputs were then compared to the outputs of another group not subjected to changes in illumination. Only when the intensity of illumination was reduced to moonlight level was there any appreciable decline in productivity. The relay assembly test room experiments were concerned with evaluating the effects of improved material conditions, methods of work, relief from fatigue, reduced monotony, and wage incentives on group output. All of these factors were found to have little effect on output. The interview program involved interviewing over 20,000 workers to gain information about their attitudes and sentiments. Out of these interviews came the first insights as to the influence of the work group on the outputs of the group's individual members. The bank wiring observation room experiments were designed to further investigate the influence of the group on individual group members. This experiment tested the effect of a group piecework incentive pay plan on the output of the work group in a bank wiring room. The researchers concluded from this experiment that output is actually a form of social behavior, and that, if a worker is to be accepted, he or she must act in accordance with the standards of the group.

Source: Alan C. Filley and Robert J. House, *Managerial Process and Organizational Behavior* (Glenview, IL: Scott, Foresman and Co., 1969), pp. 19–21. For more information on studies conducted by the National Academy of Sciences, go to their Web site at www.nas.edu.

controlled and operated. The financial managers dominated from around 1905 until the early 1930s, when the Great Depression severely weakened public confidence in business organizations.

In the late 1930s, the professional manager emerged. The **professional manager** is a career person who does not necessarily have a controlling interest in the enterprise for which he or she works. Professional managers realize their responsibility to three groups: employees, stockholders, and the public. With expanded technology and more complex organizations, the professional manager became more and more prevalent.

professional manager   Career manager who does not necessarily have a controlling interest in the organization and bears a responsibility to employees, stockholders, and the public.

CHANGING STYLES OF MANAGEMENT

As organizations grew in size and complexity, managers began stressing the importance of employees and their needs. As managers studied the employees and developed theories about employees' behavior, new styles and methods of managing emerged.

One innovative style of managing was developed by James F. Lincoln of Lincoln Electric Company in 1913. Lincoln realized that effective cooperation requires rewards. Thus, he designed a plan that coupled an incentive system with a request for cooperation. Lincoln emphasized the basic need of all individuals to express themselves. Specifically, the plan contained the following components:

1. An advisory board of employees.
2. A piece-rate method of compensation wherever possible.
3. A suggestion system.
4. Employee ownership of stock.

5. Year-end bonuses.
6. Life insurance for all employees.
7. Two weeks of paid vacation.
8. An annuity pension plan.
9. A promotion policy.

The development of Lincoln Electric Company can be attributed to its innovative management. It certainly has been successful. For several decades, Lincoln workers have consistently been among the highest paid in their industry in the world, averaging almost double the total pay of employees in competing companies. Lincoln's selling price has consistently been lower than that of any comparable product, and the company has consistently paid a dividend since 1918.

Another innovative manager, Henry Dennison (1877–1952), believed the strengths of an organization come from its members and the sources of power are the incentives, habits, and traditions that influence people in an organization.[19] Dennison believed an organization has the greatest strength if all of its members are strongly motivated; their actions do not lose effectiveness through friction, conflicts, or imbalance; and their actions move in a single direction, reinforcing one another. He believed management's primary purpose is to provide conditions under which employees work most readily and effectively. Instead of designing an organizational structure first, Dennison advocated finding "like-minded" people, grouping them, and then developing the total organizational structure. In summary, Dennison believed management's attention must focus on causes and effects in the field of human behavior. Dennison successfully practiced his management approach in the 1920s and 1930s at Dennison Manufacturing Company, which was also one of the early companies to implement the Taylor system of scientific management.

Charles McCormick and William Given, Jr., were top managers who applied a human relations philosophy to their organizations. Both McCormick's and Given's styles of management were based on worker involvement in the decision-making process.

McCormick, a manufacturer of spices and extracts, developed and made famous the **McCormick multiple-management plan**.[20] This plan used participation as a training and motivating tool by selecting 17 promising young people from various departments within the company to form a junior board of directors. The junior board met with the senior board once a month and submitted its suggestions. Besides the immediate benefit of providing suggestions, the junior board provided early identification of management talent, opened communication lines, and relieved senior board members of much of the detailed planning and research. The huge success of the junior board led to the creation of sales and factory boards that operated in much the same way.

mccormick multiple-management plan   Developed by Charles McCormick, a plan that uses participation as a training and motivational tool by selecting promising young employees from various company departments to form a junior board of directors.

Using the term **bottom-up management,** Given, president of American Brake Shoe and Foundry Company, encouraged widespread delegation of authority to gain the involvement of "all those down from the bottom up."[21] Given's approach promoted considerable managerial freedom in decision making, the free interchange of ideas, and the recognition that managerial growth involves some failure. Given believed the judgment, initiative, and creativeness of all employees in an organization provide a better end result than the autocratic administration of any single individual.

bottom-up management   Philosophy popularized by William B. Given that encouraged widespread delegation of authority to solicit the participation of all employees from the bottom to the top of the organization.

In 1938, Joseph Scanlon developed a productivity plan that gave employees a bonus for tangible savings in labor costs. The **Scanlon plan** was unique in at least three respects. First, joint management and union committees were formed to discuss and propose labor-saving techniques. Second, group rewards, rather than individual rewards, were made for suggestions. Third, employees shared in reduced costs rather than increased profits.[22] Scanlon believed participation was desirable not only to create a feeling of belonging but also to show clearly the role of employees and unions in suggesting improvements.

scanlon plan   Incentive plan developed in 1938 by Joseph Scanlon to give workers a bonus for tangible savings in labor costs.

MANAGEMENT PROCESS PERIOD

The participative forms of management developed in the 1930s gave rise to the **process approach to management** in the late 1940s.[23] This approach attempted to identify and define a process for attaining desired objectives. The process approach led management to become concerned primarily with identifying and refining the functions or components of the management process. For this reason, the process approach is sometimes referred to as the *functional approach*.

process approach to management   Focuses on the management functions of planning, controlling, organizing, staffing, and leading.

As we have said, Henri Fayol was the first management scholar to present explicitly a functional analysis of the management process. Fayol identified planning, organizing, commanding, coordination, and control as functions of management. However, Fayol's work was not readily available in English until 1949, so his ideas were virtually unknown in this country until then.

Oliver Sheldon, an Englishman, also gave an early breakdown of the management process.[24] In 1923, Sheldon defined management as the determination of business policy, the coordination of the execution of policy, the organization of the business, and the control of the executive.

In 1935, Ralph C. Davis was the first American to publish a functional breakdown of the management process.[25] He subdivided it into three functions: planning, organizing, and controlling.

All of these management scholars made early reference to a functional approach to management. But the concept was not widely accepted until Constance Starrs's translation made Fayol's work widely available in 1949. Thus, Fayol was truly responsible for founding the process approach to management.

OTHER APPROACHES

The late 1950s saw a new era in the study of management. Uneasy with the process approach to management, production managers and industrial engineering scholars began testing mathematical and modeling approaches to quantify management. As a result, mathematical and decision theory schools of thought developed for the study of management. The decision theory school was based largely on economic theory and the theory of consumer choice. The mathematical school viewed management as a system of mathematical relationships.

At about the same time the mathematical school was flourishing, behavioral scientists were studying management in terms of small-group relations; they depended heavily on psychology and social psychology. Drawing on the work of Chester Barnard and sociological theory, another school saw management as a system of cultural interrelationships. An empirical school of thought was developed by those scholars using the case approach. Their basic premise was that effective management can be learned by studying the successes and failures of other managers.

Harold Koontz was the first management scholar to discuss this fragmentation movement in detail.[26] Koontz accurately referred to this division of thought as the **management theory jungle.** Many conferences and discussions followed Koontz's analysis in an attempt to untangle the theory jungle and unite the various schools of thought. While some progress was made, a unified theory of management has yet to be realized.

management theory jungle   Term developed by Harold Koontz referring to the division of thought that resulted from the multiple approaches to studying the management process.

THE SYSTEMS APPROACH

The fragmentation period of the late 1950s and early 1960s was followed by an era of attempted integration. Many management theorists sought to use a "systems approach" to integrate the various management schools. A system is "an assemblage or combination of things or parts forming a complex or unitary whole."[27]

The **systems approach to management** was viewed as "a way of thinking about the job of managing . . . [which] provides a framework for visualizing internal and external environmental factors as an integrated whole."[28] The manager was asked to view the human, physical, and informational facets of the manager's job as linked in an integrated whole.

systems approach to management   A way of thinking about the job of managing that provides a framework for visualizing internal and external environmental factors as an integrated whole.

One popular thrust was to use a systems approach to integrate the other schools of management into the traditional functional approach. The idea was to integrate the human relations and mathematical approaches into the appropriate functional areas. Thus, while studying planning, a systems approach might include mathematical forecasting techniques.

THE CONTINGENCY APPROACH

The 1970s were characterized by the so-called contingency approach. In the **contingency approach to management,** different situations and conditions require different management approaches. Proponents believe there is no one best way to manage; the best way depends on the specific circumstances. Recognizing the rarity of a manager who thinks one way to manage works best in all situations, one might ask, "What is new about this approach?" What is new is that contingency theorists have often gone much further than simply saying "It all depends." Many contingency theories outline in detail the style or approach that works best under certain circumstances. Contingency theories, many of which are discussed in this book, have been developed in areas such as decision making, organizational design, leadership, planning, and group behavior.

contingency approach to management   Theorizes that different situations and conditions require different management approaches.

THE JAPANESE MANAGEMENT MOVEMENT AND THEORY Z

The tremendous economic success many Japanese companies enjoyed following World War II drew worldwide attention to their management practices. As management scholars studied Japanese management, they identified certain characteristics that differed somewhat from traditional American approaches. In general terms, Japanese managers encouraged more employee participation in decision making, they showed a deeper concern for the personal well-being of employees and they placed great emphasis on the quality of their products and services. Top management acted more as a facilitator of decision making than as an issuer of edicts. The flow of

FIGURE 2.4   Comparison of Japanese, American, and Theory Z Organizations

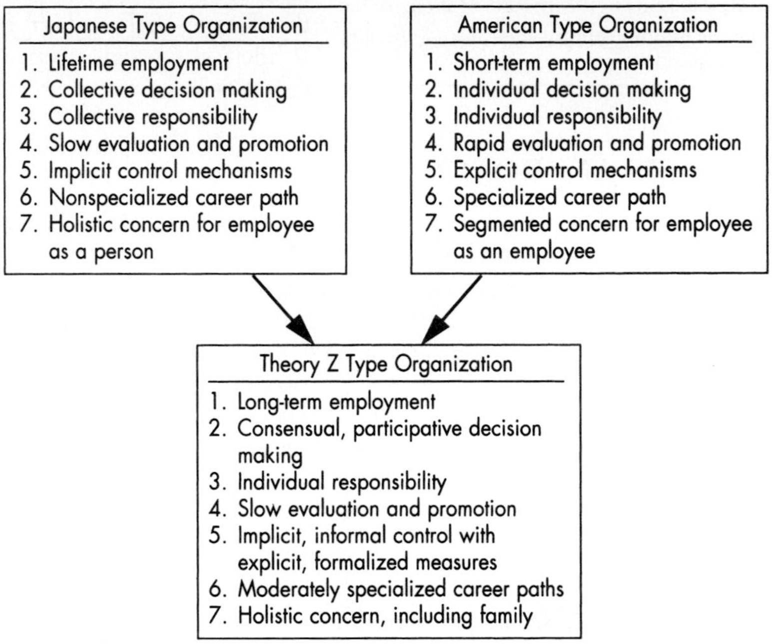

Japanese Type Organization
1. Lifetime employment
2. Collective decision making
3. Collective responsibility
4. Slow evaluation and promotion
5. Implicit control mechanisms
6. Nonspecialized career path
7. Holistic concern for employee as a person

American Type Organization
1. Short-term employment
2. Individual decision making
3. Individual responsibility
4. Rapid evaluation and promotion
5. Explicit control mechanisms
6. Specialized career path
7. Segmented concern for employee as an employee

Theory Z Type Organization
1. Long-term employment
2. Consensual, participative decision making
3. Individual responsibility
4. Slow evaluation and promotion
5. Implicit, informal control with explicit, formalized measures
6. Moderately specialized career paths
7. Holistic concern, including family

Source: Adapted from William Ouchi, *Theory Z* (Reading, MA: Addison-Wesley Publishing, Inc., 1984), pp. 58, 71–88.

information and initiatives from the bottom to the top of the organization was emphasized. Japanese organizations also tended to be characterized by lifetime employment and nonspecialized career paths for employees.

Realizing there are many valuable lessons to be learned from the Japanese, William Ouchi developed a theory, called **Theory Z,** that attempts to integrate American and Japanese management practices.[29] Theory Z combines the American emphasis on individual responsibility with the Japanese emphasis on collective decision making, slow evaluation and promotion, and holistic concern for employees. Other factors recommended by Ouchi, such as length of employment and career path characteristics, represent compromises between traditional American and Japanese practices. Figure 2.4 summarizes the profile of traditional American and Japanese organizations as well as Ouchi's Type Z organization.

theory Z   A theory developed by William Ouchi that attempts to integrate American and Japanese management practices by combining the American emphasis on individual responsibility with the Japanese emphasis on collective decision making, slow evaluation and promotion, and holistic concern for employees.

SEARCH FOR EXCELLENCE

In 1982, Thomas J. Peters and Robert H. Waterman, Jr., released a book, *In Search of Excellence,* that has since become the best-selling management-related book ever published.[30] Working as management consultants at a time when Japanese management styles were receiving worldwide attention (in the late 1970s), Peters and Waterman asked, "Can't we learn something from America's most successful companies?" Using a combination of subjective criteria and six measures of financial success covering a 20-year period (1961 through 1980), the authors identified a final subsample of 36

In Search of Excellence   Book by Thomas J. Peters and Robert H. Waterman, Jr., that identifies 36 companies with an excellent 20-year performance record. The authors identified eight characteristics of excellence after interviewing managers in each company.

FIGURE 2.5   Peters and Waterman's Eight Characteristics of Excellent Companies

Characteristics of Excellence	Description of Characteristics
1. A bias for action	A tendency to get on with things A willingness to experiment
2. Close to the customer	The provision of unparalleled quality/service A willingness to listen to the customer
3. Autonomy and entrepreneurship	Encouragement of practical risk taking and innovation Tolerance of a reasonable number of mistakes as a part of the innovative process
4. Productivity through people	Rank-and-file employees are viewed as the root source of quality and productivity gains Employees are treated with respect and dignity Enthusiasm and trust are encouraged
5. Hands on; value driven	The company philosophy and values are clearly communicated Managers take a "hands-on" approach
6. Stick to the knitting	Companies diversify only into businesses that are closely related Emphasis is on internal growth as opposed to mergers
7. Simple form; lean staff	Companies have simple structure with clear lines of authority Headquarters staff is kept small
8. Simultaneous loose-tight properties	Autonomy is pushed down to the lowest levels, but at the same time certain core values are not negotiable

Source: Thomas J. Peters and Robert H. Waterman, Jr., *In Search of Excellence* (New York: Harper & Row, 1982), pp. 13–16.

American companies. According to the authors' criteria, these companies had demonstrated excellent performance over the 20-year time frame studied. Most of the 36 companies in the final subsample were well-known companies such as IBM, McDonald's, Delta Air Lines, and Eastman Kodak. After interviewing each company in the subsample and analyzing their findings, Peters and Waterman identified eight "attributes of excellence," summarized in Figure 2.5.

While Peters and Waterman's work has been criticized as being overly subjective and not based on sound research methods, it has caused many managers to rethink their ways of doing things.[31] Specifically, Peters and Waterman reemphasized the value of on-the-job experimentation and creative thinking, the need to place the customer first, and the need to treat employees as human beings.

THE EMPHASIS ON QUALITY

Beginning in the late 1970s, gathering steam throughout the 1980s, and reaching its height in the early 1990s was an emphasis on overall quality of the product or service. The quality of American products and services had reached a low by the early 1970s. This phenomenon coupled with the quality successes of the Japanese, forced managers to look to the quality issue as one way of improving the position of American products and services.

The major change that resulted from this increased attention to quality was a shift from finding and correcting mistakes or rejects to *preventing* them. This led to the development of Total Quality Management (TQM), which is a management philosophy that emphasizes "managing the entire organization so that it excels in all dimensions of products and services that are important to the customer."[32] TQM is discussed at length in Chapter 21.

THE INTERNATIONAL AND GLOBAL MOVEMENT

In recent years, and especially in the late 1980s through 1995, many U.S. companies have turned to the international arena for new markets and profits. According to *Business Week*'s 1995 industry outlook, autos, chemicals, computers, semiconductors, and steel will all advance due to pent-up demand and improved productivity.[33] Although recently bridled by the worldwide economic slowdown, foreign investment in the United States is estimated to be between $150 billion and $200 billion. Even companies that do not trade directly in the international and global markets are often greatly affected by foreign competition, alliances, and investment. As a result, U.S. managers are being forced to think in terms of international and global rather than local or national markets. Business emphasis will likely continue to shift to the international scene throughout the 1990s. International management is discussed in greater detail in Chapter 7.

MANAGEMENT IN THE 21ST CENTURY

As summarized in this chapter, there is little doubt that significant changes occurred in the 20th century in all facets of American organizations and the manner in which they are managed. From a management perspective, what changes are likely to occur as we move into the 21st century?

The authors of the book *Beyond Workplace 2000* have made some interesting projections as to what organizations and management might look like in the 21st century.

- Most American companies will find that they no longer can gain a competitive advantage from further improvements in quality, service, cost, or speed, since the gap between rivals on these traditional measures of performance will all but close.

- Every American business and every employee who works for an American business will be forced to become agile, flexible, and highly adaptive, since the product or service they will provide and the business processes they will employ will be in a constant state of change.

- Every American company will be forced to develop a much better understanding of what it does truly well and will invest its limited resources in developing and sustaining superiority in that unique knowledge, skill, or capability.

- Organizational structures will become extremely fluid. No longer will there be departments, units, divisions, or functional groups in most American businesses. There will only be multidisciplinary and multiskilled teams, and every team will be temporary.

- There will be a meltdown of the barrier between leader and follower, manager and worker. Bosses, in the traditional sense, will all but disappear. While there will be a few permanent leaders external to work and project teams, these people will act more as coordinators of team activities than as traditional leaders.[34]

Time will tell if these predictions do, in fact, come true. One thing for certain is that the rate of change will continue to accelerate and both organizations and managers will be required to adapt to these changes.

CONCLUSION

This chapter has summarized the major events that affected management discipline from the 19th century to the present. But the discipline did not develop and mature at the same rate in all parts of the country. Similarly, it did not develop from a series of discrete happenings; rather, it grew from a series of major and minor events. Figure 2.6 presents a chronological summary of the major and related events in the management movement.

FIGURE 2.6   Major Components and Related Events of the Management Movement

Major Management Movements	Related Events
U.S. Industrial Revolution (before 1875)	Steam power (1790–1810) Railroad boom (1830–1850) Telegraph (1844)

Captains of industry (1875–1900)	Formation of corporate giants:
	  John D. Rockefeller (oil)
	  James B. Duke (tobacco)
	  Andrew Carnegie (steel)
	  Cornelius Vanderbilt (shipping and railroads)

Scientific management era (1895–1920)	Henry Towne, "The Engineer as Economist," 1886
	Frederick W. Taylor's work (1895–1915):
	  Carl Barth
	  Morris Cooke
	  Henry Lawrence Gantt
	  Frank and Lillian Gilbreth
	Henry Fayol, *Administration Industrielle et Generale*, 1916

Period of solidification (1920 to early 1930s)	Founding of professional management societies (1920s)
Human relations movement (1931 to late 1940s)	Hawthorne studies, led by Elton Mayo (1924–1932) Mary Parker Follett (1920–1933) Chester Barnard, *Functions of the Executive*, 1938
Management process period (early 1950s to early 1960s)	Starr's translation of Fayol's work (1949) Ralph Davis, *Top Management Planning*, 1951 George Terry, *Principles of Management*, 1953 Koontz and O'Donnell, *Principles of Management*, 1955
Management theory jungle (early to late 1960s)	Process approach Quantitative approaches Behavioral approaches
Systems approach (late 1960s to early 1970s)	Integrating the various approaches to the study of management.
Contingency approach (1970s)	Theorizes that different situations and conditions require different management approaches.
Theory Z (1980s)	Combines certain characteristics of traditional Japanese and American management styles.
Search for excellence (1980s)	Attempt to learn management lessons from a group of U.S. companies that experienced certain success over the 1961–80 time span.
International movement (1980s–1990s)	Increased awareness of international and global markets and of managerial approaches.
Management into 21st century	Extremely fluid organizations; multidisciplinary and multiskilled teams.

Summary

1. *Explain Why Management Did Not Emerge as a Recognized Discipline until the 20th Century.* Just as traffic lights were not needed before cars, management, as it now exists, was not needed before organizations became complex. Before the late 19th and 20th centuries, most organizations were relatively simple. Industrialization and mass production brought large and complex organizations.

2. *Describe the Three Facets of the U.S. Industrial Revolution.* The three major facets of the U.S. Industrial Revolution are: (1) power (2) transportation, and (3) communication.

3. *Discuss the Role the Captains of Industry Played in the Development of Modern Organizations.* The captains of industry, which included John D. Rockefeller, James B. Duke, Andrew Carnegie, and Cornelius Vanderbilt, built great companies. They introduced nationwide distribution and marketing methods. Because of the size and dominance of these companies, the relationship between business and government changed forever. Government passed legislation to check corporate practices in restraint of trade.

4. *Define Scientific Management and Outline the Role Frederick W. Taylor and His Contemporaries Played in Its Development.* Scientific management is a philosophy about the use of human effort. It seeks to maximize output with minimum effort through the elimination of waste and inefficiency at the operative level. Frederick W. Taylor was the major figure responsible for popularizing scientific management through his writings and consulting. Several contemporaries of Taylor helped spread Taylor's philosophy through their own efforts. The most prominent included Carl Barth, Morris Cooke, Henry Gantt, and Frank and Lillian Gilbreth.

5. *Summarize Henri Fayol's Contributions to Modern Management.* Henri Fayol made many contributions, but the most significant was his development of management principles and elements. The 14 principles Fayol developed are still applicable today, and his five management elements are very similar to today's functions of management.

6. *Discuss the Human Relations Thrust in Management, with Emphasis on the Role of the Hawthorne Experiments.* Following the Great Depression, more emphasis began to be placed on understanding workers and their needs. The Hawthorne studies, which began in 1924 and lasted until 1932, focused attention on human relations and specifically on the psychological and sociological aspects of work. Mary Parker Follett also helped to popularize the human relations movement.

7. *Define the Management Process Period, the Management Theory Jungle, the Systems Approach, and the Contingency Approach.* The management process period took place between the late 1940s and the late 1950s. During this period, management thought focused primarily on identifying and refining the functions or components of the management process. The management theory jungle, first clearly identified by Harold Koontz, referred to the many different approaches being taken to the study of management in the late 1950s and early 1960s. The systems approach attempted to integrate the various approaches to management. The systems approach is a way of thinking about the job of managing that provides a framework for visualizing internal and external environmental factors as an integrated whole. The contingency approach to management theorizes that different situations and conditions require different management approaches and that no one approach works best in all situations.

8. *Summarize the Major Points Made in Theory Z.* Theory Z attempts to integrate American and Japanese management practices. Theory Z combines the American emphasis on individual responsibility with the Japanese emphasis on collective decision making, slow evaluation and promotion, and holistic concern for employees.

9. *Summarize the Eight Characteristics of Excellent Companies Identified by Peters and Waterman.* In their book *In Search of Excellence*, Peters and Waterman identified eight characteristics of excellent companies (see Figure 2.5). In general, these eight characteristics emphasize the value of on-the-job experimentation and creative thinking, the need to place the customer first, and the need to treat employees as human beings.

10. *Explain Why the International Aspects of Management Are Currently Being Emphasized.* Many of today's U.S. companies have turned to the international arena for new markets and profits. Even those companies that do not trade internationally are often greatly affected by imports or exports from other countries. Thus, almost all companies today are affected to some degree by the international aspects of management.

11. *Discuss Some Predictions as to How Managers Might Manage in the 21st Century.* Organization structures may become extremely fluid with no structured departments, units, divisions, or functional groups. The barriers between leader and follower, manager and worker will disappear. Managers will act as coordinators of team activities.

Preview Analysis

1. What was the managerial task facing General Leslie Groves?

2. Is there a single best way to accomplish a management task? Explain

Review Questions

1. What were the three facets of the Industrial Revolution in America? Discuss the impact of each of these facets on the development of today's industry.

2. What effect did the captains of industry have on the relationships between government and industry?

3. What is scientific management? Discuss the four main principles of scientific management.

4. Discuss the major contribution to scientific management of Morris Cooke, Henry Lawrence Gantt, and Frank and Lillian Gilbreth.

5. What was Henri Fayol's major contribution to the management movement?

6. Discuss the impact of the Hawthorne studies on management thought.

7. Describe in detail the following approaches to the management process: Lincoln Electric Company, the McCormick multiple-management plan, bottom-up management, and the Scanlon plan.

8. What is the process approach to management? Discuss some of the major contributors to this approach.

9. Discuss the factors that led to the management theory jungle.

10. What is the systems approach to the management process?

11. Describe the period beginning in the late 1970s where significant emphasis was placed on the quality of products and services.

12. Describe the contingency approach to management.

13. What is Theory Z?

14. Identify the eight characteristics of successful companies reported by the authors of *In Search of Excellence.*

15. How are companies that do not trade internationally affected by international markets?

16. Discuss several predictions concerning how organizations might be structured and managed in the 21st century.

Skill-Building Questions

1. From the viewpoint of a practicing manager, what do you see as the major lessons to be learned from the evolution of management thought?

2. Why do you think many people have misinterpreted Frederick W. Taylor's scientific management principles as being inhumane?

3. Offer some general guidelines for applying scientific management principles in a manner that would be positively received by employees.

4. Discuss your views on the following statement: "The eight characteristics identified by the authors of *In Search of Excellence* are nothing more than good common sense."

SKILL-BUILDING EXERCISE 2.1

What Have We Learned?

Following are excerpts from a speech made by Frederick W. Taylor in 1911:*

> If any of you will get close to the average workman in this country—close enough to him so that he will talk to you as an intimate friend—he will tell you that in his particular trade if, we will say, each man were to turn out twice as much work as he is now doing, there could be but one result to follow: namely, that one-half the men in his trade would be thrown out of work.
>
> This doctrine is preached by almost every labor leader in the country and is taught by every workman to his children as they are growing up; and I repeat, as I said in the beginning, that it is our fault more than theirs that this fallacy prevails.
>
> While the labor leaders and the workmen themselves in season and out of season are pointing out the necessity of restriction of output, not one step are we taking to

counteract that fallacy; therefore, I say, the fault is ours and not theirs.

a. Do you think Taylor's position is equally applicable today? Be prepared to justify your answer.

The chairman of the American Productivity Center in Houston, C. Jackson Grayson, has warned that if management and labor cannot make their relationship less adversarial, "then we won't get the full, long-term kick in productivity that we desperately need."[†]

b. Looking at Taylor's and Grayson's remarks, which were made approximately 73 years apart, one has to wonder what we have learned. Many similar comparisons could be made. Why do you think managers don't seem to learn as much as they could from the past?

Scientific Management: Address and Discussions at the Conference on Scientific Management at the Amos Truck School of Administration and Finance (Norwood, Mass.: Plimpton Press, 1912), pp. 23–24.

[†]"The Revival of Productivity," *Business Week*, February 13, 1984, p. 100.

SKILL-BUILDING EXERCISE 2.2

The "Excellent Companies" Revisited

Within two years after *In Search of Excellence* was published, at least 14 of the "excellent" companies highlighted by Peters and Waterman had lost some of their luster. Peters and Waterman argue that these companies ran into trouble because they strayed from the principles that had been key to their earlier successes. The following companies were identified as having "stumbled" as early as 1984:

Atari Corporation	Fluor Corporation
Avon Products Inc.	Hewlett-Packard Co.
Caterpillar, Inc.	Levi Strauss & Co.
Chesebrough-Pond's Inc.	Revlon, Inc.

Delta Air Lines, Inc.	Texas Instruments, Inc.
Digital Equipment Co.	Tupperware
Eastman Kodak Co.	Walt Disney Co.

a.   Pick one of these companies and go to the library to research what happened to the company between 1980 and 1984. Specifically look at the company's revenues and profits for these years.

b.   Try to identify which of Peters and Waterman's eight characteristics might have been violated and thus hurt performance.

c.   Determine how the company has performed since 1984.

d.   How has the company dealt with the problems identified in *b* above?

CASE INCIDENT 2.1

Granddad's Company

J.R.V. Company, which manufactures industrial tools, was founded in 1905 by James R. Vail, Sr. Currently, James R. Vail, Jr., is the president of the company; his son Richard is executive vice president. James Jr. has run the company for the past 30 years in a fashion very similar to that of his father.

When the company was founded, James Sr. had been a big supporter of scientific management. He had organized the work very scientifically with the use of time and motion studies to determine the most efficient method of performing each job. As a result, most jobs at J.R.V. were highly specialized and utilized a high degree of division of labor. In addition, there was always a heavy emphasis on putting people in jobs that were best suited for them and then providing adequate training. Most employees are paid on a piece-rate incentive system, with the standards set by time and motion studies. James Jr. has largely continued to emphasize scientific management since he took over. All employees now receive two

weeks' paid vacation and company insurance. Also, employees are generally paid an average wage for their industry. The present J.R.V. building was constructed in 1920, but it has had several minor improvements, such as the addition of fluorescent lighting and an employees' lunchroom.

James Jr. is planning to retire in a few years. Recently he and Richard, his planned successor, have disagreed over the management of the company. Richard's main argument is that times have changed and time and motion studies, specialization, high division of labor, and other company practices are obsolete. James Jr. counters that J.R.V. has been successful under its present management philosophy for many years, and change would be "foolish."

Questions

1.   Do you agree with Richard? Why or why not?

2.   Are the principles of scientific management applicable in today's organization? Explain your answer.

CASE INCIDENT 2.2

Return to Scientific Management

Recently, a professor at State University was lecturing in a management development seminar on the topic of motivation. Each of the participants candidly discussed problems that existed in their respective organizations. Prob-

lem areas mentioned included absenteeism, turnover, and poor workmanship. The participants managed a variety of workers such as automobile assembly workers, clerical workers, computer operators, sanitation workers, and even some middle-level managers.

During the discussion, one of the participants made the following statement: "What we need to stop all of these problems is a little scientific management."

1. What do you think the person means?
2. Do you agree? Discuss.
3. Take one of the jobs in the above case and show how you could apply scientific management.

References and Additional Readings

[1]Daniel Wren, *The Evolution of Management Thought*, 2d ed. (New York: Ronald Press, 1979), p. 90.

[2]Ibid., p. 90.

[3]Alfred D. Chandler, Jr., "The Beginnings of 'Big Business' in American Industry," *Business History Review*, Spring 1959, p. 3.

[4]Harry Kelsey and David Wilderson, *The Evolution of Management Thought* (unpublished paper, Indiana University, Bloomington, IN, 1974), p. 7.

[5]Henry R. Towne, "The Engineer as Economist," *Transactions, ASME* 7 (1886), pp. 428–32.

[6]Frederick W. Taylor, "A Piece-Rate System," *Transactions, ASME* 16 (1895), pp. 856–83.

[7]Frederick W. Taylor, *Shop Management* (New York: Harper & Row, 1903); Frederick W. Taylor, *The Principles of Scientific Management* (New York: Harper & Row, 1911).

[8]*Scientific Management: Address and Discussions at the Conference on Scientific Management at the Amos Truck School of Administration and Finance* (Norwood, MA: Plimpton Press, 1912), pp. 32–35.

[9]John F. Mee, *Management Thought in a Dynamic Economy* (New York: New York University Press, 1963), p. 411.

[10]John F. Mee, *Seminar in Business Organization and Operation* (unpublished paper, Indiana University, Bloomington, IN, p. 5.

[11]Wren, *The Evolution of Management Thought*, pp. 136–40.

[12]Ibid., p. 188.

[13]Henry L. Gantt, *Organizing for Work* (New York: Harcourt Brace Jovanovich, 1919), p. 15.

[14]John F. Mee, "Management Teaching in Historical Perspective," *Southern Journal of Business*, May 1972, p. 21.

[15]For a detailed description of the Hawthorne studies, see Fritz G. Roethlisberger and William J. Dickson, *Management and the Worker* (Cambridge, MA: Harvard University Press, 1939).

[16]For example, see Alex Carey, "The Hawthorne Studies: A Radical Criticism," *American Sociological Review*, June 1967, pp. 403–16.

[17]Henry C. Metcalf and L. Urwick, eds., *Dynamic Administration: The Collected Papers of Mary Parker Follett* (New York: Harper & Row, 1940), p. 21.

[18]Chester I. Barnard, *The Functions of the Executive* (Cambridge, MA: Harvard University Press, 1938).

[19]Henry S. Dennison, *Organization Engineering* (New York: McGraw-Hill, 1931).

[20]Charles P. McCormick, *Multiple Management* (New York: Harper & Row, 1949).

[21]William B. Given, Jr., *Bottom Up Management* (New York: Harper & Row, 1949).

[22]Joseph Scanlon, "Enterprise for Everyone," *Fortune*, January 1950, pp. 41, 55–59; Wren, *The Evolution of Management Thought*, p. 330.

[23]Mee, *Management Thought*, p. 53.

[24]Oliver Sheldon, *The Philosophy of Management* (London: Sir Isaac Pitman & Sons, 1923).

[25]Ralph C. Davis, *The Principles of Business Organizations and Operations* (Columbus, OH: H. L. Hedrick, 1935), pp. 12–13.

[26]Harold Koontz, "The Management Theory Jungle," *Academy of Management Journal*, December 1961, pp. 174–88.

[27]*Webster's Collegiate Dictionary* (New York: Random House, 1991), p. 1356.

[28]Richard A. Johnson, Fremont E. Kast, and James E. Rosenzweig, *The Theory of Management Systems* (New York: McGraw-Hill, 1963), p. 3.

[29]William C. Ouchi, *Theory Z* (Reading, MA: Addison-Wesley, 1981).

[30]Thomas J. Peters and Robert H. Waterman, Jr., *In Search of Excellence* (New York: Harper & Row, 1982).

[31]For a criticism of *In Search of Excellence*, see Daniel T. Carroll, "A Disappointing Search for Excellence," *Harvard Business Review*, November–December 1983, pp. 78–88.

[32]Richard B. Chase and Nicholas J. Aquilano, *Production and Operations Management: A Life Cycle Approach*, 6th edition (Homewood, IL: Richard D. Irwin, 1992), pp. 186–87.

[33]Christopher Ferrell, "Industry Outlook," Business Week, January 9, 1995, p. 55.

[34]Joseph H. Boyett and Jimmie T. Boyett, Beyond Workplace 2000, Penguin Books, New York, 1995, pp. xiii–xiv.

3

Communication Skills

LEARNING OBJECTIVES

After studying this chapter, you should be able to:

1. Define communication.

2. Describe the interpersonal communication process.

3. Describe problems that could arise from conflicting or inappropriate assumptions made in interpersonal communication.

4. Define semantics and explain its role in interpersonal communication.

5. Define perception.

6. Explain how emotions may affect communication.

7. Explain the concept of feedback in communication.

8. Describe organizational communication.

9. Define downward communication systems.

10. Define upward communication systems.

11. Define and briefly discuss the E-mail process.

12. Describe the grapevine.

13. Discuss two factors that complicate communications in international business activities.

Chapter Preview

Consider the communications problems of today: information flow within the company and electronically linking the customer to the corporation. The Electronic Industries Association estimated that U.S. manufacturers would ship $64 billion worth of communications gear in 1995, a 24 percent gain over 1994. Interpersonal communication is fundamental to organizational communication, and networked communication is the logical extension. However, Howard Anderson of Yankee Group Research, Inc., warns that getting the most out of today's new communication network forms means giving up a certain amount of control.

Source: Adapted from Catherine Arnst, "The Networked Corporation," *Business Week,* June 26, 1995, pp. 86–89.

Communication is the act of transmitting information. Effective communication is an essential part of everything a manager does. Every function of management—planning, organizing, staffing, leading, and controlling—requires effective communication skills. For example, objectives set in the planning process must be communicated and explained to all employees. Assigning job duties and appraising an employee's job performance are carried out through communication. In fact, communication has been estimated to occupy between 50 and 90 percent of a manager's time.[1] Unfortunately, research has revealed that as much as 70 percent of all business communications fail to achieve their intended purpose.[2] Technology may help solve this problem. However, the technological aspects of communication within the modern corporation are among the biggest challenges the manager faces. Management Illustration 3.1 describes how some companies improve communication.

Communication in organizations can occur in many forms, ranging from face-to-face contact involving facial expressions and body movements to written communications in the form of memos, letters, and reports to networks in which people-to-people and people-to-equipment interactions take place. In general, communication in organizations can be examined in one of two basic perspectives: between individuals (interpersonal communication) and within the formal organizational structure (organizational communication). These two basic perspectives on communication are also interdependent because interpersonal communication is almost always part of organizational communication.

INTERPERSONAL COMMUNICATION

Effective communication between individuals, especially between a manager and subordinates, is critical to achieving organizational objectives and, as a result, to managing people effectively. Estimates vary, but it is generally agreed that since managers spend about 45 percent of their daily contact time with their staffs and subordinates, effective communication is critical to the wise and effective use of their time.

Interpersonal communication is an interactive process between individuals that involves sending and receiving verbal and nonverbal messages. The basic purpose of interpersonal communication is to transmit information so that the sender of the message is understood and understands the receiver. Figure 3.1 diagrams this dynamic and interactive process. An event or a condition generates information. The desire to share the information, or inform another person about it, creates the need to communicate. The sender then creates a message and communicates it both verbally and nonverbally. The receiver, in turn, perceives and interprets the message and (hopefully) creates a reply message as a response to it. This reply message may generate a response by the sender of the initial message, and the process continues in this fashion.

Often, however, many factors interfere and cause this process to fail. Some causes of interpersonal communication failure are conflicting or inappropriate assumptions, different interpretations of the meanings of words (semantics), differences in perception, emotions either preceding or during communication, poor listening habits, inadequate communication skills, insufficient feedback, and differences in the interpretations of nonverbal communications.

Conflicting or Inappropriate Assumptions

Have you ever thought you were being understood when you were really not? This is a common mistake made by couples, teachers, superiors, and parents. If one as-

Management Illustration 3.1
Building a Culture of Communication

Companies such as General Electric, Microsoft, British Airways, Intel, Hewlett-Packard, Coca-Cola, and Disney are among the most admired corporations in the world. They are in a league of their own and considered the "best of the best." How do merely successful corporations get to this level? The answer is by building communication into their corporate culture by promoting dialogue, feedback, interpretation and understanding.

Look at Intel, for example. Andrew Grove sits in a small cubicle much like everyone else at the company. One might be surprised to learn that Grove is the CEO of Intel which in 1995 had sales of over $11.5 billion. His cubicle among the lower level employees represents the open, proactive culture that permeates the corporation. Grove believes that his presence in the cubicle eliminates barriers between himself and his staff and has been critical in the company's success.

Grove is also interested in communication with his customers. The company has installed a perma-

nent hot line to field questions regarding Pentium. This hot line bridges the gap between consumer and manufacturer by having engineers readily available to answer questions.

GE is another example of a communications-oriented organization. CEO Jack Welch has established an Answer Center in Louisville, Kentucky that responds to consumer questions 24 hours a day, 365 days a year. The center answers approximately 15,000 calls per day through a database that holds over 650,000 responses to all types of inquiries. Welch believes that this type of response system clearly opens the lines of communication between the company and the consumer.

Sources: "Building a world-class organization," *Communication World* June/July, 1998, pp. 41–43; "The Education of Andrew Grove," *Business Week* Jan. 16, 1995, pp. 60–62.

For more information about Intel visit their Web site at: www.intel.com. For more information about GE visit their Web site at www.ge.com.

FIGURE 3.1   Interpersonal Communication Process

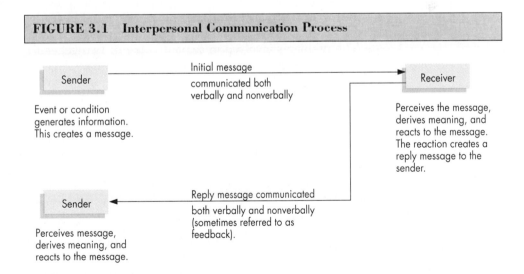

sumes that communication is flowing as intended, one tends to move on with the dialog without allowing feedback to indicate whether clarity of expression and communication has been achieved. Good managers and salespeople always seek verbal or nonverbal feedback, before continuing the communication process. Remember that interpretation of meaning can always be a problem when assumptions are

---

FIGURE 3.2   Interpretations of the Word *Fix*

An Englishman visits America and is completely awed by the many ways we use the word *fix*. For example:

1. His host asks him how he'd like his drink fixed. He meant *mixed*.

2. As he prepares to leave, he discovers he has a flat tire and calls a repairperson, who says he'll fix it immediately. He means *repair*.

3. On the way home, he is given a ticket for speeding. He calls his host, who says, "Don't worry, I'll fix it." He means *nullify*.

4. At the office the next day, he comments on the cost of living in America, and one of his colleagues says, "It's hard to make ends meet on a fixed income." She means *steady* or *unchanging*.

5. He has an argument with a co-worker. The latter says, "I'll fix you." He means *seek revenge*.

6. A cohort remarks that she is in a fix. She means *condition* or *situation*.

---

involved. Messages such as "Stop," "Do this right now," and "Please don't" never seem to have the same meanings to children that the adult sender intended. Sound communication usually flows from ensuring that the sender and the receiver see and understand assumptions in the same way.

Semantics

semantics   The science or study of the meanings of words and symbols.

Semantics is the science or study of the meanings of words and symbols. Words themselves have no real meaning. They have meaning only in terms of people's reactions to them. A word may mean very different things to different people, depending on how it is used. In addition, a word may be interpreted differently based on the facial expressions, hand gestures, and voice inflections used.

The problems involved in semantics are of two general types. Some words and phrases invite multiple interpretations. For example, Figure 3.2 shows different interpretations of the word *fix*. Another problem is that groups of people in specific situations often develop their own technical language, which outsiders may or may not understand. For example, physicians, government workers, and military employees are often guilty of using acronyms and abbreviations that only they understand.

Words are the most common form of interpersonal communication. Because of the real possibility of misinterpretation, words must be carefully chosen and clearly defined for effective communication.

Perception

perception   The mental and sensory processes an individual uses in interpreting information received.

Perception deals with the mental and sensory processes an individual uses in interpreting information she or he receives. Since each individual's perception is unique, people often perceive the same situation in different ways.

Perception begins when the sense organs receive a stimulus. The stimulus is the information received, whether it is conveyed in writing, verbally, nonverbally, or in another way. The sense organs respond to, shape, and organize the information received. When this information reaches the brain, it is further organized and interpreted, resulting in perception. Different people perceive the same information differently because no two people have the same personal experiences, memories,

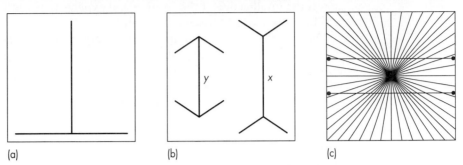

FIGURE 3.3   Illustrations of Perceptual Distortion

(a)   (b)   (c)

Source: Adapted from Jonathan L. Freedman, *Introductory Psychology*, 2d ed. (Reading, MA: Addison-Wesley, 1982), p. 58.

likes, and dislikes. In addition, the phenomenon of selective perception often distorts the intended message: People tend to listen to only part of the message, blocking out the rest for any number of reasons.

Figure 3.3 illustrates perceptual distortion. Look at the figure and answer the following questions:

1. Is the vertical line longer than the horizontal line in Figure 3.3(a)?
2. Is line *x* or *y* longer in Figure 3.3(b)?
3. Are the two horizontal lines in Figure 3.3(c) bowed or parallel?

Using a ruler, you can see that the vertical and horizontal lines in 3.3(a) are equal and that the *x* and *y* lines in 3.3(b) are also equal. The horizontal lines in 3.3(c) are also parallel. These examples illustrate the difference between the real world and the perceived world. If differences in perception exist in viewing physical objects, more subtle forms of communication such as facial expressions and hand gestures leave much room for perceptional differences.

Emotions Either Preceding or During Communication

Just as perception affects our cognitive processes during communication, emotions affect our disposition to send and receive the communication. Anger, joy, fear, sorrow, disgust, or panic (to mention only a few emotions) can all affect the way we send or receive messages. Emotional disposition is like the stage on which the communication piece plays its part: The stage can be perfectly prepared or in total disarray. The setting for the communication piece is obviously very important. Communications during periods of high emotion usually have difficulty succeeding. Therefore, managers with good communication skills strive to manage the emotional as well as the physical communication environment.

The Importance of Listening

Communication depends on the ability not only to send but also to receive messages. Hence the ability to listen effectively greatly enhances the communication process. Tests indicate that immediately after listening to a 10-minute oral presentation, the average listener has heard, comprehended, accurately evaluated, and retained about half of what was said. Within 48 hours, the effectiveness level drops another 50 percent to 25 percent. By the end of a week, that level goes down to about 10 percent or less.[3]

Effective listening is not natural to most people. How well a person listens very much depends on the listener's attitude toward the speaker. The listener who respects the intelligence of the speaker and expects to profit from the communication will be more likely to listen effectively.

Daydreaming and preoccupation with other matters also often keep individuals from listening to what a speaker is saying. It has been suggested that at any given point in a college lecture, 20 percent of both men and women are thinking about sex, 60 percent are off on some mental trip of their own, and only the remaining 20 percent are concentrating on the professor.[4]

Other barriers to effective listening include mentally arguing with points the speaker is making before he or she is finished, getting impatient with listening and preferring active involvement by talking, lack of interest in the message, and other negative reactions toward the speaker.

COMMUNICATION SKILLS

Culture, education, verbal skills, social class, and training can all affect the way a person communicates. The ability to feel confident in conversations, in presentations, or in speaking to a group are all skills that can be taught. Are you a better talker or a better listener? Actually, both skills are very important. One of the first tasks in improving an organization's communication effectiveness is to appraise the skills of the members of the organization. This assessment should provide direction on what type of training might be necessary to advance all members' communication skills.

Feedback

Effective communication is a two-way process. Information must flow back and forth between sender and receiver. The flow from the receiver to the sender is called **feedback.** It informs the sender whether the receiver has received the correct message; it also lets the receiver know if he or she has received the correct message. For example, asking a person if she or he understands a message often puts the person on the defensive and can result in limited feedback. Instead of asking if a person understands a message, it is much better to request that the receiver explain what he or she has heard.

feedback   The flow of information from the receiver to the sender.

In an experiment designed to show the importance of feedback in the communication process, one person was asked to verbally describe to a group of people the layout of the rectangles shown in Figure 3.4. The group members were required to draw the layout based on the verbal description. The group received only a verbal description of the layout. The experiment was conducted in two ways. First, the group was not allowed to ask questions while the layout was being described, and the person describing the layout was hidden from view so the group could not see the person's facial expressions or other nonverbal communications. Thus, no feedback was present. In the second trial, the group was allowed to ask questions as the layout was being described, and the speaker was openly facing the group. Thus, feedback was present. The results showed the layout was described more quickly to the group when no feedback was allowed. However, feedback greatly improved the accuracy and the group's degree of confidence in the accuracy of their drawings.

In summary, feedback in the communication process takes more time but improves the quality of communication.

FIGURE 3.4   Rectangles in Communication Experiment

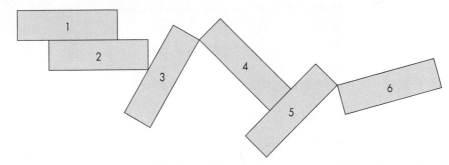

Source: Reprinted from *Managerial Psychology* by Harold J. Leavitt by permission of The University of Chicago Press © 1972 by (copyright holder).

Nonverbal Communication

People have a great capacity to convey meaning through nonverbal means of expression. One form of nonverbal communication, called **paralanguage,** includes the pitch, tempo, loudness, and hesitations in the verbal communication. People also use a variety of gestures in nonverbal communication. In America, for example, one can raise an eyebrow to indicate disapproval, interest, concern, or attention. In Japan, however, that raised eyebrow would be considered an obscene gesture.

paralanguage   Includes the pitch, tempo, loudness, and hesitations in verbal communication.

People also communicate nonverbally by how close they stand to each other. Body posture and eye contact also communicate messages. For example, lack of eye contact can communicate indifference or shyness.

In summary, nonverbal communication is an important supplement to verbal communication and sometimes can even change the meaning of verbal communication. Nonverbal communication is an effective way to communicate emotions. When combined with verbal communication, it gives managers powerful tools for transmitting information to employees.

ORGANIZATIONAL COMMUNICATION SYSTEMS

Organizational communication occurs within the formal organizational structure. In general, organizational communication systems are downward, upward, and lateral (horizontal). Overlapping these three formal systems is the informal communication system called the *grapevine.* Management Illustration 3.2 shows the communication system and basic key elements of the newly emerging horizontal corporation.

Downward Communication Systems

Traditional views of the communication processes in organizations have been dominated by **downward communication** systems. Such systems transmit information from higher to lower levels of the organization. The chain of command determines the flow of downward information. Policy manuals, bulletins,

downward communication   System that transmits information from higher to lower levels of the organization.

FIGURE 3.5   Techniques Used in Upward Communication

Informal inquiries or discussions with employees	Counseling
Exit interviews	Formal meetings with employees
Discussions with first-line supervisors	Suggestion system
Grievance or complaint procedures	Formal attitude surveys
Grapevine	Question-and-answer column in employee publication
Union representatives	Gripe boxes
Hotline system	

organizational magazines, job descriptions, and directives are all examples of downward communications.

Often downward communication systems are assumed to be better than studies indicate they actually are. For example, research has reported that the average employee understands little of the material in employee handbooks and manuals.[5]

One important choice that must be made in such systems is the medium to use. Written communication is less likely to be filtered and provides an official record, but it does not enable immediate feedback. Oral communication provides no record and is subject to filtering, but it does facilitate immediate feedback.

Upward Communication Systems

upward communication   System that transmits information from the lower levels of the organization to the top.

Upward communication systems transmit information from the lower levels of the organization to the top. An upward communication system should help managers judge the effectiveness of their downward communications and enable them to learn about organizational problems. Four major areas of information should be communicated from below: (1) the activities of subordinates in terms of their achievements, progress, and plans; (2) unresolved work problems in which subordinates may need help currently or in the future; (3) suggestions or ideas for improvements within work groups or the organization as a whole; and (4) subordinates' feelings about their jobs, associates, and the organization. Figure 3.5 lists several forms of upward communication.

The key to effective upward communication systems appears to be a manager-employee relationship in which employees believe they will not be penalized for candor. Employees often conceal or distort their real feelings, problems, opinions, and beliefs because they fear disclosure may bring on punishment. Trust in one's superior appears to be a key variable in effective upward communication systems.

Ideally, the organizational structure should provide for both upward and downward communication systems. Communication should flow in both directions through the formal organizational structure. Unfortunately, upward communication does not flow as freely as downward communication.

Some deterrents to effective upward communication include the following:

1. Management fails to respond when subordinates bring up information or problems. Failure to respond will ultimately result in no communication.
2. Managers tend to be defensive about less than perfect actions. When employees sense this defensiveness, they will withhold information.

Management Illustration 3.2

Impact of E-mail

E-mail has become a powerful tool in advancing communication throughout the organization. Perhaps the greatest advantage of E-mail is its convenience. E-mail also tends to make companies less bureaucratic, less formal and hierarchial, and more open to creative ideas and feedback from all levels of employees.

An employee at Microsoft recently said, "the phone never rings." About 99 percent of intracompany communications take place through E-mail. Some critics contend that E-mail discourages face-to-face communications, but employees at Microsoft believe that they communicate more effectively through the continual stream of E-mails that they receive every day.

Advocates of E-mail claim that this form of communication encourages creativity and has the ability to bypass the normal business hierarchy. In his 1996 book, *Only the Paranoid Survive*, Intel chief Andrew Grove credited E-mail with allowing him to detect problem areas early. He said, "I witness more arguments, I hear more business gossip, sometimes from people I have never met, than I ever did when I could walk the halls of the one building that housed all Intel employees."

Sources: "Why E-mail is Dangerous?" *Forbes* July 27, 1998, p. 94; "The Big Issue," *Forbes ASAP* December 2, 1996, p. 113. For more articles on business and business communication visit Forbes at its Web site: www.forbes.com.

3. The manager's attitude plays a critical role in the upward communication process. If the manager is truly concerned and really listens, upward communication improves.

4. Physical barriers can also inhibit the upward communication process. Separating a manager from his or her employees creates communication problems.

5. Time lags between the communication and the action can inhibit upward communication. If it takes months for the various levels of management to approve an employee's suggestion, upward communication is hindered.

6. The structure of the organization can hinder effective communication. Reporting processes and lines of authority may have been constructed with some objective other than efficient and effective communication.

7. The status and power of individuals in the communication network must be carefully considered. Accepting suggestions from a subordinate is always difficult for the ego-oriented manager.

Horizontal or Lateral Communication

The upward and downward communication systems generally follow the formal chain of command within the organization. However, greater size and complexity increase the need for communication across the lines of the formal chain of command.

horizontal or lateral communication
Communication across the lines of the formal chain of command.

This is referred to as **horizontal or lateral communication.** Horizontal communication is essential to coordination among departments and to the proper functioning of the upward and downward communication systems.

Specialized departments such as engineering, marketing research, and quality control perform functions such as gathering data, issuing reports, preparing directives, coordinating activities, and advising higher levels of management. Such specialized departments are generally quite active in horizontal communication because their activities influence several chains of command rather than one. Departments that depend on one another for achieving their respective goals also need horizontal communication.

Especially valuable to horizontal communication in today's organizations is the use of electronic mail systems, or E-mail, provided by networked and on-line systems. The E-mail system provides for high-speed exchange of written messages through the use of computerized text processing and computer-oriented communication networks. The primary advantages of this system are that it saves time, eliminates wasted effort (such as unanswered or repeat phone calls), provides written records (if necessary) of communications without the formality of memos, and enables communication among individuals who might not communicate otherwise. Management Illustration 3.2 describes the impact of E-mail on communication.

The Grapevine

Many informal paths of communication also exist in organizations. These informal channels are generally referred to as the **grapevine.** During the Civil War, intelligence telegraph lines hung loosely

grapevine   Informal channels of communication.

from tree to tree and looked like grapevines. Messages sent over these lines were often garbled; thus, any rumor was said to be "from the grapevine."[6] Grapevines develop within organizations when employees share common hobbies, home towns, lunch breaks, family ties, and social relationships. The grapevine always exists within the formal organizational structure. However, it does not follow the organizational hierarchy; it may go from secretary to vice president or from engineer to clerk. The grapevine is not limited to nonmanagement personnel; it also operates among managers and professional personnel.

The grapevine generally has a poor reputation because it is regarded as the primary source of distorted messages and rumors. However, management must recognize that the grapevine is often accurate. Management must also recognize that information in the grapevine travels more rapidly than information in the formal channels of communication.[7] Finally, management must recognize the resilience of the grapevine. No matter how much effort is spent improving the formal channels of communication, grapevines will always exist.

Because the grapevine is inevitable, management should use it to complement formal channels of communication. In utilizing the grapevine, honesty is always the best policy. Rumors and distorted messages will persist, but honest disclaimers by management will stop the spread of inaccurate information.

COMMUNICATION IN INTERNATIONAL BUSINESS ACTIVITIES

Communication in international business activities becomes more complicated in both the verbal and nonverbal communication processes. In verbal communication, the obvious problem of dealing with different languages exists. More than 3,000 languages are spoken, and about 100 of these are official languages of nations. English is the leading international language, and its leadership continues to grow. However, as anyone who has studied a foreign language knows, verbally communicating with a person in a another language complicates the communication process.

The nonverbal communication process is even more complicated. Cultural differences play a significant role in nonverbal communication. For example, in the United States, people tend to place themselves about three feet apart when standing and talking. However, in the Middle East, individuals are likely to stand only a foot or so apart while conversing. This closeness obviously could intimidate an American manager.

There are no simple answers to the problems in communicating in international business activities. However, there are two things the manager should do: (1) learn the culture of the people with whom he or she communicates and (2) write and speak clearly and simply. Most people will have learned English in school and will not understand jargon or slang. As expansion into international business continues, these simple rules will become increasingly important.[8]

Summary

1. *Define Communication.* Communication is the act of transmitting information.

2. *Describe the Interpersonal Communication Process.* Interpersonal communication occurs between individuals. It is an interactive process that involves a person's effort to attain meaning and respond to it. It involves sending and receiving verbal and nonverbal messages.

3. *Describe Problems That Could Arise from Conflicting or Inappropriate Assumptions Made in Interpersonal Communication.* Misunderstandings can occur when a speaker thinks he or she was being clear or was understood. Questions that go unanswered, points that are misunderstood, and meanings that are misinterpreted are examples of potential problems.

4. *Define Semantics and Explain Its Role in Interpersonal Communication.* Semantics is the science or study of the meanings of words and symbols. Because of the possibility of misinterpretation, words must be carefully chosen and clearly defined to enable effective communication.

5. *Define Perception.* Perception deals with the mental and sensory processes an individual uses in interpreting information received.

6. *Explain How Emotions May Affect Communication.* Emotions affect one's disposition to send and receive communication. Anger, joy, fear, sorrow, disgust, or panic can all affect the way one sends and receives messages. Communications during periods of high emotion are often subject to distortion.

7. *Explain the Concept of Feedback in Communication.* Feedback is the flow of information from the receiver to the sender. For communication to be effective, information must flow back and forth between sender and receiver.

8. *Describe Organizational Communication.* Organizational communication occurs within the formal organizational structure. In general, organizational communication systems are downward, upward, and horizontal.

9. *Define Downward Communication Systems.* Downward communication systems transmit information from higher to lower levels of the organization. The chain of command determines the flow of downward information. Policy manuals, bulletins, organizational magazines, job descriptions, and directives are all examples of downward communications.

10. *Define Upward Communication Systems.* Upward communication systems transmit information from the lower levels of the organization to the top. Four major areas of information should be communicated from below: the activities of subordinates in terms of their achievements, progress, and plans; unresolved work problems in which subordinates may need help currently or in the future; suggestions or ideas for improvements within work groups or the organization as a whole; and subordinates' feelings about their jobs, their associates, and the organization.

11. *Define and Briefly Discuss the E-mail Process.* The electronic mail, or E-mail, system provides for high-speed exchange of written messages through the use of computerized text processing and computer-oriented communication networks.

12. *Describe the Grapevine.* The grapevine consists of the informal channels of communication that develop within the organization as a result of common hobbies, home towns, lunch breaks, family ties, and social relationships among employees.

13. *Discuss Two Factors That Complicate Communications in International Business Activities.* Communicating in a foreign language complicates the communication process. Cultural differences exhibited through nonverbal communications are also complicating factors.

Preview Analysis

1. What are some communication problems in today's organizations?

2. What kind of growth is occurring in communication technology?

Review Questions

1. What is communication?

2. Define interpersonal communication.

3. Give an illustration of a conflicting assumption.

4. What is semantics?

5. What is perception, and what role does it play in communication?

6. How should one deal with emotions in communication?

7. What is feedback, and how does it affect the communication process?

8. Give some suggestions for improving listening habits.

9. Explain the importance of nonverbal communication in interpersonal communication.

10. Describe the following organizational communication systems:
    a. Downward communication system.
    b. Upward communication system.
    c. Horizontal or lateral communication system.
    d. E-mail communication system.
    e. Grapevine.

11. Describe two factors that complicate communications in international business.

Skill-Building Questions

1. Describe some ways the grapevine can be used effectively in organizations.

2. Explain why many managers frequently raise the following question: "Why didn't you do what I told you to do?"

3. Discuss the following statement: "Meanings are in people, not words."

4. "Watch what we do, not what we say." Is this a good practice in organizations? Explain.

5. Poor communication of the organization's objectives is often given as the reason for low organizational performance. Do you think this is usually a valid explanation? Why or why not?

6. What steps can be taken to form a horizontal corporation with its accompanying communications system?

SKILL-BUILDING EXERCISE 3.1

Perception Test

Take a maximum of 10 minutes to complete the following test.

1. In 1963, if you went to bed at 8 o'clock PM and set the alarm to get up at 9 o'clock the next morning, how many hours of sleep would you get?

2. If you have only one match and enter a room in which there is a kerosene lamp, an oil stove, and a wood-burning stove, which would you light first?

3. Some months have 30 days; some have 31. How many have 28 days?

4. If a doctor gave you three pills and told you to take one every half-hour, how long would they last?

5. A man builds a house with four sides, and it is rectangular in shape. Each side has a southern exposure. A big bear comes wandering by. What color is the bear?

6. I have in my hand two U.S. coins that total 55 cents in value. One is not a nickel. Please bear that in mind. What are the two coins?

7. Divide 30 by 1/2 and add 10. What is the answer?

8. Take two apples from three apples, and what do you have?

9. An archaeologist found some gold coins dated 34 BC. How old are they?

10. How many animals of each species did Moses take aboard the ark with him?

SKILL-BUILDING EXERCISE 3.2

We Americans supposedly speak the English language. However, anyone who has ever visited England knows that the English often use different words and phrases than we do. Can you identify what the English words or phrases in the left column below would be if spoken by an American?

_____ Chemist
_____ phone engaged
_____ ring-up
_____ round up
_____ wines and spirits
_____ chipped potatoes
_____ give way
_____ to let
_____ ta!
_____ its mommy's go
_____ half five
_____ mind your step
_____ a bit dear

a. Elevator
b. Mailbox
c. Orchestra Seat
d. Line
e. Can
f. Subway
g. Hood
h. Newsstand
i. Taxes
j. Suspenders
k. Aisle
l. Apartment
m. Janitor

_____ way out
_____ Bonnet
_____ Stall
_____ Flat
_____ Kiosk
_____ Ironmonger
_____ Pillar Box
_____ Porter
_____ Tin

_____ Lift
_____ Queue
_____ Lorry
_____ Rates
_____ Braces
_____ Gangway
_____ Underground

n. Hardware dealer
o. Truck
p. exit
q. drugstore
r. busy
s. too expensive
t. watch your step
u. call
v. go halfway around circle and strait up
w. liquor store
x. french fries
y. yield
z. for rent
aa. bid adieu
bb. its mommy's turn
cc. five thirty

CASE INCIDENT 3.1

Who Calls the Shots?

The financial reports for the last quarter of operations for Brighton Cabinet Company were just received by the company's president, John Branner. After looking over the reports, John decided the purchasing department was paying too much for the company's raw materials, which include plywood, paneling, and flakeboard. He immediately called Joe Scott, vice president of manufacturing, and informed him of the decision. Exhibit 1 gives a partial organizational chart for Brighton Cabinet Company.

Joe called Bill Sloane, the supervisor of purchasing, and said, "Mr. Branner is upset over the cost figures for raw materials last quarter. You were well above budget. He wants them brought down this quarter!"

As Bill hung up the phone, he asked himself who figured out the budget for his department and if they realized plywood had gone up from $6.05 to $6.75 a sheet. Bill had been instructed to cut costs, and he was determined to do so. Two days later, Bill found a supplier who would sell Brighton plywood for $5.95 a sheet. He ordered a two-week supply.

On delivery, Bill's suspicions were confirmed. The plywood was of a poorer quality, but it would work. Bill decided to continue to buy the less expensive plywood.

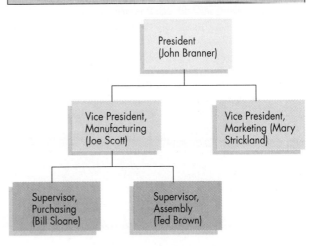

EXHIBIT 1   Partial Organization chart for Brighton Cabinet Company

A month later, Bill was approached by Ted Brown, supervisor of the assembly department, who asked, "Bill, what's with this plywood? All of a sudden, we've been having a lot of it split on us while trying to nail and staple the pieces together." Bill replied, "Well, Ted, Mr. Branner sent orders down for me to cut costs. I don't know how else to do it other than purchasing the lower-grade plywood. It was the only way out." Things were left as they were, and the quarter ended.

The financial reports for the quarter showed a drop in sales and profits. According to forecasts and trends of previous years, the profits and sales should have been higher. John Branner immediately called Mary Strickland, vice president of marketing, to his office and demanded an explanation. Mary explained, "It seems that we have lost a couple of major builders as customers. They seem to think that our competitors have something better to offer. I have investigated the situation and have found that our cabinets are splitting more on installation because we are using a lower-grade plywood now. I talked to Joe Scott. He told me you had ordered him to cut costs, and the purchase of the lower grade was one of the few ways that costs could be reduced."

John immediately ordered Joe to begin purchasing plywood of the necessary quality. Joe then informed Bill. Later that day, Bill asked Joe what should be done with the three-week supply of the lower-grade plywood. "That's your problem," Joe snapped. Apparently, he had gotten a good chewing out from Branner.

After making several calls, Bill decided the only good offer for the plywood was made by the company that sold it to Brighton. But it would pay only 60 percent of what it cost Brighton. Bill agreed to the price, wanting to get rid of it to make room for the new supplies that would be coming in.

Three days later, Bill was called into Joe's office. Joe asked, "Bill, who gave you permission to sell that plywood at that price?" "No one," Bill replied. "It was my decision. It was the best deal I could find, and I needed to get it out to make room for the new supplies coming in."

"Well, Bill, with decisions like that, this company won't last very long," Joe commented. "You should have used up the other plywood a little at a time by mixing it with the higher-grade plywood. Don't let this happen again!"

Questions

1. How did this problem begin, and how could it have been avoided?

2. Describe the communication failures that occurred in this case.

3. Is Bill really responsible? Who else, if anyone, is responsible?

4. Comment on Joe Scott's talk with Bill at the end of the case.

References and Additional Readings

[1]Henry Mintzberg, *The Nature of Managerial Work* (New York: Harper & Row, 1973), p. 38.

[2]Ralph W. Weber and Gloria E. Terry, *Behavioral Insights for Supervisors* (Englewood Cliffs, NJ: Prentice Hall, 1975), p. 138.

[3]Roger Ailes, *You Are the Message* (Homewood, IL: Dow Jones-Irwin, 1988), p. 47.

[4]David R. Hampton, Charles E. Sumner, and Ross A. Webber, *Organizational Behavior and the Practice of Management*, 4th ed. (Glenview, IL: Scott, Foresman, 1978), p. 117.

[5]See L. McCallister, "Predicted Employee Compliance to Downward Communication," *Journal of Business Communication*, Winter 1983, pp. 67–79.

[6]Keith Davis and John W. Newstrom, *Human Behavior at Work: Organizational Behavior* (New York: McGraw-Hill, 1985), p. 315.

[7]For additional information, see Jitendra Mishra, "Managing the Grapevine," *Public Personnel Management*, Summer 1990, pp. 213–28.

[8]Also see Ronald E. Dulek, John S. Fielden, and John S. Hill, "International Communication: An Executive Primer," *Business Horizons*, January–February 1991, pp. 20–25.

4

Decision-Making Skills

§⤵

LEARNING OBJECTIVES

After studying this chapter, you should be able to:

1. Explain the difference between decision making and problem solving.

2. Distinguish between programmed and nonprogrammed decisions.

3. Explain the intuitive approach to decision making.

4. Discuss two rational approaches to decision making.

5. List the different conditions under which managers make decisions.

6. Explain the role values play in making decisions.

7. Summarize the positive and negative aspects of group decision making.

8. Define creativity and innovation and outline the basic stages in the creative process.

9. Identify several specific tools and techniques that can be used to foster creative decisions.

10. List the six stages in creative decision making.

Chapter Preview

Dynamic companies and the managers who run them always seem to make great decisions at precisely the proper time. All great companies seem to have the following decision-making characteristics in common: They accept change, listen to customers, decentralize authority, hire carefully, teach continuously, and control costs. They don't do just one of these things right; they do all of them right!

To James Olson, Video Communications Division manager at Hewlett-Packard, May of 1992 looked like a scene from *Mission Impossible*. He was given the task of readying his microwave test gear division to move into the hot field of digital video. He had 11 months to get his engineers to develop a suite of products, including computers to send movies to homes, and get them to market. He accomplished this task with amazing skill. According to Olson, "We transformed ourselves from gearheads to gladiators."

Hewlett-Packard is now a leader in the field. Decisive action and a customer focus were the keys to the transformation that has competitors wondering what hit them. New-product development used to take six years, but now takes less than nine months. In addition, Olson has his team in close contact with customers, simplifying manufacturing processes and using outsourcing to speed up product development. In today's world, pleasing the marketplace and a new, creative view of decision making take precedence over tradition.

Source: Adapted from Robert D. Hof, "Go-Go Goliaths (Hewlett-Packard)," *Business Week*, February 13, 1995, pp. 66–67.

Some authors use the term *decision maker* to mean *manager.* However, although managers are decision makers, not all decision makers are managers. For example, a person who sorts fruit or vegetables is required to make decisions, but not as a manager. However, all managers, regardless of their positions in the organization, must make decisions in the pursuit of organizational goals. In fact, decision making pervades all of the basic management functions: planning, organizing, staffing, leading, and controlling. Although each of these functions requires different types of decisions, all of them require decisions. Thus, to be a good planner, organizer, staffer, leader, and controller, a manager must first be a good decision maker.

decision process   Process that involves three stages: intelligence, design, and choice. Intelligence is searching the environment for conditions requiring a decision. Design is inventing, developing, and analyzing possible courses of action. Choice is the actual selection of a course of action.

Herbert Simon, a Nobel prize winner, has described the manager's **decision process** in three stages: (1) intelligence, (2) design, and (3) choice.[1] The intelligence stage involves searching the environment for conditions requiring a decision. The design stage entails inventing, developing, and analyzing possible courses of action. Choice, the final stage, refers to the actual selection of a course of action.

The decision process stages show the difference between management and nonmanagement decisions. Nonmanagement decisions are concentrated in the last (choice) stage. The fruit/vegetable sorter has to make a choice regarding only the size or quality of the goods. Management decisions place greater emphasis on the intelligence and design stages. If the decision-making process is viewed as only the choice stage, managers spend very little time making decisions. If, however, the decision-making process is viewed as not only the actual choice but also the intelligence and design work needed to make the choice, managers spend most of their time making decisions.

DECISION MAKING VERSUS PROBLEM SOLVING

The terms *decision making* and *problem solving* are often confused and therefore need to be clarified. As indicated earlier, **decision making,** in its narrowest sense, is the process of choosing from among various alternatives. A *problem* is any deviation from some standard or desired level of performance. **Problem solving,** then, is the process of determining the appropriate responses or actions necessary to alleviate a problem. Problem solving necessarily involves decision making, since all problems can be attacked in numerous ways and the problem solver must decide which way is best. On the other hand, not all decisions involve problems (such as the person sorting fruit and vegetables). However, from a practical perspective, almost all managerial decisions do involve solving or at least avoiding problems.

decision making   In its narrowest sense, the process of choosing from among various alternatives.
problem solving   Process of determining the appropriate responses or actions necessary to alleviate a problem.

PROGRAMMED VERSUS NONPROGRAMMED DECISIONS

Decisions are often classified as programmed or nonprogrammed. **Programmed decisions** are reached by an established or systematic procedure. Normally, the decision maker knows the situation in a programmable decision. Routine, repetitive decisions usually fall into this category. Managerial decisions covered by organizational policies, procedures, and rules are programmed in that established guidelines must be followed in arriving at the decision.

programmed decisions   Decisions that are reached by following an established or systematic procedure.
nonprogrammed decisions   Decisions that have little or no precedent; they are relatively unstructured and generally require a creative approach by the decision maker.

Nonprogrammed decisions have little or no precedent. They are relatively unstructured and generally require a more creative approach by the decision maker; the decision maker must develop the procedure to be used. Generally, nonprogrammed decisions are more difficult to make than programmed decisions. Deciding on a new product, a new piece of equipment, and next year's goals are all nonprogrammed decisions.

DECISION MAKING WITH COMPUTERS

With the continuing increase in technology, computers are being used more and more to help managers make decisions. The development of artificial intelligence and related software has reached the point where computers can not only provide managers with data to help make decisions, but the computers themselves can actually execute certain managerial decisions. Chapter 5 discusses at some depth the role that computers currently play in helping managers make decisions. This chapter focuses on the non-computerized approaches that managers use to make decisions.

THE INTUITIVE APPROACH TO DECISION MAKING

When managers make decisions solely on hunches and intuition (the **intuitive approach**), they are practicing management as though it were wholly an art based only on feelings. While intuition and other forms of judgment do play a role in many decision situations, problems can occur when managers ignore available facts and rely only on feelings. When this happens, managers sometimes become so emotionally attached to certain positions that almost nothing will change their minds. They develop the "don't bother me with the facts—my mind is made up" attitude. George Odiorne isolated the following emotional attachments that can hurt decision makers:

intuitive approach   Approach used when managers make decisions based largely on hunches and intuition.

1. Fastening on unsubstantiated facts and sticking with them.
2. Being attracted to scandalous issues and heightening their significance.
3. Pressing every fact into a moral pattern.
4. Overlooking everything except what is immediately useful.
5. Having an affinity for romantic stories and finding such information more significant than any other kind, including hard evidence.[2]

Such emotional attachments can be very real and can lead to poor decisions. They most often affect managers or decision makers who are "living in the past" and either will not or cannot modernize their thinking. An example is the manager who insists on making decisions just as the founder of the company did 40 years ago.

Odiorne offers two suggestions for managers and decision makers engulfed by emotional attachments.[3] First, become aware of biases and allow for them. Undiscovered biases do the most damage. Second, seek independent opinions. It is always advisable to ask the opinion of some person who has no vested interest in the decision. Intuition does play a role in decision making. The key is to not ignore facts when they are available. "Good companies not only can learn. They've also learned to forget," says Professor C. K. Prahalad of the University of Michigan in his recent coauthored book *Competing for the Future.*[4]

RATIONAL APPROACHES TO DECISION MAKING

Approaches to decision making that attempt to evaluate factual information through the use of some type of deductive reasoning are referred to as *rational approaches*. The following sections discuss two types of rational approaches.

The Optimizing Approach

The physical sciences have provided a rational approach to decision making that can be adapted to management problems. The **optimizing approach** (sometimes called the *rational* or *scientific approach*) to decision making includes the following steps:

optimizing approach   Includes the following steps: recognize the need for a decision; establish, rank, and weigh criteria; gather available information and data; identify possible alternatives; evaluate each alternative with respect to all criteria; and select the best alternative.

1. Recognize the need for a decision.
2. Establish, rank, and weigh the decision criteria.
3. Gather available information and data.
4. Identify possible alternatives.
5. Evaluate each alternative with respect to all criteria.
6. Select the best alternative.

Once the need to make the decision is known, criteria must be set for expected results of the decision. These criteria should then be ranked and weighed according to their relative importance.

Next, factual data relating to the decision should be collected. After that, all alternatives that meet the criteria are identified. Each is then evaluated with respect to all criteria. The final decision is based on the alternative that best meets the criteria.

Limitations of the Optimizing Approach   The optimizing approach to decision making is an improvement over the intuitive approach, but it is not without its problems and limitations. The optimizing approach is based on the concept of "economic man." This concept postulates that people behave rationally and their behavior is based on the following assumptions:

1. People have clearly defined criteria, and the relative weights they assign to these criteria are stable.
2. People have knowledge of all relevant alternatives.
3. People have the ability to evaluate each alternative with respect to all the criteria and arrive at an overall rating for each alternative.
4. People have the self-discipline to choose the alternative that rates the highest (they will not manipulate the system).

Consider the following difficulties with the above approach. First, these assumptions are often unrealistic; decision makers do not always have clearly defined criteria for making decisions. Second, many decisions are based on limited knowledge of the possible alternatives; even when information is available, it is usually less than perfect. Third, there is always a temptation to manipulate or ignore the gathered information and choose a favored (but not necessarily the best) alternative.

Due to the limitations of the optimizing approach, most decisions still involve some judgment. Thus, in making decisions, the manager generally uses a combination of intuitive and rational approaches.

The Satisficing Approach

Believing the assumptions of the optimizing approach to be generally unrealistic, Herbert Simon, in attempting to understand how managerial decisions are actually made, formulated his **principle of bounded rationality**. This principle states, "The capacity of the human mind for formulating and solving complex problems is very small compared with the size of the problems whose solutions *is* re-

principle of bounded rationality   Assumes people have the time and cognitive ability to process only a limited amount of information on which to base decisions.

quired for objectively rational behavior—or even for a reasonable approximation to such objective rationality."[5] Basically, the principle of bounded rationality states that human rationality has definite limits. Based on this principle, Simon proposed a decision model of the "administrative man," which makes the following assumptions:

1. A person's knowledge of alternatives and criteria is limited.
2. People act on the basis of a simplified, ill-structured, mental abstraction of the real world; this abstraction is influenced by personal perceptions, biases, and so forth.
3. People do not attempt to optimize but will take the first alternative that satisfies their current level of aspiration. This is called *satisficing.*
4. An individual's level of aspiration concerning a decision fluctuates upward and downward, depending on the values of the most recently identified alternatives.

The first assumption is a synopsis of the principle of bounded rationality. The second assumption follows naturally from the first. If limits to human rationality do exist, an individual must make decisions based on limited and incomplete knowledge. The third assumption also naturally follows from the first assumption: If the decision maker's knowledge of alternatives is incomplete, the individual cannot optimize but can only satisfice. **Optimizing** means selecting the best possible alternative; **satisficing** means selecting the first alternative that meets the decision maker's minimum standard of satisfaction. Assumption four is based on the belief that the criteria for a satisfactory alternative are determined by the person's current level of aspiration. **Level of aspiration** refers to the level of performance a person expects to attain, and it is impacted by the person's prior successes and failures.

optimizing   Selecting the best possible alternative.
satisficing   Selecting the first alternative that meets the decision maker's minimum standard of satisfaction.
level of aspiration   Level of performance that a person expects to attain; determined by the person's prior successes and failures.

Figure 4.1 represents the satisficing approach to decision making. If the decision maker is satisfied that an acceptable alternative has been found, she or he selects that

---

FIGURE 4.1   Model of the Satisficing Approach

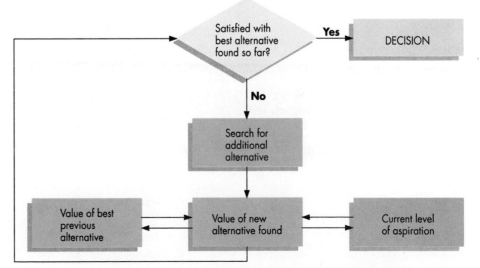

Source: Adapted from James G. March and Herbert A. Simon, *Organizations* (New York: John Wiley & Sons, 1958), p. 49.

alternative. Otherwise the decision maker searches for an additional alternative. In Figure 4.1, the double arrows indicate a two-way relationship: The value of the new alternative is influenced by the value of the best previous alternative; the value of the best previous alternative is in turn influenced by the value of the new alternative. As the arrows indicate, a similar two-way relationship exists between the value of the new alternative and the current level of aspiration. The net result of this evaluation determines whether or not the decision maker is satisfied with the alternative. Thus, the "administrative man selects the first alternative that meets the minimum satisfaction criteria and makes no real attempt to optimize.

THE DECISION MAKER'S ENVIRONMENT

A manager's freedom to make decisions depends largely on the manager's position within the organization and on its structure. In general, higher-level managers have more flexibility and discretion. The patterns of authority outlined by the formal organization structure also influence the flexibility of the decision maker.

Another important factor in decision-making style is the purpose and tradition of the organization. For example, a military organization requires a different style of decision making than a volunteer organization does.

The organization's formal and informal group structures also affect decision-making styles. These groups may range from labor unions to advisory councils.

The final subset of the environment includes all of the decision maker's superiors and subordinates. The personalities, backgrounds, and expectations of these people influence the decision maker.

Figure 4.2 shows the major environmental factors that affect decision makers in an organization. Successful managers must develop an appreciation for the different environmental forces that both influence them and are influenced by their decisions.

FIGURE 4.2   Environmental Factors Influencing Decision Making in an Organization

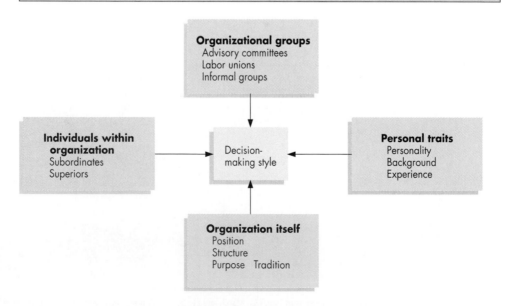

CONDITIONS FOR MAKING DECISIONS

Decisions are not always made with the same amount of available information. The best decision often depends on what happens later. Consider the simple decision of whether to take an umbrella when going outside. The more desirable alternative is determined by whether or not it rains, but this is not under the control of the decision maker. Table 4.1 gives combinations of alternatives and states of nature and their respective outcomes for the individual trying to decide whether or not to take an umbrella when going outside.

Certainty

Knowing exactly what will happen places the decision maker in a **situation of certainty.** In such a situation, the decision maker can calculate the precise outcome for each alternative. If it is raining, the person knows the outcome of each alternative and therefore can choose the best alternative (take an umbrella). Rarely, however, are decisions made in today's organizations under a condition of certainty. A manager deciding between a delivery by air (taking a set time to arrive at a set cost) or one by truck (also taking a set time to arrive at a set cost) would be an example of a decision made under a condition of certainty.

situation of certainty   Situation that occurs when a decision maker knows exactly what will happen and can often calculate the precise outcome for each alternative.

Risk

Unfortunately, the outcome associated with each alternative is not always known in advance. The decision maker can often obtain—at some cost—information regarding the different possible outcomes. The desirability of getting the information is figured by weighing the costs of obtaining the information against the information's value. A decision maker is in a **situation of risk** if certain reliable but incomplete information is available. In a situation of risk, some ideas of the relative probabilities associated with each outcome are known. If the weather forecaster has said there is a 40 percent chance of rain, the decision maker is operating in a situation of risk.

situation of risk   Situation that occurs when a decision maker is aware of the relative probabilities of occurrence associated with each alternative.

The precise probabilities of the various outcomes usually are not known. However, reasonably accurate probabilities based on historical data and past experiences often can be calculated. When no such data exist, it is difficult to estimate probabilities. In such cases, one approach is to survey individual opinions.

Under conditions of risk, the decision maker can use expected value analysis to help arrive at a decision. With this technique, the expected payoff of each known alternative is mathematically calculated based on its probability of occurrence. One

TABLE 4.1   Umbrella Decision Alternatives and Outcomes

	State of Nature	
Alternative	No Rain	Rain
Take umbrella	Dry, but inconvenient	Dry
Do not take umbrella	Dry, happy	Wet

potential shortcoming of expected value analysis is that it represents the average outcome if the event is repeated many times. That is of little help if the act occurs only once. For example, airplane passengers are not interested in average fatality rates; rather, they are interested in what happens on their particular flight.

Uncertainty

When the decision maker has very little or no reliable information on which to evaluate the different possible outcomes, he or she is operating in a situation of uncertainty. Under a **situation of uncertainty,** the decision maker has no knowledge concerning the probabilities associated with different possible outcomes. For example, a person who is going to New York and has not heard a weather forecast for New York will have no knowledge of the likelihood of rain and hence will not know whether or not to carry an umbrella.

situation of uncertainty Situation that occurs when a decision maker has very little or no reliable information on which to evaluate the different possible outcomes.

If the decision maker has little or no knowledge about which state of nature will occur, one of several basic approaches may be taken. The first is to choose the alternative whose best possible outcome is the best of all possible outcomes for all alternatives. This is an optimistic, or gambling, approach and is sometimes called the **maximax approach.** A decision maker using this approach would not take the umbrella because the best possible outcome (being dry without being inconvenienced) could be achieved only with this alternative.

maximax approach Selecting the alternative whose best possible outcome is the best of all possible outcomes for all alternatives; sometimes called the *optimistic* or *gambling approach* to decision making.
maximin approach Comparing the worst possible outcomes for each alternative and selecting the one that is least undesirable; sometimes called the *pessimistic approach* to decision making.
risk-averting approach Choosing the alternative with the least variation among its possible outcomes.

A second approach for dealing with uncertainty is to compare the worst possible outcomes for each alternative and select the one that is least bad. This is a pessimistic approach and is sometimes called the **maximin approach.** In the umbrella example, the decision maker would compare the worst possible outcome of taking an umbrella to that of not taking an umbrella. The decision maker would then decide to take an umbrella because it is better to be dry than wet.

A third approach is to choose the alternative with the least variation among its possible outcomes. This is a **risk-averting approach** and results in more effective planning. If the decision maker chooses not to take an umbrella, the outcomes can vary from being dry to being wet. Thus, the risk-averting decision maker would take an umbrella to ensure staying dry.

Table 4.2 summarizes the different approaches to making a decision under conditions of uncertainty. Management Illustration 4.1 discusses how one company uses a newly developed software package to help manage the risks associated with its business.

TIMING THE DECISION

To properly time a decision, the need for a decision must be recognized. That is not always easy. The manager may simply not be aware of what is going on, or the problem requiring a decision may be camouflaged. Some managers always seem to make decisions on the spot; others tend to take forever to decide even a simple matter. The manager who makes quick decisions runs the risk of making bad decisions. Failure to gather and evaluate available data, consider people's feelings, and anticipate the impact of the decision can result in a very quick but poor decision. Just as risky is the other extreme: the manager who listens to problems, promises to act, but never does.

Management Illustration 4.1

Managing Risks in the Dairy Business

Celsis-Lumac of Evanston, Illinois, with the assistance of Arthur D. Little, has developed a software package that dairy processors can use to help reduce the risks associated with microbial contaminated milk. The software enables users to model and quantify potential savings associated with effectively managing the risks by using rapid microbial testing systems in addition to using the traditional coliform testing systems. Rapid warning of any contamination enables a producer to contain the problem, limit the risk of contaminating end products, and shorten plant shutdown periods.

Source: "Reducing Costs by Managing Risk," *Dairy Foods*, February 1998, pg. 24. For more information about Celsis-Lumac visit their Web site at: http://microbiol.org/celsis.htm

---

TABLE 4.2   Possible Approaches to Making Decisions under Uncertainty

Approach	How It Works	Related to the Umbrella Example
Optimistic or gambling approach (maximax)	Choose the alternative whose best possible outcome is the best of all possible outcomes for all alternatives	Do not take umbrella
Pessimistic approach (maximin)	Compare the worst possible outcomes of each of the alternatives and select the alternative whose worst possible outcome is least undesirable	Take umbrella
Risk-averting approach	Choose the alternative that has the least variation among its possible alternatives	Take umbrella

---

Nearly as bad is the manager who responds only after an inordinate delay. Other familiar types are the manager who never seems to have enough information to make a decision, the manager who frets and worries over even the simplest decisions, and the manager who refers everything to superiors.

Knowing when to make a decision is complicated because different decisions have different time frames. For instance, a manager generally has more time to decide committee appointments than he or she has to decide what to do when three employees call in sick. No magic formula exists to tell managers when a decision should be made or how long it should take to make it. The important thing is to see the importance of properly timing decisions.

THE ROLE OF VALUES IN DECISION MAKING

value A conception, explicit or implicit, that defines what an individual or a group regards as desirable. People are not born with values; rather, they acquire and develop them early in life.

A **value** is a conception, explicit or implicit, defining what an individual or a group regards as desirable.[6] Values play an important role in the decision-making process. People are not born with values; rather, they acquire and develop them early in life. Parents, teachers,

---

FIGURE 4.3   George England's Major Categories of Values

Pragmatic mode	Suggests that an individual has an evaluative framework that is guided primarily by success–failure considerations
Ethical-moral mode	Implies an evaluative framework consisting of ethical considerations influencing behavior toward actions and decisions that are judged to be right and away from those judged to be wrong
Affect, or feeling, mode	Suggests an evaluative framework that is guided by hedonism: One behaves in ways that increase pleasure and decrease pain

Source: George England, "Personal Value Systems of Managers and Administrators," *Academy of Management Proceedings*, August 1973, pp. 81–94.

---

relatives, and others influence an individual's values. As a result, every manager and every employee brings a certain set of values to the workplace.

A person's values have an impact on the selection of performance measures, alternatives, and choice criteria in the decision process. Differences in values often account for the use of different performance measures. For example, a manager concerned primarily with economic values would probably measure performance differently than a manager concerned mainly with social values. The former might look only at profit; the latter might think only of customer complaints.

Differences in values may also generate different alternatives. A viable alternative to one person may be unacceptable to another because of differences in values. Because the final choice criteria depend on the performance measures used, they are also affected by values. For example, consider the question of laying off employees. Managers with dominant economic values would probably lay them off much quicker than would managers with high social values.

George England, who has conducted very extensive research on the role of values in the decision-making process, has identified three major categories of values (see Figure 4.3).[7] He reported the following:

1. Large individual differences in personal values exist within every group studied. In the different countries studied, some managers have a pragmatic orientation, some have an ethical/moral orientation, and some have an affect, or feeling, orientation. Some managers have a very small set of values; others have a large set and seem to be influenced by many strongly held values.

2. Personal value systems of managers are relatively stable. Edward Lusk and Bruce Oliver repeated one of George England's earlier studies and reported that values of managers had changed very little during the six years covered by their study.[8]

3. Personal value systems of managers are related to and/or influence the way managers make decisions. For example, those who have profit maximization as an important goal are less willing to spend money on cafeteria and restroom improvements than those who do not have profit maximization as an important value.

4. Personal value systems of managers are related to their career success as managers. Successful American managers favor pragmatic, dynamic, achievement-oriented values; less successful managers prefer more static and passive values.

5. Differences exist in the personal values of managers working in different organizational contexts. For example, the personal values of U.S. managers were found to differ from those of labor leaders.

6.   Overall, the value systems of managers in the countries studied were similar; yet some distinct differences were observed. The data suggest that cultural and social factors, as opposed to level of technological and industrial development, are more important in explaining value differences and similarities.[9]

The work of England and others clearly establishes the important role values play in managers' decision-making processes. England's and other, more recent studies show that values may differ from culture to culture and that these differences may have a profound effect on resulting decisions.[10] To make sound decisions, today's managers must not only be aware of their own values but also must know those of others inside and outside the organization. In addition, John Pearce and Richard Robinson, in their book *Strategic Management*, describe applications of Michael E. Porter's "value chain" approach to analyzing a firm's key strengths and weaknesses. The conclusion is that internal values play a great role in preparing not only the manager but the entire organization for competition.[11]

PARTICIPATION IN DECISION MAKING

Most managers have opportunities to involve their subordinates and others in the decision-making process. One pertinent question is: Do groups make better decisions than individuals? Another is: When should subordinates be involved in making managerial decisions?

Group Decision Making

Everyone knows the old axiom that two heads are better than one. Empirical evidence generally supports this view, with a few minor qualifications. Group performance is frequently better than that of the average group member.[12] Similarly, groups can often be successfully used to develop innovative and creative solutions to problems. Groups also take longer to solve problems than does the average person.[13] Thus, group decisions are generally better when avoiding mistakes is more important than speed.

Group performance is generally superior to that of the average group member for two reasons. First, the sum total of the group's knowledge is greater. Second, the group has a much wider range of alternatives in the decision process.

One facet of group decision making compares the risk people will take alone with the risk they will take in a group. Laboratory experiments have shown that unanimous group decisions are consistently riskier than the average of the individual decisions.[14] This is somewhat surprising, since group pressures often inhibit the members. Possibly people feel less responsible for the outcome of a group decision than when they act alone. More recent research has found that groups make decisions best described as more polar than do individuals acting alone.[15] "More polar" means that groups tend to make decisions that are more extreme than those they would make as individuals. Figure 4.4 summarizes the positive and negative aspects of group decision making. Management Illustration 4.2 discusses some new software designed to help decision makers solicit inputs from others.

SELECTING THE DECISION-MAKING STYLE

One key to effective decision making is the ability to select the appropriate decision-making style for each decision faced. Should group decision making be used whenever possible? Should employees be consulted in all decisions or only in certain

Management Illustration 4.2
Knowledge Networks

Many software tools are available today to help decision makers solicit inputs from others. For example, Milagro Systems, Inc., a software company located in Austin, Texas, has developed and marketed a set of computer programs and tools known as Knowledge Networks. Knowledge Networks are a means of deliberately setting up systems and processes in order to rapidly collect knowledge from individuals and then immediately use it for the benefit of other decision makers across the organization. The overall purpose of Knowledge Networks is to allow decision makers to explore issues, surface ideas, discover new insights, learn from others, be better informed to make decisions and end up with complete documentation of all the assumptions.

According to Milagro, the Knowledge Networks are simple to use and effective when:

- The decision makers believe that others might have solutions to suggest
- The decision makers feel free to ask for help
- The decision makers are willing to share information
- The decision makers want to acknowledge others for their intellect

Information on how to access Knowledge Networks can be found by E-mailing Milagro Systems at the following address: info@milagro.austin.tx.us.

Sources: Amy Doan, "Intranet Tools Foster Teamwork," *InfoWorld*, January 13, 1997, p. 48 and http://milagro.austin/tx/us/knownet/index.html.

FIGURE 4.4 Positive and Negative Aspects of Group Decision Making

Positive Aspects	Negative Aspects
1. The sum total of the group's knowledge is greater.	1. One individual may dominate and/or control the group.
2. The group possesses a much wider range of alternatives in the decision process.	2. Social pressures to conform can inhibit group members.
3. Participation in the decision-making process increases the acceptance of the decision by group members.	3. Competition can develop to such an extent that winning becomes more important than the issue itself.
4. Group members better understand the decision and the alternatives considered.	4. Groups have a tendency to accept the first potentially positive solution while giving little attention to other possible solutions.

situations? Research and practice show that no single style of decision making works best in all situations. Successful leaders learn to match the appropriate decision-making style with the situation.

Victor Vroom and Philip Yetton addressed the problem with a very practical and useful model.[16] They developed the set of alternative decision styles shown in Figure 4.5. Each style has a code and is increasingly participative: Style A1 has no subordinate participation, whereas style G11 is almost totally participative. Vroom and Yetton identified three variables bearing on the appropriateness of a given decision-making style: (1) the quality or rationality of the decision, (2) the acceptance or com-

---

FIGURE 4.5   Types of Management Decision Styles

A1: The manager makes the decision alone, with little or no input from subordinates (the *A* stands for *autocratic*).

A11: The manager asks subordinates for information that he or she needs to make the decision, but still makes the decision alone. Subordinates may or may not be informed of the decision. The role played by subordinates is clearly one of providing information as opposed to generating or evaluating alternative solutions.

C1: The manager shares the situation with selected subordinates and asks them individually for information and advice. The manager still makes the final decision, which may or may not reflect the subordinates' influence (the *C* stands for *consultative*).

C11: The manager meets with subordinates as a group to discuss the situation. Information is freely shared, although the manager still makes the final decision, which may or may not reflect the subordinates' influence.

G11: The manager and subordinates meet as a group and freely share information. The entire group makes the decision (the *G* stands for *group*).

Source: Adapted from Victor H. Vroom, "A New Look at Managerial Decision Making," *Organizational Dynamics*, Spring 1973. © 1973 by AMACOM, a division of American Management Associations, New York, p. 67. Reprinted by permission of the publisher. All rights reserved.

---

mitment by subordinates to execute the decision effectively, and (3) the amount of time required to make the decision.

Figure 4.6 shows Vroom and Yetton's model as a decision tree. The problem attributes are shown across the top of the figure. For any decision situation, start at the left-hand side and work toward the right until you reach a terminal node. When more than one decision-making style is feasible, this model chooses the style requiring the least amount of time.

Vroom and Yetton found that most leaders actually do use different decision-making styles in different situations. They also found that leaders are much more likely to break decision rules concerning acceptance of or commitment to the decision than they are those rules designed to protect the quality of rationality of the decision. One might then conclude that typical leaders' decisions are more likely to suffer from a lack of acceptance by followers than from the quality of the decision. Similarly, leaders who learn which decision styles work best in which situations usually make better decisions than those who do not.

BARRIERS TO EFFECTIVE DECISION MAKING

Although it is desirable to study how to make decisions, managers must also work to remove barriers that limit the effectiveness of those decisions. Daniel Wheeler and Irving Janis identified four basic barriers to effective decision making. Barrier one is complacency: The decision maker either does not see danger signs or opportunity or ignores data from the environment that would affect decision making. Barrier two is called *defensive avoidance:* The decision maker denies the importance of danger, the opportunity, or the responsibility for taking action. Panic is the third barrier: Frantic attempts to solve a problem rarely produce the best results. The final barrier is deciding to decide: Accepting the responsibility and challenge of decision making is critical to overall effectiveness.[17] All of these barriers must be dealt with to create an environment that stimulates effective and creative decision making.

FIGURE 4.6   Vroom and Yetton's Decision Model

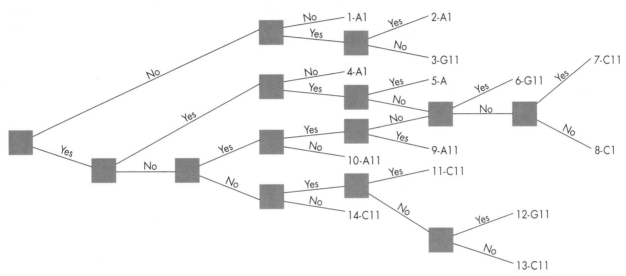

Is there a quality requirement such that one solution is likely to be more rational than another?	Do I have sufficient information to make a high quality decision?	Is the problem structured?	Is acceptance of decision by subordinates critical to effective implementation?	If you were to make the decision by yourself, is it reasonably certain that it would be accepted by your subordinates?	Do subordinates share the organizational goals to be obtained in solving the problem?	Is conflict among subordinates likely in preferred solutions?
A	B	C	D	E	F	G

Source: Victor H. Vroom, "A New Look at Managerial Decision Making," *Organizational Dynamics*, Spring 1973. © 1973 by AMACOM, a division of American Management Associations, New York, p. 70. Reprinted by permission of the publisher. All rights reserved.

MAKING CREATIVE DECISIONS

If the optimizing approach to decision making is based on unrealistic assumptions and the intuitive and satisficing approaches often result in less than optimal decisions, what can managers do to improve their decision-making process? One option that has produced positive results in numerous organizations is to encourage creative decisions and innovation at all levels. This section discusses some techniques to foster creative decisions within an organization.

The Creative Process

Creativity and innovation may seem similar but are actually quite different processes. **Creativity** is the thinking process involved in producing an idea or a concept that is new, original, useful, or satisfying to its creator or to someone else. **Innovation** refers to doing new things. Creativity involves coming up with a new idea, whereas innovation involves implementing the new idea. In the 1995 hit movie *Apollo 13*, the phrase "Houston, we have a problem" was not a simplistic one. A sound creative process and dynamic en-

creativity   Coming up with an idea that is new, original, useful, or satisfying to its creator or to someone else.
innovation   Process of applying a new and creatiave idea to a product, sevice, or method of operation.

gineering applications brought home three weary space travelers. Corporate management usually does not have to deal with life-threatening decisions such as those facing the staff and engineers of mission control. However, the development of a climate that fosters creative thinking is often very similar. The following five-step creative process is generally thought to help establish an environment for creative decision making:

1. *Preparation.* The manager investigates thoroughly to make sure that all parts of the problem are fully understood and that all facts and ideas relevant to the problem have been identified.
2. *Concentration.* The manager commits to solving the problem in a timely manner.
3. *Incubation of ideas and information.* The manager recognizes that the accepted way of solving a problem is not always the best way. (Allow the creative spark to catch fire.)
4. *Illumination.* The manager connects a problem with an acceptable solution. (This step is often called the "Eureka connection.")
5. *Verification.* The manager tests the solution and accepts the result.[18]

Although these steps often overlap, they provide a sound beginning point for the development of creative solutions that are critical to the success of the modern organization.

Establishing a Creative Environment

Probably the single most important factor that influences creativity and innovation by organizational members is the climate, or environment, in which they work. Certainly a manager's boss can have an impact on the type of climate established, but ultimately it is the individual manager who sets the tone for his or her area of responsibility. If a manager is genuinely interested in creative ideas, most employees are aware of it. The opposite is also true: Most employees realize when a manager is not interested in creativity.

People-based management skills and positive leadership can encourage a climate of creativity. To avoid hampering creativity, the manager must

- Instill trust—eliminate the fear of failure of an idea.
- Develop effective internal and external communication. Upward and lateral communication encourage innovation.
- Seek a mix of talent within the organization; a blend of different personality types and interactions encourages creative problem solving.
- Reward useful ideas and solutions.
- Allow for some flexibility in the existing organizational structure so that new ideas and creative solutions will not be eliminated by tradition.

Tools to Foster Creativity

In addition to establishing the proper environment, managers can use several techniques to encourage creativity. The following sections describe some of these techniques.

Brainstorming   Alex F. Osborn developed brainstorming as an aid to producing creative ideas for an advertising agency. Basically, **brainstorming** involves presenting a problem to a group of people and allowing them to present ideas for solution to the problem. Brainstorming is intended to produce a large quantity of ideas or alternatives and generally follows a definite procedure.

brainstorming   Presenting a problem to a group and allowing group members to produce a large quantity of ideas for its solution; no criticisms are allowed initially.

In the first phase, members of the group are asked to present ideas off the tops of their heads. Group members are told that quantity rather than quality of ideas is the goal. Questions submitted by the group leader usually include "How can we use this differently?", "How can we change?", "How can we substitute this?", or "How can we combine this?" Four basic rules for the first phase are as follows:

1. No criticism of ideas is allowed.
2. No praise of ideas is allowed.
3. No questions or discussion of ideas is allowed.
4. Combinations of and improvements on ideas that have been previously presented are encouraged.

During the second phase, the merits of each idea are reviewed. This review often leads to additional alternatives. Furthermore, alternatives with little merit are eliminated in this phase. In the third phase, one of the alternatives is selected, frequently through group consensus.

Gordon Technique   William J. J. Gordon developed a technique for the consulting firm of Arthur D. Little, Inc., to spur creative problem solving. The technique was initially devised to get creative ideas on technical problems. The **Gordon technique** differs from brainstorming in that no one but the group leader knows the exact nature of the real problem under consideration. A key word is used to describe a problem area; the group then explores that area, using the key word as a starting point. For instance, the word *conservation* may be used to start a discussion on energy conservation. The key word would direct discussion and suggestions on conservation to other areas in addition to the one under question. Proponents of the Gordon technique argue that it generates better-quality ideas because the discussion is not limited to one particular area as is the case with brainstorming.

gordon technique   Differs from brainstorming in that no one but the group leader knows the exact nature of the real problem under consideration. A key word is used to describe a problem area.

Nominal Group Technique   The **nominal group technique (NGT)** is a highly structured technique designed to keep personal interactions at a minimum. It involves the following steps:

nominal group technique (NGT)   Highly structured technique for solving group tasks; minimizes personal interactions to encourage activity and reduce pressures toward conformity.

1. *Listing.* Each group member, working alone, develops a list of probable solutions to a group task.
2. *Recording.* Each member offers an item from his or her listing in a round-robin manner to the group leader, who records the ideas on a master list in full view of the group. Some organizations today even have specially designed rooms with computers that project responses onta a large screen for all participants to see. The round-robin process continues until the leader has recorded all items on each person's list.
3. *Voting.* Each member records on an individual ballot his or her preference with respect to the priority or importance of the items appearing on the master list.

No verbal interaction is allowed during the first three steps. The results of the voting are tabulated, and scores are posted on the master list. Then the process continues as follows:

4. *Discussion.* Each item is discussed for clarification and valuation.

5. *Final voting.* Each member votes a second time with respect to the priority of the ideas generated.[19]

The NGT has been found to generate more unique ideas than brainstorming does. However, both the NGT and brainstorming suffer from the problem that occurs when the participants are so close to the problem under study that they are blind to what appear to be obvious solutions.

Brainwriting   In the **brainwriting** approach, group members are presented with a problem situation and then asked to jot their ideas on paper without any discussion. The papers are not signed. The papers are then exchanged with others, who build on the ideas and pass the papers on again until all members have had an opportunity to participate.

brainwriting Technique in which a group is presented with a problem situation and members anonymously write down ideas, then exchange papers with others, who build on ideas and pass them on until all members have participated.

synectics Creative problem-solving technique that uses metaphorical thinking to "make the familiar strange and the strange familiar."

Synectics   **Synectics** is a relatively new technique used in creative problem solving. Synectics uses metaphorical thinking to "make the familiar strange and the strange familiar." Analogies are the best method for doing this. There appear to be several basic forms from which to springboard ideas:

- *Personal analogies.* Place yourself in the role of the object. Direct analogies: Make direct comparisons.
- *Symbolic analogies.* Look at the problem in terms of symbols.
- *Fantasy analogies.* Imagine the most perfect solution.

As an illustration of the fantasy analogy method, or "goal wishing," the participants fantasize about how a particular problem could be solved if there were no physical constraints. After developing a list of wishful solutions, the participants are encouraged to come up with the most absurd solutions they can imagine. Often at least one or two of these solutions can be refined into practical solutions.

A word of caution is in order regarding all of these techniques. Much controversy exists regarding their effectiveness as aids to creativity. Two researchers addressed this issue: "The evidence on balance does not seem encouraging enough to propose that managers who are seeking an extremely creative idea to help them on a problem situation should resort to a brainstorming session."[20] On the other hand, these same researchers concluded that brainstorming may generate a wider variety of solutions to a problem.

In conclusion, none of the previously described techniques is a complete answer for improving creativity within organizations. Each should be viewed as a tool that can help in some situations when the proper environment has been established. Management Illustration 4.3 describes how some companies are using unorthodox techniques to boost creative efficiency and productivity.

A Model for Creative Decision Making

This section presents a practical model that can lead to better and more creative decisions.[21] While this model incorporates parts of the rational approach, its emphasis is on encouraging the generation of new ideas. Figure 4.7 outlines the stages of this model.

Stage 1: Recognition   When a problem or a decision situation exists, it is useful to first describe the circumstances in writing. An effective approach is to simply

Management Illustration 4.3

Encouraging Creativity

Many companies today are using unorthodox techniques to boost creative efficiency and productivity. The common thread that links these approaches is the belief that creativity comes from looking at things in a different way than normal.

Jorday Ayan, author of *Aha! 10 Ways to Free Your Creative Spirit and Find Your Great Ideas*, believes that in ordinary brainstorming sessions, participants focus solely on whatever the issue is and, thus they become locked into certain parameters in their minds. Unorthodox approaches can prompt new and unexpected participant responses and cause them to view a problem in a completely different way. Some of the unorthodox approaches being used include using toys to help people move away from rigid, adult-type thinking into a more childlike state, graphic facilitation, and creative visualization. Graphic facilitation involves graphically recording in words and pictures everything that happens in a meeting. For example, strong opinions might be recorded in red and a lightning bolt could signify an exciting idea. Creative visualization is a sort of mental dress rehearsal for an upcoming event or circumstance. Established firms such as General Motors, Hewlett-Packard, and Gillette have successfully used some of these untraditional methods.

Source: Robert Carey and Melinda Ligos, "C'mon, Everybody's Doing It," *Successful Meetings*, October 1997, pp. 42–55. For more articles found in *Successful Meetings* magazine, visit their Web site at www.successmtgs.com.

FIGURE 4.7   Model for Creative Decision Making

Stage		
1	Recognition	To investigate and eventually define a problem or decision situation
2	Fact finding	
3	Problem finding	
4	Idea finding	To generate possible alternatives or solutions (ideas)
5	Solution finding	To identify criteria and evaluate ideas generated in stage 4
6	Acceptance finding	To work out a plan for implementing a chosen idea

Source: Bruce Meyers (unpublished paper, Western Illinois University, 1987).

write out the facts in narrative form. This stage should include a description of the present situation, as well as when and where pertinent events occurred or will occur.

Stage 2: Fact Finding   After the decision situation has been described in written form, the next step is to systematically gather additional information concerning the current state of affairs. Questions asked in this stage usually begin with *who, what, where, when, how many, how much,* or similar words. The intent of the fact-finding stage is to organize available information about the decision situation.

Stage 3: Problem Finding   The fact-finding stage is concerned primarily with the present and the past; the problem-finding stage is oriented toward the future. In a sense, this stage might be viewed as problem redefining or problem analysis. The overriding purpose of this stage is to rewrite or restate the problem in a manner that will encourage more creative solutions. In light of stages 1 and 2, the decision maker should attempt to restate the problem in several different ways, with the ultimate goal of encouraging a broader range of solutions. For example, the decision situation "Shall I use my savings to start a new business?" could be restated, "In what ways might I finance my new business?" The first statement elicits a much narrower range of possible solutions than does the second. Similarly, "Shall I fire this employee?" could be restated, "Should I transfer, punish, retrain, or fire this employee, or should I give him/her another chance?"

After listing several restatements of the problem, the decision maker should select the one that most closely represents the real problem and has the greatest number of potential solutions. At this point, the decision situation should be defined in a manner that suggests multiple solutions.

Stage 4: Idea Finding   This stage aims to generate a number of different alternatives for the decision situation. In this stage, a form of brainstorming is used, following two simple rules: (1) no judgment or evaluation is allowed, and (2) all ideas presented must be considered. The purpose of these rules is to encourage the generation of alternatives, regardless of how impractical they seem at first. A good approach is for the decision maker to list as many ideas as possible that relate to the problem. The decision maker should then go back and consider what might be substituted, combined, adopted, modified, eliminated, or rearranged to transform any of the previously generated ideas into additional ideas.

Stage 5: Solution Finding   The purpose of this stage is to identify the decision criteria and evaluate the potential ideas generated in stage 4. The first step is for the decision maker to develop a list of potential decision criteria by listing all possibilities. Once a list of potential criteria has been developed, the decision maker should pare down the list by selecting the most appropriate criteria. Naturally, the decision maker should aim for a manageable number of criteria (normally fewer than seven). The next step is to evaluate each idea generated in stage 4 against the selected criteria. Usually many ideas from stage 4 can be eliminated by simple inspection. The remaining ideas should then be evaluated against each criterion using some type of rating scale. After each idea has been evaluated against all criteria, the best solution usually becomes obvious.

Stage 6: Acceptance Finding   This final stage attempts to identify what needs to be done to successfully implement the chosen idea or solution. This stage not only addresses the *who, when, where,* and *how* questions but should also attempt to anticipate potential objections to the decision.

While the above model is certainly not perfect, it does encourage managers to go beyond bounded rationality and to make better decisions than they would by following the satisficing approach.

Summary

1.   *Explain the Difference between Decision Making and Problem Solving.* In its narrowest sense, decision making is the process of choosing from among various alternatives. Problem solving is the process of determining the appropriate responses or actions necessary to alleviate a devia-tion from some standard or desired level of performance. From a practical perspective, almost all managerial decisions involve solving or avoiding problems, and therefore, it is not necessary to distinguish between managerial decision making and managerial problem solving.

2. *Distinguish between Programmed and Nonprogrammed Decisions.* Programmed decisions are reached by following an established or systematic procedure. Nonprogrammed decisions have little or no precedent and generally require a more creative approach by the decision maker.

3. *Explain the Intuitive Approach to Decision Making.* In the intuitive approach, managers make decisions based on hunches and intuition. Emotions and feelings play a major role in this approach.

4. *Discuss Two Rational Approaches to Decision Making.* One rational approach, optimizing, involves the following six steps: (1) recognize the need for a decision; (2) establish, rank, and weigh the criteria; (3) gather available information and data; (4) identify possible alternatives; (5) evaluate each alternative with respect to all criteria; and (6) select the best alternative. A second rational approach, satisficing, is based on the principle of bounded rationality. In the satisficing approach, the decision maker selects the first alternative that meets his or her minimum standard of satisfaction.

5. *List the Different Conditions under Which Managers Make Decisions.* Managers normally make decisions under the conditions of certainty, risk, or uncertainty.

6. *Explain the Role Values Play in Making Decisions.* A manager's values affect the selection of performance measures, alternatives, and choice criteria in the decision process.

7. *Summarize the Positive and Negative Aspects of Group Decision Making.* Positive aspects include the following:

(1) The sum total of the group's knowledge is greater; (2) the group possesses a much wider range of alternatives in the decision process; (3) participation in the decision-making process increases the acceptance of the decision by group members; and (4) group members better understand the decision and the alternatives considered. Negative aspects include the following: (1) One individual may dominate and/or control the group; (2) social pressures to conform can inhibit group members; (3) competition can develop to such an extent that winning becomes more important than the issue itself; and (4) groups have a tendency to accept the first potentially positive solution while giving little attention to other possible solutions.

8. *Define Creativity and Innovation and Outline the Basic Stages in the Creative Process.* Creativity is the thinking process involved in producing an idea or a concept that is new, original, useful, or satisfying to its creator or to someone else. Innovation is doing new things. The creative process generally has four stages: (1) preparation, (2) incubation, (3) illumination, and (4) verification.

9. *Identify Several Specific Tools and Techniques That Can Be Used to Foster Creative Decisions.* Tools to foster creative decisions include brainstorming, the Gordon technique, the nominal group technique, brainwriting, and synectics.

10. *List the Six Stages in Creative Decision Making.* The model for creative decision making encompasses the following six steps: (1) recognition, (2) fact finding, (3) problem finding, (4) idea finding, (5) solution finding, and (6) acceptance finding.

Preview Analysis

1. What decision-making characteristics do great companies have in common?

2. What task did James Olson of Hewlett-Packard face in May 1992?

3. What were the keys to Hewlett-Packard's transformation?

4. What three things does Olson have his team doing to increase development speed of Hewlett-Packard's products?

Review Questions

1. What are the three stages in the decision-making process?

2. What is the difference between decision making and problem solving?

3. Discuss the intuitive approach to decision making.

4. Discuss the optimizing approach to decision making.

5. What criticisms can be made concerning the optimizing approach to decision making?

6. Discuss the satisficing approach to decision making, and explain the difference between satisficing and optimizing.

7. Distinguish among the decision situations of certainty, risk, and uncertainty.

8. What are values? What relationship exists between values and managerial success?

9. Outline some positive and negative aspects of group decision making.

10. Describe the Vroom-Yetton model for selecting the most appropriate decision-making style.

11. What are the four barriers to effective decision making?

12. Describe the five-step process for creating an environment that fosters creative decision making.

13. Describe the following aids to creativity:
    a. Brainstorming
    b. Gordon technique
    c. Nominal group technique
    d. Brainwriting
    e. Synectics

14. Describe the six-stage model of creative decision making.

Skill-Building Questions

1. Identify a significant decision recently made by a major company (you might look in *Business Week* or *The Wall Street Journal*). In the decision you identify, did the manager or managers satisfice or optimize?

2. What factors do you think affect the amount of risk a manager is willing to take when making a decision?

3. Comment on the following statement: "Groups always make better decisions than individuals acting alone."

4. How many creative uses can you think of for a brick? Now ask a five-to-seven-year-old child the same question. How do you account for the differences? Why do you think children might be more creative than adults?

5. Think of a new form of a product or service to solve something that "bugs" you, for example, trash can lids that won't stay shut. (Many primary-grade creativity classes do this as a learning exercise in creativity.)

6. Illustrate each of the analogy methods described in the chapter in the discussion on synectics. Try doing the analogies with a car, a computer, a cosmetic product, and a product intended for a demographic or ethnic group other than your own.

SKILL-BUILDING EXERCISE 4.1

Lost at Sea

You are adrift on a private yacht in the South Pacific. Due to a fire of unknown origin, much of the yacht and its contents have been destroyed. The yacht is now slowly sinking. Your location is unclear because critical navigational equipment was destroyed and you and the crew were distracted in trying to bring the fire under control. Your best estimate is that you are approximately 1,000 miles south-southwest of the nearest land.

Following is a list of 15 items that are intact and undamaged after the fire. In addition to these articles, you have a serviceable rubber life raft with oars large enough to carry yourself, the crew, and all the items listed. The total contents of all survivors' pockets are a package of cigarettes, several books of matches, and five one-dollar bills.

Your task is to rank the following 15 items in terms of their importance to your survival. Place the number 1 by the most important item, the number 2 by the second most important, and so on through number 15, the least important.

_____ Sextant

_____ Shaving mirror

_____ Five-gallon can of water

_____ Mosquito netting

_____ One case of U.S. Army C rations

_____ Maps of the Pacific Ocean

_____ Seat cushion (flotation device approved by the Coast Guard)

_____ Two-gallon can of oil-gas mixture

_____ Small transistor radio

_____ Shark repellent

_____ 20 square feet of opaque plastic

_____ One quart of 160-proof Puerto Rican rum

_____ 15 feet of nylon rope

_____ Two boxes of chocolate bars

_____ Fishing kit

After everyone has completed the above rankings, your instructor will divide the class into teams or groups. Your group is to then rank the same items, using a group consensus method. This means the ranking for each of the 15 survival items must be agreed on by each group member before it becomes part of the group decision. Consensus is difficult to reach. Therefore, not every ranking will meet with everyone's complete approval. As a group, try to make each ranking one with which all group members can at least partly agree. Here are some guides to use in reaching consensus:

1. Avoid arguing for your own individual judgments. Approach the task on the basis of logic.

2. Avoid changing your mind for the sole purpose of reaching agreement and avoiding conflict. Support only solutions with which you agree at least somewhat.

3. Avoid "conflict-reducing" techniques such as majority vote, averaging, or trading.

4. View differences of opinion as a help rather than a hindrance in decision making.

Source: Adapted from John E. Jones and J. William Pfeiffer, eds., *The 1975 Annual Handbook for Group Facilitators* (La Jolla, Calif.: University Associates, Inc., 1975).

Creativity Exercise

Most of us believe we are more creative then we really are. Take a maximum of four minutes each on solving the following three problems.

A. Draw four straight lines connecting the dots in the following diagram without lifting your pencil (or pen) off the paper. You are permitted to cross a line, but you cannot retrace any part of a line.

B. What do the following words have in common (other than they are all in the English language)?

CALMNESS   FIRST

CANOPY   SIGHING

DEFT   STUN

C. Place 10 circles of the same size in five rows with four circles in each row.

After you have attempted each of the above problems be prepared to discuss the following questions:

1. Why do you think these "simple" problems were difficult for you?

2. Do you think grade school children tend to do better or worse than adults on problems such as these? Why?

CASE INCIDENT 4.1

Getting Out of the Army

Jay Abbott is confident that his future will be secure and financially rewarding if he decides to remain in the Army. He entered more than 10 years ago as a commissioned officer after completing his college education on an ROTC scholarship. At age 31, Jay has progressed to the rank of captain and is currently being considered for promotion to major. He has no reason to believe he will not be promoted. He has been successful in all of his appointments, is well liked by everyone—his peers, superiors, and subordinates—and has an unblemished record.

However, at the 10-year mark, Jay had second thoughts about staying in the Army and has been thinking about leaving ever since. He has felt more and more resentful that the Army has affected a large part of his personal life. Although he had always preferred to wear his hair shorter than most young men do, he resented the fact that even if he wanted to let it grow out or grow sideburns, he couldn't do it. It was the principle of the whole idea: the intrusion of the Army into his personal life. The fact that this intrusion extended to his wife and children bothered him even more.

Jay's wife, Ellen, was finishing her master's thesis. This took up a large portion of her free time; yet her lack of involvement in the officer's clubs was frowned on. There was just no such thing as a private family life in Jay's position. He didn't even have much time to spend with the family. His job required long hours of work, including weekend duty, which left little time for his wife and two daughters, ages seven and nine. Another problem was that Ellen, who held a degree in design engineering, was unable to pursue any kind of real career, something that was important to both of them.

These thoughts raced through Jay's mind over and over again as he tried to decide what would be best for him and his family. The Army had a lot of positive aspects, he kept reminding himself: He was already earning $34,000 a year, and with his nearly certain promotion, this would rise to $38,000. Also, he was being recommended for the Army's command and general staff college. There was little chance he would not be approved; completing the program would make his future even brighter. If he stayed, he would be able to retire in just 10 more years (at age 41) with a permanent retirement income of half his final salary plus free medical and dental coverage. By then, he figured, he would probably be a lieutenant colonel with a base pay of about $51,000; at worst, he would retire a major. At 41, he would have plenty of time to devote to a second career if he so desired.

On the other hand, regardless of how attractive the benefits seemed, salaries in the armed services had not kept pace with the rising rate of inflation: Congress had held the lid on raises at less than 5 percent, and no changes in this position were evident for the next few years. In fact, Jay had read several newspaper articles indicating that Congress was considering reducing benefits for the armed services, the 20-year retirement specifically.

After doing some checking, Jay learned that the training and experience received in the Army were valuable to civilian employers. Commissioned in the signal corps, he had vast experience in the area of telecommunications. He had recently completed a tour as an instructor in a service school. He had also been in many positions of leadership during his term in the Army. At 31, he probably had more firsthand managerial experience than most civilian managers. He knew that large organizations were currently hiring young ex-military officers at salaries $5,000 to $10,000 higher than those of recent college graduates.

Questions

1. What should Jay do?
2. What factors should Jay consider in his decision?
3. What role would values play in Jay's decision?

CASE INCIDENT 4.2

Going Abroad*

You supervise 12 engineers. Their formal training and work experience are very similar, so you can use them interchangeably on projects. Yesterday, your manager informed you that an overseas affiliate has requested four engineers to go abroad on extended loan for six to eight months. For a number of reasons, he argued and you agreed, this request should be met from your group.

All your engineers are capable of handling this assignment; from the standpoint of present and future projects, there is no special reason any one engineer should be retained over any other. Somewhat complicating the situation is the fact that the overseas assignment is in a generally undesirable location.

Questions

1. How would you select who should go abroad on extended loan?
2. Analyze this situation using the Vroom and Yetton model.

*This case is adapted from Victor H. Vroom, "A New Look at Managerial Decision Making," *Organizational Dynamics*, Spring 1973. © 1973 by AMACOM, a division of American Management Associations, New York, p. 73. Reprinted by permission of the publisher. All rights reserved.

References and Additional Readings

[1]Herbert A. Simon, The New Science of Management Decision (New York: Harper & Row, 1960), p. 2.

[2]George S. Odiorne, Management and the Activity Trap (New York: Harper & Row, 1974), pp. 128–29; George S. Odiorne, The Change Resisters (Englewood Cliffs, NJ: Prentice Hall, 1981), pp. 15–25.

[3]Odiorne, Management and the Activity Trap, pp. 142–44.

[4]"Go-Go Goliaths," Business Week, February 13, 1995, p. 66.

[5]Herbert A. Simon, Model of Man (New York: John Wiley & Sons, 1957), p. 198.

[6]William D. Guth and Renato Tagiuri, "Personal Values and Corporate Strategy," Harvard Business Review, September–October 1965, pp. 124–25.

[7]George England, "Personal Value Systems of Managers and Administrators," Academy of Management Proceedings, August 1973, pp. 81–94.

[8]Edward J. Lusk and Bruce L. Oliver, "American Managers' Personal Value Systems Revisited," Academy of Management Journal, September 1974, pp. 549–54.

[9]England, "Personal Value Systems," pp. 82–87.

[10]For example, see H. S. Badr, E. R. Gray, and B. L. Kedia, "Personal Values and Managerial Decision Making: Evidence from Two Cultures," Management International Review, Fall 1982, pp. 65–73, and H. J. Davis and S. A. Rasool, "Values Research and Managerial Behavior: Implications for Devising Culturally Consistent Managerial Styles," Management International Review, July 1988, pp. 11–19.

[11]John A. Pearce II and Richard B. Robinson, Jr., Strategic Management, 5th ed. (Burr Ridge, IL.: Richard D. Irwin, 1994), pp. 183–88.

[12]Irving Lorge, David Fox, Joel Davitz, and Marlin Brenner, "A Survey of Studies Contrasting the Quality of Group Performance and Individual Performance, 1930–1957," Psychological Bulletin, November 1958, pp. 337–72; Frederick C. Miner, Jr., "Group versus Individual Decision Making: An Investigation of Performance Measures, Decision Strategies, and Process Losses/Gains," Organizational Behavior and Human Performance, February 1984, pp. 112–24; K. L. Bettenhausen, "Five Years of Group Research: What We Have Learned and What Needs to Be Addressed," Journal of Management, June 1991, pp. 345–81.

[13]M. E. Shaw, "A Comparison of Individuals and Small Groups in the National Solution of Complex Problems," American Journal of Psychology, July 1932, pp. 491–504; Lorge, et al., "A Survey of Studies"; W. E. Watson, K. Kumar, and L. K. Michaelson, "Cultural Diversity's Impact on Interaction Process and Performance: Comparing Homogeneous and Diverse Task Groups," Academy of Management Journal, June 1993, pp. 590–602.

[14]M. Wallach, N. Kogan, and D. J. Bem, "Group Influence on Individual Risk Taking," Journal of Abnormal and Social Psychology, August 1962, pp. 75–86; N. Kogan and M. Wallach, "Risk Taking as a Function of the Situation, the Person, and the Group," in New Directions of Psychology, vol. 3, ed. G. Mardler (New York: Holt, Rinehart & Winston, 1967).

[15]D. G. Meyers, "Polarizing Effects of Social Interaction," in H. BranStatter, J. Davis, and G. Stock-Kreichgauer, eds., Group Decision Making (New York: Academic Press, 1982).

[16]Victor H. Vroom, "A New Look at Managerial Decision Making," Organizational Dynamics, Spring 1973, pp. 66–80; Victor H. Vroom and Philip W. Yetton, Leadership and Decision Making (Pittsburgh: University of Pittsburgh Press, 1973).

[17]Daniel D. Wheeler and Irving L. Janis, A Practical Guide for Making Decisions (New York: Macmillan, 1980), pp. 17–36.

[18]Graham Walles, The Art of Thought (New York: Harcourt Brace Jovanovich, 1976), p. 80.

[19]Gene E. Burton, Dev S. Pathok, and David B. Burton, "The Gordon Effect in Nominal Grouping," University of Michigan Business Review, July 1978, p. 8; Nells Zuech, "Identifying and Ranking Opportunities for Machine Vision in a Facility," Industrial Engineering, October 1992, pp. 42–44.

[20]T. Richards and B. L. Freedom, "Procedures for Managers in Idea-Deficient Situations: An Examination of Brainstorming Approaches," Journal of Management Studies, February 1978, pp. 43–55.

[21]The basis for this model and much of this discussion were contributed by Bruce Meyers, associate professor of management at Western Illinois University.

Section II

CONTEMPORARY ISSUES

5

Information Systems for Managers

᠗

LEARNING OBJECTIVES

After studying this chapter, you should be able to:

1. Recount the general evolution of computers since the early 1960s.

2. Describe the Internet and identify the two functional categories of information available on the Internet that are most useful to managers.

3. Describe an intranet.

4. Distinguish between data and information and define a management information system (MIS).

5. Define a decision support system (DSS).

6. Define an executive information system (EIS) and list the requirements for an EIS.

7. Discuss what expert systems can do.

8. List several strategies for overcoming potential problems when implementing an information system.

9. Identify and define at least four major types of illicit acts involving computers in organizations.

10. Explain what the Y2K problem is.

11. Describe an information center.

In the brief annals of doing business on the Internet, FedEx's customer World Wide Web site has become a legendary success story. Today some 12,000 customers a day click their way through the Web pages to pinpoint their parcels. Using an intranet can dramatically improve communications, unlock hidden information, and transform organizations. The Web is an inexpensive and very powerful alternative to other forms of communication. One of the obvious advantages of using the Web in this manner—E-mail—is the dramatic reduction in the need for paper. The only real stumbling block seems to be the aspect of security.

Source: Adapted from Amy Cortese, "Here Comes the Intranet," *Business Week*, February 26, 1996, pp. 76–84.

Successful implementation of the basic planning, organizing, and controlling functions of management requires that managers have adequate information. This means managers must first identify and then acquire the necessary information. Identifying and acquiring adequate information historically have been two of the biggest challenges of managers.

The advent of the "computer age" has greatly altered not only the availability of information but also the manner in which it is identified and acquired. This chapter introduces and gives an overview of information systems that can be especially useful to managers.

THE INFORMATION EXPLOSION

Until the past 25 or so years, managers almost never believed they had enough information to make decisions. Of course, information has always been available, but it has not always been easy to obtain, synthesize, and analyze. In many instances, the cost of gathering information was substantial. To many managers, the cost far outweighed the value of obtaining the information.

In the 1950s, a manager could always send a team of researchers to the local library; even then, much of the data would not be current. Other available information sources included the radio, newspapers, and professional meetings and publications. Contrast that scenario with the information age! Today's managers are often burdened, not from a lack of information but from information overload. **Information overload** is a term used to describe the current glut of print, sound, and image communication.[1]

information overload   Occurs when managers have so much information available that they have trouble distinguishing between the useful and the useless information.

Consider how television has grown from three networks to over 200 channels on some cable installations. The magazine industry has grown from a short stack of national publications into several racks of coverage in every specialized field. In addition, as discussed on the following pages, the manager is confronted with a variety of computer and image communication services and opportunities (such as software and Internet communication) that were simply not available a scant 10 years ago. From a management perspective, information overload occurs when managers have so much information that they have trouble distinguishing between the useful and the useless information. When an information system overloads, the problem is usually not with the information but with the system's method of handling the information. One focus of this chapter is to discuss systems that can help managers handle information.

The Computer Evolution

The first electronic computer, the ENIAC, was developed by the University of Pennsylvania in conjunction with the U.S. Army Ordnance Corps. The ENIAC was 8 feet high, 8 feet long, weighed 30 tons, and required about 174,000 watts of power to run.[2] On the average, it took about two days to set up ENIAC to carry out a program. It had constant maintenance problems because of its reliance on vacuum tubes and complicated wiring.

mainframe computer   Large computer system, typically with a separate central processing unit.

In the 1960s, large and very costly **mainframe computers** were in use by only the very largest companies and government organizations. Not only was the hardware for these systems expensive, but they also required highly paid operators, service personnel, programmers, and systems specialists. Because of the physical size and costs of these systems, they were almost always highly centralized and more often than not, considered an extension of the accounting function.

---

minicomputer   Small (desk-size) electronic, digital, stored-program, general-purpose computer.
microcomputer   Very small computer, ranging in size from a "computer on a chip" to a typewriter-size unit. Also called a *personal computer.*

The large computers were followed by the **minicomputers** of the 1970s. The minicomputers were much smaller in size and cost, and they were often programmed to perform specific functions for a particular business activity. Minicomputers ushered in the concept of distributed data processing, in which each operational area of an organization has control of its own computer to better respond to the needs of the area.

The decentralization first made possible by minicomputers has been taken even further by the **microcomputer** or personal computer (PC). The first commercially available personal computer was offered by Apple in 1976. Forty-four percent of all U.S. households owned a personal computer in 1997.[3] For just a few hundred dollars, a manager today can buy a microcomputer that is capable of processing mammoth amounts of data, yet occupies no more space than a typewriter!

The phenomenal improvements in computer hardware have been accompanied by improvements in software and user compatibility. Modern computers are much

---

user-friendly computer   Computer that requires very little technical knowledge to use.

---

more **user friendly** than those of the past. Managers today do not need to know sophisticated programming languages and computer jargon to use computers. In fact, the highly competitive software environment has produced many companies that are eager to build software that is highly customized for specific functional business needs. By maintaining close contact with software suppliers, the manager is the beneficiary of highly sophisticated computer specialists' knowledge and skills. For example, Visa International, the credit card giant, recently contracted with Cathy Basch and Deborah McWhinney, vice presidents of Visa's VisaVue subsidiary, to develop an electronic directory for Visa's World Wide Web site. The cost savings realized from not having to publish the material paid for the development.[4]

Computer technology improvements have also created some new problems for managers. Diverse computers and communication technologies provide a wide array of information at many different levels in the organization. Therefore, it is no longer possible to place the information function neatly on the organization chart. The need to integrate and coordinate information in an organization has led to the development of systems for doing just that.

The Internet

The Internet is a global collection of independently operating, but interconnected, computers.[5] Frequently referred to as the "information superhighway," the Internet is actually a network of computer networks. Think of the Internet as analogous to the Interstate Highway system; just as the interstate system connects to different cities via many different routes, the Internet connects computers around the world via a number of different electronic pathways.

The real value of the Internet to managers is the information that it makes available. Through the Internet, managers can access massive amounts of information by accessing computers around the world that are linked together through the Internet.

Types of Internet Resources   The type of information available and most useful for managers on the Internet can be placed into two broad functional categories: (1) conversational resources or (2) reference resources. Conversational resources allow managers to have conversations with individuals anywhere in the world. Mailing lists and newsgroups are the primary types of conversational resources. Mailing lists includes electronic mail (E-mail), whereby the user can electronically read messages to any other individual or group of individuals who have "subscribed" by having their name and electronic mail address placed on the sender's list of numbers. Newsgroups are essentially electronic bulletin boards. Anyone with Internet access can post an article to the board and anyone with Internet access can read the board.

The two types of reference-oriented resources most frequently encountered are the World Wide Web and Gopher. The World Wide Web (www or the Web) uses hypertext markup language (HTML) to transfer text, sound, graphics, and video. Hypertext is a form of text which allows the writer to link words in the text to other documents, graphic images, video, or even web pages stored anywhere in the world. Using the Web requires "browsers" to view documents and navigate through the intricate link structure. Numerous browsers are currently available, with Netscape Navigator and Microsoft Internet Explorer being the most popular.

Gopher sites are usually maintained by government agencies and educational institutions. Gopher sites contain text-only documents such as regulations, policies, and reports of governmental agencies and research reports of educational institutions. Figure 5.1 provides a summary of the internet resources most likely to be used by managers.

Intranets

An intranet is a private, corporate, computer network that uses Internet products and technologies to provide multimedia applications within organizations.[6] An intranet connects people to people and people to information and knowledge within the organization; it serves as an "information hub" for the entire organization. Most organizations set up intranets primarily for employees, but they can extend to business partners and even customers with appropriate security clearance. Research has found that the biggest applications for intranets today are internal communications followed by knowledge sharing and management information systems (management information systems are discussed in the next section).[7]

MANAGEMENT INFORMATION SYSTEMS

data   Raw material from which information is developed; composed of facts that have not been interpreted.

Before defining management information systems (MIS), we need to define some other basic terms. Many people make a clear distinction between the terms *data* and *information*. **Data** are the raw material from which information is devel-

---

FIGURE 5.1   Internet Resources Most Useful to Managers

Conversational Resources	Reference Resources
1. Mailing Lists	1. World Wide Web
2. Newsgroups	2. Gopher

Source: Adapted from Byron J. Finch, *The Management Guide to Internet Resources*, 1997 edition (New York: McGraw-Hill Companies, Inc., 1997) p. 15.

oped. Data are composed of facts that describe people, places, things, or events that have not been interpreted.[8] Data that have been interpreted and that meet the needs of one or more managers is **information**.[9] In other words, information is data that have been processed and are meaningful to one or more managers.

information   Data that have been interpreted and that meet the need of one or more managers.

management information system (MIS)   Integrated approach for providing interpreted and relevant data that can help managers make decisions.

Management Information Systems (MIS), also called management reporting systems, are designed to produce information needed for successful management of a process, department, or business.[10] MIS's support the day-to-day operational and tactical decision-making needs of managers. The information provided by an MIS provides information that managers have specified in advance as adequately meeting their information needs.[11] Usually the information made available by an MIS in the form of periodic reports, special reports, and outputs of mathematical simulations.[12]

In the broader sense, management information systems have existed for many years, even before computers. However, in most people's minds and in this chapter, the term *MIS* implies the use of computers to process data that managers will use to make operational decisions. The information an MIS provides describes the organization or one of its major parts in terms of what has happened in the past, what is happening now, and what is likely to happen in the future.[13]

Recognizing that today's management information systems involve the computer, it is important to note that MIS is not the same as data processing. **Data processing**

data processing   Capture, processing, and storage of data.

transaction-processing system   Substitutes computer processing for manual recordkeeping procedures.

is the capture, processing, and storage of data, whereas an MIS uses those data to produce information for management in making decisions to solve problems. In other words, data processing provides the database of the MIS.

Transaction-processing systems substitute computer processing for manual recordkeeping procedures. Examples include payroll, billing, and inventory record systems. By definition, transaction processing requires routine and highly structured decisions. It is actually a subset of data processing. Therefore, an organization can have a very effective transaction-processing system and not have an MIS. Figure 5.2 summarizes the characteristics of management information systems. Management Illustration 5.1 illustrates one way that MCI has effectively used a MIS.

MIS Subsystems

Many MISs have been developed for used by specific organizational subunits. Examples of MISs intended to support managers in particular functional areas include operational information systems, marketing information systems, financial information systems, and human resource information systems.

FIGURE 5.2   Characteristics of an MIS

- Uses data captured and stored as a result of transaction processing.
- Reports data and information rather than details of transaction processing.
- Assists managers in monitoring situations, evaluating conditions, and determining what actions need to be taken.
- Supports recurring decisions.
- Provides information in prespecified reports formats, either in print or on-screen.

Source: James A. Senn, *Information Technology in Business*, 2d ed. (Englewood Cliffs, NJ: Prentice Hall 1998), p. 615.

Management Illustration 5.1
MIS at MCI

MCI Communications Corporation, the public long-distance carrier, gives its customers of its "virtual network" service three different billing options. The customer can receive a record of all network transactions electronically at its designated computer center, a magnetic tape or CD-ROM can be mailed to the customer, or the customer can download data directly from the MCI mainframe billing center computer. MCI also provides customers with software that allows them to process the data and produce over 20 standard reports for their own use. These reports allow managers to take the following actions:

1. Monitor network usage and list the longest calls, the most expensive calls, and the most frequently used identification codes or calling card numbers

2. Analyze calling history and patterns by identification code, calling card, and rate period (e.g., full-price day rate or reduced evening rate).

3. Report call frequencies, isolating the most frequently called numbers and area codes.

4. Summarize calling traffic by city, state, and country.

If these reports were printed on paper, the reports for an average customer would fill 16 standard-sized boxes! By using a MIS, MCI enables its customers to obtain information in the form they desire, while also ensuring that they have the information necessary to manage their telephone use.

Source: James A. Senn, *Information Technology in Business*, 2d ed. (Englewood Cliffs, NJ: Prentice Hall 1998), pp. 615–616.

For more information about MCI Communications Corporation visit their Web site at: www.mciworldcom.com.

MIS subsystems in the operations area include computer-aided design (CAD), computer-aided manufacturing (CAM), computer-integrated manufacturing (CIM), material requirements planning (MRP). These are discussed in Chapters 9 and 21. One of the great benefits of specialized information systems is the ability to organize and coordinate information gathering and activities in critical functional areas. For example, most marketing systems focus on the product/service mix, on how the product or service is distributed, promoted, and priced, or on some types of sales analysis. Financial information systems include various auditing programs and funds management programs. Human resource information systems include job profile programs, skills inventories, and human resource planning programs.

DECISION SUPPORT SYSTEM

A decision support system (DSS) is an information system designed to assist in decision making where the decision process is relatively unstructured and only part of the information needed is structured in advance.[14] A DSS not only provides inputs to the decision process; it also becomes part of the process and makes suggestions to the decision maker. Decision support systems allow managers to use computers directly to retrieve information for decisions on semistructured problems. Such problems contain some elements that are well defined and quantifiable and some that are not. A DSS solves parts of a problem and helps to isolate points where judgment and experience are required.[15] Typically problems attacked using a DSS require the system to retrieve and process data from several files and databases and to use data provided on-line by individual decision makers simultaneously.[16] Examples of decisions that lend themselves to a DSS include plant locations, acquisitions, and new products or services.

The objective of a DSS is to provide information and decision support techniques needed to solve specific problems or pursue certain opportunities.[17] The objective

---

FIGURE 5.3   Management Information Systems Compared to Decision Support Systems

	Management Information Systems	Decision Support Systems
Information Provided		
Information form and frequency	Periodic, exception, and demand reports and responses	Interactive inquiries and responses
Information format	Prespecified, fixed format	Ad hoc, flexible, and adaptable format
Information processing methodology	Information produced by extraction and manipulation of operational data	Information produced by analytical modeling of operational and external data
Decision Support Provided		
Type of support	Provide information about the performance of the organization	Provide information, and decision support techniques to confront specific problems or opportunities
Stages of decision making supported	Support the intelligence and implementation stages of decision making	Support the intelligence, design, choice, and implementation stages of decision making
Types of decisions supported	Structured decisions for operational and tactical planning and control	Semistructured and unstructured decisions for tactical and strategic planning and control
Type of decision maker supported	Indirect support designed for many managers	Direct support tailored to the decision-making styles of individual managers

Source: James A. O'Brien, *Management Information Systems*, (Burr Ridge, IL: Richard D. Irwin, 1996), p. 374.

---

of an MIS is to provide information about the performance of basic organizational functions and processes, such as marketing, production, and finance. In comparison, a DSS focuses on providing information interactively to support specific types of decisions by individual managers. An MIS focuses on providing managers with prespecified information products that report on the performance of the organization. Figure 5.3 summarizes and contrasts the differences between a DSS and an MIS. Management Illustration 5.2 describes how one company is successfully using a DSS to improve its shipping practices.

Group Decision Support Systems

group decision support system (GDSS)   Specialized type of decision support system that combines communication, computing, and decision support technologies to facilitate problem formulation and solution in group meetings.

executive information system (EIS)   Highly interactive system that provides executives with flexible access to information for monitoring operating results and general business conditions.

A **group decision support system (GDSS)** is a specialized type of decision support system that combines communication, computing, and decision support technologies to facilitate problem formulation and solution in group meetings.[18] The idea behind a GDSS is to improve group decision making by removing common communication barriers, providing techniques for structuring decision analysis, and systematically directing the pattern, timing, or content of discussion. Both DSSs and GDSSs are evolving and will almost certainly be used more and more by managers in the future.

Management Illustration 5.2

DSS at Baxter Export

Baxter Healthcare delivers $5.5 billion worth of medical products and devices to 140 countries around the world. Baxter Export supplies Baxter subsidiaries and other customers with Baxter products sourced from the U.S. and Puerto Rico.

In order to improve customer relations and save resources, Baxter Export wanted to be able to recognize and adopt the most efficient shipping practices. It also wanted to keep its suppliers informed about trends in market demand so they could improve their own performance and efficiency. In order to realize these goals, Baxter needed extensive data gathering and analysis capabilities.

Baxter management decided to create a data warehousing and decision support system that would store shipping transaction data and provide detailed performance analysis. Data retrieval and analysis was managed by MicroStrategy's DSS Agent, which is a flexible, scalable tool that supports sophisticated analysis, while running directly against a relational database. With the click of a button, DSS Agent provides access to data at any level of detail. The efficiency and performance data provided by the system are used to identify the most efficient shipping practices.

Baxter believes that the new system not only saves money and resources, but that it provides a predictable service so customers can count on arrival times when determining their order needs and predicting reserve levels.

Source: Karen Rojek, "How Baxter Improved Data Exports," *AS/400 Systems Management*, May 1998, pp. 52–53.

For more information on Baxter Healthcare please visit their Web site at: www.baxter.com.

EXECUTIVE INFORMATION SYSTEMS

An **executive information system (EIS)** is a highly interactive system that provides executives with flexible access to information for monitoring operating results and general business conditions.[19] As opposed to the more standardized reports and analyses provided by an MIS, EIS are designed to help executives find needed information whenever they need it and in whatever form is most useful. An EIS can be viewed as a method by which executives access, on demand, information stored by management information system.[20] The essence of an EIS is to provide quick, user-friendly access to information for nontechnical, high-level executives. To be effective, an executive information system must (1) be tailored to the individual executive, (2) be able to extract and track critical data, (3) provide online access, (4) be able to access a variety of internal and external sources, and (5) be usable by the executive without intermediaries.[21]

While some people use the terms executive information systems (EIS) and executive support systems (ESS) interchangeably, others consider an ESS to be a EIS with additional capabilities to support electronic communications (E-mail, computer conferencing, etc.) And analyze data (e.g., spreadsheets, decision support systems). In this context an ESS should also include personal productivity tools such as electronic calendars, a Rolodex, and tickler files). The executive who masters both of these systems gains tremendous decision making ability and salvages precious time that can be better put to other uses.

Management Illustration 5.3
When Information Technology Alters the Workplace

As information technology spreads across corporate America, it is erasing one of the great barriers of the Industrial Age. The white-collar worker (manager) made policy, and the blue-collar worker (laborer) carried it out. Laborers were expected to do as they were told and leave the planning to higher-ups. Today information technology is dramatically changing those sharply defined roles.

The growing use of computers at all levels of the business is demanding a new type of worker who is skilled and empowered to make decisions from the flow of information that is at his or her fingertips.

Source: Adapted from James B. Treece, "Breaking the Chains of Command," *Business Week/The Information Revolution*, 1994, pp. 112–14.

EXPERT SYSTEMS

expert system Computer program that enables a computer to make an unstructured or semistructured decision that is normally made by a human with special expertise.

An **expert system** is a computer program that enables a computer to make (or give advice concerning) an unstructured or a semistructured decision that is normally made by a person with special expertise.[22] It is not unusual for a manager to need some specialized knowledge related to a particular problem. Unfortunately, not every manager can afford a staff or even an outside consultant whenever such a situation exists. Expert systems can be used in these situations. Expert systems are commonly used in such diverse areas as medical diagnosis, manufacturing quality control, and financial planning.[23]

An expert system differs from a decision support system in two major ways.[24] First, a DSS consists of computer routines that reflect how the manager thinks a problem should be solved; in other words, a DDS reflects the manager's style and capabilities. An expert system gives a manager the opportunity to make decisions that exceed his or her capabilities. Second, an expert system is able to explain why a certain line of reasoning was followed in reaching a particular solution.

IMPLEMENTATION STRATEGIES

Many organizations experience problems in implementing information systems. More often than not, implementation problems are related to the human factor. In fact, one study reported that "for the MIS practitioner, the research results in this area carry a clear message—worry less about how up-to-date your hardware is and whether or not the latest database system is in place, and worry more about how user interaction takes place, how employees are managed, and how computer resources are allocated within the organization."[25] Management Illustration 5.3 demonstrates the necessity for interaction.

To be successfully implemented, any information system must have the cooperation of many groups of people. Therefore, certain organization- and people-related factors must be considered. The following strategies have been suggested to overcome potential organization- and people-related problems.[26]

1. *Get top management involved.* Top managers must be committed to the information system if the system is to succeed. Not only must they approve the expenditures (which may be significant), but they also must outwardly exhibit interest in the project. Subordinates sense when their superiors are genuinely interested in a project, and they respond accordingly.

2. *Determine if there is a felt need for the system.* Make sure the ultimate users and those who must provide inputs to the information feel the need for it. One helpful approach is to make sure the users understand how the system can help them.

3. *Get the users involved.* Most people resist change. One of the best ways to overcome this resistance is to involve the users in the project as early as possible. Ask for their ideas and keep them fully informed as to what is going on. Involving users early in the design phase will also help ensure that the system will be compatible with the different users' needs and their organizational constraints.

4. *Provide training and education.* Users must be taught how to input data and how to get answers from the system. In addition, training should include educating users in the overall purpose of the system, what it is supposed to do, how it does it, why it needs to be done, and who must do it.

5. *Consider user attitudes.* Studies have shown that user attitudes have a great impact on system effectiveness, especially when use of the system is mandated. It is helpful to establish rewards for successful implementation of the system. These rewards do not have to be monetary but can be some form of recognition or other type of extrinsic reward.

6. *Keep the interface simple.* Even when the system is complex, the interface with users should be kept as simple as possible. Usually users do not need to see the complex flow diagrams and programming of the system design. Systems that appear very complicated to users often frighten them and make them leery of the entire system.

7. *Let the ultimate users (managers) determine information usefulness.* Information system designers should remember that what counts is what the users think is important. If users believe the information is neither useful nor important for making decisions, the system implementation will likely fail.

All of the preceding strategies are closely related to one another. They are not necessarily sequential but may be used at the same time. Also, they not only apply to the initial implementation but also should be regularly reviewed and used to improve the system after it is operational.

Research has shown, however, that the biggest problem with information systems is that most of their capability is not used strategically. It has been reported that few organizations have tapped the potential of technology to improve effectiveness (as opposed to efficiency). All too many information systems emphasize the handling of internal information rather than the delivery of better customer service and the planning of long-term strategy.[27]

Outsourcing

Many organizations find it difficult to keep up with the technology in the information system area. In addition, a significant investment is often required to establish in-house information systems. For these reasons, many organizations subcontract their information systems work to an independent outside source. This practice is referred to as **outsourcing.** Advantages of outsourcing are that the independent outside source specializes in information systems and capital expenditures are low.

outsourcing   Practice of subcontracting information systems work to an independent outside source.

Management Illustration 5.4

Hacker Insurance Now Available

The International Computer Security Association (ICSA), based in Carlisle, PA now offers "hacker insurance" as part of its TruSecure service. The basic policy costs $40,000 per year and pays $20,000 per occurrence up to a maximum of $80,000 per year. Large organizations can buy an enhanced service which will pay up to $250,000 per year. The company will pay even if the client is not financially harmed by an attack that penetrates their system.

TruSecure is a series of steps suggested by ICSA that companies must adhere to in preventing hacker attacks. ICSA performs an initial assessment of a company's computer network, identifies vulnerability, and then recommends changes to protect against hacker attacks. The insurance is part of a guarantee that no one can break into the system after the suggested changes have been made.

Source: Tony Attrino, "Security Firm Offers Hacker Insurance," *National Underwriter*, September 7, 1998, pp. 9, 55.

For more information about the International Computer Security Association visit their Web site at: www.icsa.net/.

INFORMATION SYSTEMS SECURITY

Computer abuse and misuse have recently become serious problems for many organizations. The range of illicit acts a user may perform is almost infinite. Theft, illicit use, hacking, and spreading of viruses are some of the most frequently encountered problems. Theft involves the unauthorized taking not only of hardware but also of software and data. Illicit use involves employees using the computer for unauthorized purposes that may range from playing computer games to running a private bureau service on an employer's machine. **Hacking** refers to gaining illegal access to a database. The name was derived from the notion that such people keep "hacking away" until they gain access. Once a hacker has gained access, he or she can cause considerable damage by stealing or altering data or software. A recent survey reported that the average corporate network is attacked by hackers 12 to 15 times each year.[28] Furthermore, often organizations do not realize their systems have been invaded. Many organizations are using computer security consulting firms to train their employees to recognize the tell-tale signs of a system or network invasion.

hacking   Gaining illegal access to a database.

A computer **virus** is a self-replicating block of code that enters a computer via diskette, over telephone lines, or manually.[29] Unlike "legitimate codes, a computer virus spreads an infection just as humans spread a biological virus: by contact. When "healthy" diskettes and programs come in contact with the disk drive of an infected computer, the virus merges into that disk. A virus may destroy data, reformat a disk, wear out the disk drive, or flash a harmless but unwelcome message on the screen. Many viruses consume significant memory space and can even jam the machine. Recent surveys indicate that the incidence of computer virus attacks is continuing to increase. One survey reported that virus infections had doubled in 1997 when compared to 1996.[30] Management Illustration 5.4 describes "hacker insurance" now being offered by one company.

virus   Self-replicating block of code that enters a computer via diskette, over phone lines, or manually.

THE Y2K PROBLEM

In many of today's electronic information systems, the year is represented by two digits and the twentieth century is assumed. For example, the digits 98 stands for the year 1998. When the year 2000 arrives, and even before, this will create problems because the computers will read "00" as 1900 and not the year 2000. The problem is referred to as the Y2K problem. The extent of the problems is greatly debated. At the best, operational errors will occur; at the worse entire industries may be shut down! One noted economist even predicted a 70 percent likelihood that the Y2K problem will cause a global recession.[31]

Most experts believe that few organizations will be completely prepared to handle the transition to the year 2000. These same experts recommend that organizations concentrate their resources on the most critical components to ensure that the basic processes of the organization will continue to operate.[32] Organizations should identify critical computer applications that are essential, have a high risk of failure, and cannot easily be covered by a contingency approach.

COMPUTER ETHICS

Computers can be misused to the detriment of individuals, organizations, and society. The ethical climate of the organization should establish the framework for any decisions relating to computer ethics. In other words, ethical conduct related to computers should be no different from any other ethical conduct in an organization. Computer ethics, like all ethics, are the responsibility of every manager within the company. The examples set by management tend to filter down to the employee ranks. Training sessions on the legal and illegal use of the company's computers and systems is a must. Computer usage guidelines and statements of responsibility are now standard documents in employee packets.

INFORMATION CENTERS

Learning to interact with their companies' computer systems is a major problem for many of today's managers. Most managers do not have the time or interest to become experts in data processing. What managers want and need is to be able to gain direct access to information without becoming frustrated and confused.

Many companies, including Exxon, Standard Oil of California, Bank of America, and New York Telephone, have formed internal **information centers.** At these information centers, managers learn how to interact with their information systems from staff specialists whose job is to train and support "noncomputer" people.[33] Typically, a manager contacts the center and describes the problems

information center   In-house center that a company establishes to teach managers how to use information systems.

encountered and the type of information needed. A center consultant then works one-on-one with the manager, showing how to access needed data and use the available software. The key to the information center concept is that managers use a hands-on approach and learn how to generate their own reports.

The primary difficulties faced by information center staff are overcoming managers' reluctance to trying something new, getting managers to admit they need help, and creating an environment that reduces managers' apprehension about the unknown. Once these behavioral difficulties are overcome, the information center concept generally works well.

CRITICISMS AND CAUTIONS CONCERNING INFORMATION SYSTEMS

There is little doubt that an information system can have a very positive effect on organizational performance. Yet it is still subject to frequent criticism. Much of the criticism relates to shortfalls in methods of implementation. Figure 5.4 describes some of the most frequent criticisms of information systems.

FIGURE 5.4	Criticisms of Information Systems
Weakness	**Criticism**
Inadequate information	Managers often complain that they do not get the information they need but they do get much information that is irrelevant.
Ignorance about what managers actually do	Understanding a manager's job is a natural prerequisite to providing that manager with useful information.
Centralized control of MIS	There is a tendency to centralize the development of an MIS. However, because of the large number and variety of activities that go on in an organization, this frequently leads to problems.
Complex user procedures	The rule of thumb is to keep the system as simple and user friendly as possible.
Poor communication	Any system is almost doomed to failure if there is not open communication between the users and those responsible for developing the information system.

Source: David Lynch, "MIS: Conceptual Framework, Criticisms, and Major Requirements for Success," *Journal of Business Communication*, Winter 1984, pp. 23–25.

Another frequent criticism is that computers often have a negative effect on the individuality of people.[34] Computers are often accused of dehumanizing and depersonalizing certain activities. Similarly, computerized systems frequently appear overly rigid and inflexible.

While it is true that computerized systems can be depersonalizing and inflexible, they do not have to be. Technology has advanced to the point where it is now possible to have very "people-oriented" systems.[35] The trend toward adopting these user-friendly systems will likely continue.

Tremendous strides have been made regarding computers and management information systems. Still, managers must realize that technology will never replace certain aspects of a manager's job. Managers must surely become familiar with and be able to use computerized information systems. Yet they must guard against being too dependent on any computer system. One writer notes, "Too many cut-and-dried computer printouts have usurped the human aspect and put forth the fallacy that a corporation is equal to (and not more than) the sum of its parts."[36] Information systems can be tremendously helpful in making managerial decisions. But the fact remains that successful management is still heavily dependent on human interactions and judgments.

THE CHALLENGE OF THE NEW INFORMATION AGE

The advances in digital technology are having a dramatic impact on businesses, their workers, and the suppliers and customers who deal with them.[37] Information power is getting cheaper by the day. This power will change organizations by breaking down old barriers and alter operations by shrinking cycle times, reducing defects, and cutting waste.[38] Management layers will continue to be reduced, and employees will be empowered as never before. "Virtual offices" will become commonplace.[39] Finally, customer service representatives, by tapping into companywide databases, will solve customer demands with ever-increasing quickness, efficiency, and accuracy.[40] The power of the information-based future is literally at the manager's fingertips.

Summary

1. *Recount the General Evolution of Computers Since the Early 1960s.* In the 1960s, large and costly mainframe computers were used almost exclusively by very large companies and governments. In the 1970s, the large computers were followed by minicomputers that were much smaller in size and cost. Minicomputers ushered in the concept of distributed data processing. Minicomputers were followed by microcomputers, or personal computers. Microcomputers are relatively inexpensive, take up very little space, and can process large amounts of data.

2. *Describe the Internet and Identify the Two Functional Categories of Information Available on the Internet That Are Most Useful to Managers.* The internet is a global collection of independently operating, but interconnected, computers. The two broad categories of information available on the Internet that are most useful to managers are (1) conversational resources and (2) reference resources.

3. *Describe an Intranet.* An intranet is a private, corporate computer network that uses Internet products and technologies to provide multimedia applications within organizations.

4. *Distinguish between Data and Information and Define a Management Information System (MIS).* Data are the raw materials from which information is developed; data comprise facts that describe people, places, things, or events and that have not been interpreted. Data that have been interpreted and that meet the needs of one or more managers is information. A management information system (MIS) is an integrated approach for providing interpreted and relevant data that can help managers make decisions. The term *MIS* usually implies that computers are used at some point in the system to process data.

5. *Define a Decision Support System (DSS).* A decision support system (DSS) is a system that supports a single, or a relatively small, group of managers working as a problem-solving team on the solution of a semistructured problem by providing information or suggestions concerning specific decisions. Decision support systems not only provide inputs to the decision process but actually become a part of the process and make suggestions to the decision maker.

6. *Define an Executive Information System (EIS) and List the Requirements for an EIS.* An executive information system (EIS) is a highly interactive system that provides executives with flexible access to information for monitoring operating results and general business conditions. An EIS must (1) be tailored to the individual executive, (2) be able to extract and track critical data, (3) provide online access, (4) be able to access a variety of internal and external sources, and (5) be usable by the executive without intermediaries.

7. *Discuss What Expert Systems Can Do.* An expert system is a computer program that enables a computer to make (or give advice concerning) an unstructured or semistructured decision that is normally made by a human with special expertise. Expert systems provide specialized knowledge related to a particular problem, which is especially useful when the manager cannot afford staff personnel or consultants.

8. *List Several Strategies for Overcoming Potential Problems When Implementing an Information System.* Some of the strategies available for overcoming organization- and people-related problems that can plague an information system are (1) involving top management in the project (2) determining if there is a felt need for the system, (3) getting the users involved, (4) providing training and education for the users, (5) fostering positive user attitudes, (6) keeping the interface simple, and (7) letting the ultimate users (managers) determine information usefulness.

9. *Identify and Define at Least Four Major Types of Illicit Acts Involving Computers in Organizations.* Theft, illicit use, hacking, and spreading of viruses are four major types of illicit acts involving computers in organizations. Theft involves the unauthorized taking of hardware, software, and data. Illicit use involves employees using the computer for unauthorized purposes. Hacking refers to gaining illegal access to a database. A computer virus is a code that can be self-replicating, consumes significant memory space, and can even jam a computer.

10. *Explain What the Y2K Problem Is.* In many of today's electronic information systems the year is represented by two digits and the twentieth century is assumed. When the year 2000 arrives, and even before, this will create problems because the computers will read "00" as 1900 and not the year 2000.

11. *Describe an Information Center.* An information center is an in-house center that a company establishes to teach its managers how to use its information systems. Typically, an information systems professional works one on one with a manager, showing how to use a particular system or part of a system.

Preview Analysis

1. What is the difference between the Internet and the "intranet"?

2. Using FedEx as an example, what could the intranet do for a company?

3. What is one advantage of the intranet?

4. What is the primary stumbling block to the success of the intranet?

Review Questions

1. Define information overload.
2. Distinguish between the Internet and the Intranet.
3. Distinguish between data and information.
4. What is a management information system (MIS)?
5. How does a transaction-processing system differ from an MIS?
6. Name several specific types of MIS subsystems used in operations management.
7. Distinguish among decision support systems, executive information systems, and expert systems.
8. Compare an MIS with a decision support system.
9. Briefly describe seven strategies that should be considered when developing an MIS.
10. What is outsourcing?
11. What is computer hacking?
12. What is a computer virus?
13. What is the Y2K problem?

Skill-Building Questions

1. From the viewpoint of a customer, think of a recent situation in which you were inconvenienced by an information system. What were the circumstances, and what took place? If this situation has the potential to inconvenience customers, why does the company continue to use it?
2. When you go into a fast-food store and the salesperson keys your order into the cash register, how might this information be used as part of an MIS?
3. List two companies that you have had a positive experience with one or more of their information systems. What did you like about the systems? What did you dislike about the system?
4. What do you think will be the future for systems and systems management in today's rapidly changing technological environment?
5. How do you think the World Wide Web and the Internet will affect businesses? Illustrate your comments with examples, if possible.

SKILL-BUILDING EXERCISE 5.1

What to Computerize?

This exercise may be done individually or in small groups. For each of the following potential data processing activities, state whether the data should be processed manually or a stored computer program would do the job better. Briefly justify your answer.

A. Balancing your personal checkbook.
B. Calculating a table of square root values for many numbers.
C. Preparing a list of parts and the quantity of each needed for every automobile being assembled today on the production line.
D. Controlling the pressure and flow of chemicals through several high-pressure lines at the same time (high fluctuations in pressure are extremely dangerous).
E. Calculating the grade-point average for a specific student in the college of business.
F. Calculating withholding taxes and issuing a paycheck for the net wages of all four people working for your department.
G. Controlling the operation of all traffic signals in midtown Manhattan.

SKILL-BUILDING EXERCISES 5.2

Recall*

Your instructor will read several series of digits to you. Listen carefully to each number. *When told to do so,* recall the digits and record them on a sheet of paper in their proper order as shown by the spaces provided below. Remember, do not write down the numbers until your instructor tells you to.

Did You Get It
Correct?

Yes   No

String 1: ____ ____ ____ ____ ____ ____ ____ ____ ____ ____ ____ ____ ____ ____ ____ ____ ____

String 2: ____ ____ ____ ____ ____ ____ ____ ____ ____ ____ ____ ____ ____ ____ ____ ____ ____

String 3: ____ ____ ____ ____ ____ ____ ____ ____ ____ ____ ____ ____ ____ ____ ____ ____ ____

String 4: ____ ____ ____ ____ ____ ____ ____ ____ ____ ____ ____ ____ ____ ____ ____ ____ ____

String 5: ____ ____ ____ ____ ____ ____ ____ ____ ____ ____ ____ ____ ____ ____ ____ ____ ____

String 6: ____ ____ ____ ____ ____ ____ ____ ____ ____ ____ ____ ____ ____ ____ ____ ____ ____

Compare the following sets of outcomes by noting whether you get the string correct or not.

Comparison I

Did you get String 1 correct?	Yes	No
Did you get String 2 correct?	Yes	No
Did you get String 3 correct?	Yes	No

How are 1, 2, and 3 different? _____

How does this show? _____

_____

Comparison II

Did you get String 3 correct?	Yes	No
Did you get String 5 correct?	Yes	No

How are Strings 3 and 5 different? _____

What does this show? _____

_____

Comparison III

Did you get String 4 correct?	Yes	No
Did you get String 6 correct?	Yes	No

How are Strings 4 and 6 different? _____

What does this show? _____

_____

*This exercise is adapted from Henry J. Tosi and Jerald W. Young, *Management Experiences and Demonstrations* (Burr Ridge, IL: Richard D. Irwin, 1982), pp. 154–55.

CASE INCIDENT 5.1

Held Ransom*

When a senior programmer in a multinational pharmaceutical company became worried about the security of his job, he decided to make himself indispensable to the company. He did this by altering computer programs and data files. His task was made easy for him because:

- He had unrestricted access to the operating system.

- He could access the company's mainframe by telephone from his home.

- There was no defined security management philosophy to help identify misuse of computer facilities.

This individual perpetrated his crime by introducing logic bombs into all major systems. These logic bombs were timed to go off on particular dates without his personal intervention. The result would be to destroy all data and program files and leave a message to that effect!

Questions

1. What precautions could managers take to guard against the development of situations such as described in this case?

2. Do you think situations like this are relatively isolated and unlikely to happen in most companies? Support your answer.

*Adapted from Grant Findlay, "Data Security: Reducing the Risks," *The Accountant's Magazine*, June 1987, p. 57.

References & Additional Readings

[1]Carol L. Colman and Kenneth R. Hey, "Remove Your Business Blinders—and View the Future," *Journal of Business Strategy*, July–August 1988, p. 2.

[2]Stan Augarten, Bit by Bit: *An Illustrated History of Computers* (New York: Ticknor & Fields, 1984), pp. 124–25, 128.

[3]Edward E. Furash, "Internet Mania,." *Journal of Lending & Credit Risk Management*, September 1998, pp. 88–91.

[4]Amy Cortese, "Updates? Just a Mouse Click Away," *Business Week*, February 26, 1996, p. 84.

[5]Byron J. Finch, *The Management Guide to Internet Resources*, (New York: McGraw-Hill), 1997 ed., p. 2. Much of this section is drawn from this source.

[6]Paul Barker, "The Evolving Corporate Intranet," *Telecommunications*, December 1997, pp. 67–70.

[7]Ibid.

[8]David Lynch, "MIS: Conceptual Framework, Criticisms and Major Requirements for Success," *Journal of Business Communication*. Winter 1984, p. 20.

[9]Ibid.

[10]James A. Senn, *Information Technology in Business*, 2d ed. (Englewood Cliffs, NJ: Prentice Hall), 1998, p. 615.

[11]James A. O'Brien, *Management In Systems*, 3d ed. (Burr Ridge, IL: Richard D. Irwin 1996), p. 370.

[12]Raymond McLeod, Jr., *Management Information Systems*, 4th ed. (New York: Macmillan, 1990) p. 30.

[13]Ibid.

[14]Senn, *Information Technology in Business*, p. 616.

[15]Steven Alter, *Information Systems: A Management Perspective* (Reading, MA: Addison-Wesley, 1992), p. 133.

[16]Senn, *op cit*, p. 616.

[17]O'Brien, *Management Information Systems*, p. 374.

[18]Gerardine DeSanctis and R. Brent Gallupe, *"A Foundation for the Study of Group Decision Support Systems,"* Management Science, May 1987, pp. 589–90.

[19]Alter, *Information Systems*, p. 136.

[20]James O. Hicks, Jr., *Management Information Systems: A User Perspective*, 3d ed. (Minneapolis: West, 1993), p. 158. Other parts of this section are drawn from this source.

[21]James O'Brien, *Management Information Systems* (Burr Ridge, IL: Richard D. Irwin, 1994), p. 361, as adapted from Hugh Watson, R. Kelly Ranier, and Chang Koh, "Executive Information Systems: A Framework for Development and a Survey of Current Practices," *MIS Quarterly*, March 1991, p. 14.

[22]Hicks, *Management Information Systems*, p. 171.

[23]Senn, *Information Technology in Business*, p. 625.

[24]McLeod, *Management Information Systems*, p. 411.

[25]Paul H. Cheney and Gary W. Dickson, "Organizational Characteristics of Information Systems: An Exploratory Investigation," *Academy of Management Journal*, March 1982, pp. 181–82.

[26]Jugloslan S. Multinovich and Vladimir Vlahovich, "A Strategy for a Successful MIS/DSS Implementation," *Journal of Systems Management*, August 1984, pp. 8–16.

[27]Mark G. Brown, Darcy E. Hitchcock, and Marshal L. Willard, *Why TQM Fails and What to Do About It* (Burr Ridge, IL: Richard D. Irwin, 1994), p. 203.

[28]Laura DiDio, "Do You Know If You've Been Hacked?", *ComputerWorld*, July 6, 1998, pp. 39–40.

[29]Scott W. Cullen, "The Computer Virus: Is There a Real Panacea?", *The Office*, March 1989, p. 43.

[30]Terry Corbitt, "New-Age Viruses," *Credit Management*, September 1998, pp. 34–35.

[31]David Kirkpatrick, "Could Y2K Cause a Global Recession?" *Fortune*, October 12, 1998, pp. 172–176.

[32]Ian Hayes and William Ulrich, "It's All About Managing Risk," *Software Magazine*, (Year 2000 Survival Guide Supplement), April 15, 1998, pp. 12–20.

[33]William Clarke, "How Managers with Little DP Know-How Learn to Go Online with the Company Database," *Management Review*, June 1983, pp. 9–11. Much of this section is based on this article.

[34]James A. O'Brien, *Information Systems in Business Management*, 5th ed. (Burr Ridge, IL: Richard D. Irwin, 1988), p. 604.

[35]Ibid.

[36]Robert E. McGarrah, "Ironies of Our Computer Age," *Business Horizons*, September–October 1984, p. 34.

[37]Ira Sager, "The Great Equalizer," *Business Week/The Information Revolution*, 1994, pp. 100–101.

[38]Ibid.

[39]Ibid.

[40]Ibid.

6

Legal, Ethical, and Social Responsibilities

§➤

LEARNING OBJECTIVES

After studying this chapter, you should be able to:

1. Define ethics.

2. Explain what a code of ethics is.

3. Describe three philosophical approaches that serve as a basis for codes of ethics.

4. Explain four general areas into which laws relating to business ethics can be categorized.

5. Outline the laws relating to competitive behavior, consumer protection, and product safety.

6. Outline the laws relating to environmental protection.

7. Define social responsibility.

8. Explain corporate philanthropy.

9. Describe a social audit.

Most of us are impressed when we see corporations using a business as a vehicle to do more than simply make money. Companies today are more aware of the importance of ethics and social responsibility than ever before. Take a look at two completely different corporations, Patagonia and Marriot. Patagonia is the epitome of extreme liberalism while Marriot tends to stay far to the right. Both companies, however, have one thing in common. They have recognized that the corporation is a powerful tool for social change.

Patagonia began its career as an environmental crusader in the early 1970s when the company encouraged a shift away from rock-scarring pitons. Since then, Patagonia has supported countless social and environmental causes. Today, the company manufactures jackets from recycled plastic bottles, makes clothes entirely from organic cotton, and donates 1% of its sales to environmental causes. Patagonia also encourages employees to take the courses that it offers on nonviolent activism. On top of that, the company has been known to post bail for employees who have been arrested while crusading for environmental causes. Patagonia is not only contributing profits to bring about change but also developing new business practices that will preserve the environment. Hopefully, others will follow.

Marriot may be far less liberal, but the company still consciously uses its power as a corporation to incite social change. Perhaps the best example of this is the company's "Pathways to Independence" program that finds welfare recipients, trains them in the business, and promotes them to jobs within the company. Since the program's inception in 1991, the company has employed more than 750 people, 300 of which still remain with the company. Both companies hope that their contributions, large or small, will serve as a source of inspiration in persuading other companies to follow suit.

Source: "The Foundation for Doing Good," *Inc.* December 1997, p. 41.

In all too many businesses, the principle of *caveat emptor*—let the buyer beware—unfortunately governs the decision making and behavior of managers. Scandals on Wall Street, the savings and loan bailout, and huge salaries paid to executives of failing businesses could lead one to think there are no ethics in business other than "looking out for number one."

On the positive side, the business world offers a great deal: rewarding jobs, opportunities to provide excellent products and services, and chances to contribute to society at large. On the negative side, too much can be obtained in the business world through unethical and corrupt behavior.

ETHICS IN MANAGEMENT

ethics   Principles of conduct used to govern the decision making and behavior of an individual or a group of individuals.
stakeholders   Employees, customers, shareholders, suppliers, government, and the public at large.

Ethics are principles of conduct used to govern the decision making and behavior of an individual or a group of individuals. Because management is concerned with making decisions within an organization, the ethics of the individual or group making these decisions have significant implications for the organization's **stakeholders:** employees, customers, shareholders, suppliers, the government, and the public at large.

The role of ethics in management decisions is difficult, partly because it is such an emotionally charged issue and partly because of the many and varied ethical problems managers face. For example, what are the ethical implications of the promotion and sale of cigarettes by U.S. companies in foreign countries while the U.S. government acts to diminish tobacco consumption in the United States? What about the individual manager who is aware of unethical practices in his or her company? Should the person blow the whistle and risk his or her job? Should the person quit and allow unethical practices to continue? Or should the person just ignore the practices? These are only a few of the difficult and complex ethical decisions managers face.

CODES OF ETHICS

One response by businesses to the question of ethics has been to develop a code of ethics that is communicated to all employees. A **code of ethics** is a written

code of ethics   A written document that outlines the principles of conduct to be used in making decisions within an organization.
principle of justice   Involves making decisions based on truth, a lack of bias, and consistency.
principle of individual rights   Involves making decisions based on protecting human dignity.
principle of utilitarianism   Involves making decisions directed toward promoting the greatest good for the greatest number of people.

document that outlines the principles of conduct to be used in making decisions within the organization. Codes of ethics are based on one or more of the following philosophical approaches: justice, individual rights, and utilitarianism.[1] The **principle of justice** involves making decisions based on truth, a lack of bias, and consistency. The **principle of individual rights** concerns making decisions based on protecting human dignity. For example, managers would not force employees to act in a way that is contrary to their moral beliefs. Finally, the **principle of utilitarianism** involves making decisions directed toward promoting the greatest good for the greatest number of people. Figure 6.1 summarizes these philosophical approaches.

Underlying each of these three philosophical approaches is the fundamental concept that managers must be as concerned about the interests of the organization's stakeholders as they are about their own self-interests. James F. Lincoln, founder of the highly successful Lincoln Electric Company, commented on this fundamental

---

FIGURE 6.1   Philosophical Approaches to Codes of Ethics

Principle of justice	Making decisions based on truth, lack of bias, and consistency
Principle of individual rights	Making decisions based on protecting human dignity
Principle of utilitarianism	Making decisions based on promoting the greatest good for the greatest number of people.

---

concept as follows: "Do unto others as you would have them do unto you. This is not just a Sunday school idea, but a proper labor–management policy."[2]

Codes of ethics should be formal, written, and communicated to all employees. Although codes of ethics differ in content from one industry to another and from one company to another, a general list of topics covered includes the following:

- Fundamental honesty and adherence to the law.
- Product safety and quality.
- Health and safety in the workplace.
- Conflicts of interest.
- Employment practices.
- Fairness in selling/marketing practices.
- Financial reporting.
- Supplier relationships.
- Pricing, billing, and contracting.
- Trading in securities/using inside information.
- Payments to obtain business/Foreign Corrupt Practices Act.
- Acquiring and using information about others.
- Security.
- Political activities.
- Protection of the environment.
- Intellectual property/proprietary information.[3]

Unfortunately, one of the myths about business is that being ethical and being profitable are mutually exclusive.[4] However, a reputation for honest and fair business practices is a corporate must that cannot help but contribute to profits.

Obviously, codes of ethics do not end unethical behavior, but they are a positive step in addressing the problem. However, having a written code of ethics probably does more harm than good if management does not put its precepts into practice. The adage "Actions speak louder than words" is especially true regarding ethics in business. Finally, organizations must impose sanctions on employees for ethical violations.[5]

In many instances, moral courage of the company's leadership is the real issue. Without steadfast adherence to principles and "leading by example," codes of ethics begin to break down. In his book *Organizations in Action*, James D. Thompson states that leaders must have the courage to change things even when things are going well, share authority and power, hire subordinates who are likely to outperform them, stick to their values in hard times, resist pressures to pursue short-run gains, take unpopular positions when necessary, and support subordinates who offer innovative ideas. These are not revolutionary ideas; in fact, they are not even new ideas (Thompson's book was published in 1967). They are just sound ideas for leaders who believe in ethics and codes of conduct.[6]

LAWS RELATING TO ETHICS IN BUSINESS

One outcome of unethical practices by managers has been the passage of laws to regulate behavior. Over the years, numerous laws have been enacted that directly relate to the issue of ethics in business.[7] Many of these laws apply to the general areas of competitive behavior, consumer protection, product safety, and environmental protection.

Competitive Behavior

The earliest laws relating to business ethics concerned competitive practices among businesses. Often referred to as *antitrust laws*, they were intended to maintain a favorable competitive environment. Table 6.1 provides a brief summary of the significant federal legislation.

In the 1990s, perhaps the greatest interest in competitive behavior has been in the international arena. U.S. complaints about trading partners' behavior (especially Japan and China) has led to a renewed interest in protectionism for domestic markets and industries. Protectionism is rarely good for free and open markets. Certain industries, including aviation, consumer film, semiconductors, spirits, and telecommunications, have all demanded attention to problems of unfair and anticompetitive practices in the international market. Negotiations rather than legislation seem to be

TABLE 6.1   Significant Antitrust Legislation

Legislation	Date	Effect
Sherman Act	1890	Made it illegal to enter into a contract, combination, or conspiracy in restraint of trade. Outlawed monopolies, attempts to monopolize, or conspiracies to monopolize interstate commerce.
Clayton Act	1914	Made price discrimination illegal if it tends to create a monopoly or lessen competition Made it illegal to have a contract requiring another entity to boycott a competitor if doing so substantially lessens competition or tends to create a monopoly. Prohibited mergers through purchase of stock if the effect is to substantially lessen competition or create a monopoly. Prohibited interlocking directorates.
Federal Trade Commission Act	1914	Created Federal Trade Commission (FTC). Prohibited unfair methods of competition or deceptive trade practices.
Robinson-Patman Act	1936	Prohibited price discrimination that substantially lessens competition or tends to create a monopoly.
Celler-Kefauver Amendment to Clayton Act	1950	Prohibited mergers through purchases of assets if the effect is to substantially lessen competition or create a monopoly.
Hart-Scott-Rodino Antitrust Improvement Act	1976	Required public notice of mergers before their completion. Permitted prosecution of antitrust violations by the attorneys general of individual states for damages to state citizens.

a more reasonable way to solve differences, since negotiations seek understanding and tolerance whereas legislation tends to be restrictive and protective in nature.

CONSUMER PROTECTION

Consumer protection is the object of legislation that deals with unethical practices of businesses that affect consumers of their products or services. Although the Federal Trade Commission (FTC) was originally created to enforce antitrust legislation, it was given broad authority under the Wheeler-Lea Act of 1938 to protect consumers against unethical business practices. The Food and Drug Administration (FDA) also has authority to protect consumers from adulterated, misbranded, or unsafe foods. Some of the consumer protection laws apply to credit protection, warranty protection, misbranding, and false and misleading advertising. For the astute manager, consumer protection basically revolves around the issue of trust. In dealing with the consuming public, this implies three essential activities: (1) making realistic promises in the first place, (2) keeping those promises during product and service delivery, and (3) enabling and empowering employees and service systems to deliver on the promises made.[8] Table 6.2 provides a summary of significant consumer protection legislation.

Product Safety

Motor vehicles, food products, drugs, and major consumer products must meet certain safety specifications. Government legislation for this purpose has expanded to protect consumers from latent defects in products that are increasing in complexity and diversity. Table 6.3 summarizes significant product safety legislation.

Environmental Protection

During the past 20 years, environmental protection has become an important social and economic issue. This concern has reflected itself in many laws designed to improve the environment. A significant number of those laws directly affect businesses.

The key legislation in environmental protection is the National Environmental Policy Act, passed in 1969. This law committed the government to preserving the country's ecology, established the Environmental Protection Agency (EPA) to administer the act, and established the Council on Environmental Quality, which advises the president on environmental policy and reviews environmental impact statements. *Environmental impact statements* require federal agencies to submit reports providing an environmental analysis of any actions taken by other organizations that might affect the environment. Table 6.4 summarizes significant environmental protection legislation.

Changing interpretations of the environmental regulations by the EPA and complaints that the laws are too strict and costly have made environmental protection a controversial issue for business. However, during the 1990s, environmental protection will continue to be a significant concern for businesses.

Many believe there is an overlap between environmental protection and social responsibility (discussed in the next section). For example, where do issues involving smokers' and nonsmokers' rights fit in? Are the new "social contract" ideas involving health, welfare, and entitlements purely social issues, or are they also environmental

TABLE 6.2   Significant Consumer Protection Legislation

Legislation	Date	Effect
Credit Protection		
Truth in Lending Act (also known as Consumer Credit Protection Act)	1968	Required creditors to inform consumers of the amount of finance charge and the annual interest rate. Limited credit cardholders' liability in unauthorized use of the card.
Fair Credit Reporting Act	1970	Required companies providing consumer credit reports to supply accurate information. Required companies that use credit reports and that withhold credit on the basis of the report to inform consumers of sources of credit information.
Fair Credit Billing Act	1975	Required accuracy in consumer credit billings.
Equal Credit Opportunity Act	1975	Prohibited creditors from making credit decisions on the basis of discriminatory practices.
Fair Debt Collection Act	1978	Prohibited creditors from using unreasonable debt collection tactics.
Fair Credit and Charge Card Disclosure Act	1988	Outlined requirements that charge card issuers must observe when soliciting accounts.
Home Equity Loan Consumer Protection Act	1988	Required a clear statement of all additional fees and repayment options on home equity loans (second mortgages). Required certain standards in advertising on these loans.
Warranties		
Magnuson-Moss Warranty Act	1975	Required warranty statements to be written in ordinary language. Required warranty statements to contain all terms and conditions of the warranty. Required warranty statements to be made available before purchase.
Misbranding and False and Misleading Advertising		
Food and Drugs Act	1906	Prohibited adulteration and misbranding of food/drugs in interstate commerce.
Federal Food, Drug, and Cosmetic Act	1938	Added cosmetics and therapeutic products to Food and Drug Administration's jurisdiction.
Wool Products Labeling Act	1939	Required fabric components and manufacturer's name on wool product labels.
Fur Products Labeling Act	1951	Required fur products producers to name animal of origin on label.
Textile Fiber Products Identification Act	1958	Prohibited misbranding and false advertising of fiber products.
Kefauver-Harris Drug Amendment to Food, Drug, and Cosmetic Act	1962	Required manufacturers to test effectiveness and safety of drugs before marketing them.
Federal Hazardous Substances Act	1960	Required warning labels on dangerous household chemical products.
Fair Packaging and Labeling Act	1966	Required honest and informative labeling, including quantity of contents and ingredients in products.
Country of Origin Labeling Act	1985	Required manufacturers of clothing products to indicate on the label the country of origin.

TABLE 6.3   Significant Product Safety Legislation

Legislation	Date	Effect
Flammable Fabrics Act	1953	Prohibited interstate transportation of fabrics made of highly flammable materials. Set minimum standards for the fire-retardant qualities of fabrics.
National Traffic and Motor Vehicle Safety Act	1966	Established motor vehicle safety standards. Provided mechanisms to remedy defective vehicles.
Child Protection and Toy Safety Act	1969	Required greater protection on children's toys.
Poison Prevention Packaging Act	1970	Required safety packaging on products that can be harmful to children.
Consumer Product Safety Act	1972	Created the Consumer Product Safety Commission (CPSC) and gave it broad authority to establish minimum product safety standards and to enforce regulations for noncomplying products.

TABLE 6.4   Significant Environmental Protection Legislation

Legislation	Date	Effect
National Environmental Policy Act	1969	Established national policy on environment. Created the Environmental Protection Agency (EPA) to administer the act. Created the Council on Environmental Quality to advise the president on environmental issues.
Air Pollution		
Clean Air Act (numerous amendments have been made)	1963	Provided assistance to state and local governments in formulating air pollution control programs. Amendments to the act authorized federal standards for auto exhaust emissions. Amendments to the act established nationwide air pollution standards and limited the discharge of certain pollutants into the lower atmosphere.
Solid Waste		
Solid Waste Disposal Act	1965	Provided research and assistance to state and local governments for their solid waste disposal programs.
Resource Conservation and Recovery Act	1976	Directed the EPA to regulate hazardous waste treatment, storage, transportation, and disposal. Provided technical and financial assistance for facilities for recovery of energy and other resources from solid waste.
Water Pollution		
Clean Water Restoration Act	1966	Provided technical and financial assistance in the development of waste treatment, water purification, and water quality control programs.
Water Quality Improvement Act	1970	Provided for federal cleanup of oil spills. Strengthened federal control over water pollution control.
Safe Drinking Water Act	1974	Established standards for drinking water quality.
Other Forms of Pollution		
Noise Control Act	1972	Required EPA to establish noise standards for major sources of noise such as airplanes.
Toxic Substances Control Act	1976	Required testing and use requirements on certain chemical substances.
Comprehensive Environmental Response, Compensation and Liability Act (commonly called Superfund Act)	1980	Created a trust fund (partly paid for by toxic chemical manufacturers) to clean up hazardous waste sites.

concerns? Perhaps only the courts will make the final determination. However, proactive management groups of most large corporations are currently examining these issues and their potential effects on the workplace.[9,10]

SOCIAL RESPONSIBILITY

social responsibility   The role of business in solving current social issues over and above legal requirements.

Social responsibility refers to the role of business in resolving current social issues over and above legal requirements. Today there is little doubt that business must involve itself in social issues beyond producing and selling goods and services, not only because it is the ethical thing to do but also because it is in the best interest of business.

Social Responsibility: A Historical Perspective

The idea that business has a responsibility other than producing goods and services is not new. In 1919, Henry L. Gantt stated his belief that the community would attempt to take over business if the business system neglected its social responsibilities.[11] Another early management writer who discussed social responsibility was Oliver Sheldon. Writing in 1923, Sheldon stressed that management has a social responsibility:

> It is important, therefore, early in our consideration of management in industry, to insist that however scientific management may become, and however much the full development of its powers may depend upon the use of the scientific method, its primary responsibility is social and communal.[12]

However, concern for social responsibility was rare during this early period.

Looking back, the attitudes of managers toward social responsibility seem to have gone through three historical phases.[13] Phase 1, which dominated until the 1930s, emphasized the belief that a business manager has but one objective: to maximize profits. Phase 2, from the 1930s to the early 1960s, stressed that managers are responsible not only for maximizing profits but also for maintaining an equitable balance among the competing claims of customers, employees, suppliers, creditors, and the community. Phase 3, which is still predominant today, contends that managers and organizations should involve themselves in the solution of society's major problems. For additional information on socially responsible companies, see Management Illustration 6.1.

Actions Necessary to Implement Social Responsibility

The biggest obstacle to organizations assuming more social responsibility is pressure by financial analysts and stockholders who push for steady increases in earnings per share on a quarterly basis. Concern about immediate profits makes it difficult to invest in areas that cannot be accurately measured and still have returns that are long run in nature. Furthermore, pressure for short-term earnings affects corporate social behavior; most companies are geared toward short-term profit goals. Budgets, objectives, and performance evaluations are often based on short-run considerations. Management may state a willingness to lose some short-term profit to achieve social objectives. However, managers who sacrifice profit and seek to justify these actions on the basis of corporate social goals may find stockholders unsympathetic.

Organizations should also carefully examine their cherished values, short-run profits and others, to ensure that these concepts are in tune with the values held by society. This should be a constant process, because the values society holds are ever-changing.

Management Illustration 6.1

Anita Roddick: Soap and Social Action

Anita Roddick, founder of The Body Shop chain of cosmetic and personal care stores, is continually looking for charitable causes to which she can lend a hand. The somewhat brash, self-proclaimed English housewife has successfully brought social and environmental concerns to the corporate forefront. By her own accounts, her greatest accomplishment in the corporate arena is not her 1995 sales of $650 million but rather her persistence in crusading for social change.

Roddick is the head of a company team called Values and Visions. The major efforts of this team are directed at campaigning against domestic violence towards women, against the Nigerian government for its execution of Ken Saro-Wiwa, an environmental activist among the Ogoni people, and against nuclear testing in the South Pacific. Another company team, Community Trade, is re-sponsible for checking that the company is fairly paying the sometimes impoverished developing-world suppliers of The Body Shop's raw materials. Roddick also speaks out against the use of animals for cosmetic testing and encourages women to become more politically active in their communities.

While companies have become obsessed with shareholder value, Roddick says, "The fact that we are honorable and honest is more important than somebody maximizing stockholder profit." While criticized by many as self-righteous, Roddick continues to lecture on "social audit," "values-aware management," and "the moral duties of management." This is a woman on a mission.

Source: *Worldbusiness*, Jan/Feb 1997, p. 46–47. For more information about The Body Shop visit their Web site at: www.the-body-shop.com.

Organizations should reevaluate their long-range planning and decision-making processes to ensure that they fully understand the potential social consequences. Plant location decisions are no longer merely economic matters. Environmental impact and job opportunities for disadvantaged groups are examples of other factors to consider.

Organizations should seek to aid both governmental agencies and voluntary agencies in their social efforts. This should include technical and managerial help as well as monetary support. Technological knowledge, organizational skills, and managerial competence can all be applied to solving social problems.

Organizations should look at ways to help solve social problems through their own businesses. Many social problems stem from the economic deprivation of a fairly large segment of our society. Attacking this problem could be the greatest social effort of organizations.

Another major area in which businesses are active is corporate philanthropy. Corporate philanthropy involves donations of money, property, or work by organizations to socially useful purposes. Many companies have directed their philanthropic efforts toward education, the arts, and the United Way. Contributions can be made directly by the company, or a company foundation can be created to handle the philanthropic program. For example, General Electric has the General Electric Foundation. Management Illustration 6.2 describes a new award for philanthropic companies.

The Social Audit

social audit An attempt by an organization to systematically study, survey, and evaluate its social performance rather than its economic and financial performance.

A relatively new method of measuring the success of a firm is to conduct a social audit. The **social audit** allows management to evaluate the success or lack of success of programs designed to improve the social performance of

115

Management Illustration 6.2
And the Winners Are . . .

In an attempt to honor companies' philanthropic efforts, the first annual Newman's Own/*George* award was presented in 1998. The award was presented by actor Paul Newman, who founded the not-for-profit Newman's Own food company, and John F. Kennedy Jr., president of *George* magazine. What does the winner receive? A check for $250,000 donated to the winner's favorite charity and, more importantly, the title of corporate hero.

Does the name Aaron Feuerstein ring a bell? Maybe not. But to the people of Lawrence, Massachusetts, he is a saint. When fire destroyed his Malden Mills Industries, Inc. earlier that year, Feuerstein opted to keep all employees on the payroll for months while the plant was rebuilt. Feuerstein was just one among ten corporate leaders who were in the running for the award for "innovative and significant corporate philanthropy."

Other finalists included Norwest Corp. To make the cut, this Minneapolis bank provided $300 million in low-interest mortgages and donated $16.5 million to Habitat for Humanity. EBSCO Industries,

Inc. of Birmingham, Alabama also scored a shot at becoming a corporate hero by donating $10 million to revive the Alabama Symphony. For these companies, social responsibility is as important as profits when judging corporate performance. How is that for a balanced scorecard?

The Finalists

CITIBANK
EAST CAROLINA BANK
EBSCO INDUSTRIES
HANCOCK COMMUNITIES AND THE MARTZ AGENCY
KIMBERLY-CLARK
MACY'S WEST
MALDEN MILLS
NORWEST
PATAGONIA
WORKING ASSETS LONG DISTANCE

Source: *Business Week*, April 20, 1998 p. 48.

the organization. Rather than looking exclusively at economic and financial measures, the social audit can be a beginning point for encouraging environmental and social strategies that really work.

One suggested method for accomplishing the social audit and reacting to the information includes the following steps:

1. Examine social expectations, sensitivity, and past responses.
2. Examine and then set social objectives and meaningful priorities.
3. Plan and implement strategies and objectives in each program area.
4. Set budgets for resources necessary for social action and make a commitment to acquire them.
5. Monitor accomplishments and/or progress in each program area.

To ensure that stockholders, stakeholders, and the general public know about the commitment and accomplishments of social programs, most large corporations publish their successes in their annual reports. These firms make social responsibility an integral part of their mission statements. True commitment goes beyond the self-serving and selective nature of public relations. Most experts agree that socially responsible firms will eventually be rewarded by their markets and stakeholders.[14,15]

Summary

1. *Define Ethics.* Ethics are principles of conduct used to govern the decision making and behavior of an individual or a group of individuals.

2. *Explain What a Code of Ethics Is.* A code of ethics is a written document that outlines the principles of conduct to be used in making decisions within an organization.

3. *Describe Three Philosophical Approaches That Serve as a Basis for Codes of Ethics.* The principle of justice involves making decisions based on trust, lack of bias, and consistency. The principle of individual rights involves making decisions based on protecting human dignity. The principle of utilitarianism involves making decisions directed toward promoting the greatest good for the greatest number of people.

4. *Explain Four General Areas into Which Laws Relating to Business Ethics Can Be Categorized.* Laws relating to business ethics can be categorized into competitive behavior, consumer protection, product safety, and environmental protection.

5. *Outline the Laws Relating to Competitive Behavior, Consumer Protection, and Product Safety.* Refer to Tables 6.1, 6.2, and 6.3 for summaries of these laws.

6. *Outline the Laws Relating to Environmental Protection.* The laws relating to environmental protection are the National Environmental Policy Act, Clean Air Act, Solid Waste Disposal Act, Resource Conservation and Recovery Act, Clean Water Restoration Act, Water Quality Improvement Act, Safe Drinking Water Act, Noise Control Act, Toxic Substances Control Act, and Comprehensive Environmental Response, Compensation and Liability Act.

7. *Define Social Responsibility.* Social responsibility refers to the role of business in solving current social issues over and above legal requirements.

8. *Explain Corporate Philanthropy.* Corporate philanthropy involves donations of money, property, or work by organizations to socially useful purposes.

9. *Describe a Social Audit.* A social audit is an attempt by an organization to systematically study, survey, and evaluate its social performance rather than its economic and financial performance.

Preview Analysis

1. What do you think of Patagonia's program?

2. Do you feel Marriot's program is worthwhile?

Review Questions

1. What are ethics?
2. What is a code of ethics?
3. Summarize three philosophical approaches that serve as a basis for a code of ethics.
4. Outline some topics that might be included in a code of ethics.
5. Summarize the laws relating to ethics in competitive behavior.

6. Outline the laws relating to ethics in consumer protection.
7. Outline the laws relating to ethics in product safety.
8. List the laws relating to ethics in environmental protection.
9. Define social responsibility.
10. What is corporate philanthropy?
11. What is a social audit, and what does it try to do?

Skill-Building Questions

1. Do you believe organizations and managers should be evaluated with regard to social responsibility? Explain.

2. "Profits, not social responsibility, must be the primary concern of managers." Discuss this statement.

3. What are some ethical questions you have faced in college? What basis did you use to resolve them?

4. James F. Lincoln stated, "Do unto others as you would have them do unto you. This is not just a Sunday school ideal, but a proper labor–management policy." Do you agree with this statement? Why or why not?

5. Think of an example of what Ben & Jerry's calls "caring capitalism."

6. Look in the newspaper, magazines, or the internet and identify a firm that has recently received negative press for failing to assume "social responsibility." What would you suggest that the company do differently in reacting to social issues?

SKILL-BUILDING EXERCISE 6.1

Where Do You Stand?*

Read each of the following situations and decide how you would respond. Be prepared to justify your position in a class discussion.

Situation 1: Family versus Ethics

Jim, a 56-year-old middle manager with children in college, discovers that the owners of his company are cheating the government out of several thousand dollars a year in taxes. Jim is the only employee in a position to know this. Should Jim report the owners to the Internal Revenue Service at the risk of endangering his own livelihood, or should he disregard the discovery to protect his family's livelihood?

Situation 2: The Roundabout Raise

When Joe asks for a raise, his boss praises his work but says the company's rigid budget won't allow any further merit raises for the time being. Instead, the boss suggests the company "won't look too closely at your expense accounts for a while." Should Joe take this as authorization to pad his expense account because he is simply getting the money he deserves through a different route, or should he not take this roundabout "raise"?

Situation 3: The Faked Degree

Bill has done a sound job for over a year; he got the job by claiming to have a college degree. Bill's boss learns Bill actually never graduated. Should his boss dismiss him for a false résumé? Should he overlook the false claim, since Bill is otherwise conscientious and honorable and dismissal might ruin Bill's career?

Situation 4: Sneaking Phone Calls

Helen discovers that a co-worker makes about $100 a month in personal long-distance telephone calls from an office telephone. Should Helen report the employee or disregard the calls, since many people make personal calls at the office?

Situation 5: Cover-Up Temptation

José discovers that the chemical plant he manages is creating slightly more water pollution in a nearby lake than is legally permitted. Revealing the problem will bring negative publicity to the plant, hurt the lakeside town's resort business, and scare the community. Solving the problem will cost the company well over $100,000. It is unlikely that outsiders will discover the problem. The violation poses no danger whatever to people; at most, it will endanger a small number of fish. Should José reveal the problem despite the cost to his company, or should he consider the problem as a mere technicality and disregard it?

Situation 6: Actual Salary

Dorothy finds out that the best-qualified candidate for a job really earned only $18,000 a year in his last job, not the $28,000 he claimed. Should Dorothy hire the candidate anyway, or should she choose someone considerably less qualified?

*These situations are taken from Roger Rickles, "Executives Apply Stiffer Standards Than Public to Ethical Dilemmas," *The Wall Street Journal*, November 3, 1983, p. 33.

SKILL-BUILDING EXERCISE 6.2

Truthfulness in Advertising

Advertising claims may be totally inaccurate ("sticker price is a low $11,998" may omit all transporation costs, state taxes, dealer charges, and factory options, which together add 25 percent to 30 percent to the price of a car). Other claims are greatly exaggerated ("12-hour relief from sore throat pain"), verbally misleading ("you'll have to eat 12 bowls of Shredded Wheat to get the vitamins and nutrition in 1 bowl of Total"), or visually misleading (healthy, active people shown in pleasant social situations to advertise liquor, beer, or cigarettes.

Questions

From magazines, newspapers, or television, select an advertisement you believe to be untruthful.

1. Why do you think the claims are untruthful?
2. Into what group (inaccurate, exaggeratead, or misleading) do you think they fall?

Source: La Rue Tone Hosmer. *The Ethics of Management* (Homewood, Ill.: Richard D. Irwin, 1987), p. 86.

CASE INCIDENT 6.1

Lightbulb Sellers*

You receive the following telephone call: "Hello, Mr. Smith. This is Sam. I am a handicapped person." Sam wants to sell you a high-priced lightbulb, guaranteed to last up to five years. He may also want to sell you vitamins and household cleaning solutions. The lightbulbs sold in this manner cost about twice as much as they do at a local hardware store.

However, few of the lightbulb sales organizations are charities. They are for-profit companies whose business is selling lightbulbs by phone. United Handicapped Workers, Lifeline Industries Inc., Handicapped Workers of America, United Handicapped Workers of Charlotte (North Carolina), and American Handicapped Workers are among the larger for-profit companies selling lightbulbs by phone.

The people who make the phone calls are normally paid an hourly wage, a commission, or some combination of the two. The fact that you are dealing with a for-profit business is not always clear, even though the caller may say, "We're not asking for charity or a handout."

Questions

1. Do you believe the practices of these organizations are ethical? Explain.

2. What are the pros and cons of these practices?

*Adapted from "Lightbulb Sellers' Employers Often Not Charity," *Atlanta Journal and Constitution*, May 28, 1990, p. B3.

CASE INCIDENT 6.2

Bonuses at Drexel Burnham Lambert

Drexel Burnham Lambert, former Wall Street junk bond powerhouse, filed for Chapter 11 protection from its creditors February 13, 1990. The firm's management announced its assets would be sold and it would cease doing business. The bankruptcy claim threw into jeopardy the claims of hundreds of creditors.

On February 24, 1990, it was announced that Drexel Burnham had paid out $260 million in cash and stock bonuses in the two months before it filed for bankruptcy protection. Of the total bonuses, $150 million was paid in December 1989 and $110 million was paid in January

1990. People inside the firm have said some executives were paid more than $10 million in bonuses.

Questions

1. Do creditors of Drexel Burnham have any options under present laws against the firm's actions?

2. What reasons could be offered for paying these bonuses?

Source: Adapted from Kurt Eichenwald, "Drexel Asserts Bonuses Come to $260 Million," *New York Times*, February 24, 1990, p. 37L.

References and Additional Readings

[1]George A. Steiner and John F. Steiner, *Business, Government, and Society*, 4th ed. (New York: Random House, 1985), p. 150.

[2]C. Roland Christensen, Norman A. Berg, and Malcolm S. Salter, *Policy Formulation and Administration*, 8th ed. (Homewood, IL: Richard D. Irwin, 1980), p. 591.

[3]Rena A. Gorlin, *Codes of Professional Responsibility*, 2d ed. (Washington, DC: Bureau of National Affairs, 1990), p. 52.

[4]Ibid., p. 52.

[5]John Winthrop Wright, "What Is the Status on Ethics in American Business?" *Bottomline* 6 (June 1989), pp. 11–14.

[6]James D. Thompson, *Organizations in Action* (New York: McGraw-Hill, 1967), pp. 20–23.

[7]For another view on the legal nature of ethics, see Amitai Etzioni, "Corporate Behavior: Fewer Flaws Mean Fewer Laws," *Business and Society Review*, Spring 1992, pp. 13–17.

[8]Mary Jo Bittner, "Building Service Relationships," *Journal of Academy of Marketing Science* 23, no. 4 (1995), p. 246.

[9]Linda Himelstein, "Tobacco, Does It Have a Future?" *Business Week*, July 4, 1994, pp. 24–29.

[10]Howard Gleckman, "Rewriting the Social Contract," *Business Week*, November 20, 1995, pp. 120–38.

[11]Henry Gantt, *Organization for Work* (New York: Harcourt Brace Jovanovich, 1919), p. 15.

[12]Oliver Sheldon, *The Philosophy of Management* (Marshfield, MA: Pitman Publishing, 1966), p. xv (originally published in London in 1923 by Sir Isaac Pitman and Sons).

[13]For a different perspective, see Steven L. Wartick and Philip L. Cochran, "The Evolution of the Corporate Social Performance Model," *Academy of Management Review*, October 1985, pp. 758–69.

[14]F. Luthans, R. M. Hodgetts, and K. R. Thompson, *Social Issues in Business Strategic and Public Policy Perspectives*, 6th ed. (New York: Macmillan, 1990). pp. 595–613.

[15]L. L. Carson and G. A. Steiner, *Measuring Business Social Performance: The Corporate Social Audit* (New York: Committee for Economic Development, 1974), p. 61.

7

International Business

LEARNING OBJECTIVES

After studying this chapter, you should be able to:

1. Give several reasons organizations extend their operations to other countries.

2. Define comparative advantage, competitive advantage, value-added chain, and self-reference criterion.

3. Define multinational corporation (MNC), global industry, global strategy, and strategic alliance.

4. Describe the strategies organizations use in international business.

5. Discuss the importance of cultural differences in international business.

6. Explain the foreign exchange risks in international business.

7. Define tariffs, quotas, embargoes, and subsidized protection.

8. Describe the European Union.

9. Define exporting, importing, licensing, and joint venture.

10. Outline some typical Japanese management practices.

The world is shrinking because of international trade and efficient global communication. Trading in the international marketplace can present a vast opportunity or a real danger. Managers have to consider new rules and methods of operation when going international. American entrepreneurs who work with a foreign company, whether a customer or a supplier, are far less likely to know its financial state, turnaround time, hiring and labor practices, and environmental record than they would if the company were in their own city or state. In the United States, a business must abide by certain basic rules regarding disclosure, employment practices, and contractual obligations. This is not always the case with companies abroad.

Jonathan Rosenthal of Equal Exchange, Inc. (an international trade adviser), recommends to clients that they begin the internationalization process by determining what is acceptable legally and ethically for their firms and then use the following guidelines to begin an appraisal of potential trading or supplier partners. Issues to include in the appraisal include the following:

1. Production standards: Is the facility capable of producing the required product within the desired time frame? Are instructions and specifications followed carefully?

2. Employer–worker issues: Are employees paid a decent wage? Do they have safe working conditions that basically meet our standards regarding child labor and reasonable work hours?

3. Environmental concerns: How does the company dispose of its waste products, renew the environment, affect neighboring communities, and does it recycle?

One aspect of diversity is learning to deal with customers, producers, and suppliers in the international environment. Differing positions and expectations must be resolved if efficient and safe business is to be conducted. Take your partnership seriously. Whenever possible, visit those you do business with and investigate their operations. Understanding is critical to the success of any international venture.

Source: Adapted from Erika Kottie, "Keeping Tabs," *Entrepreneur*, December 1994, p. 43. Reprinted with permission.

An important factor in the management of any organization is the increasing internationalization of business activity. International business activities range from exporting goods to establishing manufacturing operations in other nations. The internationalization of American companies has been growing dramatically. Companies such as Ford, Coca-Cola, and IBM are building large and growing international operations. Many firms are realizing increasing profit percentages from their international operations. Exxon, General Motors, Coca-Cola, Gillette, and IBM now receive over 50 percent of their net profits from foreign operations.

While not all businesses are directly involved in international activities, events that affect U.S. organizations occur almost daily in other nations. Thus, it is becoming increasingly important that all managers understand the nature of international business activity.

DECISIONS ON INTERNATIONAL BUSINESS INVOLVEMENT

Generally, the decision to extend an organization's operations to other countries is based on profits, stability, or competition. In terms of profits, international operations give organizations the chance to meet the increasing demand for goods and services in foreign countries. In addition, new sources of demand for an organization's output can stabilize the organization's production process. Finally, when competitors enter foreign markets, companies often respond in a like fashion.

The decision to enter international business activities is based on the comparative advantages of countries and the competitive advantages of the individual business. A country has a **comparative advantage** when it can produce goods more efficiently or cheaply than other countries because of its specific circumstances. Factors that determine a country's comparative advantage include the presence of material resources, the availability of labor, and the relative costs of these resources. **Competitive advantage,** sometimes called *business-specific advantage*, refers to some proprietary characteristic of the business, such as a brand name, that competitors cannot imitate without substantial cost and risk.[1]

Comparative advantage influences the decision concerning where to manufacture and market the firm's products. Competitive advantage influences the decision concerning in which activities and technologies along the value-added chain a business should concentrate its resources relative to its competitors.[2] The **value-added chain** refers to the process by which a business combines the raw material, labor, and technology into a finished product, markets the product, and distributes the product. A company may be involved in any part or all parts of the value-added chain.

The concept of the value-added chain is now expanding to include foreign operations and opportunities. Some firms, however, have difficulty realizing the benefits of merging and combining efforts because their management views the international environment with a **self-reference criterion;** that is, it views international markets, competition, management practices, organizational environments, supplier and distributor relationships, and corporate culture as though they were domestic in nature. This cultural bias can make problem solution and managerial decision making much more difficult.

comparative advantage   Exists when a country can produce goods more efficiently or cheaply than other countries because of its specific circumstance.

competitive advantage   Sometimes called *business-specific advantage*; refers to some proprietary characteristic of the business, such as a brand name, that competitors cannot imitate competitors without substantial cost and risk.

value-added chain   Process by which a business combines the raw material, labor, and technology into a finished product, markets the product, and distributes the product.

self-reference criterion   Cultural bias of viewing the international competitive and market environment as though it were domestic in nature.

MULTINATIONAL CORPORATIONS, GLOBAL INDUSTRIES, AND GLOBAL STRATEGIES

multinational corporation (MNC)   Business that maintains a presence in two or more countries, has a considerable portion of its assets invested in and derives a substantial portion of its sales and profits from international activities, considers opportunities throughout the world, and has a worldwide perspective and orientation.

A **multinational corporation (MNC)** is a business that

- Maintains a production, assembly, sales, or service presence in two or more countries.
- Has a considerable portion of its assets invested in and derives a considerable portion of its sales and profits from its international activities. For example, it has been suggested that when operations in other countries account for 35 percent of sales and profits, an organization is considered to be multinational. It has also been suggested that an organization becomes multinational when 20 percent of its assets are in other countries.
- Considers opportunities throughout the world, even if it does not do business in every region and country.
- Has a worldwide perspective and orientation in managerial decision making. In other words, the organization makes managerial decisions regarding the use of its resources—funds, technology, and business know-how—on a global basis.

global industry   Industry in which the competitive positions of firms in major geographic or national markets are fundamentally affected by their overall global positions.

A **global industry** is an industry in which the competitive positions of firms in major geographic or national markets are fundamentally affected by their overall global positions.[3] Reasons for globalization vary, but most organizations make the move because of diminishing technological advantages (such as the number of patents and innovations produced), the increased opportunity to successfully penetrate a foreign market, shrinking domestic markets, the desire to protect market share and dominance, and the ability to improve organizational performance. For example, IBM's capabilities in competing for computer sales in Germany and France were significantly enhanced by the technology and marketing skills developed elsewhere in the company, combined with a coordinated worldwide manufacturing system. Semiconductors, computers, home electronics, automobile manufacturing, banking, pharmaceuticals, and insurance are some examples of global industries.

One trend in globalization is the formation of *strategic alliances*. Management Illustration 7.1 describes and gives some examples of strategic alliances.

Global strategies are the alternatives a particular business chooses to compete in global industries on a worldwide, coordinated basis. Basically, five global strategy options are available to businesses. **Product standardization** involves producing and selling a standardized product using the same methods throughout the world. The basic idea behind this strategy is to take advantage of the economies of scale in producing the product and develop a strong worldwide system. Coca-Cola has pursued this global strategy. A **broad-line global strategy** involves competing worldwide in the full product line of the industry.[4] Product standardization can be employed in the broad-line global strategy. A **global focus strategy** involves selecting a particular segment of the industry in which the business competes on a worldwide basis. Again, product standardization can be used in the

global strategies   Alternatives a particular business chooses to compete in global industries on a worldwide, coordinated basis.
product standardization   Involves producing and selling a standardized product using the same methods throughout the world.
broad-line global strategy   Involves selecting a particular segment of the industry in which a business competes on a worldwide basis.
global focus strategy   Involves selecting a particular segment of the industry in which a business competes on a worldwide basis.

Management Illustration 7.1
Strategic Alliances

Strategic alliances, an emerging form of international competition in the 1990s, entail the pooling of specific resources and skills by the cooperating organizations to achieve common goals as well as goals specific to the individual partners. When General Mills and Nestlé (purpose: to spread General Mills cereals throughout Europe, Asia, and Africa) and Ford and Mazda (purpose: to join product development forces, share production facilities, and strengthen marketing support) joined forces, they illustrated the primary reasons for forming a strategic alliance: to gain access to new markets, accelerate the pace of entry into new markets, share research (development, manufacturing, and/or marketing), broaden or fill product lines, learn new skills, and expand the cross-cultural knowledge of management groups. These partnerships could be formed between buyers and suppliers, laterally, or even internally between competing divisions.

The payoffs from alliances are still open to question. However, the sheer number of formulations is staggering. Growth rates are estimated to be 25 percent annually. Estimates are that as many as 20,000 alliances were formed in the United States between 1988 and 1992, with IBM leading the pack with over 400. Popularity does not come without cost, however. Time spent in negotiation, implementation, and integration, along with loss of flexibility and freedom, leakage of proprietary knowledge, and atrophying of the firm's capabilities, are the most common difficulties.

Given all the international organizational forms available (joint ventures, wholly owned subsidiaries, licensing, and mergers), why are so many strategic alliances being formed in the 1990s? Two common reasons are to spread related technology and to achieve market strength. Examples include computer companies allying with consumer electronics firms, cable TV companies allying with telecommunications firms, and computer software companies joining forces with just about any firm in the entertainment industry.

In conclusion, as long as there are advantages to be gained in shared distribution (e.g., Chrysler and Mitsubishi), licensed manufacturing (Volvo and Renault sharing body parts), research and development (Boeing and Fuji), and international understanding and trust, international strategic alliances will grow in number. Management must study and prepare for these alliances and the new managerial challenges they will bring.

Sources: P. Rajan Varadarajan and Margaret H. Cunningham, "Strategic Alliances: A Synthesis of Conceptual Foundations," *Journal of Academy of Marketing Science*, Fall 1995, pp. 282–83; George S. Day, "Advantageous Alliances," *Journal of the Academy of Marketing Science*, Fall 1995, pp. 297, 300; Johny K. Johansson, "International Alliances: Why Now?" *Journal of the Academy of Marketing Science*, Fall 1995, p. 301. ©1995 by the Academy of Marketing Science. For more articles from the *Journal of the Academy of Marketing Science*, visit their Web site at: www.bus.miami.edu/ams/journal.

---

national focus strategy Involves focusing on particular national markets to take advantage of national market differences.

protected niche strategy Involves seeking out countries where government policies exclude many global competitors.

---

global focus strategy. A **national focus strategy** involves focusing on particular national markets to take advantage of national market differences. The idea is to achieve product differentiation or become the overall low-cost producer in serving the unique needs of a particular national market. Finally, a **protected niche strategy** involves seeking out countries where government policies exclude many global competitors.[5]

UNIQUE ENVIRONMENTAL INFLUENCES IN INTERNATIONAL BUSINESS

When a business decides to extend its operations into foreign markets, it must deal with some unique environmental influences in managing these activities.

Cultural Differences

To understand the differences between U.S. and international management, it is necessary to understand differences in culture. Obviously, managers from diverse countries such as the United States, France, and Germany do not see the world in the same way because they come from different cultures (remember the self-reference criterion discussed earlier). **Culture** is something that most or all members of some social group share, something the older members of the group try to pass on to the younger members, and something (as in the case of morals, laws, and customs) that shapes behavior or structures an individual's perceptions of the world.

culture   Something shared by all or almost all members of some social group, something the older members of the group try to pass on to the younger members, and something (as in the case of morals, laws, and customs) that shapes behavior or structures an individual's perception of the world.

Numerous cross-cultural differences exist among countries. Success in the international business environment requires that these differences be recognized in managing international business activities. Some important cross-cultural differences the firm must recognize, understand, and deal with are marketing practices, human resource management, social and value systems, language, and business practices.

Marketing practices for industrial products tend to be less sensitive to cultural differences and lend themselves to a product standardization strategy. Often only minor technical modifications need be made to an industrial product to meet a particular country's requirements. On the other hand, consumer goods are much more culturally influenced and generally require a national focus strategy. For example, Procter & Gamble (P&G) discovered that its All-Temperature Cheer bombed in Japan because Japanese homemakers use only cold water for laundry and need a more compact detergent package due to limited storage space. So P&G introduced cold-water Tide and outsold the leading Japanese compact cold-water detergent.[6]

Human resource management can involve a variety of issues, but contemporary management trends indicate that the following issues are particularly important:

- Employment security: Is it temporal or lifelong? How is seniority determined and used?
- Does the workplace emphasize group/and or team concepts, or is individualism the preferred style?
- How are top executives rewarded?
- What benefits does the labor force expect?

Under the Japanese system, lifelong employment (and the loyalty that accompanies it) is the norm, whereas in the United States, job changing is thought to be a normal practice, especially if it promises more personal rewards. American and European companies tend to reward senior employees with increased pay, whereas Japanese companies value performance over seniority. Group accomplishments and team building are stressed more heavily in Europe and Japan than in the United States, which emphasizes individual performance. Only in the United States do CEOs receive huge pay bonuses. Other countries tie the performances of executives to long-term gains and goal accomplishment. Social policies of the individual countries tend to set the stage for benefits for workers.

Social and value systems change slowly in the non-Western countries, where tradition is extremely important. One's relationship to the universe is very important in India and the Oriental countries. Western cultures believe that people control their own destinies. Rapid introduction of innovation is coldly received in many markets. Masculinity still predominates in most countries other than the United

States; in many of these countries, females are not emancipated in society or the workplace.

Language can bind or separate cultures. Most of the world is multilingual, whereas many American business managers expect that English will always be the predominant language. The ability to learn foreign languages is a valuable talent for the aspiring international manager. Before beginning any business undertaking in a foreign culture, it is a wise practice to learn the slang, gestures, and nuances of the culture and the subtleties of the current business jargon.

It is also extremely important to understand business protocol, such as the value of time. Americans, for example, are usually put on edge if kept waiting for an appointment, whereas many other cultures value time differently. It has been said that the successful executive must study the appointment waiting room as closely as she or he studies the marketplace. In many instances, time even becomes a powerful negotiation tool. Another example of business protocol is gift giving. Whereas Americans consider gift giving to be a euphemism for bribery (and generally illegal), in some cultures it is a common, and sometimes an expected, way of doing business.

The organizational hierarchy is another important aspect of international business. Many Western countries favor an extremely casual hierarchy, whereas Asian countries tend to enforce a somewhat rigid and ceremonial structure. However, flat organizations tend to be the norm in Japan, whereas more elaborate reporting and communication structures prevail in the United States.

Foreign Exchange Risks

International business requires exchanging currency from one country into that of another. **Foreign exchange rates**—the rates of exchange for one currency to another currency (e.g., French francs to American dollars)—present problems because the rates fluctuate in value. Currency is a form of commodity that is traded on foreign exchange markets. The exchange rate for each currency is subject to the laws of supply and demand. Because of constant fluctuations in foreign exchange rates, a certain amount of *exposure*, or risk, is inherent in any purchase or sale.

The simplest approach to reducing a firm's exposure is to have all transactions expressed in the firm's domestic currency. However, in MNCs, thousands of transactions occur daily and having all of them stated in domestic currency is impractical. One means MNCs use to reduce exposure is hedging. **Hedging** is a market transaction that allows a business to use the forward exchange rate to minimize or eliminate exposure. A **forward exchange rate** is the price agreed on today to buy or sell a foreign currency at some stated time. Firms can enter into a **forward contract agreement,** usually through an international bank, to sell at a predetermined rate currency to be received at some time in the future. These banks charge a fee for handling forward contract agreements. Therefore, the astute manager must be fully aware of all the financial implications and complications of signing contracts with international firms.

foreign exchange rates   Rate of exchange for one currency to another currency.

hedging   Market transaction that allows a business to make use of the forward exchange rate to minimize or eliminate exposure.

forward exchange rate   The price agreed on today to buy or sell a foreign currency at some stated time.

forward contract agreement   Selling currency at a predetermined rate to be received at some time in the future.

protectionist measures   Actions taken by government to protect the country's businesses from foreign competition.

Protectionist Measures

Protectionist measures are actions governments take to protect their country's businesses from foreign competition. The General Agreement on Tariffs and Trade

(GATT), established in 1947, created an international organization to negotiate and resolve protectionist measures. For example, if a country faces a protectionist barrier in another country, it can appeal to GATT. If the problem cannot be resolved by negotiations between the countries, formal hearings are held by a panel of GATT members. The panel can order the practice stopped or allow the country claiming harm to retaliate. However, this process can take years, and the offender cannot be forced to pay damages. Ninety countries belong to GATT, but some major countries, such as China, Iran, Saudi Arabia, and Mexico, remain outside GATT.

According to GATT, more than 500 types of protectionist measures exist covering 40 percent of world trade. The actions taken are varied, but generally they fall into the areas of tariffs, quotas, embargoes, subsidies, and currency restrictions.

tariffs   Government-imposed taxes charged on goods imported into a country.

quota   Establishes the maximum quantity of a product that can be imported or exported during a given period.

embargo   Involves stopping the flow of exports to or imports from a foreign country.

subsidies or subsidized protection   Widely used practice of government support of domestic industries to make their prices cheaper than the prices of imports.

Tariffs are government-imposed taxes charged on goods imported into a country. They serve to raise revenues for the country or to protect the country's businesses from the competition of imported goods. Tariffs charged on imported parts are often less than those charged on finished goods. Thus, foreign assembly operations are frequently used.

A **quota** establishes the maximum quantity of a product that can be imported or exported during a given period. A quota can be set in either physical or value terms. Quotas can be set unilaterally by a particular country, or they can be negotiated between two countries. Voluntary negotiation generally means the quotas have been negotiated with threats of even worse restrictions if voluntary cooperation is not forthcoming.

An **embargo** involves stopping the flow of exports to or imports from a foreign country. Over the years, the U.S. government has imposed embargoes on exports to countries such as China, Iraq, Iran, and Libya.

Subsidies (or **subsidized protection**) are the widely used practice of government support of domestic industries to make their prices cheaper than the prices of imports. For example, Germany, France, Britain, and Spain used government subsidies to protect their joint venture in airplane manufacturing.

Currency restrictions are also used as a barrier to trade. With one type of currency restriction, the government limits the amount of money a foreign company can take out of the country. With another type, the government limits the ability to freely exchange one currency for another at a realistic exchange rate and within a reasonable time. Currencies that cannot be easily and quickly exchanged at a fair price are inconvertible. Governments can deliberately make their currencies inconvertible by controlling supply or demand or by tightly controlling the exchange process.

Coalitions of Cooperating Countries and Trading Blocs

International businesses must also deal with coalitions of cooperating countries that are established to improve the economic conditions of the member countries. One of the most important coalitions is the European Union (formerly the European Community). Organized in 1957, the European Union's membership includes Great Britain, Italy, France, Germany, Denmark, Ireland, Greece, Belgium, Luxembourg, the Netherlands, Spain, and Portugal. Its purpose was to reduce tariffs on goods sold among member countries. The member nations were also to have eliminated the fiscal, technical, and border barriers between member countries that over several decades have increased the costs of goods and services in Europe and reduced the international competitiveness of European companies. Europe was to be a single market with exciting potential for multinational corporations. Many problems still exist in implementing the changes necessary for Europe to become one market. It also remains to be seen whether the democratic movement in Eastern Europe, the reunification of Germany, and the demise of the Soviet Union will lead some of those countries and republics to join the European Union or form a new trading bloc of some other configuration.

Another coalition is the Organization of Petroleum Exporting Countries (OPEC), which includes many of the oil-producing countries of the world. Its purpose is to control oil prices and production levels among member countries. Today OPEC's effectiveness is limited because several member countries sell and produce at levels considerably different from official OPEC standards.

It is forecasted that by the year 2000, three large trading blocs will exist: Europe; the North American Alliance of the United States, Canada, and Mexico; and Pacific Asia (Pacific Rim countries), with Japan being the dominant country in that region.[7] Other members of the Pacific Rim trading bloc are China, Korea, Taiwan, Indonesia, Malaysia, the Philippines, Thailand, Hong Kong, and Singapore. These three large trading blocs will provide many opportunities and pose many threats for multinational organizations.

Political Changes

One of the most dramatic illustrations of how political changes influence the international business environment was the breakup of the Soviet Union and the fall of communist governments in Eastern Europe in the early 1990s. The end of the Soviet Union and the creation of the Commonwealth of Independent States (CIS) is likely to lead to many opportunities for Western businesses. In addition, the political and economic upheavals in Bulgaria, Hungary, Poland, Romania, and the countries formerly known as Czechoslovakia and Yugoslavia have caused significant changes in how these countries conduct their own international business activities and how they relate to businesses from foreign countries.

Human Rights and Ethics

Should multinational firms close their plants in countries where human rights abuses are common and accepted ethical boundaries are violated? This is a valid issue, but the U.S. manager must remember that business ethics have not yet been globalized; the norms of ethical behavior continue to vary widely even in Western capitalist countries. To date, only in the United States does widespread public concern exist over the morality of business conduct.[8] Thus, questions such as "Should Coca-Cola establish minimum labor standards for all of its bottlers around the world to prevent abuses of workers in certain countries?" seems highly appropriate in this country. However, such questions present dilemmas for multinational firms that are accompanied by ethical predicaments and hard choices. In each situation, the multinational firm must strike a balance among the values and ideals of all of its various publics. No clear and easy choices exist.[9]

ORGANIZING INTERNATIONAL BUSINESS ACTIVITIES

An organization may become involved in international business activities through exporting, importing, licensing, creating joint ventures, or manufacturing in a foreign country.

FIGURE 7.1   Reasons for Exporting and Importing Goods

Why Export?

1. If the production process requires high volume to reduce cost per unit, the home market may be too small to absorb the output. Thus, the output may be sold overseas. Stoves, for example, are purchased by households only when needed to replace an old one or when a new home is built. Selling stoves only to the United States could limit the number demanded to less than the amount that is cost efficient to produce.
2. The demand for the firm's product may be seasonal and irregular. By expanding the firm's market to other countries, production costs may be lowered by more effective production scheduling.
3. All products undergo what is called the product life cycle: When the product is introduced, the demand is usually big and the introducing firm is the only supplier. As the product reaches maturity, this competitive edge is reduced and can be maintained only by creating new markets, where the product reenters the growth stage.
4. In selling goods overseas, the organization may not face competition as stiff as it does in the United States; thus, its marketing costs may be reduced. By selling its established goods in new overseas markets, the organization is also able to increase its profits without risking new-product development.

Why Import?

1. The goods may be needed but are not available in the importing country (e.g., crude oil).
2. Many foreign-made products have prestige value and are demanded by the market (e.g., French perfumes, cars from Germany).
3. Some foreign goods are less expensive because of lower production costs.

---

exporting   The selling of an organization's goods in another country.

importing   The purchasing of goods from a foreign company.

export-import manager   Serves a group of exporting/importing organizations and handles all activities involved in the exporting/importing of their goods or services.

parent organization   An organization extending its operations beyond its nation's boundaries.

host country   The country a parent organization is entering.

Exporting is the selling of an organization's goods in another country; **importing** is the purchasing of goods from a foreign company. Figure 7.1 lists some of the more common reasons for exporting and importing.[10]

Organizations that make a commitment to selling their products overseas must decide how to organize their exporting/importing activities. The organizational structure used depends on how critical these activities are to the overall organization. The organization may establish its own internal structure. This requires special expertise in international accounting, finance, marketing, and law. As a result, many organizations either cannot or will not establish such divisions. Some contract with an **export-import manager,** a person who serves a group of exporting/importing organizations and handles all activities involved in the exporting and importing of the organizations' goods or services.

Over time, many organizations discover it is economically more feasible to expand their production operations overseas than to continue exporting goods to their markets abroad. Furthermore, in recent years less developed countries have sought local production of goods. As a result, businesses are finding they must produce in these countries to maintain their overseas markets.

International organizations differ in the degree of control retained by the **parent organization,** the organization extending its operations beyond its nation's boundaries. The country it is entering is referred to as the **host country.** The parent company may set up assembly operations in a foreign country; parts are exported overseas, and the finished product is assembled

---

FIGURE 7.2   International Strategy Options

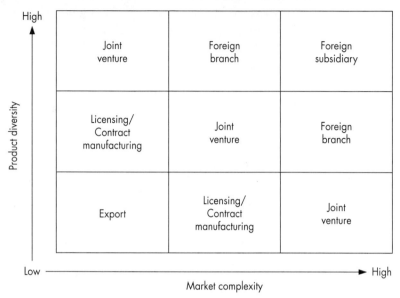

Source: Adapted from John A. Pearce II and Richard B. Robinson, Jr., *Strategic Management* (Burr Ridge, IL.: Richard D. Irwin, 1994), pp. 125–26.

there. Also, the parent organization may contract with a foreign organization to produce its product but retain control over the marketing of the product in that country. Licensing arrangements are an extension of this latter type of expansion. The parent organization enters into an agreement with a foreign organization, licensing it to produce and market the parent organization's product in return for a set percentage of sales revenues. Often the parent organization provides technical and/or managerial support to the foreign organization.

joint venture   Agreement between two or more companies to work together on a project.

Joint ventures can also be used in international business activities. A **joint venture** is an agreement between two or more companies to work together on a project. It is formed when complementary companies want to develop a product or service that takes advantage of the strengths of each company or to share the cost of a major project.

Figure 7.2 shows how strategies for firms that are attempting to move toward globalization can be categorized by the degree of complexity of each foreign market being considered and by the diversity in a company's product line.[11] Together, complexity (the number of critical success factors) and diversity (the breadth of a firm's business line) form a continuum of possible strategic choices for the strategic planner to consider.

LEARNING FROM FOREIGN MANAGEMENT PRACTICES

The success enjoyed by many foreign international companies has led to the study of their management practices to determine their applicability across national boundaries. Because of Japan's phenomenal economic success since World War II, Japanese management practices have been widely studied. Authorities cannot agree on whether there is one Japanese management style used in all Japanese companies or whether the Japanese style is better than others. However, Japanese management practices generally include the following:

- Morning physical exercise for all employees.
- Managers and workers all wearing the same company uniforms on the job.
- Morning pep talks by supervisors.
- High value placed on loyalty to the company; loyalty stressed as a condition of employment.
- Bonuses paid for extraordinary performance (although fringe benefits of all kinds are generally lower than in American-owned firms).
- Vague job classifications (Honda classifies all of its employees as "automobile assembly workers").
- Full implementation of quality circles (QCs) and zero-defect movements.
- One dining room or cafeteria for managers and workers alike (meaning a marked improvement in the quality of the food from the workers' point of view).
- No direct orders given to employees, lots of lateral communication, and bottom-up, consensus-type decision making.
- Overtime expected of all employees (at the option of management).
- Implementation and use of the just-in-time (JIT) system of inventory reduction.
- No layoffs to the greatest extent possible.
- Lawyers and lawsuits not tolerated within the enterprise.
- After-work socializing with co-workers to build company loyalty.
- Company outings and retreats for all members of an employee's family.[12]

Many people argue that Japanese management practices work because of the Japanese culture and that they cannot be readily transferred to other countries without modifications. However, the overriding theme of Japanese management appears to be that an employee is viewed as human capital that should be cultivated and developed as carefully as any trade secret. That lesson transcends national boundaries. In addition to the description of Japanese management practices previously mentioned, Figure 7.3 compares U.S. and Japanese organizational structures. These differences provide insight into the managerial style and culture of the two trading giants.

Peter Drucker has outlined six lessons he believes can be learned from foreign management, especially from Western Europe and Japan:

1. Foreign managements increasingly demand responsibility from their employees.
2. Foreign managements think through their benefits policies carefully and, especially in Japan and Germany, structure benefits according to the needs of recipients.
3. Foreign managements take marketing more seriously in that they attempt to know what constitutes value for the customer.
4. Foreign managements base marketing and innovation strategies on the systematic and purposeful abandonment of the old, the outworn, and the obsolete.
5. Foreign managements keep separate those areas where short-term results are the proper measurement and those where results should be measured over

Management Illustration 7.2

North America, Inc., Is Taking Shape

In 1995, the world will see if NAFTA (the North American Free Trade Agreement) will finally fulfill the promise of a continental market in North America. Companies from Wal-Mart to Canada's Northern Telecom Ltd. have rushed to test the promise of the world's largest market, with 370 million consumers and $6.5 trillion in output. Though the borders have hardly existed between the United States, Canada, and Mexico for some time, NAFTA will knock down commercial barriers (farming, autos, consumer goods, telecommunications, financial services, textiles, and energy) that are more traditional than legal.

Source: William C. Symonds, "Border Crossings," *Business Week*, November 22, 1993, pp. 40–42. To keep up with current information on NAFTA, visit: www.iepnt1.itaiep.doc.gov/nafta.nafta2.

FIGURE 7.3   Characteristics of Many U.S. and Japanese Organizations

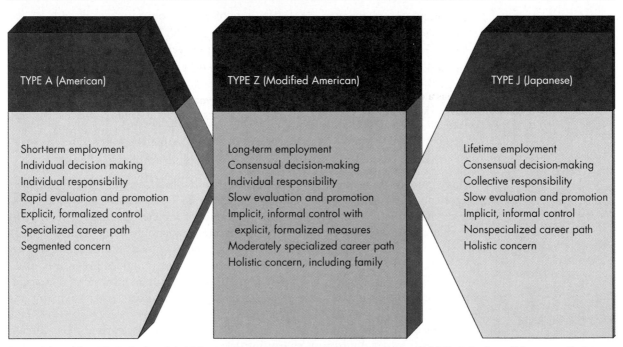

TYPE A (American)

Short-term employment
Individual decision making
Individual responsibility
Rapid evaluation and promotion
Explicit, formalized control
Specialized career path
Segmented concern

TYPE Z (Modified American)

Long-term employment
Consensual decision-making
Individual responsibility
Slow evaluation and promotion
Implicit, informal control with
    explicit, formalized measures
Moderately specialized career path
Holistic concern, including family

TYPE J (Japanese)

Lifetime employment
Consensual decision-making
Collective responsibility
Slow evaluation and promotion
Implicit, informal control
Nonspecialized career path
Holistic concern

Source: Adapted from W. G. Ouchi and A. M. Jaeger, "Type Z Organization: Stability in the Midst of Mobility," *Academy of Management Review*, 1978, pp. 305–14.

longer time spans: innovation, product development, product introduction, manager development, and so forth.

6. Managers in large Japanese, German, and French companies see themselves as national assets and leaders responsible for the development of proper policies in the national interest.[13]

Drucker readily admits that each of these lessons is American in origin. However, reexamining and possibly reinstituting practices developed earlier is always desirable, especially when foreign managements have emulated them so successfully (see Management Illustration 7.2 for an example of how lessons have been learned).

Summary

1. *Give Several Reasons Organizations Extend Their Operations to Other Countries.* Generally, the decision to extend an organization's operations to other countries is based on profits, stability, or competition.

2. *Define Comparative Advantage, Competitive Advantage, Value-Added Chain, and Self-Reference Criterion.* Comparative advantage refers to the situation in which a country can produce goods more efficiently or cheaply than other countries because of its specific circumstances. Competitive advantage refers to some proprietary characteristic of a business, such as a brand name, that competitors cannot imitate without substantial cost and risk. The value-added chain is the process by which a business combines the raw material, labor, and technology into a finished product, markets the product, and distributes the product. A self-reference criterion is the cultural bias of viewing the international competitive and market environments as though they were domestic in nature.

3. *Define Multinational Corporation (MNC), Global Industry, Global Strategy, and Strategic Alliance.* An MNC maintains a production, assembly, sales, or service presence in two or more countries, has a considerable portion of its assets invested in and derives a substantial portion of its sales and profits from its international activities, considers opportunities throughout the world, and has a worldwide perspective and orientation in managerial decision making. A global industry is one in which the competitive positions of firms in major geographic or national markets are fundamentally affected by their overall global positions. Global strategies are the alternatives chosen by a particular business to compete in global industries on a worldwide, coordinated basis. A strategic alliance entails the pooling of specific resources and skills by the cooperating organizations to achieve common goals as well as goals specific to the individual partners.

4. *Describe the Strategies Organizations Use in International Business.* Product standardization involves producing and selling a standardized product using the same methods throughout the world. A broad-line global strategy involves competing worldwide in the full product line of the industry. A global focus strategy entails selecting a particular segment of the industry in which a business competes on a worldwide basis. A national focus strategy involves focusing on particular national markets to take advantage of national market differences. A protected niche strategy involves seeking out countries where government policies exclude many global competitors.

5. *Discuss the Importance of Cultural Differences in International Business.* Culture shapes behavior and structures an individual's perceptions of the world. Numerous cross-cultural differences exist among countries. Marketing practices and human resource management are two important areas of cross-cultural differences in international business.

6. *Explain the Foreign Exchange Risks in International Business.* International business requires exchanging currency from one country to that of another. Because of constant fluctuations in foreign exchange rates, a certain amount of risk is inherent in any purchase or sale.

7. *Define Tariffs, Quotas, Embargoes, and Subsidized Protection.* Tariffs are government-imposed taxes charged on goods imported into a country. A quota establishes the maximum quantity of a product that can be imported or exported. An embargo involves stopping the flow of exports to or imports from a foreign country. Subsidized protection, or subsidies, is government support of domestic industries to make their prices cheaper than the prices of imports.

8. *Describe the European Union.* The European Union was first organized in 1957 and includes Great Britain, Italy, France, Germany, Denmark, Ireland, Greece, Belgium, Luxembourg, the Netherlands, Spain, and Portugal. Its purpose is to reduce tariffs on goods sold among member countries and to eliminate the fiscal, technical, and border barriers among member nations.

9. *Define Exporting, Importing, Licensing, and Joint Venture.* Exporting is the selling of an organization's goods in another country. Importing is the purchasing of goods from a foreign company. Licensing is an agreement allowing a foreign firm to produce and market its product in exchange for a set percentage of sales revenues. A joint venture involves an agreement between two or more companies to work together on a project.

10. *Outline Some Typical Japanese Management Practices.* Some typical Japanese management practices include morning exercise for all employees; managers and workers all wearing the same company uniforms on the job; morning pep talks by foremen or supervisors; high value placed on loyalty to the company; bonuses paid for extraordinary performance; vague job classifications; full implementation of quality circles and zero-defect programs; one dining room or cafeteria for managers and workers alike; no direct orders given to workers; overtime expected of all workers; use of the just-in-time system of inventory reduction; no layoffs to the greatest possible extent; lawyers and lawsuits not tolerated within the enterprise; afterwork socializing with co-workers; company outings and retreats for all members of an employee's family.

Preview Analysis

1. What dangers might confront a small firm that chooses to engage in international business?
2. What issues might a U.S. firm appraise when looking at a potential trading partner or foreign supplier?
3. What kinds of differing expectations might exist between trading partners? How might these differences be resolved?

Review Questions

1. What is comparative advantage? Competitive advantage? Value-added chain? Self-reference criterion?
2. Define multinational corporation, global industry, global strategy, and strategic alliance.
3. Explain five global strategies used by organizations in international business.
4. What is culture?
5. Explain the foreign exchange risk inherent in international business.
6. What is hedging? What is a forward exchange rate?
7. What is GATT, and what is its function?
8. Define tariffs, quotas, embargoes, and subsidized protection.
9. What is NAFTA? In what sectors will most opportunities for trade develop?
10. What is the European Union?
11. Define exporting, importing, licensing, and joint venture.
12. Describe several Japanese management practices.

Skill-Building Questions

1. Do you think the old saying "When in Rome, do as the Romans do" applies to international business activities? Explain your answer.
2. What problems might you face if you were asked to serve as a manager in a foreign country?
3. What are some typical U.S. management practices that would be difficult to apply in foreign countries?
4. The fastest-growing market for U.S. cigarette manufacturers is in international markets. What ethical problems do you see in exporting cigarettes to foreign markets?
5. What do you think could be some potential pitfalls of entering into a strategic alliance?
6. Do you think NAFTA is a good idea? Develop five "pro" arguments and five "con" arguments for the establishment of NAFTA. What do you think will be the next country to join the NAFTA agreement? Justify your answer.

SKILL-BUILDING EXERCISE 7.1

Blunders

Multinational corporations have occasionally experienced unexpected troubles due to culture, language, and custom differences. The following examples demonstrate problems encountered by some companies with regard to product and company names:

- When Chevrolet introduced its Nova in Puerto Rico, sales were less than brisk. When spoken, the word *Nova* sounded like "no va," which in Spanish means "it doesn't go."
- Ford introduced a low-cost truck, the Fiera, into some less developed countries and also experienced slow sales. Fiera means "ugly old woman" in Spanish.
- A private Egyptian airline, Misair, proved to be rather unpopular with French people. When pronounced in French, the name means "misery."
- The phonetic pronunciation of Esso in Japanese means "stalled car." Obviously this name did not go over well in Japan.

Questions

1. Assume you have been considering opening a McDonald's franchise in either Central America or Spain. Develop a list of internationally related factors you would need to investigate in evaluating the feasibility of this idea.
2. Prioritize the list you developed in question 1.

*These examples are taken from David A. Ricks, *Big Business Blunders: Mistakes in Multinational Marketing* (Homewood, IL.: Richard D. Irwin, 1983), pp. 37–47.

SKILL-BUILDING EXERCISE 7.2

Market Penetration

Your company is a manufacturer of consumer soaps and detergents. You have been working for the company for seven years and have recently been promoted to a new position of manager of international business activities. Presently, your company does little business in Europe.

The president of your company has recognized the vast potential of the European community and asked you to develop some recommendations for expanding into Europe—both Eastern and Western Europe. He has voiced the opinion that a plant should be built somewhere in Europe. However, he has also stated this is not essential and you are free to recommend any approach you would like to take to do business in Europe.

Your professor will break the class into teams to prepare this exercise. Prepare a 10-minute presentation on your recommendations.

CASE INCIDENT 7.1

Profiles

In the July–August 1989 issue of the *International Executive*, many statements were made as to how the Japanese viewed Americans and how they viewed themselves. Some of these included:

- Americans are too liberal, and they take too many risks. They don't always do their homework.
- We look at long-term earnings, five years ahead. Americans tend to look only at the next financial quarter or so. Japanese stockholders don't have as much involvement, power, or clout as American stockholders do.
- Americans are always identifying themselves or each other by race or religion or something. In Japan, we're just all the same.

- We are a very proud people. We do believe we are unique and different. Americans should never assume that we want to be like them.

Questions

1. Do any of these statements surprise you? If yes, why?
2. What implications would the last statement have for American business?
3. Do you have any views about the Japanese? Write down one of your views for discussion in class.

Source: Editorial of the *International Executive*, July–August 1989, pp. 39–41.

CASE INCIDENT 7.2

Impose Quotas

A labor union official of the Textile Workers of America was alleged to have made the following statement:

> Foreign imports of textiles has cost American jobs and tax revenues. In order to slow down the disruptive impacts on American society, quotas should be placed on imports into the United States for those goods and product lines that are displacing significant percentages of U.S. production and employment.

Questions

1. Do you agree with the union official? Explain.
2. Do you believe import quotas should be established for certain industries? Which ones?
3. Does the United States benefit or lose from international business activity?

- We look at long-term earnings, five years ahead. Americans tend to look only at the next financial quarter or so. Japanese stockholders don't have as much involvement, power, or clout as American stockholders do.
- Americans are always identifying themselves or each other by race or religion or something. In Japan, we're just all the same. We are a very proud people. We do believe we are unique and different. Americans should never assume that we want to be like them.

Questions

1. Do any of these statements surprise you? If yes, why?
2. What implications would the last statement have for American business?
3. Do you have any views about the Japanese? Write down one of your views for discussion in class.

Source: Editorial, *International Executive*, July–August 1989, pp. 39–41.

References and Additional Readings

[1]Bruce Kogut, "Designing Global Strategies: Comparative and Competitive Value-Added Chains," *Sloan Management Review,* Summer 1985, p. 15.

[2]Ibid., p. 15.

[3]Michael Porter, *Competitive Strategy* (New York: The Free Press, 1980), p. 275.

[4]The next four strategies are from Porter, *Competitive Strategy,* p. 294.

[5]For additional information on various global strategy options, see Sumantra Ghoshal, "Global Strategy: An Organizing Framework," *Strategic Management Journal*, September–October 1987, pp. 425–40.

[6]Joseph D. O'Brian, "Focusing on Quality in the Pacific Rim," *International Executive,* July–August 1991, p. 22.

[7]Rolf Caspers and Michael McManus, "The World in 2000: Blocs, Triangles, and Points of Light," *Business Forum* 17 (Winter 1992), pp. 60–61.

[8]David Vogel, "Is U.S. Business Obsessed with Ethics?" *Across the Board,* November–December 1993, pp. 30–33.

[9]See George G. Brenkert, "Can We Afford International Human Rights?" *Journal of Business Ethics,* July 1992, pp. 515–21.

[10]For additional information, see Mehdi Hojjat, "Four Steps to Exporting Success," *International Executive,* July–August 1991, pp. 16–20.

[11]John A. Pearce II and Richard B. Robinson, Jr., *Strategic Management* (Burr Ridge, IL.: Richard D. Irwin, 1994), pp. 125–26.

[12]Chalmers Johnson, "Japanese-Style Management in America," *California Management Review,* Summer 1988, pp. 35–36.

[13]Peter F. Drucker, "Learning from Foreign Management," *The Wall Street Journal,* June 4, 1980, p. 1.

PLANNING SKILLS

8

The Basics of Planning and Strategic Management

LEARNING OBJECTIVES

After studying this chapter, you should be able to:

1. Define planning and distinguish between formal and functional plans.

2. Contrast strategic planning with operational planning.

3. Define strategy and explain the various levels of strategies.

4. Define strategic management and explain the strategic management process.

5. Explain the differences among missions, objectives, policies, procedures, and rules.

6. Discuss the components of a SWOT analysis.

7. Define a strategic business unit (SBU).

8. Discuss what organizational factors need to be evaluated in implementing a strategic plan.

When it comes to women's progress into the ranks of management, think bits and bytes, not nuts and bolts. The computer industry, surprisingly, is where the largest gains have been made. But by no means have women shattered the invisible barrier, known as the "glass ceiling," to top offices in the Fortune 500 companies. For those who have, planning skills seem to be a recurring pattern common to successful women executives. This is especially true in banking, finance, fashion merchandising, and light manufacturing. It has been said that you cannot go anywhere in management until you can plan effectively and create strategies to move your company to higher levels of competition and profit.

For the new breed of female manager, planning skills also seem to be at the core of establishing credibility, developing strategy skills, refining a style of management, and shouldering responsibility. Proper planning procedures also help to foster candor and directness with superiors, and even an air of truthfulness and outspokenness, that is essential to creating change within the corporate system. These new female managers have also built credibility by taking serious risks and developing a team-oriented participative management style that fits perfectly with the competitive environment of the 1990s.

One high-ranking female clothing manufacturing executive explained her team-building style as a focus on a creative management vision, sharing power, and giving others responsibility: "Define clear objectives, give your people lots of leeway, stay informed on their progress, and especially, delegate and empower others to do what they need to do their job." This may be a new definition of planning that deviates from the classical concept, but many top female managers think it works. "Maybe new definitions are just what we need!" this executive said.

Sources: Lisa Mainiero, "The Longest Climb," *Psychology Today*, November–December 1994, pp. 40–43; Pamela Mendels, "How Women Have Fared," *Working Woman*, October 1995, pp. 44–45.

THE PLANNING PROCESS

planning   Process of deciding what objectives to pursue during a future time period and what to do to achieve those objectives.

Planning is the process of deciding what objectives to pursue during a future time period and what to do to achieve those objectives. It is the primary management function and is inherent in everything a manager does. This chapter discusses the basics of the planning function and how this function relates to strategic management.

Why Plan?

It is futile for a manager to attempt to perform the other management functions without having a plan. Managers who attempt to organize without a plan find themselves reorganizing on a regular basis. The manager who attempts to staff without a plan will be constantly hiring and firing employees. Motivation is almost impossible in an organization undergoing continuous reorganization and high employee turnover.

Planning enables a manager or an organization to actively affect rather than passively accept the future. By setting objectives and charting a course of action, the organization commits itself to "making it happen." This allows the organization to affect the future. Without a planned course of action, the organization is much more likely to sit back, let things happen, and then react to those happenings in a crisis mode.

Planning provides a means for actively involving personnel from all areas of the organization in the management of the organization. Involvement produces a multitude of benefits. First, input from throughout the organization improves the quality of the plans; good suggestions can come from any level in the organization. Involvement in the planning process also enhances the overall understanding of the organization's direction. Knowing the big picture can minimize friction among departments, sections, and individuals. For example, through planning, the sales department can understand and appreciate the objectives of the production department and their relationship to organizational objectives. Involvement in the planning process fosters a greater personal commitment to the plan; the plan becomes "our" plan rather than "their" plan. Positive attitudes created by involvement also improve overall organizational morale and loyalty.

Planning can also have positive effects on managerial performance. Studies have demonstrated that employees who stress planning earn very high performance ratings from supervisors.[1] They have also shown that planning has a positive impact on the quality of work produced.[2] While some have proven inconclusive, several studies have reported a positive relationship between planning and certain measures of organizational success, such as profits and goals.[3] One explanation that would fit all the findings to date is that good planning, as opposed to the mere presence or absence of a plan, is related to organizational success.

A final reason for planning is the mental exercise required to develop a plan. Many people believe the experience and knowledge gained throughout the development of a plan force managers to think in a future- and contingency-oriented manner; this can result in great advantages over managers who are static in their thinking. Management Illustration 8.1 discusses how Matsushita Electric Industrial Company of Japan has revamped its planning process to meet the challenges of the future.

Formal Planning

All managers plan. The difference lies in the methods they employ and the extent to which they plan. Most planning is carried out on an informal or casual basis. This oc-

Management Illustration 8.1
The Practice of Planning

We must plan for the future, because people who stay in the present will remain in the past.

Abraham Lincoln

One firm to which many of the benefits of planning seem to apply is Matsushita Electric Industrial Company. The late 1980s and early 1990s brought a plodding and bureaucratic management to Matsushita and made the company an also-ran to its arch-rival, Sony. President Yoichi Morishita had had enough. In a dramatic move to revamp planning functions and *risutora* (restructure), Yoichi began to break the Japanese tradition of lifetime employment and consensus management. In 1994 he adopted a U.S. model of planning that required the following steps: (1) set clear performance goals (motivate executives to boost profit margins to 5 percent); (2) reduce management layers (cut costs, improve efficiency, and reduce or transfer employees by 6,000); (3) decentralize decision making (division chiefs would have responsibility for everything from product development to financing, and all managers would have to submit their own personal three-year plans for reviving their departments or divisions); and (4) overhaul R&D (consolidate and refocus efforts by signing scientists to five-year contracts rather than lifetime employment; researchers would receive bonuses based on the success of their work, not on the company's performance. In April of 1997, Yoichi implemented a new "Year 2000 Plan" which called for a further internationalization of the company. The new plan envisioned a more balanced breakdown of the company's global business by the year 2000 with consumer, industrial, and components operations divided roughly into equal thirds (versus the current 38% consumer, 37% industrial, and 25% for components). Additional objectives include a 50%-50% domestic-international split of total sales volume and a 70%-30% split between domestic and overseas production.

Yoichi believes that in the coming decade, planning and the implementation of those plans will be critical to the success of Matsushita. To get the right plan for the right problem is the subject of his booklet, *Essential Management*, which has been distributed to all employees.

Source: Robert Neff, "Tradition Be Damned," *Business Week*, October 31, 1994, pp. 108–10, and "Matsushita", *Forbes*, January 13, 1997, p. 57.

For more information about Matsushita Electric Industrial Company go to: www.hoovers.com/capsules/41873.html.

curs when planners do not record their thoughts but carry them around in their heads. A **formal plan** is a written, documented plan developed through an identifiable process. The appropriate degree of sophistication depends on the needs of the individual managers and the organization itself. The environment, size, and type of business are factors that typically affect the planning needs of an organization.

formal plan Written, documented plan developed through an identifiable process.

Functional Plans

Plans are often classified by function or use. The most frequently encountered types of **functional plans** are sales and marketing plans, production plans, financial plans, and personnel plans. Sales and marketing plans are for developing new products or services and selling both present and future products or services. Production plans deal with producing the desired products or services on a timely schedule. Financial plans deal primarily with meeting the financial commitments and capital expenditures of the organization. Personnel plans relate to the human resource needs of the organization. Many functional plans are interrelated

functional plans Originate from the functional areas of an organization such as production, marketing, finance, and personnel.

141

and interdependent. For example, a financial plan would obviously be dependent on production, sales, and personnel plans.

The Planning Horizon: Short Range, Intermediate, and Long Range

The length of the planning horizon varies somewhat from industry to industry, depending on the specific environment and activity. What may be long range when operating in a rapidly changing environment, such as the electronics industry, may be short range when operating in a relatively static environment, such as the brick man-

short-range plans Generally cover up to one year.
long-range plans Typically span at least three to five years; some extend as far as 20 years into the future.

ufacturing industry. In practice, however, **short-range plans** generally cover up to one year, whereas **long-range plans** span at least three to five years, with some extending as far as 20 years into the future. While long-range planning is possible at any level in the organization, it is carried out primarily at the top levels.

Intermediate plans cover the time span between short-range and long-range plans. From a pragmatic standpoint, intermediate plans generally cover from one to three or one to five years, depending on the horizon covered by the long-range plan. Usually intermediate plans are derived from long-range plans and short-range plans are derived from intermediate plans. For example, if the long-range plan calls for a 40 percent growth in sales by the end of five years, the intermediate plan should outline the necessary steps to be taken over the time span covering one to five years. Short-range plans would outline what actions are necessary within the next year.

Operational versus Strategic Plans

strategic planning Analogous to top-level long-range planning; covers a relatively long period; affects many parts of the organization.
operations or tactical planning Short-range planning; done primarily by middle- to lower-level managers, it concentrates on the formulation of functional plans.

Strategic planning is analogous to top-level, long-range planning. It is the planning process applied at the highest levels of the organization, covering a relatively long period and affecting many parts of the organization. **Operations** or **tactical planning** is short-range planning and concentrates on the formulation of functional plans. Production schedules and day-to-day plans are examples of operational plans.

However, the distinctions between strategic and operations planning are relative, not absolute. The major difference is the level at which the planning is done. Strategic planning is done primarily by top-level managers; operational planning is done by managers at all levels in the organization and especially by middle- and lower-level managers.

Before studying the planning process further, it is necessary to develop a clear understanding of strategy and its various forms. These forms are discussed in the next section.

STRATEGY

strategy Outlines the basic steps management plans to take to reach an objective or a set of objectives; outlines how management intends to achieve its objectives.

The word *strategy* originated with the Greeks about 400 BC; it pertained to the art and science of directing military forces.[4] A **strategy** outlines the basic steps that management plans to take to reach an objective or a set of objectives. In other words, strategy outlines how management intends to achieve its objectives.

Levels of Strategy

Strategies exist at three primary levels in an organization and are classified according to the scope of what they are intended to accomplish. The three levels are grand, business, and functional strategies.

Grand or Corporate Strategies   Strategies that address which businesses the organization will be in and how resources will be allocated among those businesses are referred to as **grand** or **corporate strategies.** They are established at the highest levels in the organization, and they involve a long-range time horizon. Grand strategies are concerned with the overall direction of the organization, specifically tied to mission statements, and generally formulated by top corporate management. Four basic grand strategy types are recognized: growth, stability, retrenchment, and combination.

grand or corporate strategies   Address which businesses an organization will be in and how resources will be allocated among those businesses
growth strategy   Used when the organization tries to expand, as measured by sales, product line, number of employees, or similar measures.

   Growth strategies are used when the organization tries to expand in terms of sales, product line, number of employees, or similar measures. Under this concept, an organization can grow through concentration of current businesses, vertical integration, and diversification. Kellogg and McDonald's use concentration strategies—focusing on extending the sales of their current products or services—very successfully. A. G. Bass (maker of the famous "preppie" shoe, Bass Weejuns) believes vertical integration, in which a company moves into areas it previously served either as a supplier to or as a customer for its current products or services, to be a superior growth strategy. The final growth strategy is exemplified by Coca-Cola's purchase of Minute Maid Orange Juice. Diversification can take several forms, but concentric (in related fields) is the most common.

stability strategy   Used when the organization is satisfied with its present course (status quo strategy).
defensive (retrenchment) strategy   Used when a company wants or needs to reduce its operations.
combination strategy   Used when an organization simultaneously employs different strategies for different parts of the company.

   Stability strategies are used when the organization is satisfied with its present course. Management will make efforts to eliminate minor weaknesses, but generally its actions will remain the status quo. Stability strategies are most likely to be successful in unchanging or very slowly changing environments. Growth is possible under a stability strategy, but it will be slow, methodical, and nonaggressive. Most organizations elect a stability strategy by default rather than by any conscious decision or plan.

   Defensive or **retrenchment strategies** are used when a company wants or needs to reduce its operations. Most often they are used to reverse a negative trend or to overcome a crisis or problem. The three most popular types are *turnaround* (designed to reverse a negative trend and get the organization back to profitability), *divestiture* (the company sells or divests itself of a business or part of a business), and *liquidation* (the entire company is sold or dissolved). These strategies have become popular in the 1990s to reverse the excesses of the 1980s and focus on new directions for corporate growth.

   Combination strategies are used when an organization simultaneously employs different strategies for different parts of the company. Most multibusiness companies use some type of combination strategy, especially, those serving several different markets. Coca-Cola, for example, pursued a combination strategy in 1989 when it divested its Columbia Pictures division while expanding its soft-drink and orange juice businesses.

   Figure 8.1 summarizes the major types and subtypes of grand strategies.

FIGURE 8.1   Major Types and Subtypes of Grand Strategies>

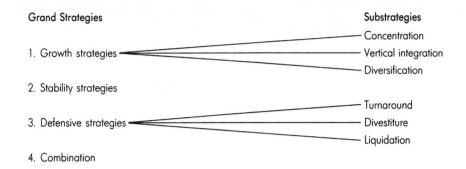

Grand Strategies

1. Growth strategies
2. Stability strategies
3. Defensive strategies
4. Combination

Substrategies

Concentration
Vertical integration
Diversification

Turnaround
Divestiture
Liquidation

---

business strategies   Focus on how to compete in a given business.

Business Strategies   **Business strategies,** the second primary level of strategy formulation, focus on how to compete in a given business. Narrower in scope than a corporate strategy, a business strategy generally applies to a single business unit. Though usually situational in nature, most of these strategies can be classified as overall cost leadership, differentiation, or focus.[5]

Overall cost leadership is a strategy designed to produce and deliver the product or service for a lower cost than the competition. Wal-Mart and Home Depot have adopted this strategy with great success.

Differentiation aims to make the product or service unique in its category. Differentiation can be achieved through a superior product (Microsoft), a quality image (Mercedes-Benz), or a brand image (Polo sportswear).

Focus is the last type of business strategy. Companies that use this method focus on, or direct their attention to, a narrow market segment. The segment may be a special buyer group, a geographical market, or one part of the product line. With a focus strategy, the firm serves a well-defined but narrow market better than competitors that serve a broader or less defined market. A "Tall Men's" clothing store is an example of a company following a focus strategy. Colgate-Palmolive, for example, has determined that to reach Hispanics successfully, it must capitalize on shared traits of this growing segment. Its 70 percent market share of toothpaste sold to Hispanics is largely attributed to understanding that three-quarters of Hispanics who watch TV or listen to radio do so with Spanish-language stations. Colgate-Palmolive has heavy sponsorship of favorite programs on these stations.[6]

Functional Strategies   The final primary level of strategy is functional strategies. **Functional strategies** deal with the activities of the different functional areas of the business—production, finance, marketing, personnel, and the like. Usually functional strategies are in effect for a relatively short period, often one year or less. These step-by-step operational or tactical plans support business-level strategies, but they are concerned mainly with "how to" issues.

functional strategies   Concerned with the activities of the different functional areas of the business.
strategic management   Formulation, proper implementation, and continuous evaluation of strategic plans; determines the long-run directions and performance of an organization. The essence of strategic management is developing strategic plans and keeping them current.

Strategic Management   The rapid rate of change in today's business world is making it increasingly necessary that managers keep their plans current. **Strategic management** is the application of the basic planning process at the highest levels of the organization. Through the strategic management process, top management determines the long-run direction and performance of the organization by ensuring careful formulation, proper implementation, and continuous evaluation of plans and strategies. The essence of strategic management is developing strategic plans and keeping them current as changes occur internally and in the environment. It is possible to prepare a formal plan with a well-defined strategy and not practice strategic management. In such a situation, the plan could become outmoded as changes occur in the environment. Practicing strategic management does not ensure that an organization will meet all changes successfully, but it does increase the odds.

Although guided by top management, successful strategic management involves many different levels in the organization. For example, top management may ask middle- and lower-level managers for input when formulating top-level plans. Once top-level plans have been finalized, different organizational units may be asked to formulate plans for their respective areas. A proper strategic management process helps ensure that plans throughout the different levels of the organization are coordinated and mutually supportive.

Organizations that consciously engage in strategic management generally follow some type of formalized process for making decisions and taking actions that affect their future direction. In the absence of a formal process, strategic decisions are made in a piecemeal fashion. An informal approach to strategy, however, does not necessarily mean the organization doesn't know what it is doing. It simply means the organization does not engage in any type of formalized process for initiating and managing strategy.

THE STRATEGIC MANAGEMENT PROCESS

The strategic management process includes setting the organization's mission; defining what business or businesses the organization will be in; setting objectives; developing, implementing, and evaluating strategies; and adjusting these components as necessary. While the basic process is similar in most organizations, differences exist in the formality of the process, levels of managerial involvement, and degree of institutionalization of the process.

Although different organizations may use somewhat different approaches to the strategic management process, most successful approaches share several common components and a similar sequence. The strategic management process is composed of three major phases: (1) formulating the strategic plan, (2) implementing the strategic plan, and (3) evaluating the strategic plan. The **formulation phase** is concerned with developing the initial strategic plan. The **implementation phase** involves implementing the strategic plan that has been formulated. The **evaluation phase** stresses the importance of continuously evaluating and updating the strategic plan after it has been implemented. Each of these three phases is critical to the success of the strategic management process. A breakdown in any one area can easily cause the entire process to fail. Management Illustration 8.2 demonstrates that the strategic management process is not a new concept and in fact may have had its roots in ancient China during the career of the warlord-philosopher Sun Tzu.

formulation phase   First phase in strategic management, in which the initial strategic plan is developed.

implementation phase   Second phase in strategic management, in which the strategic plan is put into effect.

evaluation phase   Third phase in strategic management, in which the implemented strategic plan is monitored, evaluated, and updated.

Management Illustration 8.2
Sun Tzu and the Art of War

The concept of using military strategy to improve business strategy formulation may be a relatively new idea in the Western world, but it is certainly not new to our European and Asian trading partners. In fact, most American corporations' international competitors base their theory of business acumen on sound and proven military principles rather than on what we would call "business administration." According to Scott DeGarmo, senior editor of *Success* magazine, "While Westerners study the art of the spreadsheet to prepare for business careers, Asians study *The Art of War*."

Any enlightened strategist should undertake a reading of Sun Tzu's *The Art of War*. Many consider this 2,500-year-old work by a mysterious Chinese warrior-philosopher to be "the definitive work on strategy." Many consider Japan's post World War II economic success to be an illustration of Sun Tzu's statement that "to win without fighting is best." The aim of Sun Tzu's philosophy is invincibility, victory without battle, and unassailable strength through the understanding of physics, politics, and the psychology of conflict.

Following are some of Sun Tzu's most valued ideas that can be incorporated into the formulation of modern corporate planning and strategy:

- All warfare is based on deception.
- Offer the enemy a bait to lure him; feign disorder and strike him.
- The enemy must not know where I intend to give battle. For if he does not know where I intend to give battle, he must prepare in a great many places.
- To win 100 victories in 100 battles is not the acme of skill. To subdue the enemy without fighting is the acme of skill.

- Attack an enemy's strategy, not his army.
- If you outnumber an opponent 10 to 1, surround them; 5 to 1, attack them; and 2 to 1, divide them.
- Knowing when to fight is the secret to winning.
- Surprise is a key element to victory.
- Be like a massive flood in a canyon. Direct your formation toward an objective with superior force.

With these few principles in mind, the manager of the future must prepare to relearn the rules of the corporate strategy game. The strategic management process of the future will be one of quick response and deception. According to a military expert's analysis and application of tactics that worked in the Persian Gulf war, it will be necessary to "mentally isolate your adversaries by presenting them with ambiguous, deceptive, or novel situations, as well as by operating at a tempo they can neither make out nor keep up with . . . twisting their mental images so that they can neither appreciate nor cope with what's really going on." Considering the works of Sun Tzu, maybe it is time for top managers to go into the past to find answers that will sustain their planning and strategy efforts in the future. As former Chrysler chairman Lee Iacocca has said of the aforementioned wake-up call, "For those of us who forgot, it's called being competitive."

Sources: Wong, Yim Yu, "The Strategy of an Ancient Warrior: An Inspiration for International Managers," *Multinational Business Review*, Spring 1998, pp. 83–93; John R. Brooks, Jr., "Strategic Alliances: Concepts and Examples," in Zikmund and d'Amico, *Effective Marketing: Advanced Instructional Modules* (Minneapolis/St. Paul: West, 1995), pp. 325–63; and Joseph J. Romm, "The Gospel According to Sun Tzu," *Forbes*, December 9, 1991, pp. 154–56.

Formulating Strategy

The formulation stage of the strategic management process involves developing the grand- and business-level strategies to be pursued. The strategies ultimately chosen are shaped by the organization's internal strengths and weaknesses and the threats and opportunities the environment presents.

The first part of the formulation phase is to obtain a clear understanding of the current position and status of the organization. This includes identifying the mission,

---

FIGURE 8.2   Objectives of the Company Mission

What is the mission statement designed to accomplish? According to King and Cleland, the objectives of the company mission are:

1. To ensure unanimity of purpose within the organization.
2. To provide a basis for motivating the use of the organization's resources.
3. To develop a basis, or standard, for allocating organizational resources.
4. To establish a general tone or organizational climate; for example, to suggest a businesslike operation.
5. To serve as a focal point for those who can identify with the organization's purpose and direction and to deter those who cannot do so from participating further in its activities.
6. To facilitate the translation of objectives and goals into a work structure involving the assignment of tasks to responsible elements within the organization.
7. To specify organizational purposes and the translation of these purposes into goals in such a way that cost, time, and performance parameters can be assessed and controlled.

Source: Adapted from William R. King and David I. Cleland, *Strategic Planning and Policy* (New York: Van Nostrand Reinhold, 1978), p. 124.

---

identifying the past and present strategies, diagnosing the organization's past and present performance, and setting objectives for the company's operation.

Identifying Mission

mission Defines the basic purpose(s) of an organization: why the organization exists.

An organization's mission is actually the broadest and highest level of objectives. The **mission** defines the basic purpose or purposes of the organization (for this reason, the terms *mission* and *purpose* are often used interchangeably). Basically, an organization's mission outlines why the organization exists. A mission statement usually includes a description of the organization's basic products and/or services and a definition of its markets and/or sources of revenue. Figure 8.2 outlines the objectives of a typical mission statement. Figure 8.3 presents several sample mission statements.

Defining *mission* is crucial. It is also more difficult than one might imagine. Peter Drucker emphasizes that an organization's purpose should be examined and defined not only at its inception or during difficult times but also during successful periods.[7] If the railroad companies of the early 1900s or the wagon makers of the 1800s had made their organizational purpose to develop a firm position in the transportation business, they might hold the same economic positions today that they enjoyed in earlier times.

Drucker argues that an organization's purpose is determined not by the organization itself but by its customers.[8] Customer satisfaction with the organization's product or service defines the purpose more clearly than does the organization's name, statutes, or articles of incorporation. Drucker outlines three questions that need to be answered to define an organization's present business. First, management must identify the customers: where they are, how they buy, and how they can be reached. Second, management must know what the customer buys. For instance, does the Rolls-Royce owner buy transportation or prestige? Finally, what is the customer looking for in the product? For example, does the homeowner buy an appliance from Sears, Roebuck & Company because of price, quality, or service?

Management must also identify what the future business will be and what it should be. Drucker presents four areas to investigate. The first is market potential: What does the long-term trend look like? Second, what changes in market structure might occur due to economic developments, changes in styles or fashions, or

FIGURE 8.3   Identifying Mission Statement Components: A Compilation of Excerpts from Actual Corporate Mission Statements

1. Customer-market	We believe our first responsibility is to the doctors, nurses, and patients, to mothers and all others who use our products and services. (Johnson & Johnson) To anticipate and meet market needs of farmers, ranchers, and rural communities within North America. (CENEX)
2. Product-service	AMAX's principal products are molybdenum, coal, iron, ore, copper, lead, zinc, petroleum and natural gas, potash, phosphates, nickel, tungsten, silver, gold, and magnesium. (AMAX)
3. Geographic domain	We are dedicated to the total success of Corning Glass Works as a worldwide competitor. (Corning Glass)
4. Technology	Control Data is in the business of applying microelectronics and computer technology in two general areas: computer-related hardware and computing-enhancing services, which include computation, information, education, and finance. (Control Data) The common technology in these areas relates to discrete particle coatings. (NASHUA)
5. Concern for survival	In this respect, the company will conduct its operation prudently, and will provide the profits and growth which will assure Hoover's ultimate success. (Hoover Universal)
6. Philosophy	We are committed to improve health care throughout the world. (Baxter Healthcare) We believe human development to be the worthiest of the goals of civilization and independence to be the superior condition for nurturing growth in the capabilities of people. (Sun Company)
7. Self-concept	Hoover Universal is a diversified, multi-industry corporation with strong manufacturing capabilities, entrepreneurial policies, and individual business unit autonomy. (Hoover Universal)
8. Concern for public image	We are responsible to the communities in which we live and work and to the world community as well. (Johnson & Johnson) Also, we must be responsive to the broader concerns of the public, including especially the general desire for improvement in the quality of life, equal opportunity for all, and the constructive use of natural resources. (Sun Company)

Source: John A. Pearce II and F. R. David, "Corporate Mission Statements: The Bottom Line," *Academy of Management Executive*, May 1987, pp. 109–16.

competition? For example, how have oil prices affected the automobile market structure? Third, what possible changes will alter customers' buying habits? What new ideas or products might create new customer demand or change old demands? Consider the impact of the minicalculator on sales of slide rules and hand-cranked adding machines. Finally, what customer needs are not being adequately served by available products and services? The introduction of overnight package delivery by FedEx is a well-known example of identifying and filling a current customer need.

Identifying Past and Present Strategies   In the 1980s, Ford Motor Company embarked on a conscious strategy to upgrade its product quality. Before implementing this new strategy, Ford first had to identify clearly what its strategy had been in the past. In other words, before a strategic change can be developed and implemented, the past and present strategies must be clarified.

General questions to be addressed include the following: Has past strategy been consciously developed? If not, can past history be analyzed to identify what implicit strategy has evolved? If so, has the strategy been recorded in written form? In either case, a strategy or a series of strategies, as reflected by the organization's past actions and intentions, should be identified.

Diagnosing Past and Present Performance   To evaluate how past strategies have worked and determine whether strategic changes are needed, the organization's performance record must be examined. How is the organization currently performing? How has the organization performed over the last several years? Is the performance trend moving up or down? Management must address all of these questions before attempting to formulate any type of future strategy. Evaluating an organization's performance usually involves some type of in-depth financial analysis and diagnosis.

Once management has an accurate picture of the current status of the organization, the next step in formulating strategy is to decide what the long-, intermediate-, and short-range objectives should be in light of the current mission. However, these objectives cannot be accurately established without examining the internal and external environments. Thus, establishing the long- and intermediate-range objectives and analyzing the internal and external environments are concurrent processes that influence each other.

Setting Objectives

objectives   Statements outlining what the organization is trying to achieve; give an organization and its members direction.

long-range objectives   Go beyond the current fiscal year; must support and not conflict with the organizational mission.

short-range objectives   Generally tied to a specific time period of a year or less and are derived from an in-depth evaluation of long-range objectives.

If you don't know where you are going, how will you know when you get there? **Objectives** are statements outlining what the organization is trying to achieve; they give the organization and its members direction and purpose. Few managers question the importance of objectives; they question only what the objectives should be.

Long-range objectives generally go beyond the organization's current fiscal year. Long-range objectives must support and not conflict with the organizational mission. However, they may be quite different from the organizational mission, yet still support it. For instance, the organizational mission of a fast-food restaurant might be to provide rapid, hot-food service to a certain area of the city. One long-range objective might be to increase sales to a specific level within the next four years. Obviously, this objective is quite different from the organizational mission, but it still supports the mission.

Short-range objectives should be derived from an in-depth evaluation of long-range objectives. Such an evaluation should result in a listing of priorities of the long-range objectives. Then short-range objectives can be set to help achieve the long-range objectives.

Objectives should be clear, concise, and quantified when possible. Affected personnel should clearly understand what is expected. Normally, multiple objectives should be used to reflect the desired performance of a given organizational unit or person. From a top-level perspective, objectives should span all major areas of the organization. A problem with one overriding objective is that it is often achieved at the expense of other desirable objectives. For example, if production is the only objective, quality may suffer in attempts to realize maximum production. While objectives in different areas may serve as checks on one another, they should be reasonably consistent among themselves.

Objectives should be dynamic; that is, they should be reevaluated as the environment and opportunities change. Objectives for organizations usually fall into one of four general categories: (1) profit oriented, (2) service to customers, (3) employee needs and well-being, and (4) social responsibility. Even nonprofit organizations must be concerned with profit in the sense that they generally must operate within a budget. Another scheme for classifying organizational objectives is (1) primary, (2) secondary, (3) individual, and (4) societal. Primary objectives relate directly to profit. Secondary objectives apply to specific units of the organization (e.g., depart-mental objectives). Individual objectives directly concern the organization's em-ployees. Finally, societal objectives relate to the local, national, and global communities. The following section outlines areas for establishing objectives in most organizations:[9]

1. *Profitability.* measures the degree to which the firm is attaining an acceptable level of profits; usually expressed in terms of profits before or after taxes, return on investment, earnings per share, or profit-to-sales ratios.

2. *Markets.* reflects the firm's position in its marketplace, expressed in terms of share of the market, dollar or unit volume in sales, or niche in the industry.

3. *Productivity.* measures the efficiency of internal operations expressed as a ratio of inputs to outputs, such as number of items or services produced per unit of time.

4. *Product.* describes the introduction or elimination of products or services; expressed in terms of when a product or service will be introduced or dropped.

5. *Financial resources.* reflects goals relating to the funding needs of the firm; expressed in terms of capital structure, new issues of common stock, cash flow, working capital, dividend payments, and collection periods.

6. *Physical facilities.* describes the physical facilities of the firm; expressed in terms of square feet of office or plant space, fixed costs, units of production, or similar measurements.

7. *Research and innovation.* reflects the research, development, and/or innovation aspirations of the firm; usually expressed in terms of dollars to be expended.

8. *Organization structure.* describes objectives relating to changes in the organizational structure and related activities; expressed in terms of a desired future structure or network of relationships.

9. *Human resources.* describes the human resource assets of the organization; expressed in terms of absenteeism, tardiness, number of grievances, and training.

10. *Social responsibility.* refers to the commitments of the firm regarding society and the environment; expressed in terms of types of activities, number of days of service, or financial contributions.

Policies   To help in the objective-setting process, the manager can rely to some extent on policies and procedures developed by the organization. **Policies** are broad, general guides to action that constrain or direct objective attainment. Policies do not tell organizational members exactly what to do, but they do establish the boundaries within which they must operate. For exam-ple, a policy of "answering all written customer com-plaints in writing within 10 days" does not tell a manager exactly how to respond, but it does say it must be done in writing within 10 days. Policies create an under-standing among members of a group that makes the actions of each member more predictable to other members.

policies   Broad, general guides to action that constrain or direct the attainment of objectives.
procedure   Series of related steps or tasks expressed in chronological order for a specific purpose.

Procedures and rules differ from policies only in degree. In fact, they may be thought of as low-level policies. A **procedure** is a series of related steps or tasks expressed in chronological order for a specific purpose. Procedures define in step-by-step fashion the methods through which policies are achieved. Procedures emphasize details. **Rules** require specific and definite actions to be taken or not to be taken in a given situation. Rules leave little doubt about what is to be done. They permit no flexibility or deviation. Unlike procedures, rules do not have to specify sequence. For example, "No smoking in the conference room" is a rule. In reality, procedures and rules are subsets of policies. The primary purpose is guidance. The differences lie in the range of applicability and the degree of flexibility. A no-smoking rule is much less flexible than a procedure for handling customer complaints. However, a rule can have a clear relationship to an objective. For example, a no-smoking rule may help the organization reach a stated objective of "a cleaner and safer corporate environment."

rules   Require specific and definite actions to be taken or not to be taken in a given situation.

SWOT Analysis   SWOT is an acronym for an organization's strengths, weaknesses, opportunities, and threats. A SWOT analysis is a technique for evaluating an organization's internal strengths and weaknesses and its external opportunities and threats. A major advantage of using a SWOT analysis is that it provides a general overview of an organization's strategic situation.[10] The underlying assumption of a SWOT analysis is that managers can better formulate a successful strategy after they have carefully reviewed the organization's strengths and weaknesses in light of the threats and opportunities the environment presents.

An organization's strengths and weaknesses are usually identified by conducting an internal analysis of the organization. The basic idea of conducting an internal analysis is to perform an objective assessment of the organization's current strengths and weaknesses. What things does the organization do well? What things does the organization do poorly? From a resource perspective, what are the organization's strengths and weaknesses?

The threats and opportunities presented by the environment are usually identified by methodically assessing the organization's external environment. An organization's **external environment** consists of everything outside the organization, but the focus of this assessment is on the external factors that have an impact on its business. Such factors are classified by their proximity to the organization: They are either in its broad environment or in its competitive environment. Broad environmental factors are somewhat removed from the organization but can still influence it. General economic conditions and social, political, and technological trends represent common factors in the broad environment. Factors in the competitive environment are close to the organization and come in regular contact with it. Stockholders, suppliers, competitors, labor unions, customers, and potential new entrants represent members of the competitive environment.

external environment   Consists of everything outside the organization.

Almost all managers use some method to forecast or anticipate the external environment, especially as it relates to their jobs and areas of responsibility. For example, a top-level manager may want to forecast the future demand for a certain product. A first-line supervisor may need to forecast next week's production. Generally, a forecast tells a manager what to expect in view of the current and predicted situation.

Unfortunately, many managerial forecasts are not very accurate. A review of technological forecasts appearing in the business press over the past 30 years found that about 80 percent of all technological predictions were incorrect.[11]

An assessment of the external environment emphasizes the fact that organizations do not operate in a vacuum and are very much affected by their surroundings. Table 8.1

TABLE 8.1   SWOT Analysis—What to Look for in Sizing Up a Company's Strengths, Weaknesses, Opportunities, and Threats

Potential Internal Strengths

- Core competencies in key areas
- Adequate financial resources
- Well-thought-of by buyers
- An acknowledged market leader
- Well-conceived functional area strategies
- Access to economies of scale
- Insulated (at least somewhat) from strong competitive pressures
- Proprietary technology
- Cost advantages
- Better advertising campaigns
- Product innovation skills
- Proven management
- Ahead on experience curve
- Better manufacturing capability
- Superior technological skills
- Other?

Potential External Opportunities

- Ability to serve additional customer groups or expand into new markets or segments
- Ways to expand product line to meet broader range of customer needs
- Ability to transfer skills or technological know-how to new products or businesses
- Integrating forward or backward
- Falling trade barriers in attractive foreign markets
- Complacency among rival firms
- Ability to grow rapidly because of strong increases in market demand
- Emerging new technologies

Potential Internal Weaknesses

- No clear strategic direction
- Obsolete facilities
- Subpar profitability because . . .
- Lack of managerial depth and talent
- Missing some key skills or competencies
- Poor track record in implementing strategy
- Plagued with internal operating problems
- Falling behind in R&D
- Too narrow a product line
- Weak market image
- Weak distribution network
- Below-average marketing skills
- Unable to finance needed changes in strategy
- Higher overall unit costs relative to key competitors
- Other?

Potential External Threats

- Entry of lower-cost foreign competitors
- Rising sales of substitute products
- Slower market growth
- Adverse shifts in foreign exchange rates and trade policies of foreign governments
- Costly regulatory requirements
- Vulnerability to recession and business cycle
- Growing bargaining power of customers or suppliers
- Changing buyer needs and tastes
- Adverse demographic changes
- Other?

Source: Arthur A. Thompson, Jr. and A. J. Strickland III. *Strategic Management: Concepts and Cases*, 8th ed. (Burr Ridge, IL: Richard D. Irwin, Inc. 1995), p. 94.

lists several factors that managers should consider when assessing an organization's strengths and weaknesses and the threats and opportunities posed by the environment. The most important result of a SWOT analysis is the ability to draw conclusions about the attractiveness of the organization's situation and the need for strategic action.[12]

Comparing Strategic Alternatives   The goal in this stage of the formulation process is to identify the feasible strategic alternatives (in light of everything that has been done up to this point) and then select the best alternative. Given the mission and long-range objectives, what are the feasible strategic alternatives? The results of the SWOT analysis also limit the feasible strategic alternatives. For example, the results of an internal financial analysis could severely restrict an organization's options for expansion. Similarly, the results of an external analysis of population trends might also limit an organization's expansion plans. Once a set of feasible alternatives has been defined, the final strategic choice must be made.

The evaluation and final choice of an appropriate strategic alternative involves the integration of the mission, objectives, internal analysis, and external analysis. In this phase, management attempts to select the grand strategy that offers the organization its best chance to achieve its mission and objectives through actions that are compatible with its capacity for risk and its value structure. Once the grand strategy has been identified, additional substrategies must be selected to support it.

In the case of diversified, multibusiness organizations, comparing strategic alternatives involves assessing the attractiveness of each business as well as the overall business mix. A **strategic business unit (SBU)** is a distinct business that has its own set of competitors and can be managed reasonably independently of other businesses within the organization.[13] The elements of an SBU vary from organization to organization but can be a division, a subsidiary, or a single product line. In a small organization, the entire company may be a SBU.

strategic business unit (SBU) Distinct business that has its own set of competitors and can be managed reasonably independently of other businesses within the organization.

Implementing Strategy

After the grand strategy has been carefully formulated, it must be translated into organizational actions. Given that the grand strategy and supporting substrategies have been clearly identified, what actions must be taken to implement them? Strategy implementation involves everything that must be done to put the strategy in motion successfully. Necessary actions include determining and implementing the most appropriate organizational structure, developing short-range objectives, and establishing functional strategies.

Organizational Factors   Not only does an organization have a strategic history; it also has existing structures, policies, and systems. Although each of these factors can change as a result of a new strategy, each must be assessed and dealt with as part of the implementation process.

Even though an organization's structure can always be altered, the associated costs may be very high. For example, a reorganization may result in substantial hiring and training costs for newly structured jobs. Thus, from a practical standpoint, an organization's current structure places certain restrictions on strategy implementation.

The strategy must fit with current organizational policies, or the conflicting policies must be modified. Often past policies heavily influence the extent to which future policies can be altered. For example, A. T. Cross Company, manufacturer of world-renowned writing instruments, has a policy of unconditionally guaranteeing its products for life. Because customers have come to expect this policy, Cross would find it very difficult to discontinue it.

Similarly, organizational systems that are currently in place can affect how the strategy might best be implemented. These systems can be either formal or informal. Examples include information systems, compensation systems, communication systems, and control systems.

Evaluating and Controlling the Strategic Plan

After the strategic plan has been put into motion, the next challenge is to monitor continuously the organization's progress toward its long-range objectives and mission. Is the grand strategy working, or should revisions be made? Where are problems likely to occur? The emphasis is on making the organization's managers aware of the problems that are likely to occur and of the actions to be taken if they do arise. As discussed earlier in this chapter, continuously evaluating and responding to internal and environmental changes is what strategic management is all about.

Figure 8.4 summarizes the strategic management process and its major components.

FIGURE 8.4   The Strategic Management Process

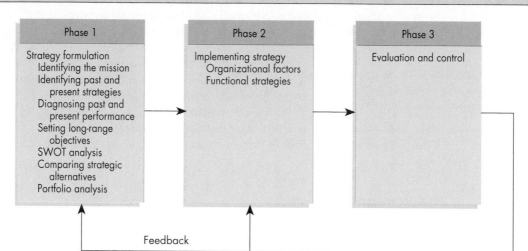

Summary

1. *Define Planning and Distinguish between Formal and Functional Plans.* Planning is the process of deciding which objectives to pursue during a future time period and what to do to achieve those objectives. Formal planning occurs when a written, documented plan is developed through an identifiable process. Functional plans originate from the functional areas of an organization, such as production, marketing, finance, and personnel.

2. *Contrast Strategic Planning with Operational Planning.* Strategic planning covers a relatively long period, affects many parts of the organization, and includes the formulation of objectives and the selection of the means for attaining those objectives. Operational or tactical planning is short range and concentrates on the formulation of functional strategies.

3. *Define Strategy and Explain the Various Levels of Strategies.* A strategy outlines the basic steps management must take to reach an objective or a set of objectives. Grand strategies (growth, stability, defensive, or combination) address what businesses an organization will be in and how resources will be allocated among those businesses. Business strategies (overall cost leadership, differentiation, and focus) concentrate on how to compete in a given business or industry. Functional strategies (production, marketing, finance, and personnel) deal with the activities of the different functional areas of the business.

4. *Define Strategic Management and Explain the Strategic Management Process.* Strategic management is the process of determining the long-run direction and performance of an organization by ensuring careful formulation, proper implementation, and continuous evaluation of plans and strategies. The major phases of the strategic management

process are (1) formulating the strategic plan, (2) implementing the strategic plan, and (3) continuously evaluating and updating the strategic plan.

5. *Explain the Differences among Missions, Objectives, Policies, Procedures, and Rules.* The organization's mission defines the basic purpose or purposes of the organization and usually includes a description of the organization's basic products and/or services and a definition of its markets and/or sources of revenue. Objectives are statements outlining what the organization is trying to achieve; they give the organization and its members direction and purpose. Objectives can be long, intermediate, or short range in nature. Policies are broad, general guides to action that constrain or direct the attainment of objectives. Policies do not tell the organization what to do, but they do establish the boundaries within which it must operate. Procedures are a series of related steps or tasks expressed in chronological order for a specific purpose. Procedures emphasize details. Finally, rules require specific and definite actions to be taken or not to be taken in a given situation. Unlike procedures, rules do not have to specify sequence; they permit no flexibility or deviation.

6. *Discuss the Components of a SWOT Analysis.* SWOT is an acronym for an organization's strengths, weaknesses, opportunities, and threats. A SWOT analysis is a technique for evaluating an organization's internal strengths and weaknesses and its external opportunities and threats. A major advantage of using a SWOT analysis is that it provides a general overview of the organization's strategic situation.

7. *Define a Strategic Business Unit (SBU).* An SBU is a distinct business that has its own set of competitors and

can be managed reasonably independently of other businesses within the organization.

8. *Discuss What Organizational Factors Need to Be Evaluated in Implementing a Strategic Plan.* Not only does an or-

ganization have a strategic history; it also has existing structures, policies, and systems. Although each of these factors can change as a result of a new strategy, each must be assessed and dealt with as part of the implementation process.

Preview Analysis

1. In the 1990s, what industry has produced the greatest advancement and career opportunities for women?

2. For female managers, planning skills seem to be at the core of developing what other managerial skills?

3. For the female manager described in the preview, what ingredients made a team-building style successful?

Review Questions

1. Define planning. What questions does planning answer?

2. Why is it necessary to plan? Distinguish between formal and functional planning. How is most planning conducted?

3. What is the difference between strategic planning and operational planning? Between long-range and short-range planning?

4. Define strategy.

5. What are the major forms of strategy?

6. What are the four types of grand strategy? What are the three forms of business strategy?

7. What are the steps in the strategic management process?

8. Define mission, objective, policy, procedure, and rule.

9. What does SWOT stand for?

10. Define a strategic business unit (SBU).

Skill-Building Questions

1. Why should one plan? What are the benefits of planning?

2. If you were serving as a strategic management consultant, how might you respond to the following question: How can I plan for next year when I don't even know what I'm going to do tomorrow?

3. What do you think are the most important of Sun Tzu's principles as summarized in Management Illustration 8.2? How could we apply these principles to business situations?

4. Comment on the following statement: "Most organizations succeed or fail based on their ability to react to environmental changes."

SKILL-BUILDING EXERCISE 8.1

Ten Most and Least Admired Companies

Every year, *Fortune* magazine publishes the results of a survey that attempts to identify the most and least admired among the largest companies in the United States.

For 1998, the survey included 469 companies. The companies identified as the 10 most admired (in descending order) were:

1   General Electric
2   Coca-Cola
3   Microsoft
4   Dell Computer
5   Berkshire Hathaway
6   Wal-Mart Stores
7   Southwest Airlines
8   Intel
9   Merck
10 Walt Disney

Those companies identified as the least admired for 1998 (in descending order) were:

460   Foundation Health Systems
461   Fruit of the Loom
462   Viad
463   Olsten
464   U.S. Industries
465   Stone Container**
466   Oxford Health Plans
467   MedPartners
468   Shoney's
469   Trump Hotels & Casinos

Looking at the above list, identify one or more trends or forces in the external environment that likely have affected the performance of these companies. Be prepared to share your list with the class.

Source: Eryn Brown, "America's Most Admired Companies," *Fortune*, Mar 1, 1999, pp 68-73.

SKILL BUILDING EXERCISE 8.2

Word Associations*

This exercise is designed to demonstrate how the establishment of a realistic and specific goal can help you improve your performance. You will be given four words and your task is to identify a fifth word that has a common association with each of the four words in a given set. For example, what word has a common association with each of the following?

    sleeping   contest   spot   shop

The answer is <u>beauty</u>.

Now that you understand the game, time yourself and see how many of the following sets you can do in *two* minutes.

1.	cross	baby	blood	ribbon	_____
2.	touch	palate	soap	sell	_____
3.	tree	cup	cake	forbidden	_____
4.	dust	movie	gaze	sapphire	_____
5.	alley	date	snow	spot	_____
6.	rest	post	linen	fellow	_____
7.	opera	no	box	stone	_____
8.	storage	shoulder	comfort	cream	_____
9.	business	suit	wrench	shine	_____
10.	bug	rest	fellow	cover	_____

Your instructor will give you the correct answers. Based on the number you got right, set the following goal for the next exercise:

If you got 1 or 2 correct, your new goal is 4.
If you got 3 or 4 correct, your new goal is 7.
If you got 5 or more correct, your new goal is 9.

Do you consider this new goal challenging? Impossible? Now, striving to make your new goal, see how many of the following sets you can do in *two* minutes.

1.	days	biscuit	collar	ear	_____
2.	play	breast	pox	wire	_____
3.	guy	crack	up	man	_____
4.	ball	trouser	fruit	house	_____
5.	dress	good	star	prayer	_____
6.	stone	jacket	fever	pages	_____
7.	bathtub	wedding	telephone	key	_____
8.	horse	brake	left	box	_____
9.	right	pike	your	stile	_____
10.	bulldog	cuff	toast	windows	_____

Your instructor will give you the correct answers. How did you do relative to your score on the first set? Do you think that having a specific goal affected your score on the second exercise?

*This exercise is adapted from Henry Tosi and Jerald W. Young, *Management Experiences and Demonstrations* (Burr Ridge, IL: Richard D. Irwin, 1982), pp. 35–38, 166, 183.

SKILL-BUILDING EXERCISE 8.3

Developing a Personal Career Plan

One of the common threads many successful people share is that they developed a sense of direction relatively early in life. At the same time, it is common for people to enter and even graduate from college with little idea of what they want to do. Similarly, many people reach middle age only to ask, "How did I end up here?"

Questions

1. Apply the concepts discussed in this chapter and develop, in outline form, a 10-year plan for your own career.

2. Your outline need only be a few pages long. Begin with a statement of mission and work down through each step in the strategic management model. Be sure and include a SWOT analysis. Make your plan as realistic as possible.

3. Identify the major assumptions and environmental trends on which you based your plan.

4. What parts of your plan do you think will be the hardest to achieve?

The following article gives great guidance for developing your own career plan: Patricia Buhler, "Managing in the 90s," *Supervision*, May 1997, pp. 24–26.

CASE INCIDENT 8.1

First in the Market

Juan Peron is a process engineer employed by Vantage Engineering, Inc., and assigned to the research laboratory in the Advanced Products Division (APD). Vantage is a well-established manufacturer of military hardware. APD's general purpose is to conduct research to improve the company's military hardware products. However, the laboratory director was recently given permission to develop spin-off products for possible sale on the open market.

Juan spent his first year in APD assisting on various project assignments. At the end of that year, he was put in charge of a special project to research a chemically processed wood for specialty applications. During the initial stages of the project, Juan spent most of his time in the laboratory becoming familiar with the basic aspects of the treatment process. However, he soon tired of the long, tedious experimental work and became more and more eager to move quickly into the promotion and marketing of the product. This desire was soon realized. An article in a recent national trade publication had generated keen interest in a similar wood product, and as a result, Vantage immediately allocated several thousand dollars to the development and marketing of the chemically processed wood. Simultaneously, a minor reorganization occurred, placing Juan and his project under the direction of Greg Waites, a close friend of Juan's. Thus, Juan had an opportunity to get out of the lab and become involved in the more desirable promotion and marketing aspects.

Juan and Greg soon began traveling nationally, discussing the new product with potential customers. Traveling enabled Juan to spend less and less time in the lab, and as a result many of the experiments required to determine the performance characteristics of the new product were left unfinished. As the number of companies demonstrating an interest in purchasing small quantities for trial applications grew, Juan suggested to Greg that a small pilot plant be constructed. In response to Greg's concerns regarding the performance characteristics of the wood, Juan assured him the preliminary tests indicated the wood could be successfully produced. Juan contended that Vantage had to get a head start on the newly created market before everyone else got into the game, that they should build the pilot plant immediately to fill the sudden influx of orders and then worry about completing the performance tests. Greg, seeing the advantages of getting into the market first, finally agreed, and construction of the pilot plant began shortly thereafter.

During construction, Juan and Greg continued traveling to promote the wood. When the pilot plant was near completion, Juan went to Vantage's personnel department and requested that three laborers be hired to operate the plant. Juan intended to personally direct the technical operations and thus saw no need to establish elaborate job descriptions for the positions.

A week later, Juan had his three employees. Due to a workload reduction in the Electronics Division of Vantage, the employees filling these positions had taken the laborer jobs to avoid being laid off. One had been a purchasing agent, and the others had been electronics technicians. At the beginning of the workday, Juan would drop by the plant and give directions to the crew for the entire day before departing to make sales calls. No formal leader had been appointed, and the three laborers, knowing little about the chemical process involved, were instructed to "use common sense and ingenuity."

A month after the plant operations had gotten under way, a major producer of archery bows requested an order for 70,000 bow handles to be delivered in time to be sold for the upcoming hunting season. It was too good to be true! Juan knew that if they accepted the order, the first year of operations would be guaranteed to be in the black. On receiving the product specifications, Juan persuaded Greg to sign the contract, arguing that they would be throwing all their hard work down the drain if they didn't. Subsequently, a crash program was established at the plant to get the order out on time.

One month after the final shipment of handles had been made, Juan hired a junior engineer, Libby Adams, to conduct the performance experiments that had been disbanded while the plant was getting the rush order out. Libby examined some of the experimental handles and discovered hairline cracks at various stress points that had not appeared during the initial examination. She immediately went to Juan's office to inform him of the problem and found Juan and Greg sitting there with a telegram from the archery company. It stated that several retail merchants had returned bows with hairline cracks in the handles and that the archery company would seek a settlement for its entire investment in the handles.

Vantage paid the settlement and subsequently canceled the wood project.

Questions

1. What caused the wood project to fail?

2. Would a more effective strategy on the part of Juan and Greg have helped ensure the success of the project?

3. At what stage of the strategic management process did the breakdown occur?

4. What general observations can be made to prevent such a situation from occurring again?

CASE INCIDENT 8.2

Hudson Shoe Company

John Hudson, president of Hudson Shoe Company, and his wife spent the month of February on a long vacation in Santo Oro in Central America. After two weeks, Mr. Hudson became restless and started thinking about an idea he had considered for several years but had been too busy to pursue—entering the foreign market.

Mr. Hudson's company, located in a midwestern city, was started some 50 years earlier by his father, now deceased. It has remained a family enterprise, with his brother David in charge of production, his brother Sam the comptroller, and his brother-in-law Bill Owens taking care of product development. Bill and David share responsibility for quality control; Bill often works with Sam on administrative matters and advertising campaigns. Many competent subordinates are also employed. The company has one of the finest reputations in the shoe industry. The product integrity is to be envied and is a source of great pride to the company.

During John's stay in Santo Oro, he decided to visit some importers of shoes. He spoke to several and was most impressed with Señor Lopez of Bueno Compania. After checking Señor Lopez's bank and personal references, his impression was confirmed. Señor Lopez said he would place a small initial order if the samples proved satisfactory. John immediately phoned his office and requested the company rush samples of its best-sellers to Señor Lopez. These arrived a few days before John left for home. Shortly after arriving home, John was pleased to receive an order for 1,000 pairs of shoes from Señor Lopez.

John stayed in touch with Lopez by telephone; within two months after the initial order, Hudson Shoe received an order for 5,000 additional pairs of shoes per month. Business continued at this level for about two years until Señor Lopez visited the plant. He was impressed and increased his monthly order from 5,000 to 10,000 pairs of shoes.

This precipitated a crisis at Hudson Shoe Company, and the family held a meeting. They had to decide whether to increase their capacity with a sizable capital investment or drop some of their customers. They did not like the idea of eliminating loyal customers but did not want to make a major investment. David suggested they run a second shift, which solved the problem nicely.

A year later, Lopez again visited and left orders for 15,000 pairs per month. He also informed them that more effort and expense was now required on his part for a wide distribution of the shoes. In addition to his regular 5 percent commission, he asked John for an additional commission of $1 per pair of shoes. When John hesitated, Lopez assured him that Hudson could raise its selling price by $1 and nothing would be lost. John felt uneasy but went along because the business was easy, steady, and most profitable. A few of Hudson's smaller customers had to be dropped.

By the end of the next year, Lopez was placing orders for 20,000 pairs per month. He asked that Hudson bid on supplying boots for the entire police force of the capital city of Santo Oro. Hudson received the contract and within a year, was supplying the army and navy of Santo Oro and three other Central American countries with their needs.

Again, several old Hudson customers could not get their orders filled. Other Hudson customers were starting to complain of late deliveries. Also, Hudson seemed to be less willing to accept returns at the end of the season or to offer markdown allowances or advertising money. None of this was necessary with its export business. However, Hudson Shoe did decide to cling to its largest domestic customer—the largest mail order chain in the United States.

In June of the following year, Lopez made a trip to Hudson Shoe. He informed John that in addition to his $1 per pair, it would be necessary to give the minister of revenue $1 per pair if he was to continue granting import licenses. Moreover, the defense ministers, who approved the army and navy orders in each country where they did business, also wanted $1 per pair. Again, selling prices could be increased accordingly. Lopez informed John that

shoe manufacturers in the United States and two other countries were most eager to have this business at any terms. John asked for 10 days to discuss this with his partners. Lopez agreed and returned home to await their decision. The morning of the meeting of the board of directors of the Hudson Shoe Company, a wire was received from the domestic chain stating it would not be buying from Hudson next season. John Hudson called the meeting to order.

Questions

1. What were the objectives of Hudson Shoe?
2. What policies existed?
3. How would you evaluate John Hudson's plans?
4. What would you do if you were John Hudson?

References and Additional Readings

[1] J. J. Hemphill, "Personal Variables and Administrative Styles," in *Behavioral Science and Educational Administration* (Chicago: National Society for the Study of Education, 1964), chap. 8.

[2] A. L. Comrey, W. High, and R. C. Wilson, "Factors Influencing Organization Effectiveness: A Survey of Aircraft Workers," *Personnel Psychology* 8 (1955), pp. 79–99.

[3] For a discussion of these studies, see John A. Pearce II, Elizabeth B. Freeman, and Richard D. Robinson, Jr., "The Tenuous Link between Formal Strategic Planning and Financial Performance," *Academy of Management Review*, October 1987, pp. 658–73.

[4] George A. Steiner, *Top Management Planning* (New York: Macmillan, 1969), p. 237.

[5] Michael E. Porter, *Comparative Strategy: Techniques for Analyzing Industries and Competitors* (New York: The Free Press, 1980).

[6] Patricia Braus, "What Does 'Hispanic' Mean?" *American Demographics*, June 1993, pp. 46–49, 58.

[7] Peter F. Drucker, *The Practice of Management* (New York: Harper & Row, 1954), p. 51.

[8] Ibid., pp. 50–57.

[9] Anthony Raia, *Managing by Objectives* (Glenview, IL: Scott, Foresman, 1974), p. 38.

[10] Arthur A. Thompson, Jr., and A. J. Strickland III, *Strategic Management: Concepts and Cases*, 7th ed. (Burr Ridge, IL: Richard D. Irwin, 1993), p. 87.

[11] Steven P. Schnaars, "Where Forecasters Go Wrong," *Across the Board*, December 1989, pp. 38–45.

[12] Thompson and Strickland, *Strategic Management*, p. 90.

[13] George A. Steiner, John B. Miner, and Edmond R. Gray, *Management Policy and Strategy*, 2d ed. (New York: Macmillan, 1982), p. 189.

9

Operations Management and Planning

LEARNING OBJECTIVES

After studying this chapter, you should be able to:

1. Define operations management.

2. Describe an operating system and identify the two basic types of operating systems.

3. Differentiate among product/service design, process selection, and site selection decisions.

4. Explain what a materials-handling system is.

5. Describe and give an example of the two basic classifications of facilities layouts.

6. Explain the sociotechnical approach to job design.

7. Describe several computer-related technologies that are currently playing major roles in production/operations management.

8. Outline the three major steps in developing an aggregate production plan.

9. Summarize the differences between resource allocation and activity scheduling.

10. Distinguish among Gantt charts, the critical path method (CPM), and the program evaluation and review technique (PERT).

When Jim Koch decided to become a microbrewer of beer (Samuel Adams brand), the market niche he targeted didn't exist. Now, despite counterattacks by his huge, supercompetitive rivals (Busch, Miller, and Coors), it does. His idea was to make a super-premium beer supported by product quality and guerrilla marketing techniques. The result is that in the last 10 years, his brewery has gone from zero to $14 million pretax profits on sales of $180 million and has achieved annualized growth of 40 percent a year.

To accomplish these feats, Koch became an expert in promotion, innovation, and operations techniques that have earned him the respect of his rivals. His promotions started small in the Boston market but are now nationwide. The basic theme was to show that he produces a better-than-theirs beer with extra-expensive, high-quality ingredients. His gimmick was the origination of "freshness dating" for beer. Now the industry standard, freshness dating got the attention of the consumer and made an inroad into the industry's market share.

Operationally, Koch began to reinvent the marketing and management of a brewing operation. Having been a consultant with the Boston Consulting Group (he earned three Harvard degrees), he applied innovative managerial techniques to compensate for a lack of capital. First, he has no brewery of his own; he outsources the brewing of his beer lines to small, underutilized breweries. Second, he delivers his own product, since no established distributor wished to offend the industry giants. Third, his 115-person national sales staff (one rep for every 500 clients) is one-half female. When asked why he hires so many women in what has been a traditionally male-dominated industry, Koch responded, "I don't hire women; I hire talented, resourceful, intelligent, energetic people. It happens that God made half of them women."

Koch has studied how to use otherwise underutilized brewers to brew and bottle his beer and how to make their manufacturing processes better. By being his own distributor, he has learned so much about product flow and movement that he is now able to get beer into any market in the country in just 24 hours. Finally, by team building and giving his employees "a piece of the action," he has developed an aggressive management pool that is the envy of his larger competitors. "We became a household word without a marketing department," says Koch. He did it with an innovative philosophy and an ability to take risks.

Source: Adapted from Robert A. Mamis, "Market Maker," *Inc.*, December 1995, pp. 54–64. Adapted with permission. © by Goldhirsh Group, Inc., 38 Commercial Wharf, Boston, MA 02110.

operations management   Application of the basic concepts and principles of management to those segments of the organization that produce its goods and/or services.

operations planning   Designing the systems of the organization that produce goods or services; planning the day-to-day operations within those systems.

Operations management, which evolved from the field of production or manufacturing management, deals with the application of the basic concepts and principles of management to those segments of the organization that produce the organization's goods and/or services. Traditionally, the term *production* brings to mind such things as smokestacks, machine shops, and the manufacture of real goods. Operations management is the management of the production function in any organization—private or public, profit or nonprofit, manufacturing or service.

Operations planning is concerned with designing the systems of the organization that produce the goods or services and with the planning of the day-to-day operations within those systems. The design of the systems that produce the goods or services is a long-range and strategic planning issue, whereas the planning of the day-to-day operations is a short-range and tactical planning issue. This chapter introduces some basic concepts related to operations management, discusses the basic design-related aspects of operations, and covers the day-to-day planning of operations.

THE IMPORTANCE OF OPERATIONS MANAGEMENT

The operations function is only one part of the total organization; however, it is a very important part. The production of goods and/or services often involves the bulk of an organization's financial assets, personnel, and expenses. The operations process also usually takes up an appreciable amount of time. Thus, because of the resources and time consumed by operations, the management of this function plays a critical role in achieving the organization's goals.

Effective operations managers directly influence employee output by (1) building group cohesiveness and individual commitment and (2) making sound technical and administrative decisions. Both tasks have become more complex and important in recent years. Society wants not only improved productivity but also an enriched work environment. Demands for expanded education, child care, enriched benefits, flextime options, and more attention to workplace safety have all caused gaps between employees and management. The human problems confronting operations management have therefore become more important and more challenging.

Most operations managers no longer manage in a stable environment with standard products. Changing technology and a strong emphasis on low costs have altered the technical and administrative problems they confront. The modern operations manager must deal not only with low costs but also with product diversity, a demand for high quality, short lead times, and a rapidly changing technology. As a result, his or her problems are now greater and require much more managerial talent than ever before.

OPERATING SYSTEMS AND ACTIVITIES

operating systems   Consist of the processes and activities necessary to turn inputs into goods and/or services.

Operating systems consist of the processes and activities necessary to turn inputs into goods and/or services. Operating systems exist in all organizations; they are made up of people, materials, facilities, and information. The end result of an operating system is to add value by improving, enhancing, or rearranging the inputs. Many operating systems take a collection of parts and form them into a

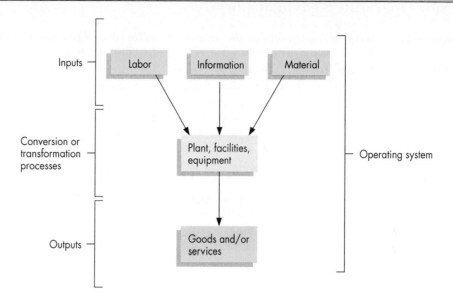

FIGURE 9.1   Simplified Model of an Operating System

more valuable whole. For example, an automobile is a group of separate parts formed into a more valuable whole.

In some situations, the operating system breaks something down from a larger quantity to smaller quantities with more value. A metal shop cuts smaller parts from larger sheets of metal; a butcher produces steaks, hamburger, and other cuts from a side of beef. Both break down a larger quantity into smaller quantities with more value.

A third type of operating system produces services by turning inputs into more useful outputs. Here more emphasis is usually placed on labor and less on materials. For example, an electronics repair shop uses some materials, but the primary value results from the repairer's labor.

Figure 9.1 presents a simplified model of an operating system. The operating system is broader and more inclusive than just the conversion or transformation process. It includes not only the design and operation of the process but also many of the activities needed to get the various inputs (such as product design and scheduling) into the transformation process. Inputs can take on numerous forms (such as managers, workers, equipment, facilities, materials, or information). Many of the activities necessary to get the outputs out of the transformation process (such as inventory control and materials distribution) are also included. Management Illustration 9.1 discusses how Chrysler has revamped its operating system with the goal of becoming the "premier" car and truck company in the world.

Basic Types of Operating Systems

There are two basic types of operating systems. One is based on continuous flows and the other on intermittent flows. Organizations with a **continuous flow system** generally have a standardized product or service. This product or service is often advertised and is immediately available to the customer. The post

continuous flow system   Operating system used by companies that produce large amounts of similar products/services flowing through similar stages of the operating system.

Management Illustration 9.1
A New Operating System at Chrysler

The most famous operating system in the automotive industry is that of Toyota. Initially established in the late 1940s, the Toyota operating system is based on the concept of "lean manufacturing". Lean manufacturing is an approach to manufacturing which attempts to minimize everything, from work in process, to part counts, to labor hours. This approach not only reduces cost, it also increases pressure to get things done more quickly as well as correctly.

Recently Chrysler has been making an aggressive effort to improve its operations with what is being called the "Chrysler Operating System" (COS). Thirty management people have designed a system based on the Toyota Operating system but tailored to Chrysler's needs. Chrysler's goal is to become the "premier" car and truck company in the world by the year 2000. The approach taken by Chrysler is to focus on the processes and practices used as opposed to the latest technology. Chrysler believes that the key to success is to focus on how the technology is applied including the human import of the technology.

Source: Gary S. Vasilash, "Going Places and Getting Things Done: Think Operating Systems," *Automotive Manufacturing and Production*, April 1998, pp. 62–65.

For more information about Chrysler visit their Web site at www.Chryslercars.com. For more information about Toyota visit their Web site at: www.toyota.com.

office, paper mills, petroleum refineries, assembly plants, and fast-food outlets with standardized products (such as McDonald's) are examples. The continuous type of operation has relatively large volumes of identical or similar products or services flowing through similar stages of the operating system.

intermittent flow system   Operating system used when customized products and services are produced.

The second type of operating system, the **intermittent flow** (or *job shop*) **system,** produces customized products and services. Because of its customized nature, organizations using an intermittent operating system usually do not keep an inventory of finished products or offer standardized services. Intermittent flow systems include special-order fabrication shops, hospitals, advertising agencies, and dental offices. Technological advances in the last several years have lowered the per-unit costs associated with many intermittent flow systems.

The continuous flow system usually results in lower unit costs than the intermittent flow system because of economies of scale, specialized labor, and high equipment use. However, continuous flow systems usually require special-purpose equipment that is less flexible and usually more expensive than general-purpose equipment. An example is the customized equipment and machinery used in an automobile assembly plant. Inputs can take on numerous forms (such as managers, workers, equipment, facilities, materials, or information).

PRODUCT/SERVICE DESIGN

An organization's product or service determines the design of its operating systems. The design of a new product/service or the redesign of an existing product/service may lead to extensive systems redesign, equipment changes, new personnel, and other modifications. Consider the redesign necessary just to change from one year's automobile models to the next year's models. The design can be functionally sound, yet not economical to produce. Of course, specific functional design objectives must be achieved; however, several alternative designs are often available. When such choices exist, production costs should certainly be one criterion used in the decision.

Historically, design engineers have encountered conflict with operations managers. Design engineers are technically oriented and sometimes lack concern for production methods and costs. On the other hand, operations managers may care more about production costs and requirements than about the functional requirements of the product. Nowhere have these differences been more pronounced than at Boeing. When Boeing recently won a $1.2 billion order from SAS, a chief component of the deal was Boeing's promise to slash the cost of its planes by one-third. However, cutting prices without knowing where the matching savings would come from was not only a gamble but an operations manager's nightmare. When asked to comment, CEO Frank Shrontz said, "We have been technically excellent but [production] process-poor, and we have to change." Now common goals and close communication between design and operations is not only a necessity at Boeing but a mandate.[1] Close communication that fosters an appreciation by both engineers and managers for the common objective of producing a functional product or service at minimum cost is certainly in the best interest of this dynamic company.

PROCESS SELECTION

process selection   Specifies in detail the processes and sequences required to transform inputs into products or services.

Process selection includes a wide range of decisions about the specific process to be used, the basic sequences of the process, and the equipment to be employed. As suggested earlier, the product/service design decisions and the process selection decisions should be closely coordinated.

The processes and equipment used can play a large role in whether the product or service is competitive. The importance of the process selection decision has become magnified in some industries with the advent of robotics. This is clearly evident in the steel and automotive industries; the Japanese steel and automotive industries have much more modern production processes than their American counterparts. At the most basic level, the types of processes that are normally considered in managerial planning can be categorized as follows: (1) conversion processes (e.g., changing iron ore into steel sheets), (2) fabrication processes (e.g., changing raw materials into some specific form, such as in making sheet metal into a car bumper), (3) assembly processes (e.g., assembling a fender to a car), and (4) testing processes (not usually functional processes but incorporated to ensure quality control).[2] Understanding which process is needed or is in operation is thought to be a key to efficiently organizing production.

Once the overall type of operations process has been selected, specific decisions are needed regarding such factors as whether to use general or special-purpose equipment, whether to make or buy the components, and how much to automate. In equipment decisions, several factors beyond normal cost should be considered:

1. Availability of operators.
2. Training required for operators.
3. Maintenance record and potential.
4. Availability of parts and services.
5. Supplier assistance in installation and debugging.
6. Compatibility with existing equipment.
7. Flexibility of equipment in handling product variation.
8. Safety of equipment.
9. Expected delivery date.
10. Warranty coverage.

In process selection, the overriding objective is to specify in detail the most economical processes and sequences required to transform the inputs into the desired product or service.

SITE SELECTION

Management should carefully consider site location. It is easy to become overly engrossed in the operating details and techniques and ignore the importance of site location. Location is an ongoing question; it does not arise only when a facility is outgrown or obsolete. Location decisions relate to offices, warehouses, service centers, and branches, as well as the parent facility. Each site selection decision involves the total production/distribution system of the organization. Therefore, not only the location of new facilities should be examined; the location of present facilities should also be regularly reviewed for the most effective production/distribution system.

Several options exist for expanding capacity when the present facility is overcrowded:

1. Subcontract work.
2. Add another shift.
3. Work overtime.
4. Move operation to a larger facility.
5. Expand the current facility.
6. Keep the current facility and add another facility elsewhere.

A decision to expand on site, move the entire operation to a larger facility, or add another facility elsewhere means management faces a location decision. A survey of Fortune 500 firms showed that 45 percent of expansions were on site, 43 percent were in new plants at new locations, and only 12 percent were relocations. The popularity of on-site expansions was thought to be due to the advantages of keeping management together, reducing construction time and costs, and avoiding splitting up operations. However, there are arguments for building new plants or relocating.[3] According to Lee Krajewski and Larry Ritzman, reasons for taking these actions might be poor materials handling, employee "job bumping," increasingly complex production control, and a simple lack of space.[4]

Two primary concerns still tend to dominate the location decision, however. The first is financial in nature. Figure 9.2 indicates the principal considerations affecting the financial decision. The second, and no less important, concern is the human relations factor. Most firms are finding out, as Saturn Corporation did when it located in Spring Hill, Tennessee, in 1985, that attractiveness of location (beauty, terrain, climate, etc.), business climate and community interest, proximity to sources of quality education, availability of well-established employee training facilities and resources, and a climate conducive to innovative entrepreneurship are factors that cannot be ignored in a location decision.[5] The final choice of the site should be a compromise on all the above factors.

FACILITIES LAYOUT

Facilities layout is essentially the process of planning the optimal physical arrangement of facilities, which includes personnel, operating equipment, storage space, office space, materials-handling equipment, and room for customer service and movement. Facilities layout integrates all of the previous planning of the design

---

FIGURE 9.2   Factors to Be Considered in Site Location

1. Revenue.
   a. Location of customers and accessibility.
   b. Location of competitors.
2. Operating costs.
   a. Price of materials.
   b. Transportation costs: materials, products, people.
   c. Wage rates.
   d. Taxes: income, property, sales.
   e. Utility rates.
   f. Rental rates.
   g. Communication costs.
3. Investment.
   a. Cost of land.
   b. Cost of construction.
4. Other limiting factors.
   a. Availability of labor with appropriate skills.
   b. Availability of materials, utilities, supplies.
   c. Union activity.
   d. Community attitudes and culture.
   e. Political situation.
   f. Pollution restrictions.
   g. Climate.
   h. General living conditions.

---

facilities layout Process of planning the optimal physical arrangement of facilities, including personnel, operating equipment, storage space, office space, materials-handling equipment, and room for customer or product movement.

process into one physical system. Facilities layout decisions are needed for a number of reasons, including

1. Construction of a new or an additional facility.
2. Obsolescence of current facilities.
3. Changes in demand.
4. Development of a new or redesigned product or process.
5. Personnel considerations: frequent accidents, poor working environment, or prohibitive supervisory costs.

Demand forecasts for the product or service must be considered in establishing the productive capacity of the organization. The costs of running short on space and equipment must be balanced against the costs of having idle space and equipment. A good approach is to match space needs with estimates of future demand but purchase equipment only as it is needed. This allows quick capacity expansion and avoids the costs of idle equipment.

Materials Handling

The materials used and how they are moved around in manufacturing a product or producing a service can have a significant influence on the facility layout. The size, shape, weight, density, and even the flexibility of the materials used can affect the layout. Some materials require special handling and storage with regard to factors such as temperature, humidity, light, dust, and vibration. A materials-handling system is the entire network that receives materials, stores materials, moves materials between processing points and between buildings, and positions the final product or service for delivery to the ultimate customer.

The design and layout of the facilities must be closely coordinated with the design of the materials-handling system. Materials-handling specialists James Apple and Leon McGinnis believe the chief difficulty in this area that needs to be overcome through innovative management is the failure to realize that this function should be a "factory integrator," the thread that ties the system together. In fact, process planning and the production scheduling and control systems should incorporate materials-handling system needs and limitations (such as wide aisles in the plant to accommodate forklifts) as part of their design and not ignore the complexity of the function. This new view of the materials-handling function would include attention to the (1) handling unit and container design, (2) micromovement (within a production workplace),

> **FIGURE 9.3   Materials-Handling Principles**
>
> 1. Materials should move through the facility in direct flow patterns, minimizing zigzagging or backtracking.
> 2. Related production processes should be arranged to provide for direct material flows.
> 3. Mechanical materials-handling devices should be designed and located, and material storage locations should be selected so that human effort expended through bending, reaching, lifting, and walking is minimized.
> 4. Heavy or bulky materials should be moved the shortest distance through locating the processes that use them near receiving and shipping areas.
> 5. The number of times each material is moved should be minimized.
> 6. Systems flexibility should allow for unexpected situations such as materials-handling equipment breakdowns, changes in production system technology, and future expansion of production capacities.
> 7. Mobile equipment should carry full loads at all times; empty and partial loads should be avoided.

Source: Norman Gaither, *Production and Operations Management*, 5th ed. © 1992 by The Dryden Press, a division of Holt, Rinehart & Winston, reprinted by permission of Wadsworth Publishing Co., p. 292.

(3) macromovement (between operations), (4) staging and storage of materials, and (5) control system for directing and tracking activity.[6]

In light of this view, consider two divergent trends currently taking place in the U.S. manufacturing environment. At one extreme is a movement toward simplicity with less mechanization (surprisingly, this trend is also occurring in Japan, which already has the advantage of flexibility). At the other extreme is the tendency to develop highly complex and automated systems. The manager must be ready to learn about and adapt to both trends.[7] While the design of any materials-handling system depends on the specifics of the situation, the principles outlined in Figure 9.3 generally apply.

Basic Layout Classifications

Most layouts are either process oriented or product oriented. Process layouts are generally used in intermittent flow operating systems. In a **process layout,** equipment or services of a similar functional type are arranged or grouped together: All X-ray

process layout Facilities layout that groups together equipment or services of a similar functional type.

machines are grouped together; all reproduction equipment is grouped together; all drilling machines are grouped together; and so forth. Custom fabrication shops, hospitals, and restaurants are usually arranged in this fashion. With a process layout, a product/customer moves from area to area in the desired sequence of functional operations. When the product or service is not standardized or when the volume of similar products or customers in service at any one time is low, a process layout is preferred because of its flexibility.

Product layouts usually occur in continuous flow operating systems. In a **product layout,** equipment or services are arranged according to the progressive steps by which the product is made or the customer is serviced. A

product layout Facilities layout that arranges equipment or services according to the progressive steps by which the product is made or the customer is served.

product layout is generally used when a standardized product is made in large quantities. The assembly line is the ultimate product layout. Automobile assembly plants, cafeterias, and standardized testing centers are normally product layout oriented. In a product layout, all the equipment or services necessary to produce a product or completely serve a customer are located in one area.

Figure 9.4 lists the major advantages of each type of layout.

FIGURE 9.4   Advantages of Process and Product Layouts

Advantages of Process Layout

1. Lower investment in equipment and personnel because of less duplication (do not need the same machine or person doing the same thing in two different areas).
2. Adaptable to demand fluctuations.
3. Worker jobs are less repetitive and routine.
4. Layout is conducive to incentive pay systems.
5. Allows for the production of a greater variety of products with a smaller capital base.
6. Failures of equipment or people do not hold up successive operations.

Advantages of Product Layout

1. Relatively unskilled labor may be utilized.
2. Training costs are low.
3. Materials-handling costs are usually low.
4. Smaller quantities of work in process.
5. Operations control and scheduling are simplified.

JOB DESIGN

job design   Designates the specific work activities of an individual or a group of individuals.

Job design specifies the work activities of an individual or a group of individuals. Job design answers the question of how the job is to be performed, who is to perform it, and where it is to be performed.

The job design process generally proceeds in three phases:

1. The specification of individual tasks.
2. The specification of the method of performing each task.
3. The combination of individual tasks into specific jobs to be assigned to individuals.[8]

Phases 1 and 3 determine the content of the job, while phase 2 indicates how the job is to be performed.

Job Content

job content   Aggregate of all the work tasks the jobholder may be asked to perform.

Job content is the sum of all the work tasks the jobholder may be asked to perform. Starting with the scientific management movement, job design focused on the most efficient way to do a job. This usually meant minimizing short-run costs by minimizing unit operation time. Thus, the number of tasks a jobholder was assigned was small. The obvious problem with this approach is that the job can become overly routine and repetitive, which leads to motivational problems in the form of boredom, absenteeism, turnover, and perhaps low performance. One fact greatly complicates the job design process: Different people react differently to similar jobs. In other words, what is boring and routine to one person is not necessarily boring and routine to another.

Recent history has shown that there are inherent advantages to job specialization. The most often cited benefit is high-speed, low-cost production.[9] Figure 9.5 illustrates the most commonly recognized advantages and disadvantages of job specialization.

FIGURE 9.5   Advantages and Disadvantages of Specialization of Labor

<table>
<tr><th colspan="2">Advantages of Specialization</th></tr>
<tr><th>To Management</th><th>To Labor</th></tr>
<tr><td>
1. Rapid training of the workforce.

2. Ease in recruiting new workers.
3. High output due to simple and repetitive work.
4. Low wages due to ease of substitutability of labor.
5. Close control over work flow and workloads.
</td><td>
1. Little or no education required to obtain work.
2. Ease in learning job.
</td></tr>
<tr><th colspan="2">Disadvantages of Specialization</th></tr>
<tr><th>To Management</th><th>To Labor</th></tr>
<tr><td>
1. Difficulty in controlling quality since no one person has responsibility for entire product.
2. Worker dissatisfaction leading to hidden costs arising from turnover, absenteeism, tardiness, grievances, and intentional disruption of production process.
3. Reduced likelihood of improving the process because of workers' limited perspective.
4. Limited flexibility to change the production process to produce new or improved products.
</td><td>
1. Boredom stemming from repetitive nature of work.

2. Little gratification from work itself because of small contribution to each item.

3. Little or no control over the workplace, leading to frustration and fatigue (in assembly-line situations).
4. Little opportunity to progress to a better job since significant learning is rarely possible on fractionated work.
</td></tr>
</table>

Source: Richard B. Chase, Nicholas J. Aquilano, and F. Robert Jacobs, *Production and Operations Management: Manufacturing and Services,* 8th ed., (Burr Ridge, IL: (Irwin McGraw-Hill, 1998), p. 416.

Job Methods

The next step in the job design process is to determine the precise methods to be used to perform the job. The optimal **job method** is a function of the manner in which the human body is used, the arrangement of the workplace, and the design of the tools and equipment used.[10] The main purpose of job method design is to find the one best way to do a job. Normally, job methods are determined after the basic process and physical layout have been established.

job method   Manner in which the human body is used, the arrangement of the workplace, and the design of the tools and equipment used.
ergonomics   Study of the interface between people and machines.

Motion study is used in designing jobs. It involves determining the necessary motions and movements to perform a job or task and then designing the most efficient method for putting these motions and movements together.

Ergonomics is the study of the interface between people and machines. A primary concern of ergonomics is that the equipment and the workplace be designed to make jobs as easy as possible.

Job methods designers have traditionally concentrated on manual tasks. However, the basic concept of finding the one best way applies to all types of jobs.

The Physical Work Environment

The physical work environment—temperature, humidity, ventilation, noise, light, color, and so on—can affect employee performance and safety. Studies clearly show that adverse physical conditions do have a negative impact on performance, but the degree of influence varies from person to person.

The importance of safety in the design process was reinforced by the **Occupational Safety and Health Act (OSHA) of 1970.** Designed to reduce job injuries, the act gives very specific federal safety guidelines for almost all U.S. organizations.

occupational safety and health act (OSHA) of 1970 Federal legislation designed to reduce job injuries; established specific federal safety guidelines for almost all U.S. organizations.

In general, the work area should allow for normal lighting, temperature, ventilation, and humidity. Baffles, acoustical wall materials, and sound absorbers should be used to reduce unpleasant noises. Exposure to less than ideal conditions should be limited to short periods. All of these measures will minimize potential physical or psychological damage to employees.[11]

Sociotechnical Approach

The sociotechnical concept was introduced in the 1950s by Eric Trist and his colleagues at the Tavistock Institute of Human Relations in London.[12] The **sociotechnical approach** rests on two premises. First, in any organization that requires people to perform certain tasks, a joint system is operating; this joint system combines the social and technological systems. Second, the environment of every sociotechnical system is influenced by a culture, its values, and a set of generally accepted practices.[13] The concept stresses that the technical system, the related social system, and the general environment should all be considered when designing jobs.

sociotechnical approach Approach to job design that considers both the technical system and the accompanying social system.

The sociotechnical approach is very situational; few jobs have identical technical requirements, social surroundings, and environments. This approach requires that the job designer carefully consider the role of the worker within the system, the task boundaries, and the autonomy of the work group. Using the sociotechnical approach, Louis Davis has developed the following guidelines for job design:

1. The need for the content of a job to be reasonably demanding for the employee in terms other than sheer endurance and yet provide some variety (but not necessarily novelty).
2. The need to be able to learn on the job and go on learning.
3. The need for some minimum area of decision making that the individual can call his or her own.
4. The need for some minimum degree of social support and recognition at the workplace.
5. The need to be able to relate what the individual does and what he or she produces to the person's social life.
6. The need to feel that the job leads to some sort of desirable future.[14]

COMPUTER TECHNOLOGY AND THE DESIGN PROCESS

In recent years, computers have come to play a major role in production/operations technology. The term *factories of the future* has become popular and generally refers to the use of computers in various parts of the operating system. **Computer-aided design**

computer-aided design (CAD) Generates various views of different components and assemblies.

Management Illustration 9.2
New CAD Approach Used at Black & Decker

Black & Decker recently introduced a new product, The Scumbuster, with half the normal work and in half the time usually required to bring a product to market. The Scumbuster is a one pound, battery-operated cleaning tool that brushes away soap, scum, mold, and mildew from bathroom tubs, tiles, and fixtures. The introduction of the Scumbuster resulted in a major change in the way Black & Decker's Household Products Group creates new products.

In developing the Scumbuster, Black and Decker used CATIA, which is a CAD system developed by Paris-based Dassault Systems and marketed worldwide by IBM. A major advantage of CATIA is that it produces 3D digital mockup and sophisticated virtual product modeling. As the company considered changes during the design process, CATIA helped it understand the implications of different changes. Before CATIA, hard prototypes, which were time consuming and costly to produce, had to be used to evaluate the implications of different design changes.

The success of the Scumbuster project resulted in a complete shift to 3D design at Black & Decker.

Source: William Cleary, "3D Speedup", *Appliance Manufacturer*, May 1998, pp. 35–37.

For more information about Black & Decker visit their Web site at: www.blackanddecker.com. For more information about CATIA visit: www.catia.ibm.com/.

(CAD) can be used in product design by generating various views of different components and assemblies. With CAD, designs can be developed, analyzed, and changed much faster than by using conventional drawing methods. Management Illustration 9.2 discusses how Black and Decker's Household Products Group has adopted CAD as a means of speeding up the development of new products.

computer-aided manufacturing (CAM) Uses stored data regarding various products to provide instructions for automated production equipment.

computer-aided engineering (CAE) Uses a product's characteristics to analyze its performance under different parameters.

computer-integrated manufacturing (CIM) Uses computer technology to incorporate all of the organization's production-related functions into an integrated computer system to assist, augment, and/or automate most functions.

Computer-aided engineering (CAE) uses a product's characteristics to analyze its performance under different parameters. For example, several designs could be subjected to different tests and comparisons made by computer instead of actually making and testing different prototypes. **Computer-aided manufacturing (CAM)** uses stored data regarding various products to provide instructions for automated production equipment. When CAD provides the design information used by CAM, the result is called *computer-aided design and manufacturing(CAD/CAM)*. Finally, **computer-integrated manufacturing (CIM)** uses computer technology to incorporate all of the organization's production-related functions into an integrated computer system to assist, augment, and/or automate most operations.[15] With CIM, the output of one activity or operation serves as the input to the next activity, and this system pervades the entire organization.

There is little doubt that operations design and planning are moving more and more toward the use of computer technology. For example, sales of mechanical CAD/CAM/CAE software increased almost 20 percent in 1996 and continued to bullish in 1997 (more recent figures are not available).[16] Many believe that in the near future, CIM will become a reality for most manufacturers. The design function of this idea may already be in place at Ford Motor Company. The Ford concept is to speed the design process and reduce costs by building interactive multimedia links among more than 100 designers at seven worldwide sites. According to designer Giuseppe Delena, "This is not about linking buildings; it's about joining minds and someday these workstations will be our window to the world."[17]

DAY-TO-DAY OPERATIONS PLANNING

Designing an effective operating system does not ensure that the system will operate efficiently. The day-to-day operations must also be planned and then carried out. This process is called **production planning** and includes aggregate production planning, resource allocation, and scheduling. Its overriding purpose is to maintain a smooth, constant flow of work from start to finish so that the product or service will be completed in the desired time at the lowest possible cost.

production planning   Concerned primarily with aggregate production planning, resource allocation, and activity scheduling.

Aggregate Production Planning

aggregate production planning   Concerned with overall operations and balancing major sections of the operating system; matches the organization's resources with demands for its goods and services.

Aggregate production planning deals with overall operations and with balancing the major parts of the operating system. Its primary purpose is to match the organization's resources with the demands for its goods or services. Specifically, the plan should find the production rates that satisfy demand requirements while minimizing the costs of workforce and inventory fluctuations. Aggregate production plans generally look 6 to 18 months into the future.

The first step in developing an aggregate production plan is to obtain a demand forecast for the organization's goods or services. The second step involves evaluating the impact of the demand forecasts on the organization's resources—plant capacity, workforce, raw materials, and the like. The final step is to develop the best plan for using the organization's current and expected resources to meet the forecast demand. The aggregate production plan determines production rates, work force needs, and inventory levels for the entire operating system over a specified period.

One of the oldest and simplest methods of graphically showing both expected and completed production is the Gantt chart. Developed by Henry L. Gantt in the early 1900s, the main feature of the **Gantt chart** is that it shows work planned and work accomplished in relation to time. Figure 9.6 presents a typical Gantt chart.

gantt chart   Planning and controlling device that graphically depicts work planned and work accomplished in their relation to each other and to time.

From a planning perspective, Gantt charts require operations managers to clearly think through the sequence of events necessary to complete the tasks being charted. From a control perspective, Gantt charts emphasize the element of time by readily pointing out any actual or potential slippages. One criticism of the Gantt chart is that it can require considerable time to incorporate scheduling changes such as rush orders. To accommodate such scheduling changes rapidly, mechanical boards using movable pegs or cards have been developed.

Resource Allocation

resource allocation   Efficient allocation of people, materials, and equipment to meet the demand requirements of the operating system.

Resource allocation is the efficient allocation of people, materials, and equipment to meet the demand requirements of the operating system. It is the natural outgrowth of the aggregate production plan. The materials needed must be determined and ordered; the work must be distributed to the different departments and workstations; personnel must be allocated; and time allotments must be set for each stage of the process.

Due to resource scarcities, resource allocation has become critical in recent times. Increased competition, both domestic and foreign, has also heightened its

FIGURE 9.6   Sample Gantt Chart

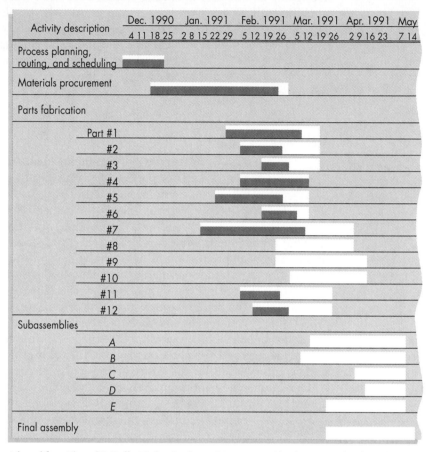

Source: Adapted from Elwood S. Buffa, *Modern Production Management*, 4th ed. (New York: John Wiley & Sons, Inc., 1973), p. 576.

importance. Proper resource allocation can mean great cost savings, which can give the needed competitive edge.

Numerous mathematical and computer-assisted tools and techniques can assist in resource allocation. Linear programming, the critical path method (CPM), and the program evaluation and review technique (PERT) are some of the most often used approaches. The last two are discussed in the following section.

critical path method (CPM)   Planning and control technique that graphically depicts the relationships among the various activities of a project; used when time durations of project activities are accurately known and have little variance.

performance evaluation and review technique (PERT)   Planning and control technique that graphically depicts the relationships among the various activities of a project; used when the durations of the project activities are not accurately known.

Critical Path Method (CPM) and Program Evaluation and Review Technique (PERT)   Network analysis focuses on finding the most time-consuming path through a network of tasks and identifying the relationships among the different tasks. The Gantt chart concept formed the foundation for network analysis.[18] The most popular network analysis approaches are the **critical path method (CPM)** and the **program evaluation and review technique (PERT).** These two techniques were developed almost simultaneously in the late 1950s. CPM grew out

FIGURE 9.7   Project Represented by Gantt Chart and a Project Network

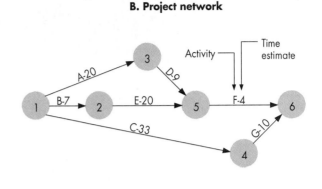

A. Gantt chart

B. Project network

of a joint study by Du Pont and Remington Rand Univac to determine how to best reduce the time required to perform routine plant overhaul, maintenance, and construction work.[19] PERT was developed by the Navy in conjunction with representatives of Lockheed Aircraft Corporation and the consulting firm of Booz, Allen, & Hamilton to coordinate the development and production of the Polaris weapons system.

CPM and PERT both result in a network representation of a project. The network is composed of sequential activities and events. An activity is the work necessary to complete a particular event, and it usually consumes time. Events denote a point in time, and their occurrence signifies the completion of all activities leading to the event. All activities originate and terminate at events. Activities are usually represented by arrows in a network, while events are represented by a circle.

The path through the network that has the longest duration (based on a summation of estimated individual activity times) is referred to as the *critical path*. If any activity on the critical path lengthens, the entire project duration lengthens.

Figure 9.7 shows the same project shown in Figure 9.6 represented by both a Gantt chart and a project network. The project network has two distinct advantages over the Gantt chart: (1) the interdependencies of the activities are noted explicitly, and (2) the activities are shown in greater detail. In addition, from a practical standpoint, Gantt charts become very difficult to visualize and work with for projects involving more than 25 activities.

The major difference between CPM and PERT concerns the activity time estimates. CPM is used for projects whose activity durations are accurately known and whose variance in performance time is negligible. PERT is used when the activity durations are more uncertain and variable. CPM is based on a single estimate for an activity duration, whereas PERT is based on three time estimates for each activity: an optimistic (minimum) time, a most likely (modal) time, and a pessimistic (maximum) time.

Project network analysis can provide information beyond simple project planning and control. By knowing the critical activities, the project manager can best allocate limited resources and can make more accurate time–cost trade-offs.

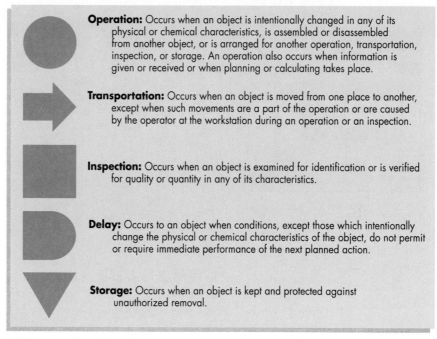

FIGURE 9.8   Flowcharting Activities

Operation: Occurs when an object is intentionally changed in any of its physical or chemical characteristics, is assembled or disassembled from another object, or is arranged for another operation, transportation, inspection, or storage. An operation also occurs when information is given or received or when planning or calculating takes place.

Transportation: Occurs when an object is moved from one place to another, except when such movements are a part of the operation or are caused by the operator at the workstation during an operation or an inspection.

Inspection: Occurs when an object is examined for identification or is verified for quality or quantity in any of its characteristics.

Delay: Occurs to an object when conditions, except those which intentionally change the physical or chemical characteristics of the object, do not permit or require immediate performance of the next planned action.

Storage: Occurs when an object is kept and protected against unauthorized removal.

Source: William R. Mullee and David B. Porter, "Process-Chart Procedures," in *Industrial Engineering Handbook*, 2d ed., ed. H.B. Maynard (New York: McGraw-Hill, 1963), pp. 2–21.

Routing

routing Finds the best path and sequence of operations for attaining a desired level of output with a given mix of equipment and personnel.
assembly chart Depicts the sequence and manner in which the various components of a product or service are assembled.
flow process chart Outlines what happens to a product or service as it progresses through the facility.

Routing finds the best path and sequence of operations for attaining a desired level of output with a given mix of equipment and personnel. Routing looks for the best use of existing equipment and personnel through careful assignment of these resources. An organization may or may not have to analyze its routing system frequently; it depends on the variety of products or services it offers.

Flowcharts and diagrams are used to locate and end inefficiencies in a process by analyzing the process in a step-by-step fashion. Most charting procedures divide the actions in a given process into five types: operations, transportations, inspections, delays, and storages. Figure 9.8 defines each of these types of actions.

Two types of charts frequently used are the assembly chart and the flow process chart. An **assembly chart** depicts the sequence and manner in which the various parts of a product or service are assembled. A **flow process chart** outlines what happens to the product as it moves through the operating facility. Flow process charts can also map the flow of customers through a service facility. Figure 9.9 shows a flow process chart for the processing of a form for an insurance company.

Activity Scheduling

activity scheduling Develops the precise timetable to be followed in producing a product or service.

Activity scheduling develops the precise timetable to be followed in producing the product or service. It also in-

FIGURE 9.9   Flow Process Chart: Present Method for Completing Authorization-to-Investigate Form

Operation __Complete authorization to__

Product __investigate form__

Depts. __Property Loss__

Drawing No. __N.A.__ Part No. __N.A.__

Quantity __One form in triplicate__

Present ✔ Proposed ____

Sheet __1__ of __1__ Sheets

Charted By __Joe Millard__

Date __9/14__

Approved By __Jim Street__

Date __9/15__

Summary		
● Operation	7
➡ Transport	4
■ Inspect	1
D Delay	1
▼ Store	—
Vertical distance	—
Horizontal distance	180 ft.
Time (min.)	11.05

No.	Distance moved (feet)	Worker time (min.)	Symbols	Description
1		.20	●➡■DV	Remove Claim Dept's. request from in-basket and identify client.
2	55	3.25	●➡■DV	Walk to filing area, locate file, and return to desk. Locate pertinent information in client file.
3		.50	●➡■DV	Type information on authorization to investigate form (form no. 3355).
4	35	.50	●➡■DV	Walk to section leader's desk.
5		.20	●➡■DV	Wait for signature.
6	35	.50	●➡■DV	Walk back to desk.
7		.20	●➡■DV	Tear form apart into separate sheets.
8		1.75	●➡■DV	Prepare regional investigator's copy for mailing; place in mail basket on desk.
9		1.50	●➡■DV	Prepare Claims Dept's. copy for routing; place in mail basket on desk.
10		.20	●➡■DV	Place one copy in client's file.
11	55	2.25	●➡■DV	Walk to filing area, refile, and return to desk.
12			●➡■DV	
13			●➡■DV	
14			●➡■DV	

Source: *Production and Operations Management:* 6th edition, by Norman Gaither. Copyright © 1994 by Harcourt Brace and Company, reprinted by permission of the publisher, p. 661.

cludes dispatching work orders and expediting critical and late orders. Scheduling does not involve deciding how long a job will take (which is part of job design); rather, it determines when the work is to be done. Scheduling is the link between system design and operations planning and control. Once the initial schedule has been set, the system is ready for operation. Of course, scheduling is an ongoing activity in an operating system.

A scheduling system design must be based on knowledge of the operating system for which it is being designed. Scheduling for intermittent systems is very complex because of the larger number of individual orders or customers that must flow through the system. Many types of scheduling tools, such as the Gantt chart, the critical path method (CPM), and the program evaluation and review technique (PERT), have been developed to help overcome scheduling problems.

Scheduling for high-volume continuous flow systems is often a process of matching the available resources to the production needs as outlined by the aggregate plan. Computer simulation is used to assist in the scheduling of continuous flow systems by estimating the impact of different scheduling decisions on the system.

Summary

1. *Define Operations Management.* Operations management is the application of the basic concepts and principles of management to those segments of the organization that produce its goods and/or services.

2. *Describe an Operating System and Identify the Two Basic Types of Operating Systems.* An operating system consists of the processes and activities necessary to transform various inputs into goods and/or services. The two basic types of operating systems are those based on continuous flows and those based on intermittent flows. Continuous flow systems generally have a standardized product or service. Intermittent flow systems usually produce customized products and services.

3. *Differentiate among Product/Service Design, Process Selection, and Site Selection Decisions.* Product/service design decisions deal with how the product or service will be designed. The design must be such that it can be economically produced. Process selection includes a wide range of decisions concerning the specific process to be used, the basic sequences of the process, and the equipment to be used. Site selection decisions are concerned with where to locate a new or an additional facility.

4. *Explain What a Materials-Handling System Is.* A materials-handling system is the entire network that receives materials, stores materials, moves materials between processing points and between buildings, and positions the final product or service for delivery to the ultimate customer.

5. *Describe and Give an Example of the Two Basic Classifications of Facilities Layouts.* The two basic types of layouts are process layouts and product layouts. With a process layout, equipment or services of a similar functional type are arranged or grouped together. Custom fabrication shops and hospitals are examples of organizations that use process layouts. With a product layout, the equipment or services are arranged according to the progressive steps by which the product is made or the customer is serviced. Automobile assembly plants and cafeterias are examples of organizations that use product layouts.

6. *Explain the Sociotechnical Approach to Job Design.* The sociotechnical approach to job design considers not only the technical system and the task to be done but also the accompanying social system.

7. *Describe Several Computer-Related Technologies That Are Currently Playing Major Roles in Production/Operations Management.* Computer-aided design (CAD) is used in product design to generate various views of different components and assemblies. Computer-aided engineering (CAE) uses a product's characteristics to analyze its performance under different parameters. Computer-aided manufacturing (CAM) uses stored data regarding various products to provide instructions for automated production equipment. Computer-integrated manufacturing (CIM) uses computer technology to incorporate all of the organization's production-related functions into an integrated computer system to assist, augment, and/or automate most operations.

8. *Outline the Three Major Steps in Developing an Aggregate Production Plan.* The first step in developing an aggregate production plan is to obtain a demand forecast for the organization's goods or services. The second step involves evaluating the impact of the demand forecasts on the organization's resources. The third step is to develop the best plan for using the organization's current and expected resources to meet the forecast demand.

9. *Summarize the Differences between Resource Allocation and Activity Scheduling.* Resource allocation is concerned with the efficient allocation of people, materials, and equipment to meet the demand requirements of the operating system. This includes distributing the workload and determining how much time should be allotted for each stage in the production process. Activity scheduling develops the precise timetable to be followed when producing the product or service. Activity scheduling does

not involve determining how long a job will take; rather, it determines when the work is to be done.

10. *Distinguish among Gantt Charts, the Critical Path Method (CPM), and the Program Evaluation and Review Technique (PERT).* Gantt charts graphically depict work planned and work accomplished in relation to time. CPM and PERT both result in a network representation of a project or a group of activities. CPM and PERT have two distinct advantages over Gantt charts: (1) The interdependencies of the activities are noted explicitly, and (2) the activities are shown in greater detail. The major difference between CPM and PERT centers around activity time estimates. CPM is used for projects whose activity durations are accurately known. PERT is used when the activity durations are more uncertain and variable.

Preview Analysis

1. What do you think were some of the marketing techniques Jim Koch used to market Samuel Adams beer?

2. What three manufacturing and sales techniques make Samuel Adams beer unique?

3. How do you think this brand will fare against the large national brands? What suggestions from the chapter can you offer that might help in planning for the brand?

Review Questions

1. What is operations management?

2. Describe an operating system.

3. Describe the two basic types of operating systems.

4. What is the overriding objective of the process selection decision?

5. At the most basic level of process selection, what are the four primary types?

6. Discuss several factors that should be considered in site location.

7. What is a process-oriented layout? A product-oriented layout?

8. What is a materials-handling system?

9. Describe the three phases of the job design process.

10. Define ergonomics.

11. What is the sociotechnical approach to job design? Using the sociotechnical approach, give some guidelines for job design.

12. Define CAD, CAE, CAM, and CIM.

13. What is production planning?

14. Define aggregate production planning.

15. What is the difference between resource allocation and activity scheduling?

Skill-Building Questions

1. Explain how you might take a production line approach (transferring the concepts and methodologies of operations management) to a service organization such as a branch bank.

2. Does process selection in service industries such as restaurants and hotels differ from process selection in manufacturing? If so, how?

3. Why should all of the phases in designing an operating system be integrated?

4. Discuss the following statement: "Most production planning is a waste of time because it all depends on demand forecasts, which are usually inaccurate."

5. What can the computer do to help with modern assembly line planning? How might simulations be used?

SKILL-BUILDING EXERCISE 9.1

Analyzing the Layout

Visit a local fast-food restaurant (McDonald's, Burger King, Hardee's, Wendy's, etc.) and sketch the basic layout of the facility on a single sheet of 8 1/2-by-11-inch paper. Observe the flow of customers and employees through the store. Identify what specific aspects of the layout you think are particularly good. Try to identify one or more aspects of the layout that you think could be improved. Why do you think this improvement has not been made previously? Write down your findings and be prepared to discuss them in class.

SKILL-BUILDING EXERCISE 9.2

Disseminating Confidential Information

Every month, you are responsible for collating and stapling 500 copies of a four-page document. The documents must then be placed in manila envelopes, sealed, and have the word *CONFIDENTIAL* written on each. The four pages are printed on one side only and are numbered sequentially.

1. Assume you have a manual stapler and a felt marker at your disposal. Draw a sketch of how you would arrange your workplace for doing this task and describe the procedure you would use.

2. Assume you have the authority (within reason) to make changes in the equipment, materials, and processes used, as long as the basic task of organizing the information and labeling it as confidential is accomplished. What suggestions would you make?

CASE INCIDENT 9.1

The Lines at Sam's

Sam Baker owns and manages a cafeteria on Main Street in Dawsonville. During his two years of operation, Sam has identified several problems he has been unable to solve. One is the line that always seems to develop at the checkout register during the rush hour. Another is customers' constant complaints that the size of the helpings and the size of the pie slices vary tremendously from customer to customer. A third problem is the frequency with which the cafeteria runs out of "choice" dishes. The final problem is that every Sunday at noon, when a large crowd arrives after church, Sam invariably runs short of seating space.

Sam had worked at other food establishments for the previous 15 years, and most of them experienced similar problems. In fact, these and other, related problems have come to be expected and are therefore accepted practice for the industry. After all, Sam's former boss used to say, "You can't please everybody all the time." Sam is wondering if he should take the industry's position and just accept these problems as an inherent part of the business.

Questions

1. Do you have any suggestions for Sam? If so, what are they?

2. What other service-oriented industries can you think of that seem to take the same view toward their problems that Sam's industry does?

CASE INCIDENT 9.2

A New Building for Tot-Two

The Tot-Two Company manufactures clothes for children up to age five. Tot-Two has been growing rapidly for the past several years and is planning to build a new plant in a recently developed industrial park on the north side of town. Shirley Shaver, the plant's operations manager, has been assigned the task of drawing up a new physical layout subject to the constraints that the new building cannot exceed 7,000 square feet including office space and that it must be a perfect rectangle to minimize construction costs. Shirley developed the following list of departments with their respective approximate space requirements:

Shipping (400 square feet)—area for shipping all finished goods.

Receiving (400 square feet)—area for receiving all materials and supplies.

Materials supply room (300 square feet)—storage area for all incoming materials.

Spreading and cutting area (1,600 square feet)—area containing three 40-foot tables for spreading and then cutting the cloth. Many layers of cloth are spread on top of each other and cut at the same time with large portable cutters.

Pattern-making area (200 square feet)—area in which patterns are made.

Assembly area (1,200 square feet)—area for sewing the various clothing parts.

Packing area (400 square feet)—area for packing the finished goods into boxes for shipping.

Finished goods storage (500 square feet)—area for storing finished goods before shipping.

Design area (200 square feet)—area occupied by designers.

Office space (800 square feet)—space for secretaries and company officers.

Wash facilities (300 square feet)—area containing men's and women's bathrooms.

Lunch/break area (400 square feet)—area with vending machines and lunch tables.

Shirley then drew up an initial layout as illustrated in Exhibit 1.

Questions

1. What are the strong points of Shirley's layout? What are the weak points?

2. Redesign the layout, based on your answers to question 1.

Designers (200 sq. ft.)	Office (800 sq. ft.)	Assembly (1,200 sq. ft.)
Lunch/break (400 sq. ft.)		
Wash facilities (300 sq. ft.)	Packing (400 sq. ft.)	
Shipping (400 sq. ft.)	Finished goods storage (500 sq. ft.)	Spreading and cutting (1,600 sq. ft.)
Pattern making (200 sq. ft.)	Material supply (300 sq. ft.) / Receiving (400 sq. ft.)	

References and Additional Readings

[1] Howard Banks, "Moment of Truth," *Forbes*, May 22, 1995, pp. 51–62.

[2] Richard B. Chase and Nicholas J. Aquilano, *Production and Operation Management*, 7th ed. (Burr Ridge, IL.: Richard D. Irwin, 1995), pp. 60–61.

[3] Lee J. Krajewski and Larry P. Ritzman, *Operation Management*, 3d ed. (Reading, MA.: Addison-Wesley, 1993), p. 348.

[4] Ibid., p. 348.

[5] James L. Lewardowski and William P. MacKinnon, "What We Learned at Saturn," *Personnel Journal*, December 1992, pp. 30–32.

[6] James M. Apple and Leon F. McGinnis, "Innovation in Facilities and Materials Handling Systems: An Introduction," *Industrial Engineering*, March 1987, pp. 33–38.

[7] Nicholas J. Aquilano, Richard B. Chase, and Mark M. Davis, *Fundamentals of Operations Management*, 2d ed. (Burr Ridge, IL.: Richard D. Irwin, 1995), pp. 594–95.

[8] Louis E. Davis, "Job Design and Productivity: A New Approach," *Personnel*, March 1957, p. 420.

[9] Chase and Aquilano, *Production and Operation Management*, p. 438.

[10] Richard A. Johnson, William T. Newell, and Roger C. Vergin, *Production and Operations Management: A Systems Concept* (Boston: Houghton Mifflin, 1974), p. 204.

[11] Ibid., p. 206.

[12] Peter B. Vaill, "Industrial Engineering and Socio-Technical Systems," *Journal of Industrial Engineering*, September 1967, p. 535.

[13] Louis E. Davis and James C. Taylor, *Design of Jobs*, 2d ed. (Santa Monica, CA: Goodyear Publishing, 1979), pp. 98–99.

[14] Louis E. Davis, *Job Satisfaction—a Socio-Technical View*, Report No. 515-1-69 (Los Angeles: University of California, 1969), p. 14.

[15] Mikell P. Groover, *Automation, Production Systems and Computer Integrated Manufacturing* (Englewood Cliffs, NJ: Prentice Hall, 1980), pp. 721–22; James B. Dilworth, *Production and Operations Management*, 5th ed. (New York: McGraw-Hill, 1993), pp. 609–13.

[16] "Mechanical CAD/CAM/CAE Up for Second Year," *Manufacturing Engineering*, April 1998, p. 22.

[17] James Daley, "There's a Future in Your Ford," *Forbes*, June 1995, p. 85.

[18] Evidence indicates there were other forerunners to CPM and PERT. See Edward R. Marsh, "The Harmonogram of Karol Adamiecki," *Academy of Management Journal*, June 1975, pp. 358–64.

[19] Joseph J. Moder and Cecil R. Phillips, *Project Management with CPM and PERT* (New York: Van Nostrand Reinhold, 1970), p. 6.

Section

IV

ORGANIZING AND STAFFING SKILLS

Chapter 10

10

Organizing Work

ॐ

LEARNING OBJECTIVES

After studying this chapter, you should be able to:

1. Define organization and differentiate between a formal and an informal organization.

2. Explain the importance of the organizing function.

3. List the attributes of a highly effective organization.

4. List the advantages and the major disadvantage of horizontal division of labor.

5. Distinguish among power, authority, and responsibility.

6. Explain the concept of centralization versus decentralization.

7. Define empowerment.

8. List four principles of organization that are related to authority.

9. Identify several reasons managers are reluctant to delegate.

10. Recount the major factors that affect a manager's span of management.

11. Name and define three workplace changes, in addition to decentralization and empowerment, that have affected the organizing function in today's organizations.

Coach Maureen O'Brien holds an M.A. degree in educational psychology and counseling from the University of Connecticut. Her extensive involvement in athletics, both as a touring professional basketball player with the Harlem Globetrotters and as coach of various teams, gives her a unique outlook on understanding organizations and appraising work teams.

O'Brien offers the following suggestions for managers who wish to formulate and understand their organizations more effectively. First, review the organization's common goals and needs for teamwork: What's your game? Second, decide why the organization exists: Do you have a noble purpose? Third, determine whether the stated goals are moving the organization in a desirable direction: Are you winning? Fourth, examine the two sides of team and organizational effectiveness (task and relationship): Are we emphasizing human doings or human beings? Finally, know what a high-performance organization looks like so you will know if you are one.

If top management seeks to become a high-performance organization, the following simple rules apply in most organizational as well as life's activities. First, always keep score: Know when you have won. Second, feel important: Achieve your goals. Third, have balance: Have quality of work and quality of life. Fourth, self-correct: Admit mistakes and change. Fifth, encourage diversity: Guard against "groupthink." Sixth, share leadership and power: Explore all ideas. Seventh, work at developing trust among team members: Deal with conflict. Finally, encourage full participation: It's an organization, not an individual. All excellent organizations learn early on how to self-examine and change. If they do not, they do not remain or ever become excellent.

Source: Adapted from Maureen O'Brien, *Who's Got the Ball?* (San Francisco: Jossey-Bass, 1995), pp. xvii–32.

organization   Group of people working together in some concerted or coordinated effort to attain objectives.

organizing   Grouping of activities necessary to attain common objectives and the assignment of each grouping to a manager who has the authority necessary to supervise the people performing the activities.

informal organization   Aggregate of the personal contacts and interactions and the associated groupings of people working within the formal organization.

Most work today is accomplished through organizations. An **organization** is a group of people working together in some type of concerted or coordinated effort to attain objectives. As such, an organization provides a vehicle for implementing strategy and accomplishing objectives that could not be achieved by individuals working separately. The process of **organizing** is the grouping of activities necessary to attain common objectives and the assignment of each grouping to a manager who has the authority required to supervise the people performing the activities.[1] Thus, organizing is basically a process of division of labor accompanied by appropriate delegation of authority. Proper organizing results in more effective use of resources.

The framework that defines the boundaries of the formal organization and within which the organization operates is the organization structure. A second and equally important element of an organization is the informal organization. The **informal organization** refers to the aggregate of the personal contacts and interactions and the associated groupings of people working within the formal organization.[2] The informal organization has a structure, but it is not formally and consciously designed.

REASONS FOR ORGANIZING

One of the primary reasons for organizing is to establish lines of authority. Clear lines of authority create order within a group. Absence of authority almost always leads to chaotic situations where everyone is telling everyone else what to do.

Second, organizing improves the efficiency and quality of work through synergism. *Synergism* occurs when individuals or groups work together to produce a whole greater than the sum of the parts. For example, synergism results when three people working together produce more than three people working separately. Synergism can result from division of labor or from increased coordination, both of which are products of good organization.

A final reason for organizing is to improve communication. A good organization structure clearly defines channels of communication among the members of the organization. Such a system also ensures more efficient communications.

Historically, the desire to organize led to the development of an organization. The use of an organization allows people to jointly (1) increase specialization and division of labor, (2) use large-scale technology, (3) manage the external environment, (4) economize on transaction costs, and (5) exert power and control.[3] When designed and coordinated effectively, these characteristics help the organization to serve its customers with a high degree of service and productivity. Management Illustration 10.1 describes efficient and effective organizations.

DIVISION OF LABOR

Organizing is basically a process of division of labor. The merits of dividing labor have been known for centuries. Taking the very simple task of manufacturing a pin, Adam Smith in 1776 demonstrated how much more efficiently the task could be performed through division of labor.[4] Smith argued that it was much more efficient to

Management Illustration 10.1

Attributes of Highly Effective Organizations

Effectiveness is doing the right thing. Efficiency is doing things right. High-performance and high-quality organizations are both effective and efficient. Though there is never one prescription for success or one predictor of what will make the organization successful, several recognized characteristics are associated with effective organizations. These characteristics not only are descriptors but also serve as guideposts for the corporate mission and goals embraced by the organization.

Highly effective organizations are

1. Externally focused and market driven.
2. Customer centered.
3. Built on and committed to maintaining strategic networks and alliances.
4. Mobilized toward a vision.
5. Dedicated to creating value in products and services.
6. Committed to positive learning and change.
7. Dedicated to fulfilling responsibilities to all stakeholders (customers, employees, suppliers, society).
8. Committed to measuring progress against world-class standards of excellence.

Two companies that consistently attempt to conform organization structure and design to these attributes are General Electric (GE) and Ford. GE's progressive program stresses the following: (1) Be lean—reduce tasks and be a cost leader; (2) be agile and delayered—create an environment that promotes fast and responsive decision making; (3) trust others; and (4) reward—recognize and compensate risk and performance. Ford takes a somewhat different approach by emphasizing (1) employee involvement in implementing the company's mission, values, and guiding principles; (2) values—people and products; and (3) adhering to quality first—this is Ford's number one focus to relate to the consumer and bind the organization together.

Author Stephen Covey's seven guiding principles of effective people summarize how to point the organization in the right direction. Without effective people, there is no effective organization. Covey describes effective people as (1) being proactive; (2) beginning with the end in mind; (3) putting first things first; (4) thinking win/win; (5) seeking first to understand, then to be understood; (6) synergizing; and (7) sharpening the saw (constantly renewing oneself and one's mental attitude). As Covey points out, excellent companies and excellent individuals really do go hand in hand.

Sources: Joseph W. Weiss, *Organizational Behavior and Change* (Minneapolis/St. Paul: West, 1996), pp. 372–75; Stephen R. Covey, *The Seven Habits of Highly Effective People: Restoring the Character Ethic* (New York: Simon & Schuster, 1990), pp. 212–13.

For more information about General Electric and Ford Motor Company visit their Web sites at: www.ge.com & www.ford.com.

divide the different tasks or operations required to make an object than it was to have each employee make the entire object individually.

Labor can be divided either vertically or horizontally. Vertical division of labor is based on the establishment of lines of authority and defines the levels that make up the vertical organization structure. In addition to establishing authority, vertical division of labor facilitates the flow of communication within the organization. To illustrate how vertical division of labor can vary from company to company, consider the automobile industry in the early 1980s. At that time, Toyota had 5 levels between the chairperson and the first-line supervisor, whereas Ford had over 15.[5] As of mid-1993, Ford had reduced this number to nine. For a more thorough description of the advantages of the "flat" organization, see Chapter 11 and Figure 11.3.

Horizontal division of labor is based on specialization of work. The basic assumption underlying horizontal division of labor is that by making each worker's task specialized, more work can be produced with the same effort through increased efficiency and quality. Specifically, horizontal division of labor can result in the following advantages:

1. Fewer skills are required per person.
2. The skills required for selection or training purposes are easier to supply.
3. Practice in the same job develops proficiency.
4. Primarily utilizing each worker's best skills promotes efficient use of skills.
5. Concurrent operations are made possible.
6. More conformity in the final product results when each piece is always produced by the same person.

The major problem with horizontal division of labor is that it can result in job boredom and even degradation of the employee. An extreme example of horizontal division of labor is the automobile assembly line. Most people working on an automobile assembly line do a small number of very simple tasks over and over again. It usually doesn't take long for these employees to become bored. Once employees become bored, their productivity often declines, absenteeism and tardiness increase, and the quality of work goes down. Solutions to the problems created by horizontal division of labor include a reexamination of job scope, implementing job rotation, and balancing job simplification with job depth.

job scope   Refers to the number of different types of operations performed on the job.
job depth   Refers to the freedom of employees to plan and organize their own work, work at their own pace, and move around and communicate as desired.

Job scope refers to the number of different types of operations performed. In performing a job with narrow scope, the employee performs few operations and repeats the cycle frequently. The negative effects of jobs lacking in scope vary with the person performing the job, but can include more errors and lower quality. Often job rotation, wherein workers shift in the planned sequence of activities, eliminates boredom and monotony and encourages multiple skills and cross-training.

Job depth refers to the freedom of employees to plan and organize their own work, work at their own pace, and move around and communicate as desired. A lack of job depth can result in job dissatisfaction and work avoidance, which in turn can lead to absenteeism, tardiness, and even sabotage.

Division of labor is not more efficient or even desirable in all situations. At least two basic requirements must exist for the successful use of division of labor. The first requirement is a relatively large volume of work. Enough volume must be produced to allow for specialization and keep each employee busy. The second requirement is stability in the volume of work, employee attendance, quality of raw materials, product design, and production technology.

POWER, AUTHORITY, AND RESPONSIBILITY

power   Ability to influence, command, or apply force.
authority   Legitimate exercise of power.
responsibility   Accountability for the attainment of objectives, the use of resources, and the adherence to organizational policy.

Power is the ability to influence, command, or apply force. Power is usually derived from the control of resources. **Authority** is power derived from the rights that come with a position and represents the legitimate exercise of power. Thus, authority is one source of power for a manager. Lines of authority link the various organizational components. Unclear lines of authority can create major confusion and conflict within an organization.

Responsibility is accountability for the attainment of objectives, the use of resources, and the adherence to organizational policy. Once responsibility is accepted, performing assigned work becomes an obligation. The term *responsibility* as used here should not be confused with the term *responsibilities* as in the context of defining job duties.

SOURCES OF AUTHORITY

As just mentioned, authority can be viewed as a function of position, flowing from top to bottom through the formal organization. According to this view, people hold authority because they occupy a certain position; once removed from the position, they lose their authority. Taking this theory one step further, one can say the American people, through the Constitution and laws, represent the ultimate source of authority in this country. The Constitution and laws guarantee the right of free enterprise. The owners of a free enterprise organization have the right to elect a board of directors and top management. Top management selects middle-level managers. This process continues down to the lowest person in the organization. This traditional view of authority is also called the *formal theory of authority*.

A second theory of authority was first outlined in 1926 by Mary Parker Follett and popularized in 1938 by Chester Barnard.[6] Called the *acceptance theory of authority*, this theory maintains that a manager's source of authority lies with his or her subordinates because they have the power to either accept or reject the manager's command. Presumably, if a subordinate does not view a manager's authority as legitimate, it does not exist. Both Follett and Barnard viewed disobeying a communication from a manager as a denial of authority by the subordinate. In summary, the acceptance theory of authority recognizes that subordinates play an active role in determining lines of authority and are not merely passive recipients in the process. This idea is somewhat similar to the contention that without followers you can have no leaders. Both elements must be present and mutually recognized for true structure to exist. Companies with a high degree of worker involvement, responsibility, and accountability appear to recognize acceptance theory as being beneficial for mutual support and encouragement between labor and management.

CENTRALIZATION VERSUS DECENTRALIZATION

There are limitations to the authority of any position. These limitations may be external, in the form of laws, politics, or social attitudes, or they may be internal, as delineated by the organization's objectives or by the job description. The tapered concept of authority states that the breadth and scope of authority become more limited as one descends the scalar chain (see Figure 10.1).

The top levels of management establish the shapes of the funnels in Figures 10.1 and 10.2. The more authority top management chooses to delegate, the less conical the funnel becomes. The less conical the funnel, the more decentralized the organization.

centralization Little authority is delegated to lower levels of management.

decentralization A great deal of authority is delegated to lower levels of management.

Centralization and **decentralization** refer to the degree of authority delegated by upper management. This is usually reflected by the numbers and kinds of decisions made by the lower levels of management. As they increase, the degree of decentralization also increases. Thus, an organization is never totally centralized or totally decentralized; rather, it falls along a continuum ranging from highly centralized to highly decentralized. In Figure 10.2, the organization represented by the diagram on the left is much more centralized than that represented by the right-hand diagram.

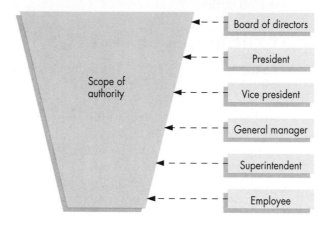

FIGURE 10.1   Tapered Concept of Authority

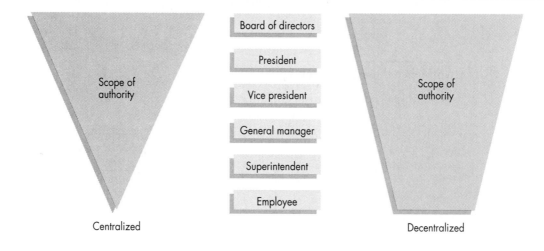

FIGURE 10.2   Centralized versus Decentralized Authority

The trend in today's organizations is toward more decentralization. Decentralization has the advantage of allowing for more flexibility and quicker action. It also relieves executives from time-consuming detail work. It often results in higher morale by allowing lower levels of management to be actively involved in the decision-making process. The major disadvantage of decentralization is the potential loss of control. Duplication of effort can also accompany decentralization. Management Illustration 10.2 describes how one company has decentralized its research efforts in order to get quicker payoffs.

EMPOWERMENT

empowerment   Form of decentralization in which subordinates have authority to make decisions.

Empowerment is a form of decentralization that involves giving subordinates substantial authority to make decisions. Under empowerment, managers express confidence in the ability of employees to perform at high levels. Employees are also encouraged

Management Illustration 10.2

Swedish Company Decentralizes

The Swedish company, L. M. Ericsson, is one of the world's largest suppliers of cellular phone equipment. Approximately 40 percent of world's mobile phone users are already hooked up to Ericsson's systems. As with most high tech companies, research and development (R&D) plays a critical role in Ericsson's success. In fiscal 1996–1997, for instance, R&D investments amounted to approximately $2.2 billion.

In 1996 Ericsson realized that its corporate R&D group wasn't close enough to the market and, as a result, wasn't flexible and fast enough to satisfy the unrelenting demands of the marketplace. To overcome these problems, Ericsson began decentralizing R&D by shifting it away from the corporate headquarters in Stockholm to its business units and customers around the globe. Today, all R&D activities are integrated into the company's 20 major business units and another 20 sub-units. Each unit has its own staff and budget. The role of the research director under the new structure is one of synchronization and facilitation. Management is confident that the new decentralized structure will enable the company to get new products to the market in much less time.

Source: John Blair, "Ericsson Decentralizes for Quicker Research Payoff," *Research-Technology Management*, March/April 1998, pp. 4–6.

For more information about L. M. Ericsson visit their Web site at: www.ericsson.se/.

to accept personal responsibility for their work. In situations where true empowerment takes place, employees gain confidence in their ability to perform their jobs and influence the organization's performance. Under true empowerment, employees can bend the rules to do whatever they have to do to take care of the customer.[7] One result of empowerment is that employees demonstrate more initiative and perseverance in pursuing organizational goals.

Organizations can take several actions to implement empowerment:[8]

- Whenever possible, restructure organizational units to be smaller, less complex, and less dependent on other units for decision making and action.
- Reduce to a minimum the number of hard rules for the organization.
- Emphasize a change throughout the organization that focuses on empowerment and personal accountability for delivering results.
- Provide the education and training necessary to enable people to respond to opportunities for improvement.

Accompanying the trend toward more decentralization in today's organizations is a trend toward increased empowerment of today's workforce. While some people believe that empowerment is praised loudly in public but seldom implemented, companies have experienced very positive results from having empowered their employees. For example, 16 of the 25 finalists nominated for *Industry Week's* America's Best Plants reported that 100 percent of their production employees participate in empowered work teams.[9] Management Illustration 10.3 discusses how one company has successfully empowered its employees.

PRINCIPLES BASED ON AUTHORITY

Because authority is a key element in managing organizations, several key concepts are relevant. Delegation, unity of command, the scalar principle, and the span of management historically have been the most important of these concepts.

Management Illustration 10.3

Empowerment at Tennalum

Tennalum is a division of Kaiser Aluminum, located in Jackson, Tennessee, which produces aluminum screw machine stock and other hand alloy machining stock for automotive and aerospace applications and other industrial uses. In 1995 Tennalum received the Shingo Prize for Excellence in Manufacturing and the Tennessee Quality Achievement Award. Prior to 1995 Tennalum received numerous other awards since it began operations in October 1989.

Tennalum's plant culture is built around employee involvement and empowerment with a strong customer focus. There are no supervisors. Work teams are empowered to make product quality decisions and also have the authority to put suspect material on hold or halt the process if they believe inferior product is being produced. Other examples of the empowered work force include:

- Annual plant safety plans are developed and written by technicians.

- Technicians participate in the interviewing of potential new hires, including hires for staff team openings.

- A cross-functional team meets monthly to suggest ideas that could impact its work environment and basic plant rules and regulations.

Since 1990 the plant has set six total production volume records with the most recent being 50 percent greater than the first. Revenues from 1991 increased 104 percent while gross profits increased 226 percent.

Source: Larry Swick, "Team-based Organizations: The Fruits of Employee Empowerment," *Hospital Material Management*, November 1997, pp. 1–3.

For more information about Tennalum and Kaiser Aluminum please visit their Web site at: www.tennalum.com/.

Delegation: The Parity Principle

According to Herbert Engel, "As an abstract idea, delegation must be as old as the human race itself."[10] The apportioning of specific duties to members of a group by a leader seems almost as natural as it is necessary. Delegation normally occurs when one needs something done that one either cannot or chooses not do oneself. The decision may be based on situations, skills, time, established order, or the expansion and growth of responsibilities as dictated by the group or the organization. Managers can delegate responsibility to subordinates in the sense of making subordinates responsible to them. However, this delegation to subordinates makes managers no less responsible to their superiors. Delegation of responsibility does not mean abdication of responsibility by the delegating manager. Responsibility is not like an object that can be passed from individual to individual.

parity principle States that authority and responsibility must coincide.

The **parity principle** states that authority and responsibility must coincide. Management must delegate sufficient authority to enable subordinates to do their jobs. At the same time, subordinates can be expected to accept responsibility only for those areas within their authority.

Subordinates must accept both authority and responsibility before the delegation process has been completed. Management sometimes expects employees to seek and assume responsibility they have not been asked to assume and then bid for the necessary authority. Such a system leads to guessing games that do nothing but create frustration and waste energy.

A manager's resistance to delegating authority is natural. There are several reasons for this reluctance:

FIGURE 10.3   Steps in the Delegation Process

1. Analyze how you spend your time.
2. Decide which tasks can be assigned.
3. Decide who can handle each task.
4. Delegate the authority.
5. Create an obligation (responsibility).
6. Control the delegation.

---

1. Fear that subordinates will fail in doing the task.
2. The belief that it is easier to do the task oneself rather than delegate it.
3. Fear that subordinates will look "too good."
4. Humans' attraction to power.
5. Comfort in doing the tasks of the previous job held.

Despite all the reasons for not delegating, there are some very strong reasons for a manager to delegate. Several phenomena occur when a manager successfully delegates. First, the manager's time is freed to pursue other tasks, and the subordinates gain feelings of belonging and being needed. These feelings often lead to a genuine commitment on the part of the subordinates. Second, delegation is one of the best methods for developing subordinates and satisfying customers. Pushing authority down the organization also allows employees to deal more effectively with customers. In its recent reengineering effort, Hallmark Cards, Inc., found that when you drive something from the top, you have to articulate clearly and communicate why it is being done.[11] By converting delegation to a shared vision, the organization has a much better chance of accomplishing its goals and objectives without resorting to adverse persuasion. Similarly, Taco Bell went from a $500 million regional company in 1982 to a $3 billion national company today because it recognized that the way to ultimately reach and satisfy customers was to empower its lower-level employees to make changes in operational strategies and tactics.[12] Successful delegation involves delegating matters that stimulate subordinates.

How to Delegate   To successfully delegate, a manager must decide which tasks can be delegated. Figure 10.3 indicates the steps the manager can follow to analyze and improve the delegation process. In addition, clearly defining objectives and standards, involving subordinates in the delegation process, initiating training that defines and encourages delegation, and supporting control efforts tends to improve the overall delegation process.

Probably the most nebulous part of the delegation process centers around the question of how much authority to delegate. As mentioned previously, management must delegate sufficient authority to allow the subordinate to perform the job. Precisely what can and cannot be delegated depends on the commitments of the manager and the number and quality of subordinates. A rule of thumb is to delegate authority and responsibility to the lowest organization level that has the competence to accept them.

exception principle   States that managers should concentrate on matters that deviate significantly from normal and let subordinates handle routine matters; also called *management by exception*.

Failure to master delegation is probably the single most frequently encountered reason managers fail. To be a good manager, a person must learn to delegate!

The **exception principle** (also known as *management by exception*) states that managers should concentrate their efforts on matters that deviate significantly from normal and let subordinates handle routine matters. The exception principle is closely related to the parity principle. The idea behind the exception principle is that managers should concentrate on those matters that require their abilities and not become bogged down with duties their subordinates should be doing. The exception principle can be hard to comply with when incompetent or insecure subordinates refer everything to their superiors because they are afraid to make a decision. On the other hand, superiors should refrain from making everyday decisions that they have delegated to subordinates. This problem is often referred to as "micro-managing."

Unity of Command

unity of command principle   States that an employee should have one, and only one, immediate manager.

The **unity of command principle** states that an employee should have one, and only one, immediate manager. The difficulty of serving more than one superior has been recognized for thousands of years. Recall the Sermon on the Mount, when Jesus said, "No man can serve two masters." In its simplest form, this problem arises when two managers tell the same employee to do different jobs at the same time. The employee is thus placed in a no-win situation. Regardless of which manager the employee obeys, the other will be dissatisfied. The key to avoiding problems with unity of command is to make sure employees clearly understand the lines of authority that directly affect them. Too often managers assume employees understand the lines of authority when in fact they do not. All employees should have a basic understanding of the organizational chart for their company and where they fit on it. An organizational chart frequently clarifies lines of authority and the chain of command.

More times than not, problems relating to the unity of command principle stem from the actions of managers rather than the actions of employees. This happens most often when managers make requests of employees who do not work directly for them.

Scalar Principle

scalar principle   States that authority in the organization flows through the chain of managers one link at a time, ranging from the highest to the lowest ranks; also called *chain of command*.

The **scalar principle** states that authority in the organization flows through the chain of managers one link at a time, ranging from the highest to the lowest ranks. Commonly referred to as the *chain of command*, the scalar principle is based on the need for communication and the principle of unity of command.

The problem with circumventing the scalar principle is that the link bypassed in the process may have very pertinent information. For example, suppose Jerry goes directly above his immediate boss, Ellen, to Charlie for permission to take his lunch break 30 minutes earlier. Charlie, believing the request is reasonable, approves it, only to find out later that the other two people in Jerry's department had also rescheduled their lunch breaks. Thus, the department would be totally vacant from 12:30 to 1 o'clock. Ellen, the bypassed manager, would have known about the other rescheduled lunch breaks.

A common misconception is that every action must painstakingly progress through every link in the chain, whether its course is upward or downward. This point was refuted many years ago by Lyndall Urwick, an internationally known management consultant:

> Provided there is proper confidence and loyalty between superiors and subordinates, and both parties take the trouble to keep the other informed in matters in which they

should have a concern, the "scalar process" does not imply that there should be no short-cuts. It is concerned with authority, and provided the authority is recognized and no attempt is made to evade or to supersede it, there is ample room for avoiding in matters of action the childish practices of going upstairs one step at a time or running up one ladder and down another when there is nothing to prevent a direct approach on level ground.[13]

As Henri Fayol stated years before Urwick, "It is an error to depart needlessly from authority, but it is an even greater one to keep to it when detriment to the business ensues."[14] Both Urwick and Fayol are simply saying that in certain instances, one can and should shortcut the scalar chain as long as one does not do so in a secretive or deceitful manner.

Span of Management

span of management Number of subordinates a manager can effectively manage; also called *span of control.*

The **span of management** (also called the *span of control*) refers to the number of subordinates a manager can effectively manage. Although the British World War I general Sir Ian Hamilton is usually credited for developing the concept of a limited span of control, related examples abound throughout history. Hamilton argued that a narrow span of management (with no more than six subordinates reporting to a manager) would enable the manager to get the job accomplished in the course of a normal working day.[15]

In 1933, V. A. Graicunas published a classic paper that analyzed subordinate—superior relationships in terms of a mathematical formula.[16] This formula was based on the theory that the complexities of managing increase geometrically as the number of subordinates increases arithmetically.

Based on his personal experience and the works of Hamilton and Graicunas, Lyndall Urwick first stated the concept of span of management as a management principle in 1938: "No superior can supervise directly the work of more than five, or at the most, six subordinates whose work interlocks."[17]

Since the publication of Graicunas's and Urwick's works, the upper limit of five or six subordinates has been continuously criticized as being too restrictive. Many practitioners and scholars contend there are situations in which more than five or six subordinates can be effectively supervised. Their beliefs have been substantiated by considerable empirical evidence showing that the limit of five or six subordinates has been successfully exceeded in many situations.[18] Urwick has suggested these exceptions can be explained by the fact that senior workers often function as unofficial managers or leaders.[19]

In view of recent evidence, the span of management concept has been revised to state that the number of people who should report directly to any one person should be based on the complexity, variety, and proximity of the jobs, the quality of the people filling the jobs, and the ability of the manager.

While much effort is given to ensuring that a manager's span of management is not too great, the opposite situation is often overlooked. All too frequently in organizations, situations develop in which only one employee reports to a particular manager. While this situation might very well be justified under certain circumstances, it often results in an inefficient and "top-heavy" organization. The pros and cons of flat organizations (wide spans of management, few levels) versus tall organizations (narrow spans of management, many levels) are discussed at length in the next chapter. Figure 10.4 summarizes the factors affecting the manager's span of management.

FIGURE 10.4	**Factors Affecting the Span of Management**	
Factor	**Description**	**Relationship to Span of Control**
Complexity	Job scope Job depth	Shortens span of control
Variety	Number of different types of jobs being managed	Shortens span of control
Proximity	Physical dispersion of jobs being managed	Lengthens span of control
Quality of subordinates	General quality of the employees being managed	Lengthens span of control
Quality of manager	Ability to perform managerial duties	Lengthens span of control

Workplace Changes in Organizations

The trends toward increased decentralization and empowerment of employees were discussed earlier in this chapter. Other trends relating to the organizing function include the use of self-directed work teams, telecommuting and downsizing.

Self-directed work teams, (also called self-regulated and self-managed work teams), are work units without a front-line manager and empowered to control their own work.[20] Although well-established in European and especially Scandinavia, self-directed work teams are relatively new but growing in the U.S. It has been predicted that as many as 40 percent of U.S. employees will be working in self-directed teams by the year 2000.[21] Self-directed work teams are discussed in more depth in Chapter 12.

Technology has made it possible to redefine where work is done. Portable and personal computers, cellular phones, and fax machines are some of the technology based items that make it possible for some employees to work at home, on the beach, in the mountains and at any time. **Telecommuting** is the process of working away from a traditional office—usually at home. In 1997 there were more than 11 million telecommuters—up 30 percent from 1995.[22] Companies such as Procter & Gamble, IBM, Hewlett-Packard, AT&T, and Compaq have partially or fully eliminated traditional offices for field sales and customer service.[23] Other companies have eliminated offices for employees, including researchers, real estate managers, and accountants.

The advantages of telecommuting include decreased real estate and operating costs, reduced employee commute time, increased morale and loyalty, and increased reputation as a great place to work. As with self-directed work teams, telecommuting is another way of decentralizing and empowering employees. All indications are that telecommuting will continue to grow in the future. Telecommuting is discussed further in Chapter 20.

Downsizing, or the laying off of large numbers of managerial and other employees, is a phenomenon that characterized many American organizations in the 1990s. A 1998 survey of 4,500 managers of major U.S. corporations reported that 61 percent of those polled had eliminated jobs since January 1990. Twenty-one percent reported that their companies then employed fewer people than in 1990.[24] Generally, downsizing has been caused by increased global competition and the growing number of mergers and acquisitions. One result of downsizing is the tendency of organizations to reduce the number of managerial levels and widen the spans of management.[25] Many people believe that the tendency to reduce managerial levels and widen spans of management is the wave of the future and not merely a temporary reaction.

Summary

1. *Define Organization and Differentiate between a Formal and an Informal Organization.* An organization is a group of people working together in some type of concerted or coordinated effort to attain objectives. As such, an organization provides a vehicle for accomplishing objectives that could not be achieved by individuals working separately. The framework that defines the boundaries of the formal organization and within which the organization operates is the organization structure. The informal organization refers to the aggregate of the personal contacts and interactions and the associated groupings of people working within the formal organization. The informal organization has a structure, but it is not formally and consciously designed.

2. *Explain the Importance of the Organizing Function.* The organizing function determines how organizational resources will be employed to achieve goals. It also establishes lines of authority, improves the efficiency and quality of work through synergism, and improves communication by defining channels of communication in the organization.

3. *List the Attributes of a Highly Effective Organization.* Highly effective organizations are usually (1) externally focused and market driven, (2) customer centered, (3) built on and committed to maintaining strategic networks and alliances, (4) mobilized toward a vision, (5) dedicated to creating value in products and services, (6) committed to positive learning and change, (7) dedicated to fulfilling responsibilities to all stakeholders (customers, employees, suppliers, society), and (8) committed to measuring progress against world-class standards of excellence.

4. *List the Advantages and the Major Disadvantage of Horizontal Division of Labor.* Horizontal division of labor can result in the following advantages: (1) fewer skills are required per person; (2) it is easier to supply the skills required for selection or training purposes; (3) practice in the same job develops proficiency; (4) primarily utilizing each worker's best skills promotes efficient use of skills; (5) concurrent operations are made possible; and (6) there is more conformity in the final product if each piece is always produced by the same person. The major disadvantage of horizontal division of labor is that it can result in job boredom and even degradation of the worker.

5. *Distinguish among Power, Authority, and Responsibility.* Power is the ability to influence, command, or apply force. Power is derived from the control of resources. Authority is power derived from the rights that come with a position; it is the legitimate exercise of power. Responsi-

bility is accountability for the attainment of objectives, the use of resources, and the adherence to organizational policy. Once responsibility is accepted, performing assigned work becomes an obligation.

6. *Explain the Concept of Centralization versus Decentralization.* Centralization and decentralization refer to the degree of authority delegated by upper management. This is usually reflected by the numbers and kinds of decisions made by the lower levels of management. As they increase, the degree of decentralization also increases. Thus, an organization is never totally centralized or totally decentralized; rather, it falls along a continuum ranging from highly centralized to highly decentralized.

7. *Define Empowerment.* Empowerment is a form of decentralization that involves giving subordinates substantial authority to make decisions.

8. *List Four Principles of Organization That Are Related to Authority.* Four principles of organization related to authority are (1) the parity principle, (2) the unity of command principle, (3) the scalar principle, and (4) span of management.

9. *Identify Several Reasons Managers Are Reluctant to Delegate.* A manager's resistance to delegating authority is natural. Several reasons managers are reluctant to delegate include the following: (1) fear of subordinates failing; (2) it is easier for the manager to do the task than to teach a subordinate how to do it; (3) fear that subordinates will look "too good"; (4) humans' attraction to power; and (5) comfort in doing those tasks that should be delegated.

10. *Recount the Major Factors That Affect a Manager's Span of Management.* The major factors that affect a manager's span of management are (1) the complexity of the job being managed, (2) the variety among the jobs being managed, (3) the physical proximity of the jobs to one another, (4) the general quality of the subordinates being managed, and (5) the ability of the manager to perform the different managerial duties.

11. *Name and define three workplace changes, in addition to decentralization and empowerment, that have affected the organizing function in today's organizations.* The use of self-directed work teams, telecommuting and downsizing have affected today's organizations. Self-directed work teams are autonomous work units without a front-line manager and empowered to control their own work. Telecommuting is the process of working away from a traditional office—usually at home. Downsizing is the laying off of large numbers of managers and other employees.

Preview Analysis

1. What suggestions does coach Maureen O'Brien offer managers who wish to formulate and understand their organizations better?

2. What simple rules must an organization follow to ensure high performance?

3. Do you think there is a relationship between managerial and coaching skills? Explain your answer

Review Questions

1. What is an organization? Define the management function of organizing. Define organization structure. What is an informal organization?

2. Discuss the reasons for organizing.

3. What is the difference between horizontal and vertical division of labor? What is the difference between job scope and job depth?

4. Define power, authority, and responsibility.

5. Discuss two approaches to viewing the sources of authority.

6. What is the difference between a highly centralized and a highly decentralized organization?

7. Explain the concept of empowerment.

8. What is the parity principle? How does the parity principle relate to the exception principle?

9. Describe three components of the delegation process.

10. Why are many managers reluctant to delegate authority?

11. What is the unity of command principle?

12. What is the scalar principle?

13. What is the span of management?

14. Define the following: self-directed work teams, telecommuting, and downsizing.

Skill-Building Questions

1. Do you think division of labor has been overemphasized in today's highly mechanized and efficient society?

2. Comment on the following statement, which is attributed to Robert Heinlein: "A human being should be able to change a diaper, plan an invasion, butcher a hog, conn a ship, design a building, write a sonnet, balance accounts, build a wall, set a bone, comfort the dying, take orders, give orders, cooperate, act alone, solve equations, analyze new problems, pitch manure, program a computer, cook a tasty meal, fight efficiently, and die gallantly. Specialization is for insects."

3. As a manager, would you prefer a relatively large (more than seven subordinates) or small (seven or fewer subordinates) span of management? Why? What are the implications of your choice?

4. Many people believe that the concept of empowerment receives a lot more talk than action. Why do you think this could be true?

5. Do you think you would like to telecommute? Why or why not?

SKILL-BUILDING EXERCISE 10.1

Promotion Possible: A Role Play

Your instructor will ask some class members to role-play either the president or the current assistant sales manager in the following scenario.

The assistant sales manager of ABC Company has been in that job for six months. Due to poor sales over the past 18 months, the sales manager (his or her boss) has just been fired. The president of ABC then offers this job to the assistant sales manager subject to the following stipulations:

- You cannot increase the advertising budget.
- You must continue to let Metro-Media, Inc., handle the advertising.
- You cannot make any personnel changes.
- You will accept full responsibility for the sales for this fiscal year (which started two months ago).

The role play will simulate a meeting between the president and the assistant sales manager to discuss the offer. You can make any reasonable assumptions you think are necessary to play the role assigned to you.

SKILL-BUILDING EXERCISE 10.2

Minor Errors

Recently you have noticed that one of the staff members on the same level as your boss has been giving you a hard time concerning reports you submit to her. Having reviewed recent reports, you have discovered a few minor errors you should have caught; but, in your opinion, they are not significant enough to warrant the kind of criticism you've been receiving. Your boss and this particular manager have a history of bad relations, which may be one reason for her attitude and actions.

As you think about how to best handle the situation, you consider these alternatives:

1. Talk to the manager in private and ask her why she is being so critical.

2. Do nothing. It is probably a temporary situation; to bring undue attention to it will only make matters worse.

3. Since your boss may get involved, discuss it with her and ask advice on what to do.

4. Work harder to upgrade the reports; make sure there will be nothing to criticize in the future.

5. Discuss it with your boss, but minimize or downplay the situation by letting her know that you believe constructive criticism of this type is usually healthy.

Other alternatives may be open to you, but assume these are the only ones you have considered.

A. *Without discussion* with anyone, decide which of these approaches you would take now. Be prepared to defend your choice.

B. What principle of organization most closely relates to this situation?

C. To what extent do you think this is an organizing problem as opposed to a personality problem?

CASE INCIDENT 10.1

A Good Manager?

Francis S. Russell is Assistant General Manager and Sales Manager for Webb Enterprises. At the moment, this self-styled perfectionist is sitting up in bed, checking his TTD sheet for tomorrow. The TTD (Things To Do) itemizes his daily activities, placing them on an exact time schedule. Never one to browbeat subordinates, Russell has his own special way of reminding people that time is money. Ever since the days when he was the best salesman the company ever had, he had worked harder than the rest. It had paid off, too, because in only two years (when old Charlie retired), he was the heir apparent to the general managership. As this thought crossed Russell's mind, his immediate pride was replaced with a nagging problem. Where was he going to find the time to do all the things his position required? He certainly couldn't afford to just maintain the status quo. Then his mind forced him to plan tomorrow's activities and the problem was pushed into the background for future consideration.

(We see below a portion of Russell's well-planned day.)

TTD—October 16th

7:15   Breakfast with Johnson (Purchasing). Get information on his cataloging system. Maybe combine with sales department and avoid duplication.

8:30   Meeting with Henry (Asst. Sales Manager). Tell him exactly how the sales meeting for out-of-state representatives should be conducted. Caution—he's shaky on questions.

9:15   Discuss progress on new office procedures manual with Charlie (General Manager). (He's irritated because I've dragged my heels on this. Let him know I've got Newman working on the problem.)

9:45   Assign Pat Newman the job of collecting data and sample copies regarding office manuals in other companies in our industry. Set up a system for him to use in analysis.

10:45   Call on Acliff Printing. A potentially big customer. (As Russell jotted down some information on this client, he reflected that it was a shame no one else on his staff could really handle the big ones the way he could. This thought was pleasing and bothersome at the same time.)

12:00   Lunch with J. Acliff (reservations at Black Angus).

3:00   Meet with Frank Lentz (Advertising Assistant) and check his progress on the new sales campaign. (Russell thought about Lentz's usual wild ideas and hoped that he had followed the general theme and rough sketches he had prepared.)

7:30   Chamber of Commerce meeting. (Look up Pierce Hansen—he may be able to help on the Acliff account.)

Assignment:

1. Do you think Francis is a highly motivated employee trying to do a good job? Explain your answer.

2. What problems do you see concerning Francis' effectiveness as a manager?

3. Assuming you were Charlie, the General Manager, what solutions would you recommend?

CASE INCIDENT 10.2

The Vacation Request

Tom Blair has a week's vacation coming and really wants to take it the third week in May, which is the height of the bass fishing season. The only problem is that two of the other five members of his department have already requested and received approval from their boss, Luther Jones, to take off that same week. Afraid that Luther would not approve his request, Tom decided to forward his request directly to Harry Jensen, who is Luther's boss and who is rather friendly to Tom (Tom has taken Harry fishing on several occasions). Not realizing that Luther has not seen the request, Harry approves it. Several weeks pass before Luther finds out, by accident, that Tom has been approved to go on vacation the third week of May.

The thing that really "bugs" Luther is that this is only one of many instances in which his subordinates have gone directly to Harry and gotten permission to do something. Just last week, in fact, he overheard a conversation in the washroom to the effect that, "If you want anything approved, don't waste time with Luther, go directly to Harry."

Questions

1. What should Harry have done?

2. Who is at fault, Harry or Tom?

3. What if Luther confronts Harry with the problem and he simply brushes it off by saying he is really only helping?

References and Additional Readings

[1]Harold Koontz and Cyril O'Donnell, *Management: A Systems and Contingency Analysis of Managerial Functions*, 6th ed. (New York: McGraw-Hill, 1976), p. 274.

[2]Chester L. Barnard, *Functions of the Executive* (Cambridge, MA: Harvard University Press, 1938), pp. 114–15.

[3]Gareth R. Jones, *Organizational Theory* (Reading, MA: Addison-Wesley, 1995), p. 9.

[4]Adam Smith, *The Wealth of Nations* (New York: Modern Library, 1917); originally published in 1776.

[5]Thomas J. Peters and Robert H. Waterman, Jr., *In Search of Excellence* (New York: Harper & Row, 1982), p. 313.

[6]Mary Parker Follett, *Freedom and Co-Ordination* (London: Management Publication Trust, 1949), pp. 1–15 (the lecture reproduced in *Freedom and Co-Ordination* was first delivered in 1926); Barnard, *Functions*, p. 163.

[7]John Tschol, "Empowerment: The Key to Customer Service," *American Salesman*, November 1997, pp. 12–15.

[8]Robert B. Shaw, "The Capacity to Act: Creating a Context for Empowerment," in *Organizational Architecture: Designs for Changing Organizations*, ed. David A. Nadler, Marc S. Gerstein, and Robert B. Shaw (San Francisco: Jossey-Bass, 1992), p. 169.

[9]Jill Jusko, "Next Stop, The Top," *Industry Week*, July 20, 1998, pp. 42–44.

[10]Herbert M. Engel, *How to Delegate* (Houston: Gulf, 1983), p. 6.

[11]Michael Hammer and James Champy, *Reengineering the Corporation* (New York: Harper Business, 1993), pp. 168, 180–81.

[12]Ibid., pp. 180–81.

[13]L. F. Urwick, *The Elements of Administration* (New York: Harper & Row, 1943), p. 46.

[14]Henri Fayol, *General and Industrial Management* (London: Sir Isaac Pitman & Sons, 1949), p. 36; first published in 1916.

[15]Sir Ian Hamilton, *The Soul and Body of an Army* (London: Edward Arnold, 1921), p. 229.

[16]V. A. Graicunas, "Relationship in Organization," *Bulletin of the International Management Institute* (Geneva: International Labour Office, 1933); reprinted in *Papers on the Science of Ad-*

ministration, ed. L. Gulick and L. F. Urwick (New York: Institute of Public Administration, 1937), pp. 181–87.

[17]L. F. Urwick, "Scientific Principles and Organizations," *Institute of Management Series No. 19* (New York: American Management Association, 1938), p. 8.

[18]For a brief discussion of such situations, see Leslie W. Rue, "Supervisory Control in Modern Management," *Atlanta Economic Review,* January–February 1975, pp. 43–44.

[19]L. F. Urwick, "V. A. Graicunas and the Span of Control," *Academy of Management Journal,* June 1974, p. 352.

[20]Renee Beckhams, "Self-Directed Work Teams: The Wave of the Future?," *Hospital Material Management Quarterly,* August 1998, pp. 48–60.

[21]Ibid.

[22]Genevieve Capowski, "Telecommuting: The New Frontier," *HR Focus,* April 1998, p. 2.

[23]Thomas H. Davenport and Keri Pearlson, "Two Cheers for the Virtual Office," *Sloan Management Review,* Summer 1998, pp. 51–65.

[24]Eric Rolfe Greenberg, "Downsizing and the Career Path," *HR Focus,* March 1998, p. 2.

[25]James M. Higgins and Julian W. Vincze, *Strategic Management: Text and Cases* (Fort Worth, TX: The Dryden Press, 1993) p. 308.

11

Organization Structure

LEARNING OBJECTIVES

After studying this chapter, you should be able to:

1. Discuss the different stages an organization goes through as it grows and matures.

2. Explain what an organization chart is.

3. List several factors that can affect which structure is the most appropriate for a given organization.

4. Describe the general relationship between an organization's strategy and its structure.

5. Explain what is meant by a flat structure versus a tall structure.

6. Describe a contingency approach to organizing.

7. Identify the different types of departmentation.

8. Distinguish among a line structure, a line and staff structure, and a matrix structure.

9. Interpret the following phrase: simple form, lean staff.

10. Define outsourcing and summarize its potential benefits as well as its potential drawbacks.

11. Describe how committees can be made more effective.

12. Explain the difference between an "inside" and an "outside" board of directors.

In business, decentralization and organizational flattening typically involve eliminating several layers of management, often leaving managers overwhelmed with as many as a dozen direct subordinates. The U.S. Marines, on the other hand, have pushed decision-making authority down the line while retaining a simple hierarchical structure. The Marines' "rule of three" states that each Marine has three, and only three, things to worry about. In terms of organizational structure, the "rule of three" means each corporal has a three-person fire team; each sergeant has a squad of three fire teams; each lieutenant and a staff sergeant have a platoon of three squads; and so on, up to generals.

From a functional viewpoint the "rule of three" dictates that each Marine should limit his or her attention to three tasks or goals. When strategizing, each Marine should boil an infinite world of possibilities down to three alternative courses of action; anything more might lead to confusion. The "rule of three" results in an organizational hierarchy that might seem extremely narrow and tall since there are typically six full layers of management in between an infantry private and the colonel commanding his or her regiment. However, when the action starts, the layers collapse on an as-needed basis. Marines at all levels begin making decisions in responses to fast-changing situations—without so much as consulting the chain of command. Even privates are expected to take whatever initiative is necessary to complete a mission. Major General John Admire, commander of an infantry division at Camp Pendleton sums up the Marines' view, "If your decision making loop is more streamlined than your enemy's, then you set the pace and course of the battle."

The Marines believe that the key to making their organizational structure work is recruiting effective decision makers for lower levels. Few organizations make hiring and training of managers as high a priority as the Marines do.

Source: David H. Freedman, "Corps Values," *Inc.*, April 1998, pp. 54–56.

organization structure   Framework that defines the boundaries of the formal organization and within which the organization operates.

Organization structure is the framework that defines the boundaries of the formal organization and within which the organization operates. The structure of an organization reflects how groups compete for resources, where responsibilities for profits and other performance measures lie, how information is transmitted, and how decisions are made. Many people believe a good manager or a competent employee should be able to perform well regardless of the organizational structure and environment. They believe that if managers or employees are good enough, they can overcome any obstacles the organization structure presents. Others believe that given the right organization structure, anyone should be able to perform in an acceptable fashion. The truth lies somewhere in between. An appropriate organizational structure certainly helps foster good performance.

ORGANIZATION GROWTH STAGES

Figure 11.1 shows in general terms the stages an organization goes through as it grows and matures. The craft or family stage is characterized by the absence of formal policies, objectives, and structure. The operations of the organization at this stage generally center around one individual and one functional area. During the entrepreneurial stage, the organization grows first at an increasing and then a decreasing rate. An atmosphere of optimism pervades the entire organization as sales and profits rise rapidly. By the third stage of growth, the entrepreneur has been replaced by or evolved into a professional manager who performs the processes of planning, organizing, staffing, motivating, and controlling.[1] Profits are realized more from internal efficiency and less from external exploitation of the market. At this stage, the organization becomes characterized by written policies, procedures, and plans.

As the organization moves through the craft stage and into the entrepreneurial stage, an organization structure must be developed. This is a critical stage for the organization. If an appropriate structure is not established and utilized, the entrepreneur may lose control and the entire organization may collapse. An organization structure must be developed that allows the organization to adapt to change in its environment.

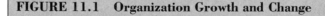

FIGURE 11.1   Organization Growth and Change

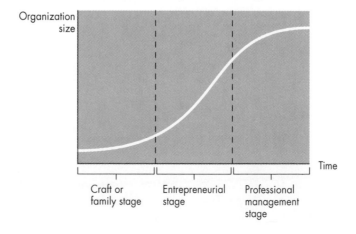

Management Illustration 11.1

Circular Organization Chart

Our Lady of the Way Hospital is a 39 bed accredited, general, acute care hospital located in Martin, Kentucky. Like most hospitals in the late 1980s and early 1990s, Our Lady of the Way exemplified a bureaucratic organization represented by the traditional "line and box organization chart." Under this structure the CEO had direct management responsibility for several functional departments. In 1992, the traditional hiearchial organization chart was replaced with a circular structure that reflected its increased reliance on team processes throughout the organization. The new structure also significantly reduced the number of people reporting to the CEO.

The circular organization is represented by a series of diagrams in which the circle, a geometric form with no beginning or end, symbolizes the ongoing nature of the team process. The circle also implies decisions are reached by consensus, and that each team member is equally responsible for the work of the team. Overlapping circles in the organization chart signify delegation of responsibility and reporting relationship. One immediate benefit of the new structure has been a streamlining of the problem-solving process. Additionally, committees and councils have become more productive.

Source: Mary M. Fanning, "A Circular Organization Chart Promotes Hospital-Wide Focus on Teams," *Hospital and Health Services Administration*, Summer 1997, pp. 243–254.

ORGANIZATION CHARTS

An organization chart uses a series of boxes connected with one or more lines to graphically represent the organization's structure. Each box represents a position within the organization, and each line indicates the nature of the relationships among the different positions. The organization chart not only identifies specific relationships but also provides an overall picture of how the entire organization fits together. As organizations become larger and more complex, it becomes increasingly difficult to represent all of the relationships accurately. Management Illustration 11.1 discusses how one organization has implemented a circular organization chart.

Central to the ability to recognize and adapt to change is management's willingness to evolve and change as well. The types of managerial talents (risk taking, creative vision, venture capital acquisition, and formulative organizational skills) that were so valuable in the craft and entrepreneurial stages are less valuable in the more mature professional management stage. It is remarkable how many entrepreneurial managers fall by the wayside in the professional management stage due primarily to the different organizational skills necessary in the higher level.

FACTORS AFFECTING STRUCTURE

Several factors can affect which structure is the most appropriate for a given organization. Strategy, size, environment, and technology are some of the important factors found to be most closely related to organization structure.

Strategy

A major part of an organization's strategy for attaining its objectives deals with how the organization is structured. An appropriate structure will not guarantee success, but it will enhance the organization's chances for success. Business leaders, athletic coaches, and military leaders all stress that to succeed one must not only have a good strategy but also be prepared to win (mentally and structurally). In addition to clarifying and defining strategy through the delegation of authority and responsibility, the organization structure can either facilitate or inhibit strategy implementation.

In a ground-breaking study of organizational strategy, Alfred D. Chandler described a pattern in the evolution of organizational structures.[2] The pattern was based on studies of Du Pont, General Motors, Sears, and Standard Oil Company, with corroborating evidence from many other firms. The pattern Chandler described was that of changing strategy, followed by administrative problems, leading to decline in performance, revised structure, and a subsequent return to economic health. In summary, Chandler concluded that structure follows strategy; in other words, changes in strategy ultimately led to changes in the organization's structure. Chandler's work related particularly to growth and to the structural adjustments made to maintain efficient performance during market expansion, product line diversification, and vertical integration.

Although subsequent research has supported the idea of a relationship between strategy and structure, it is clear that strategy is not the only variable that has a bearing on structure.[3] The process of matching structure to strategy is complex and should be undertaken with a thorough understanding of the historical development of the current structure and of other variables, including size, environment, and technology.

Size

There are many ways to measure the size of an organization, but sales volume and number of employees are the most frequently used factors. While no hard-and-fast rules exist, certain characteristics generally relate to an organization's size. Small organizations tend to be less specialized (horizontal division of labor), less standardized, and more centralized. Larger organizations tend to be more specialized, more standardized, and more decentralized. Thus, as an organization grows in size, certain structural changes naturally occur.

Environment

A landmark study relating organization to environment was conducted by Tom Burns and G. M. Stalker in the United Kingdom.[4] By examining some 20 industrial firms in both a changing industry and a more stable, established industry, Burns and Stalker focused on how a firm's pattern of organization was related to certain characteristics of the external environment. The researchers identified two distinct organizational systems. One, labeled **mechanistic systems,** is characterized by a rigid delineation of functional duties, precise job descriptions, fixed authority and responsibility, and a well-developed organizational hierarchy through which information filters up and instructions flow down. The second type, **organic systems,** are characterized by less formal job descriptions, greater emphasis on adaptability, more participation, and less fixed authority. Burns and Stalker found that successful firms in stable and established industries tended to be mechanistic in structure, whereas successful firms in dynamic industries tended to be organic in structure. See Figure 11.2 for a more complete evaluation of the structural differences between mechanistic and organic systems.

mechanistic systems   Organizational systems characterized by a rigid delineation of functional duties, precise job descriptions, fixed authority and responsibility, and a well-developed organizational hierarchy through which information filters up and instructions flow down.

organic systems   Organizational systems characterized by less formal job descriptions, greater emphasis on adaptability, more participation, and less fixed authority.

FIGURE 11.2   Structural Differences between Mechanistic and Organic Systems

Characteristics of Mechanistic and Organic Organizations	
Mechanistic	**Organic**
Work is divided into narrow, specialized tasks. Tasks are performed as specified unless changed by managers in the hierarchy.	Work is defined in terms of general tasks. Tasks are continually adjusted as needed through interaction with others involved in the task.
Structure of control, authority, and communication is hierarchical.	Structure of control, authority, and communication is a network.
Decisions are made by the specified hierarchical level.	Decisions are made by individuals with relevant knowledge and technical expertise.
Communication is mainly vertical, between superior and subordinate.	Communication is vertical and horizontal, among superiors, subordinates, and peers.
Communication content is largely instructions and decisions issued by superiors.	Communication content is largely information and advice.
Emphasis is on loyalty to the organization and obedience to superiors.	Emphasis is on commitment to organizational goals and possession of needed expertise.

Source: Adapted from Tom Burns and G. W. Stalker, *The Management of Innovation* (London: Tavistock, 1961), pp. 119–22.

Paul Lawrence and Jay Lorsch conducted a later study dealing with organizational structure and its environment.[5] Their original study included 10 firms in three distinct industrial environments. Reaching conclusions similar to those of Burns and Stalker, Lawrence and Lorsch found that to be successful, firms operating in a dynamic environment needed a relatively flexible structure, firms operating in a stable environment needed a more rigid structure, and firms operating in an intermediate environment needed a structure somewhere between the two extremes.

Numerous other studies have been conducted in the past several years investigating the relationship between organization structure and environment. In general, most have concluded that the best structure for a given organization is contingent on the organization's environment to some degree.[6] However, managerial style and corporate culture may also have an impact as interpretative agents of the environment. Microsoft's Bill Gates, Nike's Phil Knight, and Pixar's Steve Jobs have all moved their companies in the direction of the organic model so they could swiftly move into new and as yet untapped markets and product lines.

Organization and Technology

Numerous studies have also been conducted investigating potential relationships between technology and organization structure. One of the most important of these studies was conducted by Joan Woodward in the late 1950s.[7] Her study was based on an analysis of 100 manufacturing firms in the southeast Essex area of England. Woodward's general approach was to classify firms along a scale of "technical complexity" with particular emphasis on three modes of production: (1) unit or small-batch production (e.g., custom-made machines), (2) large-batch or mass production (e.g., an automotive assembly plant), and (3) continuous flow or process production (e.g., a chemical plant). The unit or small-batch production mode represents the lower end of the technical complexity scale, while the continuous flow mode represents the upper end.

After classifying each firm into one of the preceding categories, Woodward investigated a number of organizational variables. Some of her findings follow:

1. The number of levels in an organization increased as technical complexity increased.
2. The ratio of managers and supervisors to total personnel increased as technical complexity increased.
3. Using Burns and Stalker's definition of organic and mechanistic systems, organic management systems tended to predominate in firms at both ends of the scale of technical complexity, while mechanistic systems predominated in firms falling in the middle ranges.
4. No significant relationship existed between technical complexity and organizational size.

A few years later, Edward Harvey undertook a similar study.[8] Rather than using Woodward's "technical complexity" scale, Harvey grouped firms along a continuum from technical diffuseness to technical specificity. Technically diffused firms have a wider range of products, produce products that vary from year to year, and produce more "made-to-order" products. Harvey's findings were similar to Woodward's in that he found significant relationships between technology and several organizational characteristics.

The general conclusion reached in the Woodward and Harvey studies was that a relationship clearly exists between organizational technology and a number of aspects of organization structure. Many additional studies have investigated the relationship between technology and structure. While they have reported some conflicting results, most studies have found a relationship between technology and structure.[9]

FLAT VERSUS TALL STRUCTURES

The previous chapter discussed the different factors that influence a manager's span of management. A closely related concept is the idea of a flat versus a tall organization structure. Many studies have compared the relative desirability of the two structures. A **flat structure** has relatively few levels and relatively large spans of management at each level; a **tall structure** has many levels and relatively small spans of management (see Figure 11.3). A classic study in this area was conducted by James Worthy.[10] Worthy studied the morale of over 100,000 employees at Sears during a 12-year period. His study noted that organizations with fewer levels and wider spans of management offered the potential for greater job satisfaction. A wide span of management also forced the manager to delegate authority and develop more direct links of communication—another plus. On the other hand, Rocco Carzo and John Yanouzas found that groups operating in a tall structure had significantly better performance than those operating in a flat structure.[11] Other studies have also shown conflicting results. Therefore, one cannot conclude that all flat structures are better than all tall structures, or vice versa.[12]

In general, Japanese organizations historically have had fewer middle managers and flatter structures than American organizations. However, the downsizing many American organizations have experienced in the last few years has resulted in flatter structures with wider spans of control.[13]

flat structure   Organization with few levels and relatively large spans of management at each level.
tall structure   Organization with many levels and relatively small spans of management.

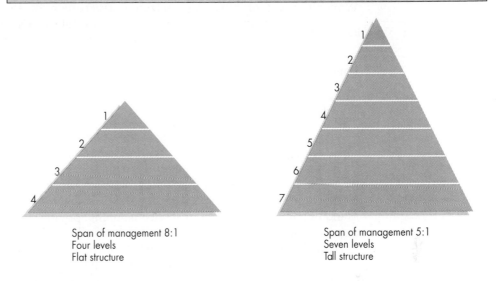

FIGURE 11.3   Flat versus Tall Structures

Span of management 8:1
Four levels
Flat structure

Span of management 5:1
Seven levels
Tall structure

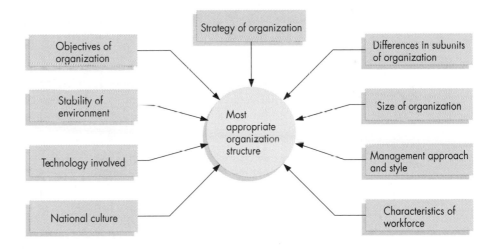

FIGURE 11.4   Variables Affecting Appropriate Organization Structure

Strategy of organization

Objectives of organization

Differences in subunits of organization

Stability of environment

Size of organization

Technology involved

Most appropriate organization structure

Management approach and style

National culture

Characteristics of workforce

A CONTINGENCY APPROACH

The previous discussions emphasize the fact that several factors affect an organization's structure. The knowledge that there is no one best way to organize (i.e., the design is conditional) has led to a **contingency (situational) approach** to organizing. Figure 11.4 shows the previously discussed variables and others that can help determine the most appropriate organization structure. The contingency approach should be viewed as a process of assessing these relevant variables and then choosing the most appropriate structure for the situation. Because most of the relevant variables are dynamic, management should periodically analyze and appraise the organization's structure in light of any relevant changes.

contingency (situational) approach to organization
structure   States that the most appropriate structure depends on the technology used, the rate of environmental change, and other dynamic forces.

DEPARTMENTATION

departmentation   Grouping jobs into related work units.

While thousands of different organization structures exist, almost all are built on the concept of departmentation. **Departmentation** involves grouping jobs into related work units. The work units may be related on the basis of work functions, product, customer, geography, technique, or time.

Work Functions

functional departmentation   Defining organizational units in terms of the nature of the work.

Functional departmentation occurs when organization units are defined by the nature of the work. Although different terms may be used, most organizations have four basic functions: production, marketing, finance, and human resources. Production refers to the actual creation of something of value, either goods, services, or both. Marketing involves product or service planning, pricing the product or service with respect to demand, evaluating how to best distribute the good or service, and communicating information to the market through sales and advertising. Any organization, whether manufacturing or service, must provide the financial structure necessary for carrying out its activities. The human resource function is responsible for securing and developing the organization's people.

Each of these basic functions may be broken down as necessary. For instance, the production department may be split into maintenance, quality control, engineering, manufacturing, and so on. The marketing department may be grouped into advertising, sales, and market research. Figure 11.5 charts a typical functional departmentation.

The primary advantage of functional departmentation is that it allows for specialization within functions. It also provides for efficient use of equipment and resources, potential economies of scale, and ease of coordination within the function itself. However, functional departmentation can have some negative effects. For ex-

FIGURE 11.5   Functional Departmentation

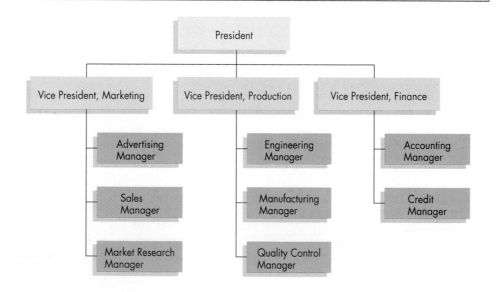

ample, suboptimization of goals occurs when members of a functional group develop more loyalty to the functional group's goals than to the organization's goals. For example, the marketing department might be overzealous in selling products even when production cannot meet any additional demand. If the group's goals and the organization's goals are not mutually supportive, such activity can lead to problems. Conflict may also develop among different departments striving for different goals. In addition, employees who are locked into their functions have a restricted view of the organization. Finally, the rather narrow functional scope of managers may be a disadvantage when a multidisciplinary approach would be more advantageous.

Product

product departmentation   Grouping all activities necessary to produce and market a product or service under one manager.

Under **product departmentation**, all the activities needed to produce and market a product or service are usually under a single manager. This system allows employees to identify with a particular product and thus develop esprit de corps. It also facilitates managing each product as a distinct profit center. Product departmentation provides opportunities for training for executive personnel by letting them experience a broad range of functional activities. Problems can arise if departments become overly competitive to the detriment of the overall organization. A second potential problem is duplication of facilities and equipment. Product departmentation adapts best to large, multiproduct organizations. Figure 11.6 illustrates how a company might be structured using product departmentation.

Geographic

geographic departmentation   Defining organizational units by territories.

Geographic departmentation is most likely to occur in organizations that maintain physically dispersed and autonomous operations or offices. Departmentation by geography permits the use of local employees and/or salespeople. This can create customer goodwill and an awareness of local feelings and desires. It can also lead to a high level of service. Of course, having too many geographic locations can be very costly.

Customer

customer departmentation   Defining organizational units in terms of customers served.

Customer departmentation is based on division by customers served. A common example is an organization that has one department to handle retail customers and one department to handle wholesale or industrial customers. Figure 11.7 shows departmentation by customer for Johnson & Johnson. This type of departmentation has the

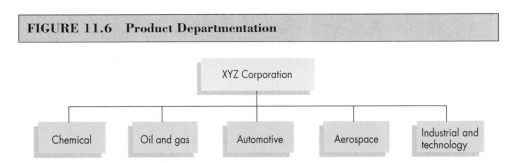

FIGURE 11.6   Product Departmentation

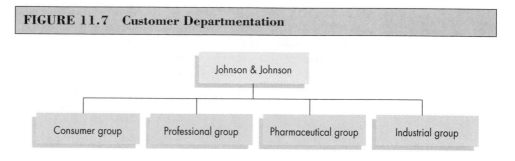

FIGURE 11.7   Customer Departmentation

same advantages and disadvantages as product departmentation. For example, if the professional group and the pharmaceutical group in Figure 11.7 became too competitive with each other for corporate resources, the organization's overall performance could suffer.

Other Types

Several other types of departmentation are possible. Departmentation by simple numbers is practiced when the most important ingredient for success is the number of employees. Organizing for a local United Way drive would be an example. Departmentation by process or equipment is another possibility. A final type of departmentation is by time or shift. Organizations that work around the clock may use this type of departmentation.

Departmentation is practiced not only to achieve division of labor but also to improve control and communications. Typically, as an organization grows in size, it adds levels of departmentation. A small organization may have no departmentation at first. As it grows, it may departmentalize first by function, then by product, then by geography. These changes, however, tend to raise the height of the organization structure and lengthen the communication distance between senior and lower-level management.

As Figure 11.8 illustrates, many different department mixes are possible for a given organization. Which one is best depends on the specific situation.

LINE STRUCTURE

line structure   Organization structure with direct vertical lines between the different levels of the organization.

The most important aspect of the **line structure** is that the work of all organizational units is directly involved in producing and marketing the organization's goods or services. This is the simplest organization structure and is characterized by vertical links between the different levels of the organization. All members of the organization receive instructions through the scalar chain. One advantage is a clear authority structure that promotes rapid decision making and prevents "passing the buck." A disadvantage is that it may force managers to perform too broad a range of duties. It may also cause the organization to become too dependent on one or two key employees who are capable of performing many duties. Because of its simplicity, line structure exists most frequently in small organizations. Figure 11.9 represents a simplified line structure.

FIGURE 11.8   Possible Departmentation Mixes for a Sales Organization

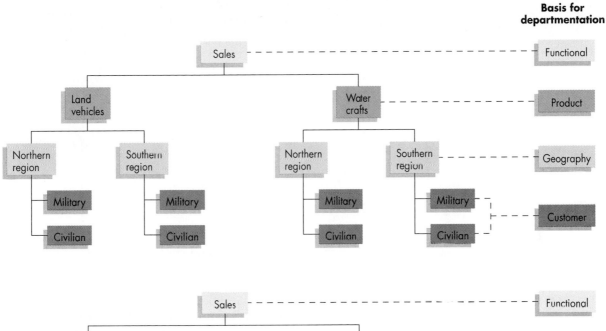

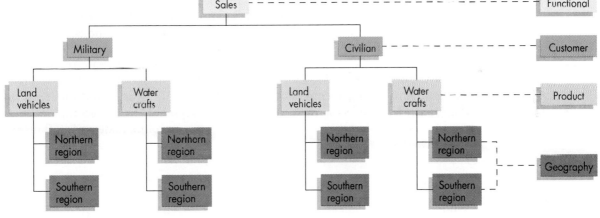

FIGURE 11.9   A Simplified Line Structure

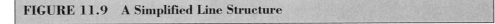
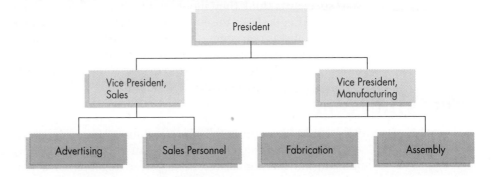

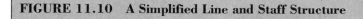

FIGURE 11.10   A Simplified Line and Staff Structure

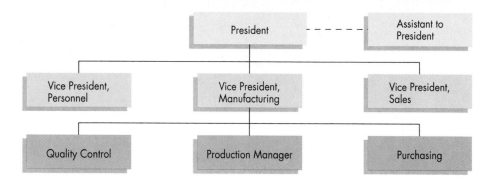

LINE AND STAFF STRUCTURE

line and staff structure   Organization structure that results when staff specialists are added to a line organization.

staff functions   Functions that are advisory and supportive in nature; designed to contribute to the efficiency and maintenance of the organization.

line functions   Functions and activities directly involved in producing and marketing the organization's goods or services.

The addition of staff specialists to a line-structured organization creates a **line and staff structure**. As a line organization grows, staff assistance often becomes necessary. **Staff functions** are advisory and supportive in nature; they contribute to the efficiency and maintenance of the organization. **Line functions** are directly involved in producing and marketing the organization's goods or services. They generally relate directly to the attainment of major organizational objectives, while staff functions contribute indirectly. Staff people are generally specialists in one field, and their authority is normally limited to making recommendations to line people. Typical staff functions include research and development, personnel management, employee training, and various "assistant to" positions. Figure 11.10 shows a simplified line and staff organization structure.

Line and Staff Conflict

The line and staff organization allows much more specialization and flexibility than does the simple line organization; however, it sometimes creates conflict. Some staff specialists resent the fact that they may be only advisers to line personnel and have no real authority over the line. At the same time, line managers, knowing they have final responsibility for the product, are often reluctant to listen to staff advice. Many staff specialists think they should not be in a position of having to sell their ideas to the line. They believe the line managers should openly listen to their ideas. If the staff specialist is persistent, the line manager often resents even more that the staff "always tries to interfere and run my department." The staff specialist who does not persist often becomes discouraged because "no one ever listens."

MATRIX STRUCTURE

The matrix (sometimes called project) form of organization is a way of forming project teams within the traditional line-staff organization. A project is "a combination of human and nonhuman resources pulled together in a temporary organization to achieve a specified purpose."[14] The marketing of a new product and the construction

FIGURE 11.11   Illustrative Matrix Structure

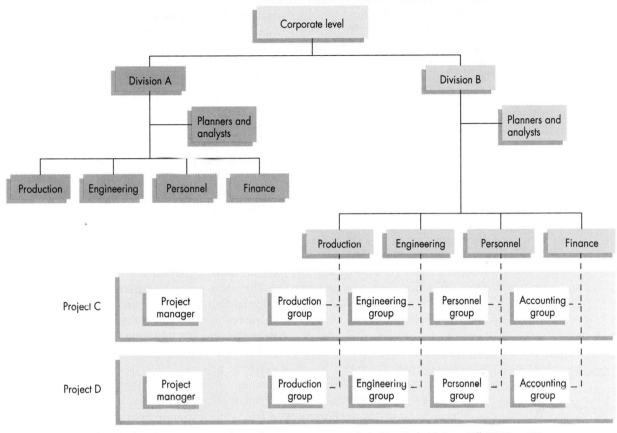

Source: David Cleland and William King, *Systems Analysis and Project Management*, 3d ed. (New York: McGraw-Hill, 1983), p. 279.

of a new building are examples of projects. Because projects have a temporary life, a method of managing and organizing them was sought so that the existing organization structure would not be totally disrupted and would maintain some efficiency.

matrix structure   Hybrid organization structure in which individuals from different functional areas are assigned to work on a specific project or task.

Under the **matrix structure,** those working on a project are officially assigned to the project and to their original or base departments. A manager is given the authority and responsibility to meet the project objectives in terms of cost, quality, quantity, and time of completion. The project manager is then assigned the necessary personnel from the functional departments of the parent organization. Thus, a horizontal-line organization develops for the project within the parent vertical-line structure. Under such a system, the functional personnel are assigned to and evaluated by the project manager while they work on the project. When the project or their individual work on it is done, the functional personnel return to their departments or begin a new project, perhaps with a new project team. Figure 11.11 shows a matrix structure.

A major advantage of matrix structure is that the mix of people and resources can readily be changed as project needs change. Other advantages include the emphasis placed on the project by use of a project team and the relative ease with which project members can move back into the functional organization once the project has ended. In addition, employees are challenged constantly and interdepartmental cooperation develops along with expanded managerial talent due to the multitude of roles the project manager must undertake.

One serious problem with the matrix structure is that it can violate the principle of unity of command. A role conflict can develop if the authority of the project manager is not clearly delineated from that of the functional managers. In such a case, the people assigned to the project may receive conflicting assignments from their project manager and their functional managers. A second problem occurs when the personnel assigned to a project are still evaluated by their functional manager, who usually has little opportunity to observe their work on the project. Third, matrix structures are often costly to implement, are only marginally accepted because they defy tradition, and put undue stress on communication networks.

Despite their drawbacks, matrix and project-oriented organizations continue to develop and spin off hybrid forms. Four new forms are the starburst, the shamrock, the pizza, and the inverted pyramid—strange names but adequate descriptions of the formats several well-known firms have chosen. Under the Starburst concept (developed by James Quinn of Dartmouth), the company splits off units and projects like shooting stars from a central core. Eastman Chemical's structure looks like a pizza with pepperoni on top. As Ernest Davenport explains, "Each pepperoni typically represents a cross-functional team responsible for managing a business, a geographic area, a function, or a core competence. The white space (the pizza) is where the collaborative interaction is supposed to occur." PepsiCo's inverted pyramid helps the firm focus on customers by putting field representatives on the top rather than on the bottom. Finally, McKinsey & Company's consulting group views the matrix as a shamrock wherein a trio of core processes linked to a common stem symbolize the multidisciplinary teams in charge of a specific process.[15] As these examples suggest, the matrix structure may go in any direction in the future. Management Illustration 11.2 describes how one hospital has implemented the use of a nursing council to overcome some of the communication problems associated with a matrix structure.

SIMPLE FORM, LEAN STAFF

As an organization grows and meets with success, it tends to evolve into an increasingly complex structure. How this occurs varies; frequently, a major cause is an increase in staff positions, especially at high levels. Many managers seem to feel a need for more staff and a more complex structure as the organization grows. They seem inclined to equate staff size with success.

In their observations, Thomas Peters and Robert Waterman found that many of the best-performing companies had maintained a simple structure with a small staff.[16] One reason is that a simple form with a lean staff allows an organization to adjust more rapidly to a fast-changing environment. It is also conducive to innovation. A simple form and a lean staff are naturally intertwined in that one breeds the other: A simple form requires fewer staff, and a lean staff results in a simple form.

Peters and Waterman outline four characteristics or practices that enable organizations to maintain a simple form and a lean staff:

1. Extraordinary divisional integrity. Each division has its own functional areas, including product development, finance, and personnel.
2. Continual formation of new divisions and rewards for this practice.

Management Illustration 11.2
Improving Communication in a Matrix Structure

St. Vincent Hospital in Green Bay, Wisconsin has developed a hospital nursing council to promote nursing in its decentralized matrix organization. The goals of the nursing council are to develop strategies for improving patient outcomes and to enhance nurse work satisfaction. Council membership is open to all nursing staff employees regardless of job description or educational background. The nursing council is composed of five smaller councils which represent the five roles of the professional nurse—manager, educator, researcher, practitioner and evaluator. Council membership gives individual staff members a forum to increase knowledge and skill in each of the five roles and also targets career advancement.

The hospital administrator, nurse directors, and non-nursing hospital directors have come to recognize the nursing council as an efficient, effective medium for communication and problem solving: changes occur more rapidly and with greater consensus; obstacles and/or barriers to acceptance of change have been significantly diminished; and recognized clinical pathways are readily available. Numerous positive changes in the patient-care delivery system have also emerged.

Source: Carolyn G. Friese, "Nursing Council—Coordination Within Decentralization," *Nursing Management*, March 1998, pp. 40–41.

3. Guidelines that determine when a new product or product line will become an independent division.
4. Moving people and even products among divisions on a regular basis without causing disruption.

Peters and Waterman postulate that the successful organizations of the future will be variations of the simple, divisionalized line and staff structure and that they will have the above characteristics. Not surprisingly, Peters and Waterman are rather negative regarding matrix organizations. They believe matrix structures tend to paralyze organizations by automatically diluting priorities and confusing employees.

OUTSOURCING

One of the most enduring management trends of the 1990s is the practice of subcontracting certain work functions to an outside entity. This practice is called **outsourcing.** Whether outsourcing is a response to downsizing or a natural extension of downsizing, it is a practice that will significantly affect the workplace and organizational charts. Work functions that are frequently being outsourced include accounting and finance functions, human resources, information technology and even contract manufacturing. According to the Outsourcing Institute, outsourcing expenditure of all types is predicted to reach $318 billion by the year 2001.[17] Numerous studies indicate that outsourcing is growing in the previously mentioned areas.[18]

Outsourcing has numerous potential benefits including the following:[19]

- Allowing the organization to emphasize its core competencies by not spending time on routine areas that can be outsourced.
- Reducing operating costs by utilizing others who can do the job more efficiently.
- Accessing top talent and state-of-the-art technology without having to own it.

Management Illustration 11.3
Outsourcing and White Collar Temps

Few companies have an outsourcing strategy as obvious as that of TopsyTail. This small Texas company, which has sold $100 million worth of hair care products since 1991, has virtually no permanent employees of its own. Owner Tomina Edmark says that everything, including design, marketing, manufacturing, distribution, and packaging, is handled by subcontractors. Talk about a flat organization chart! This technique is great for small, capital-poor companies that have a keen sense of "core competencies" that don't include management fat. The advantage to the small company is that this is a way to reduce risk and grow rapidly without taking on extra fixed costs.

A new trend seems to be popularity of hiring white-collar temps to fill executive ranks. Of the 1 million temporary employees working on any given day in the United States, about 12 percent are executives. Therefore, outsourcing (which shifts responsibilities and accountability outside the organization structure) and the temporary employee (which turns the organizational chart box into a temporary dotted line) may radically alter the organizational diagram of the future. With executive temp assignments typically lasting only four to six months, Fortune 500 executives are becoming much more open to temporarily hiring the specialist who solves a problem (often with fresh external insight) and then departs or is put on an extended temporary contract. "Have gun, will travel" will take on new meaning in the upper management circles of the future if this trend continues.

Sources: "The Outing of Outsourcing," *The Economist*, November 25, 1995, pp. 57–58; Julia Lawlor, "More Firms Hire White-collar Temps," *USA Today*.

For more articles about management trends visit *The Economist* at its Web site: www.economist.com

- Fewer personnel headaches.
- Improving resource allocation by allowing growth to take place more quickly.

Of course there are potential drawbacks to outsourcing.[20]

- Loss of control and being at the mercy of the vendor.
- Loss of in-house skills.
- Threat to the morale of the workforce if too many areas are dominated by outside vendors.

As with most management approaches, outsourcing is not a cure-all. Care must be taken that a long-term strategy evolves out of the use of outsourcing, not just a short-term fix to reduce costs. In the right situations outsourcing can work well but it almost always requires good management, good contracts, and realistic expectations. Management Illustration 11.3 discusses new trends in outsourcing as well as how one company has successfully used outsourcing.

COMMITTEES

committee Organization structure in which a group of people are formally appointed, organized, and superimposed on the line or line and staff structure to consider or decide certain matters.

Committees represent an important part of most organization structures. A **committee** is a group of people formally appointed and organized to consider or decide certain matters. From a structural standpoint, committees are superimposed on the existing line, line and staff, or matrix structure. Committees can be permanent (standing) or temporary (ad hoc) and are usually in charge of, or supplementary to, the line and staff functions.

FIGURE 11.12   Methods of Selecting Committees

Method	Advantages/Disadvantages
Appointment of chairperson and members	Promotes sense of responsibility for all. May result in most capable members. Members may not work well together.
Appointment of chairperson who chooses members	Will probably get along well. Lack of sense of responsibility by members. May not be most capable or representative.
Appointment of members who elect chairperson	Lack of sense of responsibility by chairperson. May not choose best chairperson for the job. Election of chairperson may lead to split in the committee.
Volunteers	Will get those who have greatest interest in the outcome for those who are least busy. Lack of responsibility. Potential for splits among committee members is great.

Using Committees Effectively

Managers can do many things to avoid the pitfalls and increase the efficiency of a committee. The first step is to define clearly its functions, scope, and authority. Obviously, the members must know the purpose of the committee to function effectively. If it is a temporary committee, the members should be informed of its expected duration. This will help avoid prolonging the life of the committee unnecessarily. Those responsible for establishing a committee should carefully communicate the limits of the committee's authority. This should be done very soon after the committee has been established.

In addition, careful thought should go into the selection of the committee members and chairperson. Size is always an important variable; generally, committees become more inefficient as they grow in size. A good rule of thumb is to use the smallest group necessary to get the job done. It is more important to select capable members than representative members. It is also important to pick members from the same approximate organizational level. Members from higher levels may inhibit the actions and participation of the other members. Figure 11.12 lists several methods for selecting committee members and chairpeople and outlines advantages and disadvantages for each method.

Boards of Directors

board of directors   Carefully selected committee that reviews major policy and strategy decisions proposed by top management.

A **board of directors** is really a type of committee that is responsible for reviewing the major policy and strategy decisions proposed by top management. A board of directors can be characterized as either an inside or an outside board. On an inside board, a majority of the members hold management positions in the organization; on an outside board, a majority of the members do not hold or have not held a position with the organization. While insiders who are members of a board ordinarily have other duties related to the strategic management process by virtue of their corporate position, the role the board plays as an entity should be basically the same for both types. Board members do not necessarily need to own stock; they should be chosen primarily for what they can and will contribute to the organization.

Although most boards of directors restrict their inputs to the policy and strategy level and do not participate in the day-to-day operations of the organization, their degree of involvement varies widely from board to board. For many years boards were used primarily as figureheads in many organizations, contributing little to the organization. However, this trend has been changing over the last several years. Recent lawsuits against boards of directors concerning their liabilities regarding the day-to-day operation of the organization have increased the risks of serving on boards.[21] Because of this, boards are becoming more active than they have been in the past. Moreover, some people now require liability insurance coverage before they will serve on a board of directors. An even more recent development is the tendency of shareholders to demand that the chairperson of the board be an outsider who is not employed in another capacity by the organization. Every diligent board of directors should address itself on behalf of the shareholders to this key issue: What is the standard of performance of the company's management—not what the company earned last year or this year, but what it *should* have earned?[22]

Summary

1. *Discuss the Different Stages an Organization Goes Through as It Grows and Matures.* The first stage an organization goes through is the craft or family stage, which is characterized by the absence of formal policies, objectives, and structure. Operations at this stage generally center around one individual and one functional area. The second stage is the entrepreneurial stage, in which the organization grows first at an increasing and then at a decreasing rate. By the third stage, the entrepreneur has been replaced by a professional manager and profits are realized more from internal efficiency and less from a rapidly growing market.

2. *Explain What an Organization Chart Is.* An organization chart uses a series of boxes connected with one or more lines to graphically represent the organization's structure.

3. *List Several Factors That Can Affect Which Structure Is the Most Appropriate for a Given Organization.* Some of the most important variables that can affect an organization's structure are strategy, size, environment, and technology.

4. *Describe the General Relationship between an Organization's Strategy and Its Structure.* Early research by Chandler reported that changes in strategy ultimately lead to changes in an organization's structure. Although subsequent research has supported the idea of some relationship between strategy and structure, it is clear that strategy is not the only variable that affects structure.

5. *Explain What Is Meant by a Flat Structure versus a Tall Structure.* A flat structure has relatively few levels and relatively large spans of management at each level; a tall structure has many levels and relatively small spans of management.

6. *Describe a Contingency Approach to Organizing.* The contingency approach to organization states that the most appropriate structure depends on many situational variables, including strategy, environment, size, technology, and employee characteristics. When taking a contingency approach, a manager should first analyze these variables and design a structure to fit the situation.

7. *Identify the Different Types of Departmentation.* Departmentation refers to the grouping of activities into related work units. Departmentation may be undertaken on the basis of work function, product, customer, geography, or time worked (shift).

8. *Distinguish among a Line Structure, a Line and Staff Structure, and a Matrix Structure.* A line structure is the simplest organization structure; it has direct vertical links between the different organizational levels. The addition of staff specialists to a line organization creates a line and staff structure. Staff functions are advisory and supportive in nature; line functions are directly involved in producing and marketing the organization's products or services. A matrix structure is a hybrid structure in which individuals from different functional areas are assigned to work on a specific project or task. Under a matrix structure, those working on a project are officially assigned to the project and to their original or base departments.

9. *Interpret the Following Phrase: Simple Form, Lean Staff.* An organization with a simple form and lean staff is better able to adjust to a fast-changing environment. Because of the absence of bureaucracy, this type of structure is also conducive to innovation and new ideas.

10. *Define outsourcing and summarize its potential benefits as well as its potential drawbacks.* Outsourcing is the practice of subcontracting certain work functions to an outside entity. The potential benefits of outsourcing include: allowing the organization to emphasize its core competencies, reducing operating costs, fewer personal headaches, accessing top talent and state-of-the-art technology, and improving resource allocations. Potential drawbacks include: loss of control, loss of in-house skills, and threats to the morale of employees.

11. *Describe How Committees Can Be Made More Effective.* The first step is to define clearly the committee's functions, scope, and authority. The next step is to carefully review who will serve on the committee. Size and member capability are extremely important.

12. *Explain the Difference between an "Inside" and an "Outside" Board of Directors.* With an inside board, a majority of the members hold management positions in the organization; with an outside board, a majority of the members do not hold or have not held a position with the organization.

Preview Analysis

1. Would you describe the Marines' organizational structure as flat or tall? Why?
2. Do you think the Marines' structure, as described in the preview, has captured the best points of both flat and tall organizations? Explain your answer.

3. If you were a Marine, how would you know when to consult the chain of command?

Review Questions

1. Describe the different stages an organization goes through as it grows and matures.
2. What is an organization chart?
3. What four major factors can affect an organization's structure?
4. Discuss the relationship between an organization's strategy and its structure.
5. Discuss the relationship between an organization's technology and its structure.
6. What are the advantages of a flat structure? What are the advantages of a tall structure?
7. What is the contingency approach to organizing?
8. Describe the following:
   a. Functional departmentation.
   b. Product departmentation.

   c. Geographic departmentation.
   d. Customer departmentation.
9. Explain the following:
   a. Line structure
   b. Line and staff structure
   c. Matrix structure
10. What factors contribute to potential conflict between line and staff personnel in a line and staff organization?
11. Describe four characteristics or practices that enable organizations to maintain a simple form and a lean staff.
12. What is outsourcing?
13. How can committees be made more effective?

Skill-Building Questions

1. As a practicing manager, how could you justify the use of a matrix structure given that it potentially violates the unity of command principle?
2. Do you think the contingency approach to organizing is a useful concept that can be implemented, or is it really a "cop-out"?
3. Discuss this statement: "When the appropriate organization structure is determined and implemented, a firm no longer has to worry about structure."

4. Recognizing that most organizations' staffs expand considerably as the organization grows, how would you respond to the following statement: "There is no way to grow and keep the corporate staff small"?
5. If you were an employee and your company embarked on a large-scale outsourcing program, how do you think you would react?
6. What do you think should be the role of the board of directors? What would you do to make the board of directors better for the average company?

SKILL-BUILDING EXERCISE 11.1

Applied Departmentation

Suppose you have just been hired as the vice president in charge of sales at COMBO Enterprises, Inc. COMBO manufactures, sells, and distributes both land and water vehicles. The land vehicles are bicycles powered by a two-horsepower, two-cycle engine. Basically, you have developed a method to adapt an off-the-shelf chain saw motor to a popular French-produced bicycle. The water

vehicles use the same chain saw motor adapted to a standard canoe, which is fitted with a special propeller and rudder.

The advantage over the existing competition is that, due to the light weight of the motor being used, the bicycles and canoes can also be used manually with very little loss of efficiency compared to nonmotorized bicycles and canoes. Your market surveys have shown that a large market exists for such a product.

COMBO serves both civilian and military markets for both the land and water vehicles. Presently COMBO has a plant in a medium-size eastern city and one in a medium-size western city. The eastern plant handles all business east of the Mississippi River, while the western plant handles business west of the Mississippi.

1. Design what you think would be the best way to organize the sales (marketing) division of the company.

2. Design an alternative structure for your division.

3. Why do you prefer one structure over the other?

4. Design a matrix structure for this situation (if you did not use one in question 1 or 2). What would be the pros and cons of such a structure in this situation?

SKILL-BUILDING EXERCISE 11.2

The Composition of Boards

Referring to the lists of most admired and least admired companies as identified by *Fortune* magazine (see Skill-Building Exercise 8.1, page 155), go to the library or get on the Internet and research the board of directors for any five companies from the most admired list and five from the least admired list. Determine how many outside directors and how many inside directors are serving each company. This information can be found in each company's annual report or in *Standard & Poor's Register of Corporations*, which is published annually.

A. Do most of these large, publicly-held companies have a majority of inside or outside directors?

B. Are there any obvious differences in the composition of the boards of those companies from the "most admired" list as compared to those from the "least admired" list?

C. Do you think the trend in large companies is toward more inside or more outside directors?

CASE INCIDENT 11.1

Who Dropped the Ball?

In October 1995, Industrial Water Treatment Company (IWT) introduced KELATE, a new product that was 10 times more effective than other treatments in controlling scale buildup in boilers. The instantaneous demand for KELATE required that IWT double its number of service engineers within the following year.

The sudden expansion caused IWT to reorganize its operations. Previously, each district office was headed by a district manager who was assisted by a chief engineer and two engineering supervisors. In 1996, this structure changed. The district manager now had a chief engineer and a manager of operations. Four engineering supervisors (now designated as group leaders) were established. They were to channel all work assignments through the manager of operations, while all engineering-related problems were to be handled by the chief engineer. Each group leader supervised 8 to 10 field service engineers (see Exhibit 1).

Bill Marlowe, district manager for the southeast district, has just received a letter from an old and very large customer, Sel Tex, Inc. The letter revealed that when Sel Tex inspected one of its boilers last week, it found the water treatment was not working properly. When Sel Tex officials contacted Wes Smith, IWT's service engineer for the area, they were told he was scheduled to be working in the Jacksonville area the rest of the week but would get

someone else down there the next day. When no one showed up, Sel Tex officials were naturally upset; after all, they were only requesting the engineering service they had been promised.

Bill Marlowe, upset over the growing number of customer complaints that seemed to be crossing his desk in recent months, called Ed Jones, chief engineer, into his office and showed him the letter he had received from Sel Tex.

Ed: Why are you showing me this? This is a work assignment foul-up.

Bill: Do you know anything about this unsatisfactory condition?

Ed: Sure, Wes called me immediately after he found out. Their concentration of KELATE must have gone up, since they're getting corrosion and oxygen on their tubes. I told Peter Adinaro, Wes's group leader, about it, and I suggested he schedule someone to visit Sel Tex.

Bill: OK, Ed, thanks for your help. [Bill then calls Peter Adinaro into his office.] Peter, two weeks ago Ed asked you to assign someone to visit Sel Tex because of a tube corrosion problem they are having. Do you remember?

Peter: Oh, sure! As usual, Wes Smith called Ed instead of me. I left a message for Dick to assign someone there because my whole group was tied up and I couldn't

EXHIBIT 1   Partial Organizational Chart for IWT

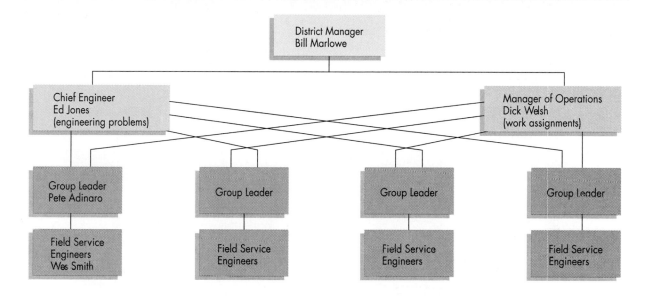

spare anyone. I thought Dick would ask another group leader to assign someone to check it out.

Bill: Well, thanks for your help. Tell Dick to come on in here for a second.

Dick Welsh, manager of operations, came into Bill's office about 20 minutes later.

Bill: Dick, here's a letter from Sel Tex. Please read it and tell me what you know about the situation.

Dick: [After reading the letter] Bill, I didn't know anything about this.

Bill: I checked with Pete, Wes's group leader, and he tells me he left a message for you to assign someone since his group was all tied up. Didn't you get the message?

Dick: Have you taken a look at my desk lately? I'm flooded with messages. Heck, I'm the greatest message handler of all times. If I could schedule my people

without having all the engineering headaches unloaded on me, I wouldn't have all these messages. Sure, it's possible that he left a message, but I haven't seen it. I will look for it, though. Anyway, that letter sounds to me like they've got an engineering problem, and Ed should contact them to solve it.

Bill: I'll write Sel Tex myself and try to explain the situation to them. You and I will have to get together this afternoon and talk over some of these difficulties. See you later, Dick.

Questions

1.   What problems does Bill Marlowe face?

2.   Are the problems related to the way IWT is organized, or are they related to the employees?

3.   How could these problems be resolved?

CASE INCIDENT 11.2

A New Organizational Structure

Yesterday, Tom Andrews was officially promoted to his new job as hospital administrator for Cobb General Hospital. Cobb General is a 600-bed hospital located in a suburban area of New Orleans. Tom is extremely excited about the promotion but at the same time has some serious doubts about it.

Tom has worked at Cobb General for three years and had previously served as the associate administrator of the hospital. Although associate administrator was his official

job title, he was really more of an "errand boy" for the former administrator, Bill Collins. Because of Tom's educational background (which includes a master of hospital administration degree) and his enthusiasm for the hospital, Tom was offered the administrator's job last week after the hospital's board of directors had asked for Bill Collins's resignation.

Tom was now looking at the organization chart for the hospital, which had been pieced together over the years

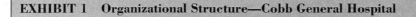

EXHIBIT 1   Organizational Structure—Cobb General Hospital

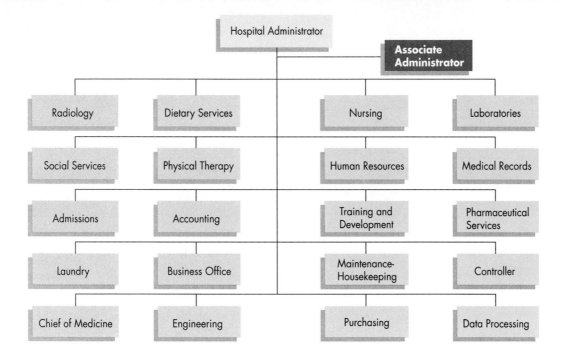

by Bill Collins (see Exhibit 1). In reality, each time a new unit had been added or a new function started, Bill merely had the person report directly to him. Tom is worried about his ability to handle all of the people currently reporting to him in his new position.

Questions

1. Do you agree with Tom's concern? Why?
2. How would you redraw the organizational chart?

References and Additional Readings

[1]Alan Filley and Robert House, *Managerial Process and Organizational Behavior* (Glenview, IL.: Scott, Foresman, 1969), pp. 443–55.

[2]A. D. Chandler, *Strategy and Structure* (Cambridge, MA: MIT Press, 1962).

[3]Some relevant research includes J. Child, "Organization Structure, Environment, and Performance: The Role of Strategic Choice," *Sociology* 6 (1972), pp. 1–22; R. Rumelt, *Strategy, Structure, and Economic Performance* (Boston: Harvard Business School, Division of Research, 1974); and Stephen P. Robins, *Organization Theory: Structure Design, and Application* (Englewood Cliffs, NJ: Prentice Hall, 1990).

[4]Tom Burns and G. M. Stalker, *The Management of Innovation* (London: Tavistock Institute, 1962).

[5]Paul Lawrence and Jay Lorsch, "Differentiation and Integration in Complex Organizations," *Administrative Science Quarterly*, June 1967, pp. 1–47; Paul Lawrence and Jay Lorsch, *Organization and Environment* (Burr Ridge, IL: Richard D. Irwin, 1969).

Originally published in 1967 by Division of Research, Graduate School of Business Administration, Harvard University.

[6]Robins, *Organization Theory*.

[7]Joan Woodward, *Industrial Organization: Theory and Practice* (London: Oxford University Press, 1965).

[8]Edward Harvey, "Technology and the Structure of Organizations," *American Sociological Review*, April 1968, pp. 247–59.

[9]Robins, *Organization Theory*.

[10]James Worthy, "Organization Structure and Employee Morale," *American Sociological Review* 15 (1956), pp. 169–79.

[11]Rocco Carzo, Jr., and John Yanouzas, "Effects of Flat and Tall Organization Structure," *Administrative Science Quarterly* 114 (1969), pp. 178–91.

[12]Dan R. Dalton, William D. Todor, Michael J. Spendolini, Gordon J. Fielding, and Lyman W. Porter, "Organization Structure and Performance: A Critical Review," *Academy of Management Review*, January 1980, pp. 49–54.

[13]James M. Higgins and Julian W. Vincze, *Strategic Management: Text and Cases* (Fort Worth, TX: The Dryden Press, 1993), p. 308.

[14]David Cleland and William King, *Systems Analysis and Project Management*, 3d ed. (New York: McGraw-Hill, 1983), p. 187.

[15]John A. Byrne, "The Horizontal Corporation," *Business Week*, December 20, 1993, pp. 80–81.

[16]Thomas J. Peters and Robert W. Waterman, Jr., *In Search of Excellence* (New York: Harper & Row, 1982), pp. 306–17.

[17]Jennifer J. Salopek, "Outsourcing, Insourcing, and In-Between Sourcing," *Training and Development*, July 1998, pp. 51–54.

[18]For example see, Genevieve Capowski, "Outsourcing Comes to HR," *HR Focus*, May 1998, p. 2; Jennifer Salopek, *op. cit*, p. 51; Celia J. Renner and Darin Tebbe, "Who is Outsourcing and Why?", *Management Accounting*, July 1998, pp. 45–47; and Yule S. Peterson, "Outsourcing: Opportunity or Burden?" *Quality Progress*, June 1998, pp. 63–64.

[19]Laure Edwards, "When Outsourcing is Appropriate," *Wall Street & Technology*, July 1998, pp. 96–98.

[20]Ibid.

[21]Richard M. Miller, "The D&O Liability Dilemma," *Chief Executive*, November–December 1988, pp. 34–39.

[22]Harold Geneen, *Managing* (Garden City, NY: 1984), p. 259.

12

Understanding Work Groups

LEARNING OBJECTIVES

After studying this chapter, you should be able to:

1. Describe formal and informal work groups.

2. Discuss the Hawthorne effect.

3. Define group norm.

4. Explain group cohesiveness.

5. Define group conformity.

6. Outline the conditions under which individual members tend to conform to group norms.

7. Explain idiosyncrasy credit.

8. Define groupthink.

9. Describe general conclusions that can be reached regarding informal group leadership.

10. Discuss suggestions for effective team building.

11. Describe a quality circle.

In late 1991, successful Honda design engineer Ron Shriver was already worrying about a new model Honda Civic sedan planned for 1995. To solve the problem, Shriver put together a 12-member team that would spend the next 18 months interrogating Honda's U.S. suppliers and its Ohio factory workers for ideas to make the next Civic model cheaper to build. The result of the combined team effort was a host of money-saving manufacturing tricks (such as a $1.2 million savings on bumper design) that would save the company millions of dollars at the manufacturing level.

Source: Adapted from Edith Hill Updike, David Woodruff, and Larry Armstrong, "Honda's Civic Lesson," *Business Week*, September 18, 1995, pp. 71 76.

In any organization, employees belong to two basic groups: formal and informal work groups. **Formal work groups** are established in the organizing function of management. Their membership and structure are established and formally recognized by the management of the organization. Overlapping the formal work groups in organizations are informal work groups. These groups are not established by the organizing function of management, yet all organizations have them.

formal work group   Work group established and formally recognized by the organizing function of management.

informal work group   Work group that results from personal contacts and interactions among people and is not formally recognized by the organization.

Informal work groups result from personal contacts and interactions among people and are not formally recognized by the organization. Groups of employees that regularly lunch together and office cliques are examples of informal work groups.

The key difference between formal and informal groups is that formal groups, once they are established by the organization, have public recognition, an identity, and goals and purposes, whereas informal groups are usually formed for reasons such as friendship, common interests, or proximity of members to one another (e.g., neighbors or co-workers). Either type of group can exist for varying lengths of time. A formal group can have a duration that is brief (a meeting) or extended (a committee or project team); an informal group can become formal if the structure changes (e.g., friends become partners in business).

The importance of belonging to a group and the effects of group membership on human behavior in organizations were documented early by Elton Mayo in the famous Hawthorne studies. The studies were carried out to find conditions that could maximize productivity of work groups at the Hawthorne plant of Western Electric. The study showed that every change, such as increasing or reducing the lighting or raising or lowering the wage scale, seemed to increase group productivity. This unpredictable result led to the coining of the term **Hawthorne effect,** meaning that giving special attention to a group of employees (such as involving them in an experiment and letting them interact with the researchers) changes their behavior.[1] The Hawthorne researchers concluded that employees react to the psychological and social conditions at work as well as to the physical conditions and that group pressures directly affect an employee's actions.[2] Later research, however, concluded that the so-called Hawthorne effect wore off as workers became accustomed to the researchers and their experiments, and critics doubt whether any real effect on worker performance occurred to begin with.[3]

hawthorne effect   States that giving special attention to a group of employees (such as involving them in an experiment) changes their behavior.

WHY EMPLOYEES JOIN INFORMAL WORK GROUPS

Work is a social experience and provides an opportunity for employees to fulfill many needs. When people are brought together in an office or a plant, they interact and work together in their formal job duties. Friendships naturally emerge out of these continuous contacts and from areas of common interest. As mentioned previously, mutual interests, friendships, and the need to fulfill social needs are three reasons that help to explain both the formation of informal work groups and the desire of employees to become members of such groups.

Work environment conditions such as the need for security (e.g., a shared sense of loyalty), physical proximity (e.g., office cubicles), technology (e.g., computer workstations and networks), people performing similar functions (such as the accounting department), and an us-against-them attitude on the part of employees (e.g., common complaints and fears) all encourage the formation of informal groups in the modern workplace. The important point is that overlapping the formal work groups in an organization are informal work groups that can have a significant impact on both individual and organizational performance.

GROUP NORMS AND BEHAVIORAL FACTORS

Managers must decide in the early stages of policy formulation whether group or individual decision making is in the best interest of productivity. John Sherwood and Florence Hoylman believe the choice between individual and group decision making depends on (1) the nature of the task itself, (2) the importance of general acceptance of the solution to implementation, (3) the value placed on the quality of the decision, (4) the competence of the persons involved, and (5) the anticipated operating effectiveness of the proposed group.[4] In addition, they conclude that groups are valuable assets because they provide greater total knowledge and information, a greater variety of approaches to problem solution, and a reduction in communication problems.[5] The following sections discuss the factors underlying group behavior and how they can be managed effectively.

Group Norms

group norms   Informal rules a group adopts to regulate and regularize group members' behavior.

Group norms are the informal rules a group adopts to regulate and regularize group members' behavior.[6] The various forms informal group norms take are limitless. One example of informal group norms that relates to the workplace is setting certain performance levels that may be either above, below, or the same as those set by management. Unfortunately, little is known about what factors determine whether an informal group will establish pro- or antiorganization norms.[7] However, a significant factor that determines whether group members closely adhere to group norms is the group's cohesiveness.[8]

Group Cohesiveness

group cohesiveness   Degree of attraction each member has for the group, or the "stick-togetherness" of the group.

Group cohesiveness basically refers to the degree of attraction each member has for the group, or the "stick-togetherness" of the group. Cohesiveness is important for the group, because the greater the cohesiveness, the more likely members are to pursue group rather than individual norms; that is, the greater the cohesiveness, the greater the individual members' conformity to group norms.

One variable that affects the cohesiveness of the group is its size. Individuals in the group must interact for the group to exist; this interaction requirement limits the size of the group. Group cohesiveness decreases as the size of the group increases. It is possible to specify an upper limit on the size of informal work groups. However, the interaction requirement generally limits the size of the group to a maximum of 15 to 20 members. If the informal work group becomes larger than 20, subgroups begin to form.

The success and status of the informal group also play an important part in group cohesiveness. The more successful a group is in achieving its goals, the more cohesive the group becomes. The relationship is circular in that success breeds cohesiveness and cohesiveness, in turn, breeds more success. Numerous factors contribute to the status of work groups. Some of these include the skill required in performing the job (skilled versus semiskilled jobs), opportunities for promotion (some groups develop reputations such as "the way to the top is through marketing"), the degree of supervision required (groups requiring less supervision have a higher status), and the type of work the group performs (the more dangerous or more financially rewarding the work, the higher the status). The important point is that groups that successfully achieve their goals and have higher status generally exhibit more cohesiveness.

Outside pressures, stability of membership, the ability to communicate, and the degree of physical isolation also influence group cohesiveness. For instance, if informal work groups perceive management's demands or requests as threats, group cohesiveness increases to offset the perceived threat. Higher cohesion results from stable membership in the group, because the group members have a longer time to know one another, learn the norms of the group, and learn how to behave according to group norms. Production lines and office layouts designed to inhibit conversation can reduce group cohesiveness. On the other hand, coal miners, who tend to be geographically isolated from the rest of the country, have demonstrated in numerous strikes the cohesiveness that can result from physical isolation from other groups.

Group cohesiveness has significant implications for managers. If the goals of a highly cohesive group are compatible with the organization's productivity goals, the group's output will be above average. However, if the group's goals are incompatible with the organization's performance goals, the group's output will be below average.[9]

Group Conformity

group conformity   Degree to which the members of the group accept and abide by the norms of the group.

Group conformity is the degree to which the members of the group accept and abide by the group's norms. Informal work groups seek to control the behavior of their members for many reasons. For example, a group desires uniform, consistent behavior from each member so that other members can predict with reasonable certainty how the individual member will behave. This certainty is necessary to achieve some degree of coordination in working toward the group's goals. On the other hand, groups are organizations in and of themselves; as a result, conformity is often required to maintain the group. Individualistic behavior among group members can threaten the survival of the group by causing internal dissension. Individual members tend to conform to group norms under the following conditions:

1. When the norm is congruent with the personal attitudes, beliefs, and behavioral predispositions of the members.
2. When the norm is inconsistent with the personal attitudes, beliefs, or behavioral predispositions but strong pressures to comply are exerted by the group and the rewards for complying are valued or the sanctions imposed for noncompliance are devalued.[10]

One study of the influence of group pressures on individuals placed college students in groups of seven to nine people.[11] Group members were told they would be comparing lengths of lines on white cards. Figure 12.1 shows the cards and lines. The subjects were then asked to pick the line on the second card that was identical in length to the line on the first card.

All but one member of each group were told to pick one of the two wrong lines on card 2. In addition, the uninformed member of the group was positioned to always be one of the last individuals to respond. Under ordinary circumstances, mistakes on the line selection occur less than 1 percent of the time. However, in this experiment, the uninformed member made the wrong selection in 36.8 percent of the trials. An uninformed member confronted with only a single individual who contradicted the choice continued to answer correctly in almost all trials. When the opposition was increased by two, incorrect responses increased to 31.8 percent.

FIGURE 12.1 Cards in Experiment

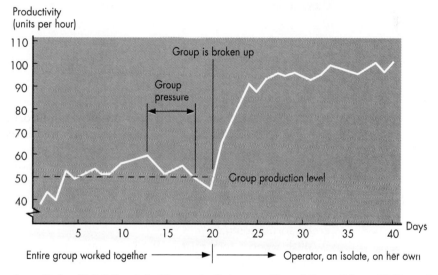

FIGURE 12.2 Effect of Group Norms on an Isolated Member's Productivity

Source: Lester Coch and J. R. P. French, Jr., "Overcoming Resistance to Change," *Human Relations* (1948), pp. 519–20.

The experiment demonstrated that the group's behavior affected the behavior of the individual members; although some individuals remained independent in their judgments, others acquiesced on almost every judgment. Overall, group pressure caused individuals to make incorrect judgments in more than one-third of the cases. The experiment also showed that the larger the number of members who disagreed with the individual, the more likely the individual was to succumb to the judgment of the group.

Lester Coch and John R. P. French conducted a classic study on the influence of groups at Harwood Manufacturing Company, a textile firm in Marion, Virginia.[12] Figure 12.2 illustrates a major finding of their study. In this case, a textile employee started to exceed the group norm of 50 units per day. On the 13th day, the group began to exert pressure on the employee, and she quickly reduced her output to conform to the group norm. On the 20th day, the group was disbanded by moving all group members except this individual to other jobs. Once again, her production quickly climbed to almost double the group norm.

While evidence of conformity abounds in all group situations, some members of groups deviate from group norms and are allowed to do so by group members. Certain members who have made or are making significant contributions to the group's goals are allowed to take some liberties within the group. This phenomenon has been called **idiosyncrasy credit**.[13]

idiosyncrasy credit   Phenomenon that occurs when certain members who have made or are making significant contributions to the group's goals are allowed to take some liberties within the group.

People who contribute a great deal to the group also play a major role in developing group norms. Consequently, the group's norms largely reflect the attitudes of the major givers. This means that those who accumulate the most idiosyncrasy credit do not have to use it; the group norms largely reflect their own attitudes. People who make large contributions to the group are allowed to deviate from the group norms, but they are not likely to do so because of the similarity between their norms and the group norms. Conversely, those members who make little or no contribution to the group must learn to conform to norms they had little or no part in establishing. Conformity therefore may be more difficult for and more rigorously demanded from these members.

Influencing Group Cohesiveness and Conformity

Since managers are now analyzing work performance by groups in different ways than in the past, there may come a time when managers desire to encourage or discourage the formulation of groups. Suggestions for building group cohesiveness include (1) making the group smaller, (2) encouraging agreement with group goals, (3) stimulating competition with other groups, (4) giving rewards to the group rather than to individuals, and (5) isolating the group. To discourage group cohesiveness, the manager can (1) make the group larger (so that contact becomes more difficult), (2) disband the group, (3) give rewards to individuals only, (4) encourage disagreement with group goals, and (5) refrain from isolating the group (mix them with other group formations).[14]

With respect to the issue of conformity, an interesting question is: How do you change it in a positive direction? W. Edwards Deming suggests, through his "system of common cause variation," that people really are different and the manager should explore the reasons for lack of conformity within a group. If an employee consistently outperforms his or her group (as in the example in the previous section), find out why and then develop strategies to raise the group level to the higher performer's level. Conversely, if a worker is consistently performing below the group level, find out why and develop strategies to raise the employee's performance level to that of the group.[15]

Groupthink

Irving Janis describes groupthink as the "deterioration of mental efficiency, reality testing, and moral judgment in the interest of group solidarity."[16] **Groupthink** demands conformity at the expense of critical thinking and good judgment by the group. Members become unwilling to criticize one another or the group, even if the actions of the individual or group are inherently wrong (a common

groupthink   Dysfunctional syndrome that cohesive groups experience that causes the group to lose its critical evaluative capabilities.

characteristic of teenage gangs). Maintaining group solidarity at any expense is a goal, and pressures to conform are enormous. Janis suggests the following symptoms of groupthink: illusions of group invulnerability, rationalizing actions, a belief in group morality (only the group is right, outsiders are wrong), negative stereotyping of outsiders, and application of pressure to deviants within the group.[17] Managers who find that groupthink situations are developing are encouraged to resolve the situation before decision making within the organization becomes myopic and out of focus.

INFORMAL WORK GROUP LEADERSHIP

Generally, two types of leaders exist in organizations. One is the formal or appointed leader (manager) who is assigned to the position by managers at higher levels of the organizational hierarchy; the other, the informal leader, is chosen by the group itself. Each type of leader relies on different sources of authority in performing the role. Note, however, that appointed leaders may or may not be informal leaders.

The leader of an informal group is the one the group sees as being most capable of satisfying its needs. The authority of the leader can be removed, reduced, or increased, depending on the group's perceived progress toward its goals. The leader's authority may also be threatened by the emergence of different or additional objectives.

A simple example of this point follows. Suppose a group of people were shipwrecked on a desolate island. The group's first goal would probably be to ensure their survival by finding food, water, and shelter. The person selected by the group as the leader would be the person the group saw as the one who could best help the group survive. However, after this need was met, other needs would emerge. The need to escape from the island would probably emerge rather quickly. The person first selected as leader may not be perceived as the one most capable of directing attainment of this new goal. In this case, the group might select a new leader. This process of changing leaders might continue, depending on the group's view of its needs. This example shows an elective, or emergent, style of leadership. Under this system, the leader must know the needs of the group and must be seen by the group as being the one most capable of meeting those needs. In other words, the source of authority for the leader of the informal work group is the group being led.

Informal group leadership has been the subject of numerous research studies. Two general conclusions reached regarding informal group leadership are as follows:

1. The individual who emerges as the leader is the one the group perceives as having the most competence in helping the group achieve its objectives.
2. The emergent leader will have strong communication skills, especially in the areas of setting objectives for the group, giving direction, and summarizing information for the group.[18]

Many informal work groups may also require two leaders, a task leader and a social leader. The task leader pushes the group toward the accomplishment of its objectives; the social leader is concerned primarily with maintaining harmony within the group.

TEAM BUILDING IN FORMAL WORK GROUPS

As indicated in previous sections of this chapter, members of informal work groups often develop feelings of loyalty, comradeship, and a common sense of values. Unfortunately, formal work groups sometimes do not develop these characteristics. Helping to develop these characteristics among the members of formal work groups is a key responsibility of management.

Rensis Likert has proposed the *linking-pin concept* to describe management's role in work groups. Likert suggests that an individual's interactions with the organization

FIGURE 12.3   Linking-Pin Concept

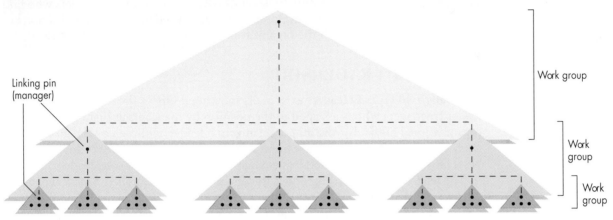

Source: Rensis Likert, *New Patterns of Management* (New York:McGraw-Hill, 1961), p. 104.

should contribute to maintaining a sense of personal worth and importance. Both formal and informal work groups are important sources of satisfaction in maintaining an employee's sense of personal worth and importance. Likert concludes:

> Management will make full use of the potential capacities of its human resources only when each person in an organization is a member of one or more effectively functioning work groups that have a high degree of group loyalty, effective skills of interaction, and high performance goals.[19]

Likert further contends that management should consciously strive to build these types of groups. Managers have overlapping group memberships and link the various formal work groups to the total organization. Thus, the manager is viewed as a linking pin in the organization. Figure 12.3 depicts the linking-pin concept. For an interesting application of this concept, see Management Illustration 12.1.

team building   Process by which the formal work group develops an awareness of those conditions that keep it from functioning effectively and then requires the group to eliminate those conditions.

Building effective formal work groups is often called team building. **Team building** is a process in which the formal work group develops an awareness of those conditions that keep it from functioning effectively and then requires the formal work group to take action to eliminate those conditions.[20]

To build an effective team, the manager must establish a working environment that is seen as being fair and equitable. This cannot be done by one manager alone; all levels of management must contribute. However, if a manager fails to establish this environment in the formal work group, the efforts of higher levels of management will usually be wasted. In addition, employee participation in working out changes and keeping employees informed about what is taking place also help to build an effective team.

An effective manager also attempts to see and understand issues from the employees' point of view. However, the manager needs to be careful here. A manager who always sides with the employees and takes an attitude of "it's us against them" can create a negative environment. The point is not to side with employees against management but to attempt to understand the issues from the employees' point of view. Management Illustration 12.2 addresses the issue of loyalty and team spirit.

The manager should also strive to gain acceptance as the group's leader. Certainly a manager has formal authority that is delegated from higher levels of management. However, formal authority does not guarantee effective team building.

Management Illustration 12.1
Zen and the Art of Teamwork

Former Chicago Bulls coach Phil Jackson has built a career on being different. From his Grateful Dead decal on the lamp in his office to his readings of poetry to his team before playoff games, his approach to management is a philosophy based partly on Zen Buddhism and partly on team building. Team building and Zen Buddhism, according to Jackson, delivered three back-to-back NBA championships to Chicago as of 1995.

When asked the obvious question of what Zen has to do with managing, Jackson replies, "Whether on the court or off, what I call for in my people is full awareness and attention." "That's what Zen is really all about—waking up and being mindful," says the coach. With this philosophy, individuals come to police themselves; they take responsibility for their own actions.

Does this altered consciousness have any benefits? Jackson believes the players (or, in fact, any team members) learn how to subjugate themselves to the needs of the team. Many nights Michael Jordan might score 50 points, but the team might lose. High individual performance but poor team performance is not what winning is all about, whether in professional sports or in business.

To motivate individuals to do their best, Jackson recommends that the manager understand which side of the person to appeal to, materialistic or spiritual. Phil Jackson prefers the spiritual, wherein individuals surrender their own egos, so that the end result is bigger than the sum of its parts. If you can also impress on the team members that they all need to grow for the team to be successful, the sum of the parts is an expanding concept.

Finally, Jackson advocates that the manager create a balance between structure and freedom. Structure provides a foundation so that the individual and the team do not lose their focus, and freedom gives them the ability to act and to create. Picture the difference between five fingers working independently and five fingers working in concert as a hand. Modern managers will learn that by following Jackson's concepts, coordination and action will be the end result and winning will come naturally.

Source: Adapted from Ron Lieber, "Zen and the Art of Teamwork," *Fortune*, December 25, 1995, p. 218. Reprinted by permission of Fortune © 1995 Time, Inc. All Rights Reserved.

For more information about the Chicago Bulls visit their Web site at :www.nba.com/bulls/.

Figure 12.4 summarizes these suggestions for effective team building.

Finally, a relatively new approach to managing work teams is **self-directed work teams (SDWT)**. SDWT are empowered to control the work they do without a formal supervisor. Each SDWT has a leader who normally comes from the employees on the team. Most of these teams plan and schedule their work, make operational and personnel decisions, solve problems, set priorities, determine what employee does what work, and share leadership responsibilities.

self-directed work teams (SDWT) Teams in which members are empowered to control the work they do without a formal supervisor.

QUALITY CIRCLES

One use of a formal work group is the quality circle, which originated in Japan. A **quality circle** is composed of a group of employees (usually from 5 to 15 people) who are members of a single work unit, section, or department. The unit's supervisor or manager is usually included as a member of the quality circle. These employees have a common bond; they perform a similar service or function by turning out a product, part of a product, or a service. Membership in a quality circle is

quality circle Composed of a group of employees (usually from 5 to 15 people) who are members of a single work unit, section, or department; the basic purpose of a quality circle is to discuss quality problems and generate ideas that might help improve quality.

235

Management Illustration 12.2
Secrets to Building Employee Loyalty and Team Spirit

According to Geoffrey Brewer, "Today's employees are mad as hell, and they're not going to take it any more." They are cynical about the future and the promises their employers make to them. Can you blame them? Downsizing, restructuring, or furlough may make good sense to top management and shareholders, but it's a disaster for the security-conscious employee. Performance under these conditions is bound to suffer.

The best companies have found that the surest answer to employee uncertainty is to just be honest. The new statement in the employee manual will probably read, "We can't promise you security; we can only promise you development and rewards and a sense of excitement and self-esteem within the context of a rapidly changing environment. We will help you prepare for the future." Does this make any sense? Surprisingly, it does to many of today's disenchanted employees. What, then, are the secrets that can cause this shift in attitude?

First, set high expectations. Stryker Corporation, a medical equipment company in Michigan, expects each of its division's profits to grow by 20 percent a year. "Winners love this environment," says Stryker's vice president of human resources. Second, communicate constantly. Springfield Remanufacturing Company has a turnover rate of less than 7 percent because all employees understand how they individually affect the profit-and-loss statement. As an employee-based company, the employees decide whether the company succeeds or fails. Third, empower, empower, empower! Hewlett-Packard stresses that its success in recent years is due to its policy of giving employees and teams the right to make decisions without management always looking over their shoulders. Fourth, invest in employees' financial security. Instead of pension funds, give the employees stock. Fifth, recognize people as often as possible. Letting employees know they have done a good job gets more jobs done well. Sixth, counsel employees on their careers. Honeywell constantly gives its employees guidance so that they will always be moving where the jobs of the future will be. Finally, educate employees. Increased education makes an employee more valuable and an employee who is more likely to be retained.

Strong management programs have shown that loyalty and the team spirit it builds are a two-way street—a street that employee and manager alike must travel for a company to succeed in this rapidly changing work environment. Loyalty and team spirit should be more than a phrase or a slogan. It should be a true commitment. As Laura Avakian of Beth Israel HealthCare of Boston says, "It's time for management to sell the organization to [employees]. Loyalty should begin before they even get in the door."

Source: Adapted from Geoffrey Brewer, "Seven Secrets to Building Employee Loyalty," *Performance*, December 1995, pp. 20–27.

For more information on Stryker Corporation visit their Web site at: www.strykercorp.com. For more information on Hewlett-Packard visit their Web site at: www.hp.com. For more information on Honeywell Inc. visit their Web site at: www.honeywell.com.

FIGURE 12.4 Suggestions for Effective Team Building

1. Establish a working environment that employees consider to be fair and equitable.
2. Practice participation: Listen to employees' ideas and get employees involved in planning.
3. Show employees that you, the manager who represents higher levels of management, also see issues from the employees' side.
4. Attempt to gain acceptance as the group's leader.

---

almost always voluntary. The basic purpose of a quality circle is to discuss quality problems and generate ideas that might help improve quality.

A quality circle usually begins by exposing the members to specialized training relating to quality. Meetings of a quality circle are normally held once or twice per

FIGURE 12.5   Potential Benefits of a Quality Control Circle

1. Problems, including some that have existed for years, do get solved.
2. Employees participate in changing things for the better.
3. Employees and managers broaden and develop as they receive special training and put it into practice.
4. Morale improves and is maintained as people become involved in helping to improve their work lives and fulfill their potential.
5. The channel for upward and downward communication is strengthened.
6. Greater trust is built between levels in the organization and among units.
7. Managers are relieved of many worries and concerns without releasing control or having any of their authority diluted.
8. Quality circles are relatively inexpensive to start.
9. Circles can evolve into other forms of employee participation.

Sources: Rich Tewell, "How to Keep Quality Circles in Motion," *Business*, January–March 1982, pp. 48–49; Edward E. Lawler III and Susan A. Mohrman, "Quality Circle after the Fad," *Harvard Business Review*, January–February 1985, pp. 65–71.

month and last for one to two hours. After the initial training, a quality circle begins by discussing specific quality problems that are brought up by either management representatives or the circle members. The circle may call on staff experts as needed. Figure 12.5 outlines the potential benefits of a quality circle. As with other forms of participative management, the underlying objective of quality circles is to get employees actively involved.[21]

Author Tom Peters suggests that U.S.-based management has much to learn from the experts on quality circles.[22] The whole point of the quality circle, according to Peters, is to create an environment where employees constantly talk and compare notes on quality. "Me" becomes "us" in a good quality circle. Since most American workers do not like meetings, the idea of a quality circle has to be "sold" diplomatically.

Summary

1. *Describe Formal and Informal Work Groups.* Formal work groups are established by the organizing function. Their structure and membership are established and recognized by management. Informal work groups result from personal contacts and interactions of people within the organization and are not formally recognized by the organization.

2. *Discuss the Hawthorne Effect.* The Hawthorne effect states that giving special attention to a group of employees (such as involving them in an experiment) changes their behavior.

3. *Define Group Norm.* Group norms are the informal rules a group adopts to regulate and regularize group members' behavior.

4. *Explain Group Cohesiveness.* Group cohesiveness refers to the degree of attraction each member has for the group, or the "stick-togetherness" of the group.

5. *Define Group Conformity.* Group conformity is the degree to which the members of a group accept and abide by the norms of the group.

6. *Outline Conditions under Which Individual Members Tend to Conform to Group Norms.* Members tend to conform to group norms when the norms are congruent with their personal attitudes, beliefs, and behavioral predispositions; when the norms are inconsistent with their personal attitudes, beliefs, or behavioral predispositions but the group exerts strong pressures to comply; and when the rewards for complying are valued or the sanctions imposed for noncompliance are devalued.

7. *Explain Idiosyncrasy Credit.* Idiosyncrasy credit refers to a phenomenon that occurs when certain members of a group who have made or are making significant contributions to the group's goals are allowed to take some liberties within the group.

8. *Define Groupthink.* Groupthink is a dysfunctional syndrome that cohesive groups experience that causes the group to lose its critical evaluative capabilities.

9. *Describe General Conclusions That Can Be Reached Regarding Informal Group Leadership.* The individual who emerges as the leader is the one the group perceives as

having the most competence in helping the group achieve its objectives. The emergent leader will usually have strong communication skills.

10.   *Discuss Suggestions for Effective Team Building.* Suggestions for effective team building include establishing a fair and equitable working environment, practicing participation, seeing issues from the employees' point of view, and gaining acceptance as the group leader.

11.   *Explain self-directed work team.* An SDWT is empowered to control the work they do without a formal supervisor.

12.   *Describe a Quality Circle.* A quality circle is composed of a group of employees (usually from 5 to 15 people) who are members of a single work unit, section, or department and whose basic purpose is to discuss quality problems and generate ideas to help improve quality.

Preview Analysis

1.   How did the U.S. engineer Ron Shriver approach the company's cost problem?

2.   Describe one of the money-saving ideas generated by team spirit at Honda.

Review Questions

1.   Describe a formal work group.
2.   Describe an informal work group.
3.   What is the Hawthorne effect?
4.   What is a group norm?
5.   What is group cohesiveness?
6.   What is group conformity?
7.   What are some suggestions for building group cohesiveness?

8.   Outline the conditions under which individual members of a group tend to conform to group norms.
9.   What is idiosyncrasy credit?
10.   Describe two general conclusions that can be reached regarding informal group leadership.
11.   Explain the linking-pin concept.
12.   What is team building?
13.   What is a self-directed work team?
14.   What is a quality circle?

Skill-Building Questions

1.   Do you think it is possible to eliminate the need for informal work groups? Explain.
2.   Discuss the following statement: "The goals of informal work groups are never congruent with the goals of the formal organization."
3.   Some employees are described as "marching to the beat of a different drummer." In light of the discussion in this chapter, what does this statement mean to you?

4.   Cite one business example and one social example of what you perceive to be "groupthink" mentality.
5.   Why do you think quality circles can be effective?

SKILL-BUILDING EXERCISE 12.1

Characteristics of Effective Work Groups

You have been a member of many groups in your lifetime. Some of these groups include both formal and informal groups. Examples of such groups might include your Sunday school class, your neighborhood playmates when you were younger, your soccer or baseball team, and your co-workers at your summer job. Whether a formal or informal work group, all of us have been members of a group at some time. Some of the groups have been quite effective, and some have been quite ineffective.

Recall the most effective and the most ineffective groups of which you have been a member. Prepare a description of the characteristics of both groups. Be prepared to make a five-minute presentation of these characteristics in class.

SKILL-BUILDING EXERCISES 12.2

Crash Project

You are told that you and your work group have two weeks to implement a new program. You think two weeks are insufficient and you and your employees would have to work around the clock to complete it in that time. Morale has always been high in your group; yet you know some people just don't like overtime. As you think about how best to handle the situation, you consider these alternatives:

1. Tell your group the company is being pretty unreasonable about this. "I don't see what the big rush is. But it's got to be done, so let's all pitch in and help, shall we?"

2. Tell your group that you have told Bob Smith (your boss) you have a superb group of people and, "If anyone in the company could get the job done, we could."

3. Tell the group your job is on the line and if they want you around for a while, they will have to make a heroic effort.

4. Tell your group you don't want to hear any griping. This is the nature of the job, and anyone who thinks he or she can't devote the extra time had better start looking for another job.

5. Tell the group the job must be done and ask them to make suggestions on how it can be completed within the deadline.

Other alternatives may be open to you, but assume these are the only ones you have considered.

WITHOUT DISCUSSION with anyone, decide which of these approaches you would take and be prepared to defend your choice.

CASE INCIDENT 12.1

One of the Gang?

Recently Ruth Brown was appointed as the supervisor of a group of word processors in which she was formerly one of the rank-and-file employees. When she was selected for the job, the department head told her the former supervisor was being transferred because she could not get sufficient work out of the group. He also said the reason Ruth was selected was that she appeared to be a natural leader, she was close to the group, and she knew the tricks they were practicing to restrict output. He told Ruth he believed she could lick the problem and he would stand behind her.

He was right about Ruth knowing the tricks. When she was one of the gang, not only did she try to hamper the supervisor, but she was the ringleader in the group's efforts to make life miserable for her. None of them had anything personal against the supervisor; all of them considered it a game to pit their wits against hers. There was a set of signals to inform the employees the supervisor was coming so that everyone would appear to be working hard. As soon as she left the immediate vicinity, everyone would take it easy. Also, the employees would act dumb to get the supervisor to go into lengthy explanations and demonstrations while they stood around. They complained constantly, and without justification, about materials and the equipment.

At lunchtime, the employees would ridicule the company, tell the latest fast one they had pulled on the super-visor, and plan new ways to harass her. All of this seemed to be a great joke. Ruth and the rest of the employees had a lot of fun at the expense of the supervisor and the company.

Now that Ruth has joined the ranks of management, it is not so funny. She is determined to use her managerial position and knowledge to win the group over to working for the company instead of against it. She knows that if this can be done, she will have a top-notch group. The employees know their stuff, have a very good team spirit, and, if they would use their brains and efforts constructively, could turn out above-average production.

Ruth's former colleagues are rather cool to her now; but this seems natural, and she believes she can overcome it in a short time. What concerns her is that Joe James is taking over her old post as ringleader of the group, and the group is trying to play the same tricks on her that it did on the former supervisor.

Questions

1. Did the company make a good selection in Ruth? Explain.

2. What suggestions would you make to Ruth?

3. Are work groups necessarily opposed to working toward organizational goals? Explain.

CASE INCIDENT 12.2

Talkative Mike

Mike was an exceptionally friendly and talkative man—to the extent that he bothered his supervisor by frequently stopping the whole work crew to tell them a joke or a story. It didn't seem to bother Mike that it was during working hours or that somebody other than his crew might be watching. He just enjoyed telling stories and being the center of attention. The trouble was that the rest of the crew enjoyed him too.

The supervisor had just recently taken over the department, and he was determined to straighten the crew out. He thought he would have no problem motivating such a friendly person as Mike. Because the crew was on a group incentive, the supervisor believed he could get them to see how much they were losing by standing around and talking. But there was no question about it: Mike was the informal leader of the crew, and they followed him just as surely as if he were the plant manager.

Mike's crew produced extremely well. When they worked—and that was most of the time—their output could not be equaled. But the frequent nonscheduled storytelling breaks did bother the supervisor. Not only could that nonproductive time be converted to badly needed production, but they also were setting a poor example for the other crews and the rest of the department.

The supervisor called Mike in to discuss the situation. His primary emphasis was on the fact that Mike's crew could make more money by better using their idle time. Mike's contention was, "What good is money if you can't enjoy it? You sweat your whole life away to rake in money, and then all you've got to show for it is a lot of miserable years and no way of knowing how to enjoy what's left. Life's too short to spend every minute trying to make more money." The discussion ended with Mike promising the group would quiet down; if their production didn't keep up, the supervisor would let him know.

Things did improve for a while; but within a week or so, the old pattern was right back where it had been. The supervisor then arranged to talk with the other members of the crew individually. Their reactions were the same as Mike's. As before, some improvements were noted at first; then the crew gradually reverted to the old habits.

Questions

1. Do you agree with Mike and his group?

2. Does the supervisor really have a complaint in light of the fact that Mike's group produces well above average?

3. If you were the supervisor, what would you do next?

References and Additional Readings

[1]Robert L. Kahn, "In Search of the Hawthorne Effect," in *Man and Work in Society*, ed. Eugene Louis Cass and Frederick G. Zimmer (New York: Van Nostrand Reinhold, 1974), p. 51.

[2]Elton Mayo, *The Human Problems of an Industrial Civilization* (Cambridge, MA: Harvard University Graduate School of Business Administration, 1946).

[3]Daniel A. Wren, *The Evolution of Management Thought*, 4th ed. (New York: John Wiley & Sons, 1994), p. 248.

[4]Florence M. Stone, *The AMA Handbook of Supervisory Management* (New York: American Management Association, 1989), p. 433.

[5]Ibid., pp. 435–36.

[6]Daniel C. Feldman, "The Development and Enforcement of Group Norms," *Academy of Management Review*, January 1984, p. 47.

[7]J. Richard Hackman, "Group Influences on Individuals," in *Handbook of Industrial and Organizational Psychology*, ed. Marvin D. Dunnette (New York: John Wiley & Sons, 1983), p. 1517.

[8]Ibid.

[9]For a further discussion of components of group cohesion, see Joseph P. Stokes, "Components of Group Cohesion: Intermem-

ber Attraction, Instrumental Value, and Risk Taking," *Small Group Behavior*, May 1983, pp. 163–73.

[10]Hackman, "Group Influences," p. 1503.

[11]Solomon Asch, "Opinions and Social Pressure," *Scientific American*, November 1955, pp. 31–34.

[12]Lester Coch and John R. P. French, Jr., "Overcoming Resistance to Change," *Human Relations* (1948).

[13]E. P. Hollander, "Conformity, Status, and Idiosyncrasy Credit," *Psychological Review*, January 1958, pp. 117–27.

[14]James L. Gibson, John M. Ivancevich, and James H. Donnelly, Jr., *Organizations*, 8th ed. (Burr Ridge, IL: Richard D. Irwin, 1994), p. 323.

[15]Brian L. Joiner and Marie A. Gaudard, "Variation, Measurement, and W. Edwards Deming," *Quality Progress*, December 1990, p. 34.

[16]Irving Janis, *Victims of Groupthink: A Psychological Study of Foreign Policy Decisions and Fiascos* (Boston: Houghton Mifflin, 1973), p. 9.

[17]Ibid.

[18]Beatrice Schultz, "Predicting Emergent Leaders: An Exploratory Study of the Salience of Communicative Functions," *Small Group Behavior*, February 1978, pp. 109–14.

[19]Rensis Likert, *New Patterns of Management* (New York: McGraw-Hill, 1961), p. 104.

[20]See Paul E. Brauchle and David W. Wright, "Fourteen Team-Building Tips," *Training & Development Journal*, January 1992, pp. 32–36. Also see Mahmoud Salem, Harold Lazarus, and Joseph Cullen, "Developing Self-Managing Teams: Structure and Performance," *Journal of Management Development* 11 (1992), pp. 24–32.

[21]Everett E. Adam, Jr., "Quality Circle Performance," *Journal of Management*, March 1991, pp. 25–39.

[22]Tom Peters, *Thriving on Chaos* (New York: Alfred A. Knopf, 1987), p. 216.

13

Staffing

LEARNING OBJECTIVES

After studying this chapter, you should be able to:

1. Outline the human resource planning process.

2. Define job analysis, job description, job specification, and skills inventory.

3. Define equal employment opportunity.

4. Describe the recruitment process.

5. Define affirmative action plan.

6. Discuss reverse discrimination.

7. Define tests, test validity, and test reliability.

8. Discuss the different types of employment interviews.

9. Discuss potential problems in the interviewing process.

Chapter Preview

Staffing is not only important at Nike, the world's leading athletic shoe company, it is one of the primary reasons for its success. Founder Phil Knight has encouraged Nike's president, Thomas E. Clarke, to adopt a collaborative management style to allow Nike to go forward in the highly competitive athletic shoe industry by stressing lines of communication, reducing management layers, and facilitating decision making. To succeed, Nike has had to commit itself to reengaging, or jump-starting and reinventing its model for international competition. For example, in the Japanese division, Yukihiro Akimoto was hired to bring a healthy lifestyle to Nike's Japanese employees.

Source: Adapted from Dori Jones Yang, Michael Oncal, Charles Hoots, and Robert Neff, "Can Nike Just Do It?" *Business Week*, April 18, 1994, pp. 86–90.

The staffing function of management involves securing and developing people to perform the jobs created by the organizing function. The goal of staffing is to obtain the best available people for the organization and to develop the skills and abilities of those people. Obtaining the best available people generally involves forecasting personnel requirements and recruiting and selecting new employees. Developing the skills and abilities of an organization's employees involves employee development as well as the proper use of promotions, transfers, and separations. The staffing function is complicated by numerous government regulations. Furthermore, many of these regulations are subject to frequent change.

Unfortunately, many staffing activities have traditionally been conducted by human resource/personnel departments and have been considered relatively unimportant by line managers. However, securing and developing qualified personnel should be a major concern of all managers because it involves the most valuable asset of an organization: human resources.

HUMAN RESOURCE PLANNING

human resource planning (HRP)   Process of "getting the right number of qualified people into the right job at the right time." Also called *personnel planning*.

Human resource planning (HRP), also referred to as *personnel planning*, has been defined as the process of "getting the right number of qualified people into the right job at the right time.[1] Put another way, HRP is "the system of matching the supply of people—internally (existing employees) and externally (those to be hired or searched for)—with the openings the organization expects to have for a given time frame.[2]

HRP involves applying the basic planning process to the human resource needs of the organization. Once organizational plans are made and specific objectives set, the HRP process attempts to define the human resource needs to meet the organization's objectives.[3]

The first basic question addressed by the planning process is: Where are we now? Human resource planning frequently answers this question by using job analyses and skills inventories.

Job Analysis and Skills Inventory

job analysis   Process of determining, through observation and study, the pertinent information relating to the nature of a specific job.
job description   Written statement that identifies the tasks, duties, activities, and performance results required in a particular job.
job specification   Written statement that identifies the abilities, skills, traits, or attributes necessary for successful performance in a particular job.

Job analysis is the process of determining, through observation and study, the pertinent information relating to the nature of a specific job. The end products of a job analysis are a job description and a job specification. A **job description** is a written statement that identifies the tasks, duties, activities, and performance results required in a particular job. The job description should be used to develop fair and comprehensive compensation and reward systems. In addition, the accuracy of the job description can help or hinder recruiters in their efforts to attract qualified applicants for positions within the company. A **job specification** is a written statement that identifies the abilities, skills, traits, or attributes necessary for successful performance in a particular job. In general, a job specification identifies the qualifications of an individual who could perform the job. Job analyses are frequently conducted by specialists from the human resource department. However, managers should have input into the final job descriptions for the jobs they are managing. Figure 13.1 shows the relationship among job analysis, human resource planning, recruitment, and selection.

FIGURE 13.1   Relationship among Job Analysis, Human Resource Planning, Recruitment, and Selection

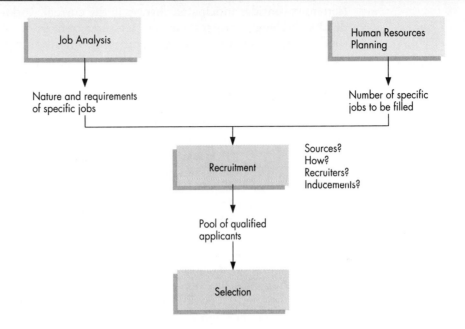

Through conducting job analyses, an organization defines its current human resource needs on the basis of existing and/or newly created jobs. A **skills inventory** consolidates information about the organization's current human resources. The skills inventory contains basic information about each employee of the organization, giving a comprehensive picture of the individual. Through analyzing the skills inventory, the organization can assess the current quantity and quality of its human resources.

skills inventory Consolidates information about the organization's current human resources.

Thomas Patten has outlined seven broad categories of information that may be included in a skills inventory:[4]

1. Personal data history: age, sex, marital status, etc.
2. Skills: education, job experience, training, etc.
3. Special qualifications: memberships in professional groups, special achievements, etc.
4. Salary and job history: present salary, past salary, dates of raises, various jobs held, etc.
5. Company data: benefit plan data, retirement information, seniority, etc.
6. Capacity of individual: scores on tests, health information, etc.
7. Special preferences of individual: location or job preferences, etc.

The primary advantage of a computerized skills inventory is that it offers a quick and accurate evaluation of the skills available within the organization. Combining the information provided by the job analysis and the skills inventory enables the organization to evaluate the present status of its human resources.[5]

Specialized versions of the skills inventory can also be devised and maintained. One example would be the management inventory, which would separately evaluate the specific skills of managers such as strategy development, experiences (e.g., international experience or language skill), and successes or failures at administration or leadership.

In addition to appraising the current status of its human resources, the organization must consider anticipated changes in the current workforce due to retirements, deaths, discharges, promotions, transfers, and resignations. Certain changes in personnel can be estimated accurately and easily, whereas other changes are more difficult to forecast.

Forecasting

The second basic question the organization addresses in the planning process is: Where do we want to go? **Human resource forecasting** attempts to answer this question with regard to the organization's human resource needs. It is a process that attempts to determine the future human resource needs of the organization in light of the organization's objectives. Some of the many variables considered in forecasting human resource needs include sales projections, skills required in potential business ventures, composition of the present workforce, technological changes, and general economic conditions. Due to the critical role human resources play in attaining organizational objectives, all levels of management should be involved in the forecasting process.

human resource forecasting Process that attempts to determine the future human resource needs of the organization in light of the organization's objectives.

Human resource forecasting is presently conducted largely on the basis of intuition; the experience and judgment of the manager are used to determine future human resource needs. This assumes all managers are aware of the future plans of the total organization. Unfortunately, this is not true in many cases.

Transition

In the final phase of human resource planning, the transition, the organization determines how it can obtain the quantity and quality of human resources it needs to meet its objectives as reflected by the human resource forecast. The human resource forecast results in a statement of what the organization's human resource needs are in light of its plans and objectives. The organization engages in several transitional activities to bring its current level of human resources in line with forecast requirements. These activities include recruiting and selecting new employees, developing current and/or new employees, promoting or transferring employees, laying off employees, and discharging employees. Given the current trend of downsizing in many organizations, some human resource departments now maintain a replacement chart for each employee. This confidential chart shows a diagram of each position in the management hierarchy and a list of candidates who would be qualified to replace a particular person should the need arise. Generally, the coordination of all the activities mentioned earlier is delegated to a human resource or personnel department within the organization.

Legal Considerations

Due to discriminatory personnel practices by many organizations, government regulation now plays a vital role in human resource planning. The following paragraphs describe the significant government bills and laws that have affected human resource planning.

equal pay act of 1963 Prohibits wage discrimination on the basis of sex.

title vii of the civil rights act of 1964 Designed to eliminate employment discrimination related to race, color, religion, sex, or national origin in organizations that conduct interstate commerce.

The **Equal Pay Act of 1963,** which became effective in June 1964, prohibits wage discrimination on the basis of sex. The law states, "No employer . . . shall . . . discriminate . . . between employees on the basis of sex by paying wages . . . at a rate less than the rate at which he pays wages to employees of the opposite sex . . . for equal work on jobs the performance of which requires equal skill, effort, and responsibility and which are performed under similar working conditions."[6]

Title VII of the Civil Rights Act of 1964 is designed to eliminate employment discrimination related to race, color, religion, sex, or national origin in organizations that conduct interstate commerce. The 1978 Civil Rights Act Amendment to Title VII prohibits discrimination in employment due to pregnancy, childbirth, or related medical conditions. The act as amended covers the following types of organizations:

1. All private employers of 15 or more people.
2. All educational institutions, public and private.
3. State and local governments.
4. Public and private employment agencies.
5. Labor unions with 15 or more members.
6. Joint labor–management committees for apprenticeship and training.

Congress passed the Civil Rights Act to establish guidelines for ensuring equal employment opportunities for all people. **Equal employment opportunity** refers to the right of all people to work and to advance on the bases of merit, ability, and potential. One major focus of equal employment opportunity efforts has been to identify and eliminate discriminatory employment practices. Such practices are any artificial, arbitrary, and unnecessary barriers to employment when the barriers operate to discriminate on the basis of sex, race, or another impermissible classification.

equal employment opportunity The right of all people to work and to advance on the bases of merit, ability, and potential.

Great strides in promoting diversity have been made since 1964. However, to Debra D. Richards, an African American communications manager for a large insurance company, change has been very slow. "At times, I think we're making progress toward a multi-cultural environment, but on a day to day level, all I have to do is look around me and look at the people in leadership positions," she says. To many people, race and sex still color a supervisor's perception of abilities.[7]

age discrimination in employment act Passed in 1968, initially designed to protect individuals ages 40 to 65 from discrimination in hiring, retention, and other conditions of employment. Amended in 1978 to include individuals up to age 70. Specifically, forbids mandatory retirement at 65 except in certain circumstances.

rehabilitation act of 1973 Prohibits discrimination in hiring of persons with disabilities by federal agencies and federal contractors.

americans with disabilities act (ADA) Gives individuals with disabilities sharply increased access to services and jobs.

The **Age Discrimination in Employment Act** went into effect on June 12, 1968. Initially it was designed to protect individuals 40 to 65 years of age from discrimination in hiring, retention, compensation, and other conditions of employment. In 1978, the act was amended and coverage was extended to individuals up to age 70. Specifically, the act now forbids mandatory retirement at age 65 except in certain circumstances.

The **Rehabilitation Act of 1973** prohibits discrimination in hiring of individuals with disabilities by federal agencies and federal contractors. The **Americans with Disabilities Act (ADA) of 1990** gives individuals with disabilities sharply increased access to services and jobs. Both acts have given citizens with disabilities protection in the workplace and increased opportunities to compete for jobs.

civil rights act of 1991 Permits women, persons with disabilities, and persons who are religious minorities to have a jury trial and sue for punitive damages if they can prove intentional hiring and workplace discrimination. Also requires companies to provide evidence that the business practice that led to the discrimination was not discriminatory but was related to the performance of the job in question and consistent with business necessity.

The **Civil Rights Act of 1991** permits women, minorities, persons with disabilities, and persons who are religious minorities to have a jury trial and sue for punitive damages of up to $300,000 if they can prove they are victims of intentional hiring or workplace discrimination. The law covers all employers with 15 or more employees. Prior to the passage of this law, jury trials and punitive damages were not permitted except in intentional discrimination lawsuits involving racial discrimination. The law places a cap on the amount of damages a victim of nonracial, intentional discrimination can collect. The cap is based on the size of the employer.

A second aspect of this act concerned the burden of proof for companies with regard to intentional discrimination lawsuits. In a series of Supreme Court decisions beginning in 1989, the court began to ease the burden-of-proof requirements on companies. This act, however, requires that companies provide evidence that the business practice that led to the discrimination was not discriminatory but was related to the performance of the job in question and consistent with business necessity.

The results of discrimination are not always as obvious as hiring and firing practices. Communication, managerial and promotional career paths, and networking that are essential to employees' success in the workplace can be also affected by indirect discrimination. Herminia Ibarra found that minority managers had more racially heterogeneous and fewer intimate network relationships, different advancement potential because of different network configurations, fewer high-status ties, and generally fewer career benefits.[8]

Figure 13.2 summarizes the laws related to equal employment opportunity.

PROMOTION FROM INTERNAL AND EXTERNAL SOURCES

An organization that has been doing an effective job of selecting employees has one of the best sources of supply for filling job openings: its own employees. Promotion from within is very popular with growing and dynamic organizations. If internal sources prove to be inadequate, external sources are always available. Though usually more costly and time consuming to pursue, external sources such as employment agencies, consulting firms, employee referrals, and employment advertisements can be valuable resources for an organization. Figure 13.3 summarizes the advantages and disadvantages of using internal and external sources for human resource needs.

With respect to internal promotions, one interesting proposition is the so-called Peter Principle. Proposed by Laurence J. Peter, the **Peter Principle** states that in a hierarchy such as a modern organization, individuals tend to rise to their levels of incompetence.

peter principle Tendency of individuals in a hierarchy to rise to their levels of incompetence.

tence.[9] In other words, people routinely get promoted in organizations and ultimately reach a level at which they are unable to perform. Organizations that maintain tight control in the human resource area, adhere to skills inventories, and conduct careful job analyses can minimize this effect.

RECRUITMENT

recruitment Seeking and attracting a supply of people from which qualified candidates for job vacancies can be selected.

Recruitment involves seeking and attracting a supply of people from which qualified candidates for job vacancies can be selected. The amount of recruitment an organization must do is determined by the difference between the

FIGURE 13.2 Summary of Equal Opportunity Laws

Law	Year	Intent	Coverage
Title VII, Civil Rights Act (as amended in 1972)	1964	Prohibits discrimination based on race, sex, color, religion, or national origin.	Private employers with 15 or more employees for 20 or more weeks per year, educational institutions, state and local governments, employment agencies, labor unions, and joint labor-management committees.
Age Discrimination in Employment Act (ADEA)	1967	Prohibits discrimination against individuals who are 40 years of age and older.	Private employers with 20 or more employees for 20 or more weeks per year, labor organizations, employment agencies, state and local governments, and federal agencies with some exceptions.
Equal Pay Act	1963	Prohibits sexual-based discrimination in rates of pay for men and women working in the same or similar jobs	Private employers engaged in commerce or in the production of goods for commerce and with two or more employees; labor organizations.
Rehabilitation Act (as amended)	1973	Prohibits discrimination against persons with disabilities and requires affirmative action to provide employment opportunity for these individuals.	Federal contractors and subcontractors with contracts in excess of $2,500, organizations receiving federal financial assistance, federal agencies.
Vietnam-Era Veterans Readjustment Assistance Act	1974	Prohibits discrimination in hiring disabled veterans with 30 percent or more disability rating, veterans discharged or released for a service-connected disability, and veterans on active duty between August 5, 1964, and May 7, 1975. Also requires written affirmative action plans for certain employers.	Federal contractors and subcontractors with contracts in excess of $10,000. Employers with 50 or more employees and contracts in excess of $50,000 must have written affirmative action plans.
Pregnancy Discrimination Act (PDA)	1978	Requires employers to treat pregnancy just like any other medical condition with regard to fringe benefits and leave policies.	Same as Title VII, Civil Rights Act.
Immigration Reform and Control Act	1986	Prohibits hiring of illegal aliens.	Any individual or company.
Americans with Disabilities Act	1990	Increases access to services and jobs for persons with disabilities.	Private employers with 15 or more employees.
Civil Rights Act	1991	Permits women, minorities, persons with disabilities, and persons who are religious minorities to have a jury trial and to sue for punitive damages if they can prove intentional hiring and workplace discrimination. Also requires companies to provide evidence that the business practice that led to the discrimination was not discriminatory but was related to the position in question and consistent with business necessity.	Private employers with 15 or more employees.

FIGURE 13.3   Advantages and Disadvantages of Internal and External Sources

Advantages	Disadvantages
Internal	
▲ Morale of Promotee	▲ Inbreeding
▲ Better assessment of abilities	▲ Possible morale problems of those not promoted
▲ Lower cost for some jobs	▲ "Political" infighting for promotions
▲ Motivator for good performance	▲ Need strong management-development program
▲ Causes a succession of promotions	
▲ Have to hire only at entry level	
External	
▲ "New blood" bringing new perspectives	▲ May not select someone who will "fit" the job or organization
▲ Cheaper and faster than training professionals	▲ May cause morale problems for internal candidates not selected
▲ No group of political supporters in organization already	▲ Longer "adjustment" or orientation time
▲ May bring industry insights	

Source: Adapted from R. L. Mathis and J. H. Jackson, *Personnel: Contemporary Perspectives and Applications* (St. Paul, MN: West, 1992). Reprinted by permission from page 210 from *Human Resource Management* 7/e, by Mathis and Jackson. © 1994 by West Publishing Company. All rights reserved.

forecasted human resource needs and the talent available within the organization. After the decision to recruit has been made, the sources of supply must be explored.

Legal Influences

The previously discussed legislation has also had a profound impact on the recruitment activities of organizations. For example, the courts have ruled reliance on "word of mouth" or "walk-in" methods of recruitment to be a discriminatory practice where females and minorities are not well represented at all levels within the organizations.[10]

The Equal Employment Opportunity Commission (EEOC) offers the following suggestions to help eliminate discrimination in recruitment practices:[11]

- Maintain a file of unhired female and minority applicants who are potential candidates for future openings. Contact these candidates first when an opening occurs.
- Utilize females and minorities in recruitment and in the entire human resource process.
- Place classified ads under "Help Wanted" or "Help Wanted, Male–Female" listings. Be sure the content of ads does not indicate any sex, race, or age preference or qualification for the job.
- Advertise in media directed toward women and minorities.
- All advertising should include the phrase "equal opportunity employer."

Research has shown that organizations that are aware of protective legislation and EEOC guidelines are more likely to promote diversity, conform to accepted hiring practices, be identity conscious in their recruitment efforts, and generally go beyond symbolic efforts to improve conditions for protected groups.[12] The diverse workplace is a reality, and growth-oriented companies use that fact as a positive rather than a negative influence on the staffing of their organizations.

SELECTION

The selection process chooses from those available the individuals most likely to succeed in the job. The process is dependent on proper human resource planning and recruitment. Only when an adequate pool of qualified candidates is available can the selection process function effectively. The ultimate objective of the selection process is to match the requirements of the job with the qualifications of the individual.

Who Makes the Decision?

The responsibility for hiring is assigned to different levels of management in different organizations. Often the human resource/personnel department does the initial screening of recruits, but the final selection decision is left to the manager of the department with the job opening. Such a system relieves the manager of the time-consuming responsibility of screening out unqualified and uninterested applicants. Less frequently, the human resource/personnel department is responsible for both the initial screening and the final decision. Many organizations leave the final choice to the immediate manager, subject to the approval of higher levels of management. In small organizations, the owner or the top manager often makes the choice.

An alternative approach is to involve peers in the selection decision. Traditionally, peer involvement has been used primarily with professionals and those in upper levels of management, but it is becoming more popular at all levels of the organization. With this approach, co-workers have an input into the final selection decision.

Legal Considerations in the Selection Process

The selection process has been of primary interest to the government, as evidenced by the number of laws and regulations in effect that prohibit discrimination in the selection of employees. One action frequently required of organizations is the development of an affirmative action plan. An **affirmative action plan** is a written document outlining specific goals and timetables for remedying past discriminatory actions.

affirmative action plan   Written document outlining specific goals and timetables for remedying past discriminatory actions.

All federal contractors and subcontractors with contracts over $50,000 and 50 or more employees are required to develop and implement written affirmative action plans, which are monitored by the Office of Federal Contract Compliance Programs (OFCCP). While Title VII and the EEOC require no specific type of affirmative action plan, court rulings have often required affirmative action when discrimination has been found.

A number of basic steps are involved in the development of an effective affirmative action plan. Figure 13.4 presents the EEOC's suggestions for developing an affirmative action plan.

Organizations without affirmative action plans will find it makes good business sense to identify and revise employment practices that have discriminatory effects before the federal government requires such action. Increased legal action and the record of court-required affirmative action emphasize the advantage of writing and instituting an affirmative action plan. Refer to Management Illustration 13.1 for more information on affirmative action practices in the workplace.

However, the growing number of reverse discrimination suits may have a significant impact on affirmative action programs. **Reverse discrimination** is providing preferential treatment for one group (e.g., minority or female) over another group (e.g., white male) rather than merely providing equal opportunity. The first real test case in this area was the Bakke case

reverse discrimination   Providing preferential treatment for one group (e.g., minority or female) over another group (e.g., white male) rather than merely providing equal opportunity.

FIGURE 13.4   EEOC's Suggestions for Developing an Affirmative Action Plan

1. The chief executive officer of an organization should issue a written statement describing his or her personal commitment to the plan, legal obligations, and the importance of equal employment opportunity as an organizational goal.
2. A top official of the organization should be given the authority and responsibility to direct and implement the program. In addition, all managers and supervisors within the organization should clearly understand their own responsibilities for carrying out equal employment opportunity.
3. The organization's policy and commitment to the policy should be publicized both internally and externally.
4. Present employment should be surveyed to identify areas of concentration and underutilization and to determine the extent of underutilization.
5. Goals and timetables for achieving the goals should be developed to improve utilization of minorities, males, and females in each area where underutilization has been identified.
6. The entire employment system should be reviewed to identify and eliminate barriers to equal employment. Areas for review include recruitment, selection, promotion systems, training programs, wage and salary structure, benefits and conditions of employment, layoffs, discharges, disciplinary action, and union contract provisions affecting these areas.
7. An internal audit and reporting system should be established to monitor and evaluate progress in all aspects of the program.
8. Company and community programs that are supportive of equal opportunity should be developed. Programs might include training of supervisors regarding their legal responsibilities and the organization's commitment to equal employment and job and career counseling programs.

Source: *Affirmative Action and Equal Employment*, vol. 1 (Washington, DC: U.S. Equal Employment Opportunity Commission, 1974), pp. 16–64.

---

of 1978.[13] Allen Bakke, a white male, brought suit against the medical school of the University of California at Davis. He charged he was unconstitutionally discriminated against when he was denied admission to the medical school while some minority applicants with lower qualifications were accepted. The Supreme Court ruled in Bakke's favor, but at the same time upheld the constitutionality of affirmative action programs.

In another case in 1979, the Supreme Court heard a challenge, brought by a white worker, Brian F. Weber, to an affirmative action plan collectively bargained by a union and an employer.[14] This case questioned whether Title VII of the Civil Rights Act of 1964 as amended prohibited private employers from granting racial preference in employment practices. The Court, in a 5-to-2 opinion, held that it did not and that the voluntary quota was permissible. The Weber decision also hinted at the Court's criteria for a permissible affirmative action plan: (1) The plan must be designed to break down old patterns of segregation; (2) it must not involve the discharge of innocent third parties; (3) it must not have any bars to the advancement of white employees; and (4) it must be a temporary measure to eliminate discrimination. However, in a 1989 case (*Martin* v. *Wilks*), the Supreme Court ruled that white employees could bring reverse discrimination claims against court-approved affirmative action plans.[15]

As these examples indicate, human resource managers must stay abreast of legislation and court rulings in this area, because constant changes and revised interpretations appear to be inevitable. For example, recent legislation in states such as Texas and California have been directed at eliminating affirmative action programs in educational institutions.

Management Illustration 13.1
Strategies for Breaking the Glass Ceiling

Equal employment opportunity, affirmative action, discrimination, and "glass ceilings"—what are they all about? They are all about jobs. In 1996, one group that has had difficulty in the above areas is finally starting to make some progress. Specifically, women are being hired and promoted with increasing frequency in computing and information technology positions. What is the secret to advances in these fields? Women agree that a strong network built on business relationships and a dogged confidence in themselves, rather than federal legislation, are the primary reasons.

Women who have succeeded in computing and information technology's management game have tended to work for companies where diversity is appreciated and encouraged (e.g., the financial investment industry, telecommunications, and high-tech components of computing and information technology). Betsy McNeil, vice president of ExecuComp Systems Corporation, says, "In these companies, CEOs are more open-minded and younger, and the opportunities for women are certainly there." "The organizations that value women attempt to cultivate an atmosphere of toleration and appreciation of different communication styles," says Elizabeth Miu-Lan Young, partner in Inter-change Consultants.

Cheryl Currid, consultant and former executive with Coca-Cola, believes that "a woman who becomes a leader overcomes this perception (being fluffy) by holding a deeper knowledge of the technology than any of the people who report to her. To become a CIO, she has to be bilingual enough to translate easily between technology speak and business speak." Simply put, a woman has to work harder and have focus and drive. As an example, one female executive said she attended a workshop made up of 50 percent men and 50 percent women at which the men agreed that the goal for the company should be to increase revenue by 2 percent. The women said they wanted to change the world; anyone can increase revenue by 2 percent!

In the late 1990s, companies are beginning to recognize that a diverse pool of employees is crucial for business survival. Companies that are looking to women as their future leaders tend to value the determination, perspective, and unique communication skills female leaders bring to the table. Overcoming the problems of the "glass ceiling" are necessary for these opportunities to become real.

Lisa Osborne Ross, a representative of the Federal Glass Ceiling Commission, suggests that human resource managers interested in leveling the field for women interested in careers and promotions in the computing and technology fields consider the following strategies for breaking the "glass ceiling":

1. *Look at the bottom line.* The more women and minorities are brought into decision-making roles, the better the bottom line will be in most companies.

2. *Cast a wider net.* Bring in a more diverse pool of talent by going beyond traditional recruiting sources.

3. *Offer more than lip service.* Institute truly effective mentoring and diversity programs.

4. *Vive la différence.* Break the mold of hiring just men.

5. *Offer flexibility.* Offer creative work environments such as flextime and telecommuting policies.

6. *Sponsor corporate women's groups.* Provide a forum whereby women can get professional support, encouragement, and mentoring from their peers.

Source: Adapted from Bronwyn Fryer, "What It Takes," *Women in Computing,* Special Report 1996, pp. 8–11. Reprinted by permission of *Fortune* © 1996 Time, Inc, all rights reserved.

For more information about the "glass ceiling" go to: www.library.unt.edu/info/willis/govdoc/glass.html.

FIGURE 13.5   Steps in the Selection Process

Steps in Selection Process	Possible Criteria for Eliminating Potential Employee
Preliminary screening from application blank, résumé, employer records, etc.	Inadequate educational level or performance/experience record for the job and its requirements
Preliminary interview	Obvious disinterest and unsuitability for job and its requirements
Testing	Failure to meet minimum standards on job-related measures of intelligence, aptitude, personality, etc
Reference checks	Unfavorable reports from references regarding past performance
Employment interview	Inadequate demonstration of ability or other job-related characteristics
Physical examination	Lack of physical fitness required for job
Personal judgment	Intuition and judgment resulting in the selection of a new employeeInadequate demonstration of ability or other job-related characteristics

Selection Procedure

Figure 13.5 presents a suggested procedure for selecting employees. The preliminary screening and preliminary interview eliminate candidates who are obviously not qualified for the job. In the preliminary screening of applications, personnel data sheets, school records, work records, and similar sources are reviewed to determine characteristics, abilities, and the past performance of the individual. The preliminary interview is then used to screen out unsuitable or uninterested applicants who passed the preliminary screening phase.

Testing

tests   Provide a sample of behavior used to draw inferences about the future behavior or performance of an individual.

aptitude tests   Measure a person's capacity or potential ability to learn.

psychomotor tests   Measure a person's strength, dexterity, and coordination.

job knowledge tests   Measure the job-related knowledge possessed by a job applicant.

proficiency tests   Measure how well the applicant can do a sample of the work that is to be performed.

interest tests   Determine how a person's interests compare with the interests of successful people in a specific job.

psychological tests   Attempt to measure personality characteristics.

polygraph tests   Record physical changes in the body as the test subject answers a series of questions; popularly known as "lie detector tests."

One of the most controversial areas of staffing is employment testing. **Tests** provide a sample of behavior that is used to draw inferences about the future behavior or performance of an individual. Many tests are available to organizations for use in the selection process.[16] Tests used by organizations can be grouped into the following general categories: aptitude, psychomotor, job knowledge and proficiency, interests, psychological, and polygraphs.

Aptitude tests measure a person's capacity or potential ability to learn. **Psychomotor tests** measure a person's strength, dexterity, and coordination. **Job knowledge tests** measure the job-related knowledge possessed by a job applicant. **Proficiency tests** measure how well the applicant can do a sample of the work to be performed. **Interest tests** are designed to determine how a person's interests compare with the interests of successful people in a specific job. **Psychological tests** attempt to measure personality characteristics. For an interesting twist on the application of psychological testing, see Management Illustration 13.2. **Polygraph tests,** popularly known as "lie detector tests," record physical changes in the body as the test subject answers a series of questions. By studying recorded

Management Illustration 13.2

Do You Have an EQ?

Are you smart enough to keep your job? In today's marketplace and office suite, IQ and scores on standardized personnel tests may not be enough to ensure security. Daniel Goleman, author of *Emotional Intelligence*, says the EQ or emotional intelligence (the power not only to control our emotions but also perceive them) is extremely important to overall corporate as well as individual success. For example, knowing when to laugh at the boss's jokes, when to trust a co-worker with a confidence, and knowing when someone is on the verge of a nervous breakdown are as important as knowing facts and figures.

Goleman believes EQ has five dimensions: knowing one's own emotions and controlling them; recognizing emotions in others (empathy) and controlling them; and self-motivation. "Empathy—the ability to see life as somebody else sees it—is a fundamental skill of management," according to Goleman. Unlike IQ, which we cannot change very much, EQ is mutable: It can be increased, stimulated, practiced, and perfected.

Since ours is an age of groups, we see that IQ alone may not be the answer to success in management. According to psychologist Robert Sternberg, "When we consider IQ in groups, groups may never work smarter than the members' strengths but the group can certainly work dumber because of friction and in-fighting." Given that the modern executive must master diverse skills in marketing, finance, accounting, and communication to be successful, she or he must also learn how to work emotionally smart, individually and collectively.

Employers have begun to screen for EQ attributes. When asked to come up with a test for measuring EQ, Kaplan Educational Centers generated analogies tests similar to a famous child marshmallow test wherein a child is placed in an isolated environment and told not to eat a marshmallow that is placed before him or her because the child will receive a reward at the end of the test period. The ability to restrain impulse and go for long-term gain was found to be a predictor of eventual academic and SAT success.

A business example of the application of EQ principles and testing includes Met Life's tests for salesperson optimism (high-optimism salespersons sold 37 percent more insurance over a two-year period). New research is under way to formulate key emotional variables that are indicative of success in managerial endeavors. Companies have also recognized that a developed EQ can aid in "reading people's gestures", assisting in problem solving and decision making, and enhancing group and team skills. It has also been found that people who lack particular emotional skills (especially empathy) can degrade group and team skills. If the above ideas are true, the prediction and understanding of EQ may be an even more important tool in the future than human resource managers have suspected.

Source: Adapted from Alan Franham, "Are You Smart Enough to Keep Your Job?" *Fortune*, January 15, 1996, pp. 34–48. For more articles from *Forbes*, visit their Web site at: www.forbes.com.

physiological measurements, the polygraph examiner then makes a judgment as to whether the subject's response was truthful or deceptive.

Employment testing is legally subject to the requirements of validity and reliability. **Test validity** refers to the extent to which a test predicts a specific criterion. For organizations, the criterion usually used is performance on the job. Thus, test validity generally refers to the extent to which a test predicts future job success or performance. The selection of criteria to define job success or performance is a difficult process, and its importance cannot be overstated. Obviously, test validity cannot be measured unless satisfactory criteria exist.

Test reliability refers to the consistency or reproducibility of the results of a test. Three methods are commonly used to determine the reliability of a test. The first method, called test-retest, involves testing a group of people and then retesting them later. The degree of similarity between the sets of scores determines the reliability of

test validity   Extent to which a test predicts a specific criterion.

test reliability   Consistency or reproducibility of the results of a test.

the test. The second method, called parallel forms, entails giving two separate but similar forms of the test. The degree to which the sets of scores coincide determines the reliability of the test. The third method, called split halves, divides the test into two halves to determine whether performance is similar on both halves. Again, the degree of similarity determines the reliability. All of these methods require statistical calculations to determine the degree of reliability of the test.

In the past, organizations have frequently used tests without establishing their validity or reliability. As a result of such practices, testing came under a great deal of attack. The previously discussed Civil Rights Act of 1964 includes a section specifically related to the use of tests:

> nor shall it be an unlawful employment practice for an employer to give and to act upon the results of any professionally developed ability test provided that such a test, its administration, or action upon the results is not designed, intended, or used to discriminate because of race, color, religion, sex, or national origin.[17]

Two Supreme Court decisions have had a profound impact on the use of testing by organizations. First, in the case of *Griggs* v. *Duke Power Company*, the Court ruled that any test that has an adverse impact on female or minority group applicants must be validated as job related, regardless of whether an employer intended to discriminate.[18] In *Albermarle Paper Company* v. *Moody*, the Supreme Court placed the burden on the employer to show that its tests are in compliance with EEOC guidelines for testing.[19]

Finally, in 1978, the EEOC, the Civil Service Commission, the Department of Justice, and the Department of Labor adopted a document titled "Uniform Guidelines on Employee Selection Procedures."[20] These guidelines established the federal government's position concerning discrimination in employment practices. The guidelines explain what private and public employers must do to prove their selection procedures, including testing, are nondiscriminatory.[21]

Polygraph and Drug Testing

Another type of test that can be used for screening job applicants is the polygraph test. The **polygraph,** popularly known as the lie detector, is a device that records physical changes in the body as the test subject answers a series of questions. The polygraph records fluctuations in blood pressure, respiration, and perspiration on a moving roll of graph paper. On the basis of the recorded fluctuations, the polygraph operator makes a judgment as to whether the subject's response was truthful or deceptive.

polygraph   a device that records physical changes in the body as the test subject answers a series of questions.

The use of a polygraph test rests on a series of cause-and-effect assumptions: stress causes certain physiological changes in the body; fear and guilt cause stress; lying causes fear and guilt. The use of a polygraph test assumes that a direct relationship exists between the subject's responses to questions and the physiological responses recorded on the polygraph. However, the polygraph itself does not detect lies; it only detects physiological changes. The operator must interpret the data that the polygraph records. Thus, the real lie detector is the operator, not the device.

Serious questions exist regarding the validity of polygraph tests. Difficulties arise if a person lies without guilt (a pathological liar) or lies believing the response to be true. Furthermore, it is hard to prove that the physiological responses recorded by the polygraph occur only because a lie has been told. In addition, some critics argue that the use of the polygraph violates fundamental principles of the Constitution: the right of privacy, the privilege against self-incrimination, and the presumption of innocence. As a result of these questions and criticisms, Congress passed the Employee Polygraph Protection Act of 1988 that severely restricts the commercial use of polygraph tests. Those exempt from this restrictive law are (1) all local, state, and federal employees (however, state laws can be passed to restrict the use of polygraphs); (2) industries with national defense or security contracts; (3) businesses with nuclear power-related contracts with the Department of Energy; and (4) businesses and consultants with access to highly classified information.

Private businesses are also allowed to use polygraphs under certain conditions: when hiring private security personnel; when hiring persons with access to drugs; and during investigations of economic injury or loss by the employer.

In the past few years, there has also been a proliferation of drug-testing programs. Such programs have been instituted not only to screen job applicants but also to test current employees for drug use. It has been estimated that about 20 percent of the Fortune 500 companies have either instituted drug-testing programs or are contemplating their institution.

Numerous lawsuits have been filed to contest the legality of such programs. Generally, a drug-testing program is on stronger legal ground if it is limited to job applicants. Furthermore, current employees should not be subjected to drug testing on a random basis. A probable cause for drug testing, such as a dramatic change in behavior or a sudden increase in accident rates, should be established before testing. In addition, the results of drug testing should be protected to ensure confidentiality.

Employment Interview

The employment interview is used by virtually all organizations as an important step in the selection process. Its purpose is to supplement information gained in other steps in the selection process to determine the suitability of an applicant for a specific opening in the organization. It is important to remember that all questions asked during an interview must be job related. Equal employment opportunity legislation has placed limitations on the types of questions that can be asked during an interview.

Types of Interviews   Organizations use several types of interviews. The structured interview is conducted using a predetermined outline. Through the use of this outline, the interviewer maintains control of the interview so that all pertinent information on the applicant is covered systematically. Structured interviews provide the same type of information on all interviewees and allow systematic coverage of all questions deemed necessary by the organization. Furthermore, research studies have recommended the use of a structured interview to increase reliability and accuracy.[22]

Two variations of the structured interview are the semistructured and the situational interview. In the semistructured interview, the interviewer prepares the major questions in advance, but has the flexibility to use techniques such as probing to help assess the applicant's strengths and weaknesses. The situational interview uses projective techniques to put the prospective employee in action situations that might be encountered on the job. For example, the interviewer may wish to see how the applicant might handle a customer complaint or observe certain important decision-making characteristics. With either method, however, interviewer bias must be guarded against.

Unstructured interviews are conducted using no predetermined checklist of questions. This type of interview uses open-ended questions such as "Tell me about your previous job." Interviews of this type pose numerous problems, such as a lack of systematic coverage of information, and are very susceptible to the personal biases of the interviewer. This type of interview, however, does provide a more relaxed atmosphere.

Organizations have used three other types of interviewing techniques to a limited extent. The stress interview is designed to place the interviewee under pressure. In the stress interview, the interviewer assumes a hostile and antagonistic attitude toward the interviewee. The purpose of this type of interview is to detect whether the person is highly emotional. In the board (or panel) interview, two or more interviewers conduct the interview. The group interview, which questions several interviewees together in a group discussion, is also sometimes used. Board interviews and group interviews can involve either a structured or an unstructured format.

Problems in Conducting Interviews   Although interviews have widespread use in selection procedures, they can pose a host of problems. The first and one of the most significant problems is that interviews are subject to the same legal requirements of validity and reliability as other steps in the selection process. Furthermore, the validity and reliability of most interviews are questionable. One reason seems to be that it is easy for the interviewer to become either favorably or unfavorably impressed with the job applicant for the wrong reasons.

Several common pitfalls may be encountered in interviewing a job applicant. Interviewers, like all people, have personal biases, and these biases can play a role in the interviewing process. For example, a qualified male applicant should not be rejected merely because the interviewer dislikes long hair on males.

halo effect   Occurs when the interviewer allows a single prominent characteristic to dominate judgment of all other traits.

Closely related is the problem of the **halo effect,** which occurs when the interviewer allows a single prominent characteristic to dominate judgment of all other traits. For instance, it is often easy to overlook other characteristics when a person has a pleasant personality. However, merely having a pleasant personality does not ensure that the person will be a qualified employee.

Overgeneralizing is another common problem. An interviewee may not behave exactly the same way on the job that she or he did during the interview. The interviewer must remember that the interviewee is under pressure during the interview and that some people just naturally become nervous during an interview.

Conducting Effective Interviews   Problems associated with interviews can be partially overcome through careful planning. The following suggestions are offered to increase the effectiveness of the interviewing process.

First, careful attention must be given to the selection and training of interviewers. They should be outgoing and emotionally well-adjusted people. Interviewing skills can be learned, and the people responsible for conducting interviews should be thoroughly trained in these skills.

Second, the plan for the interview should include an outline specifying the information to be obtained and the questions to be asked. The plan should also include room arrangements. Privacy and some degree of comfort are important. If a private room is not available, the interview should be conducted in a place where other applicants are not within hearing distance.

Third, the interviewer should attempt to put the applicant at ease. The interviewer should not argue with the applicant or put the applicant on the spot. A brief conversation about a general topic of interest or offering the applicant a cup of coffee can help ease the tension. The applicant should be encouraged to talk. However, the interviewer must maintain control and remember that the primary goal of the interview is to gain information that will aid in the selection decision.

Fourth, the facts obtained in the interview should be recorded immediately. Generally, notes can and should be taken during the interview.

Finally, the effectiveness of the interviewing process should be evaluated. One way to evaluate effectiveness is to compare the performance ratings of individuals who are hired against assessments made during the interview. This cross-check can serve to evaluate the effectiveness of individual interviewers as well as that of the overall interviewing program.

Personal Judgment

The final step in the selection process is to make a personal judgment regarding which individual to select for the job. (Of course, it is assumed that at this point more than one applicant will be qualified for the job.) A value judgment using all of the data obtained in the previous steps of the selection process must be made in selecting the best individual for the job. If previous steps have been performed correctly, the chances of making a successful personal judgment improve dramatically.

The individual making the personal judgment should also recognize that in some cases, none of the applicants is satisfactory. If this occurs, the job should be redesigned, more money should be offered to attract more qualified candidates, or other actions should be taken. Caution should be taken against accepting the "best" applicant if that person is not truly qualified to do the job.

TRANSFERS, PROMOTIONS, AND SEPARATIONS

The final step in the human resource planning process involves transfers, promotions, and separations. A **transfer** involves moving an employee to another job at approximately the same level in the organization with basically the same pay, performance requirements, and status. Planned transfers can serve as an excellent development technique. Transfers can also be helpful in balancing varying departmental workload requirements. The most common difficulty relating to transfers occurs when a "problem" employee is unloaded on an unsuspecting manager. Training, counseling, or corrective discipline of the employee may eliminate the need for such a transfer. If the employee cannot be rehabilitated, discharge is usually preferable to transfer.

transfer Moving an employee to another job at approximately the same level in the organization, with basically the same pay, performance requirements, and status.

promotion Moving an employee to a job involving higher pay, higher status, and thus higher performance requirements.

separation Voluntary or involuntary termination of an employee.

layoff Occurs when there is not enough work for all employees; employees will be called back if and when the workload increases.

A **promotion** moves an employee to a job involving higher pay, higher status, and thus higher performance requirements. The two basic criteria used by most organizations in promotions are merit and seniority. Union contracts often require that seniority be considered in promotions. Many organizations prefer to base promotions on merit as a way to reward and encourage performance. Obviously, this assumes the organization has a method for evaluating performance and determining merit. An organization must also consider the requirements of the job in question, not just the employee's performance in previous jobs. Success in one job does not automatically ensure success in another job. Both past performance and potential must be considered. This also lessens the probability that the Peter Principle effect will occur.

A **separation** involves either voluntary or involuntary termination of an employee. In voluntary separations, many organizations attempt to determine why the employee is leaving by using exit interviews. This type of interview provides insights into problem areas that need to be corrected in the organization. Involuntary separations involve terminations and layoffs. **Layoffs** occur when there is not enough work for all employees. Laid-off employees are called back if and when the workload increases. A **termination** usually occurs when an employee is not performing his or her job or has broken a company rule. Terminations should be made only as a last resort. When a company has hired an employee and invested resources in the employee, termination results in a low return on the organization's investment. Training and counseling often are tried before firing an individual. However, when rehabilitation fails, the best action is usually termination because of the negative impact a disgruntled or misfit employee can have on others in the organization.

termination   Usually occurs when an employee is not performing his or her job or has broken a company rule.

Summary

1. *Outline the Human Resource Planning Process.* Human resource planning (HRP) is the process of "getting the right number of qualified people into the right jobs at the right time." Once organizational plans are made and specific objectives are set, human resource planning attempts to define the human resource needs to meet the organization's objectives.

2. *Define Job Analysis, Job Description, Job Specification, and Skills Inventory.* Job analysis is the process of determining, through observation and study, the pertinent information relating to the nature of a specific job. A job description is a written statement that identifies the tasks, duties, activities, and performance results required in a particular job. A job specification is a written statement that identifies the abilities, skills, traits, or attributes necessary for successful performance in a particular job. A skills inventory contains basic information about all employees of the organization.

3. *Define Equal Employment Opportunity.* Equal employment opportunity refers to the right of all people to work and to advance on the bases of merit, ability, and potential.

4. *Describe the Recruitment Process.* Recruitment involves the activities of seeking and attracting a supply of people from which to select qualified candidates for job vacancies.

5. *Define Affirmative Action Plan.* An affirmative action plan is a written document outlining specific goals and timetables for remedying past discriminatory actions.

6. *Discuss Reverse Discrimination.* Reverse discrimination is the provision of alleged preferential treatment for one group (e.g., minority or female) over another group (e.g., white male) rather than merely providing equal opportunity.

7. *Define Tests, Test Validity, and Test Reliability.* Tests provide a sample of behavior used to draw inferences about the future behavior or performance of an individual. Test validity refers to the extent to which a test predicts a specific criterion. Test reliability refers to the consistency or reproducibility of the results of a test.

8. *Discuss the Different Types of Employment Interviews.* A structured interview is conducted using a predetermined outline. Unstructured interviews are conducted using no predetermined checklist of questions. In the stress interview, the interviewer assumes a hostile and antagonistic attitude to place the interviewee under stress. In the board (or panel) interview, two or more interviewers conduct the interview. In a group interview, several interviewees are questioned together in a group discussion.

9. *Discuss Potential Problems in the Interviewing Process.* The biggest problem concerns validity and reliability; the interviewer may be legally required to show that the interviewing method used was valid, reliable, and not discriminatory. Second, the interviewer may be favorably or unfavorably impressed with the prospective employee for the wrong reasons and let personal biases enter into his or her judgment of the applicant. Third, the halo effect can cause the interviewer to make judgments based on a dominant favorable characteristic and therefore fail to see the "total" individual. Finally, overgeneralizing can be a problem. The interviewer must remember that the interview is different from the job itself and that the interviewee is likely to be nervous during the interview.

Preview Analysis

1. How would you characterize the "collaborative management" style at Nike?

2. What is meant by the term *reengaging*?

3. What do you think Nike must do to be successful in the next five years?

Review Questions

1. How does staffing relate to the organizing function?
2. What is human resource planning?
3. What is a job analysis? A job description? A job specification? A skills inventory?
4. What is human resource forecasting?
5. Describe a model of the human resource planning process.
6. Describe the purposes of the following government legislation:
   a. Equal Pay Act of 1963.
   b. Civil Rights Act of 1964.
   c. Age Discrimination in Employment Act of 1968, as amended in 1978.
   d. Rehabilitation Act of 1973.
   e. Americans with Disabilities Act of 1990.
   f. Civil Rights Act of 1991.
7. What is equal employment opportunity?
8. Define affirmative action plan.
9. What is recruitment? Describe some sources of recruitment.
10. What is selection? Describe the steps in the selection process.
11. What is test validity?
12. What is test reliability? What methods are commonly used to determine test reliability?
13. Describe two basic types of interviews.
14. Discuss some common pitfalls in interviewing.
15. What is a transfer? A promotion? A separation?

Skill-Building Questions

1. Discuss the following statement: "An individual who owns a business should be able to hire anyone and shouldn't have to worry about government interference."
2. Discuss your feelings about reverse discrimination.
3. Many managers believe line managers should not have to worry about human resource needs and this function should be handled by the human resource department. What do you think?
4. One common method of handling problem employees is to transfer them to another department of the organization. What do you think about this practice?
5. What is EQ? How do you think you might rate on this characteristic? For what types of jobs would a high EQ be useful?

SKILL-BUILDING EXERCISE 13.1

Affirmative Action Debate

Your instructor will break the class into teams of four to five students. Each team should then prepare to debate one of the following statements:

1. The federal government should not require affirmative action programs for private enterprise organizations that are federal contractors or subcontractors.

2. Affirmative action programs have been very helpful to minorities and women. Private enterprise organizations should be required to have affirmative action programs.

After the debate, the instructor will list on the board the points made by each team and discuss the issues involved.

SKILL-BUILDING EXERCISE 13.2

The Layoff

Two years ago, your organization experienced a sudden increase in its volume of work. At about the same time, it was threatened with an equal employment opportunity suit that resulted in an affirmative action plan. Under this plan, additional women and minority members have been recruited and hired.

Presently, the top level of management in your organization is anticipating a decrease in volume of work. You have been asked to rank the clerical employees of your section in the event a layoff is necessary.

Below you will find biographical data for the seven clerical people in your section. Rank the seven people according to the order in which they should be laid off, that is, the person ranked first is to be laid off first, etc.

Burt Green: White male, age 45. Married, four children; five years with the organization. Reputed to be an alcoholic; poor work record.

Nan Nushka: White female, age 26. Married, no children, husband has a steady job; six months with the organization. Hired after the affirmative action plan went into effect; average work record to date. Saving to buy a house.

Johnny Jones: Black male, age 20. Unmarried; one year with organization. High performance ratings. Reputed to be shy—a "loner"; wants to start his own business some day.

Joe Jefferson: White male, age 24. Married, no children but wife is pregnant; three years with organization. Going to college at night; erratic performance attributed to work/study conflicts.

Livonia Long: Black female, age 49. Widow, three grown children; two years with the organization. Steady worker whose performance is average.

Ward Watt: White male, age 30. Recently divorced, one child; three years with the organization. Good worker.

Rosa Sanchez: Hispanic female, age 45. Six children, husband disabled one year ago; trying to help support her family; three months with the organization. No performance appraisal data available.

1. What criteria did you use for ranking the employees?
2. What implications does your ranking have in the area of affirmative action?

CASE INCIDENT 13.1

Accept Things as They Are?

Jane Harris came to work at the S&J department store two years ago. In Jane's initial assignment in the finance department, she proved to be a good and hard worker. It soon became obvious to both Jane and her department head, Rich Jackson, that she could handle a much more responsible job than the one she presently held. Jane discussed this matter with Rich. It was obvious to him that if a better position could not be found for Jane, S&J would lose a good employee. As there were no higher openings in the finance department, Rich recommended her for a job in the accounting department. She was hired.

Jane joined the accounting department as payroll administrator and quickly mastered her position. She became knowledgeable in all aspects of the job and maintained a good rapport with her two employees. A short time later, Jane was promoted to assistant manager of the accounting department. In this job, Jane continued her outstanding performance.

Two months ago, Bob Thomas suddenly appeared as a new employee in the accounting department. Ralph Simpson, vice president of administration for S&J, explained to Jane and Steve Smith, head of the accounting department, that Bob was a trainee. After Bob had learned all areas of the department, he would be used to take some of the load off both Jane and Steve and also to undertake special projects for the department. Several days after Bob's arrival, Jane learned that Bob was the son of a politician who was a close friend of the president of S&J. Bob had worked in his father's successful election campaign until shortly before he joined S&J.

Last week, Steve asked Jane to help him prepare the accounting department's budget for next year. While working on the budget, Jane got a big surprise. She found that Bob had been hired at a salary of $2,400 per month. At the time of Bob's hiring, Jane, as assistant manager of the accounting department, was making only $2,000 per month.

After considering her situation for several days, Jane went to see Ralph Simpson, the division head, about the problem. She told Ralph she had learned of the difference in salary while assisting Steve with the budget and stated it was not right to pay a trainee more than a manager. She reminded Ralph of what he had said several times: that Jane's position should pay $26,000 to $28,000 per year considering her responsibility, but S&J just could not afford to pay her that much. Jane told Ralph that things could not remain as they were at present, and she wanted to give S&J a chance to correct the situation. Ralph told Jane he would get back to her in several days.

About a week later, Ralph gave Jane a reply. He stated that while the situation was unfair, he did not think S&J could do anything about it. He told her that sometimes one has to accept things as they are, even if they are wrong. He further stated that he hoped this would not cause S&J to lose a good employee.

Questions

1. What options does Jane have?
2. What influence, if any, would the federal government have in this case?

CASE INCIDENT 13.2

The Employment Interview

Jerry Sullivan is the underwriting manager for a large insurance company located in the Southwest. Recently, one of his best employers had given him two weeks' notice of her intention to leave. She was expecting a baby soon, and she and her husband had decided she was going to quit work and stay home with her new baby and her other two young children.

Today Jerry was scheduled to start interviewing applicants for this job. The first applicant was Barbara Riley. She arrived at the company's office promptly at 9 A.M., the time scheduled for her interview. Unfortunately, just before she arrived, Jerry received a phone call from his boss, who had just returned from a three-week vacation. He wanted Jerry to bring him up to date on what had been going on. The telephone conversation lasted 30 minutes. During that time, Barbara Riley was seated in the company's reception room.

At 9:30, Jerry went to the reception room and invited her into his office. The following conversation occurred:

Jerry: Would you like a cup of coffee?
Barbara: No, I've already had one.
Jerry: You don't mind if I have a cup, do you?
Barbara: No, go right ahead. *[Jerry pauses, and rings his secretary Dorothy Cannon.]*
Jerry: Dorothy, would you fix me a cup of coffee?
Dorothy: I'll bring it in shortly. You have a call on Line 1.
Jerry: Who is it?
Dorothy: It's Tom Powell, our IBM representative. He wants to talk to you about the delivery date on our new word processor.
Jerry: I'd better talk to him. *[Turning to Barbara.]* I'd better take this call. I'll only be a minute. *[He picks up his phone.]* Well, Tom, when are we going to get our machines?

This phone conversation goes on for almost 10 minutes. After hanging up, Jerry turns again to Barbara to resume the interview.

Jerry: I'm sorry, but I needed to know about those machines. We really do need them. We only have a short time, so why don't you just tell me about yourself.

At that point, Barbara tells Jerry about her education, which includes an undergraduate degree in psychology and an M.B.A., which she will be receiving shortly. She explains to Jerry that this will be her first full-time job. Just then the phone rings, and Jerry's secretary tells him that his next interviewee is waiting.

Jerry: [Turns to Barbara.] Thank you for coming in. I'll be in touch with you as soon as I interview two more applicants for this job. However, I need to ask you a couple of quick questions.
Barbara: OK.
Jerry: Are you married?
Barbara: I am divorced.
Jerry: Do you have children?
Barbara: Yes, two boys.
Jerry: Do they live with you?
Barbara: Yes.
Jerry: The reason I am asking is that this job requires some travel. Will this pose a problem?
Barbara: No.
Jerry: Thanks, and I'll be in touch with you.

Questions

1. Outline the inadequacies of this interview.
2. What information did Jerry learn?
3. What do you think of Jerry's last questions?

References and Additional Readings

[1] C. F. Russ, Jr., "Manpower Systems: Part I," *Personnel Journal*, January 1982, p. 41.

[2] Ibid.

[3] For a description of how Robbins & Meyers, Inc., does human resource planning, see David R. Leigh, "Business Planning Is People Planning," *Personnel Journal*, May 1984, pp. 44–45.

[4] Thomas H. Patten, *Manpower Planning and the Development of Human Resources* (New York: John Wiley & Sons, 1971), p. 243.

[5] For a detailed discussion of skills inventories, see Donald C. Doele and Carlton W. Dukes, "Skills Inventories and Promotion Systems," in *Handbook of Human Resources Administration*, 2d ed., ed. Joseph J. Famularo (New York: McGraw-Hill, 1986), pp. 18–1 through 18–21.

[6] "Equal Pay for Equal Work under the Fair Labor Standards Act," *Interpractices Bulletin* (Washington, DC: U.S. Department of Labor, 1967), Title 29, pt. 800.

[7] Wendy Zellner, "Pioneer: The Race Battle Never Ends," *Business Week*, October 17, 1994, p. 98.

[8] Herminia Ibarra, "Race, Opportunity, and Diversity of Social Circles in Managerial Networks," *Academy of Management Journal* 38, no. 3 (1995), p. 673.

[9]Laurence J. Peter and R. Hall, *The Peter Principle* (New York: Bantam Books, 1969). See also Laurence J. Peter, *Why Things Go Wrong* (New York: William Morrow and Company, 1985).

[10]*Parham* v. *Southwestern Bell Telephone Company*, 433 F2d 421 (8th Cir. 1970).

[11]*Affirmative Action and Equal Employment*, vol. 1 (Washington, DC: U.S. Equal Employment Opportunity Commission, 1974), pp. 30–31.

[12]Alison M. Konrad and Frank Linnehan, "Formalized HRM Structures: Coordinating Equal Employment Opportunity or Concealing Organizational Practices?" *Academy of Management Journal* 38, no. 3 (1995), p. 787.

[13]*University of California Regents* v. *Bakke*, 483 U.S. 265 (1978).

[14]*United Steelworkers* v. *Weber*, 99 S. Ct. 2721 (1979).

[15]*Martin* v. *Wilks*, 104 LEd 2d. 835.

[16]For a detailed description of a large number of tests, see *Tests and Reviews* (Highland Park, NJ: Gryphon Press, 1974).

[17]Title VII, Section 703(h), Civil Rights Acts of 1964.

[18]*Griggs* v. *Duke Power Company*, U.S. Supreme Court (1971).

[19]Thaddeus Holt, "A View from Albermarle," *Personnel Psychology*, Spring 1977, p. 71. Also see "EEOC Guidelines on Employment Testing," *Federal Register*, August 1, 1970, p. 12333.

[20]"Uniform Guidelines on Employee Selection Procedures," *Federal Register*, August 25, 1978, pp. 38290–315.

[21]For a more in-depth discussion of the current state of testing, see Dale Yoder and Paul D. Staudohar, "Testing and EEO: Getting Down to Cases," *Personnel Administrator*, February 1984, pp. 67–74.

[22]E. D. Pursell, M. A. Champion, and S. R. Gaylord, "Structured Interviewing: Avoid Selection Problems," *Personnel Journal*, November 1980, p. 908.

14

Developing Employees and Managers

LEARNING OBJECTIVES

After studying this chapter, you should be able to:

1. Define human asset accounting.

2. Describe the orientation process.

3. Define training.

4. Define needs assessment.

5. Discuss vestibule training, apprenticeship training, and computer-based instruction.

6. List and define the most popular methods of management development.

7. Describe an assessment center.

8. List the steps involved in the evaluation of training and management development.

U.S. corporations spent roughly $51 billion on formal training programs in 1995. Organizations are quickly learning that training programs are essential in developing the desired skills and attitudes necessary for the success of corporate initiatives.

In 1992, the American Society for Training and Development (ASTD) awarded Arthur Andersen Worldwide Organizations the top prize for its successful training program. While the Clinton Administration recently recommended that 1.5 percent of corporate revenues be dedicated to the education of employees, Andersen invests about $300 million—roughly 6 percent—of its annual revenues to formal training.

That money helped build four Centers for Professional Education around the world. At these education centers, new employees must complete 570 hours of general and specific training that combine formal classes, multimedia computer programs, job assignments, and informal networking sessions. This training constitutes what is referred to as a "major." The employees then undergo an additional 200 training hours in a "minor," which is industry specific and supplements the major. Executives at Andersen claim that the extensive training ensures that the quality of service is rendered uniform worldwide.

Source: "Five Top Corporate Training Programs," *Successful Meetings* February 1995, pp. 56–62.

On an organization's balance sheet, such factors as cash, buildings, and equipment are listed as assets. One asset that is not listed is the value of the organization's human resources. However, businesses make huge investments in recruiting, hiring, training, and developing their human resources. **Human asset accounting** involves determining and recording the value of an organization's human resources in its statement of financial condition.[1] Although human asset accounting is not an acceptable accounting practice for tax or financial reporting purposes, it does recognize that the quality of an organization's human resources is an important asset.

human asset accounting   Determining and recording the value of an organization's human resources in its statement of financial condition.

HUMAN RESOURCE DEVELOPMENT STRUCTURE

Enhancing the quality of an organization's human resources involves many activities. Newly hired employees must be introduced to the organization and to their jobs. They must be trained to perform their jobs. Employee assistance and union relations (if applicable) must be planned and managed. Also, current employees must regularly have their skills updated and must learn new skills. A business must also be concerned about developing the skills of its management team. Developing employee skills is a key managerial responsibility.

FIGURE 14.1   Human Resource Wheel

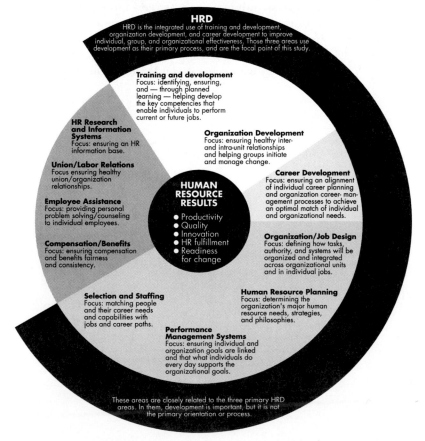

Source: Adapted from P. A. McLagan, "Models for HRD Practice," *Training and Development Journal* 41 (1989), p. 53.

As Figure 14.1 shows, the human resource development process has many steps and functions. Most of these steps are not independent or mutually exclusive tasks. Instead, in the rapidly changing organization of the 1990s, the human resource department is a blend of all the needs that affect the company's workforce. The human resource department is at the heart of many important managerial decisions because of the increasing reliance on the department's skills in understanding, training, and providing tools with which to build and maintain a competitive workforce.

ORIENTATION

orientation   Introduction of new employees to the organization, their work units, and their jobs.

Orientation is the introduction of new employees to the organization, their work units, and their jobs. Orientation comes from co-workers and the organization. The orientation from co-workers is usually unplanned and unofficial, and it can provide the new employee with misleading and inaccurate information. This is one reason it is important that the organization provide an orientation. An effective orientation program has an immediate and lasting impact on the new employee and can make the difference between a new employee's success or failure.[2]

Job applicants get some orientation to the organization even before they are hired. Sometimes the orientation comes through the organization's reputation: how it treats employees and the types of products or services it provides. Also, during the selection process, applicants often learn about other general aspects of the organization and what their duties, working conditions, and pay will be. Commonly cited objectives of company orientation programs are (1) reduction of new employee stress, (2) lower start-up costs of integrating the new employee into the organization, (3) eventual reduction of turnover due to failure to understand the rules and culture of the organization, (4) reduced time required to integrate the employee into the job, and (5) helping the employee adjust to his or her work team or work environment more quickly.

After the employee is hired, the organization's formal orientation program begins. For all types of organizations, orientation usually should be conducted at two distinct levels:

1. General organizational orientation: presents topics of relevance and interest to all employees.
2. Departmental and job orientation: covers topics unique to the new employee's specific department and job.

Normally, the general orientation is given by the human resource department. Departmental and job orientation are generally handled by the new employee's manager. Each new employee should receive a kit or packet of information to supplement the general organizational orientation program. This **orientation kit** is usually prepared by the human resource department and provides a wide variety of materials. It should be designed with care and provide only essential information. The orientation kit may include the following:

orientation kit   Normally prepared by the human resource department, provides a wide variety of materials to supplement the general organizational orientation.

- Organizational chart.
- Map of the organization's facilities.
- Copy of policy and procedures handbook.
- List of holidays and fringe benefits.
- Copies of performance appraisal forms and procedures.
- Copies of other required forms (e.g., expense reimbursement form).

- Emergency and accident prevention procedures.
- Sample copy of company newsletter or magazine.
- Telephone numbers and locations of key company personnel (e.g., security).
- Copies of insurance plans.

Many organizations require employees to sign a form stating they have received and read the orientation kit. In unionized organizations, this protects the company if a grievance arises and the employee claims not to be aware of certain company policies and procedures. It is equally important that a form be signed in nonunionized businesses, particularly in light of an increase in wrongful discharge litigation. Whether signing a form actually encourages new employees to read the orientation kit is questionable, however.

Orientations do pose some difficulties. Commonly cited problems include information overload for the new employee, too much paperwork, unnecessary information, too much "selling" of the organization, lack of support of existing employees (e.g., seasoned co-workers telling new employees not to listen to the company line), lack of a long-term orientation (many orientations are done in only one day), lack of accurate follow-up, and failure to correct weaknesses in the orientation program. Reducing these difficulties is a real challenge for the human resource department.

Organizations should realize that the orientation, whether from co-workers or from the organization, will have a strong impact on the performance of new employees. Thus, it is in the company's best interest to have a well-planned, well-executed orientation program.[3]

TRAINING EMPLOYEES

training   Acquiring skills or learning concepts to increase the performance of employees.

Training involves the employee acquiring skills or learning concepts to increase his or her performance. Generally, the new employee's manager has primary responsibility for training in how to perform the job. Sometimes this responsibility is delegated to a senior employee in the department. Regardless, the quality of this initial training can greatly influence the employee's job attitude and productivity.

Economic, social, technological, and governmental changes also influence the skills an organization needs. Changes in these areas can make current skills obsolete in a short time. Also, planned organizational changes and expansions can make it necessary for employees to update their skills or acquire new ones. Management Illustration 14.1 demonstrates the importance of retraining employees.

Needs Assessment

Training must be directed toward the accomplishment of some organizational objective, such as more efficient production methods, improved quality of products or services, or reduced operating costs. This means an organization should commit its resources only to those training activities that can best help in achieving its objec-

needs assessment   Systematic analysis of the specific training activities a business requires to achieve its objectives.

tives. **Needs assessment** is a systematic analysis of the specific training activities a business requires to achieve its objectives. In general, a needs assessment can be conducted in three ways: organizational analysis, functional unit or departmental analysis, and individual employee analysis.

At the organizational level, records on absenteeism, turnover, tardiness, and accident rates provide objective evidence of problems within the organization. When

Management Illustration 14.1
Training and the Turnaround Entrepreneur

In 1995, Joanna Lau was voted *Inc.* magazine's Turnaround Entrepreneur of the Year, an award given to an individual whose management, training, and leadership skills have resurrected or repositioned a declining company. Lau was a 30-year-old General Electric–bred engineer looking for a manufacturing operation she could run on her own when she did a management case study on Bowmar/ALI for her M.B.A. studies. This small subsidiary of Bowmar Instrument Corporation had fallen on hard times and had been milked of its earnings by the parent company (losses of $1.5 million on sales of $7 million). Instead of seeing failure, Lau saw opportunity.

With some rather creative financing, family loans, minority grants, and a lot of courage, she persuaded 24 of the company's 60 employees to join her in buying the company. Once this was done, the new owners, under Lau's leadership, set about reinventing the company. The first step in resurrecting the company and pursuing highly competitive defense contracts was to cross-train the owner-employees so that smaller was actually better. Lau's idea was that the more that you knew about your peers' jobs, the more contribution and teamwork would occur. She was right. New confidence and dedication quickly followed.

Once that confidence had been restored in the employees, she set about restoring suppliers' and the Defense Department's confidence in the now renamed Lau Technologies. After touring the plant, contractors and customers were impressed with the owner-employees' commitment to total quality and training. Business began to build.

In five years, revenues have grown from $7 million to $60 million and losses of $1.5 million have become profits of $2.7 million. Lau's company was one of the first to answer the speed-up production call during the Gulf War. Her training procedures allowed the company to set up 24-hour production with 70 new temporary workers (all of whom could be trained quickly because of the previous cross-training commitment on the part of the company). Having your workers also be owners revives the "can do" spirit necessary for intense growth periods.

By supplying a critical component for the Bradley fighting vehicle, Lau Technologies greatly aided the manufacturing and distribution process that enabled many of these vehicles to be rushed to the battle theater. The company received the U.S. Army Contractor Excellence Award for doing a job in 10 weeks that normally would have taken a year. At Lau Technologies, employees were empowered to be owners, managers, and workers, all wearing the same hat. Training and commitment provided the additional ingredients that ensured the success of this up-and-coming company.

Source: Adapted with permission from Leslie Brokaw, "Case In Point," *Inc.*, December 1995, pp. 88–92. © 1995 by Goldhirsh Group, Inc., 38 Commercial Wharf, Boston, MA 02110.

For more information about Lau Technologies visit their Web site at: www.lautechnologies.com.

problems occur, these records should be examined carefully to determine if the problems could be partially resolved through training. Employee attitude surveys can also be used to uncover training needs at both the organizational and functional unit levels. Normally, most organizations bring in an independent party to conduct and analyze the survey.

Consumer or customer surveys can also indicate problem areas that may not be obvious to the employees of the organization. Responses to a customer survey may indicate areas of training for the organization as a whole or within functional units of the organization.

A popular approach to planning the assessment process includes the following steps:

1. Define the objectives of the assessment process (what is the purpose?).
2. Identify data necessary to conduct the assessment.

3. Select a method for gathering the data (questionnaires, interviews, surveys, etc.).
4. Gather the data.
5. Analyze and verify the data.
6. Prepare a final report.[4]

These steps may be customized to fit the individual needs of the company, but a plan always helps to produce favorable results.

Establishing Training Objectives

After training needs have been determined, objectives must be established for meeting these needs. Unfortunately, many organizational training programs have no objectives. "Training for training's sake" appears to be the maxim. This philosophy makes it virtually impossible to evaluate the strengths and weaknesses of a training program.

Effective training objectives should state what the organization, department, or individual is to be like when the training is completed. The outcomes should be in writing. Training objectives can be categorized as follows:

1. Instructional objectives:
   - What principles, facts, and concepts are to be learned in the training programs?
   - Who is to be taught?
   - When are they to be taught?
2. Organizational and departmental objectives:
   - What impact will the training have on organizational and departmental outcomes, such as absenteeism, turnover, reduced costs, and improved productivity?
3. Individual performance and growth objectives:
   - What impact will the training have on the behavioral and attitudinal outcomes of the individual trainee?
   - What impact will the training have on the personal growth of the individual trainee?

When clearly defined objectives are lacking, it is impossible to evaluate a program efficiently. However, sound training objectives can usually unlock the potential of the employee by identifying skill deficiencies and developmental opportunities, making good performance better, overcoming skill deficits, and helping the employee prepare for the future.[5]

Methods of Training

Several methods can be used to satisfy the organization's training needs and accomplish its objectives. Some of the more commonly used methods include on-the-job training, job rotation, vestibule training, apprenticeship training, classroom training, and computer-assisted instruction. As Figure 14.2 indicates, multimedia and visual approaches to training are gaining in popularity, according to a survey conducted by *Training* magazine.

FIGURE 14.2   Percentage of Organizations Using Various Methods for Employee Training

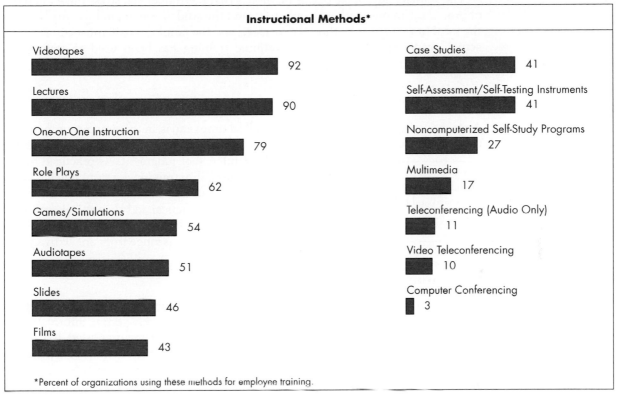

Instructional Methods*

Method	Percent
Videotapes	92
Lectures	90
One-on-One Instruction	79
Role Plays	62
Games/Simulations	54
Audiotapes	51
Slides	46
Films	43
Case Studies	41
Self-Assessment/Self-Testing Instruments	41
Noncomputerized Self-Study Programs	27
Multimedia	17
Teleconferencing (Audio Only)	11
Video Teleconferencing	10
Computer Conferencing	3

*Percent of organizations using these methods for employee training.

Source: Adapted from B. Filipczak, "What Employers Teach," *Training* 29, no. 10 (1992) p. 46. Reprinted with permission. © 1992 Lakewood Publications, Minneapolis, MN. All rights reserved.

On-the-Job Training and Job Rotation

on-the-job training (OJT)   Normally given by a senior employee or supervisor, training in which the trainee is shown how to perform the job and allowed to do it under the trainer's supervision.

On-the-job training (OJT) is normally given by a senior employee or supervisor. The trainee is shown how to perform the job and allowed to do it under the trainer's supervision.

One form of on-the-job training is *job rotation* (sometimes called *cross-training*). In job rotation, an employee learns several different jobs within a work unit or department and performs each job for a specified period. One main advantage of job rotation is that it allows flexibility in the department. For example, when one member of a work unit is absent, another can perform that job.

One advantage of OJT is that it requires no special facilities. Also, the new employee does productive work during the learning process. A major disadvantage is that the pressures of the workplace can cause training to be haphazard or neglected.

Vestibule Training

vestibule training   System in which procedures and equipment similar to those used in the actual job are set up in a special working area called a vestibule.

In **vestibule training,** procedures and equipment similar to those used in the actual job are set up in a special working area called a *vestibule.* The trainee is then taught how to perform the job by a skilled person and is able to learn the job at a comfortable pace without the pressures of production schedules.

The primary advantage of this method is that the trainer can stress theory and use of proper techniques rather than output, and the student can learn by actually doing the job. However, this method is expensive, and the employee still must adjust to the actual production environment. Vestibule training has been used to train word processor operators, bank tellers, clerks, and others in similar jobs.

Apprenticeship Training

Apprenticeship training dates back to biblical times and is, in the simplest terms, training in those occupations requiring a wide and diverse range of skills and knowledge as well as independence of judgment. As practiced by organizations, **apprenticeship training** is a system in which an employee is given instruction and experience, both on and off the job, in all of the practical and theoretical aspects of the work required in a skilled occupation, craft, or trade. Most apprenticeship programs range from one to five years.

apprenticeship training System in which an employee is given instruction and experience, both on and off the job, in all of the practical and theoretical aspects of the work required in a skilled occupation, craft, or trade.

Classroom Training

Classroom training is conducted off the job and is probably the most familiar method of training. Classroom training is an effective means of quickly getting information to large groups with limited or no knowledge of the subject being presented. It is useful for teaching actual material, concepts, principles, and theories. Portions of orientation programs, some aspects of apprenticeship training, and safety programs are usually presented with some form of classroom instruction. However, classroom training is used more frequently for technical, professional, and managerial employees. The most common classroom methods used for the general workforce are lecture, discussion, audiovisual methods, experiential methods, and computer-based training.

The lecture method is the simplest and least costly. A lecturer gives an oral presentation on a subject to an audience. The primary problems concern the skill of the lecturer and the ability of the audience to listen effectively. The lecture method is more effective when discussion is not only allowed but encouraged.

If expertise or lecture skills are lacking, audiovisual techniques can bring outside experts to the classroom via video or film. The method is most effective if a moderator allows periodic discussion or hands-on demonstration to complement the audiovisual presentation.

Occasionally, experiential methods, such as case studies or role playing, are effective for the general workforce. Though most commonly associated with management training, this method usually emphasizes creative thinking, problem solution, and human behavior skills.

computer-based training Training that allows the trainee to absorb knowledge from a preset computer program and advance his or her knowledge in a self-paced format.

Computer-based training allows the employee to absorb information from a preset computer program and advance his or her knowledge in a self-paced format. This method is more effective than the old workbook method of answering questions, but it requires the use and understanding of computer equipment. Highly technical and computer-based manufacturing processes lend themselves to this method. The advantages of being able to use the full capabilities (especially the visually attractive CD-ROM feature) of the computer for learning usually outweigh the disadvantages associated with limited computer skills. One growing method of training is Internet-based training.

Making Training Meaningful

To make all types of training more meaningful, a manager should avoid several common pitfalls. Lack of reinforcement is one. An employee who is praised for doing a job well is likely to be motivated to do it well again. Praise and recognition can very effectively reinforce an employee's learning. Feedback regarding progress is critical to effective learning. Setting standards for trainees and measuring performance against the standards encourage learning.

The adage "practice makes perfect" definitely applies to the learning process. Too many managers try to explain the job quickly, then expect the person to do it perfectly the first time. Having trainees perform a job or explain how to perform it focuses their concentration and enhances learning. Repeating a job or task several times also helps. Learning is always aided by practice and repetition.

Managers sometimes also have preconceived and inaccurate ideas about what certain people or groups of people can or cannot do. A manager should realize that different people learn at different rates. Some learn rapidly; some learn more slowly. A manager should not expect everyone to "catch on" to the job right away. The pace of the training should be adjusted to the trainee. Also, a person who is not a fast learner will not necessarily always be a poor performer. The manager should take the attitude that all people can learn and want to learn.

Author Tom Peters believes modern managers should "train everyone—lavishly." A prescription for success is to model the company's training program after successful companies such as IBM (where every employee spends at least 40 hours per year in the classroom), Disney (where all employees are trained as though they will be career employees), or Nissan (which spent an estimated $63 million on training workers when it opened a new plant). Peters believes successful corporations have learned that employees will be more effective and loyal when they receive high-quality and up-to-date training.[6]

MANAGEMENT DEVELOPMENT

management development   Process of developing the attitudes and skills necessary to become or remain an effective manager.

Management development is concerned with developing the attitudes and skills necessary to become or remain an effective manager. To succeed, it must have the full support of the organization's top executives. Management development should be designed, conducted, and evaluated on the basis of the objectives of the organization, the needs of the managers involved, and probable changes in the organization's management team.

Needs Assessment

Numerous methods have been proposed for use in assessing management development needs. The management development needs of any organization are composed of the aggregate, or overall, needs of the organization and the development needs of each manager within the organization.

Organizational Needs   The most common method for determining organizational management development needs is an analysis of problem areas within the organization. For example, increases in the number of grievances or accidents within an area of the organization often signal the need for management development. High turnover rates, absenteeism, or tardiness may also indicate management development needs. Projections based on the organization's objectives and on changes in

Management Illustration 14.2

Success Is No Mystery—It's Simply a Matter of Discipline

Motivational speaker Jim Rohn has a consistent theme in his presentations to managers. "Either you design your future or somebody else will design it for you," says Rohn. He should know. When he was 25 with only pennies in his pocket, Rohn discovered that his philosophy was all wrong. "I was preventing myself from succeeding and I needed to adopt new disciplines for sharpening my skills and goals," says this now millionaire management success guru.

Rohn swims against the positive-thinking success school and teaches a tough-love formula. There are no quick and easy answers to managerial development and prosperity. There are, however, new disciplines that will pave the way up if one works hard enough at expanding one's talents and those of one's peers (after all, success in business is a team effort in many cases). "We cannot change circumstances," says Rohn, "we can only change ourselves and what we do."

How do we change, and what new disciplines should become part of our critical thinking? Jim Rohn suggests the following:

1. *Expand your guidance system.* Your guidance system is like your philosophy. Learn from books, seminars, other people's experiences to discard errors we have been making, or you will stay stuck with the system you were handed. Change must be constant. Change must have purpose.

2. *Use disgust as a personal motivator.* Disgust is a powerful motivator. If you are truly disgusted with a current personal or business situation, you can change it with an adherence to discipline.

3. *See the truth about your true condition.* Don't delude yourself. If you are unhappy with your performance, recognize the need to adopt new disciplines to change your life (adopt health over smoking, for example).

4. *Try new things.* Discipline is trying things that lead to progress. The more you learn and train, the more you grow.

5. *Don't see rest as an objective.* The true business objective is productivity; rest is what is earned after the objective is accomplished. Rest is a reward, not an objective.

6. *Decide what you want, write it down, and check off progress (no matter how small) toward the objective.* Progress is made one step at a time. Mentally see yourself accomplishing the objective.

7. *The twin killers of success are greed and impatience.* Have the discipline not to give in to them. Work toward something that serves others. By helping enough people get what they want, you will get what you want. Also, remember that it takes time to reach a worthy objective. Be patient.

Rohn finishes his thoughts to aspiring executives who seek development and inspiration in their lives by reminding them that anybody can take steps toward success. Success isn't magical, mysterious, or profound. It's easy if one adds disciplines (new thoughts or experiences), accomplishes small objectives on the path to larger ones, and works hard to grow and change.

Source: Adapted from Robert McGarvey, "Just Do It," *Entrepreneur*, January 1996, pp. 142–47. Reprinted with permission.

For more articles from *Entrepreneur* magazine, visit their Web site at: www.EntrepreneurMag.com.

its management team are also used to determine overall management development needs. Undertaking new business ventures, increased competitive threat (new competitors with new strategies), and a revised corporate vision or mission all usually call for a reevaluation of current management development. Top management must move forward through constant training, or it will begin to move backward and will lose its competitive edge that is so critical to successful business operation.

Needs of Individual Managers   The performance of the person is the primary indicator of individual development needs. Performance evaluations of each manager should be examined to determine areas that need strengthening. The existence of problem situations within a manager's work unit can also signal needs. Planned promotions or reassignments also often indicate the need for development. Outside motivators and consultants often can assist with the personal development and growth of the manager. Management Illustration 14.2 gives an example of the power of self-development.

Establishing Management Development Objectives

After the management development needs of the organization have been determined, objectives for the overall management development program and for individual programs must be established to meet those needs. Both types of objectives should be expressed in writing and should be measurable. As mentioned earlier in this chapter, training objectives can be categorized within three broad areas: instructional, organizational and departmental, and individual performance and growth. This categorization scheme can also be used for management development objectives.

Instructional objectives might incorporate targets relating to the number of trainees to be taught, hours of training, cost per trainee, and time required for trainees to reach a standard level of knowledge. Furthermore, objectives are needed for the principles, facts, and concepts to be learned in the management development program(s). Organizational and departmental objectives are concerned with the impact the programs will have on organizational and departmental outcomes, such as absenteeism, turnover, safety, and number of grievances. Individual and personal growth objectives relate to the impact on the behavioral and attitudinal outcomes of the individual. They may also relate to the impact on the personal growth of the individuals involved in the programs.

After the overall management development objectives have been established, individual program objectives must be identified that specify the skills, concepts, or attitudes that should result. After these objectives are developed, course content and method of instruction can be specified. Figure 14.3 shows the relationship among needs assessment, objectives, identification of overall management development objectives, and identification of objectives for each individual management development program.

METHODS USED IN MANAGEMENT DEVELOPMENT

After the company's needs have been assessed and its objectives stated, management development programs can be implemented. This section examines some of the more frequently used methods of management development. As with employee training, management development can be achieved both on and off the job. Figure 14.4 summarizes some of the more commonly used methods of management development.

Understudy Assignments

Generally, *understudy assignments* are used to develop an individual's capabilities to fill a specific job. An individual who will eventually be given a particular job works for the incumbent. The title of the heir to the job is usually assistant manager, administrative assistant, or assistant to a particular manager.

The advantage of understudy assignments is that the heir realizes the purpose of the training and can learn in a practical and realistic situation without being directly

FIGURE 14.3   Relationship between Needs Assessment and Objectives in Management Development

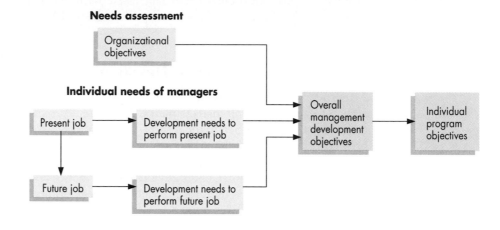

Needs assessment

Organizational objectives

Individual needs of managers

Present job → Development needs to perform present job

Future job → Development needs to perform future job

Overall management development objectives → Individual program objectives

FIGURE 14.4   Methods Used in Management Development

On the Job	Off the Job
Understudy assignments	Classroom training
Coaching	Lectures
Job rotation	Case studies
Special projects and committee assignments	Role playing
	In-basket techniques
	Business games
	Assessment centers

responsible for operating results. On the negative side, the understudy learns the bad as well as the good practices of the incumbent. In addition, understudy assignments maintained over a long period can become expensive. If an understudy assignment system is used, it generally should be supplemented with one or more of the other management development methods.

Coaching

coaching   Carried out by experienced managers, emphasizes the responsibility of all managers for developing employees.

Coaching is carried out by experienced managers and emphasizes the responsibility of all managers for developing employees. Under this method of management development, experienced managers advise and guide trainees in solving managerial problems. The idea behind coaching should be to allow the trainees to develop their own approaches to management with the counsel of a more experienced person.

One advantage of coaching is that trainees get practical experience and see the results of their decisions. However, there is a danger that the coach will neglect the training responsibilities or pass on inappropriate management practices. The coach's expertise and experience are critical to the success of this method.

Job Rotation

Job rotation is designed to give an individual broad experience through exposure to many different areas of the organization. With understudy assignments, coaching, and experience, the trainee generally receives training and development for one particular job. With **job rotation,** the trainee goes from one job to another within the organization, generally remaining in each job from six months to a year. This technique is used frequently by large organizations for training recent college graduates.

job rotation Process in which the trainee goes from one job to another within the organization, generally remaining in each job from six months to a year.

One advantage of job rotation is that the trainees can see how management principles can be applied in a cross-section of environments. Also, the training is practical and allows the trainee to become familiar with the entire operation of the company. One serious disadvantage of this method is that the trainee is frequently given menial assignments in each job. Another disadvantage is the tendency to leave the trainee in each job longer than necessary. Both of these disadvantages can produce negative attitudes.

Special Projects and Committee Assignments

Special projects require the trainee to learn about a particular subject. For example, a trainee may be told to develop a training program on safety. This would require learning about the organization's present safety policies and problems and the safety training procedures used by other companies. The individual must also learn to work with and relate to other employees. However, it is critical that the special assignments provide a developmental and learning experience for the trainee and not just busywork.

Committee assignments, which are similar to special projects, can be used if the organization has regularly constituted or ad hoc committees. In this approach, an individual works with the committee on its regularly assigned duties and responsibilities. Thus, the person exercises skills in working with others and learns through the activities of the committee.

Classroom Training

With classroom training, the most familiar type of training, several methods can be used. Classroom training is used not only in management development programs but also in the orientation and training activities discussed earlier in this chapter. Therefore, some of the material in this section is also applicable to those activities.

Lectures   With lecturing, instructors have control over the situation and can present the material exactly as they desire. Although the lecture is useful for presenting facts, its value in changing attitudes and teaching skills is somewhat limited.[7]

case study Training technique that presents real and hypothetical situations for the trainee to analyze.

Case Studies   The **case study,** a technique popularized by the Harvard Business School, presents real and hypothetical situations for the trainee to analyze. Ideally, the case study should force the trainee to think through problems, propose solutions, choose among the alternatives, and analyze the consequences of the decision.

One primary advantage of the case method is that it brings a note of realism to the instruction. However, case studies often are simpler than the real situations managers face. Another drawback is that when cases are discussed, the participants often lack emotional involvement; thus, attitudinal and behavioral changes are less likely to occur. Also, the success of the case study method depends heavily on the skills of the instructor.[8]

One variation of the case study is the *incident method*. The trainee is initially given only the general outline of a situation. The instructor then provides additional information as the trainee requests it. Theoretically, the incident method makes students probe the situations and seek additional information, much as they would be required to do in real life.

Role Playing   With role playing, trainees are assigned different roles and required to act out these roles in a realistic situation. The idea is for the participants to learn from playing out the assigned roles. The success of this method depends on the ability of participants to assume the roles realistically. Videotaping allows for review and evaluation of the exercise to improve its effectiveness.

in-basket technique   Simulates a realistic situation by requiring each trainee to answer one manager's mail and telephone calls.

In-Basket Techniques   The **in-basket technique** simulates a realistic situation by requiring each trainee to answer one manager's mail and telephone calls. Important duties are interspersed with routine matters. For instance, one call may come from an important customer who is angry, while a letter from a local civic club may request a donation. The trainees analyze the situations and suggest alternative actions. They are evaluated on the basis of the number and quality of decisions and on the priorities assigned to each situation. The in-basket technique has been used not only for management development but also in assessment centers, which are discussed later in this chapter.

business game   Generally provides a setting of a company and its environment and requires a team of players to make decisions involving company operations.

Business Games   **Business games** generally provide a setting of a company and its environment and require a team of players to make decisions involving company operations. They also normally require the use of computer facilities. In a business game, several teams act as companies within a type of industry. This method forces individuals not only to work with other group members but also to function in an atmosphere of competition within the industry.

Advantages of business games are that they simulate reality, decisions are made in a competitive environment, feedback is provided concerning decisions, and decisions are made using less than complete data. The main disadvantage is that many participants simply attempt to determine the key to winning. When this occurs, the game is not used to its fullest potential as a learning device.[9]

Management Education

In addition to traditional on- and off-the-job training, manager development can occur within the confines of the academic or special (seminar) education environment. Expert training can occur within additional undergraduate, M.B.A., executive M.B.A., or special seminar programs. These methods rely on sources outside the corporation to control and design the educational material for managers who wish to receive additional training. At their best, these programs can provide fresh ideas, strategies, and perspectives for the manager-student. At their worst, they may lack real-world application and be a waste of time. Among the chief complaints regarding the university-based programs are that they are too lengthy, drain the energy of employees, and may encourage career moves and employment changes. The last is a particularly distressing problem considering that many companies pay 80 percent of the tuition for advanced or additional degrees. Internet-based college courses are increasing rapidly.

Assessment Centers

assessment center   Utilizes a formal procedure to simulate the problems a person might face in a real managerial situation to evaluate the person's potential as a manager and determine the person's development needs.

An **assessment center** utilizes a formal procedure to evaluate an employee's potential as a manager and determine that employee's developmental needs. Assessment centers are used for making decisions about promoting, evaluating, and training managerial personnel.[10] Basically, these centers simulate the problems a person might face in a real managerial situation. In the typical center, 10 to 15 employees of about equal organizational rank are brought together for three to five days to work on individual and group exercises typical of a managerial job. Business games, in-basket techniques, and role playing are used to simulate managerial situations. These exercises involve the participants in decision making, leadership, written and oral communication, planning, organizing, and motivating. Assessors observe the participants, rate their performance, and provide feedback to them about their performance and developmental needs.

Assessors are often selected from management ranks several levels above those of the participants. Also, psychologists from outside the organization often serve as assessors. For a program to be successful, the assessors must be thoroughly trained in the assessment process, the mechanics of the exercises to be observed, and the techniques of observing and providing feedback.

Some operational problems can arise in using assessment centers. First, the organization must recognize that they are often more costly than other methods of management assessment. Problems can also occur when employees come from different levels in the organization. When their differences become apparent, lower-level participants often defer to those at higher levels during the group exercises; thus, the assessment results are biased. Finally, certain "canned" exercises may be only remotely related to the on-the-job activity at the organization in question. Care must be taken to ensure that exercises used in the assessment center bring out the specific skills and aptitudes needed in the position for which participants are being assessed.

EVALUATING EMPLOYEE TRAINING AND MANAGEMENT DEVELOPMENT ACTIVITIES

When the results of employee training and management development are evaluated, certain benefits accrue. Less effective programs can be withdrawn to save time and effort. Weaknesses within programs can be identified and remedied. Evaluation of training and management development activities can be broken down into four areas:[11]

1. *Reaction.* How well did the trainees like the program?
2. *Learning.* What principles, facts, and concepts were learned in the program?
3. *Behavior.* Did the job behavior of the trainees change because of the program?
4. *Results.* What were the results of the program in terms of factors such as reduced costs or reduction in turnover?

Even when great care is taken in designing evaluation procedures, it is difficult to determine the exact effects of training on learning, behavior, and results. Because of this, the evaluation of training is still limited and often superficial. However, if the management development programs are carefully tied to the focus of the corporate mission, related to the organization's strategic plan, and supported with sincere commitment on the part of senior management, they provide great benefits and move the organization in the direction of positive growth. Motivating employees usually is a function of opportunities for advancement and a corporate culture that encourages change and growth. In-house training, updated knowledge of computer technology, increased ability to create and implement strategy, and empowerment are no longer extras in which only some companies are interested. They are mandates for successful competition.

Summary

1. *Define Human Asset Accounting.* Human asset accounting involves determining and recording the value of an organization's human resources in its statement of financial condition.

2. *Describe the Orientation Process.* Orientation is the introduction of new employees to the organization, their work units, and their jobs.

3. *Define Training.* Training is a process that involves acquiring skills or learning concepts to increase the performance of employees.

4. *Define Needs Assessment.* Needs assessment is a systematic analysis of the specific training activities required to achieve the organization's objectives.

5. *Discuss Vestibule Training, Apprenticeship Training, and Computer-Based Training.* In vestibule training, procedures and equipment similar to those used in the actual job are set up in a special working area called a vestibule, where the trainee learns the job at a comfortable pace without the pressures of production schedules. Apprenticeship training generally lasts from two to five years and requires the trainee to work under the guidance of a skilled worker over this period. Computer-based training allows the trainee to absorb information from a preset computer program in a self-paced format.

6. *List and Define the Most Popular Methods of Management Development.* Understudy assignments require the person who will someday have a specific job to work for the incumbent to learn the job. With coaching, experienced managers advise and guide trainees in solving management problems. Job rotation exposes a manager to broad experiences in many different areas of the organization. Role playing requires trainees to act out assigned roles in a realistic situation. In-basket techniques require the trainee to answer one manager's mail and telephone calls. Business games generally provide settings of the company and its environment and require a team of players to make operating decisions.

7. *Describe an Assessment Center.* An assessment center utilizes a formal procedure to simulate the problems a person might face in a real managerial situation to evaluate the person's potential as a manager and determine the person's development needs.

8. *List the Steps Involved in the Evaluation of Training and Management Development.* The four steps in the evaluation of training and management development are (1) reaction (how well did the trainees like the program?), (2) learning (what principles, facts, and concepts were learned in the program?), (3) behavior (did the job behavior of the trainees change because of the program?), and (4) results (what were the results of the program in terms of factors such as reduced costs or reduced turnover?).

Preview Analysis

1. What courses do you feel would be most appropriate for Arthur Andersen employees?

2. Describe a course that would be helpful to you in pursuing your career.

Review Questions

1. What is human asset accounting?
2. What is orientation?
3. Describe the two distinct levels at which orientation is normally conducted within organizations.
4. What is training?
5. Describe the following methods of training:
   a. On-the-job.
   b. Job rotation.
   c. Vestibule.
   d. Apprenticeship.
   e. Computer-based training.
6. What is management development?
7. Describe the following methods used in management development:
   a. Understudy assignments.
   b. Coaching.
   c. Job rotation.
   d. Special projects and committee assignments.
   e. Classroom training.
8. What is an assessment center?
9. Describe four areas in the evaluation of training and management development.

Skill-Building Questions

1. Discuss the following statement: "Why should we train our employees? It is a waste of money because they soon leave and another organization gets the benefits."
2. Outline a system for evaluating a development program for supervisors.
3. Discuss the following statement: "Management games are fun, but you don't really learn anything from them."
4. Why are training programs generally one of the first areas to be eliminated when an organization must cut its budget?
5. Using the seven suggestions of motivational speaker Jim Rohn in Management Illustration 14.2, design a new guidance system for yourself. Make five new plans that will help you change in a positive direction, and describe a system for implementing the changes. Carry them out!

SKILL-BUILDING EXERCISE 14.1

Training Methods

Summarized below are some methods that can be used in training both operative and managerial employees. Your professor will assign one of these methods for you to explain to your class. You are to prepare a five-minute presentation describing the method, how it works, and its strengths and weaknesses.

- Role playing
- Sensitivity training
- Simulation exercises
- Wilderness training
- In-basket technique
- Incident method
- Vestibule training
- Apprenticeship training

SKILL-BUILDING EXERCISES 14.2

OJT

Assume you are training director for a large, local retail company. The company has seven department stores in your city. One of your biggest problems is adequately training new salesclerks. Because salesclerks represent your company to the public, the manner in which they conduct themselves is highly important. Especially critical aspects of their job include knowledge of the computerized cash register system, interaction with the customers, and knowledge of the particular products being sold.

A. Design a three-day orientation/training program for these salesclerks. Be sure to outline the specific topics (subjects) to be covered and the techniques to be used.

B. Specify what methods could be used to evaluate the success of the program.

C. Be prepared to present your program to the class.

CASE INCIDENT 14.1

Starting a New Job

Jack Smythe, branch manager for a large computer manufacturer, has just been told by his marketing manager, Bob Sprague, that Otis Brown has given two weeks' notice. When Jack had interviewed Otis, he had been convinced of the applicant's tremendous potential in sales. Otis was bright and personable, an honor graduate in electrical engineering from Massachusetts Institute of Technology who had the qualifications the company looked for in computer sales. Now he was leaving after only two months with the company. Jack called Otis into his office for an exit interview.

Jack: Come in, Otis, I really want to talk to you. I hope I can change your mind about leaving.
Otis: I don't think so.
Jack: Well, tell me why you want to go. Has some other company offered you more money?
Otis: No. In fact, I don't have another job. I'm just starting to look.
Jack: You've given us notice without having another job?
Otis: Well, I just don't think this is the place for me!
Jack: What do you mean?
Otis: Let me see if I can explain. On my first day at work, I was told that my formal classroom training in computers would not begin for a month. I was given a sales manual and told to read and study it for the rest of the day.

The next day I was told that the technical library, where all the manuals on computers are kept, was in a mess and needed to be organized. That was to be my responsibility for the next three weeks.

The day before I was to begin computer school, my boss told me that the course had been delayed for another month. He said not to worry, however, because he was going to have James Chess, the branch's leading salesperson, give me some on-the-job training. I was told to accompany James on his calls. I'm supposed to start the computer school in two weeks, but I've just made up my mind that this place is not for me.

Jack: Hold on a minute, Otis. That's the way it is for everyone in the first couple months of employment in our industry. Any place you go will be the same. In fact, you had it better than I did. You should have seen what I did in my first couple of months.

Questions

1.   What do you think about the philosophy of this company on a new employee's first few months on the job?

2.   What suggestions do you have for Jack to help his company avoid similar problems of employee turnover in the future?

CASE INCIDENT 14.2

A New Computer System

John Brown, 52, has been at State Bank for 30 years. Over the past 20 years, he has worked in the bank's investment department. During his first 15 years in the department, it was managed by Lisa Adams. The department consisted of Lisa, John, and two other employees. Lisa made all decisions, while the others performed manual recordkeeping functions. When Lisa retired five years ago, John held the position of assistant cashier.

Tom Smith took over the investment department after Lisa Adams retired. Tom, 56, has worked for State Bank for the past 28 years. Shortly after taking control of the department, Tom recognized that it needed to be modernized and staffed with people capable of giving better service to the bank's customers. As a result, he increased the department workforce to 10 people and installed two different computer systems. Of the 10 employees, only John and Tom are older than 33.

When Tom took over the department, John was a big help because he knew all about how the department had

been run in the past. Tom considered John to be a capable worker; after about a year, he promoted John to assistant vice president.

After he had headed the department for about a year and a half, Tom purchased a computer package to handle the bond portfolio and its accounting. When the new system was implemented, John said he did not like the computer system and would have nothing to do with them.

Over the next two years, further changes came about. As the other employees in the department became more experienced, they branched into new areas of investment work. The old ways of doing things were replaced by new, more sophisticated methods. John resisted these changes; he refused to accept or learn new methods and ideas. He slipped more and more into doing only simple but time-consuming activities.

Presently, a new computer system is being acquired for the investment section, and another department is being put under Tom's control. John has written Tom a letter stating he wants no part of the new computer systems but would like to be the manager of the new department. In his letter, John said he was tired of being given routine tasks while the "young people" got all the exciting jobs. John contended that since he has been with the bank longer than anyone else, he should be given first shot at the newly created job.

Questions

1. What suggestions do you have to motivate John to train on the new computer systems?

2. What methods of training would you recommend for John?

References and Additional Readings

[1]For a more in-depth discussion of human asset accounting, see Roger N. Hermanson, *Accounting for Human Assets: Research Monograph No. 99* (Atlanta: Georgia State University, Business Publishing Division, 1986).

[2]Carol A. Sales, Eliahu Levahoni, and Robert Knoop, "Employee Performance as a Function of Job Orientation and Job Design," *Industrial Relations* (Canadian), Spring 1989, pp. 90–91.

[3]See Jeffrey P. Davidson, "Starting the New Hire on the Right Foot," *Personnel*, August 1989, pp. 67–71.

[4]Laura K. Fleming and Ann M. Apking, "The Supervisor's Role in a Training Needs Analysis," *Supervisory Management*, May 1986.

[5]Craig Eric Schneier, David McCoy, and Seymour Burchman, "Unlocking Employee Potential: Developing Skills," *Management Solutions*, February 1988.

[6]Tom Peters, *Thriving on Chaos* (New York: Alfred A. Knopf, 1987), pp. 323–26.

[7]See Ricky W. Griffen and William E. Cashin, "The Lecture and Discussion Method for Management Education: Pros and Cons," *Journal of Management Development* 8, no. 2 (1989), pp. 25–32.

[8]For more information on the case method, see Chimezie A. B. Osigweh, "Casing the Case Approach in Management Development," *Journal of Management Development* 8, no. 2 (1989), pp. 41–57. Also see William E. Fulmer, "Using Cases in Management Development Programs," *Journal of Management Development* 11 (1992), pp. 33–37.

[9]For additional information, see Stephen A. Stumpf and Jane E. Dutton, "The Dynamics of Learning through Simulations: Let's Dance," *Journal of Management Development* 9, no. 2 (1990), pp. 7–15. Also see Bernard Keys and Joseph Wolfe, "The Role of Management Games in Education and Research," *Journal of Management* 16 (June 1990), pp. 307–36, and Peggy A. Golden and Jerald R. Smith, "Utilizing Simulation Games: Three Consulting Experiences," *Journal of Management* 9 (1990), pp. 16–21.

[10]George Munchas III and Barbara McArthur, "Revisiting the Historical Use of the Assessment Center in Management Selection and Development," *Journal of Management Development* 11 (1992), pp. 33–37.

[11]D. I. Kirkpatrick, "Evaluation of Training," in *Training and Development Handbook*, ed. R. L. Craig and L. R. Bittel (New York: McGraw-Hill, 1986), p. 18-2.

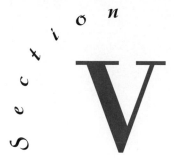

DIRECTING SKILLS

15

Motivation

§🐘

LEARNING OBJECTIVES

After studying this chapter, you should be able to:

1. Define motivation.

2. Describe the scientific management approach to motivation.

3. Explain the equity theory of motivation.

4. Explain the hierarchy of needs.

5. Discuss the achievement-power-affiliation approach to motivation.

6. Discuss the motivation-maintenance approach to motivation.

7. Discuss the expectancy approach to motivation.

8. Explain reinforcement theory.

9. Define job satisfaction and organizational morale.

In the fall of 1996, Lucent Technologies paid for its employee, Joseph Freund, to fly to Florida for two weeks. Surprisingly, the free air fare and car rental were not part of an expense paid business trip. They were actually a reward, which also included tickets for his wife, daughter, and mother-in-law. Why such generosity from Lucent? Freund was part of a team that devised a way to reduce the costs associated with product-liability testing. Under the incentive program, these cost savings are translated into "points," which can be redeemed for everything from golf clubs to home appliances.

Lucent's vice president of human resources, Pam Vosmik, says, "The program works for two reasons—because the incentives are fun and because employees experience tangible rewards for coming up with good business ideas." In the first year, 54 percent of the total workforce at Lucent participated in the program. Of the 6,000 ideas submitted, 2,100 were approved and implemented. The employee incentive program generated more than $20 million in cost savings in the first year alone.

Source: "Spreading Out the Carrots," *Industry Week*, May 19, 1997, pp. 20–24.

Statements and questions such as the following are often expressed by managers: Our employees are just not motivated. Half the problems we have are due to a lack of personal motivation. How do I motivate my employees?

The problem of motivation is not a recent development. Research conducted by William James in the late 1800s indicated the importance of motivation.[1] James found that hourly employees could keep their jobs by using approximately 20 to 30 percent of their ability. He also found that highly motivated employees will work at approximately 80 to 90 percent of their ability. Figure 15.1 illustrates the potential influence of motivation on performance. Highly motivated employees can bring about substantial increases in performance and substantial decreases in problems such as absenteeism, turnover, tardiness, strikes, and grievances.

THE MEANING OF MOTIVATION

motivation   Comes from the Latin word *movere*, which means to move.

The word **motivation** comes from the Latin word *movere*, which means to move. Numerous definitions are given for the term. Usually included are such words as *aim, desire, end, impulse, intention, objective,* and *purpose*. These definitions normally include three common characteristics of motivation. First, motivation is concerned with what activates human behavior. Second, motivation is concerned with what directs this behavior toward a particular goal. Third, motivation is concerned with how this behavior is sustained.[2]

Motivation can be analyzed using the following causative sequence:

Needs → Drives or motives → Achievement of goals

In motivation, needs produce motives, which lead to the accomplishment of goals. Needs are caused by deficiencies, which can be either physical or psychological. For instance, a physical need exists when an individual goes without sleep for 48 hours. A psychological need exists when an individual has no friends or companions. Individual needs will be explored in much greater depth later in this chapter.

A motive is a stimulus that leads to an action that satisfies the need. In other words, motives produce actions. Lack of sleep (the need) activates the physical

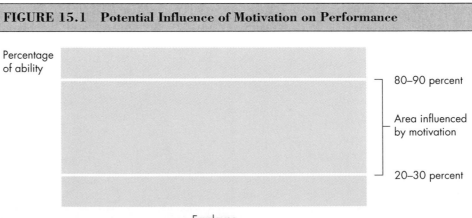

FIGURE 15.1   Potential Influence of Motivation on Performance

Source: Paul Hersey and Kenneth H. Blanchard, *Management of Organizational Behavior: Utilizing Human Resources.* 4th ed. (Englewood Cliffs, NJ: Prentice Hall, 1982), p. 4. Copyright © 1982 by Prentice Hall, Inc. Adapted by permission.

changes of fatigue (the motive), which produces sleep (the action or, in this example, inaction).

Achievement of the goal satisfies the need and reduces the motive. When the goal is reached, balance is restored. However, other needs arise, which are then satisfied by the same sequence of events. Understanding the motivation sequence in itself offers a manager little help in determining what motivates people. The approaches to analyzing motivation described in this chapter help to provide a broader understanding of what motivates people. They include the following: scientific management, equity, need hierarchy, achievement-power-affiliation, motivation-maintenance, expectancy, and reinforcement.

SCIENTIFIC MANAGEMENT APPROACH

The scientific management approach to motivation evolved from the work of Frederick W. Taylor and the scientific management movement that took place at the turn of this century. Taylor's ideas were based on his belief that existing reward systems were not designed to reward individuals for high production. He believed that when highly productive people discover they are being compensated basically the same as less productive people, then the output of highly productive people will decrease. Taylor's solution was quite simple. He designed a system whereby an employee was compensated according to individual production.

One of Taylor's problems was determining a reasonable standard of performance. Taylor solved the problem by breaking jobs down into components and measuring the time necessary to accomplish each component. In this way, Taylor was able to establish standards of performance "scientifically."

Taylor's plan was unique in that he had one rate of pay for units produced up to the standard. Once the standard was reached, a significantly higher rate was paid, not only for the units above the standard but also for all units produced during the day. Thus, under Taylor's system, employees could in many cases significantly increase their pay for production above the standard.

The scientific management approach to motivation is based on the assumption that money is the primary motivator. Financial rewards are directly related to performance in the belief that if the reward is great enough, employees will produce more.

EQUITY THEORY

equity theory Motivation theory based on the idea that people want to be treated fairly in relationship to others.

inequity Exists when a person perceives his or her job inputs and outcomes to be less than the job inputs and outcomes of another person.

inputs What an employee perceives are his or her contributions to the organization (i.e., education, intelligence, experience, training, skills, and the effort exerted on the job).

Proposed by J. Stacey Adams, **equity theory** is based on the idea that people want to be treated fairly in relationship to others.[3] **Inequity** exists when a person perceives his or her job inputs and outcomes to be less than the job inputs and outcomes of another person. The important point to note in this definition is that it is the person's *perception* of inputs and outcomes, not necessarily the actual inputs and outcomes. Furthermore, the other person in the comparison can be an employee in the person's work group or in another part of the organization.

Inputs are what an employee perceives are his or her contributions to the organization (i.e., education, intelligence, experience, training, skills, and the effort exerted on the job). Outcomes are the rewards received by the employee (i.e., pay, rewards intrinsic to the job, seniority benefits, and status).

Equity theory also postulates that the presence of inequity in a person creates tension in a person that is proportional to the magnitude of the inequity. Furthermore, the tension will motivate the person to achieve equity or reduce inequity. The strength of the motivation varies directly with the amount of inequity. A person might take several actions to reduce inequity:

1. Increase inputs on the job if his or her inputs are low relative to the other person. For example, a person might work harder to increase his or her inputs on the job.
2. Reduce inputs if they are high relative to the other person's inputs and to his or her own outcomes.
3. Quit the job.
4. Request a pay increase.

NEED HIERARCHY

need hierarchy   Based on the assumption that individuals are motivated to satisfy a number of needs and that money can directly or indirectly satisfy only some of these needs.

The **need hierarchy** is based on the assumption that individuals are motivated to satisfy a number of needs and that money can directly or indirectly satisfy only some of these needs. The need hierarchy is based largely on the work of Abraham Maslow.[4]

Maslow's Need Hierarchy

hierarchy of needs   The organization of individual's needs into five levels (physiological, safety, social, esteem or ego, and self-actualization.

Maslow thought that several different levels of needs exist within individuals and that these needs relate to each other in the form of a hierarchy. Maslow's **hierarchy of needs** consists of the five levels shown in Figure 15.2.

The physiological needs are basically the needs of the human body that must be satisfied in order to sustain life. These needs include food, sleep, water, exercise, clothing, shelter, and so forth.

Safety needs are concerned with protection against danger, threat, or deprivation. Since all employees have (to some degree) a dependent relationship with the organization, safety needs can be critically important. Favoritism, discrimination, and arbitrary administration of organizational policies are all actions that arouse uncertainty and therefore affect the safety needs.

The third level of needs is composed of the social needs. Generally categorized at this level are the needs for love, affection, belonging—all are concerned with establishing one's position relative to others. This need is satisfied by the development of meaningful personal relations and by acceptance into meaningful groups of individuals. Belonging to organizations and identifying with work groups are means of satisfying these needs in organizations.

The fourth level of needs is composed of the esteem needs. The esteem needs include both self-esteem and the esteem of others. These needs influence the development of various kinds of relationships based on adequacy, independence, and the giving and receiving of indications of esteem and acceptance.

The highest-order need is concerned with the need for self-actualization or self-fulfillment—that is, the need of people to reach their full potential in applying their abilities and interests to functioning in their environment. This need is concerned with the will to operate at the optimum. The need for self-actualization or self-fulfillment is never completely satisfied; one can always reach one step higher. Management Illustration 15.1 presents a unique description of one of the higher order needs.

FIGURE 15.2   Maslow's Need Hierarchy

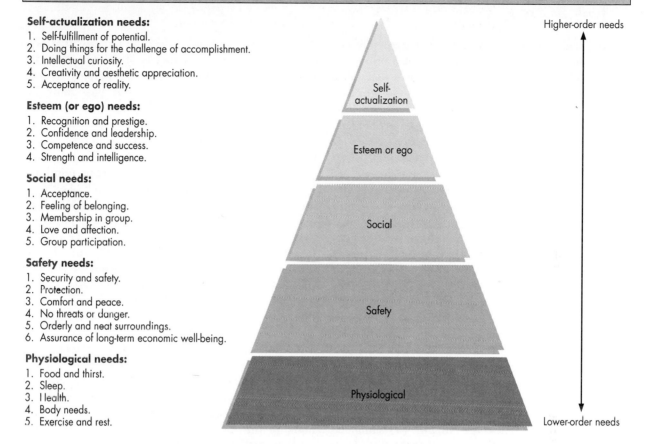

Self-actualization needs:
1. Self-fulfillment of potential.
2. Doing things for the challenge of accomplishment.
3. Intellectual curiosity.
4. Creativity and aesthetic appreciation.
5. Acceptance of reality.

Esteem (or ego) needs:
1. Recognition and prestige.
2. Confidence and leadership.
3. Competence and success.
4. Strength and intelligence.

Social needs:
1. Acceptance.
2. Feeling of belonging.
3. Membership in group.
4. Love and affection.
5. Group participation.

Safety needs:
1. Security and safety.
2. Protection.
3. Comfort and peace.
4. No threats or danger.
5. Orderly and neat surroundings.
6. Assurance of long-term economic well-being.

Physiological needs:
1. Food and thirst.
2. Sleep.
3. Health.
4. Body needs.
5. Exercise and rest.

(Pyramid labels, top to bottom: Self-actualization; Esteem or ego; Social; Safety; Physiological. Right side: Higher-order needs; Lower-order needs.)

Need Hierarchy—Other Considerations

The need hierarchy shown in Figure 15.2 adequately describes the general order or ranking of most people's needs. However, there are several other possibilities to be considered. First, although the needs of most people are arranged in the sequence shown in Figure 15.2, differences in the sequence can occur, depending on an individual's learning experience, culture, social upbringing, and numerous other personality aspects. Second, the strength or potency of a person's needs may shift back and forth under different situations. For instance, during bad economic times, physiological and safety needs might tend to dominate an individual's behavior; in good economic times, higher-order needs might dominate an individual's behavior.

The unconscious character of the various needs should be recognized. In addition, there is a certain degree of cultural specificity of needs. In other words, the ways by which the various needs can be met tend to be controlled by cultural and societal factors. For example, the particular culture may dictate one's eating habits, social life, and numerous other facets of life.

Finally, different methods can be used by different individuals to satisfy a particular need. Two individuals may be deficient in relation to the same physiological need; however, the way in which each chooses to satisfy that need may vary considerably.

As far as motivation is concerned, the thrust of the need hierarchy is that the lowest-level unsatisfied need causes behavior. The hierarchy represents what Maslow thought was the order in which unsatisfied needs would activate behavior.

Management Illustration 15.1

I Think I Can

Having high hopes is extremely important for entrepreneurs and managers. Hope is also an excellent motivator for employees. Hope is a sustaining force when all of Murphy's laws seem to be working against us. Psychologist C. R. Snyder of the University of Kansas believes high-hope people are more likely to reach their goals. Snyder's research has shown that "abilities are important, but often hope is the factor that energizes you so you get where you want to go." "Hope is a powerful predictor of outcomes in every area we've looked at," says Snyder.

Since it is estimated that only 40 percent of employees can be considered as having "very hopeful" attitudes, managers need to learn techniques to stimulate the majority of the "not-so-hopeful" class so productivity will increase. The how-to's of hope instillation would include the following: (1) *Set clear goals*—high-hope people have more goals and most are realistic; (2) *break goals down into bite-size steps*—the all-or-nothing approach to setting goals is rarely successful; (3) *keep a victory log*—the best hope booster is seeing what you have already accomplished and being able to rely on those accomplishments when times are tough; (4) *minimize negatives in your position*—concentrate on positives; and (5) *surround yourself with a support network*—high-hope people call on their peers for support, team building, and spirit.

Professor Rob Gilbert ("Mister Motivation"), in his book *Gilbert on Greatness*, believes that not only do hope and winning go hand in hand, but hope leads to winning. Therefore, to instill a winning spirit in the modern workplace amid the depression that sometimes prevails, a manager must understand the "will to win." Using the phrase "If It Is to Be, It Is Up to Me," managers should consider the following advice for motivating employees and themselves: (1) "Winners are not passionate because they are successful; they are successful because they are passionate"; (2) "Be an action person—don't wait to get motivated before you do something—do something and you'll get motivated"; (3) "What you conceive in your mind and believe in your heart, you will achieve"; (4) "Nothing positive will come from being negative, and nothing negative will come from being positive"; (5) "Winners look for ways things can be done—losers look for reasons they can't"; (6) "Losers visualize the penalties of failure—winners visualize the rewards of success"; and (7) ask yourself the following question: "If you were on trial for living the life of a winner, would the jury have enough evidence to convict you?"

In the children's classic *The Little Engine That Could* by Watty Piper, "I Think I Can" became "I Thought I Could" with belief and effort. To motivate and give hope to today's overstressed employees, the effective manager-leader might include the book in the new-employee packet and then diligently practice and teach the same principles to employees that we commonly teach to our children: Have hope, never give up, believe in yourself, and go for your goals!

Sources: Robert McGarvey, "High Hopes," *Entrepreneur*, June 1995, pp. 76–79; Susan Ungaro, "From the Editor . . .," *Family Circle*, January 9, 1996, p. 6.

For more articles on entrepreneurs and management visit *Entrepreneur* at www.entrepreneurmag.com/misc/.

Many of today's organizations are applying the logic of the need hierarchy. For instance, compensation systems are generally designed to satisfy the lower-order needs—physiological and safety. On the other hand, interesting work and opportunities for advancement are designed to appeal to higher-order needs. So the job of a manager is to determine the need level an individual employee is attempting to satisfy and then provide the means by which the employee can satisfy that need. Obviously, determining the need level of a particular person can be difficult. All people do not operate at the same level on the need hierarchy. All people do not react similarly to the same situation.

Little research has been conducted to test the validity of the need hierarchy theory.[5] Its primary value is that it provides a structure for analyzing needs and, as will be seen later in this chapter, is used as a basis for other theories of motivation.

ACHIEVEMENT-POWER-AFFILIATION APPROACH

The achievement-power-affiliation approach to motivation was primarily developed by David McClelland.[6] While recognizing that people have many different needs, this approach to motivation focused on three needs: (1) need to achieve, (2) need for power, and (3) need for affiliation. The use of the term *need* in this approach is different from the need hierarchy approach in that, under this approach, the three needs are assumed to be learned, whereas Maslow saw needs as inherent.

The need for achievement is a desire to do something better or more efficiently than it has been done before—to achieve. The need for power is basically a concern for influencing people—to be strong and influential. The need for affiliation is a need to be liked—to establish or maintain friendly relations with others.

McClelland maintains that most people have developed a degree of each of these needs, but the level of intensity varies among people. For example, an individual may be high in the need for achievement, moderate in the need for power, and low in the need for affiliation. This individual's motivation to work will vary greatly from that of another person who has a high need for power and low needs for achievement and affiliation. An employee with a high need for affiliation would probably respond positively to demonstrations of warmth and support by a manager; an employee with a high need for achievement would likely respond positively to increased responsibility. Finally, under this approach to motivation, when a need's strength has been developed, it motivates behaviors or attracts employees to situations where such behaviors can be acted out. However, this does not satisfy the need; it is more likely to strengthen it further.

MOTIVATION-MAINTENANCE APPROACH

motivation maintenance   An approach to work motivation that associates factors of high-low motivation with either the work environment or the work itself.

Frederick Herzberg, Bernard Mausner, and Barbara Snyderman developed an approach to work motivation that has had wide acceptance in management circles.[7] The approach is referred to by several names: **motivation-maintenance,** dual-factor, or motivation-hygiene approach.

Initially, the development of the theory involved extensive interviews with approximately 200 engineers and accountants from 11 industries in the Pittsburgh area. In the interviews, researchers used what is called the critical incident method. This involved asking subjects to recall work situations in which they had experienced periods of high and low motivation. They were asked to recount specific details about the situation and the effect of the experience over time.

Analysis of the interviewees' statements showed that different factors were associated with good and bad feelings. The findings fell into two major categories. Those factors that were most frequently mentioned in association with a favorably viewed incident concerned the work itself. These factors were achievement, recognition, responsibility, advancement, and the characteristics of the job. But when subjects felt negatively oriented toward a work incident, they were more likely to mention factors associated with the work environment. These included status; interpersonal relations with supervisors, peers, and subordinates; technical aspects of supervision; company policy and administration; job security; working conditions; salary; and aspects of their personal lives that were affected by the work situation.

FIGURE 15.3   Hygiene–Motivator Factors

Hygiene Factors (Environmental)	Motivator Factors (Job Itself)
Policies and administration	Achievement
Supervision	Recognition
Working conditions	Challenging work
Interpersonal relations	Increased responsibility
Personal life	Opportunities for advancement
Money, status, security	Opportunities for personal growth

The latter set of factors was called "hygiene" or "maintenance" factors because the researchers thought that they are preventive in nature. In other words, they do not produce motivation but can prevent motivation from occurring. Thus, proper attention to hygiene factors is a necessary but not sufficient condition for motivation. The first set of factors were called "motivators." The researchers contended that these factors, when present in addition to the hygiene factors, provide true motivation.

In summary, the motivation-maintenance approach contends that motivation comes from the individual, not from the manager. At best, proper attention to the hygiene factors keeps an individual from being highly dissatisfied but does not make that individual motivated. Both hygiene and motivator factors must be present in order for true motivation to occur. Figure 15.3 lists some examples of hygiene and motivator factors.

Job enrichment programs have been developed in an attempt to solve motivational problems by using the motivation-maintenance theory. Unlike **job enlargement,** which merely involves giving an employee more of a similar type of operation to perform, or **job rotation,** which is the practice of periodically rotating job assignments, **job enrichment** involves an upgrading of the job by adding motivator factors. Designing jobs that provide for meaningful work, achievement, recognition, responsibility, advancement, and growth is the key to job enrichment.

job enlargement   Involves giving an employee more of a similar type of operation to perform.
job rotation   The practice of periodically rotating job assignments.
job enrichment   Involves an upgrading of the job by adding motivator factors.

As can be seen from Figure 15.4, the motivation-maintenance approach is very closely related to the need hierarchy approach to motivation and so is subject to many of the same criticisms.

EXPECTANCY APPROACH TO MOTIVATION

expectancy approach   Based on the idea that employee beliefs about the relationship among effort, performance, and outcomes as a result of performance and the value employees place on the outcomes determine their level of motivation.
expectancy   The employee's belief that his or her effort will lead to the desired level of performance.

The **expectancy approach** to motivation was developed by Victor H. Vroom.[8] It is based on the idea that employee beliefs about the relationship among effort, performance, and outcomes as a result of performance and the value employees place on the outcomes determine their level of motivation. Figure 15.5 outlines the expectancy approach to motivation.

The expectancy approach postulates that an employee's level of motivation depends on three basic beliefs: expectancy, instrumentality, and valence. **Expectancy** refers to the employee's belief that his or her effort will lead to the desired level of performance. **Instrumentality** refers to the employee's belief that attaining the de-

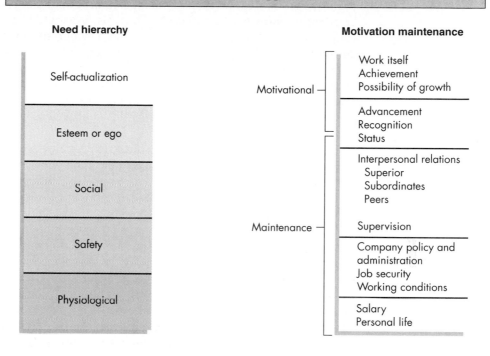

FIGURE 15.4   Comparison of the Need Hierarchy with the Motivation-Maintenance Approach

Need hierarchy

Self-actualization

Esteem or ego

Social

Safety

Physiological

Motivation maintenance

Motivational —

Work itself
Achievement
Possibility of growth

Advancement
Recognition
Status

Maintenance —

Interpersonal relations
  Superior
  Subordinates
  Peers

Supervision

Company policy and
administration
Job security
Working conditions

Salary
Personal life

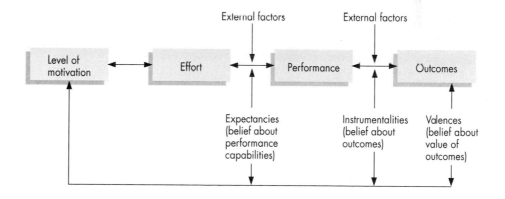

FIGURE 15.5   Expectancy Approach to Motivation

External factors   External factors

Level of motivation ⟷ Effort ⟷ Performance ⟷ Outcomes

Expectancies
(belief about
performance
capabilities)

Instrumentalities
(belief about
outcomes)

Valences
(belief about
value of
outcomes)

instrumentality   The employee's belief that attaining the desired level of performance will lead to desired outcomes.

valence   The employee's belief about the value of the outcome.

sired level of performance will lead to certain outcomes. **Valence** refers to the employee's belief about the value of the outcomes. External factors are beyond the employee's control and often negatively influence expectancies and instrumentalities because they introduce uncertainty into the relationship. Company policies and efficiency of the equipment being used are examples of external factors.

The following example is intended to illustrate the expectancy approach. Assume John Stone is an insurance salesman for the ABC Life Insurance Company. John has learned over the years that he completes one sale for approximately every six calls he makes. John has a high expectancy about the relationship between his effort and performance. Since John is on a straight commission he also sees a direct relationship between performance and rewards. Thus, his expectation that increased effort will lead to increased rewards is relatively high. Further, suppose that John's income is currently in a high tax bracket such that he gets to keep, after taxes, only 60 percent of his commissions. This being the case, he may not look on the additional money he gets to keep (the outcome) as being very attractive. The end result is that John's belief about the value of the additional money (valence) may be relatively low. Thus, even when the expectation of receiving the additional money is high, his motivation to do additional work may be relatively low.

Each of the separate components of the expectancy approach can be affected by the organization's practices and management. The expectancy that increased effort will lead to increased performance can be positively influenced by providing proper selection, training, and clear direction to the work force. The expectancy that increased performance will lead to desired outcomes is almost totally under the control of the organization. Does the organization really attempt to link rewards to performance? Or are rewards based on some other variable, such as seniority? The final component—the preference for the rewards being offered—is usually taken for granted by the organization. Historically, organizations have assumed that whatever rewards are provided will be valued by employees. Even if this were true, some rewards are certainly more valued than others. Certain rewards, such as a promotion that involves a transfer to another city, may be viewed negatively. Organizations should solicit feedback from their employees concerning the types of rewards that are valued. Since an organization is going to spend a certain amount of money on rewards (salary, fringe benefits, and so on), it should try to get the maximum return from its investment.

REINFORCEMENT THEORY

reinforcement theory   The consequences of a person's present behavior influence future behavior.

positive reinforcement   Involves providing a positive consequence as a result of desired behavior.

avoidance   Also called negative reinforcement; involves giving a person the opportunity to avoid a negative consequence by exhibiting a desired behavior.

extinction   Involves providing no positive consequences or removing previously provided positive consequences as a result of undesirable behavior.

punishment   Involves providing a negative consequence as a result of undesired behavior.

The development of the **reinforcement theory** of motivation (something called *operant conditioning*) is generally credited to B. F. Skinner.[9] The general idea behind reinforcement theory is that the consequences of a person's present behavior influence future behavior. For example, behavior that leads to a positive consequence is likely to be repeated, while behavior that leads to a negative consequence is unlikely to be repeated.

The consequences of an individual's behavior are called reinforcement. Basically, four types of reinforcement exist—positive reinforcement, avoidance, extinction, and punishment. These are summarized in Figure 15.6. **Positive reinforcement** involves providing a positive consequence as a result of desired behavior. **Avoidance,** also called negative reinforcement, involves giving a person the opportunity to avoid a negative consequence by exhibiting a desired behavior. Both positive reinforcement and avoidance can be used to increase the frequency of desired behavior.

Extinction involves providing no positive consequences or removing previously provided positive consequences as a result of undesirable behavior. In other words, behavior that no longer pays is less likely to be repeated. **Punishment** in-

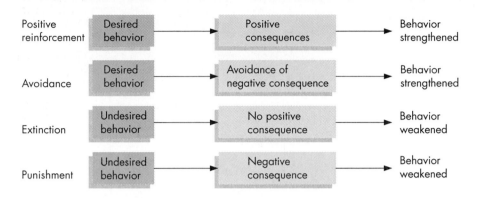

FIGURE 15.6   Types of Reinforcement

volves providing a negative consequence as a result of undesired behavior. Both extinction and punishment can be used to decrease the frequency of undesired behavior.

The current emphasis on the use of reinforcement theory in management practices is concerned with positive reinforcement. Examples include increased pay for increased performance, and praise and recognition when an employee does a good job. Generally, several steps are to be followed in the use of positive reinforcement. These steps include:

1. Selecting reinforcers that are strong and durable enough to establish and strengthen the desired behavior.
2. Designing the work environment in such a way that the reinforcing events are contingent on the desired behavior.
3. Designing the work environment so that the employee has the opportunity to demonstrate the desired behavior.[10]

The key to successful positive reinforcement is that rewards must result from performance. Several suggestions for the effective use of reinforcement have been proposed. These include the following:

1. All people should not be rewarded the same. In other words, the greater the level of performance by an employee, the greater should be the rewards.
2. Failure to respond to an employee's behavior has reinforcing consequences.
3. A person must be told what can be done to be reinforced.
4. A person must be told what he or she is doing wrong.
5. Reprimands should not be issued in front of others.
6. The consequences of a person's behavior should be equal to the behavior.[11]

In addition, positive reinforcement generally is more effective than negative reinforcement and punishment in producing and maintaining desired behavior.[12]

INTEGRATING THE APPROACHES TO MOTIVATION

All of the approaches to motivation previously presented contain the common thread that motivation is goal-directed behavior. Although the approaches may appear to be quite different, most of them are not in conflict with one another. Rather, each looks at a different segment of the overall motivational process or at the same segment from

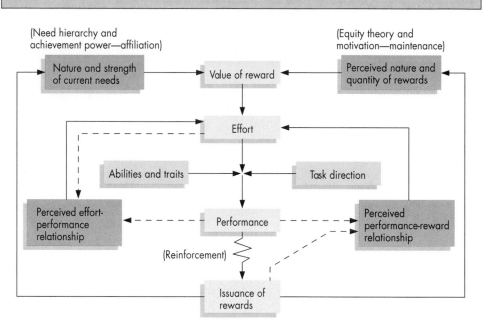

FIGURE 15.7   The Overall Motivational Process

a different perspective. Figure 15.7 presents a model that reflects the overall motivational process and indicates relationships among major motivational approaches.

Vroom's expectancy approach is shown at the heart of the model by the three factors that are shown to influence effort; note the arrows leading to the effort box. Maslow's need hierarchy and the achievement-power-affiliation approach are represented in the upper left-hand corner of the model by the variable labeled "Nature and strength of current needs." The nature and strength of current needs reflect the individual's needs, which in turn affect the value the person places on the reward being offered. If the reward matches the individual's needs, that person will place more value on the reward than if it does not match the need level. Equity theory comes into play in the individual's perception of the nature and quantity of rewards as compared to those received by other people. Good performance that is rewarded reinforces the likelihood that good performance will be repeated. The motivation-maintenance approach is represented by the variable "perceived nature and quantity of rewards," which is found in the upper right-hand corner of the model. Both of these variables reflect the need for rewards to consist of both hygiene and motivator factors. For example, if only hygiene factors are provided, then the perceived nature and quantity of the rewards would only be marginal, which in turn would result in a marginal or low value placed on the reward by the individual. Issuance of rewards based on performance reinforces the person's behavior. As suggested by Figure 15.7 no single approach to motivation provides all the answers. Management Illustration 15.2 describes the importance of charisma to motivation and leadership.

JOB SATISFACTION

Closely related to motivation is the concept of job satisfaction. In fact, managers often view motivated employees as being synonymous with satisfied employees. There are, however, important differences between motivated employees and satisfied employees.

Management Illustration 15.2
How Important Is Charisma to Leadership and Motivation?

The new department head doesn't have an M.B.A., ten years' experience, or seniority. How do such people just bypass their more experienced peers in the promotion cycle? They have charisma! They persuade people—subordinates, peers, customers, and even bosses—to do things they would rather not do. The old phrases ring true for the stimulation provided by the charismatic leader: People charge over the hill for them, run through fire, and walk barefoot on broken glass. They don't just demand attention, they command it! To many, charisma is what truly makes a leader.

Whether it's Michael Jordan, Jack Welch of General Electric, Ted Turner of Turner Enterprises, the late Congresswoman Barbara Jordan, or former president John Kennedy, the charismatic leader inspires followers in what she or he believes in, raises the followers' level of enthusiasm and productivity, and gets the team or the company to perform—if not to its best, at least better. These types of leaders are not always saints (remember, Adolph Hitler was charismatic) and can often lead their followers over the brink to disaster. For this type of leader, what begins as a mission can become an obsession. According to John Thompson of Human Factors, "Leaders [of this type] can cut corners on values and become driven by self-interest; then they may abuse anyone who makes a mistake."

However, history has shown that charisma is an extremely important leadership trait in business. Its role has, however, been played down in most business schools, according to Jeffrey Sonnefield of Emory University. He says, "Most leadership courses focus on followership, compliance, and consensus management instead of leadership—the result is a sort of guerrilla war against charisma." "Dentists, CPAs, morticians, engineers, architects, and bankers don't need it," says Gerard Roche, an executive headhunter, "but, by contrast, it's enormously important for managers in startups, turn-arounds, or whenever a business is ripping through rapid, unpredictable change."

The traits of charismatic leaders include the following: (1) *Simplify and exaggerate*—they have a remarkable ability to distill complex ideas into simple messages; (2) *romanticize risk*—they relish risk (in fact, to many, that may be what the game is all about); (3) *defy the status quo*—they are rebels who fight convention and their oddball image enhances their charisma; (4) *step into another's shoes*—they are able to see things from another person's perspective; and (5) *spar and rule*—they goad, challenge, poke, and prod (they test your courage and intellect). In the end, charisma can be learned and developed. But no matter whether you have it or would like to develop it, it's what gives the action and fun to the business game for many executives.

Source: Adapted from Patricia Sellers, "What Exactly Is Charisma?" *Fortune*, January 15, 1996, pp. 68–75. Reprinted by permission of *Fortune*© 1996 Time, Inc. All rights reserved.

---

job satisfaction An individual's general attitude about his or her job.

Job satisfaction is an individual's general attitude about his or her job. The five major components of job satisfaction are: (1) attitude toward work group, (2) general working conditions, (3) attitude toward company, (4) monetary benefits, and (5) attitude toward supervision. Other major components that should be added to these five are the individual's attitudes toward the work itself and toward life in general. The individual's health, age, level of aspiration, social status, and political and social activities can all contribute to job satisfaction. Therefore, job satisfaction is an attitude that results from other specific attitudes and factors.

Job satisfaction refers to the individual's mental set about the job. This mental set may be positive or negative, depending on the individual's mental set concerning the major components of job satisfaction. Job satisfaction is not synonymous with organizational morale. **Organizational morale** refers to an individual's feeling

organizational morale An individual's feeling of being accepted by, and belonging to, a group of employees through common goals, confidence in the desirability of these goals, and progress toward these goals.

of being accepted by, and belonging to, a group of employees through common goals, confidence in the desirability of these goals, and progress toward these goals. Morale is related to group attitudes, while job satisfaction is more of an individual attitude. However, the two concepts are interrelated in that job satisfaction can contribute to morale and morale can contribute to job satisfaction.

The Satisfaction–Performance Controversy

For many years, managers have believed for the most part that a satisfied worker will automatically be a good worker. In other words, if management could keep all the workers "happy," good performance would automatically follow. Charles Greene has suggested that many managers subscribe to this belief because it represents "the path of least resistance."[13] Greene's thesis is that increasing employees' happiness is far more pleasant for the manager than confronting employees with their performance if a performance problem exists.

Research evidence generally rejects the more popular view that employee satisfaction leads to improved performance. The evidence does, however, provide moderate support for the view that performance causes satisfaction. The evidence also provides strong indications that : (1) rewards constitute a more direct cause of satisfaction than does performance; and (2) rewards based on current performance cause subsequent performance.[14]

Research has also investigated the relationship between intrinsic and extrinsic satisfaction and performance for jobs categorized as being either stimulating or nonstimulating.[15] The studies found that the relationship did vary, depending on whether the job was stimulating or nonstimulating. These and other studies further emphasize the complexity of the satisfaction-performance relationship. One relationship that has been clearly established is that job satisfaction does have a positive impact on turnover, absenteeism, tardiness, accidents, grievances, and strikes.[16]

In addition, recruitment efforts by employees are generally more successful if the employees are satisfied. Satisfied employees are preferred simply because they make the work situation a more pleasant environment. So, even though a satisfied employee is not necessarily a high performer, there are numerous reasons for cultivating satisfied employees.

A wide range of both internal and external factors affect an individual's level of satisfaction. The top portion of Figure 15.8 summarizes the major factors that determine an individual's level of satisfaction (or dissatisfaction). The lower portion of the figure shows the organizational behaviors generally associated with satisfaction and dissatisfaction. Individual satisfaction leads to organizational commitment, while dissatisfaction results in behaviors detrimental to the organization (turnover, absenteeism, tardiness, accidents, etc.). For example, employees who like their jobs, supervisors, and other job-related factors will probably be very loyal and devoted employees. However, employees who strongly dislike their jobs or any of the job-related factors will probably be disgruntled and will often exhibit these feelings by being late, absent, or by taking more covert actions to disrupt the organization.

Satisfaction and motivation are not synonymous. Motivation is a drive to perform, while satisfaction reflects the individual's attitude or happiness with the situation. The factors that determine whether an individual is satisfied with the job differ from those that determine whether the individual is motivated. Satisfaction is largely determined by the comfort offered by the environment and the situation. Motivation,

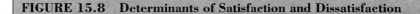

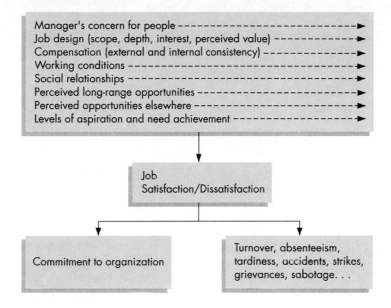

FIGURE 15.8   Determinants of Satisfaction and Dissatisfaction

Manager's concern for people
Job design (scope, depth, interest, perceived value)
Compensation (external and internal consistency)
Working conditions
Social relationships
Perceived long-range opportunities
Perceived opportunities elsewhere
Levels of aspiration and need achievement

Job Satisfaction/Dissatisfaction

Commitment to organization

Turnover, absenteeism, tardiness, accidents, strikes, grievances, sabotage. . .

on the other hand, is largely determined by the value of rewards and their contingency on performance. The result of motivation is increased effort, which in turn increases performance if the individual has the ability and if the effort is properly directed. The result of satisfaction is increased commitment to the organization, which may or may not result in increased performance. This increased commitment will normally result in a decrease in problems, such as absenteeism, tardiness, turnover, and strikes.

Summary

1. *Define Motivation.* Motivation is concerned with what activates human behavior, what directs this behavior toward a particular goal, and how this behavior is sustained.

2. *Describe the Scientific Management Approach to Motivation.* The scientific management approach to motivation is based on the assumption that money is the primary motivation of people: if the monetary reward is great enough, employees will work harder and produce more.

3. *Explain the Equity Theory of Motivation.* The equity theory of motivation is based on the idea that people want to be treated fairly in relationship to others.

4. *Explain the Hierarchy of Needs.* The five levels of needs are physiological, safety, social, ego, and self-actualization. The physiological needs include food, sleep, water, exercise, clothing, and shelter. Safety needs are concerned with protection against danger, threat, or deprivation. Social needs are the needs for love, affection, and belonging. Ego needs include both self-esteem and the esteem of others.

Self-actualization is the need of people to reach their full potential in applying their abilities and interests to functioning in their environment.

5. *Discuss the Achievement-Power-Affiliation Approach to Motivation.* This approach focuses on three needs of people: achievement, power, and affiliation. The level of intensity of these needs varies among individuals, and people are motivated in situations that allow them to satisfy their most intense needs.

6. *Discuss the Motivation-Maintenance Approach of Motivation.* This approach postulates that all work-related factors can be grouped into two categories. The first category, maintenance factors, will not produce motivation but can prevent it. The second category, motivators, encourages motivation.

7. *Discuss the Expectancy Approach to Motivation.* This approach holds that motivation is based on a combination of the individual's expectancy that increased effort will lead to increased performance, the expectancy that

increased performance will lead to increased rewards, and the individual's preference for those rewards.

8. *Explain Reinforcement Theory.* This theory is an approach to motivation based on the idea that behavior that appears to lead to a positive consequence tends to be repeated, while behavior that appears to lead to a negative consequence tends not to be repeated.

9. *Define Job Satisfaction and Organizational Morale.* Job satisfaction is an individual's general attitude about his or her job. Organizational morale refers to an individual's feeling of being accepted by, and belonging to, a group of employees through common goals, confidence in the desirability of these goals, and progress toward these goals.

Preview Analysis

1. What do you think of Lucent's approach to motivation?

2. Do you think this approach to motivation will work on a regular basis?

Review Questions

1. Explain the motivation sequence.
2. Describe the following approaches to motivation:
   a. Scientific management.
   b. Equity.
   c. Need hierarchy.
   d. Achievement-power-affiliation.
   e. Motivation-maintenance.
   f. Expectancy.
   g. Reinforcement.

3. What is job satisfaction? What are the major components of job satisfaction?
4. What is organizational morale?
5. Discuss the satisfaction–performance controversy.
6. From a managerial standpoint, what are the real benefits of having satisfied employees?

Skill-Building Questions

1. Discuss your views on this statement: Most people can be motivated with money.

2. Do you think a very loyal employee is necessarily a good employee?

3. As a manager, would you prefer a motivated or a satisfied group of employees? Why?

4. The XYZ Company has just decided to take all of its 200 employees to Las Vegas for a three-day expense-paid weekend to show its appreciation for their high level of performance this past year. What is your reaction to this idea?

5. Discuss the following statement: A satisfied employee is one that is not being pushed hard enough.

SKILL-BUILDING EXERCISE 15.1

Motivation-Maintenance

This exercise is designed to illustrate Herzberg's motivation-maintenance theory in terms of your personal experiences.

A. Think of a time when you were extremely motivated or "turned on" by a job (the instance could have taken place yesterday or several years ago and it could have been on a full- or part-time job) and write a brief two- or three-sentence description of the situation. After you have completed the description, list the reasons this situation had a motivational effect on you. Don't sign your name, but do pass your paper forward.

B. After completing the above, repeat the same procedure, for a situation that was highly demotivating. After all the papers have been passed forward, your instructor will help you analyze them.

SKILL-BUILDING EXERCISE 15.2

Does Money Motivate?

You will be divided into groups of three people each. Your group will be assigned one of the two following statements:

1. Money is the primary motivator of people.
2. Money is not the primary motivator of people.

Your assignment is to prepare for a debate with another group on the validity of the statement that your group has been assigned. You will be debating a group that has the opposing viewpoint.

At the end of the debate, prepare a brief statement summarizing the key points made by your opposing group.

CASE INCIDENT 15.1

Our Engineers Are Just Not Motivated

You are a consultant to the manager of mechanical engineering for a large company (8,000 employees, $200 million annual sales) that manufactures industrial equipment. The manager has been in this position for six months, having moved from a similar position in a much smaller company.

Manager: I just can't seem to get these people to perform. They are all extremely competent, but they just don't seem to be willing to put forth the kind of effort that we expect and need if this company is going to remain successful.

Consultant: What type of work do they do?

Manager: Primarily designing minor modifications to existing equipment lines to keep up with our competition and to satisfy special customer requirements.

Consultant: How do you evaluate their performance?

Manager: Mainly on whether they meet project deadlines. It's hard to evaluate the quality of their work, since most of it is fairly routine and the designs are frequently altered later by the production engineers to facilitate production processes.

Consultant: Are they meeting their deadlines reasonably well?

Manager: No, that's the problem. What's worse is that they don't really seem too concerned about it.

Consultant: What financial rewards do you offer them?

Manager: They are all well-paid—some of the best salaries for mechanical engineers that I know of anywhere. Base pay is determined mainly on the basis of seniority, but there is also a companywide profit-sharing plan. At the end of each year, the company distributes 10 percent of its profits after taxes to the employees. The piece of the pie that you get is in proportion to your basic salary. This kind of plan was used in the company I used to work for, and it seemed to have a highly motivating effect for them. They also get good vacations, insurance plans, and all the other usual goodies. I know of no complaints about compensation.

Consultant: How about promotion possibilities?

Manager: Well, all I know is that I was brought in from the outside.

Consultant: If they are so lackadaisical, have you considered firing any of them?

Manager: Are you kidding? We need them too much, and it would be difficult and expensive to replace them. If I even threatened to fire any of them for anything short of blowing up the building, my boss would come down on me like a ton of bricks. We are so far behind on our work as it is. Besides, I'm not sure that it's really their fault entirely.

Questions

1. Why are the engineers not motivated?
2. What should management do to correct the situation?

CASE INCIDENT 15.2

ᕽᕽ

The Long-Term Employee

Bill Harrison is 57 years old and has been with Ross Products for 37 years. He is on a top-paying machine-operator job and has been for the last 20 years. Bill is quite active in community affairs and takes a genuine interest in most employee activities. He is very friendly and well liked by all employees, especially the younger ones, who often come to him for advice. He is extremely helpful to these younger employees and never hesitates to help when asked. When talking with the younger employees, Bill never talks negatively about the company.

Bill's one shortcoming, as his supervisor Alice Jeffries sees it, is his tendency to spend too much time talking with other employees. This not only causes Bill's work to suffer but also, perhaps more importantly, hinders the output of others. Whenever Alice confronts Bill with the problem, Bill's performance improves for a day or two. It never takes long, however, for Bill to slip back into his old habit of storytelling and interrupting others.

Alice considered trying to have Bill transferred to another area where he would have less opportunity to interrupt others. However, Alice concluded she needs Bill's experience, especially since she has no available replacement for Bill's job.

Bill is secure in his personal life. He owns a nice house and lives well. His wife works as a librarian, and their two children are grown and married. Alice has sensed that Bill thinks he is as high as he'll ever go in the company. This doesn't seem to bother him since he feels comfortable and likes his present job.

Questions

1. What would you do to try to motivate Bill if you were Alice Jeffries?

2. Suppose Alice could transfer Bill. Would you recommend that she do it?

References and Additional Readings

[1] Cited in Paul Hersey and Kenneth H. Blanchard, *Management of Organizational Behavior: Utilizing Human Resources*, 4th ed. (Englewood Cliffs, NJ: Prentice Hall, 1982), p. 4.

[2] Richard M. Steers and Lyman W. Porter, *Motivation and Human Behavior* (New York: McGraw-Hill, 1983), pp. 3–4.

[3] J. Stacey Adams, "Toward an Understanding of Inequity," *Journal of Abnormal and Social Psychology*, November 1963, pp. 422–36. Also see Richard C. Huseman, John D. Hatfield, and Edward W. Miles, "A New Perspective on Equity Theory: The Equity Sensitivity Construct," *Academy of Management Review*, October 1987, pp. 322–34.

[4] Abraham H. Maslow, *Motivation and Personality*, 2nd ed. (New York: Harper & Row, 1970).

[5] Edwin A. Locke, "The Nature and Causes of Job Satisfaction," in *Handbook of Industrial and Organizational Psychology*, ed. Marvin D. Dunnette (New York: John Wiley & Sons, 1983).

[6] David C. McClelland, *The Achievement Motive* (New York: Halsted Press, 1976).

[7] Frederick Herzberg, Bernard Mausner, and Barbara Snyderman, *The Motivation to Work* (New York: John Wiley & Sons, 1959).

[8] Victor H. Vroom, *Work and Motivation* (New York: John Wiley & Sons, 1967).

[9] B. F. Skinner, *Science and Human Behavior* (New York: MacMillan, 1953) and *Beyond Freedom and Dignity* (New York: Knopf, 1972).

[10] Steers and Porter, *Motivation*, pp. 123–24.

[11] Ibid., pp. 162–63.

[12] P. M. Podsakoff, William D. Tudor, and Richard Skov, "Effects of Leader Contingent and Noncontingent Reward and Punishment Behaviors on Subordinate Performance and Satisfaction," *Academy of Management Journal*, December 1982, pp. 810–21.

[13] Charles N. Greene, "The Satisfaction–Performance Controversy," *Business Horizons*, October 1972, p. 31. Also see D. R. Norris and R. E. Niebuhr, "Attributional Influences on the Job Performance–Job Satisfaction Relationship," *Academy of Management Journal*, June 1984, pp. 424–31.

[14] Greene, "The Satisfaction–Performance Controversy," p. 40.

[15] John M. Ivancevich, "The Performance to Satisfaction Relationship: A Causal Analysis of Stimulating and Nonstimulating Jobs," *Organizational Behavior and Human Performance* 22 (1978), pp. 350–64.

[16] Donald P. Schwab and Larry L. Cummings, "Theories of Performance and Satisfactions: A Review," *Industrial Relations*, October 1970, pp. 408–29. Also see Locke, "Job Satisfaction," p. 1343, for a complete summary of the related research.

16

Leadership

ॐ

LEARNING OBJECTIVES

After studying this chapter, you should be able to:

1. Define power.

2. Describe the sources of power in organizations.

3. Define leadership.

4. Describe the self-fulfilling prophecy in management.

5. Define the trait theory of leadership.

6. List and define the basic leadership styles.

7. Understand the Managerial Grid.®

8. Define the contingency approach to leadership.

9. Explain the path–goal theory of leadership.

10. Define the life-cycle theory of leadership.

11. Define transactional and transformational leadership.

12. Discuss some of the lessons that can be learned from leadership research.

Chapter Preview

Business observers believe George Fisher has cleaned up Kodak by creating a new spirit and developing a willingness to compete. The steps he has prescribed for the company include (1) implementing a new, focused strategy, (2) creating a new, dynamic digital imaging unit, (3) repairing the balance sheet, (4) improving morale, and (5) overhauling the organization culture and leadership by stressing accountability, quality, and cycle time transformations. Fisher believes Kodak has been suffering from "paralysis by analysis" because the executives take forever to study a problem. Quoting from Machiavelli's *The Prince:* "Taking the lead in new things is always difficult."

Source: Mark Maremont, "Kodak's New Focus," *Business Week*, January 30, 1995, pp. 62–68.

Leadership is probably researched and discussed more than any other topic in the field of management. New suggestions, methods, and tips for improving leadership skills are offered each year. Everyone seems to acknowledge the importance of leadership to managerial and organizational success. This chapter reviews the research on leadership and offers perspectives on leadership processes and styles.

POWER, AUTHORITY, AND LEADERSHIP

Before undertaking a study of leadership, a clear understanding must be developed of the relationships among power, authority, and leadership. **Power** is a measure of a person's potential to get others to do what he or she wants them to do, as well as to avoid being forced by others to do what he or she does not want to do.[1] Figure 16.1 summarizes several sources of power in organizations. The use of or desire for power is often viewed negatively in our society because power is often linked to the concepts of punishment, dominance, and control.

power   a measure of a person's potential to get others to do what he or she wants them to do, as well as to avoid being forced by others to do what he or she does not want to do.

David C. McClelland has observed, "In American society in general, individuals are proud of having a high need to achieve, but dislike being told they have a high need for power."[2] McClelland's work, which was briefly described in Chapter 15, led him to study managers at AT&T where he found that managers high in need for power when they joined the company were more successful 16 years later if they were low in need for affiliation and high in self-control. McClelland concluded power can have both a positive and negative form. Positive power results when the exchange is voluntary and both parties feel good about the exchange. Negative power results when the individual is forced to change. Power in organizations can be exercised upward, downward, or horizontally. It does not necessarily follow the organizational hierarchy from top to bottom.

Authority, which is the right to issue directives and expend resources, is related to power but is narrower in scope. Basically, the amount of authority a manager has depends on the amount of coercive, reward, and legitimate power the manager can exert. Authority is a function of position in the organizational hierarchy, flowing from the top to the bottom of the organization. An individual can have power—expert or referent—without having formal authority. Furthermore, a manager's authority can be diminished by reducing the coercive and reward power in the position.

authority   is the right to issue directives and expend resources, related to power but narrower in scope.
leadership   the ability to influence people to willingly follow one's guidance or adhere to one's decisions.

Leadership is the ability to influence people to willingly follow one's guidance or adhere to one's decisions. Obtaining followers and influencing them in setting and

FIGURE 16.1   Sources of Power

Organizational Sources	Basis
Reward power	Capacity to provide rewards.
Coercive power	Capacity to punish.
Legitimate power	Person's position in the organizational hierarchy.

Personal Sources	Basis
Expert power	The skill, expertise, and knowledge an individual possesses.
Referent power	The personal characteristics of an individual that make other people want to associate with the person.

leader   one who obtains followers and influences them in setting and achieving objectives.

achieving objectives makes a **leader.** Leaders use power in influencing group behavior. For instance, political leaders often use referent power. Informal leaders in organizations generally combine referent power and expert power. Some managers rely only on authority, while others use different combinations of power.

LEADERSHIP AND MANAGEMENT

Leadership and management are not necessarily the same but are not incompatible. Effective leadership in organizations creates a vision of the future that considers the legitimate long-term interests of the parties involved in the organization, develops a strategy for moving toward that vision, enlists the support of employees to produce the movement, and motivates employees to implement the strategy. Management is a process of planning, organizing, staffing, motivating, and controlling through the use of formal authority.[3] In practice, effective leadership and effective management must ultimately be the same.

LEADER ATTITUDES

Douglas McGregor developed two attitude profiles, or assumptions, about the basic nature of people. These attitudes were termed **Theory X** and **Theory Y;** they are summarized in Figure 16.2. McGregor maintained that many leaders in essence subscribe to either Theory X or Theory Y and behave accordingly. A Theory X leader would likely use a much more authoritarian style of leadership than a leader who believes in Theory Y assumptions. The real value of McGregor's work was the idea that a leader's attitude toward human nature has a large influence on how that person behaves as a leader.[4]

FIGURE 16.2   Assumptions about People

Theory X

1. The average human being has an inherent dislike of work and will avoid it if possible.
2. Because of their dislike of work, most people must be coerced, controlled, directed, or threatened with punishment to get them to put forth adequate effort toward the achievement of organizational objectives.
3. The average human being prefers to be directed, wishes to avoid responsibility, has relatively little ambition, and wants security above all.

Theory Y

1. The expenditure of physical and mental effort in work is as natural as play or rest.
2. External control and the threat of punishment are not the only means for bringing about effort toward organizational objectives. Workers will exercise self-direction and self-control in the service of objectives to which they are committed.
3. Commitment to objectives is a function of the rewards associated with their achievement.
4. The average human being learns, under proper conditions, not only to accept but to seek responsibility.
5. The capacity to exercise a relatively high degree of imagination, ingenuity, and creativity in the solution of organizational problems is widely, not narrowly, distributed in the population.
6. Under the conditions of modern industrial life, the intellectual potentialities of the average human being are only partially utilized.

Source: Douglas McGregor, *The Human Side of Enterprise* (New York: McGraw-Hill, 1960), pp. 33–34 and 47–48. Copyright © 1960 by McGraw-Hill, Inc. Used with permission of McGraw-Hill Book Company.

FIGURE 16.3   Framework for Classifying Leadership Studies

Focus		Approach	
		Universal	**Contingent**
	Traits	Trait theory	Fiedler's contingency theory
	Behaviors	Leadership styles Ohio State studies Michigan studies Managerial Grid®	Path-goal theory Life-cycle theory

Source: Adapted from Arthur G. Yago, "Leadership Perspectives in Theory and Practice," *Management Science,* arch 1982, p. 316.

The relationship between a leader's expectations and the resulting performance of subordinates has received much attention. Generally, it has been found that if a manager's expectations are high, productivity is likely to be high. On the other hand, if the manager's expectations are low, productivity is likely to be poor. McGregor called this phenomenon the **self-fulfilling prophecy.** It has also been called *Pygmalion in management.*

self-fulfilling prophecy   The relationship between a leader's expectations and the resulting performance of subordinates.

FRAMEWORK FOR CLASSIFYING LEADERSHIP STUDIES

Many studies have been conducted on leadership. One useful framework for classifying these studies is shown in Figure 16.3.[5] *Focus* refers to whether leadership is to be studied as a set of traits or as a set of behaviors. *Traits* refer to what characteristics the leader possesses, whereas *behaviors* refer to what the leader does. The second—dimension—approach refers to whether leadership is studied from a universal or contingent approach. The universal approach assumes there is one best way to lead regardless of the circumstances. The contingent approach assumes the best approach to leadership is contingent on the situation. Each of the studies shown in Figure 16.3 is discussed in the following sections.

Trait Theory

trait theory   stressed what the leader was like rather than what the leader did.

Early research efforts devoted to leadership stressed what the leader was *like* rather than what the leader *did*—a **trait theory** of leadership. Many personality traits (such as originality, initiative, persistence, knowledge, enthusiasm), social traits (tact, patience, sympathy, etc.), and physical characteristics (e.g., height, weight, attractiveness) have been examined to differentiate leaders.[6]

At first glance, a few traits do seem to distinguish leaders from followers. These include being slightly superior in such physical traits as weight and height and in a tendency to score higher on tests of dominance, intelligence, extroversion, and adjustment. But the differences seem to be small, with much overlap.

Thus, the research in this area has generally been fruitless—largely because the traits related to leadership in one case usually did not prove to be predictive in other cases. In general, it can be said that traits may to some extent influence the capacity

Management in Action 16.1
Leadership Qualities of CEOs of Winning Companies

A leadership quality of CEOs of winning companies is the emphasis they place on developing other leaders. Noel M. Tichy, professor at the University of Michigan Business School states as follows: "Great Leaders have to be great teachers. Many companies rely on consultants or executive-education programs to develop their leaders. But the really outstanding CEOs realize that their company's future is too important to outsource. They take a personal role in it." Tichy estimates that Jack Welch, General Electric's chairman and CEO spends 30% of his time on leadership develop-ment. Welch even teaches a development program for senior leaders once a week. Andy Grove, CEO of Intel Corporation personally teaches the company's orientation program for managers and requires his managers to teach. When PepsiCo's CEO Roger Enrico was vice chairman of the firm, he spent 110 days over an 18-month period coaching high-potential executives and honing their ideas.

Source: Adopted from Industry Week, "The Stuff of Leadership," August 18, 1997, p. 100.

to lead. But these traits must be analyzed in terms of the leadership situation (described in detail later in this chapter). Management Illustration 16.1 discusses one leadership quality that has been found in several of today's successful CEO's.

Basic Leadership Styles

Other studies dealt with the style of the leader. They found three basic leadership styles: autocratic, laissez-faire, and democratic. The main difference among these styles is where the decision-making function rests. Generally, the **autocratic leader** makes more decisions for the group; the **laissez-faire leader** allows people within the group to make all decisions, and the **democratic leader** guides and encourages the group to make decisions. More detail about each of the leadership styles is given in Figure 16.4. (Figure 16.4 implies that the democratic style is the most desirable and productive. However, current research on leadership, discussed later in this chapter, does not necessarily support this conclusion.) The primary contribution of this research was identifying the three basic styles of leadership.

autocratic leader makes most decisions for the group.
laissez-faire leader allows people within the group to make all decisions.
democratic leader guides and encourages the group to make decisions.

Ohio State Studies

A series of studies on leadership was conducted at Ohio State University to find out the most important behaviors of successful leaders. The researchers wanted to find out what a successful leader does, regardless of the type of group being led: a mob, a religious group, a university, or a business organization. To do this, they developed a questionnaire called the **Leader Behavior Description Questionnaire (LBDQ)**. Both the original form and variations of it are still used today.

In using the questionnaire, two leader behaviors emerged consistently as being the most important: consideration and initiating structure. The term **consideration** refers to the leader behavior of showing concern for individual group

leader behavior description questionnaire (LBDQ) a questionnaire to determine what a successful leader does, regardless of the type of group being led.
consideration leader behavior of showing concern for individual group members and satisfying their needs.

313

FIGURE 16.4   Relationship between Styles of Leadership and Group Members

Autocratic Style

Leader
1. The individual is very conscious of his or her position.
2. He or she has little trust and faith in members of the group.
3. This leader believes pay is a just reward for working and the only reward that will motivate employees.
4. Orders are issued to be carried out, with no questions allowed and no explanations given.

Group members
1. No responsibility is assumed for performance, with people merely doing what they are told.
2. Production is good when the leader is present, but poor in the leader's absence.

Laissez-Faire Style

Leader
1. He or she has no confidence in his or her leadership ability.
2. This leader does not set goals for the group.

Group members
1. Decisions are made by whomever in the group is willing to do it.
2. Productivity generally is low, and work is sloppy.
3. Individuals have little interest in their work.
4. Morale and teamwork generally are low.

Democratic Style

Leader
1. Decision making is shared between the leader and the group.
2. When the leader is required or forced to make a decision, his or her reasoning is explained to the group.
3. Criticism and praise are given objectively.

Group members
1. New ideas and change are welcomed.
2. A feeling of responsibility is developed within the group.
3. Quality of work and productivity generally are high.
4. The group generally feels successful.

Source: Adapted from Leland B. Bradford and Ronald Lippitt, "Building a Democratic Work Group," *"Personnel 22,* no. 3 (November 1945). Copyright © 1945 by American Management Association, Inc. Reprinted by permission of the publisher.

initiating structure   leader behavior of structuring the work of group members and directing the group toward the attainment of the group's goals.

members and satisfying their needs. The term **initiating structure** refers to the leader behavior of structuring the work of group members and directing the group toward the attainment of the group's goals.

Since the Ohio State research, many other studies have been done on the relationship between the leader behaviors of consideration and initiating structure and their resulting effect on leader effectiveness. The major conclusions that can be drawn from these studies are:[7]

1. Leaders scoring high on consideration tend to have more satisfied subordinates than do leaders scoring low on consideration.

2. The relationship between the score on consideration and leader effectiveness depends on the group being led. In other words, a high score on consideration was positively correlated with leader effectiveness for managers

and office staff in a large industrial firm, whereas a high score on consideration was negatively correlated with leader effectiveness for production foremen.

3. There is also no consistent relationship between initiating structure and leader effectiveness; rather, the relationship varies depending on the group that is being lead.

University of Michigan Studies

The Institute for Social Research of the University of Michigan conducted studies to discover principles contributing both to the productivity of a group and to the satisfaction derived by group members. The initial study was conducted at the home office of the Prudential Insurance Company in Newark, New Jersey.

Interviews were conducted with 24 section heads or supervisors and 419 non-supervisory personnel. Results of the interviews showed that supervisors of high-producing work groups were more likely:

1. To receive general rather than close supervision from their superiors.
2. To like the amount of authority and responsibility they have in their job.
3. To spend more time in supervision.
4. To give general rather than close supervision to their employees.
5. To be employee oriented rather than production oriented.

Supervisors of low-producing work groups had basically opposite characteristics and techniques. They were production oriented and gave close supervision.

Rensis Likert, then director of the institute, published the results of his years of research in the book *New Patterns of Management*, which is a classic in its field.[8] Likert believes there are four patterns or styles of leadership or management employed by organizations. He has identified and labeled these styles as follows:

System 1: Exploitative authoritative. Authoritarian form of management that attempts to exploit subordinates.

System 2: Benevolent authoritative. Authoritarian form of management, but paternalistic in nature.

System 3: Consultative. Manager requests and receives inputs from subordinates but maintains the right to make the final decision.

System 4: Participative. Manager gives some direction, but decisions are made by consensus and majority, based on total participation.

Likert used a questionnaire to determine the style of leadership and the management pattern employed in the organization as a whole. The results of his studies indicated that System 4 was the most effective style of management and that organizations should strive to develop a management pattern analogous to this system.

The Managerial Grid

Robert Blake and Jane Mouton have also developed a method of classifying the leadership style of an individual.[9] The **Managerial Grid**®, depicted in Figure 16.5, is a two-dimensional framework rating a leader on the basis of concern for people and concern for production. (Notice that these activities closely relate to the leader activities from the Ohio State studies—consideration and initiating

managerial grid® a two-dimensional framework rating a leader on the basis of concern for people and concern for production.

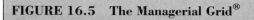

FIGURE 16.5   The Managerial Grid®

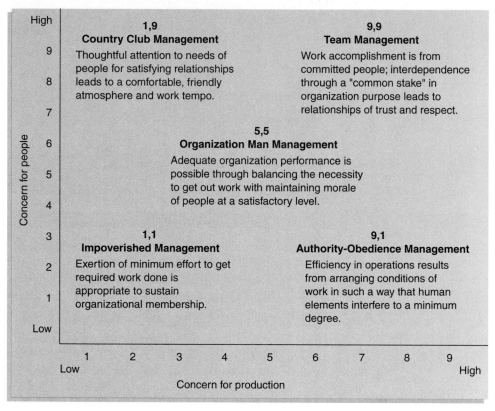

Source: Robert R. Blake and Jane Srygley Mouton. *The New Managerial Grid®* (Houston: Gulf Publishing, 1978), p. 11. Copyright © 1978 by Gulf Publishing Company. Reproduced by permission.

structure.) A questionnaire is used to locate a particular style of leadership or management on the grid.

Blake and Mouton identified five basic styles of management, using the Managerial Grid. *Authority-obedience*—located in the lower right-hand corner (9,1 position)—assumes that efficiency in operations results from properly arranging the conditions at work with minimum interference from other people. The opposite view, *country club management*—located in the upper left-hand corner (1,9 position)—assumes that proper attention to human needs leads to a comfortable organizational atmosphere and workplace. *Team management*—in the upper right-hand corner (9,9)—combines a high degree of concern for people with a high degree of concern for production. The other two styles on the grid are *impoverished management* (1,1) and *organization man management* (5,5). The Managerial Grid is intended to serve as a framework for managers to learn what their leadership style is and to develop a plan to move toward a 9,9 team management style of leadership.

Fiedler's Contingency Studies of Leadership

The leadership studies discussed so far are similar in that they did not specifically address the complex differences between groups (such as production workers versus accountants) and their influences on leader behavior. To imply that a manager should be employee oriented rather than production oriented (Michigan studies) or that the manager should exhibit concern for both production and people (Blake and Mouton) does not say much about what the manager should do in particular situations. Nor does it offer much guidance for daily leadership situations. As a result, research began to focus on the style of leadership that is most effective in particular situations.[10] This is called the **contingency approach to leadership.**

contingency approach to leadership focuses on the style of leadership that is most effective in particular situations.

One of the first studies using the contingency approach was conducted by Fred Fiedler.[11] He studied the match between the leader's personality and the situation. Fiedler defined two basic leader personality traits—task and relationship motivation. Task-motivated leaders gain satisfaction from the performance of a task. Relationship-motivated leaders gain satisfaction from interpersonal relationships. Fiedler viewed task versus relationship as a leader trait that was relatively constant for any given person.

A scale, called the least preferred coworker scale (LPC), was used to measure whether a person is a task- or relationship-oriented leader. Respondents were asked to think of all the people they had worked with and select the person with whom they could work least effectively. The respondents then described their least preferred coworker on the LPC. Three sample items on the LPC are:[12]

Pleasant	8	7	6	5	4	3	2	1	Unpleasant
Friendly	8	7	6	5	4	3	2	1	Unfriendly
Cooperative	8	7	6	5	4	3	2	1	Uncooperative

A person who described a least preferred co-worker in fairly favorable terms was presumed to be motivated to have close interpersonal relations with others; Fiedler classified these people as relationship-motivated leaders. On the other hand, people who rejected co-workers with whom they had difficulties were presumed to be motivated to accomplish or achieve the task; they were classified as task-oriented leaders.[13]

Fiedler next turned to the situation in which the leader was operating. He placed leadership situations along a favorable-unfavorable continuum based on three major dimensions: leader-member relations, task structure, and position power. **Leader-member relations** refer to the degree others trust and respect the leader and to the leader's friendliness. This compares somewhat to referent power. **Task structure** is the degree to which job tasks are structured. For example, assembly-line jobs are more structured than managerial jobs. **Position power** refers to the power and influence that go with a job. A manager has more position power who is able to hire, fire, and discipline. Position power compares to coercive, reward, and legitimate power. Using these three dimensions, an eight-celled classification scheme was developed. Figure 16.6 shows this scheme along the continuum.

leader-member relations the degree that others trust and respect the leader and the leader's friendliness.
task structure the degree to which job tasks are structured.
position power the power and influence that go with a job.

Figure 16.7 shows the most productive style of leadership for each situation. In both highly favorable and highly unfavorable situations, a task-motivated leader was found to be more effective. In highly favorable situations, the group is ready to be directed and is willing to be told what to do. In highly favorable situations, the group welcomes having the leader make decisions and direct the group. In moderately favorable situations, a relationship-motivated leader was found to be more effective. In Situation 7 (moderately poor leader-member relations, unstructured task, and strong position power), the task and relationship styles of leadership were equally productive.

FIGURE 16.6   Fiedler's Classification of Situations

Situation	1	2	3	4	5	6	7	8
Leader-member relations	Good	Good	Good	Good	Poor	Poor	Poor	Poor
Task structure	Structured	Structured	Unstructured	Unstructured	Structured	Structured	Unstructured	Unstructured
Position power	Strong	Weak	Strong	Weak	Strong	Weak	Strong	Weak
	Favorable for leader						Unfavorable for leader	

FIGURE 16.7   Relationship of Leadership Style to Situation

Situation	1	2	3	4	5	6	7	8
Leader-member relations	Good	Good	Good	Good	Poor	Poor	Poor	Poor
Task structure	Structured	Structured	Unstructured	Unstructured	Structured	Structured	Unstructured	Unstructured
Leader position power	Strong	Weak	Strong	Weak	Strong	Weak	Strong	Weak
	Favorable for leader						Unfavorable for leader	
Most productive leadership style	Task	Task	Task	Relation	Relation	No data relation	Task or	Task

Continuum of Leader Behaviors

Robert Tannenbaum and Warren Schmidt also contend that different combinations of situational elements require different styles of leadership. They suggest that there are three important factors, or forces, involved in finding the most effective leadership style: forces in the manager, the subordinate, and the situation.[14] Furthermore, all of these forces are interdependent.

Figure 16.8 describes in detail the forces that affect leadership situations. Since these forces differ in strength and interaction in differing situations, one style of leadership is not effective in all situations.

In fact, Tannenbaum and Schmidt argue that there is a continuum of behaviors that the leader may employ, depending on the situation (see Figure 16.9). These authors further conclude that successful leaders are keenly aware of the forces that are most relevant to their behavior at a given time. Successful leaders accurately understand not only themselves but also the other persons in the organizational and social environment, and they are able to behave correctly in light of these insights.

Path–Goal Theory of Leadership

path–goal theory of leadership attempts to define the relationships between a leader's behavior and the subordinates' performance and work activities.

The **path–goal theory of leadership** attempts to define the relationships between a leader's behavior and the subordinates' performance and work activities.[15] Leader behavior is acceptable to subordinates to the degree that they see it as a source of satisfaction now or as a step toward future satisfaction. Leader behavior influences the motivation of subordinates when it makes the satisfaction of their needs contingent on successful performance; and it provides the guidance, support, and rewards needed for effective performance (but that are not already present in

FIGURE 16.8   Forces Affecting the Leadership Situation

Forces in the Manager	Forces in the Subordinates	Forces in the Situation
Value system: How the manager personally feels about delegating, degree of confidence in subordinates. Personal leadership inclinations. Authoritarian versus participative. Feelings of security in uncertain situations.	Need for independence: Some people need and want direction, while others do not. Readiness to assume responsibility: Different people need different degrees of responsibility. Tolerance for ambiguity: Specific versus general directions. Interest and perceived importance of the problem: People generally have more interest in, and work harder on, important problems. Degree of understanding and identification with organizational goals: A manager is more likely to delegate authority to an individual who seems to have a positive attitude about the organization. Degree of expectation in sharing in decision making: People who have worked under subordinate-centered leadership tend to resent boss-centered leadership.	Type of organization: Centralized versus decentralized. Work group effectiveness: How effectively the group works together. The problem itself: The work group's knowledge and experience relevant to the problem. Time pressure: It is difficult to delegate to subordinates in crisis situations. Demands from upper levels of management. Demands from government, unions, and society in general.

FIGURE 16.9   Continuum of Leader Behavior

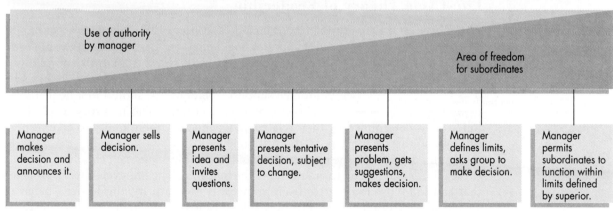

Source: Robert Tannenbaum and Warren H. Schmidt, "How to Choose a Leadership Pattern," *Harvard Business Review*, May–June 1973. Copyright © 1973 by the President and Fellows of Harvard College; all rights reserved.

the environment). The path–goal theory of leadership and the expectancy theory of motivation, which was described in the previous chapter, are closely related in that leader behaviors can either increase or decrease employee expectancies.

In path–goal theory, leader behavior falls into one of the four basic types—role classification, supportive, participative, and autocratic. *Role classification leadership*

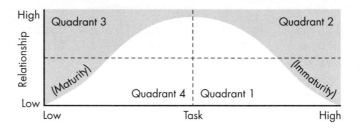

FIGURE 16.10 Life-Cycle Theory of Leadership

lets subordinates know what is expected of them, gives guidance as to what should be done and how, schedules and coordinates work among the subordinates, and maintains definite standards of performance. *Supportive leadership* has a friendly, approachable leader who attempts to make the work environment more pleasant for subordinates. *Participative leadership* involves consulting with subordinates and asking for their suggestions in the decision-making process. *Autocratic leadership* comes from a leader who gives orders that are not to be questioned by subordinates.

Under this theory, each of these leadership behaviors results in different levels of performance and subordinate satisfaction, depending on the structure of the work tasks. Role clarification leads to high satisfaction and performance for subordinates engaged in unstructured tasks. Supportive leadership brings the most satisfaction to those who work on highly structured tasks. Participative leader behavior enhances performance and satisfaction for subordinates engaged in ambiguous tasks. Autocratic leadership behavior has a negative effect on both satisfaction and performance in both structured and unstructured task situations.

Life-Cycle Theory of Leadership

Paul Hersey and Kenneth Blanchard include maturity of the followers as an important factor in leader behavior.[16] According to the **life-cycle theory of leadership,** as the level of maturity of followers increases, structure (task) should be reduced while socioemotional support (relationship) should first be increased and then gradually decreased. The maturity level of the followers is determined by their relative independence, their ability to take responsibility, and their achievement–motivation level.

life-cycle theory of leadership as the level of maturity of followers increases, structure should be reduced while socioemotional support should first be increased and then gradually decreased.

Figure 16.10 shows the cycle of the basic leadership styles that should be used by the leader, depending on the maturity of the followers. The life-cycle theory proposes that as the followers progress from immaturity to maturity, the leader's behavior should move from: (1) high task–low relationships to (2) high task–high relationships to (3) low task–high relationships to (4) low task–low relationships.

Transformational and Transactional Leaders

One final approach to the analysis of leadership has been based on how leaders and followers influence one another. Under this approach, leadership is viewed as either a transactional or transformational process. **Transactional leader-**

transactional leadership takes the approach that leaders engage in a bargaining relationship with their followers.

Management Illustration 16.2
Transformational Leadership

Jason replaced Ron, a solid, steady supervisor who had kept things under control and produced reliable results. Ron had a breadth of knowledge and was highly respected by his organization. As a result, his instructions were rarely questioned or challenged. He did not take risks, and little had been done to expand the unit for several years.

Shortly after Jason became supervisor, his new boss set a difficult challenge for the group. Jason called a meeting of the work group and laid out the challenge. The meeting started out badly. Everyone knew that the challenge was well beyond the current status and seemed out of reach. Jason said to the group, "Look, we might not meet the challenge, but let's see what we can do. You guys are the experts. How can I help?" One employee, John, said, "I've had some ideas in the past, but Ron didn't want to hear them." However, John laid out his ideas, others pitched in, and soon they developed an action plan. Then Jason took responsibility for ensuring that his team had the resources necessary to accomplish the plan.

Ultimately, the team met the challenge. After that, the team felt there was nothing they couldn't do. They set several more production records and improved safety levels. Jason exhibited the following leadership behaviors: clear goals, open communications and generation of team motivation, prudent risk taking, confidence building, shared responsibility, and winning together. These are also called transformational leadership behaviors.

Source: Adapted from "An Example of Transformational Leadership," *Business Quarterly*, Summer 1997, p. 63. For more information about *Business Quarterly*, visit its Web site at: www.cmpa.co/b3.html.

ship takes the approach that leaders engage in a bargaining relationship with their followers. Under this approach, the leader (manager):

1. Tells employees what they need to do to obtain rewards.
2. Takes corrective action only when employees fail to meet performance objectives.

transformational leader cultivates employee acceptance of the group mission.

The **transformational leader** (manager) cultivates employee acceptance of the group mission. The manager-employee relationship is one of mutual stimulation and is characterized by charisma on the part of the leader, inspiration by the leader, consideration by the leader of individual needs, and intellectual stimulation between the leader and followers.[18] Transformational leaders go beyond transacting with their followers and transform not only the situation but also the followers. Management Illustration 16.2 presents an example of transformational leadership.

LESSONS FROM LEADERSHIP STUDIES

How can all of these leadership theories be made relevant to the organization's need for effective managers? First, given the situational factors discussed in this chapter, it appears unlikely that a selection process will be developed to accurately predict successful leaders. The dynamic, changing nature of managerial roles further complicates the situation. Even if the initial process could select effective leaders, the dynamics of the managerial situation might make the selection invalid. Further, contrary to the conclusions of many studies, most leadership training today seems to assume there is one best way to lead.

However, leadership training designed to help leaders or potential leaders identify the nature of the leadership situation appears to have potential in developing more effective leaders. Such training is not so much a process of changing individual traits as it is one of ensuring that the person is operating in an appropriate situation or of teaching the individual how to act in a given situation. The following points on effective leadership can tentatively be made:

1. High consideration and initiating structure often provide a successful leadership style.
2. Under emergency or high-pressure situations, emphasis on initiating structure is desirable and often preferred by subordinates.
3. When the manager is the only information source for subordinates regarding their tasks, they often expect the manager to structure their behavior.
4. Subordinates have differing preferences regarding the degree of consideration and initiating structure exhibited by their managers.
5. Higher management often has set preferences regarding the leadership styles employed by lower-level managers.
6. Some managers can adjust their behavior to fit the situation; while others, in attempting to make this adjustment, appear to be fake and manipulative.

Summary

1. *Define Power.* Power is a measure of a person's potential to get others to do what he or she wants them to do, as well as to avoid being forced by others to do what he or she does not want to do.

2. *Describe the Sources of Power in Organizations.* The sources of power in organizations are reward, coercive, legitimate, expert, and referent.

3. *Define Leadership.* Leadership is the ability to influence people to willingly follow one's guidance or adhere to one's decisions.

4. *Describe the Self-Fulfilling Prophecy in Management.* The self-fulfilling prophecy basically postulates that what a manager expects of subordinates and the way he or she treats subordinates influences their performance and career progress.

5. *Define the Trait Theory of Leadership.* The trait theory of leadership emphasizes what the leader is like rather than what the leader does. Personality traits and physical characteristics are examined to differentiate leaders. Few studies have been able to support this theory.

6. *List and Define the Basic Leadership Styles.* The autocratic leader makes most decisions for the group. The laissez-faire leader allows people within the group to make all decisions. The democratic leader guides and encourages the group to make decisions.

7. *Understand the Managerial Grid.* The Managerial Grid is a two-dimensional framework rating a leader on the basis of concern for people and concern for production.

8. *Define the Contingency Approach to Leadership.* The contingency approach to leadership defines two basic styles of leadership—task motivated and relationship motivated. In both highly favorable and highly unfavorable situations, a task-motivated leader was found to be more effective. In moderately favorable situations, a elationship-motivated leader was found to be more effective.

9. *Explain the Path–Goal Theory of Leadership.* The path–goal theory of leadership attempts to define the relationships between a leader's behavior and the subordinates' performance and work activities. Leader behavior influences the motivation of subordinates when it makes the satisfaction of their needs contingent on successful performance; and it provides the guidance, support, and rewards needed for effective performance.

10. *Define the Life-Cycle Theory of Leadership.* According to the life-cycle theory of leadership, as the maturity of followers increases, structure (task) should be reduced while socioemotional support (relationship) should first be increased and then gradually decreased.

11. *Define Transactional and Transformational Leadership.* Transactional leadership takes the approach that leaders engage in a bargaining relationship with their followers. Transformational leadership involves cultivating employee acceptance of the group mission.

12. *Discuss Some of the Lessons That Can Be Learned from Leadership Research.* The following lessons can be learned from leadership research:

High consideration and initiating structure often provide a successful leadership style.

Under emergency or high-pressure situations, emphasis on initiating structure is desirable and often preferred by subordinates.

When the manager is the only information source for subordinates regarding their tasks, they often expect the manager to structure their behavior.

Subordinates have differing preferences regarding the degree of consideration and initiating structure exhibited by their managers.

Higher management often has set preferences regarding the leadership styles employed by lower-level managers.

Some managers can adjust their behavior to fit the situation; while others, in attempting to make this adjustment, appear to be fake and manipulative.

Preview Analysis

1. How did George Fisher create a new spirit at *Kodak?*
2. What had been *Kodak's* problem in the past?
3. What do you think would be George Fisher's approach to leadership?
4. What does the quote from Machiavelli's *The Prince* mean to you?

Review Questions

1. Define power.
2. Describe sources of power in organizations.
3. Define leadership.
4. Describe in detail the following three leadership styles:
   a. Autocratic.
   b. Laissez-faire.
   c. Democratic.
5. What was the purpose of the Ohio State leadership studies? What were the results of the Ohio State studies?
6. What was the purpose of the University of Michigan leadership studies? Explain the results of the Michigan studies.
7. Describe the Managerial Grid.®
8. What is Fiedler's contingency approach to leadership?
9. Describe three important forces, or factors, that Tannenbaum and Schmidt think should be considered in determining which leadership style is most effective.
10. What is the path–goal theory of leader effectiveness?
11. What is the life-cycle theory of leadership?
12. Define transactional and transformational leadership.
13. Describe some of the implications of the studies on leadership for organizations and managers.

Skill-Building Questions

1. Discuss the following statement: Leaders are born and cannot be developed.
2. Do you agree or disagree with this statement: Leaders must have courage. Why?
3. Do you think the variance in leadership styles of such people as Adolf Hitler, Franklin D. Roosevelt, and Martin Luther King, Jr., can be explained by any of the theories discussed in this chapter? Elaborate on your answer.
4. Explain what people mean when they use this statement: Leaders lead by example. Do you believe it? Explain your answer.

SKILL-BUILDING EXERCISE 16.1

Insubordination?

The company installed a new performance management system this year. You distributed the information and forms several weeks ago, and they were due to be completed two weeks ago. One manager reporting to you has not yet returned his. This morning, you ran into him in the parking lot and asked him about it. He reacted angrily with: "I haven't had time to do it—I don't have enough time to get my job done as it is, much less to take the time necessary to have my people write a bunch of meaningless information."

You asked him to stop by your office later to discuss it. As you think about how to handle this situation in the meeting, you consider several alternatives.

1. In view of his attitude and behavior, it clearly is appropriate to exercise your authority. Tell him, in no uncertain terms, that this must be done if he expects to continue as a supervisor.

2. Tell him why this program is important and use your best persuasion technique to sell him on doing it willingly.

3. Remind him that no salary increases, including his own, will be processed until the forms are completed.

Establish another deadline and let him know you expect it to be done then.

4. Explain to him that appraising employee performance is a part of every supervisor's job and that he himself is being evaluated on his performance in implementing this program.

5. Tell him you understand the difficulties of his job and the shortage of time available to do it, but remind him that this is a mandatory program that has top management's backing.

Other alternatives may be open to you, but assume these are the only ones you have considered. WITHOUT DISCUSSION with anyone, choose one of them and be prepared to defend your choice.

SKILL-BUILDING EXERCISE 16.2

Leadership Situations

Under the situational approach to leadership, different situations call for different leadership styles. Assuming this approach is correct, outline specific situations in which you would employ an autocratic style of leadership. In addition, outline situations in which you would employ a participative style of leadership. Be very specific in describing the situation. Be prepared to present your list of situations for both leadership styles to the class.

SKILL-BUILDING EXERCISE 16.3

Test Your Leadership Style

Read both statements in each entry in the following list and circle either *a* or *b* to indicate whichever best describes you—or is the least incorrect about you. You must answer every question to arrive at a proper score.

1. *a.* You are the person people most often turn to for help.
   b. You are aggressive and look after your best interests first.
2. *a.* You are more competent and better able to motivate others than most people.
   b. You strive to reach a position where you can exercise authority over large numbers of people and sums of money.
3. *a.* You try hard to influence the outcome of events.
   b. You quickly eliminate all obstacles that stand in the way of your goals.
4. *a.* There are few people you have as much confidence in as yourself.
   b. You have no qualms about taking what you want in this world.
5. *a.* You have the ability to inspire others to follow your lead.
   b. You enjoy having people act on your commands and are not opposed to making threats if you must.

6. *a.* You do your best to influence the outcome of events.
   b. You make all the important decisions, expecting others to carry them out.
7. *a.* You have a special magnetism that attracts people to you.
   b. You enjoy dealing with situations requiring confrontation.
8. *a.* You would enjoy consulting on the complex issues and problems that face managers of companies.
   b. You would enjoy planning, directing, and controlling the staff of a department to ensure the highest profit margins.
9. *a.* You want to consult with business groups and companies to improve effectiveness.
   b. You want to make decisions about other people's lives and money.
10. *a.* You could deal with level upon level of bureaucratic red tape and pressure to improve performance.
    b. You could work where money and profits are more important than other people's emotional well-being.

11. *a.* You typically must start your day before sunrise and continue into the night six to seven days a week.

   b. You must fire unproductive employees regularly and expediently to achieve set targets.

12. *a.* You must be responsible for how well others do their work (and you will be judged on their achievements, not yours).

   b. You have a workaholic temperament that thrives on pressure to succeed.

13. *a.* You are a real self-starter and full of enthusiasm about everything you do.

   b. Whatever you do, you have to do it better than anyone else.

14. *a.* You are always striving to be the best, the tops, the first at whatever you do.

   b. You have a driving, aggressive personality and fight hard and tough to gain anything worth having.

15. *a.* You have always been involved in competitive activities, including sports, and have won several awards for outstanding performance.

   b. Winning and succeeding are more important to you than playing just for enjoyment.

16. *a.* You will stick to a problem when you are getting nowhere.

   b. You quickly become bored with most things you undertake.

17. *a.* You are naturally carried along by some inner drive or mission to accomplish something that has never been done.

   b. Self-demanding and a perfectionist, you are always pressing yourself to perform to the limit.

18. *a.* You maintain a sense of purpose or direction that is larger than yourself.

   b. Being successful at work is the most important think to you.

19. *a.* You would enjoy a job requiring hard and fast decisions.

   b. You are loyal to the concepts of profit, growth, and expansion.

20. *a.* You prefer independence and freedom at work to a high salary or job security.

   b. You are comfortable in a position of control, authority, and strong influence.

21. *a.* You firmly believe that those who take the most risks with their own savings should receive the greatest financial rewards.

   b. There are few people's judgment you would have as much confidence in as your own.

22. *a.* You are seen as courageous, energetic, and optimistic.

   b. being ambitious, you are quick to take advantage of new opportunities.

23. *a.* You are good at praising others and you give credit readily when it's due.

   b. You like people, but have little confidence in their ability to do things the right way.

24. *a.* You usually give people the benefit of the doubt, rather than argue openly with them.

   b. Your style with people is direct, "tell it like it is" confrontation.

25. *a.* Although honest, you are capable of being ruthless if others are playing by devious rules.

   b. You grew up in an environment that stressed survival and required you to create your own rules.

Find Your Score

Count all the *a* responses you circled and multiply by 4 to get your percentage for leadership traits. Do the same with *b* answers to arrive at manager traits.

   Leader (number of *a*'s) _____ × 4 = _____%
   Manager (number of *b*'s) _____ × 4 = _____%

Interpret Your Score

Consider yourself a leader if you score more than 65 percent in the leader tally above; consider yourself a manager if you score more than 65 percent in the manager tally. If your scores cluster closer to a 50-50 split, you're a leader/manager.

The Leader

Your idea of fulfilling work is to motivate and guide coworkers to achieve their best and to reach common goals in their work by functioning in harmony. You are the sort of person who simply enjoys watching people grow and develop. You are commonly described as patient and encouraging in your dealings with people and a determined self-starter in your own motivation. Since you have a natural ability for inspiring top performances, there's usually little turnover among your employees, and staff relations are harmonious. At times, however, you may be too soft on people or overly patient when their performance lags. Where people are concerned, you may be too quick to let emotions get in the way of business judgments. Overall, you're the visionary type, not the day-to-day grinder.

The Manager

You are capable of getting good work out of people, but your style can be abrasive and provocative. You are especially competent at quickly taking charge, bulldozing through corporate red tape, or forcing others to meet tough work demands. Driven partly by a low threshold for boredom, you strive for more complexity in your work.

But you love the "game" of power and the sense of having control over others. Also, your confidence in your own ideas is so strong that you may be frustrated by working as part of a team. Your tendency to see your progress as the battle of a great mind against mediocre ones is not the best premise for bringing out the best in others. Therefore, the further up the corporate ladder you go, the more heavily human-relations problems will weigh against you.

The Leader/Manager Mix

As a 50–50 type, you probably do not believe in the need to motivate others. Instead, you maintain that the staff should have a natural desire to work as hard as you do,

without needing somebody to egg them on. You do your job well, and you expect the same from your subordinates. This means that while your own level of productivity is high, you are not always sure about how to motivate others to reach their full potential. Generally, however, you do have the ability to get others to do as you wish, without being abrasive or ruffling feathers. You may pride yourself on being surrounded by a very competent, professional staff that is self-motivated, requiring little of your own attention. But don't be too sure: almost everyone performs better under the right sort of encouraging leadership.

Source: Adapted from Michael Clugston, "Manager." *Canadian Business*, June 1988, pp. 268, 270.

CASE INCIDENT 16.1

Changes in the Plastics Division

Ed Sullivan was general manager of the Plastics Division of Warner Manufacturing Company. Eleven years ago, Ed hired Russell (Rusty) Means as a general manager of the Plastics Division's two factors. Ed trained Rusty as a manager and thinks Rusty is a good manager, an opinion based largely on the fact that products are produced on schedule and are of such quality that few customers complain. In fact, for the past eight years, Ed has pretty much let Rusty run the factories independently.

Rusty believes strongly that his job is to see that production runs smoothly. He feels that work is work. Sometimes it is agreeable, sometimes disagreeable. If an employee doesn't like the work, he or she can either adjust or quit. Rusty, say the factory personnel, "runs things. He's firm and doesn't stand for any nonsense. Things are done by the book, or they are not done at all." The turnover in the factories is low; nearly every employee likes Rusty and believes that he knows his trade and that he stands up for them.

Two months ago, Ed Sullivan retired and his replacement, Wallace Thomas, took over as general manager of the Plastics Division. One of the first things Thomas did was call his key management people together and announce some major changes he wanted to implement. These included: (1) bring the operative employees into the decision-making process; (2) establish a planning committee made up of three management members and three operative employees; (3) start a suggestion system; and (4) as quickly as possible, install a performance appraisal program agreeable to both management and the

operative employees. Wallace also stated he would be active in seeing that these projects would be implemented without delay.

After the meeting, Rusty was upset and decided to talk to Robert Mitchell, general manager of sales for the Plastics Division.

Rusty: Wallace is really going to change things, isn't he?

Robert: Yeah, maybe it's for the best. Things were a little lax under Ed.

Rusty: I liked them that way. Ed let you run your own shop. I'm afraid Wallace is going to be looking over my shoulder every minute.

Robert: Well, let's give him a chance. After all, some of the changes he's proposing sound good.

Rusty: Well, I can tell you our employees won't like them. Having them participate in making decisions and those other things are just fancy management stuff that won't work with our employees.

Questions

1. What different styles of leadership are shown in this case?

2. What style of leadership do you think Wallace will have to use with Rusty?

3. Do you agree with Rusty? Discuss.

CASE INCIDENT 16.2

Does the Congregation Care?

You are talking with a young pastor of an independent church with 300 adult members. The pastor came directly to the church after graduating from a nondenominational theological school and has been in the job for eight months.

Pastor: I don't know what to do. I feel as if I've been treading water ever since the day I got here; and frankly, I'm not sure that I will be here much longer. If they don't fire me, I may leave on my own. Maybe I'm just not cut out for the ministry.

You: What has happened since you came to this church?

Pastor: When I arrived, I was really full of energy and wanted to see how much this church could accomplish. The very first thing I did was to conduct a questionnaire survey of the entire adult membership to see what types of goals they wanted to pursue. Unfortunately, I found that the members had such mixed (and perhaps apathetic) feelings about the goals that it was hard to draw any conclusions. There were also a few who strongly favored more emphasis on internal things, such as remodeling the sanctuary, developing our music program, and setting up a day-care center for the use of the members. Most of the members, however, didn't voice any strong preferences.

A lot of people didn't return the questionnaire, and a few even seemed to resent my conducting the survey.

You: What have you done since you took the survey?

Pastor: To be honest about it, I've kept a pretty low profile, concentrating mainly on routine duties. I haven't tried to implement or even push any major new programs. One problem is that I've gotten the impression, through various insinuations, that my being hired was by no means an overwhelmingly popular decision. Evidently, a fairly substantial segment of the congregation was skeptical of my lack of experience and felt that the decision to hire me was railroaded through by a few members of the Pastoral Search Committee. I guess I am just reluctant to assume a strong leadership role until some consensus has developed concerning the goals of the church and I've had more time to gain the confidence of the congregation. I don't know how long that will take, though; and I'm not sure I can tolerate the situation much longer.

Questions

1. Analyze and explain the situation using any of the theories of leadership discussed in this chapter.

2. What would you recommend the young pastor do?

References and Additional Readings

[1]John P. Kotter, *Power in Management,* (New York: American Management Association, 1979) p. i.

[2]David C. McClelland, *Power: The Inner Experience* (New York: John Wiley & Sons, 1975), p. 255.

[3]John P. Kotter, *The Leadership Factor* (New York: The Free Press, 1988), pp. 25–26.

[4]For another view on Theory X and Theory Y, see T. C. Carbone, "Theory X and Theory Y Revisited," *Managerial Planning,* May–June 1981, pp. 24–27.

[5]Arthur G. Jago, "Leadership: Perspectives in Theory and Research," *Management Science,* March 1982, pp. 315–36.

[6]J. D. Barrow, "The Variables of Leadership: A Review and Conceptual Framework," *Academy of Management Review,* April 1977, p. 232.

[7]Victor H. Vroom, "Leadership," in *Handbook of Industrial & Organizational Psychology,* ed. Marvin D. Dunnette (Skokie, IL: Rand McNally, 1976), p. 1531.

[8]Rensis Likert, *New Patterns of Management* (New York: McGraw-Hill, 1961).

[9]Robert R. Blake and Jane Srygley Mouton, *The New Managerial Grid* (Houston: Gulf Publishing, 1978); Robert R. Blake and Jane S. Mouton, "How to Choose a Leadership Style," *Training and Development Journal,* February 1982, pp. 38–45.

[10]C. L. Graeff, "The Situational Leadership Theory: A Critical Review," *Academy of Management Review,* April 1983, pp. 285–91.

[11]Fred E. Fiedler, *A Theory of Leadership Effectiveness* (New York: McGraw-Hill, 1967)

[12]Ibid., p. 269.

[13]For more analysis on this subject, see Ramadhar Singh, "Leadership Style and Reward Allocation: Does Least Preferred Co-Worker Scale Measure Task and Relation Orientation?" *Organizational Behavior and Human Performance,* October 1983, pp. 178–97.

[14]Robert Tannenbaum and Warren Schmidt, "How to Choose a Leadership Pattern," *Harvard Business Review,* July–August 1986, p. 129.

[15]For an in-depth analysis of the path–goal theory, see J. F. Schriesheim and C. A. Schriesheim, "Test of the Path–Goal Theory of Leadership and Some Suggested Directions for Future Research," *Personnel Psychology,* Summer 1980, pp. 349–71; and Janet Falk and Eric R. Wendler, "Dimensionality of Leader–Subordinate Interactions: A Path–Goal Investigation," *Organizational Behavior and Human Performance,* October 1982, pp. 241–64.

[16]Paul Hersey and Kenneth Blanchard, "Life-Cycle Theory of Leadership," *Training and Development Journal,* June 1979, pp. 94–100.

[17]B. M. Bass, *Leadership and Performance beyond Expectations* (New York: Free Press, 1985).

[18]Ronald J. DeLuga, "Relationship of Transformational and Transactional Leadership with Employee Influencing Strategies," *Group and Organizational Studies,* December 1988, p. 457.

17

Managing Conflict and Stress

LEARNING OBJECTIVES

After studying this chapter, you should be able to:

1. Define conflict.

2. Discuss the useful effects of conflict.

3. Outline the stages of conflict development.

4. Present an approach for analyzing conflict.

5. Name five approaches of resolving interpersonal conflict.

6. Define stress.

7. Define burnout.

8. Outline the basic elements of a violence-prevention program.

9. Explain the three basic types of employee assistance programs.

10. Explain wellness programs.

The abuse began about ten years ago. Sally was verbally assaulted, beat-up, and thrown out of a moving vehicle. Even after divorcing her abusive husband and obtaining a restraining order, Sally was unable to escape his abuse. He began to stalk and follow her to the grocery store, to friends' houses and to her job at Massachusetts General Hospital. Sally turned to the hospital's employee assistance program for help. Initially Sally told the counselor that she was afraid for her child, who was also being abused. Through more intense questioning, it became clear that Sally was also a victim and that the threat of violence was escalating.

Source: Bonnie S. Michelman, Nancy P. Robb, and Leah Marie Coviello, "A Comprehensive Approach to Workplace Violence," *Security Management*, July 1998, pp. 28–35.

conflict   Overt behavior that results when an individual or a group of individuals thinks a perceived need or needs of the individual or group has been blocked or is about to be blocked.

Conflict is an overt behavior that results when an individual or group of individuals thinks a perceived need or needs of the individual or group has been blocked or is about to be blocked. Conflict occurs because individuals have different perceptions, beliefs, and goals. From an organizational perspective, conflict can be viewed as anything which disrupts the "normal" routine.[1]

Conflict in organizations is often assumed to be unnatural and undesirable, something to be avoided at all costs. Conflict can lead to rigidity in the system in which it operates, distort reality, and debilitate the participants in the conflict situation. Therefore, many organizations approach the management of conflict with the following assumptions:

1. Conflict is avoidable.
2. Conflict is the result of personality problems within the organization.
3. Conflict produces inappropriate reactions by the persons involved.
4. Conflict creates a polarization within the organization.

However, conflict is perfectly natural and should be expected to occur. Management must know when to eliminate conflict and when to build on it. Today's managers must accept the existence of conflict and realize that to attempt to stop all conflict is a mistake. The general consensus is that conflict itself is not undesirable; rather, it is a phenomenon that can have constructive or destructive effects.[2]

For example, in a struggle between two people for a promotion, the winner will probably think the conflict was most worthwhile, while the loser will likely reach the opposite conclusion. However, the impact of the conflict on the organization must also be considered. If the conflict ends in the selection and promotion of the better-qualified person, the effect is good from the organization's viewpoint. If, by competing, the parties have produced more or made improvements within their areas of responsibility, the effect is also positive. At the same time, there may be destructive effects. The overall work of the organization may have suffered during the conflict. The loser may resign or withdraw as a result of the failure. The conflict may become chronic and inhibit the work of the organization. In extreme cases, the health of one or both participants may be impaired.

The destructive effects of conflict are often obvious, whereas the constructive effects may be more subtle. The manager must be able to see these constructive effects and weigh them against the costs. Some potentially useful effects of conflict include the following:

1. Conflict energizes people. Even if not all of the resulting activity is constructive, it at least wakes people up and gets them moving.
2. Conflict is a form of communication; the resolution of conflict may open new and lasting channels.
3. Conflict often provides an outlet for pent-up tensions, resulting in catharsis. With the air cleansed, the participants can again concentrate on their primary responsibilities.
4. Conflict may actually be an educational experience. The participants may become more aware and more understanding of their opponents' functions and the problems with which they must cope.

Management Illustration 17.1 describes one management pioneer who was ahead of her time, especially in her views about conflict.

Management Illustration 17.1
Ahead of Her Time

Mary Parker Follett, born three years after the Civil War, had the vision that harmony could result from the proper use of conflict. This notion collided with the male-dominated society of her day who believed that the objective was not to resolve the conflict but rather to conquer it; men sought unconditional surrender.

In 1900, Follett embarked on a career as a Boston social worker. When she was in her late 50s, she used her experiences gained from running vocational guidance centers to lecture and write about management and leadership in business.

Follett challenged the psychologists of her day for "assuming that you cannot be a good leader unless you are aggressive, masterful, dominating. But I think not only that these characteristics are not the qualities essential to leadership but, on the contrary, that they often militate directly against leadership." Follett had many other views which were novel for her times but which are readily accepted today.

Peter Drucker, one of the century's leading management writers, has described Follett as "the brightest star in the management firmament" of her time. A collection of Follett's work has recently been published.

Source: "A Guru Ahead of Her Time," *Nation's Business*, May 1997, p. 24. To read more from *Nation's Business*, visit their Web site at: www.nationsbusiness.org.

PROGRESSIVE STAGES OF CONFLICT

A manager must be aware of conflict's dynamic nature. Conflict usually does not appear suddenly. It passes through a series of progressive stages as tensions build. These stages of development are as follows:

1. Latent conflict: At this stage, the basic conditions for conflict exist but have not yet been recognized. For example, racial differences may preclude basic communication channels between two employees.

2. Perceived conflict: One or both participants recognize the cause of the conflict. For example, an employee begins to complain that his or her manager doesn't like him or her.

3. Felt conflict: Tension is beginning to build between the participants, although no real struggle has begun. When employees become short-tempered with one another, this form of conflict begins to emerge.

4. Manifest conflict: The struggle is under way, and the behavior of the participants makes the existence of the conflict apparent to others not directly involved. Arguments or damaged feelings are no longer privately held. Disruptions begin to arise in public.

5. Conflict aftermath: The conflict has been ended through resolution or suppression. This establishes new conditions that will lead either to more effective cooperation or to a new conflict that may be more severe than the first. This form of conflict can result in firings, punishments, or future difficulties. In some instances, resolution can be positive and serve to end the issue.

Conflict does not always pass through all of these stages. Furthermore, the parties in conflict may not be at the same stage simultaneously. For example, one participant may be at the manifest stage of conflict while the other is at the perceived stage.

ANALYZING CONFLICT

Conflict can be analyzed from many different perspectives. One approach is based on the party or parties involved: intrapersonal, interpersonal, and intergroup. The following sections examine these three perspectives in more detail.

Intrapersonal Conflict

intrapersonal conflict   Conflict internal to the individual.

Intrapersonal conflict is internal to the individual. It is probably the most difficult form of conflict to analyze. Intrapersonal conflict can result when barriers exist between the drive and the goal. Such conflict may also result when goals have both positive and negative aspects and when competing and conflicting goals exist. For example, when Jon Howard, a flight attendant with Trans World Airlines, had to choose between job security and salary, he chose security. The company offered its employees part ownership in the company and job security but reduced their salaries by 40 percent and increased their work hours. The conflict and the decision Howard chose has given him many sleepless nights and grave concern about his future.[3]

When a drive or a motive is blocked before the goal is reached, frustration and anxiety can occur. Barriers can be either overt (rules and procedures) or covert (mental hang-ups). When a barrier exists, people tend to react with defense mechanisms, which are behaviors used to cope with frustration and anxiety. Figure 17.1 lists some typical defense mechanisms.

Responses to frustration and anxiety vary and can be expressed through withdrawal behavior (higher absenteeism and turnover rates), aggression (sabotage and other destructive work acts), excessive drinking, drug abuse, and more subtle responses such as ulcers or heart trouble.

Goal conflict occurs when a goal has both positive and negative features or when two or more competing goals exist. Three major forms of conflicting goals are (1) mutually exclusive positive goals (conflict occurs because a person has to choose between two or more positive goals at the same time), (2) positive–negative goals (the person tries to achieve a goal that has both positive and negative aspects), and (3) negative–negative aspects (the person tries to avoid two or more negative, mutually exclusive goals). Since goal conflict forces the person to make a decision, decision making often creates a feeling of conflict within the individual. This

dissonance   Feeling of conflict felt by individual trying to make a decision.

dissonance or disharmony is a danger sign that managers must watch for, since it can lead to a loss of mental concentration and productivity in the workplace.

An extension of goal conflict is *cognitive conflict*, in which ideas or thoughts are perceived as incompatible in a given situation, and *affective conflict*, in which feelings or emotions are incompatible and the result is usually anger at the other person. In addition, task interdependence (too many jobs), scarce rewards, communication failures, individual differences, and inadequate reward systems can increase the level and amount of conflict. Managing all of these occurrences is a constant challenge for the manager.

Interpersonal Conflict

interpersonal conflict   Conflict between two or more individuals.

Interpersonal conflict, or conflict between two or more individuals, may result from many factors. Opposing personalities often result in interpersonal conflict. Some people simply rub each other the wrong way. The extrovert and the introvert, the boisterous

FIGURE 17.1   Reactions to Frustration and Anxiety

Adjustive Reactions	Psychological Process	Illustration
Compensation	Individual devotes himself or herself to a pursuit with increased vigor to make up for some feeling of real or imagined inadequacy.	Zealous, hardworking president of the Twenty-Five Year Club who has never advanced very far in the company hierarchy.
Conversion	Emotional conflicts are expressed in muscular, sensory, or bodily symptoms of disability, malfunctioning, or pain.	A disabling headache keeping a staff member off the job the day after a cherished project has been rejected.
Displacement	Redirects pent-up emotions toward persons, ideas, or objects other than the primary source of the emotion.	Roughly rejecting a simple request from a subordinate after receiving a rebuff from the boss.
Fantasy	Daydreaming or other forms of imaginative activity provide an escape from reality and imagined satisfactions.	An employee's daydream of the day in the staff meeting when he corrects the boss' mistakes and is publicly acknowledged as the real leader of the group.
Negativism	Active or passive resistance, operating unconsciously.	The manager who, having been unsuccessful in getting out of a committee assignment, picks apart every suggestion anyone makes in the meetings.
Rationalization	Justifies inconsistent or undesirable behavior, beliefs, statements, and motivations by providing acceptable explanations for them.	Padding the expense account because "everybody does it."
Regression	Individual returns to an earlier and less mature level of adjustment in the face of frustration.	A manager, having been blocked in some administrative pursuit, busies himself with clerical duties or technical details more appropriate for his subordinates.
Repression	Completely excludes from consciousness impulse, experiences, and feelings that are psychologically disturbing because they arouse a sense of guilt or anxiety.	An employee "forgetting" to tell his boss the circumstances of an embarrassing situation.
Resignation, apathy, and boredom	Breaks psychological contact with the environment, withholding any sense of emotional or personal involvement.	Employee who, receiving no reward, praise, or encouragement, no longer cares whether or not he does a good job.
Flight or withdrawal	Leaves the field in which frustration, anxiety, or conflict is experienced, either physically or psychologically.	The salesman's big order falls through, and he takes the rest of the day off; constant rebuff or rejection by superiors and colleagues pushes an older employee toward being a loner and ignoring whatever friendly gestures are made.

Source: Timothy W. Costello and Sheldon S. Zalkind, *Psychology in Administration: A Research Orientation* (Englewood Cliffs, NJ: Prentice Hall, 1963), pp. 148–149. Copyright © 1963 by Prentice-Hall, Inc. Reprinted by permission of the publisher.

individual and the reserved one, the optimist and the pessimist, the impulsive person and the deliberate person are but a few possible combinations that may spark conflict.

Prejudices based on personal background or ethnic origin can also cause interpersonal conflict. Obvious examples are racial and religious conflicts, but other, more subtle, prejudices exist. Examples include the college graduate versus the person with only a high school education, the married person versus the divorced person, and the long-time employee versus the new hire.

Another cause of interpersonal conflict arises when individuals are dissatisfied with their roles relative to the roles of others. An employee may be compatible with both his or her manager and co-workers. However, when a peer is promoted to a management job, the employee may no longer accept his or her role in relation to the former peer.

In a classic discussion of role conflict, Robert L. Kahn revealed that each individual organizational member has numerous roles to play. In many instances, role conflict occurs because of job overload (especially at the managerial level). In attempting to deal with role conflict, employees may cut themselves off from peers and support groups, suffer high anxiety, reduce their productivity, and eventually become demotivated.[4]

Intergroup (Structural) Conflict

intergroup (structural) conflict   Conflict that results from the organizational structure; may be relatively independent of the individuals occupying the roles within the structure.

The organizational structure may be the cause of **intergroup** or **structural conflict.** Such conflict may be relatively independent of the individuals occupying the roles within the structure. For example, structural conflict between marketing and production departments is fairly common. The marketing department, being customer oriented, may believe some exceptions can and should be made in production for the sake of current and future sales. The production department may view such exceptions as unreasonable and not in the best interests of the organization. Hence, a structural conflict occurs. The conflict situation can be even more intense if the managers of each department are also experiencing interpersonal conflict. The following sections discuss various types of structural conflict.

Goal Segmentation and Rewards   Each functional unit of an organization has different functional goals. These can cause conflict that, when it emerges, may seem to be personality clashes. The classic problem of inventory levels illustrates this dilemma. The marketing department would like to keep finished-goods inventories high to supply all of the customers' needs on short notice. The finance department would like to keep inventories low because of the cost of maintaining these inventories. The end result is often a conflict between departments.

The reward system is a key method for reducing this type of conflict. A reward system that stresses the separate performances of the departments feeds the conflict. However, rewarding the combined efforts of the conflicting departments reduces the conflict.

Nevertheless, inadequate reward systems that lead to conflict are still very common. Four factors generally inhibit implementing effective reward systems:

- Insistence on an objective criterion (i.e., rewards are linked to one objective when in fact many objectives come into play).
- Overemphasis on highly visible behaviors (for example, difficult to observe concepts such as team building are rarely rewarded).
- Hypocrisy (having a reward system that actually encourages one type of behavior while claiming to encourage another).
- Emphasis on morality or equity rather than efficiency (many situations are not just "either-or" situations).[5]

Mutual Departmental Dependence   Sometimes two departments or units of an organization are dependent on each other to accomplish their respective goals, creating a potential for structural conflict. For instance, the marketing department's sales depend on the volume of production from the production department; at the same time, the production department's quotas are based on the sales of the marketing department. This type of mutual dependence exists in many organizations.

Unequal Departmental Dependence   Often departmental dependence is unequal and fosters conflict. In most organizations, for instance, staff groups are more dependent on line groups. The staff generally must understand the problems of the line, cooperate with the line, and sell ideas to the line. However, the line does not have to reciprocate. One tactic in this form of conflict is an attempt by the more dependent unit to interfere with the work performance of the independent group. In doing so, the more dependent group hopes the other group will cooperate once it realizes how the dependent group can hinder progress.

Functional Unit and the Environment   Functional units obviously perform different tasks and cope with different parts of the environment. Research has shown that the more the environments served by functional units differ, the greater the potential for conflict. Paul Lawrence and Jay Lorsch have developed four basic dimensions to describe these differences: (1) structure—the basic type of managerial style employed; (2) environment orientation—the orientation of the unit to the outside world; (3) time span orientation—the unit's planning-time perspectives; and (4) interpersonal orientation—the openness and permissiveness of interpersonal relationships.[6]

Role Dissatisfaction   Role dissatisfaction may also produce structural conflict. Professionals in an organizational unit who receive little recognition and have limited opportunities for advancement may initiate conflict with other units. Purchasing agents often demonstrate this form of conflict.

Role dissatisfaction and conflict often result when a group that has low perceived status sets standards for another group. For example, within academic institutions, administrators—whom the faculty may view as having less status—often set standards of performance and make administrative decisions that affect the faculty.

Role Ambiguity   Ambiguities in the description of a particular job can lead to structural conflict. When the credit or blame for the success or failure of a particular assignment cannot be determined between two departments, conflict is likely to result. For instance, improvements in production techniques require the efforts of the engineering and production departments. After the improvements are made, credit is difficult to assign; thus, conflict often results between these two departments.

Common Resource Dependence   When two organizational units are dependent on common but scarce resources, potential for conflict exists. This often occurs when two departments are competing for budget money. Each naturally believes its projects are more important and should be funded.

Communication Barriers   Semantic differences can cause conflict. For instance, purchasing agents and engineers generally use different language to describe similar materials, which leads to conflict. Communication-related conflict also occurs when a physical or organizational barrier to effective communication exists. Company headquarters and branch offices frequently suffer from this problem.

Figure 17.2 summarizes types of intergroup or structural conflict.[7]

Political Conflict

Intrapersonal, interpersonal, and structural conflict generally are not planned; they simply develop as a result of existing circumstances. But political (sometimes called *strategic*) conflict is started purposely and is often undertaken with an elaborate battle plan. Such conflict usually results from the promotion of self-interests on the part of an individual or a group. The instigator(s) has a clear goal, and those who stand in the

FIGURE 17.2   Summary of Types of Intergroup (or Structural) Conflict

Type	Example
Goal segmentation and rewards	Different inventory levels are desired by different functional departments.
Mutual departmental dependence	Marketing department's sales are dependent on the volume of production from the production department.
Unequal departmental dependence	Staff departments are generally more dependent on line departments.
Functional unit and environment	The environment faced by an applied research department and a sales department are different and can lead to conflict between these departments.
Role dissatisfaction	Professionals in an organizational unit who receive little attention.
Role ambiguities	When the credit or blame for the success or failure of a particular assignment cannot be determined between two departments.
Common resource dependence	Two departments competing for computer time.
Communication barriers	Purchasing agents and engineers may use different language to describe similar materials, and conflict can result from those semantic differences.

way are the adversary. In organizations, the goal is usually to gain an advantage over the opponent within the reward system. The potential reward may be a bonus or commission, a choice assignment, a promotion, or an expansion of power. Whatever it is, usually one of the participants will receive it (or the greatest portion of it). As an example, the vice presidents of an organization may find themselves in a political conflict situation as the retirement of the president nears. An ambitious vice president, in an attempt to better his or her personal chances for the presidency, may create a political conflict with one or more of the other vice presidents.

Political conflict does not always imply that the participants are dishonest or unethical. Indeed, rewards are there to be pursued with vigor. But such conflicts can degenerate into unfair play because the participants cannot resist the temptation to win at all costs.

MANAGING CONFLICT

As described earlier, conflict is an inherent part of any organization. Even though some conflict may be beneficial to an organization, unresolved conflict or conflict that is resolved poorly usually results in negative consequences such as job withdrawal behaviors, unionization activity, low morale and lower levels of goal attainment.[8] Successful resolution of conflict among employees often depends on the employees' immediate manager or managers. The objective of the manager is not to resolve the conflict but to act as a referee and counselor in helping the participant(s) reach an acceptable solution. Understanding the type of conflict—intrapersonal, structural, interpersonal, or political—and the stage of the conflict cycle will aid the manager.

Approaches to Resolving Conflict Situations

Five general approaches can be used to resolve interpersonal conflict situations: (1) withdrawal of one or more of the participants, (2) smoothing over the conflict, (3) compromising, (4) forcing the conflict to a conclusion through third-party in-

---

FIGURE 17.3   Tactics for Managing Interpersonal Conflict with Difficult People

Hostile-aggressives:

Stand up for yourself.
Give them time to run down.
Use self-assertive language.
Avoid a direct confrontation.

Complainers:

Listen attentively.
Acknowledge their feelings.
Avoid complaining with them.
State the facts without apology.
Use a problem-solving mode.

Clams:

Ask open-ended questions.
Be patient in waiting for a response.
Ask more open-ended questions.
If no response occurs, tell clams what you plan to do, because no discussion has taken place.

Superagreeables:

In a nonthreatening manner, work hard to find out why they will not take action.
Let them know you value them as people.
Be ready to compromise and negotiate, and do not allow them to make unrealistic commitments.
Try to discern the hidden meaning in their humor.

Negativists:

Do not be dragged into their despair.
Do not try to cajole them out of their negativism.
Discuss the problem thoroughly, without offering solutions.
When alternatives are discussed, bring up the negative side yourself.
Be ready to take action alone, without their agreement.

Know-it-alls:

Bulldozers:
Prepare yourself.
Listen and paraphrase their main points.
Use the questioning form to raise problems.
Balloons:
State facts or opinions as your own perceptions of reality.
Find a way for balloons to save face.
Confront balloons alone, not in public.

Indecisive Stallers:

Raise the issue of why they are hesitant.
If you are the problem, ask for help.
Keep the action steps in your own hands.
Possibly remove the staller from the situation.

Source: R. M. Bramson, *Coping With Difficult People* (New York. Dell, 1981). © 1981 by Robert Bramson. Used with permission of Doubleday, a division of Bantam Doubleday Dell Publishing Group, Inc.

---

tervention, and (5) confrontation between the participants in an effort to solve the underlying source of conflict. Withdrawal of one or more of the participants involves actions such as firing, transferring, or having an employee quit. Smoothing over the conflict happens when the manager pretends the conflict does not exist. Compromising occurs when both sides give up some of what they want. Third-party intervention occurs when the manager steps in and forces a solution on the parties in conflict. Confrontation occurs when both parties confront each other with what is really bothering them.

While each of these can work in certain situations, confrontation is generally considered to be the most effective method of resolving conflict, while third-party intervention has been found to be the least effective method.[9] One reason for this is that resolutions reached through confrontation tend to be more long lasting.

In some instances, however, the profiles of the parties involved in conflict fall into the category of "difficult people." Figure 17.3 suggests some rather interesting tactics for dealing with these personalities. The general rule for the manager is to ensure that each situation involving interpersonal conflict is dealt with based on the individual's and the situation's basic characteristics.[10]

Much structural conflict results from interdependencies among organizational units that are inherent in the organizational structure. Some of this conflict potential may be removed by decoupling the conflicting units by reducing their common resource dependencies; giving each control over its own resources; introducing buffer inventories; or invoking impersonal, straightforward rules for resource allocation. Decoupling may also occur by duplicating facilities for dependent departments. However, this approach may be too expensive for the organization. A more affordable approach to reducing interdependencies is the use of a "linking" position between dependent departments. The purpose is to ease communication and coordination among interdependent and potentially conflicting departments. Another approach is to design the work flow so that the system reflects more logical and complete work units in which responsibility and authority are more consistent. Finally, the matrix organization can offer a means for constructive confrontation, which, as stated earlier, is the most effective method of conflict resolution.[11]

The Conflict Interface

Besides acting as referees in enforcing these rules, managers can give valuable assistance to the participant(s) without interfering with their responsibility to resolve the conflict. Managers can help the participants understand why the conflict exists and what underlying issues must be resolved. They can also help obtain information needed to reach a solution. To maximize the constructive aspects of the conflict and speed its resolution while minimizing the destructive consequences, the manager should make sure the participants are aware of the following ground rules for constructive confrontations:

1. Review past actions and clarify the issues before the confrontation begins.
2. Communicate freely; do not hold back grievances.
3. Do not surprise the opponent with a confrontation for which she or he is unprepared.
4. Do not attack the opponent's sensitive spots that have nothing to do with the issues of the conflict.
5. Keep to specific issues; do not argue aimlessly.
6. Maintain the intensity of the confrontation and ensure that all participants say all they want to say. If the basic issues have been resolved at this point, agree on what steps are to be taken toward resolving the conflict.

In interpersonal conflict, managers can regulate somewhat the frequency of contacts between the participants and perhaps establish a problem-solving climate when they meet. A manager's most important contribution, however, is to keep the individuals working toward a true resolution of the conflict. Confrontation of the conflict situation within the ground rules just described should encourage constructive conflict within the organization.[12]

WORKPLACE STRESS

Just as conflict is an integral part of organizational life, so is stress. Stress is part of living and can contribute to personal growth, development, and mental health. However, excessive and prolonged stress generally becomes quite negative. For example, experts have estimated the workplace stress is the cause of more than one million days of absenteeism and more than $20 billion in workers' compensation costs in the U.S. each year.[13] A 1996 survey by the Gallup Organization found that 16.7 percent of 1,000 working adults surveyed reported that stress interfered with their ability to concentrate at work either all of the time or quite a bit.[14]

stress   Mental and/or physical condition that results from a perceived threat of danger (physical or emotional) and the pressure to remove it.

Stress is the mental and/or physical condition that results from a perceived threat of danger (physical or emotional) and the pressure to remove it. The potential for stress exists when an environmental situation presents a demand that threatens to exceed the person's capabilities and resources for meeting it, under conditions in which the person expects a substantial difference in rewards and costs resulting from meeting the demand versus not meeting it.

In its earliest stages, stress manifests itself in exaggerated behavior such as cynical attitudes, increased use of alcohol, tobacco and medications.[15] If allowed to continue, stress affects employees on the job in several ways, including increased absenteeism, job turnover, lower productivity, and mistakes on the job. In addition, prolonged excessive stress can result in both physical and emotional problems. Some common stress-related disorders include tension and migraine headaches; coronary heart disease; high blood pressure; and muscle tightness in the chest, neck, and lower back. From a psychological perspective, inordinate or prolonged stress can impair concentration, memory, sleep, appetite, motivation, mood, and the ability to relate to others. In addition, recent studies have shown that stress at work is carried to the home environment. Soon the employee becomes surrounded by stress and becomes dysfunctional.[16]

Stress strikes all levels of workers. While there is no single course of workplace stress, much of today's stress-related illnesses world-wide is the result of added demands placed on employees because of downsizing and the difficulties that women in particular force in juggling the demands of work and family.[17] In the face of reductions in workforces due to downsizing and reengineering, many employees have had to increase their job scopes and responsibilities. Those who experience "good job fit" do not seem to experience as much stress as those who are mismatched or overmatched in their expanded positions.[18] Figure 17.4 lists some of the more common sources and suggested causes of job-related stress.

The Workplace Stress Audit

The first step in managing workplace stress is to determine what the specific sources of stress are since they can and usually do vary from situation to situation. One method of doing this is to undertake a stress audit. A stress audit attempts to identify any work-related causes of stress. A stress audit can be undertaken by outside consultants or by internal personnel. When a company undertakes a stress audit, management is acknowledging that the workplace can be a source of stress and that it is not just the individual employees' personal problems.

Once the sources of stress have been identified, solutions for reducing the stress should be explored. For example, in the case of North Sea oil rig workers, audits discovered that major sources of stress included long amounts of time away from the family, the foul weather and its effect on transporting and working conditions, living conditions and a lack of opportunity for relaxing and exercising during free time.[19] While all of these sources of stress seemed inherent to the job, remedies were discovered. The shift system could be rearranged, exercise facilities, no-smoking areas, quiet rooms, and more private sleeping areas could be provided. Even the stress of having to fly back and forth to the rigs could be lessened by providing more information about the safety of helicopters.

Managing Personal Stress

In addition to reducing stress inherent in the industry and job, managers should learn to personally manage stress on a daily basis. The old strategy of waiting for an annual

FIGURE 17.4   Common Sources and Suggested Causes of Organizational Stress

Common Sources	Suggested Causes
Job mismatch	Job demands skills or abilities the employee does not possess (job incompetence).
	Job does not provide opportunity for the employee to fully utilize skills or abilities (underutilization).
Conflicting expectations	The formal organization's concept of expected behavior contradicts the employee's concept of expected behavior.
	The informal group's concept of expected behavior contradicts the employee's concept.
	The individual employee is affected by two (or more) strong influences.
Role ambiguity	Employee is uncertain or unclear about how to perform on the job.
	Employee is uncertain or unclear about what is expected in the job.
	Employee is unclear or uncertain about the relationship between job performance and expected consequences (rewards, penalties, and so forth).
Role overload	Employee is incompetent at job.
	Employee is asked to do more than time permits (time pressure).
Fear/responsibility	Employee is afraid of performing poorly or failing.
	Employee feels pressure for high achievement.
	Employee has responsibility for other people.
Working conditions	The job environment is unpleasant; there is inadequate lighting or improper regulation of temperature and noise, for example.
	The requirements of the job may unnecessarily produce pacing problems, social isolation, and so forth.
	The machine design and maintenance procedures create pressure.
	The job involves long or erratic work hours.
Working relationships	Individual employees have problems relating to, and/or working with, superiors, peers, and/or subordinates.
	Employees have problems working in groups.
Alienation	There is limited social interaction.
	Employees do not participate in decision making.

Source: Adapted from Charles R. Stoner and Fred L. Fry, "Developing a Corporate Policy for Managing Stress," *Personnel*, May–June 1983, p. 70.

vacation to "wind-down" is no longer a solution.[20] One or two weeks off rarely counterbalances 50 weeks of stress. Furthermore, many people don't take vacation time, even when it is available. According to one national stress survey, one out of four took no vacation. Of those who did take a vacation, people with lower levels of stress, averaged 2.2 weeks of vacation while those with higher levels of stress averaged only 1.4 weeks of vacation per year.

The first step is reducing personal stress to determine if your life is reasonably balanced. The following behaviors are indications that your life may be out-of-balance:

- Hurrying everywhere; walking, talking, driving faster.
- Feeling depressed, apathetic or bored most of the time.
- Changes in sleeping or eating patterns.
- Difficulty enjoying social activities.
- Emphasis on how much you get done, rather than how well you do it.
- Inability to accept praise or affection, even when you want it.
- More frequent accidents than usual.[21]

FIGURE 17.5   The Path to Professional Burnout

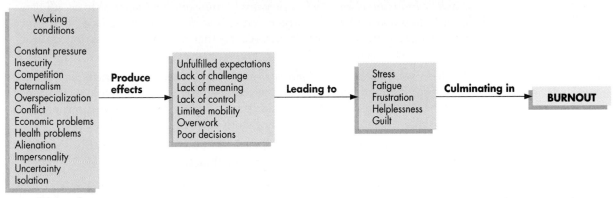

Source: Reprinted by permission from *Business* Magazine, "Helping Employees Cope with Burnout," by Donald P. Rogers, October–December 1984. Copyright © 1984 by the College of Business Administration, Georgia State University, Atlanta.

Recognizing the above signs in your life will let you know that you should search for ways of restoring balance. The following five-step approach can help you regain your balance:

1. Counter every "yes" with a "No." If you add a new unscheduled activity to your day, cancel another. If you decide to make an unscheduled stop at the grocery store, reschedule your plan to stop at the post office.

2. Schedule only 80 percent of your time. Leave some breathing space for unpredictable events; remember most things take longer than you think.

3. Practice giving in. Constantly making decisions places demands on your time and energy. Occasionally giving in and letting someone else make the decisions can take the pressure off.

4. Be realistic. Set realistic deadlines and workloads. Usually, no one expects as much of you as yourself.

5. Focus on the Five F's. To find balance, focus on faith, family, finances, friends, and fitness. Examine each of these areas and balance your schedule each week by including activities in all five areas.[22]

Burnout

burnout   Condition that occurs when work is no longer meaningful to a person.

Burnout occurs when work is no longer meaningful to a person. Research has shown that chronic stress, rather than acute crises, and prolonged personal contact tend to bring about the highest degrees of burnout.[23] Figure 17.5 illustrates the sequence of events that often leads to professional burnout. As burnout has become more recognized, certain related myths have surfaced.[24]

Myth 1: Burnout is just a newfangled notion that gives lazy people an excuse not to work. Although *burnout* is a relatively new term, the behavior has been around for centuries. History abounds with examples of workers, such as writers, artists, and scientists, who gradually or suddenly stopped producing.

Myth 2: As long as people really enjoy their work, they can work as long and hard as they want and never experience burnout. Any work that inherently includes significant and continuing frustration, conflict, and pressure can lead to burnout.

Myth 3: Individuals know when they are burning out, and when they do, all they need to do is take off for a few days or weeks and then they will be as good as new. Unfortunately, most people do not realize that burnout is occurring until it reaches its later stages.

Myth 4: Individuals who are physically and psychologically strong are unlikely to experience burnout. Physically and psychologically strong individuals may indeed be able to work harder than less strong people. However, without proper stress skills, the inordinate amount of work can cause serious damage.

Myth 5: Job burnout is always job related. Burnout usually results from a combination of work, family, social, and personal factors.

Since chronic stress is one of the major causes of burnout, following the guidelines previously discussed for reducing workplace and personal stress should reduce burnout. A second step in reducing burnout is to identify those jobs with the highest potential for burnout. Certain jobs are more likely to lead to burnout than others. Once those jobs have been identified, several actions are possible. Some of the possibilities include redesigning the jobs, clarifying expectations, improving physical working conditions, and training the jobholders.

For top- and mid-level managers, a chief source of burnout is the "career plateau" (the point at which further promotion or advancement no longer seems possible). Studying career resilience, examining how one gains insight or learns about a career, and carefully matching individuals with their careers through career identity can dramatically reduce burnout. Figure 17.6 identifies several methods for increasing career motivation.

Workplace Violence

Violence in the workplace has recently become a real concern. Reports show that some form of violence has occurred in nearly one-third of all companies within the last five years.[25] These same reports indicate that approximately one million workplace incidences of violence result in some two million victims annually.

For many organizations, the danger from workplace violence comes not only from extreme violence, like shootings, but from non-fatal assaults, verbal threats, harass-

---

FIGURE 17.6   Methods for Increasing Career Motivation

1. Review your accomplishments and give yourself credit for them.
2. Take a moderate risk—one from which there will be some benefit.
3. Show others you can cooperate but that you also have your own ideas.
4. Inquire about how well you are doing.
5. Ask for information about career opportunities.
6. Set specific career goals for next year and general goals for the next five years.
7. Create your own job challenge by redesigning your job and generating new assignments.
8. If you want to be a leader, try it. Initiate and delegate work.
9. Take actions toward your goals.

Sources: Adapted from M. London and E. M. Moore, *Career Management and Survival in the Workplace* (San Francisco: Jossey-Bass, 1987), p. 5; K. N. Wexley and J. Hinricks, eds., *Developing Human Resources* (Washington, DC: BNA Books, 1991), pp. 51–59.

ment and intimidation, sexual harassment, and other erratic behaviors suggesting emotional instability.

While there is no way to guarantee that an organization will not be victimized, the establishment of a workplace violence prevention program can greatly reduce the probability of a problem. A comprehensive workplace violence prevention program should include the following elements:[26]

- A written policy statement that communicates a clear commitment to promoting a workplace safe from violence, that prohibits threats and violence of every sort, and that requires employees to immediately report to management all circumstances that create a concern for safety from violence.

- A Management Response Team that represents diverse segments of the organization, trained and charged with the responsibility of investigating and managing all reports of circumstances that raise a concern for an employee.

- A meaningful reporting and response mechanism that establishes clear lines of communication and responsibility for issues involving violence and ensures that the organization is both promptly notified of potential security risks and can take immediate steps to resolve underlying concerns.

- Clear standards of behavior that prohibit threats and violence of every sort, and require prompt, appropriate discipline of employees who breach safety rules.

- A wide array of other security, employment, legal, and administrative practices can help an organization prevent and manage on-site threats and violence. Such practices include a security inventory to assess the particular risks faced by the organization from violence; the development of security protocols to manage threats and violence; pre-employment background checks; and the pursuit of legal remedies such as restraining orders (when needed) to guard against third-party threats.

- A system of periodic employee training addressing such issues such as workplace policies; warning signs of violence; the requirement that employees report threats to management; methods for properly investigating complaints made under the workplace violence policy; defusing hostile situations; and strategies for addressing domestic violence.

Management Illustration 17.2 describes a violence-prevention program recently implemented by the United States Postal Service.

Employee Assistance Programs (EAPs)

Many large organizations and a growing number of smaller ones are attempting to help employees with stress, burnout, and other personal problems that include not only alcohol and drug abuse but also depression, anxiety, domestic trauma, financial problems, and other psychiatric/medical problems. This help is not purely altruistic; it is based largely on cost savings. The help is generally offered in the form of **employee assistance programs (EAPs).**

employee assistance program (EAP) Program sponsored by the organization that attempts to help employees with stress, burnout, and other personal problems that include alcohol and drug abuse, depression, anxiety, domestic trauma, financial problems, and other psychiatric/medical problems.

A primary result of personal problems brought to the workplace is reduced productivity. Absenteeism and tardiness also tend to increase. Increased costs of insurance programs, including sickness and accident benefits, are a direct result of personal problems brought to the workplace. Lower morale, more friction among employees, more friction between supervisors and employees, and more

Management Illustration 17.2
Violence Prevention at the Postal Service

After several well-publicized tragedies a few years ago, the U.S. Postal Service (USPS) implemented a violence-prevention plan in the Fall of 1997. Within a year of the plan's implementation, 61,000 supervisors, managers, craft and union officials went through eight hours of violence awareness training. This training was also supplemented with anger-management training given to thousands of employees through health and wellness seminars.

After implementing a zero-tolerance policy at the national and local level, USPS created threat-assessment core teams at each of its 85 districts. These core teams consist of human resource managers who serve as team leaders, senior labor relations specialists, medical staff members, employee assistance program professionals, district managers, and plant managers. Situational advisors, composed of postal inspectors, outside mental health professionals and the postal service's law department, can be called in as the core team sees a need.

The core teams are advertised so people know whom to call if they see something inappropriate. Upon receiving a call, the human resource manager assesses when to intervene. The core team members then go out and investigate. Following its investigation, the core team meets to assess the risk and assigns a risk priority to the situation. The highest risk assessment number is 1, which indicates there is a clear and immediate threat of violence. A rating of 4 indicates a situation in which there is no perceived risk of violence. If the risk assessment is greater than 1, the team develops a risk-abatement plan for the individual. If the risk assessment is a 1, the individual is immediately terminated.

Source: Carla Joinson, "Controlling Hostility," *HR Magazine*, August 1998, pp. 65–70. To read more about HR issues, visit the Society for Human Resource Management Web site at: www.shrm.org.

grievances also result from troubled employees. Permanent loss of trained employees due to disability, retirement, and death is also associated with troubled employees. Frequently cited work-related stress problems that affect the employee's feeling of self-worth are lack of supervisor trust and respect, help disincentives (misdirected credit), conflict between job performance and reward, job communication, supervisor action or inaction, and job nonperformance (lack of control over job).[27] An intangible but very real cost associated with troubled employees is the loss of business and damaged public image.

Until recently, organizations attempted to avoid employees' problems that were not job related. Although aware of the existence of these problems, organizations did not believe they should interfere with employees' personal lives. In the past, organizations tended to get rid of troubled employees. In recent years, however, cost considerations, unions, and government legislation have altered this approach. The accepted viewpoint today is that employees' personal problems are private until they begin affecting their job performance. When and if that happens, personal problems become a matter of concern for the organization.

Studies have shown that absenteeism can be significantly reduced by employee assistance programs. EAPs have also been found to help reduce on-the-job accidents and grievances. Workers' compensation premiums, sickness and accident benefits, and trips to the infirmary also tend to decrease with an EAP.

Several types of employee assistance programs exist. In one type, which is rarely used, diagnosis and treatment of the problem are provided directly by the organization. In a second type of program, the organization hires a qualified person to diagnose the employee's problem; then the employee is referred to the proper agency or clinic for treatment. The third and most common type of program employs a coordinator who evaluates the employee's problem only sufficiently to make a referral to the proper agency or clinic for diagnosis. Sometimes the coordinator serves only as a

FIGURE 17.7   Ten Critical Elements of an EAP

Element	Significance
Management backing	Without this at the highest level, key ingredients and overall effect are seriously limited.
Labor support	The EAP cannot be meaningful if it is not backed by the employees' labor unit.
Confidentiality	Anonymity and trust are crucial if employees are to use an EAP.
Easy access	For maximum use and benefit.
Supervisor training	Crucial to employees needing understanding and support during receipt of assistance.
Union steward training	A critical variable is employees' contact with the union— the steward.
Insurance involvement	Occasionally assistance alternatives are costly, and insurance support is a must.
Breadth of service components	Availability of assistance for a wide variety of problems (e.g., alcoholism, family, personal, financial, grief, medical).
Professional leadership	A skilled professional with expertise in helping who must have credibility in the eyes of the employee.
Follow-up and evaluation	To measure program effectiveness and overall improvement.

Source: Adapted from F. Dickman and W. G. Emener, "Employee Assistance Programs: Basic Concepts, Attributes, and an Evaluation," *Personnel Administrator*, August 1982, p. 56.

consultant to the organization and is not a full-time employee. This type of program is especially popular with smaller employers and branch operations of large employers.

To be successful, an EAP must first be accepted by the employees; they must not be afraid to use it. Experience has shown that certain elements are critical to the success of an EAP. Figure 17.7 summarizes several of the most important characteristics of an EAP.

Wellness Programs

In addition to the EAPs discussed in the previous section, many companies have installed programs designed to prevent illness and enhance employee well-being. These

wellness program   Company-implemented program designed to prevent illness and enhance employee well-being.

programs are referred to as **wellness programs** and include such things as periodic medical exams, stop-smoking clinics, education on improved dietary practices, hypertension detection and control, weight control, exercise and fitness, stress management, accident-risk reduction, immunizations, and cardiopulmonary resuscitation (CPR) training. Some of the documented results of wellness programs include fewer sick days, reduced coronary heart disease, and lower major medical costs. Many also believe that employee productivity increases for employees who participate in exercise and fitness programs. Numerous studies have reported a very attractive return on investment for most types of wellness programs.[28] Experts in the wellness field report that even small companies can offer wellness programs and that such programs do not have to be expensive.

One example of the many organizations now adopting wellness programs is Adolph Coors Company. Coors claims that its 25,000-square-foot wellness facility, designed for employees and their spouses, has helped the company save over $2 million annually in medical claims and other health-related factors. The Coors program is designed around a six-step behavioral change model: awareness, education, incentives, programs, self-education, and follow-up and support. Chief among the elements that are critical for successful wellness programs are CEO support and direction, accessibility, inclusion of family, needs assessment, staffing with specialists, and establishment of a separate budget for wellness activities.[29]

Summary

1. *Define Conflict.* Conflict is overt behavior that results when an individual or a group of individuals think a perceived need or needs of the individual or group has been blocked or is about to be blocked.

2. *Discuss the Useful Effects of Conflict.* Some potentially useful effects of conflict are that it energizes people; is a form of communication; often provides an outlet for pent-up tensions, resulting in catharsis; and may actually be an educational experience.

3. *Outline the Stages of Conflict Development.* The stages of conflict development are latent conflict, perceived conflict, felt conflict, manifest conflict, and conflict aftermath.

4. *Present an Approach for Analyzing Conflict.* One approach to analyzing conflict is based on the party or parties involved: intrapersonal, interpersonal, or intergroup.

5. *Name Five Methods of Resolving Interpersonal Conflict.* There are five general methods of resolving interpersonal conflict: (1) withdrawal of one or more of the participants; (2) smoothing over the conflict and pretend it does not exist; (3) compromising for the sake of ending the conflict; (4) forcing the conflict to a conclusion through third-party intervention; and (5) forcing a confrontation between the participants in an effort to solve the underlying source of conflict.

6. *Define Stress.* Stress is the mental and/or physical condition that results from a perceived threat of danger (physical or emotional) and the pressure to remove it.

7. *Define Burnout.* Burnout is a condition that occurs when work is no longer meaningful to a person.

8. *Outline the Basic Elements of a Violence-Prevention Program.* The basic elements of a comprehensive violence-prevention program are a written policy statement communicating a clear commitment to promoting a workplace safe from violence, a Management Response Team, a meaningful reporting and response mechanisms, clear standards of behavior, a wide array of other security, employment, legal, and administrative practices, and a system of periodic employee training covering violence-prevention issues.

9. *Explain the Three Basic Types of Employee Assistance Programs.* In one type of EAP, diagnosis and treatment of the problem are provided directly by the organization. In a second type, the organization hires a qualified person to diagnose the employee's problem and then refers the employee to a proper agency or clinic for treatment. The third and most common type employs a coordinator who evaluates the employee's problem only sufficiently to make a referral to the proper agency or clinic for diagnosis.

10. *Explain Wellness Programs.* Wellness programs are company-implemented programs designed to prevent illness and enhance employee well-being.

Preview Analysis

1. Should a company get involved with the personal conflicts of its employees? Why or why not?

2. What specific actions, if any, would you recommend that Sally's EAP take regarding Sally's situation?

Review Questions

1. What is conflict?
2. What two basic viewpoints can be used to analyze conflict?
3. Identify the five stages of conflict.
4. What causes intrapersonal conflict?
5. What are some typical defense mechanisms used when an individual is frustrated?
6. What are some causes of interpersonal conflict?
7. Name at least four types of intergroup conflict.
8. What is political conflict?
9. Describe some of the useful effects of conflict.
10. What are some methods that can be used to resolve interpersonal conflict?

11. Outline some key questions that need to be answered in conflict resolution.

12. Name several ways that stress can manifest itself in the workplace.

13. What is a workplace stress audit?

14. What is burnout?

15. What is a workplace violence-prevention program?

16. What are three basic types of employee assistance programs (EAPs)?

17. What is a wellness program?

Skill-Building Questions

1. Should managers attempt to avoid conflict at all times? Explain.

2. "Conflict is inevitable." Do you agree or disagree with this statement? Discuss.

3. How can managers reduce destructive stress in organizations?

4. How would you handle a situation in which you have two people working for you who "just rub each other the wrong way"?

5. Examine your personal situation and identify some ways you that you might reduce stress in your day-to-day activities.

SKILL-BUILDING EXERCISE 17.1

Self-Evaluation: The Glazer Stress Control Lifestyle Questionnaire*

As you can see, each scale below is composed of a pair of adjectives or phrases separated by a series of horizontal lines. Each pair has been chosen to represent two contrasting behaviors. Each of us belongs somewhere along the line between the two extremes. Since most of us are neither the most competitive nor the least competitive person we know, put a check mark where you think you belong between the two extremes.

*The source of this questionnaire is unknown to the authors.

	1	2	3	4	5	6	7	
1. Doesn't mind leaving things temporarily unfinished	___	___	___	___	___	___	___	Must get things finished once started
2. Calm and unhurried about appointments	___	___	___	___	___	___	___	Never late for appointments
3. Not competitive	___	___	___	___	___	___	___	Highly competitive
4. Listens well, lets others finish speaking	___	___	___	___	___	___	___	Anticipates others in conversation (nods, interrupts, finishes sentences for the other)
5. Never in a hurry, even when pressured	___	___	___	___	___	___	___	Always in a hurry
6. Able to wait calmly	___	___	___	___	___	___	___	Uneasy when waiting
7. Easygoing	___	___	___	___	___	___	___	Always going full speed ahead
8. Takes one thing at a time	___	___	___	___	___	___	___	Tries to do more than one thing at a time, thinks about what to do next
9. Slow and deliberate in speech	___	___	___	___	___	___	___	Vigorous and forceful in speech (uses a lot of gestures)
10. Concerned with satisfying himself or herself, not others	___	___	___	___	___	___	___	Wants recognition by others for a job well done
11. Slow doing things	___	___	___	___	___	___	___	Fast doing things (eating, walking, etc.)
12. Easygoing	___	___	___	___	___	___	___	Hard driving
13. Expresses feelings openly	___	___	___	___	___	___	___	Holds feelings in
14. Has a large number of interests	___	___	___	___	___	___	___	Few interests outside work
15. Satisfied with job	___	___	___	___	___	___	___	Ambitious, wants quick advancement on job
16. Never sets own deadlines	___	___	___	___	___	___	___	Often sets own deadlines
17. Feels limited responsibility	___	___	___	___	___	___	___	Always feels responsible
18. Never judges things in terms of numbers	___	___	___	___	___	___	___	Often judges performance in terms of numbers (how much, how many)
19. Casual about work	___	___	___	___	___	___	___	Takes work very seriously (works weekends, brings work home)
20. Not very precise	___	___	___	___	___	___	___	Very precise (careful about detail)

Scoring

Assign a value from 1 to 7 for each score. Total them. The categories are as follows:

Total score   110–140:   Type A_1.   If you are in this category, and especially if you are over 40 and smoke, you are likely to have a high risk of developing cardiac illness.

Total score   80–109:   Type A_2.   You are in the direction of being cardiac prone, but your risk is not as high as the A1. You should, nevertheless, pay careful attention to the advice given to all Type As.

Total score   60–79:   Type AB.   You are an admixture of A and B patterns. This is a healthier pattern than either A1 or A2, but you have the potential for slipping into A behavior and you should recognize this.

Total score   30–59:   Type B_2.   Your behavior is on the less-cardiac-prone end of the spectrum. You are generally relaxed and cope adequately with stress.

Total score   0–29:   Type B_1.   You tend to the extreme of noncardiac traits. Your behavior expresses few of the reactions associated with cardiac disease.

SKILL-BUILDING EXERCISE 17.2

Social Readjustment Rating Scale

Everybody is confronted by both major and minor changes in the workplace and in their private lives. Some of these changes are predictable and some are not; some can be controlled and others cannot. The following list contains 43 life events. Please record the frequency with which you have confronted each of these within the past 12 months.

Social Readjustment Rating Scale

Life Events	Life Change Units		Number of Events in Past 12 Months		Total
Death of spouse	100	×	_____	=	_____
Divorce	73	×	_____	=	_____
Marital separation	65	×	_____	=	_____
Jail term	63	×	_____	=	_____
Death of close family member	63	×	_____	=	_____
Personal injury or illness	53	×	_____	=	_____
Marriage	50	×	_____	=	_____
Fired at work	47	×	_____	=	_____
Marital reconciliation	45	×	_____	=	_____
Retirement	45	×	_____	=	_____
Change in health of family member	44	×	_____	=	_____
Pregnancy	40	×	_____	=	_____
Sex difficulties	39	×	_____	=	_____
Gain of new family member	39	×	_____	=	_____
Business readjustment	39	×	_____	=	_____
Change in financial state	38	×	_____	=	_____
Death of a close friend	37	×	_____	=	_____
Change to different line of work	36	×	_____	=	_____
Change in number of arguments with spouse	35	×	_____	=	_____
Mortgage over $100,000*	31	×	_____	=	_____
Foreclosure of mortgage or loan	30	×	_____	=	_____
Change in responsibility at work	29	×	_____	=	_____
Son or daughter leaving home	29	×	_____	=	_____

Social Readjustment Rating Scale *(Continued)*

Life Events	Life Change Units		Number of Events in Past 12 Months		Total
Trouble with in-laws	29	×	_____	=	_____
Outstanding personal achievement	28	×	_____	=	_____
Spouse begins or stops work	26	×	_____	=	_____
Begin or end school	26	×	_____	=	_____
Change in living conditions	25	×	_____	=	_____
Revision of personal habits	24	×	_____	=	_____
Trouble with boss	23	×	_____	=	_____
Change in work hours or conditions	20	×	_____	=	_____
Change in residence	20	×	_____	=	_____
Change in schools	20	×	_____	=	_____
Change in recreation	19	×	_____	=	_____
Change in church activities	19	×	_____	=	_____
Change in social activities	18	×	_____	=	_____
Mortgage or loan less than $100,000*	17	×	_____	=	_____
Change in sleeping habits	16	×	_____	=	_____
Change in number of family get-togethers	15	×	_____	=	_____
Change in eating habits	15	×	_____	=	_____
Vacation	13	×	_____	=	_____
Christmas or High Holy Days	12	×	_____	=	_____
Minor violations of the law	11	×	_____	=	_____
Life change units total				=	_____

Source: T. H. Holmes and R. H. Rahe, "The Social Readjustment Rating Scale," *Journal of Psychosomatic Research* 11 (1967), pp. 213–18, for complete wording of the items. Reproduced by permission.
*Figures adjusted by authors to reflect inflation.

After you have gone through the list, compute your score by multiplying the assigned points times the number of times a specific event has occurred and summing the totals. Use the following information to interpret your score:

Score	More Susceptible to Illness Than Following Percentage of General Population
350–400	90%
300–349	80%
200–299	50%
150–199	37%
Up to 150	Low Stress Level

If your total score is under 150, your level of stress, based on life change, is low. If your score is between 150 and 300, your stress levels are borderline—you should minimize other changes in your life at this time. If your score is over 300, your life change level of stress is high—you should not only minimize any other changes in your life and work but should strive to practice some stress intervention techniques.

CASE INCIDENT 17.1

ઙ૰

The Young College Graduate and the Old Superintendent

You are a consultant to the manager of a garment manufacturing plant in a small southern town. The manager has been having trouble with two employees: Ralph, the plant superintendent, and Kevin, the production scheduler. Ralph is 53 years old and has been with the company since he was released from military duty after World War II. He started in the warehouse with a sixth-grade education and worked his way up through the ranks. Until recently, Ralph handled—along with his many other duties—the production scheduling function. He was proud of the fact that he could handle it all "in my head." As the volume of production and the number of different products grew, however, the plant manager thought significant savings could be attained through a more sophisticated approach to scheduling. He believed he could save on raw materials by purchasing in larger quantities and on production setup time by making longer runs. He also wanted to cut down on the frequency of finished-goods stock-outs; when backlogs did occur, he wanted to be able to give customers more definite information as to when goods would be available. He wanted to have a planned schedule for at least two months into the future, with daily updates.

Kevin is 24 years old and grew up in the Chicago area. This is his first full-time job. He earned a master of science degree in industrial engineering from an eastern engineering school. He jumped right into the job and set up a computer-assisted scheduling system, using a time-sharing service with a teletype terminal in his office. The system is based on the latest production scheduling and inventory control technology. It is very flexible and has proven to be quite effective in all areas that were of interest to the plant manager.

Plant manager: Sometimes I just want to shoot both Ralph and Kevin. If those two could just get along with each other, this plant would run like a well-oiled machine.

Consultant: What do they fight about?

Manager: Anything and everything that has to do with the production schedule. Really trivial things in a lot of cases. It all seems so completely senseless!

Consultant: Have you tried to do anything about it?

Manager: At first, I tried to minimize the impact of their feuds on the rest of the plant by stepping in and making decisions that would eliminate the point of controversy. I also tried to smooth things over as if the arguments were just friendly disagreements. I thought that after they had a chance to get accustomed to each other, the problem would go away. But it didn't. It got to the point that I was spending a good 20 percent of my time stopping their fights. Furthermore, I began to notice that other employees were starting to take sides. The younger people seemed to support Kevin; everybody else sided with Ralph. It began to look as if we might have our own little war.

Consultant: What's the current situation?

Manager: I finally told them both that if I caught them fighting again, I would take very drastic action with both of them. I think that move was a mistake though, because now they won't even talk to each other. Kevin just drops the schedule printouts on Ralph's desk every afternoon and walks away. Ralph needs some help in working with those printouts, and Kevin needs some feedback on what's actually going on in the plant. Frankly, things aren't going as well production-wise now as when they were at each other's throats. And the tension in the plant as a whole is even worse. They are both good people and outstanding in their respective jobs. I would really hate to lose either of them, but if they can't work together, I may have to let one or both of them go.

Questions

1. Why is this conflict occurring?

2. What method did the manager use in dealing with this conflict situation? Was it effective?

3. Recommend an approach for resolving the conflict.

CASE INCIDENT 17.2

ઙ૰

Problems at the Hospital

Smith County is a suburban area near a major midwestern city. The county has experienced such a tremendous rate of growth during the past decade that local governments have had difficulty providing adequate service to the citizens.

Smith County Hospital has a reputation for being a first-class facility, but it is inadequate to meet local needs. During certain periods of the year, the occupancy rates exceed the licensed capacity. There is no doubt in anyone's mind that the hospital must be expanded immediately.

At a recent meeting of the Hospital Authority, the hospital administrator, Kaye Austin, presented the group with a proposal to accept the architectural plans of the firm of Watkins and Gibson. This plan calls for a 100-bed addition adjacent to the existing structure. Kaye announced that after reviewing several alternative plans, she believed the Watkins and Gibson plan would provide the most benefit for the expenditure.

At this point, Randolph (Randy) Lewis, the board chairperson, began questioning the plan. Randy made it clear he would not go along with the Watkins and Gibson plan. He stated that the board should look for other firms to serve as the architects for the project.

The ensuing argument became somewhat heated, and a 10-minute recess was called to allow those attending to get coffee as well as allow tempers to calm down. Kaye was talking to John Rhodes, another member of the Hospital Authority board, in the hall and said, "Randy seems to fight me on every project."

Randy, who was talking to other members of the board, was saying, "I know that the Watkins and Gibson plan is good, but I just can't stand for Kaye to act like it's her plan. I wish she would leave so we could get a good administrator from the community whom we can identify with."

Questions

1. Is Randy's reaction uncommon? Explain.
2. What type of conflict exists between Kaye and Randy?
3. What methods would you use to reduce or resolve the conflict?
4. Could Kaye have done anything in advance of the meeting to maximize her chances of success? Explain.

References and Additional Readings

[1]Adapted from William Cottringer, "Conflict Management," *Executive Excellence*, August 1997, p. 6.

[2]See Kenneth Thomas, "Conflict and Conflict Management," in *Handbook of Industrial and Organizational Psychology*, ed. Marvin D. Dunnette (New York: John Wiley & Sons, 1983).

[3]Susan Chandler, "Solo Flyer," *Business Week*, October 17, 1994, pp. 97–98.

[4]Robert L. Kahn, "Role Conflict and Ambiguity in Organizations," *Personnel Administrator*, March–April 1964, pp. 8–13.

[5]Steven Kerr, "On the Folly of Rewarding A. While Hoping for B," *Academy of Management Journal* 18 (1975), pp. 769–83.

[6]P. R. Lawrence and J. W. Lorsch, *Organization and Environment* (Boston: Harvard Business School, Division of Research, 1967).

[7]For more information, see Dean Tjosvold, Valerie Dann, and Choy Wong, "Managing Conflict between Departments to Serve Customers," *Human Relations*, October 1992, pp. 1035–54.

[8]Julie Olson-Buchanan, Fritz Drasgow, Philip J. Moberg, Alan D. Mead, et al., "Interactive Video Assessment of Conflict Resolution Skills," *Personnel Psychology*, Spring 1998, pp. 1–24.

[9]See also Philip B. DuBose and Charles D. Pringle, "Choosing a Conflict Management Technique," *Supervision*, June 1989, pp. 10–12.

[10]R. M. Bramson, *Coping with Difficult People* (New York: Dell, 1981).

[11]See also Evert Van de Vliert and Boris Kabanoff, "Toward Theory-Based Measures of Conflict Management," *Academy of Management Journal*, March 1990, pp. 199–209.

[12]See also Kenneth Thomas, "Conflict and Conflict Management: Reflections and Update," *Journal of Organizational Behavior*, May 1992, pp. 263–74.

[13]Cecilia MacDonald, "Managing Stress is a Balancing Act," *Credit Act*, July/August 1997, pp. 35–37.

[14]Sacha Cohen, "De-Stress for Success," *Training and Development*, November 1997, pp. 76–80.

[15]"How to Reduce Workplace Stress," *Worklife Report*, Vol 10 No. 3, 1997, pp. 4–5.

[16]Victoria J. Doby and Robert D. Caplan, "Organizational Stress as Threat to Reputation: Effects on Anxiety at Work and Home," *Academy of Management Journal* 38, no. 4 (1995), pp. 1105–23.

[17]"Workplace Stress Equals Health Distress," *Worklife Report*, Vol 11, No. 1, 1997, p. 10.

[18]Jia Lin Xie and Gary Johns, "Job Scope and Stress: Can Job Scope Be Too High?" *Academy of Management Journal* 38, no. 5 (1995), pp. 1288–1309.

[19]"How to Reduce Workplace Stress," op cit.

[20]Much of this section is drawn from: Cecilia MacDonald, "Frayed to the Breaking Point," *Credit Union Management*, June 1996, pp. 30–31.

[21]Ibid.

[22]Ibid.

[23]C. Maslach, *Burnout—The Cost of Caring.* (Englewood Cliffs, NJ: Prentice-Hall, Inc) 1982.

[24]Michael E. Cavanagh, "What You Don't Know about Stress," *Personnel Journal*, July 1988, pp. 56–57.

[25]Barry Brandman, "Fight Workplace Violence," *Transportation and Distribution*, September 1997, pp. 87–92.

[26]Rebecca A. Speer, "Can Workplace Violence Be Prevented?", *Occupational Hazards*, August 1998, pp. 26–30.

[27]H. Richard Priesmeyer, *Organization and Chaos* (Westport, Conn.: Quorum Books, 1992), pp. 164–65.

[28]For example, see Fred W. Schott and Sandra Wendel, "Wellness with a Track Record," *Personnel Journal*, April 1992, pp. 98–104.

[29]Shari Caudron and Michael Rozek, "The Wellness Payoff," *Personnel Journal*, July 1990, pp. 54–62, as described in John M. Ivancevich, *Human Resource Management* (Burr Ridge, IL: Richard D. Irwin, 1995), pp. 636–37.

Managing Change, Culture, and Diversity

❧

LEARNING OBJECTIVES

After studying this chapter, you should be able to:

1. Identify the three major categories of organizational change.

2. List the three major barriers to managing change.

3. Discuss several reasons employees resist change.

4. Identify several prescriptions for reducing resistance to change.

5. List the three steps in Lewin's model for change.

6. Summarize the four phases of an organizational development (OD) program.

7. Define corporate culture.

8. Describe the generic types of organizational culture.

9. Define diversity management.

10. List several guidelines for managing a diverse workforce.

Chapter Preview

According to Calhoun W. Wick, president of Wick & Company, a Wilmington, Delaware–based research and consulting firm, "A work environment that buoys rather than debases employees results in a double gain: people are fulfilled and the company is more profitable in the long run." He believes that such an environment "fosters diversity, promotes a sense of security, makes people feel optimal, and encourages risk taking." Many firms have misread the change, culture, and diversity issues of the 1980s and 1990s as mandates to avoid legal penalties. Instead, perhaps Wick's view is correct: Diversity, change, and cultural reengineering are good for people and good for business.

When Jamie Houghton took over as CEO at Corning, Inc., he made it clear that the company's future was to be directly tied to how well the firm promoted diversity within the workplace. He said in one of his many speeches to the rank and file, "We were losing women and blacks at twice the rate of white males. The baby boom is over and statistics say only 15 percent of the people entering the workforce in the year 2000 will be white males." "If you only want to deal with 15 percent of the talent out there, that's fine," he added, "but we realized that we had to do something different because Corning has never had a hard time hiring women and minorities—only in keeping them because of the glass ceiling—we will change that!"

The company has hired a chief diversity officer and begun a campaign to assess and then change people's attitudes. It has been made clear to every employee that the differences, not the similarities, in the workforce are where the new approaches and fresh ideas come from. The day of the company clone is dead at Corning. The basic idea is that if the company can be a leader in diversity, it will naturally be a leader in products, customer service, and competitive strategy because of the talent it will attract and keep. Corning's idea is certainly one whose time has come!

Source: Adapted from Calhoun W. Wick and Lu Stanton Leon, *The Learning Edge* (New York: McGraw-Hill, 1993), pp. 151–52.

In his book *Thriving on Chaos*, Tom Peters stresses the importance of change to the modern corporation: "To up the odds of survival, leaders at all levels must become obsessive about change."[1] He adds, "Change must become the norm, not cause for alarm."[2] What does *change* mean from his perspective? Simply put, it means that unless managers have changed something, they have not earned their paychecks. This bold view is somewhat foreign to most companies today.

Today managing change and dealing with its impact on the corporate culture are essential skills that the manager must master if the organization is to compete globally. Furthermore, the manager must learn these skills rapidly, since change is occurring at an ever-increasing rate. The new bottom line for the late 1990s will be to assess each and every action in light of its contribution to an increased corporate capacity for change.[3]

MANAGING CHANGE

Organizations today are beset by change. Many managers find themselves unable to cope with an environment or an organization that has become substantially different from the one in which they received their training and gained their early experience. Other managers have trouble transferring their skills to a new assignment in a different industry. A growing organization, a new assignment, and changing customer needs may all be encountered by today's managers. To be successful, managers must be able to adapt to these changes.

Change as it applies to organizations can be classified into three major categories: (1) technological, (2) environmental, and (3) internal to the organization. **Technological changes** include such things as new equipment and new processes. The technological advances since World War II have been dramatic, with computers and increased speed of communication being the most notable. **Environmental changes** are all the nontechnological changes that occur outside the organization. New government regulations, new social trends, and economic changes are all examples of environmental change. Changes **internal** to the organization include such changes as budget adjustments, policy changes, diversity adjustments, and personnel changes. Figure 18.1 lists several examples of each major type of change affecting today's organizations.

technological changes Changes in such things as new equipment and new processes.
environmental changes All nontechnological changes that occur outside the organization.
internal changes Budget adjustments, policy changes, personnel changes, and the like.

Any of these types of changes can greatly affect a manager's job. Different people react in different ways to changes, and this complicates the manager's job.

FIGURE 18.1   Types of Changes Affecting Organizations

Technological	Environmental	Internal
Machines	Laws	Policies
Equipment	Taxes	Procedures
Processes	Social trends	New methods
Automation	Fashion trends	Rules
Computers	Political trends	Reorganization
New raw materials	Economic trends	Budget adjustment
Robots	Interest rates	Restructuring of jobs
	Consumer trends	Personnel
	Competition	Management
	Suppliers	Ownership
	Population trends	Products/services sold

Employee Reactions to Change

How an employee perceives a change greatly affects how that person reacts to the change. While many variations are possible, four basic situations can occur:

1. If employees cannot foresee how the change will affect them, they will resist the change or be neutral at best. Most people shy away from the unknown, believing that change may make things worse.

2. If employees perceive that the change does not fit their needs and hopes, they will resist the change. In this instance, employees are convinced the change will make things worse.

3. If employees see that the change is inevitable, they may first resist and then resign themselves to the change. The first reaction is to resist. Once the change appears imminent, employees often see no other choice but to go along with it.

4. If employees view the change as being in their best interests, they will be motivated to make the change work. The key here is for the employees to feel sure the change will make things better. Three out of four of these situations result in some form of resistance to change. Also, the way in which employees resist change can vary greatly. For example, an employee may not actively resist a change but may never actively support it. Similarly, an employee may mildly resist by acting uninterested in the change. At the other extreme, an employee may resist by trying to sabotage the change.

Barriers to Managing Change

A recent study of 9,144 working Americans by Watson Wyatt Worldwide in San Francisco concluded the three biggest barriers to managing change are lack of management visibility and support, inadequate management skills, and employee resistance to change.[4] A lack of management visibility and support often has a negative effect on employees' perceptions about whether or not the company is well managed. When employees don't see top management, they tend to assume that top management is unconcerned about what they are doing. Regarding inadequate management skills, only 28 percent of the respondents to the study said that managers do a good job of explaining the rationale for decisions and only 27 percent reported that they were involved in decisions that affect them. Furthermore, only 36 percent believe that their managers are good facilitators, good coaches (33 percent) or good about keeping people informed (38 percent). Resistance to change is a natural human phenomenon and is discussed at length in the next section.

Resistance to Change

Most people profess to be modern and up to date. However, they still resist change. This is most often true when the change affects their jobs. Resistance to change is a natural, normal reaction; it is not a reaction observed only in troublemakers. For example, when Ken Iverson, chairman of Nucor Corporation (a mini-mill steel specialist), handed over the reigns of the company in 1996 to John D. Correnti, employees were sullen because they feared the unknown (Iverson had run the company for several decades). The adjustments Correnti will implement will affect all the employees, and therefore uncertainty rather than optimism rules, especially because of Correnti's nonsupportive attitude toward unions.[5] All change requires adjustment; in fact, the adjustment may concern employees more than the actual change.

Resistance to change may be very open, or it may be very subtle. The employee who quits a job because of a change in company policy is showing resistance to change in a very open and explicit manner. For example, two of the original founders left Manugistics, a software and services company based in Maryland, when the company decided to go global.[6] Other employees who stay but become very sullen are resisting in a more passive manner.

Reasons for Resisting Change   Employees resist change for many reasons. Some of the most frequent reasons are as follows:

1. *Fear of the unknown.* It is natural human behavior to fear the unknown. With many changes, the outcome is not foreseeable. When it is, the results are often not made known to all of the affected employees. For example, employees may worry about and resist a new computer if they are not sure what its impact will be on their jobs. Similarly, employees may resist a new manager simply because they don't know what to expect. A related fear is the uncertainty employees may feel about working in a changed environment. They may fully understand the change, yet really doubt whether they will be able to handle it. For example, an employee may resist a change in procedure because of a fear of being unable to master it.

2. *Economics.* Employees fear any change they think threatens their jobs or incomes. The threat may be real or only imagined. In either case, the result is resistance. For example, a salesperson who believes a territory change will result in less income will resist the change. Similarly, production workers will oppose new standards they believe will be harder to achieve.

3. *Fear that skills and expertise will lose value.* Everyone likes to feel valued by others, and anything that has the potential to reduce that value will be resisted. For example, an operations manager may resist implementation of a new, more modern piece of equipment for fear the change will make him or her less needed by the organization.

4. *Threats to power.* Many employees, and especially managers, believe a change may diminish their power. For example, a manager may perceive a change to the organization's structure as weakening his or her power within the organization.

5. *Additional work and inconvenience.* Almost all changes involve work and many result in personal inconveniences to the affected employees. If nothing else, they often have to learn new ways. This may mean more training, school, or practice. A common reaction by employees is that "it isn't worth the extra effort required."

6. *Threats to interpersonal relations.* The social and interpersonal relationships among employees can be quite strong. These relationships may appear unimportant to everyone but those involved. For example, eating lunch with a particular group may be very important to the involved employees. When a change, such as a transfer, threatens these relationships, the affected employees often resist. Employees naturally feel more at ease when working with people they know well. Also, the group may have devised methods for doing the work based on the strengths and weaknesses of group members. Any changes in the group would naturally disrupt the routine.

Reducing Resistance to Change   Most changes come from management. The way in which management implements a change often has a great impact on acceptance of the change. Figure 18.2 shows how employees normally respond to

FIGURE 18.2   Employee Response Model

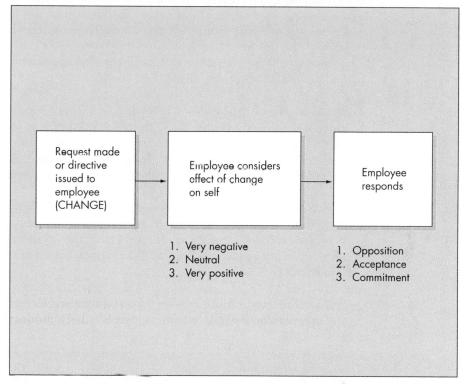

Source: Adapted from Waldron Berry, "Overcoming Resistance to Change," *Supervisory Management*, February 1983.

change. Before the manager can reduce the resistance to the change, she or he must know how the employees will react to the change. The following steps are recommended before issuing a directive:

1. Determine the response needed from the employee to accomplish the task effectively.
2. Estimate the expected response if the directive is simply published or orally passed to the employee (as many are).
3. If a discrepancy exists between the needed response and the estimated response, determine how the two responses can be reconciled (opposition is never an acceptable response).[7]

The following paragraphs present several suggestions for reducing resistance to change and helping employees to accept and even commit themselves to change.

Build Trust   If employees trust and have confidence in management, they are much more likely to accept change. If an air of distrust prevails, change is likely to be strongly resisted. Management's actions determine the degree of trust among employees. Managers can go a long way toward building trust if they discuss upcoming changes with employees and actively involve employees in the change process.

Discuss Upcoming Changes   Fear of the unknown is one of the major barriers to change. This fear can be greatly reduced by discussing any upcoming changes with the affected employees. During this discussion, the manager should be as open and honest as possible. The manager should explain not only what the change will be but also why the change is being made. The manager should also outline the impact of the change on each affected employee. Figure 18.3 presents a classical approach to change resistance that can help a manager who is attempting to explain and discuss an upcoming change.

Involve the Employees   Involving employees means more than merely discussing the upcoming changes with them. The key is to involve employees personally in the entire change process. It is natural for employees to want to go along with a change they have helped devise and implement. A good approach is to ask for employees' ideas and input as early as possible in the change process.

Make Sure the Changes Are Reasonable   The manager should always do everything possible to ensure that any proposed changes are reasonable. Often proposals for changes come from other parts of the organization. These proposals are sometimes not reasonable because the originator is unaware of all the pertinent circumstances.

Avoid Threats   The manager who attempts to force change through the use of threats is taking a negative approach. This is likely to decrease rather than increase

---

FIGURE 18.3   Methods of Overcoming Resistance to Change

Approach	Commonly Used in Situations	Advantages	Drawbacks
Education + communication	Where there is a lack of information or inaccurate information and analysis	Once persuaded, people will often help with the implementation of the change	Can be very time-consuming if lots of people are involved
Participation + involvement	Where the initiators do not have all the information they need to design the change, and where others have considerable power to resist	People who participate will be committed to implementing change, and any relevant information they have will be integrated into the change plan	Can be very time-consuming if participators design an inappropriate change
Facilitation + upport	Where people are resisting because of adjustment problems	No other approach works as well with adjustment problems	Can be time-consuming and expensive and still fail
Negotiation + agreement	Where someone or some group will clearly lose out in a change, and where that group has considerable power to resist	Sometimes it is a relatively easy way to avoid major resistance	Can be too expensive in many cases if it alerts others to negotiate for compliance
Manipulation + co-optation	Where other tactics will not work or are too expensive	It can be relatively quick and inexpensive solution to resistance problems	Can lead to future problems if people feel manipulated
Explicit + implicit coercion	Where speed is essential and the change initiators possess considerable power	It is speedy and can overcome any kind of resistance	Can be risky if it leaves people mad at the initiators

Source: Reprinted by permission of Harvard Business Review. An exhibit from "Choosing Strategies for Change," by John P. Kotter and Leonard A. Schlesinger, March–April 1979, © 1979 by the President and Fellows of Harvard College. All rights reserved.

Management Illustration 18.1
Change at Wang Labs

Following its Chapter 11 bankruptcy-induced departure from the world of minicomputers, Wang Laboratories reinvented itself as an imaging-software provider. To head up this dramatic change, Wang brought in Jose Ofman as president and chief operating officer. Prior to being hired by Wang, Ofman had spent the previous 25 years at EDS Corporation where he dealt with change on a regular basis. Riz Rizhavi, a former colleague at EDS, describes Ofman as keeping up with the latest ideas but being able to temper his passion for new ideas with a certain amount of judgment.

As far as managing change, Ofman believes the key is in developing a good management team,

"the most important thing is to have the right team, and listen to them, and get them to operate as a team and not as individuals." In describing the team he has put together at Wang, Ofman said, "The team at the top has all come from different companies. We all have a view of the world that is substantially different. We all share the same view for Wang."

Source: William Terdoslavich, "Jose Ofman: Wang Laboratories," *Computer Reseller News*, November 10, 1997, p. 145.

For more information about Wang Laboratories visit their Web site at: www.wang.com/.

employee trust. Most people resist threats or coercion. Such tactics also usually have a negative impact on employee morale.

Follow a Sensible Time Schedule   A manager can often influence the timing of changes. Some times are doubtless better than others for making certain changes. If nothing else, the manager should always use common sense when proposing a time schedule for implementing a change.

program of planned change   Deliberate design and implementation of a structural innovation, a new policy or goal, or a change in operating philosophy, climate, and style.

Planned Change

Often the need for a change can be foreseen and plans made. In such a case, it is desirable to develop a program of planned change. A **program of planned change** has been defined as "the deliberate design and implementation of a structural innovation, a new policy or goal, or a change in operating philosophy, climate, and style."[8] A program of planned change is most needed when the change will influence most or all of the organization rather than only a small segment of it.

A program of planned change usually involves a change agent, the person responsible for coordinating and overseeing the change process. A change agent can be an employee of the organization or an outside consultant.

Implementing a Planned Change   Basically, three elements of an organization can be altered to make a change: its organizational structure, its technology, and/or its human resources.[9] Usually a change in one element affects the others. For example, a structural change in the form of a reorganization would affect the organization's human resources. Structural and technological changes would be fairly simple to make except for their impact on the organization's human resources. Management Illustration 18.1 describes how Wang Laboratories has attempted to implement major changes in its business.

Lewin's Three-Step Model for Change

Kurt Lewin was one of the great social scientists of modern times. His Field Force Analysis theory, developed some 50 years ago, views the change process as the dynamics of restraining forces versus driving forces, i.e., forces that resist change and those that encourage it. As part of his force field analysis, Lewin developed a three-step model for successfully implementing change:

1. Lewin's first step, unfreezing, deals with breaking down the forces supporting or maintaining the old behavior. These forces can include such variables as the formal reward system, reinforcement from the work group, and the individual's perception of proper role behavior.

2. The second step, presenting a new alternative, involves offering a clear and attractive option representing new patterns of behavior.

3. The third step, refreezing, requires that the changed behavior be reinforced by the formal and informal reward systems and by the work group. It is in this step that the manager can play a pivotal role by positively reinforcing employee efforts to change.

Most of the suggestions offered earlier in this chapter for reducing resistance to change deal with the first two parts of Lewin's model: unfreezing and presentation of a new alternative.

Implicit in Lewin's three-step model is the recognition that the mere introduction of change does not ensure the elimination of the prechange conditions or that the change will be permanent. Unsuccessful attempts to implement lasting change can usually be traced to a failure in one of Lewin's three steps. Management Illustration 18.2 describes one of Lewin's early applications of his theory.

ORGANIZATIONAL DEVELOPMENT

organizational development (OD)
Organizationwide, planned effort, managed from the top, to increase organizational performance through planned interventions.

Organizational development (OD) is an organizationwide, planned effort managed from the top, with a goal of increasing organizational performance through planned interventions in the organization. In particular, OD looks at the human side of organizations. It seeks to change attitudes, values, and management practices in an effort to improve organizational performance. The ultimate goal of OD is to structure the organizational environment so that managers and employees can use their skills and abilities to the fullest.

An OD effort starts with a recognition by management that organizational performance can and should be improved. Following this, most OD efforts include the following phases:

1. Diagnosis
2. Change planning
3. Intervention/education
4. Evaluation

Diagnosis involves gathering and analyzing information about the organization to determine the areas in need of improvement. Information is usually gathered from employees through the use of questionnaires or attitude surveys. Change planning involves developing a plan for organization improvement based on the data obtained. This planning identifies specific problem areas in the organization and out-

Management Illustration 18.2
Changing Eating Habits

One of Kurt Lewin's most significant examples of his theory at work occurred as a result of a commission from the U.S. government to develop a program to change the eating habits of American families during World War II. To help the war effort, the government was encouraging families and especially housewives, to buy more of the visceral organs and less of the more normal muscle cuts of beef. The government attempted to explain the facts and logically tell the housewives why it was necessary to support this program—patriotism, economy, and nutrition. However, the government underestimated the restraining forces; people were simply not used to preparing or eating tongue, heart, and lungs. As a result, the housewives resisted the change until Lewis came in and developed a program to counteract the restraining forces. The cornerstone of the program was a grassroots campaign that organized discussion groups throughout the country where housewives could meet and discuss the issue. Once housewives actually got involved with the nature of the problem, they gradually broadened their thinking and came to understand how their change of diet could help the war effort. The result was that they did change their buying habits.

Source: Stephen Coney, "Work It Out Together," *Incentive*, April, 1997, p. 26. To read more from *Incentive* magazine, visit their web site at: www.incentivemag.com.

lines steps to take to resolve the problems. Intervention/education involves the sharing of diagnostic information with the people affected by it and helping them to realize the need for change. The intervention/education phase often involves the use of outside consultants working with individuals or employee groups. It can also involve the use of management development programs. The evaluation phase in effect repeats the diagnostic phase. In other words, after diagnosis, strategy planning, and education, data are gathered to determine the effects of the OD effort on the total organization. This information can then lead to more planning and education. For a more elaborate view, including pre- and poststeps in this process, see Figure 18.4.

Diagnosis

The first decision to be made in the OD process is whether the organization has the talent and available time necessary to conduct the diagnosis. If not, an alternative is to hire an outside consultant. Once the decision has been made regarding who will do the diagnosis, the next step is to gather and analyze information. Some of the most frequently used methods for doing this are the following:

1. *Review available records.* The first step is to review any available records or documents that may be pertinent. Personnel records and financial reports are two types of generally available records that can be useful.
2. *Survey questionnaires.* The most popular method of gathering data is through questionnaires filled out by employees. Usually the questionnaires are intended to measure employee attitudes and perceptions about certain work-related factors.
3. *Personal interviews.* In this approach, employees are individually interviewed regarding their opinions and perceptions and certain work-related factors. This method takes more time than the survey questionnaire method but can result in better information.
4. *Direct observation.* In this method, the person conducting the diagnosis observes firsthand the behavior of organizational members at work. One advantage of

FIGURE 18.4   Model for the Management of Organizational Development

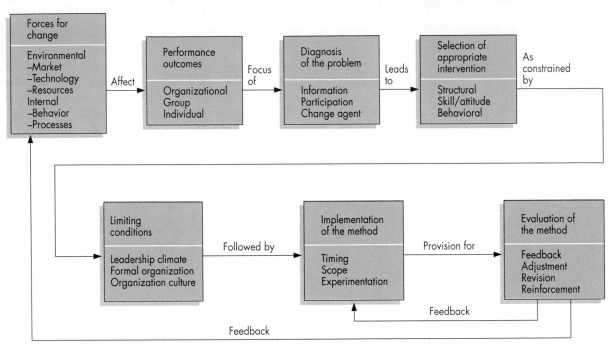

Source: Adapted from James L. Gibson, John M. Ivancevich, and James H. Donnelly, Jr., *Organizations* (Burr Ridge, IL: Richard D. Irwin, 1994), p. 668.

this method is that it allows observation of what people actually do as opposed to what they say they do.

In the diagnosis stage, one should collect data for a reason. A plan for analyzing the data should be developed even before the data are collected. Too often data are collected simply because they are available and with no plan for analysis.

Change Planning

The data collected in the diagnosis stage must be carefully interpreted to determine the best plan for organizational improvement. If a similar diagnosis has been done in the past, it can be revealing to compare the data and look for any obvious differences. Because much of the collected data are based on personal opinions and perceptions, there will always be areas of disagreement. The key to interpreting the data is to look for trends and areas of general agreement. The end result of the change-planning process is to identify specific problem areas and outline steps for resolving the problems.

Intervention/Education

The purpose of the intervention/education phase is to share the information obtained in the diagnostic phase with the affected employees and help them realize the need for change. A thorough analysis in the change-planning phase often results in the identification of the most appropriate intervention/education method to use. Some of the most frequently used intervention/education methods are discussed next.

direct feedback   Process in which the change agent communicates the information gathered through diagnosis directly to the affected people.

team building   Process by which a work group develops awareness of conditions that keep it from functioning effectively and takes action to eliminate these conditions.

sensitivity training   Method used in OD to make one more aware of oneself and one's impact on others.

Direct Feedback   With the **direct feedback** method, the change agent communicates the information gathered in the diagnostic and change-planning phases to the involved parties. The change agent describes what was found and what changes are recommended. Then workshops are often conducted to initiate the desired changes.

Team Building   The objective of **team building** is to increase the group's cohesiveness and general group spirit. Team building stresses the importance of working together. Some of the specific activities used include (1) clarifying employee roles, (2) reducing conflict, (3) improving interpersonal relations, and (4) improving problem-solving skills.[10]

Sensitivity Training   **Sensitivity training** is designed to make one more aware of oneself and one's impact on others. Sensitivity training involves a group, usually called a *training group* or *T-group*, that meets and has no agenda or particular focus. Normally the group has between 10 and 15 people who may or may not know one another. With no planned structure and/or no prior common experiences, the behavior of individuals in trying to deal with the lack of structure becomes the agenda. While engaging in group dialogue, members are encouraged to learn about themselves and others in the nonstructured environment.

Sensitivity training has been both passionately criticized and vigorously defended as to its relative value for organizations. In general, the research shows that people who have undergone sensitivity training tend to show increased sensitivity, more open communication, and increased flexibility.[11] However, these same studies indicate that while the outcomes of sensitivity training are beneficial in general, it is difficult to predict exactly the outcomes for any one person.

Evaluation

Probably the most difficult phase in the OD process is the evaluation phase.[12] The basic question to be answered is: Did the OD process produce the desired results? Unfortunately, many OD efforts begin with admirable but overly vague objectives such as improving the overall health, culture, or climate of the organization. Before any OD effort can be evaluated, explicit objectives must be determined. Objectives of an OD effort should be outcome oriented and should lend themselves to the development of measurable criteria.

A second requirement for evaluating OD efforts is that the evaluation effort be methodologically sound. Ideally, an OD effort should be evaluated using hard, objective data. One approach is to compare data collected before the OD intervention against data collected after the OD intervention. An even better approach is to compare "before" and "after" data with similar data from a control group. When using this approach, two similar groups are identified, an experimental group and a control group. The OD effort is then implemented with the experimental group but not with the control group. After the OD intervention has been completed, the before and after data from the experimental group are compared with the before and after data from the control group. This approach helps to rule out changes that may have resulted from factors other than the OD intervention.

From a practical standpoint, it may be desirable to use different personnel to evaluate an OD effort than those who implemented the effort. However, the people who implemented the effort may not be capable of objectively evaluating it.

Change as a Global Issue

As mentioned previously, one of the driving pressures for change is the desire to compete globally. Since America's global trading partners (notably Japan, China, and Europe) have adopted change as an essential ingredient of their long-term strategies, corporate America must follow suit. When asked about change in the international environment, Eric A. Cronson, vice president and managing director of Thomas Group Europe, commented, "Change has to be radical—if you stay in your comfort zone, you will not be internationally competitive."[13] Similarly, Joseph V. Marulli, president of information services at Eunetcom, commented at an international conference on change, "Transformation has to be in the leader's heart, in your heart, and in the hearts of all the senior people."[14] From comments such as these, the manager must understand that the challenge to compete is really the challenge to change.

MANAGING ORGANIZATION CULTURE

The word *culture* is derived in a roundabout way from the Latin verb *colere*, which means "to cultivate."[15] In later times, *culture* came to indicate a process of refinement and breeding in domesticating a particular crop. The modern-day meaning draws on this agricultural derivation: It relates to society's control, refinement, and domestication of itself. A contemporary definition of **culture** is "the set of important understandings (often unstated) that members of a community share in common."[16]

culture   Set of important understandings (often unstated) that members of a community share.

Culture in an organization compares to personality in a person. Humans have fairly enduring and stable traits that help them protect their attitudes and behaviors. So do organizations. In addition, certain groups of traits or personality types are known to consist of common elements. Organizations can be described in similar terms. They can be warm, aggressive, friendly, open, innovative, conservative, and so forth. An organization's culture is transmitted in many ways, including long-standing and often unwritten rules; shared standards regarding what is important; prejudices; standards for social etiquette and demeanor; established customs for relating to peers, subordinates, and superiors; and other traditions that clarify to employees what is and is not appropriate behavior. Thus, corporate culture communicates how people in the organization should behave by establishing a value system conveyed through rites, rituals, myths, legends, and actions. Simply stated, **corporate culture** means "the way we do things around here."[17]

corporate culture   Communicates how people in an organization should behave by establishing a value system conveyed through rites, rituals, myths, legends, and actions.

Cultural Forms of Expression

Culture has two basic components: (1) substance, the meanings contained in its values, norms, and beliefs; and (2) forms, the practices whereby these meanings are expressed, affirmed, and communicated to members.[18]

How Does Culture Originate?

There is no question that different organizations develop different cultures. What causes an organization to develop a particular type of culture? Many organizations trace their culture to one person who provided a living example of the major values of the organization. Robert Wood Johnson of Johnson & Johnson, Harley Procter of

Procter & Gamble, Walt Disney of Walt Disney Company, and Thomas J. Watson, Sr., of IBM all left their imprints on the organizations they headed. Research indicates, however, that fewer than half of a new company's values reflect the values of the founder or chief executive. The rest appear to develop in response both to the environment in which the business operates and to the needs of the employees.[19] Four distinct factors contribute to an organization's culture: its history, its environment, its selection process, and its socialization processes.[20]

History   Employees are aware of the organization's past, and this awareness builds culture. Much of the "way things are done" is a continuation of how things have always been done. The existing values that a strong leader may have established originally are constantly and subtly reinforced by experiences. The status quo is also protected by the human tendency to fervently embrace beliefs and values and to resist changes. Executives at Walt Disney Company reportedly pick up litter on the grounds without thinking because of the Disney vision of an immaculate Disneyland.

Environment   Because all organizations must interact with their environments, the environment plays a role in shaping their cultures. Deregulation of the telecommunications industry in the 1980's dramatically altered its environment. Before deregulation, the environment was relatively risk averse and noncompetitive. Increases in costs were automatically passed on to customers. As a result of deregulation, the environment changed overnight to become highly competitive and much more dynamic. No longer sheltered by a regulated environment, the cultures of the telecommunications companies were forced to change.

Staffing   Organizations tend to hire, retain, and promote people who are similar to current employees in important ways. A person's ability to fit in can be important in these processes. This "fit" criterion ensures that current values are accepted and that potential challengers of "how we do things" are screened out. Adjustment has to be carefully managed. For example, when Bill George took over Medronic, a leading producer of pacemakers, in 1991, he quickly found out that to survive in the rapidly growing high-tech health care business, he needed a change—but not at the expense of what had historically worked for the company. He opted for a merger with another company. The merger brought in "new blood" that was free-spirited and experimental in nature and teamed them with a highly disciplined, methodical existing culture. Though it was hard work, empowerment of people and a merger of cultures helped the company halve its development time and remain competitive in the industry.[21]

Entry Socialization   While an organization's values, norms, and beliefs may be widely and uniformly held, they are seldom written down. The new employee, who is least familiar with the culture, is most likely to challenge it. It is therefore important to help the newcomer adopt the organization's culture. Companies with strong cultures attach great importance to the process of introducing and indoctrinating new employees. This process is called **entry socialization.** Entry socialization not only reduces threats to the organization from newcomers but also lets new employees know what is expected of them. It may be handled in a formal or informal manner, as well as on an individual or group basis.

entry socialization   Adaptation process by which new employees are introduced and indoctrinated into the organization.

Identifying Culture

Researchers have identified seven characteristics that, taken together, capture the essence of an organization's culture:[22]

1. *Individual autonomy.* The degree of responsibility, independence, and opportunities for exercising initiative that individuals in the organization have.
2. *Structure.* The number of rules and regulations and the amount of direct supervision that is used to oversee and control employee behavior.
3. *Support.* The degree of assistance and warmth provided by managers to their subordinates.
4. *Identification.* The degree to which members identify with the organization as a whole rather than with their particular work group or field of professional expertise.
5. *Performance–reward.* The degree to which reward allocations (i.e., salary increases, promotions) in the organization are based on performance criteria.
6. *Conflict tolerance.* The degree of conflict present in relationships between peers and work groups, as well as the willingness to be honest and open about differences.
7. *Risk tolerance.* The degree to which employees are encouraged to be aggressive, innovative, and risk seeking.

Each of these traits should be viewed as existing on a continuum ranging from low to high. A picture of the overall culture can be formed by evaluating the organization on each of these characteristics.

There are as many distinct cultures as there are organizations. Most can be grouped into one of four basic types, determined by two factors: (1) the degree of risk associated with the organization's activities and (2) the speed with which the organization and its employees get feedback indicating the success of decisions.[23] Figure 18.5 shows in matrix form the four generic types of culture.

tough person, macho culture   Characterized by individuals who take high risks and get quick feedback on whether their decisions are right or wrong.

Tough Person Macho Culture   The **tough person macho culture** is characterized by individualists who regularly take high risks and get quick feedback on whether their decisions are right or wrong. Teamwork is not important, and every colleague is a potential rival. In this culture, the value of cooperation is ignored; there is no chance to learn from mistakes. People who do best in this culture are those who need to gamble and who can tolerate all-or-nothing risks because

FIGURE 18.5   Generic Types of Organization Culture

		Degree of Risk	
		High	Low
Speed of Feedback	Rapid	Tough person, macho culture	Work-hard/play-hard culture
	Slow	Bet-your-company culture	Process culture

they need instant feedback. Companies that develop large scale advertising programs for major clients would be characterized by the tough person, macho culture; these advertising programs are usually high budget with rapid acceptance or failure.

work-hard/play-hard culture   Encourages employees to take few risks and to expect rapid feedback.
bet-your-company culture   Requires big-stakes decisions; considerable time passes before the results are known.
process culture   Involves low risk with little feedback; employees focus on how things are done rather than on the outcomes.

Work-Hard/Play-Hard Culture   The **work-hard/play-hard culture** encourages employees to take few risks and to expect rapid feedback. In this culture, activity is the key to success. Rewards accrue to persistence and the ability to find a need and fill it. Because of the need for volume, team players who are friendly and outgoing thrive. Companies that are sales based such as real estate companies often have a work-hard/play-hard culture.

Bet-Your-Company Culture   The **bet-your-company culture** requires big-stakes decisions, with considerable time passing before the results are known. Pressures to make the right decisions are always present in this environment. Companies involved in durable goods manufacturing are often characterized by a bet-your-company culture.

Process Culture   The **process culture** involves low risk coupled with little feedback; employees must focus on how things are done rather than on the outcomes. Employees in this atmosphere become cautious and protective. Those who thrive are orderly, punctual, and detail oriented. Companies in regulated or protected industries often operate in this type of culture.

Changing Culture

Implicit in this discussion has been the fact that strong cultures can contribute greatly to an organization's success. A strong culture in this context means one that is clearly defined, reinforces a common understanding about what is important, and has the support of management and employees. Weak cultures have the opposite characteristics and can inhibit success. Figure 18.6 summarizes some characteristics of a weak culture.

Executives who have successfully changed organization cultures estimate that the process usually takes from 6 to 15 years.[24] Because organization culture is difficult and time consuming to change, any attempts should be well thought out.

FIGURE 18.6   Characteristics of a Weak Culture

- Organizational members have no clear values or beliefs about how to succeed in their business.
- Organizational members have many beliefs as to how to succeed but cannot agree on which are most important.
- Different parts of the organization have fundamentally different beliefs about how to succeed.
- Those who personify the culture are destructive or disruptive and don't build on any common understanding about what is important.
- The rituals of day-to-day organizational life are disorganized and/or working at cross-purposes.

Source: Terrence E. Deal and Allan A. Kennedy, *Corporate Cultures: The Rites and Rituals of Corporate Life* (Reading, MA: Addison-Wesley, 1982), pp. 135–36.

Allan Kennedy, an expert on organization culture, believes only five reasons justify a large-scale cultural change:[25]

1. The organization has strong values that do not fit into a changing environment.
2. The industry is very competitive and moves with lightning speed.
3. The organization is mediocre or worse.
4. The organization is about to join the ranks of the very large companies.
5. The organization is small but growing rapidly.

Some organizations attempt to change their cultures only when they are forced to do so by changes in their environments or economic situations; others anticipate a necessary change. While massive cultural reorientation may be reasonable in most situations, it is usually possible to strengthen or fine-tune the current situation. A statement of corporate mission consistently reinforced by systems, structures, and policies is a useful tool for strengthening the culture.

Because of the cost, time, and difficulty involved in changing culture, many people believe it is easier to change, or physically replace, the people. This view assumes most organizations promote people who fit the prevailing norms of the organization. Therefore, the easiest if not the only way to change an organization's culture is to change its people.

MANAGING DIVERSITY

One of the more prevalent changes in today's work environment is the increasing diversification of the workforce. Diversity of the workforce encompasses many different dimensions, including sex, race, religion, age, and types of disability. Compared to a workforce that historically was dominated by white males, today's workforce is very diverse and projected to become more so.

Workforce 2000, the widely referenced study published in 1987 by the Hudson Institute and undertaken by a grant from the Employment and Training Administration of the U.S. Department of Labor, projected that only one-third of the workforce in the year 2000 would be native-born, white males.[26] More recent projections estimate that white males will represent approximately 38 percent of the U.S. workforce by the year 2005.[27] This is down from 60 percent in 1960. The major reason that males no longer dominate the workforce is that women have entered the workforce in record numbers in recent years. The Bureau of Labor Statistics estimates that by the year 2000 over 60 percent of all women over age 16 will be in the workforce. This single dimension of diversity alone has many ramifications for organizations. Child care, spouse relocation assistance programs, pregnancy leave programs, flexible hours, and work-at-home jobs are all directly affected by the increasing number of women in the workforce.

The fastest growing segment of the U.S. workforce is projected to be Asians and Pacific Islanders.[28] This group is expected to increase fivefold over the next few years. Non-Caucasians were projected to constitute 29 percent of labor force entrance throughout the 1990s. In addition, some 600,000 legal and illegal immigrants are expected to enter the United States each year. Of these numbers, two-thirds are expected to join the workforce. In addition to the possibility of a limited educational background, minority and immigrant employees are likely to have language, attitude, and cultural problems. Organizations must begin now to successfully integrate these people into their workforces. A survey published by Olsten Corporation in 1992 emphasized that these changes would apply to small businesses as well as to large ones.[29]

Almost everyone has heard the phrase "the graying of America." It is projected that the average age of U.S. employees will continue to rise. The authors of *Workforce 2000* predicted that the average age of U.S. employees would rise from 36 in 1987 to 39 by the year 2000. Others predicted that the number of people aged 45–59 would increase by 40 percent by the year 2000.[30] The older workforce will likely be more experienced, reliable, and stable but also less adaptable to change and retraining. One direct result of this trend is that retirement age is already increasing. A variety of work alternatives, such as flexible benefits, sabbatical leaves, job sharing, and part-time work, may become necessary to hire and hold good employees.

Guidelines for Managing Diversity

Companies competing in today's fast-paced global markets tend to define diversity in very broad terms that encompass differences in gender, racioethnicity, age, physical abilities, qualities and sexual orientation, as well as differences in attitudes, perspectives and background.[31] Diversity management has been defined as "the process by which a company (or manager, or human resource department, or any individual) incorporates the dissimilarities of its workforce into the decision-making process in order to motivate, direct, lead, organize, plan, and staff more efficiently."[32] From an overall viewpoint, managers must get away from the tradition of fitting employees into a single corporate mold. Not everyone will look and act the same way. New policies must be created to explicitly recognize and respond to the unique needs of individual employees. Specifically, today's managers should follow certain guidelines for managing within and among a diverse workforce:[33]

1. *Focus on observable behavior.* Don't jump to conclusions; rather, focus on actual observations. Resist saying things like "There goes Mary again" or "Joe looks like he hasn't heard a thing I said for the last two hours."

2. *Avoid stereotyping.* One suggestion is to use people's names even when thinking about them. It is easy to stereotype people when they are thought of in terms of "types," but it is hard to do so when using an individual's name. For example, think "What can I expect from John and Tom?" as opposed to "What can I expect from them?"

3. *Evaluate output, not input.* Results are what counts. Don't worry about minor habits and idiosyncrasies, especially when the work is getting done.

4. *Don't make assumptions about nonstandard behavior.* Begin with the fact that a nonstandard behavior is different but not necessarily inappropriate. Remember the old saying "there is more than one way to skin a cat."

5. *Provide feedback based on observations.* Let employees know how you see certain behaviors or events. Often others do not perceive things the same way the manager does. Don't dismiss dysfunctional behavior as either unimprovable or deliberately inappropriate. Often the person's perception is simply different, and in the absence of feedback to the contrary, he or she will continue to think so.

6. *Don't tolerate nonbehavioral assumptions from anyone.* Regardless of how unpopular it might be at the time, confront any form of stereotyping. One approach is to point out that the accuser is really describing behavior in which everyone in the workplace engages to some extent.

7. *Test your own behaviors.* Ask employees for feedback to determine what effects your own behaviors have on others, and look for what you might do to improve.

Greater diversity can be expected to create certain specific challenges but also some important contributions. Communication problems are certain to occur. These include misunderstandings between employees and managers. There may also be a need to translate verbal and written materials into several languages. Additional training, including remedial work in very basic skills such as writing and problem solving, will be necessary. Organizational factionalism can be expected to increase. This will require dedicating increasing amounts of time to dealing with special-interest and advocacy groups.

In addition to creating the above challenges, greater diversity presents new opportunities. Diversity contributes to an organization culture that is more tolerant of different behavioral styles and wider views. This often leads to better business decisions. Other advantages include cost savings, winning the competition for better talent, and increasing business growth.[34] Costs associated with poor diversity management include higher turnover among women and minorities, higher absenteeism rates and more discrimination-based lawsuits. Winning the competition for talent involves attracting, retaining, and promoting the best employees from different demographic groups. Business growth can be enhanced by leveraging opportunities associated with increased marketplace understanding, greater creativity, higher quality team problem-solving, improved leadership effectiveness, and better global relations.

The increasing diversification of the workforce is a fact. Not only are the demographics of today's workforce different, but so are its attitudes, expectations, and needs. Learning to effectively manage a diverse workforce should be viewed as an investment in the future. The current trend in diversity management is to empower human resource managers to focus on recruitment, career development, diversity training, upward mobility, diverse input and feedback, self-help, accountability, systems accommodation (develop respect), and outreach as methods to help the organization make strides in fostering and coping with a diverse workforce.[35]

Summary

1. *Identify the Three Major Categories of Organizational Change.* The three major categories of organizational change are technological changes, environmental changes, and changes internal to the organization.

2. *List the Three Major Barriers to Managing Change.* The three major barriers to managing change are: lack of management visibility and support, inadequate management skills, and employee resistance to change.

3. *Discuss Several Reasons Employees Resist Change.* Employees resist change for many reasons. Six of the most frequently encountered reasons are (1) fear of the unknown, (2) economics, (3) fear that expertise and skills will lose value, (4) threats to power, (5) inconvenience, and (6) threats to interpersonal relations.

4. *Identify Several Prescriptions for Reducing Resistance to Change.* Just as there are many reasons employees resist change, there are many approaches for reducing resistance to change. Several suggestions for reducing resistance to change include (1) building trust between management and employees; (2) discussing upcoming changes with af-

fected employees; (3) involving employees in the change process as early as possible; (4) ensuring that the proposed changes are reasonable; (5) avoiding threats; (6) following a sensible time schedule for implementing the change; and (7) implementing the change in the most logical place.

5. *List the Three Steps in Lewin's Model for Change.* Lewin's model for change involves three steps: unfreezing, presenting a new alternative, and refreezing.

6. *Summarize the Four Phases of an Organizational Development (OD) Program.* Most OD efforts include a diagnosis phase, a change-planning phase, an intervention/education phase, and an evaluation phase. Diagnosis involves gathering and analyzing information to determine the areas of the organization in need of improvement. Change planning involves developing a plan for organization improvement. Intervention/education involves the sharing of diagnostic information with the people affected by it and helping them to realize the need for change. The evaluation phase attempts to determine the effects the OD effort has had on the organization.

7. *Define Corporate Culture.* Corporate culture communicates how people in the organization should behave by establishing a value system conveyed through rites, rituals, myths, legends, and actions. Simply stated, corporate culture means "the way we do things around here."

8. *Describe the Generic Types of Organizational Culture.* The tough-guy, macho culture is characterized by individualists who regularly take high risks and get quick feedback on whether they are right or wrong. The work-hard/play-hard culture encourages employees to take few risks and to expect rapid feedback. The bet-your-company culture requires big-stakes decisions with considerable time lags before the results are known. The process culture involves low risk coupled with little feedback; employees must focus on how things are done rather than on the outcomes.

9. *Define Diversity Management.* Diversity management is the process by which a company (or manager, or human resource department, or any individual) incorporates the dissimilarities of its workforce into the decision-making process to motivate, direct, lead, organize, plan, and staff more efficiently.

10. *List Several Guidelines for Managing a Diverse Workforce.* Seven specific guidelines for managing within and among a diverse workforce are: (1) focus on observable behavior, (2) avoid stereotyping, (3) evaluate output, not input, (4) don't make assumptions about nonstandard behavior, (5) provide feedback based on observations, (6) don't tolerate nonbehavioral assumptions from anyone, and (7) test your own behaviors.

Preview Analysis

1. According to Calhoun W. Wick, what should a work environment do for the employee?

2. What is Wick's view on diversity?

3. What has happened at Corning regarding the diversity issue?

4. What do you think might be some of the duties of a diversity officer?

Review Questions

1. Name the three major categories of change that apply to organizations.

2. Describe the four basic reactions of employees to change.

3. Name six common barriers (reasons for resistance) to change.

4. Discuss six approaches to reducing resistance to change.

5. What is a program of planned change?

6. Describe Lewin's model for change.

7. What is organizational development (OD)?

8. What organizational characteristics determine corporate culture?

9. How is corporate culture originated and maintained?

10. Name and briefly define the four generic types of corporate culture.

11. What is meant by the term *managing diversity?*

12. Discuss several guidelines for managing within and among a diverse workforce.

13. Discuss three positive reasons for doing a good job of managing diversity in an organization.

Skill-Building Questions

1. Take a position and be prepared to defend it with regard to the following statement: "Most people resist change, not because the change is harmful but because they are lazy."

2. Check recent literature (*Business Week, The Wall Street Journal,* and other library sources) and identify two or three industries that are currently experiencing major changes. How is each industry responding to the changes? Are these industries likely to be stronger or weaker as a result of these changes?

3. Pick an organization or industry you think will need to change its culture if it is to thrive in the future (as the telecommunication companies had to do in the 1980s). Be prepared to explain why you think this change must occur.

4. Do you think most people would like to work within and among a diverse workforce? Why or why not?

5. What are the biggest problems a diverse work environment can create? What aspects do you think would be the hardest to deal with or manage?

SKILL-BUILDING EXERCISE 18.1

Sexist/Nonsexist Language

As part of communicating that an organization is truly committed to supporting a highly qualified and diverse work force, managers should take every opportunity to demonstrate the use of nonsexist language.

A. Try to identify a nonsexist word to use in place of each of the following words that may carry a sexist connotation:

Man-hours	Salesman
Watchman	Spokesman
Girl Friday	Foreman
Repairman	Draftsman
Layout man	Policeman
Manmade	Freshman

B. List additional words or terms that you think might carry a sexist connotation.

SKILL-BUILDING EXERCISE 18.2

Resisting Change

One of the problems you face involves mistakes being made by employees who perform a particular operation. The same mistakes seem to occur in more than one department. You believe a training program for the people concerned will help reduce errors.

You are aware, however, that your supervisors may defend existing procedures simply because the introduction of training may imply criticism of the way they have been operating. You realize, too, that the supervisors may fear resistance by employees afraid of not doing well in the training program. All in all, you plan to approach the subject carefully.

1. Add to the agenda of your weekly staff meeting a recommendation that training be undertaken to help reduce errors.

2. Talk to all your supervisors individually and get their attitudes and ideas about what to do before bringing the subject up in the weekly staff meeting.

3. Ask the corporate training staff to come in, determine the training needs, and develop a program to meet those needs.

4. Since this training is in the best interests of the company, tell your supervisors they will be expected to implement and support it.

5. Appoint a team to study the matter thoroughly, develop recommendations, then bring it before the full staff meeting.

Other alternatives may be open to you, but assume these are the only ones you have considered. WITHOUT DISCUSSION with anyone, choose one of them and be prepared to defend your choice.

CASE INCIDENT 18.1

The Way We Do Things

Fitzgerald Company manufactures a variety of consumer products for sale through retail department stores. For over 30 years, the company has held a strong belief that customer relations and a strong selling orientation are the keys to business success. As a result, all top executives have sales backgrounds and spend much of their time outside the company with customers. Because of the strong focus on the customer, management at Fitzgerald emphasizes new-product development projects and growth in volume. The company rarely implements cost reduction or process improvement projects.

Between 1975 and 1985, Fitzgerald's 10 percent share of the market was the largest in the industry. Profitability was consistently better than the industry average. However, in the last 10 years, the markets for many of Fitzgerald's products have matured, and Fitzgerald has dropped from market share leader to the number three company in the industry. Profitability has steadily declined since 1991, although Fitzgerald offers a more extensive line of products than any of its competitors. Customers are complaining that Fitzgerald's prices are higher than those of other companies.

In June 1996, Jeff Steele, president of Fitzgerald Company, hired Valerie Stevens of Management Consultants, Inc., to help him improve the company's financial performance. After an extensive study of Fitzgerald Company and its industry group, Valerie met with Jeff and said, "Jeff, I believe the Fitzgerald Company may have to substantially change its culture."

Questions

1. Describe, in general terms, the corporate culture at Fitzgerald Company.

2. What does Valerie mean when she says Fitzgerald Company may have to change its culture? What are some of the necessary changes?

3. Discuss the problems the company may encounter in attempting to implement changes.

CASE INCIDENT 18.2

Upgrading Quality

Judy Franklin, the plant manager of Smart Manufacturing Company, was reviewing the Quality Control Department figures with despair. Once again, the department's figures indicated quality improvements were not being made. Judy was annoyed. "I don't understand it," she thought. "I've been stressing to my staff for over a year that I want to see some quality improvements, but it just doesn't seem to be happening. Quality may actually be worse now than it was a year ago!"

Judy called in David Berg, the quality control manager, and production manager Stuart Lewicki. "Look," Judy said, "I told both of you over a year ago I wanted to see some improvements in quality around here, and we've talked about it at every staff meeting since then. But nothing has happened. What's going on?"

David spoke up. "My department just inspects the products. The quality problems occur in production. All I can do is what I've been doing all along—tell Stuart about

the problems we are seeing. I've already told him that 50 percent of the quality problems are caused by worker carelessness."

"I know," said Stuart. "I don't understand it. I've been stressing to my shift supervisors that we need to see quality improvements. They have all told me they are coming down really hard on quality problems and are telling their people they need to work harder on getting out a quality product. Just the other day, Frances Stanfield threatened to fire Joe Duncan if she got any more complaints from quality control about Joe's work."

Questions

1. Why have efforts to improve quality failed?

2. Design a quality improvement program that would have a better chance of being successful if used by Judy.

References and Additional Readings

[1]Tom Peters, *Thriving on Chaos* (New York: Alfred A. Knopf, 1987), p. 464.

[2]Ibid.

[3]Ibid., p. 274.

[4]Margaret Boles and Brenda Paik Sunoo, "Three Barriers to Managing Change," *Workforce*, January 1998, p. 25.

[5]Stephen A. Baker, "From Blueprints To Grand Design," *Business Week*, January 8, 1996, p. 34.

[6]Gillian Flynn, "HR Translates Ideology Into Action," *Workforce*, February 1997, p. 52.

[7]Waldron Berry, "Overcoming Resistance to Change," *Supervisory Management*, February 1983.

[8]John M. Thomas and Warren G. Bennis, eds., *The Management of Change and Conflict* (New York: Penguin Books, 1972), p. 109.

[9]Harold J. Leavitt, "Applied Organization Change in Industry; Structural, Technical, and Human Approaches," in *New Perspectives in Organization Research*, ed. W. W. Cooper, H. J. Leavitt, and M. W. Shelly II (New York: John Wiley & Sons, 1964), pp. 55–71.

[10]Arthur G. Bedeian, *Management* (Hinsdale, IL: The Dryden Press, 1986).

[11]Michael Beer, "The Technology of Organization Development," in *Handbook of Industrial and Organizational Psychology*, ed. Marvin D. Dunnette (New York: John Wiley & Sons, 1983), p. 941; Michael Beer, *Organization Change and Development: A Systems View* (Santa Monica, CA: Goodyear Publishing, 1980), pp. 194–95.

[12]Much of this section is drawn from David E. Terpstra, "The Organization Development Evaluation Process: Some Problems and Proposals." Human Resource Management, Spring 1981, p. 24.

[13]"The 1995 *Business Week* Europe Forum of Financial Directors," *Business Week*, January 15, 1996.

[14]Ibid.

[15]Roy Wagner, *The Invention of Culture*, rev. ed. (Chicago: University of Chicago Press, 1981), p. 21.

[16]Vijay Sathe, "Implications of Corporate Culture: A Manager's Guide to Action," *Organizational Dynamics*, Autumn 1983, p. 6.

[17]Terrence E. Deal and Allan A. Kennedy, *Corporate Cultures: The Rites and Rituals of Corporate Life* (Reading, MA: Addison-Wesley, 1982), p. 4.

[18]Harrison M. Trice and Jance M. Beyer, "Studying Organizational Cultures through Rites and Ceremonials," *Academy of Management Review* 9, no. 4 (1984), p. 645.

[19]"The Corporate Culture Vultures," *Fortune*, October 17, 1983, p. 72.

[20]Stephen P. Robbins, *Essentials of Organizational Behavior* (Englewood Cliffs, NJ: Prentice Hall, 1984), pp. 174–76.

[21]Ron Stodghill, "One Company, Two Cultures," *Business Week*, January 22, 1996, p. 88.

[22]Stephen P. Robbins, *Essentials of Organizational Behavior*, © 1984, p. 171. Reprinted by permission of Prentice Hall, Inc., Englewood Cliffs, NJ.

[23]This section is drawn from Deal and Kennedy, *Corporate Cultures*, pp. 107, 129–35.

[24]"The Corporate Culture Vultures," p. 70.

[25]Ibid.

[26]William B. Johnston and Arnold H. Parker, *Workforce 2000: Work and Workers for the 21st Century* (Indianapolis: Hudson Institute Inc., 1987).

[27]Joseph H. Boyett and Jimmie T. Boyett, *Beyond Workplace 2000*, (New York: Dutton Books) 1995, pp. 79–81.

[28]B. Bremmer and J. Weber, "A Spicier Stew in the Melting Pot," *Business Week*, December 21, 1995, p. 29.

[29]Ellyn E. Spragins, "The Diverse Workforce," *Inc.*, January 1993, p. 33.

[30]Rick Fischer, "Tomorrow's Workforce—Predictions, Projections and Implications," *Public Relations Quarterly*, Spring 1995, pp. 12–16.

[31]Gail Robinson and Kathleen Dechant, "Building a Business Case for Diversity," *Academy of Management Executive*, August 1997, pp. 21–31.

[32]David S. Gold, "Managing Diversity . . . Defined," in *Managing Diversity*, vol. 1, no. 2 (Jamestown, NY: Jamestown Area Labor Management Committee, 1992), p. 3.

[33]These guidelines are adapted from Alan Weiss, "Understanding Behavior in Managing Diversity," in *Managing Diversity*, vol. 1, no. 2 (Jamestown, NY: Jamestown Area Labor Management Committee, 1992), pp. 6–7.

[34]Much of this section is drawn from Gail Robinson and Kathleen Dechant, *op. cit.*

[35]Adapted from L. Copeland, "Valuing Diversity, Part 2: Pioneers and Champions of Change," *Personnel*, July 1988, p. 48; H. Jain, B. M. Pitts, and G. De Santis, eds., *Equality for All: National Conference on Racial Equality in the Workplace—Retrospect and Prospect* (Hamilton, Ontario: McMaster University and IRRA, Hamilton and District Chapter, 1991); and A. Dastmalchian, P. Blyton, and R. Adamson, *The Climate of Workplace Relations* (New York: Rutledge, a Division of Rutledge, Chapman, and Hall, 1991).

Section

VI

CONTROLLING SKILLS

19

Controlling

LEARNING OBJECTIVES

After studying this chapter, you should be able to:

1. Explain why management controls are necessary.

2. Describe a feedback system.

3. Discuss the basic requirements of the control process.

4. Describe the Control Pyramid.

5. Identify the factors that affect how much control should be exercised in an organization.

6. Discuss the two categories of control methods.

7. Differentiate among preliminary, concurrent, and postaction controls.

8. List several methods or systems of control commonly used by managers.

9. List the four basic types of financial ratios.

10. Discuss the basic purpose of a break-even chart.

Mike Doyle, former marketing services director of Abbey National Bank in England, was sentenced in 1997 to eight years in jail for fraud. In his job as marketing services director, Doyle had a big say in how the bank's £ 35 million (approximately $56 million U.S. dollars) marketing budget was spent. The fraud only came to light when the bank's sales promotions manager, Gary Brown, complained that he was not being consulted about payments being made to some of the firms that were apparently supplying the marketing department. Doyle was convicted of receiving bribes from suppliers by putting through excessive or bogus invoices.

Source: Jon Rees, "Tricksters of the Trade," *Marketing Week*, July 3, 1997.

The basic premise of organizations is that all activities will function smoothly; however, the possibility that this will not be the case gives rise to the need for control.

control   Process of ensuring that organizational activities are going according to plan; accomplished by comparing actual performance to predetermined standards or objectives, then taking action to correct any deviations.

Control simply means knowing what is actually happening in comparison to preset standards or objectives and then making any necessary corrections. The overriding purpose of all management controls is to alert the manager to an existing or a potential problem before it becomes critical. Control is accomplished by comparing actual performance to predetermined standards or objectives and then taking action to correct any deviations from the standard. However, control is a sensitive and complex part of the management process.

Controlling is similar to planning. It addresses these basic questions: Where are we now? Where do we want to be? How can we get there from here? But controlling takes place after the planning is completed and the organizational activities have begun. Whereas most planning occurs before action is taken, most controlling takes place after the initial action has been taken. This does not mean control is practiced only after problems occur. Control decisions can be preventive, and they can also affect future planning decisions.

WHY PRACTICE MANAGEMENT CONTROL?

As we just noted, management controls alert the manager to potentially critical problems. At top management levels, a problem occurs when the organization's goals are not being met. At middle and lower levels, a problem occurs when the objectives for which the manager is responsible are not being met. These may be departmental objectives, production standards, or other performance indicators. All forms of management controls are designed to give the manager information regarding progress. The manager can use this information to do the following:

1. *Prevent crises.* If a manager does not know what is going on, it is easy for small, readily solvable problems to turn into crises.
2. *Standardize outputs.* Problems and services can be standardized in terms of quantity and quality through the use of good controls.
3. *Appraise employee performance.* Proper controls can provide the manager with objective information about employee performance.
4. *Update plans.* Even the best plans must be updated as environmental and internal changes occur. Controls allow the manager to compare what is happening with what was planned.
5. *Protect the organization's assets.* Controls can protect assets from inefficiency, waste, and pilferage.

TWO CONCERNS OF CONTROL

When practicing control, the manager must balance two major concerns: stability and objective realization. To maintain stability, the manager must ensure that the organization is operating within its established boundaries of constraint. The boundaries of constraint are determined by policies, budgets, ethics, laws, and so on. The second concern, objective realization, requires constant monitoring to ensure that enough progress is being made toward established objectives.

A manager may become overly worried about one concern at the expense of another. Most common is a manager who becomes preoccupied with the stability of the operation and neglects the goal. This manager is overly concerned with day-to-day rules and policies and forgets about his or her goals. A manager who is obsessed with the manner or style in which a job is done is an example. On the other hand, a manager may lose sight of stability and have glamorous but short-lived success. A manager who sets production records by omitting safety checks is an example of this behavior.

The above concerns create a paradox. According to author Tom Peters, "control is an illusion. . . no one really controls anything. . . most success is due to luck."[1] This "illusion of control," according to Peters, leads to "the control paradox" wherein "you are out of control when you are 'in control' and you are in control when you are 'out of control.'"[2] He explains this rather interesting view by giving the example of the executive who "knows everything" (such executives are surrounded by layers of management and tons of paper documents telling them what is going on) but is inept because she or he is so removed from reality as to be really "out of control." In contrast is the manager who is "in control" despite the thousands of things going on (people taking initiatives, plans being made at various levels, and people exceeding their job descriptions as a part of tactical and operational decision making) because he or she sticks to the assigned task and/or plan and sees it to completion.[3] Using Peters's ideas, managers would do well to understand that control is as much an attitude as a physical reality.

THE MANAGEMENT CONTROL PROCESS

Figure 19.1 is a simple model of the management control process. Outputs from the activity are monitored by some type of sensor and compared to preset standards (normally set during the planning process). The manager acts as the regulator; he or she takes corrective action when the outputs do not meet the standards. The manager's actions may be directed at the inputs to the activity or at the activity itself.

feedback system   System in which outputs from the system affect future inputs or future activities of the system.

Such a system, in which outputs from the system affect future inputs into or future activities of the system, is called a **feedback system.** In other words, a feedback system is influenced by its own past behaviors. The heating

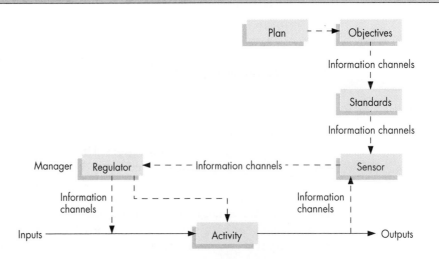

FIGURE 19.1   The Control Process

system of a house is a common example of a mechanical feedback system. The thermostat sensor compares the temperature resulting from heat previously generated by the system to some predetermined standard (the desired temperature setting) and responds accordingly. Feedback is a vital part of the control process. Although preventive, before-the-fact steps can often aid the control process, total control cannot be practiced without feedback. Managers may receive and act on facts about the inputs or the activity itself. But in the end, they must know what is happening in the organization; feedback gives them this information. Extensions of the feedback concept are described in Management Illustration 19.1.

Three Requirements for Control

The process of control has three basic requirements: (1) establishing standards, (2) monitoring results and comparing them to standards, and (3) correcting deviations. The first step, setting standards, comes from the planning process, while the latter two, monitoring and correcting, are unique to the control process. All three are essential to effective control.

standard   Value used as a point of reference for comparing other values.

Setting Standards   A **standard** is a value used as a point of reference for comparing other values. As such, a standard outlines what is expected of the job and/or the individual. When used in management control, standards often come directly from objectives. In some instances, objectives may be used directly as standards. In other instances, performance indicators may be derived from the objectives. In certain situations, a standard may be determined by methods analysts, industrial engineers, or recognized experts. In any case, standards should be easy to measure and define. The more specific and measurable an objective is, the more likely it can be directly used as a standard. Standards may deal with output per hour, quality level, inventory level, or other indicators of individual and/or organizational performance.

Monitoring Performance   Obviously, the overall control system is no better than the information on which it operates, and much of this information is gathered from the monitoring process. Monitoring is often considered to be synonymous with control. In fact, it is only one part of the total control process. The main purpose of monitoring performance is to gather data and detect problem areas. The type of standards used often dictates the type of checks to be made.

The major problem in monitoring performance is deciding when, where, and how often to inspect or check. Checks must be made often enough to provide needed information. However, some managers become obsessed with the checking process. Monitoring can be expensive if overdone, and it can result in adverse reactions from employees. Timing is equally important. The manager must recognize a problem in time to correct it.

Correcting for Deviations   Too often, managers set standards and monitor results but do not follow up with actions. The first two steps are of little value if corrective action is not taken. The action needed may be simply to maintain the status quo. Action of this type would depend on standards being met in a satisfactory manner. If standards are not being met, the manager must find the cause of the deviation and correct it. It is not enough to treat only the symptoms. This action is comparable to replacing a car battery when the real problem is a faulty generator. In a short time, the battery will go dead again. It is also possible that a careful analysis of the deviation

Management Illustration 19.1

The Feedback Loop: The First Control Device

It is estimated that the feedback loop ("the giving or feeding back of information about the control subject to some analysis mechanism which then uses the information for decision making") is one of the original control devices, since there are abundant examples of its function in biology (e.g., control of body temperature). In biology, numerous organisms have evolved a full set of devices out of which they build a closed loop. These devices are (1) a sensing device (sensor or receptor), which detects what is going on and transmits information to a (2) control center (collator), which compares what is going on to some concept of a standard and then issues orders to a (3) motor device (effector), which takes action to bring results into line with the standard. For example, using body temperature, humans note that they are hot (by feelings or sweating) and then decide to cool themselves in some way until a balance or comfort zone is restored.

In organizations, management makes extensive use of the same simple concept. The concept stays simple as long as the manager understands exactly what the steps are to construct a "feedback loop" and how to use the concept for control. By thinking of the concept in steps, the manager is better able to see how this control device operates; make sure that, if different individuals are interacting or implementing the separate steps, tight process control is kept over them; and control the process itself. The sequence of the feedback loop is as follows:

1. *Carefully choose the control subjects.* What do we intend to regulate? A variety of choices are available such as level of sales, complaints, expenses, production sequences, etc.

2. *Define the critical unit of measure.* Don't just use terms such as *good, high,* or *low.* These terms lack preciseness and can mean different things to different people. Create adjectives that everyone agrees on (or are the industry standard), and make sure they clearly and directly tie into the concept being measured.

3. *Establish a standard level of performance.* This must match the unit of measure. This standard can come from history, competition, or some new idea, but it specifies the level that is to be obtained or held.

4. *Create sensory devices.* These devices measure the actual performance in terms of the unit of measure. These devices could be mechanical or just paperwork (sales reports or records) that describes the event. The only real requirements are that the devices be understood by all and that all are able to read performance from them.

5. *Mobilize for measurement.* Create the organizational and mechanical machinery for using the sensory devices to measure and report actual performance. This step is critical to the success of the technique.

6. *Compare actual performance with the standard.* To work, this must go on at all levels of the company. Each division or department must understand how its function meshes with the overall operation or function.

7. *Decide on action needed when there is a difference between actual and standard performance.* This step is where the manager shows his or her leadership and true worth. What form of change (from doing nothing to changing and making corrections) is necessary and warranted?

8. *Take the action.* This may be as simple as correcting a small problem (throwing a switch) or as complicated as revising a major decision or procedure.

The conclusion for the manager who desires to learn about control is to start with the simple and work to the more complex. The feedback loop is a great place to start. In other words, if the manager knows how to control (by mastering the concept of the feedback loop), she or he can control anything.

Source: Adapted from J. M. Juran, *Managerial Breakthrough*, rev. ed. (New York: McGraw-Hill, 1995), pp. 199–203.

> **FIGURE 19.2   Potential Causes of Performance Deviations**
>
> - Faulty planning.
> - Lack of communication within the organization.
> - Need for training.
> - Lack of motivation.
> - Unforeseen forces outside the organization, such as government regulation or competition.

will require a change in the standard. The standard may have been improperly set, or changing conditions may dictate a change in standard. Figure 19.2 lists some potential causes of deviations between desired and actual performance.

Tools used to correct for deviations should have the following characteristics:

1. The tools should be used to eliminate the root causes of a problem (as in the battery example above).
2. Tools should be capable of correcting defects (which are bound to occur).
3. Tools should be relatively simple and straightforward so that all employees can use them (e.g., monitoring a gauge, turning a dial, reading a simple report).
4. Tools should be easy for employees to tie to goals or standards for improvement.
5. Tools should be applied totally, not piecemeal.[4]

Control Tolerances

Actual performance rarely conforms exactly to standards or plans. A certain amount of variation will normally occur. Therefore, the manager must set limits on the acceptable degree of deviation from the standard. In other words, how much variation from standard is tolerable? For example, by how much can expenses be allowed to exceed expectations before the manager becomes alarmed? The manner in which the manager sets **control tolerances** depends on the standard and methods being used. If sampling is being used to monitor the activity, statistical control techniques can be used. The tolerance levels may be formalized, or they may merely exist in the mind of the manager. The important point is that the manager must develop some guidelines as to what deviation is acceptable (in control) and what is not acceptable (out of control).

control tolerances   Variation from the standard that is acceptable to the manager.

The Control Pyramid

The Control Pyramid, provides a method for implementing controls in the organization.[5] The idea is to implement simple controls first and then move to more complex controls at a later time. The first area to be considered using this method would be *foolproof controls*, wherein the control deals with repetitive acts and requires little thought (e.g., turning off lights). Surprisingly, many of these acts and controls already exist in an organization's normal course of business. The second area to consider is *automatic controls*, wherein a feedback loop can exist without much human interaction (e.g., regulation of plant temperature). These systems require monitoring, but the control can be machine or computer based. The third area is *operator controls*, which require a human response (e.g., a salesperson checking records). The key to this form of control is to make it meaningful for the controller. The fourth area is *su-*

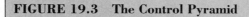

FIGURE 19.3   The Control Pyramid

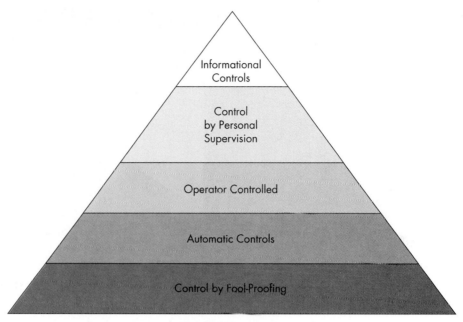

The Control pyramid.

Source: Adapted from J. M. Juran, *Managerial Breakthrough*, rev. ed. (New York: McGraw-Hill, 1995), p. 205.

pervisory control, the layer that controls the person or persons implementing the controls, (e.g., a department head checking an employee's reports). The organization must make sure that this form of control gets results and is not redundant. The final area is *informational controls* (e.g., report summaries). This is the ultimate feedback loop, wherein the manager must pull together all the information provided by the other controls.[6] Seeing the process as a whole helps the manager get a feel for how interrelated the control process is and how it must be synchronized. See Figure 19.3 for an explanatory diagram of this process.

How Much Control?

When deciding how much control should be exercised in an organization, three major factors must be appraised: (1) economic considerations and (2) behavioral considerations and (3) flexibility and innovation considerations.

Economic Considerations   Installing and operating control systems cost money. A good quality control system, for instance, requires additional labor, if nothing else. The equipment costs of sophisticated electronic and mechanical control systems can be very high. Ideally, control systems should be installed as long as they save more than they cost. Figure 19.4 shows the general relationship between control costs and the benefits gained. The straight, upward sloping line represents the costs associated with implementing and maintaining the controls (up-front installation expenses, labor costs, etc). The S-shaped curve represents the performance or benefits received as a result of having the controls. Analyzing Figure 19.4 several points can be seen:

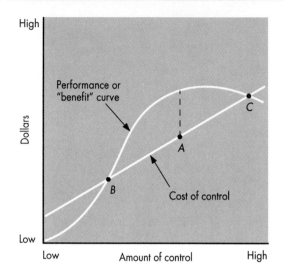

FIGURE 19.4   **General Relationship between Control Cost and Benefits**

- There is some minimum amount of control necessary before the benefits of more control outweigh the costs (point A).
- There is some optimal amount of control (point B).
- There is some maximum amount of control that, if exceeded, can be very costly (point C).

The costs of implementing a control system can usually be estimated or calculated much more accurately than the benefits. For example, it is difficult to quantify and measure the true benefits of a quality control system. A good quality control system supposedly increases goodwill; but how does one measure this attribute? The decision is obviously much easier when the costs of not maintaining control are either very high or very low. For example, because the cost of low quality control is so high, airlines go to great expense to ensure high control of quality. Despite the measurement problems, management should regularly undertake such a study to ensure that gross misapplications do not occur.

Behavioral Considerations   Managers need to be aware of the potential impact of the control system on employees. Most people do not like to work where they think their every move is being watched or questioned. For example, most salespeople do not like to have to account for every penny spent on meals and entertainment. At the same time, however, very few people like to work where no control exists; an absence of control creates an environment in which people do not know what is expected of them.

Flexibility and Innovation Considerations   Too much control may restrict the flexibility and innovation required to be competitive. Overly restrictive controls often stifle the entrepreneurial spirit of employees and discourage them from trying new and creative options. The key is to maintain control without squelching innovation.

Many managers tend to increase controls whenever things are not going according to plan. Figure 19.5 shows a simplified version of a model developed by Alvin

FIGURE 19.5   Simplified Gouldner Model of Organization Control

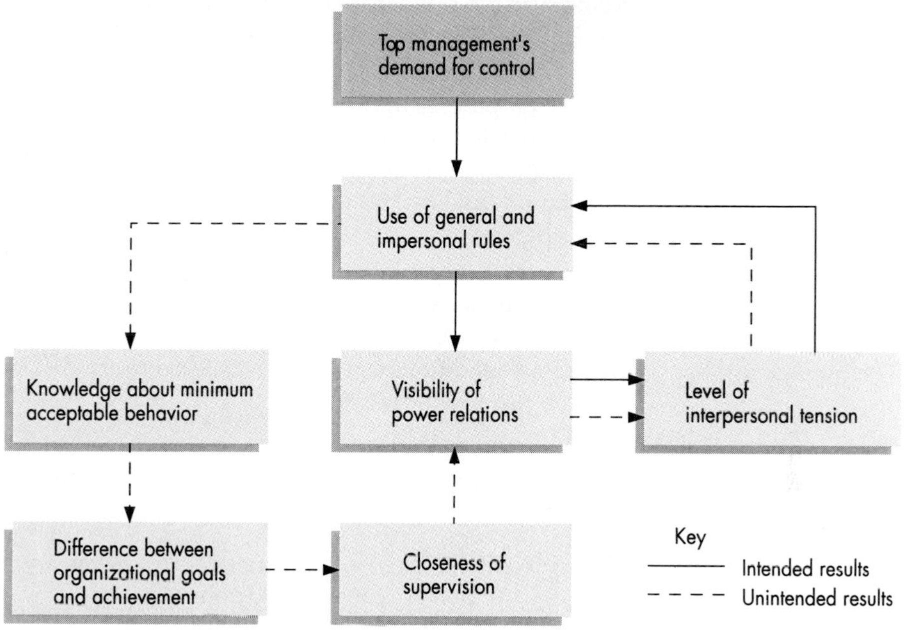

Source: James G. March and Herbert A. Simon, *Organizations* (New York: John Wiley & Sons, 1958), p. 45.

Gouldner that explains this behavior. Gouldner's model begins with top management's demand for control over operations. This is attempted through the use and enforcement of general and impersonal rules regarding work procedures. These rigid rules are meant to be guides for the behavior of the organization members; they also have the unintended effect of showing minimum acceptable behavior. In organizations where there is little congruence between individual and organizational objectives or acceptance of organizational objectives is not high, the effect is a reduction of performance to the lowest acceptable level: People who are not highly committed to organizational objectives will perform at the lowest acceptable level. Managers view such behavior as resulting from inadequate control; they therefore respond with closer supervision. This increases the visibility of power, which in turn raises the level of interpersonal tension in the organization. Raising the tension level brings even stricter enforcement of the general and impersonal formal rules. Hence, the cycle repeats itself. The overall effect is increased control, increased interpersonal tension, and a lowering of performance.

One problem in deciding on the right degree of control is that different people react differently to similar controls. Research suggests that reactions differ according to personality and prior experiences.[7] Problems can occur from unforeseen reactions to control due to both compliance and resistance.[8] Problems from compliance arise when people adhere to the prescribed behavior even when it is inappropriate. The salesperson who will not vary from prescribed procedures to satisfy a customer complaint is an example of this. Problems resulting from resistance to controls arise when individuals attempt to preempt, work around, or sabotage the controls. Distorting a report and padding the budget are forms of control resistance.

Several things can be done to lessen negative reactions to controls. Most approaches are based on good common sense. However, they require a concerted effort by the manager. The tendency is to take these suggestions for granted. The guidelines are as follows:

1. Make sure the standards and associated controls are realistic. Standards set too high or too low turn people off. Make sure the standards are attainable yet challenging.

2. Involve employees in the control-setting process. Many of the behavioral problems associated with controls result from a lack of understanding of the nature and purpose of the controls. People naturally resist anything new, especially if they do not understand why it is being used. Solicit and listen to suggestions from employees.

3. Use controls only where needed. As the Gouldner model suggests, there is a strong tendency to overcontrol. Periodically evaluate the need for different controls. A good rule of thumb is to evaluate every control at least annually. Changing conditions can make certain controls obsolete. Remember, overcontrol can produce negative results.

Management Illustration 19.2 describes how one company turned around its fortunes by improving the controls exercised over its sales people.

Where Should Control Reside?

For years, it was believed that control in organizations is a fixed commodity that should rest only in the hands of top management. This viewpoint naturally favored a highly centralized approach to decision making and controlling. However, as decentralized organizations have become more common, controls have been pushed farther and farther down the hierarchy. It is now recognized that where the controls reside is an important factor in how much control is desirable.

Author James Champy believes the modern approach to control should involve more "enabling" or learning to control at lower levels.[9] Supporting this idea, Leon Royer, director of Learning Services at 3M, found that learning and enabling go hand in hand. Lower-level employees are valuable controllers if they are allowed to learn how to control.[10] The difficulty with enabling, however, is that it means senior management must be willing to relinquish control. Tom Hardeman, ramp manager for FedEx at DFW Airport in Dallas, believes that once roadblocks are removed, line personnel are some of the most valuable controllers because they are close to actual situations that need control.[11] In summary, enabling enhances control and its efficiency.

Building on this material, evidence favors relatively tight controls as long as they are placed as far down in the organization as possible.[12] This approach has several advantages. First, it keeps higher-level managers from getting too involved in details. Second, it shows why the control is necessary. Third, it elicits commitment from lower-level managers. When controls are spread through many levels of an organization, caution must be taken to ensure that there are no disagreements about how the controls are distributed. In other words, managers at every level should clearly understand their authority and responsibility.

TYPES OF CONTROL

behavior (personal) control Based on direct, personal surveillance.

There are two categories of control methods: behavior control and output control. **Behavior** or **personal control** is based on direct, personal surveillance. The first-line super-

Management Illustration 19.2
Reassurance at Pearl Assurance

In 1995 Pearl Assurance of the United Kingdom was on the brink of disaster. Insurance industry regulations had just fined the company for failing to comply with industry regulations and were threatening to close it down unless things rapidly improved. Like many of the UK's other leading insurance companies, Pearl was also implicated in a pensions mis-selling scandal. Employee morale and sales were both at an all-time low.

Within two years, Pearl's fortunes had been reversed. New sales for the first quarter of 1997 were almost double the previous year and employee turnover had fallen from 28 percent to 12 percent. Pearl was also listed as one of the 100 most attractive firms to work for in *Britain's Best Employers*, published by the Corporate Research Foundation.

What happened to get Pearl into trouble and how did management reverse the trend? Gary Brandon, manager of sales training, believes that much of the problem stemmed from a lack of control relating to the sales personnel. Today Pearl uses a much more comprehensive selection procedure to ensure that salespeople have both the skills and integrity necessary to deal with clients. Salespeople today specialize in either general insurance or financial advice, before sales representatives tended to deal with all aspects of insurance.

For every team of 12 salespeople, Pearl now has a district manager and two training and competence managers (TCMs). Once the salespeople are hired, they are subjected to a rigorous 7–12 week training program depending on previous experience. The training does not end there. New salespeople are accompanied and coached by their TCMs on their first 10 customer visits. After the first 10 weeks the frequency of observations by the TCM gradually drops to once a quarter.

Before 1995, Pearl was much less selective in its hiring practices, its sales force was less specialized, and training was much less intense. Brandon believes that the new controls in place at Pearl put the company in position "to guard against any problems."

Source: Anat Arkin, "Assurer Foundation," *People Management*, September 11, 1997, pp. 40–41. To learn more about the Corporate Research Foundation, visit their Web site at: www.crf-online.co.za.

---

output (impersonal) control Based on the measurement of outputs.

---

visor who maintains a close personal watch over employees is using behavior control. **Output** or **impersonal control** is based on the measurement of outputs Tracking production records and monitoring sales figures are examples of output controls.

Research shows that these two categories of control are not substitutes for each other in the sense that a manager uses one or the other.[13] The evidence suggests that output control occurs in response to a manager's need to provide an accurate measure of performance. On the other hand, behavior control is exerted when performance requirements are well known and personal surveillance is needed to promote efficiency and motivation. In most situations, organizations need to use a mix of output and behavior controls because each serves different organizational needs.

Preliminary, Concurrent, or Postaction Control?

In general, methods for exercising control can be described as either preliminary, concurrent, or postaction. **Preliminary control** methods, sometimes called **steering controls,** attempt to prevent a problem from occurring. Requiring prior approval for purchases of all items over a certain dollar value is an example. **Concurrent controls,** also called **screening controls,** focus on things that happen as inputs are being transformed into outputs. They

---

preliminary (steering) control Method of exercising control to prevent a problem from occurring.

concurrent (screening) control Focuses on process as it occurs; designed to detect a problem when it occurs.

---

postaction control   Designed to detect an existing or a potential problem before it gets out of hand.

are designed to detect a problem as it occurs. Personal observation of customers being serviced is an example of a concurrent control. **Postaction control** methods are designed to detect existing problems after they occur but before they reach crisis proportions. Written or periodic reports represent postaction control methods. Most controls are based on postaction methods.

Budgetary Control

budget   Statement of expected results or requirements expressed in financial or numerical terms.

Budgets are probably the most widely used control devices. A **budget** is a statement of expected results or requirements expressed in financial or numerical terms. Budgets express plans, objectives, and programs of the organization in numerical terms. Preparation of the budget is primarily a planning function; however, its administration is a controlling function.

Many different types of budgets are in use. Figure 19.6 outlines some of the most common types. Some may be expressed in terms other than dollars. For example, an equipment budget may be expressed in numbers of machines; material budgets may be expressed in pounds, pieces, gallons, and so on. Budgets not expressed in dollars can usually be translated into dollars for inclusion in an overall budget.

While budgets are useful for planning and control, they are not without their dangers. Perhaps the greatest danger is inflexibility. This is a special threat to organizations operating in an industry with rapid change and high competition. Rigidity in the budget can also lead to ignoring organizational goals for budgetary goals. The financial manager who won't go $5 over budget to make $500 is a classic example. Budgets can hide inefficiencies. The fact that a certain expenditure has been made in the past often becomes justification for continuing the practice even when the situation has greatly changed. Managers may also pad budgets because they anticipate that their budgets will be cut by superiors. Since the manager is never sure how severe the cut will be, the result is often an inaccurate, if not unrealistic, budget.

The answer to effective budget control may be to make the manager and any concerned employees accountable for their budgets. Performance incentives can be tied to budget control, accuracy, and fulfillment. In other words, if it is worth budgeting, it is worth budgeting right! Others believe budgets should also be tied not only to financial data but also to customer satisfaction. Budget for what it takes to satisfy the customer would be the rule of thumb for this logic. Ron Rittenmeyer of Frito-Lay cautions that organizations can get so hung up on measuring themselves by sticking

---

FIGURE 19.6   Types and Purposes of Budgets

Type of Budget	Purpose
Revenue and expense budget	Provides details for revenue and expense plans
Cash budget	Forecasts cash receipts and disbursements
Capital expenditure budget	Outlines specific expenditures for plant, equipment, machinery, inventories, and other capital items
Production, material, or time budget	Expresses physical requirements of production, or material, or the time requirements for the budget period
Balance sheet budgets	Forecasts the status of assets, liabilities, and net worth at the end of the budget period

to their own sets of rules, focusing internally, and watching their budgets that they forget their customers.[14] Yet the customer is what business is all about.

Zero-Base Budgeting   Zero-base budgeting was designed to stop basing this year's budget on last year's budget. **Zero-base budgeting** requires each manager to justify an entire budget request in detail. The burden of proof is on each manager to justify why any money should be spent. Under zero-base budgeting, each activity under a manager's discretion is identified, evaluated, and ranked by importance. Then each year every activity in the budget is on trial for its life and is matched against all the other claimants for an organization's resources.

zero-base budgeting   Form of budgeting in which the manager must build and justify each area of a budget. Each activity is identified, evaluated, and ranked by importance.

Financial Controls

In addition to budgets, many managers use other types of financial information for control purposes. These include balance sheets, income statements, and financial ratios. Regardless of the type of financial information used, it is meaningful only when compared with either the historical performance of the organization or the performances of similar organizations. For example, knowing that a company had net income of $100,000 last year doesn't reveal much by itself. However, when compared to last year's net income of $500,000 or to an industry average of $500,000, much more can be determined about the company's performance.

Financial Ratio Analysis   Financial ratios can be divided into four basic types: profitability, liquidity, debt, and activity ratios. Profitability ratios indicate the organization's operational efficiency, or how well the organization is being managed. Gross profit margin, net profit margin, and return on investment (ROI) are all examples of profitability ratios. Liquidity ratios are used to judge how well an organization will be able to meet its short-term financial obligations. The current ratio (current assets divided by current liabilities) and the quick ratio (current assets minus inventories divided by current liabilities) are examples of liquidity ratios. Debt (sometimes called leverage) ratios measure the magnitude of owners' and creditors' claims on the organization and indicate the organization's ability to meet long-term obligations. The debt to equity ratio and total debt to total assets ratio are two common debt ratios. Activity ratios evaluate how effectively an organization is managing some of its basic operations. Asset turnover, inventory turnover, average collection period, and accounts receivable turnover represent some commonly used activity ratios.

As mentioned earlier, financial ratios are meaningful only when compared to past ratios and to ratios of similar organizations. Also, financial ratios reflect only certain specific information, and therefore they should be used in conjunction with other management controls. Figure 19.7 presents a summary of several financial ratio calculations.

Direct Observation

A store manager's daily tour of the facility, a company president's annual visit to all branches, and a methods study by a staff industrial engineer are all examples of control by direct observation. Although time consuming, personal observation is sometimes the

FIGURE 19.7   Summary of Financial Ratio Calculations

Ratio	Calculation	Purpose
Profitibility Ratios		
Gross profit margin	$\dfrac{\text{Sales} - \text{Cost of goods sold}}{\text{Sales}} \times 100$	Indicates efficiency of operations and product pricing
	$\dfrac{\text{Net profit after tax}}{\text{Sales}} \times 100$	Indicates efficiency after all expenses are considered
Return on assets (ROA)	$\dfrac{\text{Net profit after tax}}{\text{Total assest}} \times 100$	Shows productivity of assets
Return on equity (ROE)	$\dfrac{\text{Net profit after tax}}{\text{Stockholders' equity}} \times 100$	Shows earnings power of equity
Liquidity Ratios		
Current ratio	$\dfrac{\text{Current assets}}{\text{Current liabilities}}$	Shows short-run debt paying ability
Quick ratio	$\dfrac{\text{Current assets} - \text{inventories}}{\text{Current liabilities}}$	Shows short-term liquidity
Debt Ratios		
Debt to equity	$\dfrac{\text{Total liabilities}}{\text{Stockholders' equity}}$	Indicates long-term liquidity
Total debt to total assets (debt ratio)	$\dfrac{\text{Total liabilities}}{\text{Total assets}}$	Shows percentage of assets financed through borrowing
Activity Ratios		
Asset turnover	$\dfrac{\text{Sales}}{\text{Total assets}}$	Shows efficiency of asset utilization
Inventory turnover	$\dfrac{\text{Cost of goods sold}}{\text{Average inventory}}$	Shows management's ability to control investment in inventory
Average collection period	$\dfrac{\text{Receivables} \times 365 \text{ days}}{\text{Annual credit sales}}$	Shows effectiveness of collection and credit policies
Accounts receivable turnover	$\dfrac{\text{Annual credit sales}}{\text{Receivables}}$	Shows effectiveness of collection and credit policies

only way to get an accurate picture of what is really happening. One hazard is that employees may misinterpret a superior's visit and consider such action meddling or eavesdropping. A second hazard is that behaviors change when people are being watched or monitored. Another potential inaccuracy lies in the interpretation of the observation. The observer must be careful not to read into the picture events that did not actually occur. Visits and direct observation can have very positive effects when viewed by employees as a display of the manager's interest.

Written Reports

Written reports can be prepared on a periodic or an "as necessary" basis. There are two basic types of written reports: analytical and informational. Analytical reports interpret the facts they present; informational reports present only the facts. Preparing a report is a four- or five-step process, depending on whether it is informational or analytical. The steps are (1) planning what is to be done, (2) collecting the facts, (3) organizing the facts, (4) interpreting the facts (this step is omitted with informational reports), and (5) writing the report.[15] Most reports should be prepared for the benefit of the reader and not the writer. In most cases, the reader wants useful information not previously available.

Audits

Audits can be conducted by either internal or external personnel. External audits are normally done by outside accountants and are limited to financial matters. Most are conducted to certify that the organization's accounting methods are fair, are consistent, and conform to existing practices. Internal audits are performed by the organization's own personnel.

audit Method of control normally involved with financial matters; also can include other areas of the organization.

management audit Attempts to evaluate the overall management practices and policies of the organization.

An audit that looks at areas other than finance and accounting is known as a management audit. **Management audits** attempt to evaluate the overall management practices and policies of the organization. They can be conducted by outside consultants or inside staff; however, a management audit conducted by inside staff can easily result in a biased report.

Break-Even Charts

break-even chart Depicts graphically the relationship of volume of operations to profits.

Break-even charts depict graphically the relationship of volume of operations to profits. The break-even point (BEP) is the point at which sales revenues exactly equal expenses. Total sales below the BEP result in a loss; total sales above the BEP result in a profit.

Figure 19.8 shows a typical break-even chart. The horizontal axis represents output; the vertical axis represents expenses and revenues. Though not required, most break-even charts assume there are linear relationships and all costs are either fixed or variable. Fixed costs do not vary with output, at least in the short run.

FIGURE 19.8   Break-Even Chart

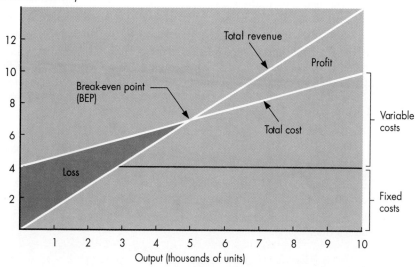

They include rent, insurance, and administrative salaries. Variable costs vary with output. Typical variable costs include direct labor and materials. The purpose of the chart is to show the break-even point and the effects of changes in output. A break-even chart is useful for showing whether revenue and/or costs are running as planned.

Time-Related Charts and Techniques

Gantt charts, the critical path method (CPM), and the program evaluation and control technique (PERT) (discussed in Chapter 8) are tools used to plan and schedule. These same tools can also be used for controlling once the plans have been put into action. By tracking actual progress compared to planned progress, activities that fall behind schedule can quickly be spotted.

Summary

1. *Explain Why Management Controls Are Necessary.* The overriding purpose of all management controls is to alert the manager to an existing or a potential problem before it becomes critical. Specifically, management controls can be used to (1) prevent crises, (2) standardize outputs, (3) appraise employee performance, (4) update plans, and (5) protect an organization's assets.

2. *Describe a Feedback System.* Any system in which the outputs from the system affect future inputs or future activities of the system is called a feedback system; in other words, a feedback system is influenced by its own past behavior.

3. *Discuss the Basic Requirements of the Control Process.* The control process has three basic requirements: (1) establishing standards, (2) monitoring results and comparing them to standards, and (3) correcting for any deviations between the standard and actual results.

4. *Describe the Control Pyramid.* The control pyramid is a method for implementing control in the organization. It consists of control through foolproofing, automatic controls, operator control, control by personal supervision, and informational controls.

5. *Identify the Factors That Affect How Much Control Should Be Exercised in an Organization.* When deciding how much control should be exercised in an organization, two major factors must be appraised: (1) economic considerations and (2) behavioral considerations.

6. *Discuss the Two Categories of Control Methods.* Control methods can be either of two kinds: (1) behavior control or (2) output control. Behavior (or personal) control is based on direct, personal surveillance. Output (or impersonal) control is based on the measurement of outputs.

7. *Differentiate among Preliminary, Concurrent, and Postaction Controls.* Preliminary (steering) controls are designed to prevent a problem from occurring. Concurrent (screening) controls focus on things that happen as inputs are being transformed into outputs. They are designed to detect a problem as it occurs. Postaction controls are designed to detect existing or potential problems after they occur but before they reach crisis proportions.

8. *List Several Methods or Systems of Control Commonly Used by Managers.* Many control methods or systems are in use today. Some of the most popular control methods/systems include all types of budgets, financial controls (balance sheets, income statements, and financial ratios), direct observations, written reports, audits, break-even charts, and time-related charts and techniques.

9. *List the Four Basic Types of Financial Ratios.* The four basic types of financial ratios are profitability, liquidity, debt, and activity ratios.

10. *Discuss the Basic Purpose of a Break-Even Chart.* A break-even chart graphically depicts the relationship of volume of operations to profits.

Preview Analysis

1. How might Abbey National have prevented the problems regarding its marketing department?

2. Why would a "quite well-paid" executive such as Doyle become a thief?

3. Why do you think that a bank like Abbey National might not have adequate controls?

Review Questions

1. What is management control? What are the two major concerns in management control?
2. Describe a model of the management control process.
3. Outline the three basic requirements of control.
4. How much control should be exercised in an organization?
5. Describe the two categories of control methods.
6. Define preliminary, concurrent, and postaction controls.
7. Describe the following control methods and systems:
   a. Budgets
   b. Financial ratios
   c. Direct observation
   d. Written reports
   e. Audits
   f. Break-even charts

Skill-Building Questions

1. If you were implementing a new control system designed to track more closely the expenses of your salespeople, what actions might you take to minimize negative reactions?
2. Why are many managers reluctant to take the actions necessary to correct for deviations?
3. How should you deal with managers who are so "married" to their departmental budgets that they will not let you spend $1 to make $10?
4. Give an example of how you might "enable" a subordinate to control something at the line level. What might be the benefits of "enabling"?

SKILL-BUILDING EXERCISE 19.1

Breaking Even*

As of January 1, 1998, UND Family Health Service Center had 15 employees with a total annual salary budget of $400,000. The annual maintenance cost was estimated at $80,000. Based on 1997 data, the monthly patient service in 1998 is forecast as 180 patients per month. For each patient serviced, the average variable cost incurred (e.g., paperwork, treatment materials, equipment depreciation, utility consumption) is estimated at $10, and average revenue per patient is projected to be $230.

A. Based on the above information, do you think the center manager can balance annual costs and annual revenues? Explain. What would you suggest to the manager?

B. If, by implementing more efficient operations management, the center's operating (variable) cost can be reduced to $8 per patient, do you think the center could balance its annual budget?

C. If dismissing employees becomes necessary to balance the budget, how many employees would you recommend be let go? Why?

D. At the end of June 1998, the manager showed you the following report:

	Jan.	Feb.	March	April	May	June
Number of patients	150	140	152	145	130	145

What comments would you make to the manager?

*This exercise was written by Jiaqin Yang, assistant professor, the University of North Dakota.

SKILL-BUILDING EXERCISE 19.2

Staying on Budget

As manager of the Ace Division of the Triple-A Company, you agreed to the following budget at the beginning of the current fiscal year: This budget was based on forecast sales of 30,000 units during the year.

Fixed costs	$80,000
Subcontracting costs (variable, per unit)	$4
Other variable costs (per unit)	$2
Sales price	$10

You are six months into the fiscal year and have collected the following sales data:

Month	Actual Sales (Units)
1	2,000
2	2,200
3	1,700
4	1,800
5	2,300
6	2,200

By shopping around, you have held your subcontracting costs to an average of $3.60 per unit. The fixed and other variable costs are conforming to budgets.

A. What was the break-even point based on the original forecast in sales for the Ace Division?

B. What is the revised break-even point?

C. What trends in the above information, if any, concern you?

D. Based on the preceding information, prepare a brief report for your boss, summarizing the current status of the Ace Division.

CASE INCIDENT 19.1

"Bird Dogging" the Employee

Ace Electronics, Inc., is a small company located in Centerville. It is owned and operated by Al Abrams, a highly experienced electronics person who founded the company.

Ace's basic product is a walkie-talkie that is sold primarily to the U.S. military. The walkie-talkie units are relatively simple to produce; Ace merely purchases the parts—cables, wires, transistors, and so on—and assembles them with hand tools. Due to this moderate level of complexity, Ace employs semiskilled workers at low wage rates.

Although Ace has made a profit each year since it started production, Al Abrams was becoming increasingly concerned. Over the past six years, he had noticed a general decline in employee morale; furthermore, he had observed a decline in his employees' productivity and his company's profit margin.

As a result of his concern, Al asked his supervisors to keep a closer watch on the workers' hour-to-hour activities. In the first week, they discovered two workers in the restroom reading magazines. This "bird dogging" technique, as management called it, or "slave driving," as the workers called it, failed to increase either production or productivity.

Al recognized that the lack of performance on the part of some employees was affecting the production of everyone. This phenomenon was caused by the balanced assembly line under which the walkie-talkies were assembled. If an employee next to a normally productive employee did not work fast enough, walkie-talkies would back up on the line. Instead of having a back-up, however, the assembly line was usually readjusted to the production rate of the slower employees.

In addition, another situation developed to lower productivity and increase unit costs. Ace was required by the government to meet monthly production and delivery schedules. If it failed, a very substantial financial penalty could result. In recent years, the production and delivery schedule had become more difficult to meet. For the last eight months, Al had scheduled overtime to meet the production and delivery schedule and thus avoid the financial penalty. This overtime increased unit production costs and caused another problem: Many employees began to realize that if they worked more slowly at the beginning of the month, they could receive more overtime at the end of the month. Even the senior employees were slowing down to increase their overtime wages.

Al was very reluctant to fire employees, especially senior employees. Even if he was inclined to do so, it was difficult to catch employees slowing down or provide any reasonable evidence for such a rash action. Al was frustrated and perplexed.

Questions

1. Describe in detail the control dilemma at Ace Electronics.

2. Are Al Abrams and the employees getting the same feedback? Why or why not?

3. What should Al do?

CASE INCIDENT 19.2

Mickey Mouse Controls

Jean: Hey, John, I could sure use some help. We regional supervisors are caught in the middle. What do you do about all this red tape we're having to put up with? The accounting department is all bothered about the way people are padding their expenses and about the cost of luncheons and long-distance calls. You know—their answer is nothing but more red tape.

John: Well, Jean, I don't know. I'm feeling the heat too. Upper management wants us to maintain our contacts with our brokers and try to get the money out in loans. So we push the district supervisors to see our best contacts or at least call them frequently. Yet lately, I've been having a heck of a time getting my people reimbursed for their expenses. Now the accounting department is kicking because we spend a few bucks taking someone to lunch or making a few long-distance calls.

Jean: I really don't know what to do, John. I'll admit that some of my people tend to charge the company for expenses that are for their personal entertainment. But how can I tell whether they're buttering up a broker or just living it up on the company? The accounting department must have some receipts and records to support expenses. Yet I think that getting a receipt from a parking lot attendant is carrying this control stuff too far. As a matter of fact, the other day, I caught a taxi at the airport and failed to get a receipt—I'll bet I have a hard time getting that money from the company even if I sign a notarized affidavit.

John: Well, the way I handle those things is to charge the company more for tips than I actually give—and you know they don't require receipts for tips. I just don't know how to decide whether those reimbursement receipts that I sign for my people are legitimate. If I call people up and ask about some items on a reimbursement request, they act as though I'm making a charge of grand larceny. So far, I've decided to sign whatever requests they turn in and leave the accounting department to scream if it wants to. The trouble is that I don't have any guidelines as to what is reasonable.

Jean: Yeah, but I don't want to ask questions about that because it would just result in more controls! It isn't up to me to be a policeman for the company. The accounting department sits back looking at all those figures—it should watch expenses. I ran into someone from the department the other day on what she called an internal audit trip, and she told me that they aren't in a position to say whether a $40 lunch at a restaurant is necessary to sell a loan. She said that the charge was made by one of my people and that I should check it out! Am I a regional production person or am I an accountant? I've got enough to do meeting my regional quota with my five district salespeople. I can't go snooping around to find out whether they're taking advantage of the company. They may get the idea that I don't trust them, and I've always heard that good business depends on trust. Besides, our department makes the company more money than any other one. Why shouldn't we be allowed to spend a little of it?

John: Well, I say that the brass is getting hot about a relatively small problem. A little fudging on an expense account isn't going to break the company. I learned the other day that the accounting department doesn't require any receipts from the securities department people. They just give them a per diem for travel and let them spend it however they want to, just so long as they don't go over the allotted amount for the days that they're on trips.

Jean: Now that sounds like a good idea. Why can't we do that? It sure would make my life easier. I don't want to get a guilt complex about signing reimbursement requests that may look a little out of line. Why should I call an employee on the carpet for some small expense that may be the reason we got the deal? Performance is our job, so why can't the company leave us alone? They should let us decide what it takes to make a deal. If we don't produce the loans, we should catch flak about something that's important—not about these trifling details.

John: Jean, I've got to run now. But honestly, if I were you, I wouldn't worry about these Mickey Mouse controls. I'm just going to do my job and fill in the form in order to stay out of trouble on the details. It's not worth getting upset about.

Questions

1. Has the company imposed overly restrictive controls? Explain why or why not.
2. Do you think the company has a good conception of control tolerances? Why or why not?
3. What should Jean do?

References

[1]Tom Peters, *Liberation Management* (New York: Alfred A. Knopf, 1992), pp. 486, 488.

[2]Ibid., pp. 465–66.

[3]Ibid.

[4]Jermy Main, *Quality Wars* (New York: The Free Press, 1994), pp. 132–33.

[5]J. M. Juran, *Managerial Breakthrough*, rev. ed. (New York: Mc-Graw-Hill, 1995), pp. 203–5.

[6]Ibid.

[7]For a discussion of some relevant studies, see Arnold S. Tannenbaum, "Control in Organizations: Individual Adjustment in Organization Performance," *Administering Science Quarterly*, September 1962, pp. 241–46; Klaus Bartolke, Walter Eschweiler, Dieter Flechsenberger, and Arnold S. Tannenbaum, "Worker Participation and the Distribution of Control as Perceived by Members of Ten German Companies," *Administrative Science Quarterly* 27 (1982), pp. 380–97.

[8]Gene W. Dalton and Paul R. Lawrence, *Motivation and Control in Organizations* (Homewood, IL.: Richard D. Irwin, 1971), p. 8.

[9]James Champy, *Reengineering Management* (New York: Harper Business, 1995), p. 130.

[10]Ibid.

[11]Ibid., pp. 130–31.

[12]Timothy J. McMahon and G. W. Perritt, "Toward a Contingency Theory of Organizational Control," *Academy of Management Journal*, December 1973, pp. 624–35.

[13]William G. Ouchi and Mary Ann Maguire, "Organizational Control: Two Functions," *Administrative Science Quarterly*, December 1975, pp. 559–71; William G. Ouchi, "The Transmission of Control through Organizational Hierarchy," *Academy of Management Journal*, June 1978, pp. 174–76.

[14]Champy, *Reengineering Management*, p. 140.

[15]C. W. Wilkinson, Dorothy Wilkinson, and Gretchen Vik, *Communicating through Letters and Reports*, 9th ed. (Homewood, IL: Richard D. Irwin, 1986).

20

Appraising and Rewarding Performance

LEARNING OBJECTIVES

After studying this chapter, you should be able to:

1. Define performance appraisal.

2. Define performance.

3. Explain the determinants of performance.

4. List and describe the nine major performance appraisal methods.

5. Define job analysis.

6. Explain the contents of a job description.

7. Discuss common errors made in performance appraisal interviews.

8. Suggest ways to make performance appraisal systems more legally acceptable.

9. Define compensation.

10. Outline desirable preconditions for implementing a merit pay program.

In years past, companies that wished to redesign their incentive and performance pay systems went to Cleveland-based Lincoln Electric Company for a model of radical performance pay systems. The Lincoln plan rewards employees as much as 100 percent of their wages in annual performance-linked bonuses. Each of its 3,400 employees is a self-managing entrepreneur who has minimal supervision. However, because of recent bad management decisions in the international arena, the company has had to borrow money to pay employee bonuses. This is in spite of the fact that the company has experienced record sales. The system may have to change in the future.

Source: Zachary Schiller, "A Model Incentive Plan Gets Caught in a Vice," *Business Week*, January 22, 1996, pp. 89, 92.

Performance appraisal systems that are directly tied to an organization's reward system provide a powerful incentive for employees to work diligently and creatively toward achieving organizational objectives. When properly conducted, performance appraisals not only let employees know how well they are presently performing but also clarify what needs to be done to improve performance.[1]

performance appraisal   Process that involves determining and communicating to employees how they are performing their jobs and establishing a plan for improvement.

Performance appraisal is a process that involves determining and communicating to employees how they are performing their jobs and establishing a plan for improvement. Some of the more common uses of performance appraisals are to make decisions related to merit pay increases, promotions, layoffs, and firings. For example, the present job performance of an employee is often the most significant consideration for determining whether to promote the person. While successful performance in the present job does not necessarily mean an employee will be an effective performer in a higher-level job, performance appraisals do provide some predictive information.

Performance appraisal information can also provide needed input for determining both individual and organizational training and development needs. For example, it can be used to identify individual strengths and weaknesses. These data can then be used to help determine the organization's overall training and development needs. For an individual employee, a completed performance appraisal should include a plan outlining specific training and development needs.

Another important use of performance appraisals is to encourage performance improvement. In this regard, performance appraisals are used as a means of communicating to employees how they are doing and suggesting needed changes in behavior, attitude, skill, or knowledge. This type of feedback clarifies for employees the job expectations the manager holds. Often this feedback must be followed by coaching and training by the manager to guide an employee's work efforts.

To work effectively, performance appraisals must be supported by documentation and a commitment by management to make them fair and effective. Typical standards for the performance appraisal process are that it be fair, accurate (facts, not opinions, should be used), include as much direct observation as possible, be consistent, and contain as much objective documentation as possible.[2] The amount and types of documentation necessary to support decisions made by management vary, but the general rule of thumb is to provide enough varied documentation to allow anyone evaluating the performance of an employee to generally come to the same conclusion as the manager.

An additional concern in organizations is how often to conduct performance appraisals. No real consensus exists on this question, but the usual answer is as often as necessary to let employees know what kind of job they are doing and, if performance is not satisfactory, the measures they must take to improve. For many employees, this cannot be accomplished through one annual performance appraisal. Therefore, it is recommended that for most employees, informal performance appraisals should be conducted two or three times a year in addition to the annual performance appraisal.

How does one know when the performance appraisal process is working as it should? According to General Electric CEO Jack Welch, "If we get the right people in the right job (and keep them there) we've won the game."[3] Performance appraisal is one of the primary tools for helping the organization's management to meet its goals and objectives and effectively compete internationally.

UNDERSTANDING PERFORMANCE

performance   Degree of accomplishment of the tasks that make up an employee's job.

Performance refers to the degree of accomplishment of the tasks that make up an employee's job. It reflects how well an employee is fulfilling the requirements of the job. Often confused with effort, which refers to energy expended, performance is measured in terms of results. Because many American corporations have become very results oriented in the last decade more and more emphasis is being placed on measuring performance.

Determinants of Performance

Job performance is the net effect of an employee's effort as modified by abilities, role perceptions, and results produced. This implies that performance in a given situation can be viewed as resulting from the interrelationships among effort, abilities, role perceptions, and results produced.

effort   Results from being motivated; refers to the amount of energy an employee uses in performing a job.
abilities   Personal characteristics used in performing a job.
role perception   Direction in which employees believe they should channel their efforts on their jobs.

Effort, which results from being motivated, refers to the amount of energy an employee uses in performing a job. **Abilities** are personal characteristics used in performing a job. Abilities usually do not fluctuate widely over short periods of time. **Role perception** refers to the direction in which employees believe they should channel their efforts on their jobs. The activities and behavior employees believe are necessary in the performance of their jobs define their role perceptions. The results produced are usually measured by standards created by the degree of attainment of management-directed objectives.

To attain an acceptable level of performance, a minimum level of proficiency must exist in each of the performance components. Similarly, the level of proficiency in any one of the performance components can place an upper boundary on performance. Studies indicate that the level of performance can be improved and boundaries raised if management empowers employees to become more active in determining and evaluating their performance measures and standards.[4] To accomplish this, however, management has to erase the natural fear of and resistance to empowerment and become advocates of employee involvement.[5]

PERFORMANCE APPRAISAL METHODS

An early method of performance appraisal used in the United States was described as follows:

> On the morning following each day's work, each workman was given a slip of paper informing him in detail just how much work he had done the day before, and the amount he had earned. This enabled him to measure his performance against his earnings while the details were fresh in his mind.[6]

This method of performance appraisal was effective in that it gave immediate feedback and tied pay to performance. Since then, the number and variety of performance appraisal methods have dramatically increased. Management Illustration 20.1 describes one of the more current approaches to performance appraisal. The following sections describe the performance appraisal methods used in businesses today.

Management Illustration 20.1
360-Degree Feedback

A comprehensive way to evaluate employee feedback is through 360-degree feedback. It is used by some of the most successful companies in America, including UPS, AT&T, Amoco, General Mills, and Procter & Gamble. Traditionally, companies evaluate employee performance by relying almost exclusively on supervisor ratings that generally follow two types: measuring personality characteristics and technical abilities or appraisal by objectives. The first type of evaluation is usually in the form of a questionnaire with the evaluator ultimately making a subjective judgment. The second type of evaluation places emphasis on the achievement of recognized goals rather than personal characteristics.

With 360-degree feedback, a person's job performance is evaluated by his or her immediate supervisor as well as other individuals who have either direct or indirect contact with the person's work. The person also conducts a self-assessment of his or her performance. Co-workers also evaluate the person. Additionally, subordinates, customers, clients (internal as well as external), and anyone else who has contact with the person make an evaluation. Thus, a full circle (360 degrees) of evaluations is made by those people above, below, inside, outside, and anywhere in between. These evaluations are typically made by having all of the above mentioned individuals complete a lengthy, anonymous questionnaire.

Source: Adapted from Marc Marchese, "Industry: The Poser of the 360-Degree Feedback," *Pennsylvania CPA Journal*, December 1995. For more information on UPS, visit its Web site at: www.ups.com. For AT&T, visit www.att.com. For Amoco, visit www.amoco.com. For General Mills, visit www.generalmills.com. For Procter & Gamble, visit www.pg.com.

Goal Setting, or Management by Objectives (MBO)

In addition to being a useful method for directing the organization's objective-setting process, management by objectives (MBO) can also be used in the performance appraisal process. The value of linking the MBO program to the appraisal process is that employees tend to support goals if they agree the goals are acceptable and if they expect to be personally successful in their efforts.[7] Employee acceptance (by giving the employee a stake in the MBO process) is certainly a powerful motivator for considering the MBO process. The typical MBO process consists of

1. Establishing clear and precisely defined statements of objectives for the work an employee is to do.
2. Developing an action plan indicating how these objectives are to be achieved.
3. Allowing the employee to implement this action plan.
4. Appraising performance based on objective achievement.
5. Taking corrective action when necessary.
6. Establishing new objectives for the future.

If an employee is to be evaluated on the objectives set in the MBO process, several requirements must be met. First, objectives should be quantifiable and measurable; objectives whose attainment cannot be measured or at least verified should be avoided where possible. Objectives should also be challenging, yet achievable, and they should be expressed in writing and in clear, concise, unambiguous language. Figure 20.1 lists some sample objectives that meet these requirements.

Production Standards

The **production standards approach** to performance appraisal is most frequently used for employees who are involved in physically producing a product and is basi-

---

FIGURE 20.1   Sample Objectives

To answer all customer complaints in writing within three days of receipt of complaint.
To reduce order-processing time by two days within the next six months.
To implement the new computerized accounts receivable system by August 1.

FIGURE 20.2   Frequently Used Methods for Setting Production Standards

Method	Areas of Applicability
Average production or work	When tasks performed by all employees are the same or approximately the same
Performance of specially selected employees	When tasks performed by all employees are basically the same and it would be cumbersome and time consuming to use the group average
Time study	Jobs involving repetitive tasks
Work sampling	Noncyclical types of work in which many different tasks are performed and there is no set pattern or cycle
Expert opinion	When none of the more direct methods (described above) applies

---

production standards approach   Performance appraisal method most frequently used for employees who are involved in physically producing a product; is basically a form of objective setting for these employees.

cally a form of objective setting for these employees. It involves setting a standard or an expected level of output and then comparing each employee's performance to the standard. Generally, production standards should reflect the normal output of an average person. Production standards attempt to answer the question of what is a fair day's output. Several methods can be used to set production standards. Figure 20.2 summarizes some of the more common methods.

An advantage of the production standards approach is that the performance review is based on highly objective factors. Of course, to be effective, the standards must be viewed by the affected employees as being fair. The most serious criticism of production standards is a lack of comparability of standards for different job categories.

Essay Appraisal

essay appraisal method   Requires the manager to describe an employee's performance in written narrative form.

The **essay appraisal method** requires the manager to describe an employee's performance in written narrative form. Instructions are often provided to the manager as to the topics to be covered. A typical essay appraisal question might be "Describe, in your own words, this employee's performance, including quantity and quality of work, job knowledge, and ability to get along with other employees. What are the employee's strengths and weaknesses?"

The primary problem with essay appraisals is that their length and content can vary considerably (depending on the manager) and the method can be very subjective (whereas objective measures are more defensible). For instance, one manager may write a lengthy statement describing an employee's potential and saying little about past performance; another manager may concentrate on the employee's past performance. Thus, essay appraisals are difficult to compare. The writing skill of a manager can also affect the appraisal. An effective writer can make an average employee look better than the actual performance warrants.

Critical-Incident Appraisal

critical-incident appraisal   Requires the manager to keep a written record of incidents, as they occur, involving job behaviors that illustrate both satisfactory and unsatisfactory performance of the employee being rated.

The **critical-incident appraisal** method requires the manager to keep a written record of incidents, as they occur, involving job behaviors that illustrate both satisfactory and unsatisfactory performance of the employee being rated. As they are recorded over time, the incidents provide a basis for evaluating performance and providing feedback to the employee.

The main drawback to this approach is that the manager is required to jot down incidents regularly, which can be a burdensome and time-consuming task. Also, the definition of a critical incident is unclear and may be interpreted differently by different managers. Some believe this method can lead to friction between the manager and employees when the employees think the manager is keeping a "book" on them.

Graphic Rating Scale

graphic rating scale   Requires the manager to assess an employee on factors such as quantity of work, dependability, job knowledge, attendance, accuracy of work, and cooperativeness.

With the **graphic rating scale** method, the manager assesses an employee on factors such as quantity of work, dependability, job knowledge, attendance, accuracy of work, and cooperativeness. Graphic rating scales include both numerical ranges and written descriptions. Figure 20.3 gives an example of some of the items that might be included on a graphic rating scale that uses written descriptions.

The graphic rating scale method is subject to some serious weaknesses. One potential weakness is that managers are unlikely to interpret written descriptions in the same manner because of differences in background, experience, and personality. Another potential problem relates to the choice of rating categories. It is possible to choose categories that have little relationship to job performance or omit categories that have a significant influence on job performance.

Checklist

checklist   Requires the manager to answer yes or no to a series of questions concerning the employee's behavior.

With the **checklist** method, the manager answers yes or no to a series of questions concerning the employee's behavior. Figure 20.4 lists some typical questions. The checklist can also have varying weights assigned to each question.

Normally, the scoring key for the checklist method is kept by the human resource department; the manager is generally not aware of the weights associated with each question. But because the manager can see the positive or negative connotation of each question, bias can be introduced. Additional drawbacks to the checklist method are that it is time consuming to assemble the questions for each job category; a separate listing of questions must be developed for each job category; and the checklist questions can have different meanings for different managers.

FIGURE 20.3   Sample Items on a Graphic Rating Scale Evaluation Form

Quantity of work (the amount of work an employee does in a workday)

( )　　　　　( )　　　　　( )　　　　　( )　　　　　( )

| Does not meet requirements. | Does just enough to get by. | Volume of work is satisfactory. | Very industrious, does more than is required. | Superior production record. |

Dependability (the ability to do required jobs with a minimum of supervision)

( )　　　　　( )　　　　　( )　　　　　( )　　　　　( )

| Requires close supervision; is unreliable. | Sometimes requires prompting. | Usually completes necessary tasks with reasonable promptness. | Requires little supervision, is reliable. | Requires absolute minimum of supervision. |

Job knowledge (information that an employee should have on work duties for satisfactory job performance)

( )　　　　　( )　　　　　( )　　　　　( )　　　　　( )

| Poorly informed about work duties. | Lacks knowledge of some phases of job. | Moderately informed, can answer most questions about the job. | Understands all phases of job. | Has complete mastery of all phases of job. |

Attendance (faithfulness in coming to work daily and conforming to work hours)

( )　　　　　( )　　　　　( )　　　　　( )　　　　　( )

| Often absent without good excuse, or frequently reports for work late, or both. | Lax in attendance or reporting for work on time, or both. | Usually present and on time. | Very prompt, regular in attendance. | Always regular and prompt, volunteers for overtime when needed. |

Accuracy (the correctness of work duties performed)

( )　　　　　( )　　　　　( )　　　　　( )　　　　　( )

| Makes frequent errors. | Careless, often makes errors. | Usually accurate, makes only average number of mistakes. | Requires little supervision, is exact and precise most of the time. | Requires absolute minimum of supervision, is almost always accurate. |

FIGURE 20.4   Sample Checklist Questions

	Yes	No
1. Does the employee lose his or her temper in public?	____	____
2. Does the employee play favorites?	____	____
3. Does the employee praise people in public when they have done a good job?	____	____
4. Does the employee volunteer to do special jobs?	____	____

Behaviorally Anchored Rating Scales (BARS)

behaviorally anchored rating scale (BARS)   Assesses behaviors required to successfully perform a job.

The **behaviorally anchored rating scale (BARS)** method of performance appraisal is designed to assess behaviors required to successfully perform a job. The focus of BARS (and, to some extent, the graphic rating scale and checklist methods) is not on performance outcomes but on functional behaviors demonstrated on the job. The assumption is that these functional behaviors result in effective performance on the job (notice, however, that this concept can somewhat conflict with the results-oriented approach introduced at the beginning of the chapter).

To understand the use and development of BARS, several key terms must be understood. First, most BARS use the term *job dimension* to mean those broad categories of duties and responsibilities that make up a job. Each job is likely to have several job dimensions, and separate scales must be developed for each one.

Figure 20.5 illustrates a BARS written for rating hotel managers' communication skills. Scale values appear on the left side of the table and define specific categories of performance. Anchors, which appear on the right side of the table, are specific written statements of actual behaviors that, when exhibited on the job, indicate the level of performance on the scale opposite that particular anchor. As the anchor statements appear beside each scale value, they are said to "anchor" the respective scale values along the scale.

Rating performance using BARS requires the manager to read the list of anchors on each scale to find the group of anchors that best describes the employee's job behavior during the period being reviewed. The scale value opposite that group of anchors is then checked. This process is followed for all of the identified dimensions on the job. A total evaluation is obtained by combining the scale values checked for all of the job dimensions.

A BARS is normally developed through a series of meetings attended by both the manager and employees who are actually performing the job. Three steps are usually followed:

1. Manager and job incumbents identify the relevant job dimensions for the job.
2. Manager and job incumbents write behavioral anchors for each job dimension. As many anchors as possible should be written for each dimension.
3. Manager and job incumbents reach a consensus concerning the scale values to be used and the grouping of anchor statements for each scale value.

FIGURE 20.5   BARS Scale for Rating Hotel Managers' Communication Skills

Relevant behavior: Attending departmental staff meetings and involving subordinates in discussions; visiting with executive committee regularly on personal basis; using memos to communicate special instructions and policies to departments; disseminating financial and other operating information to subordinates; conducting periodic meetings with employees.

Scale Values		Anchors
Communicates effectively with staff members and attends meetings frequently.	7.00 | 6.00	This manager calls a "town hall" meeting to explain why the hotel will be cutting back staff. Employees are permitted to ask questions and discuss why certain positions in the hotel are being eliminated.
	| 5.00	During a busy expansion program, this manager increases the frequency of policy committee meetings to improve communications and coordination of the project.
Communicates satisfactorily with staff members and attends some meetings.	| 4.00	Once a week, this manager invites several line employees into his or her office for an informal talk about hotel activities.
	| 3.00	This manager neglects to discuss with his or her front-office manager the problem of overstaffed bellmen during certain periods of the day, yet expresses concern to the resident manager.
Experiences difficulty in communicating with staff members and attends meetings infrequently.	| 2.00 | 1.00	This manager misses departmental meetings and fails to visit with subordinates individually, but leaves memos around the hotel with instructions on what should be done.
		During weekly executive committee meetings, this manager dismisses most subordinate comments as stupid.

Source: Terry W. Umbreit, Robert W. Eder, and Jon P. McConnell, "Performance Appraisals: Making Them Fair and Making Them Work," *Cornell Hotel & Restaurant Administration Quarterly*, February 1986, p. 65.

The use of BARS can result in several advantages. First, BARS are developed through the active participation of both the manager and the job incumbents. This increases the likelihood that the method will be accepted. Second, the anchors are developed from the observations and experiences of employees who actually perform the job. Finally, BARS can be used to provide specific feedback concerning an employee's job performance. One major drawback to the use of BARS is that they take considerable time and commitment to develop. Furthermore, separate rating scales must be developed for different jobs.

Forced-Choice Rating

forced-choice rating   Requires the manager to rank a set of statements describing how an employee carries out the duties and responsibilities of the job.

Many variations of the **forced-choice rating** method exist. The most common practice requires the manager to rank a set of statements describing how an employee carries out the duties and responsibilities of the job. Figure 20.6 illustrates a group of forced-choice statements. The statements are normally weighted, and the weights are generally not known to the manager. After the manager ranks all of the forced-choice statements, the human resource department applies the weights and computes a score. This method attempts to eliminate bias by forcing the manager to rank statements that are seemingly indistinguishable or unrelated. However, the forced-choice method can irritate managers who think they are not being trusted. Furthermore, the results of the forced-choice appraisal can be difficult to communicate to employees.

Ranking Methods

When it becomes necessary to compare the performance of two or more employees, ranking methods can be used. Three of the more commonly used ranking methods are alternation, paired comparison, and forced distribution.

Alternation Ranking   In this ranking method, the names of the employees to be evaluated are listed down the left side of a sheet of paper. The manager is then asked to choose the most valuable employee on the list, cross that name off the left-hand list, and put it at the top of the column on the right side of the paper. The manager is then asked to select and cross off the name of the "least valuable" employee from the left-hand column and move it to the bottom of the right-hand column. The manager then repeats this process for all of the names on the left-hand

---

FIGURE 20.6   Sample Forced-Choice Set of Statements

Instructions: Rank the following statements according to how they describe the manner in which this employee carries out duties and responsibilities. Rank 1 should be given to the most descriptive and Rank 4 to the least descriptive. No ties are allowed.

Rank	Description
_____	Easy to get acquainted with
_____	Places great emphasis on people
_____	Refuses to accept criticism
_____	Thinks generally in terms of money
_____	Makes decisions quickly.

side of the paper. The resulting list of names in the right-hand column gives a ranking of the employees from most to least valuable.

Paired Comparison Ranking   This method is best illustrated with an example. Suppose a manager is to evaluate six employees. The names of these employees are listed on the left side of a sheet of paper. The manager then compares the first employee with the second employee on a chosen performance criterion, such as quantity of work. If the manager thinks the first employee has produced more work than the second employee, she or he places a check mark by the first employee's name. The first employee is then compared to the third, fourth, fifth, and sixth employee on the same performance criterion. A check mark is placed by the name of the employee who produced the most work in each of these paired comparisons. The process is repeated until each employee has been compared to every other employee on all of the chosen performance criteria. The employee with the most check marks is considered to be the best performer. Likewise, the employee with the fewest check marks is the lowest performer. One major problem with the paired comparison method is that it becomes unwieldy when comparing large numbers of employees.

Forced Distribution   This method requires the manager to compare the performances of employees and place a certain percentage of employees at various performance levels. It assumes the performance level in a group of employees is distributed according to a bell-shaped, or "normal," curve. Figure 20.7 illustrates how the forced distribution method works. The manager is required to rate 60 percent of the employees as meeting expectations, 20 percent as exceeding expectations, and 20 percent as not meeting expectations.

One problem with the forced distribution method is that for small groups of employees, a bell-shaped distribution of performance may not be applicable. Even where the distribution approximates a normal curve, it is probably not a perfect curve. This means some employees will probably not be rated accurately. Also, ranking methods differ dramatically from the other methods in that one employee's performance evaluation is a function of the performance of other employees in the job.

FIGURE 20.7   Forced Distribution Curve

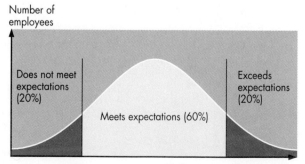

SELECTING A PERFORMANCE APPRAISAL METHOD

Whatever performance appraisal method an organization uses, it must be job related. Therefore, before selecting a performance appraisal method, job analyses must be conducted and job descriptions written.[8] Job analysis is a formal process of determining and reporting information relating to the nature of a specific job. It determines the tasks the job comprises and the skills, knowledge, abilities, and responsibilities required for successful performance of the job. Normally, job analyses are performed by trained specialists with the organization's human resource department or by outside consultants. Figure 20.8 summarizes the information a job analysis provides.

Job analysis involves not only determining job content but also reporting the results of the analysis. One product of a job analysis is a job description, a formal written document, usually one to three pages long, that should include the following:

- Date written.
- Job status (full-time or part-time).
- Job title.
- Supervision received (to whom the jobholder reports).
- Supervision exercised (who reports to this employee).
- Job summary (a synopsis of the job responsibilities).
- Detailed list of job responsibilities.
- Principal contacts (in and outside the organization).
- Competency or position requirements.
- Required education or experience.
- Career mobility (position or positions employee may qualify for next).[9]

After a job description is written, the most appropriate performance appraisal method can be determined.

FIGURE 20.8   Information Provided by Job Analysis

Area of Information	Contents
Job title and location within company	
Organizational relationship	A brief explanation of the number of persons supervised (if applicable) and the job title(s) of the position(s) supervised. A statement concerning supervision received.
Relation to other jobs	Describes and outlines the coordination required by the job.
Job summary	Condensed explanation of the content of the job.
Information concerning job requirements	Varies greatly from job to job and from organization to organization. Typically includes information on such topics as machines, tools, and materials; mental complexity and attention required; physical demands; and working conditions.

POTENTIAL ERRORS IN PERFORMANCE APPRAISALS

leniency   Grouping of ratings at the positive end of the scale instead of spreading them throughout the scale.

central tendency   Tendency of voters to rate most employees as doing average or above-average work.

recency   Occurs when performance evaluations are based on work performed most recently, generally work performed one to two months before evaluation.

halo effect   Occurs when managers allow a single prominent characteristic of an employee to influence their judgment on each separate item in the performance appraisal.

Several common errors have been identified in performance appraisals. **Leniency** is the grouping of ratings at the positive end of the performance scale instead of spreading them throughout the scale. **Central tendency** occurs when performance appraisal statistics indicate that most employees are evaluated similarly as doing average or above-average work. **Recency** occurs when performance evaluations are based on work performed most recently, generally work performed one to two months before evaluation. Leniency, central tendency, and recency errors make it difficult, if not impossible, to separate the good performers from the poor performers. In addition, these errors make it difficult to compare ratings from different managers. For example, it is possible for a good performer who is evaluated by a manager committing central tendency errors to receive a lower rating than a poor performer who is rated by a manager committing leniency errors.

Another common error in performance appraisals is the **halo effect**.[10] This occurs when managers allow a single prominent characteristic of an employee to influence their judgment on each separate item in the performance appraisal. This often results in the employee receiving approximately the same rating on every item.

Personal preferences, prejudices, and biases can also cause errors in performance appraisals. Managers with biases or prejudices tend to look for employee behaviors that conform to their biases. Appearance, social status, dress, race, and sex have influenced many performance appraisals. Managers have also allowed first impressions to influence later judgments of an employee. First impressions are only a sample of behavior; however, people tend to retain these impressions even when faced with contradictory evidence.

Because of all the potential problems just cited, some critics of the traditional process suggest that there may be a better way to evaluate employees. Author Tom Peters suggests that job descriptions and traditional evaluations are relevant only in stable, predictable, and very vertically oriented (functional) organizations.[11] Peters believes organizations that are better able to respond to dynamic competition are adopting "fluidity" concepts and are seriously reviewing the traditional forms of control (performance standards, MBO, and job descriptions).[12] Why? The reasoning is as follows. First, the focus should be on what is important (e.g., flexibility rather than rigidity). Second, the processes should be "living" ones that will encourage change on the part of both the organization and the employee. Third, a simple written contract will encourage creativity and reduce unnecessary and costly layers of bureaucracy.[13] Time will determine whether these ideas have merit.

OVERCOMING ERRORS IN PERFORMANCE APPRAISALS

A promising approach to overcoming errors in performance appraisals is to improve the skills of managers. Suggestions on the specific training managers should receive are often vague, but they usually emphasize that managers should be given training to observe behavior more accurately and judge it fairly.

More research is needed before a definitive set of topics for manager training can be established. However, at a minimum, managers should receive training in (1) the performance appraisal method(s) of the company, (2) the importance of the manager's role in the total appraisal process, (3) the use of performance appraisal information, and (4) the communication skills necessary to provide feedback to the employee.[14]

General "do's" and "don'ts" of the performance appraisal process can help managers to not only prevent but reduce the errors that always seem to plague the process. The "do's" include the following:

1. Base performance appraisal on job performance only and not other factors unrelated to the job.
2. Use only those rating scales that are relevant to the job itself and are indicators of objective performance and attainment.
3. Sincerely work at the appraisal interview process.
4. Be problem solving oriented.

The "don'ts" include the following:

1. Don't criticize. Be proactive.
2. Carefully avoid the halo effect and leniency errors.
3. Dominate conversations about performance. Encourage employees to speak and to address issues in the evaluation process themselves.
4. Avoid general prescriptions to fix performance. Always present concrete and realizable objectives. Performance goals are the foundation of productivity.[15]

PROVIDING FEEDBACK THROUGH THE APPRAISAL INTERVIEW

After one of the previously discussed methods for developing an employee's performance appraisal has been used, the results must be communicated to the employee. Unless this interview is properly conducted, it can and frequently does result in an unpleasant experience for both manager and employee. Following are some of the more important factors influencing success or failure of appraisal interviews:

• The more employees participate in the appraisal process, the more satisfied they are with the appraisal interview and with the manager and the more likely they are to accept and strive to meet performance improvement objectives.

• The more a manager uses positive motivational techniques (e.g., recognizing and praising good performance), the more satisfied the employee is likely to be with the appraisal interview and with the manager.

• The mutual setting by the manager and the employee of specific performance improvement objectives results in more improvement in performance than does a general discussion or criticism.

• Discussing and solving problems that may be hampering the employee's current job performance improve the employee's performance.

• Areas of job performance needing improvement that are most heavily criticized are less likely to be improved than similar areas of job performance that are less heavily criticized.

• The more employees are allowed to voice their opinions during the interview, the more satisfied they will be with the interview.

• The amount of thought and preparation employees independently devote before the interview increases the benefits of the interview.

• The more the employee perceives that performance appraisal results are tied to organizational rewards, the more beneficial the interview will be.

Management Illustration 20.2
Performance Evaluation of the Poor Performer

A recent arbitration case illustrates some considerations in performance evaluation of the poor performer. An employee was moved to a different job after 21 years of service without any significant performance problems. The employee was in the new job for two years, during which period she had three different supervisors. Although the supervisors had expressed concerns about her performance and developed plans of action to provide her training, performance evaluations, and feedback, they neglected to follow through with these plans. In addition, the employee did not get along well with her assigned trainers, which hampered the instruction she received in the new job.

The employee was put on a 30-day probation that called for her termination if she did not improve her job performance. When she failed to meet her supervisor's expectations during this period, she was discharged. She filed a grievance protesting her discharge. The arbitrator did not award any back pay to the employee but directed management to reinstate her for a 12-week probationary period. He directed management to make sure that the employee received proper training and close performance monitoring during the 12-week probationary period.

Source: Adapted from William E. Lissy, "Labor Law for Supervisors: Incompetence," *Supervision*, July 1996. For more information about labor law topics, visit the U.S. Department of Labor at its Web site: www.dol.gov.

The interviewer must also be aware that many employees are very skeptical about the appraisal process because of its potential association with punishment. Research has shown that this most often happens because the employee does not trust the manager's motivation; the feedback is unclear; the employee does not respect the manager's judgment; the feedback is inconsistent with the opinions of others; and the employee has had negative past experiences with the evaluation, appraisal, or feedback process.[16] Most of these problems can be overcome by simply accentuating the positive as the basis for the interview, feedback, and correction processes.

Management Illustration 20.2 gives some considerations in evaluating poor performers.

PERFORMANCE APPRAISAL AND THE LAW

Title VII of the Civil Rights Act permits the use of a bona fide performance appraisal system. Performance appraisal systems generally are not considered to be bona fide when their application results in adverse effects on minorities, women, or older employees.[17]

Many suggestions have been offered to make performance appraisal systems more legally acceptable. Some of these include (1) deriving the content of the appraisal system from job analyses; (2) emphasizing work behaviors rather than personal traits; (3) ensuring that the results of the appraisals are communicated to employees; (4) ensuring that employees are allowed to give feedback during the appraisal interview; (5) training managers in conducting proper evaluations; (6) ensuring that appraisals are written, documented, and retained; and (7) ensuring that personnel decisions are consistent with the performance appraisals.[18]

REWARDING PERFORMANCE

The previously described systems and methods of appraising employee performance are useful only if they are closely tied to the organization's reward system. Appraising performance without a system that ties the results of the appraisal to the organization's reward system creates an environment where employees are poorly motivated.

Organizational Reward System

The organizational reward system consists of the types of rewards the organization offers. **Organizational rewards** include all types of rewards, both intrinsic and extrinsic, that are received as a result of employment by the organization. **Intrinsic rewards** are internal to the individual and are normally derived from involvement in work activities. Job satisfaction and feelings of accomplishment are examples of intrinsic rewards. Most extrinsic rewards are directly controlled and distributed by the organization and are more tangible than intrinsic rewards. Figure 20.9 provides examples of both intrinsic and extrinsic rewards.

organizational rewards   All types of rewards, both intrinsic and extrinsic, received as a result of employment by the organization.

intrinsic rewards   Rewards internal to the individual and normally derived from involvement in work activities.

Though intrinsic and extrinsic rewards are different, they are also closely related. Often an extrinsic reward provides the recipient with intrinsic rewards. For example, an employee who receives an extrinsic reward in the form of a pay raise may also experience feelings of accomplishment (an intrinsic reward) by interpreting the pay raise as a sign of a job well done.

Compensation consists of the extrinsic rewards offered by the organization and includes the base wage or salary, any incentives or bonuses, and any benefits employees receive in exchange for their work. The base wage or salary is the hourly, weekly, or monthly pay employees receive for their work. Incentives are rewards offered in addition to the base wage or salary and are usually directly related to performance. Benefits are rewards employees receive because of their employment with the organization. Paid vacations, health insurance, and retirement plans are examples of benefits.

compensation   Composed of the extrinsic rewards offered by the organization and consists of the base wage or salary, any incentives or bonuses, and any benefits employees receive in exchange for their work.

Relating Rewards to Performance

The free enterprise system is based on the premise that rewards should depend on performance. This performance-reward relationship is desirable not only at the corporate level but also at the individual employee level. The underlying theory is that

FIGURE 20.9   Intrinsic versus Extrinsic Rewards

Intrinsic Rewards	Extrinsic Rewards
Sense of achievement	Formal recognition
Feelings of accomplishment	Fringe benefits
Informal recognition	Incentive payments
Job satisfaction	Base wages
Personal growth	Promotion
Status	Social relationships

employees will be motivated when they believe good performance will lead to rewards. Unfortunately, many extrinsic rewards provided by organizations do not lend themselves to being related to performance. For example, paid vacations, insurance plans, and paid holidays are usually determined by organizational membership and seniority rather than by performance.

Other rewards, such as promotion, can and should be related to performance. However, opportunities for promotion may occur only rarely. When available, the higher positions may be filled on the basis of seniority or by someone outside the organization.

A key organizational variable that can be used to reward individuals and reinforce performance is basing an employee's annual pay raise on his or her performance (often referred to as *merit pay*). Even though many U.S. companies have some type of merit pay program, most do a poor job of relating pay and performance.[19] Surveys repeatedly show that neither top management nor rank-and-file employees have much confidence that a positive relationship exists between performance and pay.[20]

If relating rewards to performance is desirable, why is it not more widespread? One answer is that it is not easy to do; it is much easier to give everybody the same thing, as evidenced by the ever-popular across-the-board pay increase. Relating rewards to performance requires that performance be accurately measured, and this is not easy. It also requires discipline to actually match rewards to performance. Another reason is that many union contracts require that certain rewards be based on totally objective variables, such as seniority. While no successful formula for implementing a merit pay program has been developed, a number of desirable preconditions have been identified and generally accepted:[21]

1. *Trust in management.* If employees are skeptical of management, it is difficult to make a merit pay program work.
2. *Absence of performance constraints.* Because pay-for-performance programs are usually based on individual ability and effort, the job must be structured so that an employee's performance is not hampered by factors beyond his or her control.
3. *Trained managers.* Managers must be trained in setting and measuring performance standards.
4. *Good measurement systems.* Performance should be based on criteria that are job specific and focus on results achieved.
5. *Ability to pay.* The merit portion of the salary-increase budget must be large enough to get employees' attention.
6. *Clear distinction among cost of living, seniority, and merit pay.* In the absence of strong evidence to the contrary, employees will naturally assume a pay increase is an economic or a longevity increase.
7. *Well-communicated total pay policy.* Employees must have a clear understanding of how merit pay fits into the total pay picture.
8. *Flexible reward schedule.* It is easier to establish a credible pay-for-performance plan if all employees do not receive pay adjustments on the same date.

Summary

1. *Define Performance Appraisal.* Performance appraisal involves determining and communicating to an employee how he or she is performing the job and establishing a plan for improvement.

2. *Define Performance.* Performance refers to the degree of accomplishment of the tasks that make up an employee's job.

3. *Explain the Determinants of Performance.* Job performance is the net effect of an employee's effort in terms of abilities, role perceptions, and results produced. This implies that performance in a given situation can be viewed as resulting from the interrelationships among effort, abilities, role perceptions, and results produced. Effort refers to the amount of energy an employee expends in performing a job. Abilities are personal characteristics used in performing a job. Role perception refers to the direction in which employees believe they should channel their efforts on their jobs.

4. *List and Describe the Nine Major Performance Appraisal Methods.*

    1. Evaluation by objectives involves using the objectives set in the management-by-objectives process as a basis for performance appraisal.
    2. The production standards approach involves setting a standard or expected level of output and then comparing each employee's performance to the standard.
    3. The essay appraisal method requires the manager to describe an employee's performance in written narrative form.
    4. The critical-incident appraisal method requires the manager to keep a written record of incidents, as they occur, involving job behaviors that illustrate both satisfactory and unsatisfactory performance by the employee being rated.
    5. The graphic rating scale method requires the manager to assess an individual on factors such as quantity of work, dependability, job knowledge, attendance, accuracy of work, and cooperativeness.
    6. The checklist method requires the manager to answer yes or no to a series of questions concerning the employee's behavior.
    7. The behaviorally anchored rating scale (BARS) method is designed to assess behaviors required to successfully perform a job.
    8. The forced-choice rating method requires the manager to rank a set of statements describing how an employee carries out the duties and responsibilities of the job.
    9. Ranking methods (alternation, paired comparison, and forced distribution) require the manager to compare the performance of an employee to the performance of other employees.

5. *Define Job Analysis.* Job analysis is a formal process of determining and reporting information related to the nature of a specific job.

6. *Explain the Contents of a Job Description.* A job description should include the following: date written, job status, job title, supervision received, supervision exercised, job summary, detailed list of job responsibilities, principal contacts, competency or position requirements, required education or experience, and career mobility.

7. *Discuss Common Errors Made in Performance Appraisal Interviews.* Leniency is the grouping of ratings at the positive end of the performance scale instead of spreading them throughout the scale. Central tendency occurs when performance appraisal statistics indicate that most employees are evaluated similarly as doing average or above-average work. Recency occurs when performance evaluations are based on work performed most recently. The halo effect occurs when managers allow a single prominent characteristic of an employee to influence their judgment on each separate item in the performance appraisal.

8. *Suggest Ways to Make Performance Appraisal Systems More Legally Acceptable.* Some suggestions include deriving the content of the appraisal system from job analyses; emphasizing work behaviors rather than personal traits; ensuring that the results of the appraisals are communicated to employees; ensuring that employees are allowed to give feedback during the appraisal interview; training managers in conducting proper evaluations; ensuring that appraisals are written, documented, and retained; and ensuring that personnel decisions are consistent with performance appraisals.

9. *Define Compensation.* Compensation consists of the extrinsic rewards offered by the organization and includes the base wage or salary, any incentives or bonuses, and any benefits employees receive in exchange for their work.

10. *Outline Desirable Preconditions for Implementing a Merit Pay Program.* Desirable preconditions are trust in management; absence of performance constraints; trained managers; good measurement systems; ability to pay; a clear distinction among cost of living, seniority, and merit pay; a well-communicated total pay policy; and a flexible reward schedule.

Preview Analysis

1. Describe the unique performance pay plan at Lincoln Electric.

2. Why have things begun to change at Lincoln Electric?

3. Have performance-based systems failed at Lincoln Electric?

4. Would you like to work under a performance-based pay system? Why or why not?

Review Questions

1. Define performance appraisal.

2. What is performance? What factors influence an employee's level of performance?

3. Identify at least three uses of performance appraisal information.

4. Describe the following methods used in performance appraisal:
   a. Evaluation by objectives.
   b. Production standards.
   c. Essay.
   d. Critical incident.
   e. Graphic rating scale.
   f. Checklist.
   g. Behaviorally anchored rating scale.
   h. Forced-choice rating.
   i. Ranking methods.

5. Define the following types of performance appraisal errors:
   a. Leniency.
   b. Central tendency.
   c. Recency.
   d. Halo effect.

6. Outline some factors that influence the success or failure of performance appraisal interviews.

7. Describe some suggestions for making performance appraisal systems more legally acceptable.

8. Identify three basic components of compensation and give examples of each.

9. Outline some preconditions for implementing a merit pay program.

Skill-Building Questions

1. What are your thoughts on discussing salary raises and promotions during the performance appraisal interview?

2. Which method of performance appraisal do you think is the fairest? Why? (You may have to cite an example to explain your reason.) Under which method would you like to work? Why?

3. It has been said that incentive plans work for only a relatively short time. Do you agree or disagree? Why?

4. Why do you think management frequently uses across-the-board pay increases?

SKILL-BUILDING EXERCISE 20.1

Developing a Performance Appraisal System

A large public utility has been having difficulty with its performance evaluation program. The organization has an evaluation program in which all operating employees and clerical employees are evaluated semiannually by their supervisors. The form they have been using is given in Exhibit 1. It has been in use for 10 years. The form is scored as follows: excellent = 5; above average = 4; average = 3; below average = 2; and poor = 1. The scores for each facet are entered in the right-hand column and are totaled for an overall evaluation score.

In the procedure used, each supervisor rates each employee on July 30 and January 30. The supervisor discusses the rating with the employee and then sends the rating to the personnel department. Each rating is placed in the employee's personnel file. If promotions come up, the cumulative ratings are considered at that time. The ratings are also supposed to be used as a check when raises are given.

The system was designed by Joanna Kyle, the personnel manager, who retired two years ago. Her replacement was Eugene Meyer. Meyer graduated 15 years ago with a degree in commerce from the University of Texas. Since then he's had a variety of experiences, mostly in utilities. For about five of these years, he did personnel work.

Eugene has been reviewing the evaluation system. Employees have a mixture of indifferent and negative feelings about it. An informal survey has shown that about 60 percent of the supervisors fill out the forms, give about three minutes to each form, and send them to personnel without discussing them with the employees. Another 30 percent do a little better. They spend more time completing the forms but communicate about them only briefly and superficially with their employees. Only about 10 percent of the supervisors seriously try to do what was intended.

EXHIBIT 1   Performance Evaluation Form

Performance Evaluation

Supervisors: When you are asked to do so by the personnel department, please complete this form on each of your employees. The supervisor who is responsible for 75 percent or more of an employee's work should complete this form on him or her. Please evaluate each facet of the employee separately.

Facet	Rating					Score
Quality of work	Excellent	Above average	Average	Below average	Poor	
Quantity of work	Poor	Below average	Average	Above average	Excellent	
Dependability at work	Excellent	Above average	Average	Below average	Poor	
Initiative at work	Poor	Below average	Average	Above average	Excellent	
Cooperativeness	Excellent	Above average	Average	Below average	Poor	
Getting along with co-workers	Poor	Below average	Average	Above average	Excellent	

Total _____

Supervisor's signature _____

Employee name _____

Employee number _____

Eugene also found that the forms were rarely used for promotion or pay raise decisions. Because of this, most supervisors may have thought the evaluation program was a useless ritual. In his previous employment, Eugene had seen performance evaluation as a much more useful experience. It included giving positive feedback to employees, improving future employee performance, developing employee capabilities, and providing data for promotion and compensation.

Eugene has had little experience with design of performance evaluation systems. He believes he should seek advice on the topic.

Write a report summarizing your evaluation of the strengths and weaknesses of the present appraisal system. Recommend some specific improvements or data-gathering exercises to develop a better system for Eugene Meyer.

SKILL BUILDING EXERCISE 20.2

Who Are "Normal" Employees?

Assume your company has just adopted the form shown in Skill-Building Exercise 20.1 for its performance evaluation system. Assume further that your company has also instituted a policy that every manager's performance appraisals must conform to the bell-shaped curve shown below. Using this curve, a manager that has 10 employees would have one that would be ranked as excellent, one that would be ranked above average, six that would be ranked average, one that would be ranked as below average, and one that would be ranked as below average, and one that would be ranked unsatisfactory.

Prepare a 10-minute presentation summarizing the problems, advantages, and disadvantages of using such a system.

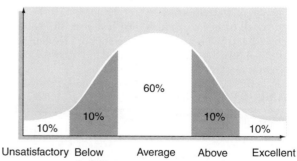

CASE INCIDENT 20.1

Determining Pay Raises

About four months ago, Judy Holcomb was promoted to supervisor of the Claims Department for a large, eastern insurance company. It is now time for all supervisors to make their annual salary increase recommendations. Judy doesn't feel comfortable in making these recommendations because she has been in her job only a short time. To further complicate the situation, the former supervisor has left the company and is unavailable for consultation.

There are no formal company restrictions on the kind of raises that can be given, but Judy's boss has said the total amount of money available to Judy for raises would be 8 percent of Judy's payroll for the past year. In other words, if the sum total of the salaries for all of Judy's employees was $200,000, then Judy would have $16,000 to allocate for raises. Judy is free to distribute the raises any way she wants, within reason.

Summarized below is the best information on her employees that Judy can find from the files of the former supervisor of the Claims Department. This information is supplemented by feelings Judy has developed during her short time as supervisor.

John Thompson: John has been with Judy's department for only five months. In fact, he was hired just before Judy was promoted into the supervisor's job. John is single and seems to be a carefree bachelor. His job performance, so far, has been above average, but Judy has received some negative comments about John from his coworkers. Present salary, $28,000.

Carole Wilson: Carole has been on the job for three years. Her previous performance appraisals have indicated superior performance. However, Judy does not believe the previous evaluations are accurate. She thinks Carole's performance is, at best, average. Carole appears to be well liked by all of her coworkers. Just last year, she became widowed and is presently the sole support for her five-year-old child. Present salary: $29,000.

Evelyn Roth: Evelyn has been on the job for four years. Her previous performance appraisals were all average. In addition, she had received below-average increases for the past two years. However, Evelyn recently approached Judy and told her she believes she was discriminated against in the past due to both her age and sex. Judy thinks Evelyn's work so far has been satisfactory but not superior. Most employees don't seem to sympathize with Evelyn's accusations of sex and age discrimination. Present salary: $27,000.

Jane Simmons: As far as Judy can tell, Jane is one of her best employees. Her previous performance appraisals also indicate she is a superior performer. Judy knows Jane badly needs a substantial salary increase because of some personal problems. She appears to be well respected by her coworkers. Present salary: $28,500.

Bob Tyson: Bob has been performing his present job for eight years. The job is very technical, and he would be difficult to replace. However, as far as Judy can discern, Bob is not a good worker. He is irritable and hard to work with. Despite this, Bob has received above-average pay increases for the past two years. Present salary: $23,000.

Questions

1. Indicate the size of the raise you would give each of these employees.

2. What criteria did you use in determining the size of the raise?

3. What do you think would be the feelings of the other people in the group if they should find out what raises you recommend?

4. Do you think the employees would eventually find out what raises others received? Would it matter?

CASE INCIDENT 20.2

Conducting a Performance Appraisal

Plant manager Paul Dorn wondered why his boss, Leonard Hech, had sent for him. Paul thought Leonard had been tough on him lately; he was slightly uneasy at being asked to come to Leonard's office at a time when such meetings were unusual. "Close the door and sit down, Paul," invited Leonard. "I've been wanting to talk to you." After preliminary conversation, Leonard said that because Paul's latest project had been finished, he would receive the raise he had been promised on its completion.

Leonard went on to say that since it was time for Paul's performance appraisal, they might as well do that now. Leonard explained that the performance appraisal was based on four criteria: (1) the amount of high-quality merchandise manufactured and shipped on time, (2) the quality of relationships with plant employees and peers, (3) progress in maintaining employee safety and health, and (4) reaction to demands of top management. The first criterion had a relative importance of 40 percent; the rest had a weight of 20 percent each.

On the first item, Paul received an excellent rating. Shipments were at an all-time high, quality was good, and few shipments had arrived late. On the second item, Paul also was rated excellent. Leonard said plant employees and peers related well to Paul, labor relations were excellent, and there had been no major grievances since Paul had become plant manager.

However, on attention to matters of employee safety and health, the evaluation was below average. His boss stated that no matter how much he bugged Paul about improving housekeeping in the plant, he never seemed to produce results. Leonard also rated Paul below average on meeting demands from top management. He explained that Paul always answered yes to any request and then disregarded it, going about his business as if nothing had happened.

Seemingly surprised at the comments, Paul agreed that perhaps Leonard was right and that he should do a better job on these matters. Smiling as he left, he thanked Leonard for the raise and the frank appraisal.

As weeks went by, Leonard noticed little change in Paul. He reviewed the situation with an associate. "It's frustrating. In this time of rapid growth, we must make constant changes in work methods. Paul agrees but can't seem to make people break their habits and adopt more efficient ones. I find myself riding him very hard these days, but he just calmly takes it. He's well liked by everyone. But somehow, he's got to care about safety and housekeeping in the plant. And when higher management makes demands he can't meet, he's got to say, 'I can't do that and do all the other things you want, too.' Now he has dozens of unfinished jobs because he refuses to say no."

As he talked, Leonard remembered something Paul had told him in confidence once. "I take Valium for a physical condition I have. When I don't take it, I get symptoms similar to a heart attack. But I only take half as much as the doctor prescribed." Now, Leonard thought, I'm really in a spot. If the Valium is what is making him so lackadaisical, I can't endanger his health by asking him to quit taking it. And I certainly can't fire him. Yet, as things stand, he really can't implement all the changes we need to fulfill our goals for the next two years.

Questions

1. Do you think a raise was justified in Paul's situation? Explain.

2. What could have been done differently in the performance appraisal session?

3. What can be done now to change the situation?

References and Additional Readings

[1] For more discussion on effective performance appraisals, see Dean Elmuti, Yunus Kathawala, and Robert Wayland, "Traditional Performance Appraisal Systems: The Deming Challenge," *Management Decision* 30, pp. 42–48.

[2] Michael Smith, "Documenting Employee Performance," *Supervisory Management*, September 1979.

[3] Tim Smart and Judith H. Dobrzynski, "Jack Welch on the Art of Thinking Small," *Business Week/Enterprise*, 1993, pp. 212–16.

[4] Dori Jones Young, "Letting Go Is Hard to Do," *Business Week/Enterprise*, 1993, pp. 218–19.

[5] Ibid.

[6] Frederick W. Taylor, *Scientific Management* (New York: Harper & Row, 1911), p. 52.

[7] Bob Wooten, "Using Appraisals to Set Objectives," *Supervisory Management*, November 1981.

[8] James A. Buford, Bettye B. Burkhulter, and Grover T. Jacobs, "Link Job Descriptions to Performance Appraisals," *Personnel Journal*, June 1988, pp. 132–40.

[9] Judith A. DeLapa, "Job Descriptions That Work," *Personnel Journal*, June 1989, p. 156.

[10] For a more in-depth discussion of the halo effect, see William K. Blazer and Lorne M. Sulsky, "Halo and Performance Appraisal Research: A Critical Examination," *Journal of Applied Psychology*, December 1992, pp. 976–85.

[11] Tom Peters, *Thriving on Chaos* (New York: Alfred A. Knopf, 1987), p. 500.

[12] Ibid., p. 501.

[13] Ibid., p. 494.

[14] For additional information on training for performance appraisals, see Robert N. Buckham, "Appraisal Training: Not Just for Managers," *Training and Development Journal*, June 1990, pp. 18, 21.

[15] Edward L. Levine, "Let's Talk: Discussing Job Performance," *Supervisory Management*, October 1980.

[16] Michael Smith, "Feedback as a Performance Management Technique," *Management Solutions*, April 1987.

[17] For an update on the legal status of performance appraisals, see David C. Martin and Kathryn M. Bartol, "The Legal Ramifications of Performance Appraisals: An Update," *Employee Relations Law Journal*, Autumn 1991, pp. 257–86.

[18] Ginger C. Reed, "Employers' New Burden of Proof in Discrimination Cases," *Employment Relations Today*, Summer 1989, p. 112.

[19] Frederick S. Hills, Robert M. Madigan, K. Dow Scott, and Steven E. Markham, "Tracking the Merit of Merit Pay," *Personnel Administrator*, March 1987, p. 50.

[20] E. James Brennan, "The Myth and the Reality of Pay for Performance," *Personnel Journal*, March 1985, p. 73.

[21] The following preconditions are drawn from Hills et al., "Tracking the Merit," pp. 56–57.

Operations Control

LEARNING OBJECTIVES

After studying this chapter, you should be able to:

1. Understand the basic requirements for controlling operating costs.

2. Define quality from the perspective of an operations manager.

3. Explain the concept of quality assurance.

4. Explain the concept of total quality management (TQM).

5. Define continuous improvement and Kaizen.

6. Describe ISO 9000 and the zero-defects approaches to quality.

7. Identify and define the two major types of quality control.

8. Recount the major reasons for carrying inventories.

9. Explain the concept of just-in-time (JIT) inventory.

10. Describe the ABC classification system for managing inventories.

11. Summarize the economic order quantity (EQQ) concept.

12. Describe the basic purposes of material requirements planning (MRP).

Varian Vacuum Products' (VVP) plant in Lexington, Massachusetts manufactures vacuum pumps, leak detection, vacuum gauges and controllers, and vacuum valves and hardware. The VVP—Lexington plant is 100,000 square feet, is a nonunion facility, and has about 40,000 customers worldwide. A decade ago VVP—Lexington was in serious trouble. Business was dropping 10 to 20 percent a year and the parent company had twice tried, without success, to sell the company. Vice-president and general manager Peter Frasso estimates that VVP—Lexington was within two to three years of being out of business.

The turnaround began in 1989. A total quality management system was put into place. Some dramatic results followed. Scrap and rework costs fell from 15 percent of sales to less than 1 percent of sales. Inventory turnover increased from 0.6 to 3.9. On-time delivery improved to 90 percent, up from 22 percent. On top of all this profitability increased.

Source: John S. McClenahen, "Varian Vacuum Products," *Industry Week,* Oct 20, 1997, pp. 79–82.

There are two aspects to an effective operating system: design and control. These aspects are related in that after a system has been designed and implemented, day-to-day operations must be controlled. With respect to efficient operation, the system processes must be monitored; quality must be assured; inventories must be managed; and all of these tasks must be accomplished within cost constraints. In addition to ensuring that things do not get out of control, good operations control can be a substitute for resources. For example, good quality control can reduce scrap and wasted materials, thus cutting costs. Similarly, effective inventory control can reduce the investment costs in inventories.

Effective operations control is attained by applying the basic control concepts to the operations function of the organization. Operations controls generally relate to one of three areas: costs, quality, or inventories.

CONTROLLING OPERATIONS COSTS

Ensuring that operating costs do not get out of hand is one of the primary jobs of the operations manager. The first requirement for controlling costs is to understand the organization's accounting and budgeting systems. Operations managers are primarily concerned with costs relating to labor, materials, and overhead. Figure 21.1 describes the major components of each of these costs. **Variable overhead expenses** change with the level of production or service. **Fixed overhead expenses** do not change appreciably with the level of production or service.

variable overhead expenses   Expenses that change in proportion to the level of production or service.
fixed overhead expenses   Expenses that do not change appreciably with fluctuations in the level of production or service.

Normally, operations managers prepare monthly budgets for each of the major cost areas. Once these budgets have been approved by higher levels of management, they are put into effect. By carefully monitoring the ensuing labor, material, and overhead costs, the operations manager can compare actual costs to budgeted costs. The methods used to monitor costs naturally vary, but typically they include direct observation, written reports, break-even charts, and so on.

Usually a cost control system indicates only when a particular cost is out of control; it does not address the question of *why* it is out of control. For example, suppose an operations manager determines from the monthly cost report that the labor costs

---

FIGURE 21.1   Budget Costs: The Basis for Cost Control

Type of Cost	Components
Direct labor—variable	Wages and salaries of employees engaged in the direct generation of goods and services. This typically does not include wages and salaries of support personnel.
Materials—variable	Cost of materials that become a tangible part of finished goods and services.
Production overhead—variable	Training new employees, safety training, supervision and clerical, overtime premium, shift premium, payroll taxes, vacation and holiday, retirement funds, group insurance, supplies, travel, repairs and maintenance.
Production overhead—fixed	Travel, research and development, fuel (coal, gas, or oil), electricity, water, repairs and maintenance, rent, depreciation, real estate taxes, insurance.

Source: Adopted from *Production and Operations Management* by Norman Gaither. Copyright © 1980 by The Dryden Press. Reprinted by permission of Wadsworth Publishing Co.

on product X are exceeding budget by 20 percent. The manager must then attempt to determine what is causing the cost overrun. The causes could be many, including unmotivated employees, several new and untrained employees, low-quality raw materials, and equipment breakdown. The wise manager not only investigates the cause but also plans for prevention. The logical conclusion of a monitoring process is the implementation of prevention measures.[1]

Determining the cause may require only a simple inspection of the facts, or it may call for an in-depth analysis. Whatever the effort required, the operations manager must ultimately identify the source of the problem and then take the necessary corrective action. If the same cost problems continue to occur, chances are the manager has not correctly identified the true cause of the problem or the necessary corrective action has not been taken.

QUALITY MANAGEMENT

Quality is a relative term that means different things to different people. The consumer who demands quality may have a different concept than the operations manager who demands quality. The consumer is concerned with service, reliability, performance, appearance, and so forth. The operations manager's primary concern is that the product or service specifications be achieved, whatever they may be. For the operations manager, **quality** is determined in relation to the specifications or standards set in the design stages.

quality   For the operations manager, quality is determined in relation to the specifications or standards set in the design stages—the degree or grade of excellence specified.

The quality of an organization's goods and services can affect the organization in many ways. Some of the most important of these areas are (1) loss of business, (2) liability, (3) costs, and (4) productivity.[2] The reputation of an organization is often a direct reflection of the perceived quality of its goods and/or services. In today's legalistic environment, an organization's liability exposure can be significant and the associated costs can be high. Higher-quality goods and services generally have less liability exposure than lower-quality goods and services. In addition to liability costs, quality can affect other costs, including scrap, rework, warranty, repair, replacement, and other, similar costs. Productivity and quality are often closely related.[3] Poor-quality equipment, tools, parts, or subassemblies can cause defects that hurt productivity. Similarly, high-quality equipment, tools, parts, and subassemblies can boost productivity.

Because of the many different ways quality can affect an organization, it is often difficult to determine precisely the costs associated with different quality levels. Also, it must be realized that consumers and customers are willing to pay for quality only up to a point. In response, many firms have instituted a total customer response program in which quality in the workplace is transferred to dealings with customers. To implement the program, firms must (1) develop a new attitude toward customers, (2) reduce management layers so that managers are in contact with customers, (3) link quality and information systems to customer needs and problems, (4) train employees in customer responsiveness, (5) integrate customer responsiveness throughout the entire distribution channel, and (6) use customer responsiveness as a marketing tool.[4]

Quality Assurance

For years, the responsibility for quality in almost all organizations rested with a quality control department.[5] The idea under this approach was to identify and remove defects and/or correct mistakes before they got to the customer. Some systems emphasized finding and correcting defects at the end of the line; others focused on detecting defects during the production process. Both approaches focused on only the production part of the process; they gave little or no consideration to the design of the products/services or to working with suppliers. Suppliers were usually treated as adversaries.

Today's quality management emphasizes the prevention of defects and mistakes rather than finding and correcting them. The idea of "building in" quality as opposed to "inspecting it in" is also known as *quality assurance*. This approach views quality as the responsibility of all employees rather than the exclusive domain of a quality control department. Furthermore, suppliers are treated as partners.

While there have been many individuals who have championed the prevention approach to quality, W. Edwards Deming is perhaps most responsible. Deming was statistics professor at New York University in the 1940s who went to Japan after World War II to assist in improving quality and productivity. While he became very much revered in Japan, Deming remained almost unknown to U.S. business leaders until the 1980s when Japan's quality and productivity attracted the attention of the world.

Total Quality Management

Total quality management (TQM) is a management philosophy that emphasizes "managing the entire organization so that it excels in all dimensions of products and services that are important to the customer."[6] TQM, in essence, is an organization-wide emphasis on quality as defined by the customer. Under TQM, everyone from the CEO on down to the lowest-level employee must be involved. TQM can be summarized by the following actions:[7]

1. Find out what customers want. This might involve the use of surveys, focus groups, interviews, or some other technique that integrates the customer's voice in the decision-making process.

2. Design a product or service that will meet (or exceed) what customers want. Make it easy to use and easy to produce.

3. Design a production process that facilitates doing the job right the first time. Determine where mistakes are likely to occur, and try to prevent them. When mistakes do occur, find out why so that they are less likely to occur again. Strive to "mistake-proof" the process.

4. Keep track of results, and use those results to guide improvement in the system. Never stop trying to improve.

5. Extend these concepts to suppliers and to distribution.

As stated previously, TQM is an organizationwide emphasis on quality as defined by the customer. It is not a collection of techniques but a philosophy or way of thinking about how people view their jobs and quality throughout the organization.

Implementing TQM   Today's managers are bombarded with advice and literature telling them how to implement TQM. Three of the most popular approaches for implementing TQM are the Deming method, the Juran method and the Crosby method, each named after the person who championed the respective approach. The Deming method emphasizes statistical quality control through employee empowerment. The Juran method emphasizes the reformulation of attitudes, comprehensive controls and annual objective reviews. The Crosby method emphasizes conformance to requirements and zero defects. All of these approaches are sound; however the best approach for implementing TQM is to custom-tailor the process for each application. In a study conducted by Frank Mahoney, the following initiatives were those most often cited by senior executives who had successfully implemented TQM.[8]

1. Demonstrate top-down commitment and involvement-push.
2. Set *tough* improvement goals, not just stretch goals.
3. Provide appropriate training, resources, and human resource backup.
4. Determine critical measurement factors; benchmark and track progress.
5. Spread success stories, especially those about favorable benchmarking; always share financial progress reports.
6. Identify the costs of quality and routes to improvement; prove the case that quality costs decline with quality progress.
7. Rely on teamwork, involvement, and all-level leadership.
8. Respect the "gurus," but tailor every initiative for a good local fit.
9. Allow time to see progress, analyze the system's operation, reward contributions, and make needed adjustments.
10. Finally, recognize that the key internal task is a culture change and the key external task is a new set of relationships with customers and suppliers.

Although it would seem to make good sense to transform an organization in the direction of total quality management, there is still resistance from the traditionalists. Figure 21.2 compares traditional organizations with those using TQM. The most often cited barriers to adopting TQM are (1) a lack of consistency of purpose on the part of management, (2) an emphasis on short-term profits, (3) an inability to modify personnel review systems, (4) mobility of management (job hopping), (5) lack of commitment to training and failure to instill leadership that is change oriented, and (6) excessive costs.[9]

FIGURE 21.2   Comparison of Traditional Organizations with Those Using TQM

Aspect	Traditional	TQM
Overall mission	Maximize return on investment	Meet or exceed customer satisfaction
Objectives	Emphasis on short term	Balance of long term and short term
Management	Not always open; sometimes inconsistent objectives	Open; encourages employees input; consistent objectives
Role of manager	Issue orders; enforce	Coach, remove barriers, build trust
Customer requirements	Not highest priority; may be unclear	Highest priority; important to identify and understand
Problems	Assign blame; punish	Identify and resolve
Problem solving	Not systematic; by individuals	Systematic; by teams
Improvement	Erratic	Continual
Suppliers	Adversarial	Partners
Jobs	Narrow, specialized; much individual effort	Broad, more general; much team effort
Focus	Product oriented	Process oriented

Source: William J. Stevenson, *Production/Operation Management*, 4th ed. (Homewood, IL: Richard D. Irwin, 1993), p. 107.

Continuous Improvement/Kaizen   *Continuous improvement* in general refers to an ongoing effort to make improvements in every part of the organization relative to all of its products and services.[10] With regard to TQM, it means focusing on continuous improvement in the quality of the processes by which work is accomplished. The idea here is that the quest for better quality and better service is never ending.

kaizen   "Good change;" a process of continuous and relentless improvement.

Kaizen is a philosophy for improvement that originated in Japan and that has recently enjoyed widespread adoption throughout the world. The word *Kaizen* comes from two Japanese words: *Kai*, meaning "change", and *zen*, meaning "good."[11] Hence, Kaizen literally means "good change," and in today's context it describes a process of continuous and relentless improvement. Kaizen is not based on large technical leaps but on the incremental refining of existing processes. Kaizen is basically a system of taking small steps to improve the workplace. Kaizen is based on the belief that the system should be customer driven and involve all employees through systematic and open communication. Under Kaizen, employees are viewed as the organization's most valued asset. This philosophy is put into practice through teamwork and extensive employee participation. In summary, Kaizen applies the principles of participatory management toward incremental improvement of the current methods and processes. Kaizen does not focus on obtaining new and faster machines but rather on improving the methods and procedures used in the existing situation. Management Illustration 21.1 describes how Dana Corporation has successfully implemented Kaizen.

Quality at the source refers to the philosophy of making each employee responsible for the quality of his or her work.[12] In effect, this approach views every employee as a quality inspector for his or her own work. A major advantage of this approach is that it removes the adversarial relationship that often exists between quality control inspectors and production employees. It also encourages employees to take pride in their work.

Reengineering   Some people confuse the concept of reengineering with TQM. **Reengineering,** also called business process engineering, is "the search for and im-

reengineering   Searching for and implementing radical change in business processes to achieve breakthroughs in costs, speed productivity, and service.

plementation of radical change in business processes to achieve breakthrough results in costs, speed, productivity, and service."[13] Unlike TQM, reengineering is not a program for making marginal improvements in existing procedures. Reengineering is rather a one-time concerted effort, initiated from the top of the organization, to make major improvements in processes used to produce products or services. The essence of reengineering is to start with a clean slate and redesign the organization's processes to better serve its customers.

Other Quality Standards

While TQM is a highly effective, organizationwide philosophy about quality, there are other techniques and approaches that organizations may adopt to encourage quality. Most of these can be used alone or in conjunction with TQM. Quality circles were discussed in Chapter 11. Two additional approaches are discussed below.

Management Illustration 21.1
Kaizen Blitz at Dana Corporation

Dana Corporation is a manufacturer and distributor of products and systems for vehicular, industrial and offhighway markets. In 1995 Dana adapted kaizen blitz from the Toyota production system. According to Roger Harnishfeger, Dean of Dana University's Technical School, Dana's kaizen blitz is a process that encompasses half a day dedicated to instruction of the basic kaizen philosophies and three full days spent developing and implementing ideas for improvement. According to Harnishfeger, "there's a tremendous amount of implementation that goes on during the blitz. It's not a case where you'll learn some new techniques and maybe someday you might use them."

The kaizen blitz process has generated as much as 400 percent improvement in one plant. Other specific examples include the reduction of the travel distance of people and parts in one plant from 2,072 feet to 166 feet, the reduction of floor space required for one operation from 216 square feet to 60 square feet, the reduction in work-in-process by more than 75 percent, and the reduction in labor required to get the same output by 80 percent.

Dana has also used the kaizen blitz in nonmanufacturing environments, having successfully applied the concept in warehousing and with one plant's office staff. Currently Dana has trained more than 30 of its employees to lead kaizen blitzes. Many of Dana's divisions are doing blitzes once a month.

Source: Leigh Ann Klaus, "Kaizen Blitz Proves Effective for Dana Corporation," *Quality Progress*, May 1998, p. 8. For more information about Dana Corporation visit their Web site at: www.dana.com.

ISO 9000 ISO 9000 is a set of quality standards created in 1987 by the International Organization for Standardization (ISO), in Geneva, Switzerland. ISO currently is composed of the national standards bodies of over 90 countries with the major objective of promoting the development of standardization and facilitating the international exchange of goods and services. The American National Standards Institute (ANSI) is the member body representing the United States in the ISO.

ISO 9000 A set of quality standards for international business.

Originally the ISO published five international standards designed to guide internal quality management programs and to facilitate external quality assurance endeavors. In essence, ISO 9000 outlines the quality system requirements necessary to meet quality requirements in varying situations. ISO 9000 focuses on the design and operation processes, not on the end product or service. ISO 9000 requires extensive documentation in order to demonstrate the consistency and reliability of the processes being used. In summary, ISO certification does not relate to the quality of the actual end product or service, but it guarantees that the company has fully documented its quality control procedures.

While ISO issues the standards, it does not regulate the program internationally; regulation is left to national accreditation organizations such as the U.S. Register Accreditation Board (RAB). RAB and other such boards then authorize registrars to issue ISO 9000 certificates.

Zero-Defects The name *zero-defects* is somewhat misleading in that this approach doesn't literally try to cut defects or defective service to zero. This would *zero-defects program*   Increasing quality by increasing everyone's impact on quality.

obviously be very cost ineffective in many situations. A **zero-defects program** attempts to create a positive attitude toward the prevention of low quality. The objective of a zero-defects program is to heighten awareness of quality by making everyone aware of his or her potential impact on quality. Naturally, this should lead to more attention to detail and concern for accuracy.

Most successful zero-defects programs have the following characteristics:

1. Extensive communication regarding the importance of quality—signs, posters, contests, and so on.
2. Organizationwide recognition—publicly granting rewards, certificates, and plaques for high-quality work.
3. Problem identification by employees—employees point out areas where they think quality can be improved.

The Malcolm Baldrige National Quality Award

In 1987, the U.S. Congress passed the Malcolm Baldrige National Quality Improvement Act. The purpose of this legislation was to inspire increased efforts by U.S. businesses to improve the quality of their products and services. The **Malcolm Baldrige Award** is named after the late Malcolm Baldrige who was a successful businessman and a former U.S. secretary of commerce. The award is administered by the National Institute of Standards and Technology and can only be awarded to businesses located in the United States. The purpose of the award is to encourage efforts to improve quality and to recognize the quality achievements of U.S. companies. A maximum of two awards are given each year in each of three categories: large manufacturer, large service organization, and small business (500 or less employees).

Malcolm Baldrige Award   Recognition of U.S. companies' achievements in quality.

Types of Quality Control

Quality control relating to the inputs or outputs of the system is referred to as **product quality control** (sometimes called *acceptance control*). Product quality control is used when the quality is being evaluated with respect to a batch of products or services that already exists, such as incoming raw materials or finished goods. Product quality control lends itself to acceptance sampling procedures, in which some portion of a batch of outgoing items (or incoming materials) is inspected to ensure that the batch meets specifications with regard to the percentage of defective units that will be tolerated in the batch. With acceptance sampling procedures, the decision to accept or reject an entire batch is based on a sample or group of samples.

product quality control   Relates to inputs or outputs of the system; used when quality is evaluated with respect to a batch of existing products or services.
process control   Relates to equipment and processes used during the production process; used to monitor quality while the product or service is being produced.

Process control concerns monitoring quality while the product or service is being produced. Process control relates to the control of the equipment and processes used during the production process. Under process control, periodic samples are taken from a process and compared to a predetermined standard. If the sample results are acceptable, the process is allowed to continue. If the sample results are not acceptable, the process is halted and adjustments are made to bring the machines or processes back under control.

Acceptance Sampling **Acceptance sampling** is a method of predicting the quality of a batch or a large group of products from an inspection of a sample or group of samples taken from the batch. Acceptance sampling is used for one of three basic reasons:

acceptance sampling   Statistical method of predicting the quality of a batch or a large group of products by inspecting a sample or group of samples.

1. The potential losses or costs of passing defective items are not great relative to the cost of inspection; for example, it would not be appropriate to inspect every match produced by a match factory.
2. Inspection of some items requires destruction of the product being tested, as is the case when testing flash bulbs.
3. Sampling usually produces results more rapidly than does a census.

Acceptance sampling draws a random sample of a given size from the batch or lot being examined. The sample is then tested and analyzed. If more than a certain number (determined statistically) are found to be defective, the entire batch is rejected, as it is deemed to have an unacceptably large percentage of defective items. Because of the possibility of making an incorrect inference concerning the batch, acceptance sampling always involves risks. The risk the producer is willing to take of rejecting a good batch is referred to as the *producer's risk*. The risk of accepting a bad batch is referred to as the *consumer's risk*. Obviously, one would desire to minimize both the producer's risk and the consumer's risk. However, the only method of simultaneously lowering both of these risks is to increase the sample size, which also increases the inspection costs. Therefore, the usual approach is to decide on the maximum acceptable risk for both the producer and the consumer and design the acceptance sampling plan around these risks.

Process Control Charts A **process control chart** is a time-based, graphic display that shows whether a machine or a process is producing output at the expected quality level. If a significant change in the variable being checked is detected, the machine is said to be out of control. Control charts do not attempt to show why a machine is out of control, only whether it is out of control.

process control chart   Time-based graphic display that shows whether a machine or a process is producing items that meet preestablished specifications.

The most frequently used process control charts are called *mean* and *range charts*. Mean charts (also called *X-charts*) monitor the mean or average value of some characteristic (dimension, weight, etc.) of the items produced by a machine or process. Range charts (also called *R-charts*) monitor the range of variability of some characteristic (dimension, weight, etc.) of the items produced by a machine or process.

The quality control inspector, using control charts, first calculates the desired level of the characteristic being measured. The next step is to calculate statistically the upper and lower control limits, which determine how much the characteristic can vary from the desired level before the machine or process is considered to be out of control. Once the control chart has been set up, the quality control inspector periodically takes a small sample from the machine or process outputs. Depending on the type of chart being used, the mean or range of the sample is plotted on the control chart. By plotting the results of each sample on the control chart, it is easy to identify quickly any abnormal trends in quality. Figure 21.3 shows a sample mean chart. A range chart looks like a mean chart; the only difference is that the range, as opposed to the mean, of the characteristic being monitored is plotted.

FIGURE 21.3   Mean Chart

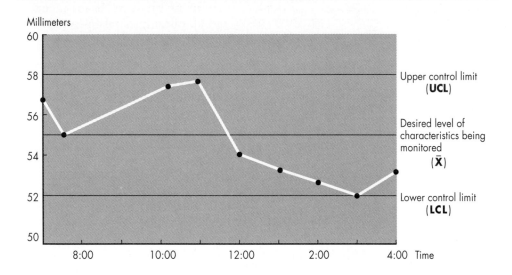

Millimeters

Upper control limit
(**UCL**)

Desired level of
characteristics being
monitored
(**X̄**)

Lower control limit
(**LCL**)

A mean or range chart used by itself can easily lead to false conclusions. For example, the upper and lower control limits for a machined part might be 0.1000 millimeters and 0.0800 millimeters, respectively. A sample of four parts of 0.1200, 0.1100, 0.0700, and 0.0600 would yield an acceptable mean of 0.0900; yet every element of the sample is out of tolerance. For this reason, when monitoring variables, it is usually desirable to use mean and range charts simultaneously to ensure that a machine or a process is under control.

INVENTORY CONTROL

Inventories serve as a buffer between different rates of flow associated with the operating system. **Inventories** are generally classified into one of three categories, depending on their location within the operating system: (1) raw material, (2) in process, or (3) finished goods. Raw material inventories serve as a buffer between purchasing and production. In-process inventories are used to buffer differences in the rates of flow through the various production processes. Finished-goods inventories act as a buffer between the final stage of production and shipping.

inventory   Quantity of raw materials, in-process goods, or finished goods on hand; serves as a buffer between different rates of flow associated with the operating system.

Inventories add flexibility to the operating system and allow the organization to do the following:

1.   Purchase, produce, and ship in economic lot sizes rather than in small jobs.
2.   Produce on a smooth, continuous basis even if the demand for the finished product or raw material fluctuates.
3.   Prevent major problems when forecasts of demand are in error or when unforeseen slowdowns or stoppages in supply or production occur.

If it were not so costly, every organization would attempt to maintain very large inventories to facilitate purchasing, production scheduling, and distribution.

However, many costs are associated with carrying inventory. Potential inventory costs include such factors as insurance, property taxes, storage costs, obsolescence costs, spoilage, and the opportunity cost of the money invested in the inventory. The relative importance of these costs depends on the specific inventory being held. For example, with women's fashions, the obsolescence costs are potentially very high. Similarly, the storage costs for dangerous chemicals may be very high. Thus, management must continually balance the costs of holding the inventory against the costs of running short of raw materials, in-process goods, or finished goods.

Just-in-Time Inventory Control

just-in-time inventory control (JIT) Inventory control system that schedules materials to arrive and leave as they are needed.

Just-in-time inventory control (JIT) was pioneered in Japan but has recently become popular in the United States. JIT systems are sometimes referred to as *zero inventory systems, stockless systems,* or *Kanban systems.* JIT is actually a philosophy for production to ensure that the right items arrive and leave as they are needed. Traditionally, incoming raw materials are ordered in relatively few large shipments and stored in warehouses until needed for production or for providing a service.

Under JIT, organizations make smaller and more frequent orders of raw materials. JIT depends on the elimination of set-up time between the production of different batches of different products. JIT can be viewed as an operating philosophy whose basic objective is to eliminate waste. In this light, waste is "anything other than the minimum amount of equipment, materials, parts, space, and workers' time which are absolutely essential to add value to the product or service."[15]

The JIT philosophy applies not only to inventories of incoming raw materials but also to the production of subassemblies or final products. The idea is not to produce an item or a subassembly until it is needed for shipment. JIT is called a *demand pull system* because items are produced or ordered only when they are needed (or pulled) by the next stage in the production process. Figure 21.4 summarizes the benefits of JIT. One potential hazard is that the entire production line can be shut down if the needed parts or subassemblies are not available when needed. JIT has been successfully implemented by many American companies, including Hewlett-Packard, Motorola, Black & Decker, General Motors, Ford, Chrysler, General Electric, Goodyear, and IBM.[16]

Despite the popularity of JIT in American business, it is not a quick fix for all the quality and operations problems a company may face. In fact, JIT may take many years to really catch hold in a company. Beginning in the early 1960s, it took Toyota over 20 years to fully implement the concept.[17] Although JIT was a key to Toyota's lean production system, it also exposed many defects in the inventory system, because JIT enables easier detection of defective inventory. Fixing these forms of defects (finding where and how the defects occurred) is sometimes time consuming and difficult to accomplish.

Author Tom Peters offers a new twist on JIT. Peters believes that instead of using JIT just to assist suppliers in improving their products (i.e., resulting in fewer defective parts), a company can push JIT forward in the distribution channel to proactively seek out opportunities to assist customers (using some variant of JIT as a marketing strategy) and link them to the company's processes. In other words, by examining and solving customers' problems by supplying them with exactly what they need, the company not only improves its quality control but also builds ties to its

---

FIGURE 21.4   Benefits of JIT System

1. Inventory levels are drastically lowered.
2. The time it takes products to go through the production facility is greatly reduced. This enables the organization to be more flexible and more responsive to changing customer demands.
3. Product/service quality is improved and the cost of scrap is reduced because defective parts and services are discovered earlier.
4. With smaller product batches, less space is occupied by inventory and materials-handling equipment. This also allows employees to work closer together, which improves communication and teamwork.

Source: Adapted from Norman Gaither, *Production and Operations Management*, 5th ed. (Fort Worth, TX: The Dryden Press, 1992), p. 377. Reprinted by permission of Wadsworth Publishing Co.

customer base.[18] Management Illustration 21.2 describes one JIT system recently implementing by Chrysler Corporation.

Independent versus Dependent Demand Items

independent demand items   Finished goods ready to be shipped out or sold.

dependent demand items   Subassembly or component parts used to make a finished product; their demand is based on the number of finished products being produced.

Independent demand items are finished goods or other end items. For the most part, independent demand items are sold or shipped out as opposed to being used in making another product. Examples of independent demand environments include most retail shops, book publishing, and hospital supplies.[19] **Dependent demand items** are typically subassemblies or component parts that will be used in making some finished product. In these cases, the demand for the items depends on the number of finished products being produced. An example is the demand for wheels for new cars. If the car company plans to make 1,000 cars next month, it knows it must have 5,000 wheels on hand (allowing for spares).[20] With independent demand items, forecasting plays an important role in inventory stocking decisions. With dependent demand items, inventory stocking requirements are determined directly from the production plan.

ABC Classification System

ABC classification system   Method of managing inventories based on their total value.

One of the simplest and most widely used systems for managing inventories is the ABC approach. The **ABC classification system** manages inventories based on the total value of their usage per unit of time. In many organizations, a small number of products or materials, group A, accounts for the greatest dollar value of the inventory; the next group of items, group B, accounts for a moderate amount of the inventory value; and group C accounts for a small amount of the inventory value. Figure 21.5 illustrates this concept. The dollar value reflects both the cost of the item and the item's usage rate. For example, an item might be put into group A through a combination of either low cost and high usage or high cost and low usage.

Grouping items in this way establishes appropriate control over each item. Generally, the items in group A are monitored very closely; the items in group B are monitored with some care; and the items in group C are checked only occasionally. Items in group C are usually not subject to the detailed paperwork of items in groups A and B. In an automobile service station, gasoline would be considered a group A item and

Management Illustration 21.2

JIT Order System at Chrysler

Chrysler Corporation has recently moved from a manual parts acquisition system to a just-in-time system in its two Proving Grounds warehouse locations. Previously, inquirers had to fill out a requisition form or send a request through internal mail to the stock room. Employees then had to physically search for the part and bring it to the stock room. This process could result in a turnaround of several days. Another problem was that there was no way to know if a part was out of stock without physically checking.

Chrysler's new warehouse management system (WMS), from AllPoints Systems, is a just-in-time supply system where engineers can order parts for its vehicle testing facilities. With the WMS, orders are placed into the system and the information is then sent to one of the Symbol Technologies handheld radio frequency (RF) scanners used in the warehouse. A warehouse employee then picks the parts, scans them for a bar-code and either takes them to the front desk of the stock room or has them delivered directly to the person who placed the order. When Chrysler receives an incoming shipment of parts, the order is entered into the system, which then generates the bar code label. The label is applied to the part and scanned when the parts are put up.

With the new system, turnaround time on receiving parts has improved tremendously and engineers always know what quantities of each part are available. The system automatically generates order lists and paperwork when inventory reaches minimum levels.

Source: "Auto Manufacturer Keeps Engine Parts Moving with RF System," *Automatic I.D. News*, May 1998, p. 20.

For more information about the Chrysler Corporation visit their Web site at www.Chrysler.com.

FIGURE 21.5   ABC Inventory Classification (Inventory value for each group versus the group's portion of the total list)

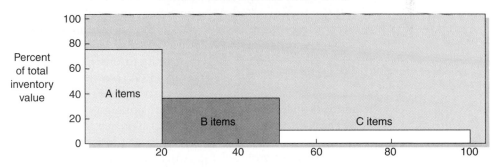

Percent of total list of different stock items

Source: Richard B. Chase, Nicholas J. Aquilano, and F. Robert Jacobs, *Production and Operations Management—Manufacturing and Services*, 8th ed. (Burr Ridge, IL: Irwin McGraw-Hill, 1998) p. 608.

---

be monitored daily. Tires, batteries, and transmission fluid would be group B items and might be checked weekly or biweekly. Valve stems, windshield wiper blades, radiator caps, hoses, fan belts, oil and gas additives, car wax, and so forth would be group C items and might be checked and ordered only every two or three months.[21]

One potential shortcoming of the ABC method is that although the items in group C may have very little cost/usage value, they may be critical to the operation. It is possible, for instance, for a very inexpensive bolt to be vital to the production of a costly piece of machinery. One way to handle items such as this is to designate them as group A or B items regardless of their cost/usage value. The major advantage of the ABC method is that it concentrates on controlling those items that are most important to the operation.

With computer technology and information systems becoming increasingly commonplace in small and medium-size firms, the ABC method can be computerized and categories can be monitored or changed with greater skill and accuracy. An additional value of computerizing the operation and control of the classification system is the power it brings to ordering cycles and stock control.

Safety Stocks

safety stocks   Inventory maintained to accommodate unexpected changes in demand and supply and allow for variations in delivery time.

Most organizations maintain **safety stocks** to accommodate unexpected changes in demand and supply and allow for variations in delivery time. The optimal size of the safety stock is determined by the relative costs of a stock-out of the item versus the costs of carrying the additional inventory. The cost of a stock-out of the item is often difficult to estimate. For example, the customer may choose to go elsewhere rather than wait for the product. If the product is available at another branch location, the stock-out cost may be simply the cost of shipping the item from one location to another.

The Order Quantity

Most materials and finished products are consumed one by one or a few units at a time; however, because of the costs associated with ordering, shipping, and handling inventory, it is usually desirable to purchase materials and products in large lots or batches.

When determining the optimal number of units to order, the ordering costs must be balanced against the cost of carrying the inventory. Ordering costs include such things as the cost of preparing the order, shipping costs, and setup costs. Carrying costs include storage costs, insurance, taxes, obsolescence, and the opportunity costs of the money invested in the inventory. The smaller the number of units ordered, the lower the carrying costs (because the average inventory held is smaller) but the higher the ordering costs (because more orders must be placed). The optimal number of units to order, referred to as the **economic order quantity (EOQ),** is determined by the point at which ordering costs equal carrying costs, or where total cost (ordering costs plus carrying costs) is at a minimum.

economic order quantity (EOQ)   Optimal number of units to order at one time.

The greatest weakness of the EOQ approach is the difficulty in accurately determining the actual carrying and ordering costs. However, research has shown that the total costs associated with order sizes that are reasonably close to the economic order quantity do not differ appreciably from the minimum total costs associated with the EOQ.[22] Thus, as long as the estimated carrying and ordering costs are "in the ballpark," this approach can yield meaningful results. Variations of this basic model have been developed to take into account such things as purchase quantity and other special discounts.

Material Requirements Planning

material requirements planning (MRP)   Dependent inventory planning and control system that schedules the right amount of materials needed to produce the final product on schedule.

Material requirements planning (MRP) is a special type of inventory system in which the needed amount of each component of a product is figured on the basis of the amount of the final product to be produced. When each component is needed depends on when the final assembly is needed and the lead time required to incorporate the component into the assembly.

FIGURE 21.6   Potential Advantages of Material Requirements Planning (MRP)

1. Reduces the average amount of inventory for dependent demand items (raw material, parts, and work-in-progress inventory).
2. Improves work flow, resulting in reduced elapsed time between the start and finish of jobs.
3. Enables delivery promises to be more reliable.
4. Minimizes parts shortages.
5. Keeps priorities of work items up to date so that shop work is more effective and appropriate.
6. Helps plan the timing of design changes and aids in their implementation.
7. Can simulate and evaluate changes in the master schedule.
8. Tells management ahead of time if desired delivery dates appear achievable.
9. Changes (expedites or deexpedites) due dates for orders.
10. Facilitates capacity requirements planning.

Source: Adopted from James B. Dilworth, *Production and Operations Management*, 4th ed. (New York: Random House, 1989), p. 317.

The purpose of MRP is to get the right materials to the right places at the right times. It does little good to have some of the parts needed to produce a product if the organization does not have all of them. Because carrying parts that are not being used is costly, the idea behind MRP is to provide either all or none of the necessary components. Figure 21.6 outlines some of the advantages of MRP.

Japanese organizations have used MRP to support their highly productive manufacturing and assembly process. Their planning systems include strategic industrial outsourcing. Under this concept, help with the MRP process is gained by relying on strategic partners to supply critical components. From their traditional vertically integrated system, entry and exit of resources and products are extremely efficient. Most suppliers' modernization attempts have been aided by the parent manufacturer so that the outsourcer and the manufacturer's systems match. Once the MRP systems are in alignment, significant gains can be made in cost savings and production efficiency.[23]

Almost all MRP systems, regardless of the competitive system in which they operate, utilize a computer because of its ability to store inventory records, production sequences, and production lead times and then rapidly convert these data into period-by-period production schedules and inventory levels.

MRP utilizes three basic documents: (1) the master production schedule, (2) the bill of materials, and (3) the inventory status file. The *master production schedule* is derived from the aggregate production plan and forecasts the number of end products to be produced for a given period. The *bill of materials* is a listing of all parts and subassemblies that make up each end product. The *inventory status file* is a record of parts currently in inventory.

The MRP system uses these three files to create schedules that identify the specific parts and materials required to produce end items, the precise numbers needed, and the dates when orders for these materials should be placed and be received or completed. For example, if the master production schedule determines that a manufacturer needs to have 100 end items assembled and ready for shipment by June, the company may need to order some subcomponents in April and make additional subcomponent orders in May. Use of an MRP system allows a production planner to take the requirements for end items and "back schedule" the production and ordering of subcomponents. The MRP printout would indicate how much of each subcomponent and when to order so as to meet the end item production requirements. Figure 21.7 presents an overall view of the inputs to and the reports generated by a basic MRP system.

MRP differs from JIT in that MRP generally produces to forecasts (a push system) rather than to actual demands (a pull system). MRP allows for large batch production of parts, whereas JIT strives for very small batches. Many companies combine elements of both MRP and JIT.[24] In these instances, companies use basic MRP for ordering purposes and materials management and then execute using JIT procedures. Figure 21.8 provides a general comparison between JIT and MRP.

FIGURE 21.7   Overall View of the Inputs to a Standard Material Requirements Planning Program and the Reports Generated by the Program

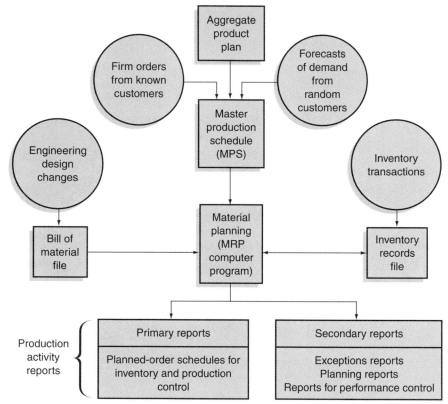

Source: Richard B. Chase, Nicholas J. Aquilano, and F. Robert Jacobs, *Production and Operations Management—Manufacturing and Services*, 8th ed. (Burr Ridge, IL: Irwin McGraw-Hill, 1998) p. 634.

FIGURE 21.8   Differences between JIT and MRP

Operating System Characteristics	JIT	MRP
Focus	Physical operations	Information system
Rates of output	Level schedule	Variable production plan
Work authorization	Kanban pull	Master schedule push
Data philosophy	Minimize data captured	Capture all data
Problem response	Resolve and fix	Regenerate
Clerical personnel	Decreased	Increased
Forms of control	Shop floor, visual, line workers	Middle management, reports, staff
Capacity adjustment	Visual, immediate	Capacity requirements planning, deferred

Source: Nicholas J. Aquilano and Richard B. Chase, *Fundamentals of Operations Management* (Burr Ridge, IL: Richard D. Irwin, 1991), p. 582.

Summary

1. *Understand the Basic Requirements for Controlling Operating Costs.* The first requirement for controlling costs is to understand the organization's accounting and budgeting system. Once the budgets have been put into effect, they must be carefully monitored for any unexpected cost variances. Any cost variances detected must then be analyzed to determine the cause.

2. *Define Quality from the Perspective of an Operations Manager.* The operations manager's primary concern is that the product or service specifications be achieved. For the operations manager, quality is determined in relation to the specifications or standards set in the design stages.

3. *Explain the Concept of Quality Assurance.* Quality assurance refers to the idea of "building in" quality as opposed to "inspecting it in."

4. *Explain the Concept of Total Quality Management (TQM).* Total quality management is a management philosophy that emphasizes managing the entire organization so that it excels in all dimensions of products and services that are important to the customer. In essence, TQM is an organizationwide emphasis on quality as defined by the customer.

5. *Define Continuous Improvement and Kaizen.* Continuous improvement refers to an ongoing effort to make improvements in every part of the organization relative to all of its products and services. Kaizen is a philosophy for improvement that originated in Japan and that literally means "good change." Kaizen is basically a system of taking small steps to improve the workplace.

6. *Describe ISO 9000 and the Zero-Defects Approach to Quality.* ISO 9000 is a set of quality standards established in 1987 by the International Organization for Standardization (ISO). ISO 9000 focuses on the design and operations processes and not on the end product or service. ISO 9000 requires extensive documentation in order to demonstrate the consistency and reliability of the processes being used. A zero-defects program attempts to create a positive attitude toward the prevention of low quality.

7. *Identify and Define the Two Major Types of Quality Control.* The two major types of quality control are product quality control and process control. Product quality control is used when the quality is being evaluated with respect to a batch of products or services that already exist, such as incoming raw materials or finished goods. Under process control, machines and/or processes are periodically checked to detect significant changes in the quality produced by the process.

8. *Recount the Major Reasons for Carrying Inventories.* Inventories add flexibility to the operating system and allow the organization to do the following:

- Purchase, produce, and ship in economic lot sizes rather than in small jobs.
- Produce on a smooth, continuous basis even if the demand for the finished product or raw material fluctuates.
- Prevent major problems when forecasts of demand are in error or when unforeseen slowdowns or stoppages in supply or production occur.

9. *Explain the Concept of Just-in-Time (JIT) Inventory.* JIT is a philosophy for scheduling so that the right items arrive and leave at the right time. The basic idea under JIT is to have materials arrive just as they are needed.

10. *Describe the ABC Classification System for Managing Inventories.* The ABC classification system is a method of managing inventories based on the total value of their usage per unit of time. In many organizations, a small number of products, group A, accounts for the greater dollar value of the inventory; the next group of items, group B, accounts for a moderate amount of the inventory value; and group C accounts for a small amount of the inventory value. The purpose of grouping items in this way is to establish appropriate control over each item. Generally, the items in group A are monitored very closely; the items in group B are monitored with some care; and the items in group C are checked only occasionally.

11. *Summarize the Economic Order Quantity (EOQ) Concept.* When determining the optimal number of units to order, the ordering costs must be balanced against the cost of carrying the inventory. Ordering costs include such things as the cost of preparing the order, shipping costs, and setup costs. Carrying costs include storage costs, insurance, taxes, obsolescence, and the opportunity costs of the money invested in the inventory. The smaller the number of units ordered, the lower the carrying costs (because the average inventory held is smaller) but the higher the ordering costs (because more orders must be placed). The optimal number of units to order, referred to as the economic order quantity (EOQ), is determined by the point where ordering costs equal carrying costs, or where total cost (ordering costs plus carrying costs) is at a minimum.

12. *Describe the Basic Purposes of Material Requirements Planning (MRP).* Material requirements planning is a special type of inventory system in which the needed amount of each component of a product is figured on the basis of the amount of the final product to be produced. When each component is needed depends on when the final assembly is needed and the lead time required to incorporate the component into the assembly. The purpose of MRP is to get the right materials to the right places at the right times.

Preview Analysis

1. What aspects of TQM do you suspect might have helped VVP-Lexington realize such dramatic results?
2. Do you think that most of the ideas and methods presented in this chapter are applicable to small business or only to large businesses such as VVP-Lexington? Explain.

Review Questions

1. Name the three major categories of costs that usually concern operations managers from a control standpoint. Give several examples of each category.
2. What is the difference between fixed and variable overhead expenses?
3. Define quality assurance.
4. Explain the concept of total quality management (TQM).
5. What is reengineering?
6. Explain the trust of ISO 9000.
7. What is the objective of a zero-defects program?
8. What is the Malcolm Baldrige Award?
9. Define continuous improvement and Kaizen. How are they related?
10. What is the meaning of "quality at the source"?
11. Differentiate between product quality control and process quality control.
12. What are the purposes of inventories?
13. What is just-in-time inventory control?
14. Explain the difference between independent and dependent demand items.
15. How does the ABC classification system work?

Skill-Building Questions

1. Given that quality is a relative concept, how does a manager ever know if the quality level is optimal?
2. Total quality management (TQM) has gotten a lot of attention over the last several years. How do you account for this phenomenon? Do you think it is justified or just a lot of hype about nothing new?
3. What do you think are the most significant barriers to the implementation of TQM programs? What would you recommend to fix the problems?
4. Suppose you are manager of a drive-in restaurant and your business fluctuates dramatically from season to season as well as from day to day within a season. Discuss the production control problems such a situation presents.
5. It has been said that good inventory management can make the difference between success and failure in certain industries. Name several industries in which this statement is particularly applicable, and discuss the reasons for your answer.

SKILL-BUILDING EXERCISE 21.1

Out of Control?*

Situation 1

The manager of a fast-food hamburger chain must ensure that the hamburger advertised as a quarter-pounder is actually 4 ounces, more or less. The company policy states that the quarter-pounder must come within 3/10 of an ounce of being 4 ounces in order to be used. The following chart reflects the expected weight of the patty (4 ounces), the upper control limit (4.3 ounces), and the lower control limit (3.7 ounces). A sample of patties has been taken each day for the last eight days, and the average weight recorded for each day is recorded on the chart.

A. Should the patty preparation process be investigated?
B. Why do you think so?

Situation 2

You are the owner of a car repair shop that specializes in tune-ups. On each work order, the mechanic records the time at which he began the tune-up and the time when finished. From these data, you can determine how long

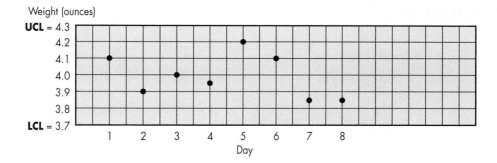

each mechanic spends on each job. You expect each job to take about 40 minutes; however, you know that if someone were in a hurry, the job could be done in as few as 20 minutes. Also, you believe that under no circumstances should a tune-up take over one hour. A recently hired mechanic has recorded the times shown on the following chart for his last 11 tune-up jobs:

A. Should you have a talk with this mechanic? Is there a problem?

B. Why do you think so?

*This exercise is adapted from Henry L. Tosi and Jerald W. Young, *Management Experiences and Demonstrations* (Burr Ridge, IL: Richard D. Irwin, 1982), pp. 45–47.

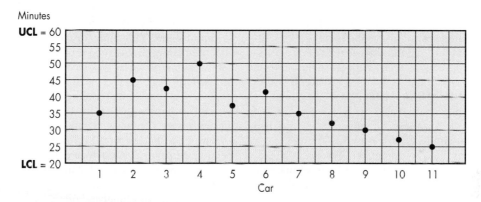

CASE INCIDENT 21.1

Production Problems

Braddock Company of Sea Shore City fabricates stamped metal parts used in the production of wheelbarrows. Braddock fabricates two basic styles of wheelbarrow trays: One is for a deep, four-cubic-foot construction model, and the other is for a shallow, two-cubic-foot homeowner's model. Braddock's process is simple. Raw metal sheets are picked up from inventory (Braddock presently maintains about 7 days' worth of the large metal sheets for the construction model and about 10 days' worth of the smaller sheets for the homeowner model) and fed into a large machine that bends and shapes the metal into the desired tray. The trays are then inspected and packaged, 10 to a box, for shipping.

In the past few days, Braddock has been experiencing quality problems with both tray styles. Undesirable creases have been forming in the corners following the stamping operation. However, the problem with the construction model tray is more pronounced and appeared almost three full days before it did on the homeowner's model.

Several incidents have occurred at Braddock during the past week that Hal McCarthy, the operations manager, thinks may have a bearing on the problem. Shorty McCune, a machine operator and labor activist, was accused of drinking on the job and released a few days before the problem began. Since his release, Shorty has been seen in and around the plant talking to several other employees. About two weeks ago, Braddock also began receiving raw metal from a new supplier because of an attractive price break.

The only inspection the company performs is the postfabrication inspection.

Questions

1. What do you think is causing Braddock's problem?

2. Why is the problem more pronounced on the construction model than on the homeowner model?

3. How can Braddock eliminate its problem?

CASE INCIDENT 21.2

ॐ

The Purchasing Department

The buyers for a large airline company were having a general discussion with the manager of purchasing in her office Friday afternoon. The inspection of received parts was a topic of considerable discussion. Apparently, several parts had recently been rejected six months or more of all parts, including stock and nonstock items. The company employs an inspector who is supposedly responsible for inspecting all aircraft parts, in accordance with FAA regulations. However, the inspector has not been able to check those items purchased as nonaircraft parts because he is constantly overloaded. Furthermore, many of the aircraft parts are not being properly inspected because of insufficient facilities and equipment.

One recent example of the type of problem being encountered was the acceptance of a batch of plastic forks that broke easily when in use. The vendor had shipped over 100 cases of the forks of the wrong type. Unfortunately, all the purchase order specified was "forks." Another example was the acceptance of several cases of plastic cups with the wrong logo. The cups were put into use for in-flight service and had to be used because no other cups were available. A final example was the discovery that several expensive radar tubes in stock were found to be defective and with expired warranty. These tubes had to be reordered at almost $900 per unit.

It was apparent that the inspection function was inadequate and unable to cope with the volume of material being received. Purchasing would have to establish some guidelines as to what material should or should not be inspected after being processed by the material checker. Some of the buyers thought the material checker (who is not the inspector) should have more responsibility than simply checking quantity and comparing the packing sheet against purchase orders. Some believed the checker could and should have caught the obvious errors in the logo on the plastic cups. Furthermore, if the inspector had sampled the forks, they would have been rejected immediately. As for the radar tubes, they should have been forwarded by the inspector to the avionics shop for bench check and then after being received. Such a rejection delay was costing the company a considerable amount of money, since most of the items were beyond the standard 90-day warranty period. The current purchasing procedures state that the department using the parts is responsible for the inspection placed in stock. Some buyers thought the inspector should be responsible for inspection of all materials received, regardless of its function or usage. It was pointed out, however, that several landing gears had been received from the overhaul/repair vendor and tagged by the inspector as being acceptable. These gears later turned out to be defective and unstable and had to be returned for repair. This generated considerable discussion concerning the inspector's qualifications, testing capacity, work load, and responsibility for determining if the unit should be shop checked.

Much of the remaining discussion centered around what purchasing should recommend for the inspection of material. One proposal was that everything received be funneled through the Inspection Department. Another proposal was that all material be run through inspection except as otherwise noted on the purchase order. Other questions were also raised. If purchasing required all material to be inspected, would this demand additional inspection personnel? Who would be responsible for inspection specifications? Furthermore, who should determine what items should be shop checked?

The meeting was finally adjourned until the following Friday.

Questions

1. What do you think of the current system of inspection?

2. Do you think the inspector is at fault? Explain.

3. What would you suggest happen at the meeting next Friday?

References and Additional Readings

[1]Y. S. Chang, George Labovitz, and Victor Rosansky, *Making Quality Work* (New York: Harper Business, 1993), p. 65.

[2]William J. Stevenson *Production/Operations Management*, 4th ed. (Burr Ridge, IL: Richard D. Irwin, 1993), p. 99.

[3]Ibid., p. 100.

[4]Tom Peters, *Thriving on Chaos* (New York: Alfred A. Knopf, 1987), pp. 118–19.

[5]Parts of this section were drawn from Stevenson, *Production/Operations Management*, p. 101.

[6]Richard B. Chase and Nicholas J. Aquilano, *Production and Operations Management: A Life Cycle Approach*, 6th ed. (Burr Ridge, IL: Richard D. Irwin, 1992), p. 677.

[7]Stevenson, *Production/Operations Management*, pp. 104–5.

[8]Adapted from Francis X. Mahoney and Carl G. Thor, *The TQM Trilogy* (New York: AMACOM, 1994), pp. 132–37. Excerpted by permission of the publisher. All rights reserved.

[9]Mahoney and Thor, *The TQM Trilogy*, p. 134.

[10]Chase and Aquilano, *Production and Operations Management*, p. 196; other parts of this section are drawn from this section.

[11]Vivienne Walker, "Kaizen—The Art of Continual Improvement," *Personnel Management*, August 1993, pp. 36–38.

[12]Stevenson, *Production/Operations Management*, p. 105; other parts of this section are drawn from this source: Chase and Aquilano, *Production and Operations Management*, p. 202.

[13]Thomas B. Clark, "Business Process Reengineering," Working Paper, Georgia State University, November 1997, p. 1.

[14]Richard B. Chase and Nicholas J. Aquilano, *Production and Operations Management: A Life Cycle Approach*, 3rd ed. (Burr Ridge, IL: Richard D. Irwin, 1981), pp. 654–655.

[15]Nicholas J. Aquilano and Richard B. Chase, *Fundamentals of Operations Management* (Burr Ridge, IL: Richard D. Irwin, 1991), p. 586.

[16]Norman Gaither, *Production and Operations Management*, 5th ed. (Fort Worth, TX: The Dryden Press, 1992). p. 377.

[17]Jeremy Main, *Quality Wars* (New York: The Free Press, 1994). p. 115.

[18]Tom Peters, *Thriving on Chaos*, p. 117.

[19]Richard B. Chase and Nicholas J. Aquilano, *Production and Operations Management: A Life Cycle Approach*, 4th ed. (Burr Ridge, IL: Richard D. Irwin, 1985), p. 481.

[20]William J. Stevenson, *Production/Operations Management*, 4th ed. (Burr Ridge, IL: Richard D. Irwin, 1993), p. 585.

[21]Richard B. Chase and Nicholas J. Aquilano, *Production and Operations Management: A Life Cycle Approach*, 6th ed. (Burr Ridge, IL: Richard D. Irwin, 1992), p. 677.

[22]John F. Magee, "Guides to Inventory Policy: I. Functions and Lot Size," *Harvard Business Review*, January–February 1956, p. 49–60.

[23]Adapted from a book review by Paul Shrivastava found in the *Academy of Management Review* 21, no. 1 (1996), p. 286, of Toshibiro Nishiguchi, *Strategic Industrial Sourcing: The Japanese Advantage* (New York: Oxford University Press, 1994).

[24]Aquilano and Chase, *Fundamentals of Operations Management*, p. 581.

Glossary of Key Terms

A

ABC classification system   Method of managing inventories based on their total value.

abilities   Personal characteristics used in performing a job.

acceptance sampling   Statistical method of predicting the quality of a batch or a large group of products by inspecting a sample or group of samples.

activity scheduling   Develops the precise timetable to be followed in producing a product or service.

affirmative action plan   Written document outlining specific goals and timetables for remedying past discriminatory actions.

Age Discrimination in Employment Act   Passed in 1968, initially designed to protect individuals ages 40 to 65 from discrimination in hiring, retention, and other conditions of employment. Amended in 1978 to include individuals up to age 70. Specifically, forbids mandatory retirement at 65 except in certain circumstances.

aggregate production planning   Concerned with overall operations and balancing major sections of the operating system; matches the organization's resources with demands for its goods and services.

Americans with Disabilities Act (ADA)   Gives individuals with disabilities sharply increased access to services and jobs.

apprenticeship training   System in which an employee is given instruction and experience, both on and off the job, in all of the practical and theoretical aspects of the work required in a skilled occupation, craft, or trade.

aptitude tests   Measure a person's capacity or potential ability to learn.

assembly chart   Depicts the sequence and manner in which the various components of a product or service are assembled.

assessment center   Utilizes a formal procedure to simulate the problems a person might face in a real managerial situation to evaluate the person's potential as a manager and determine the person's development needs.

audit   Method of control normally involved with financial matters; also can include other areas of the organization.

authority   Legitimate exercise of power; right to issue directives and expend resources; related to power but narrower in scope.

autocratic leader   Makes most decisions for the group.

avoidance   Giving a person the opportunity to avoid a negative consequence by exhibiting a desirable behavior. Also called *negative reinforcement*.

B

behavior (personal) control   Based on direct, personal surveillance.

behaviorally anchored rating scale (BARS)   Assesses behaviors required to successfully perform a job.

bet-your-company culture   Requires big-stakes decisions; considerable time passes before the results are known.

board of directors   Carefully selected committee that reviews major policy and strategy decisions proposed by top management.

bottom-up management   Philosophy popularized by William B. Given that encouraged widespread delegation of authority to solicit the participation of all employees from the bottom to the top of the organization.

brainstorming   Presenting a problem to a group and allowing group members to produce a large quantity of ideas for its solution; no criticisms are allowed initially.

brainwriting   Technique in which a group is presented with a problem situation and members anonymously write down ideas, then exchange papers with others, who build on ideas and pass them on until all members have participated.

break-even chart   Depicts graphically the relationship of volume of operations to profits.

broad-line global strategy   Involves competing worldwide in the full product line of the industry.

budget   Statement of expected results or requirements expressed in financial or numerical terms.

burnout   Condition that occurs when work is no longer meaningful to a person.

business game   Generally provides a setting of a company and its environment and requires a team of players to make decisions involving company operations.

business strategies   Focus on how to compete in a given business.

C

case study   Training technique that presents real and hypothetical situations for the trainee to analyze.

central tendency   Tendency of raters to rate most employees as doing average or above-average work.

442

centralization Little authority is delegated to lower levels of management.

checklist Requires the manager to answer yes or no to a series of questions concerning the employee's behavior.

Civil Rights Act of 1991 Permits women, persons with disabilities, and persons who are religious minorities to have a jury trial and sue for punitive damages if they can prove intentional hiring and workplace discrimination. Also requires companies to provide evidence that the business practice that led to the discrimination was not discriminatory but was related to the performance of the job in question and consistent with business necessity.

coaching Carried out by experienced managers, emphasizes the responsibility of all managers for developing employees.

code of ethics A written document that outlines the principles of conduct to be used in making decisions within an organization.

combination strategy Used when an organization simultaneously employs different strategies for different parts of the company.

committee Organization structure in which a group of people are formally appointed, organized, and superimposed on the line or line and staff structure to consider or decide certain matters.

communication The act of transmitting information.

comparative advantage Exists when a country can produce goods more efficiently or cheaply than other countries because of its specific circumstance.

compensation Composed of the extrinsic rewards offered by the organization and consists of the base wage or salary, any incentives or bonuses, and any benefits employees receive in exchange for their work.

competitive advantage Sometimes called *business-specific advantage*; refers to some proprietary characteristic of the business, such as a brand name, that competitors cannot imitate without substantial cost and risk.

computer-aided design (CAD) Generates various views of different components and assemblies.

computer-aided engineering (CAE) Uses a product's characteristics to analyze its performance under different parameters.

computer-aided manufacturing (CAM) Uses stored data regarding various products to provide instructions for automated production equipment.

computer-based training Training that allows the trainee to absorb knowledge from a preset computer program and advance his or her knowledge in a self-paced format.

computer-integrated manufacturing (CIM) Uses computer technology to incorporate all of the organization's production-related functions into an integrated computer system to assist, augment, and/or automate most functions.

conceptual skills Involve understanding the relationship of the parts of a business to one another and to the business as a whole. Decision making, planning, and organizing are specific managerial activities that require conceptual skills.

concurrent (screening) control Focuses on process as it occurs; designed to detect a problem when it occurs.

conflict Overt behavior that results when an individual or a group of individuals thinks a perceived need or needs of the individual or group has been blocked or is about to be blocked.

consideration Leader behavior of showing concern for individual group members and satisfying their needs.

contingency approach to leadership Focuses on the style of leadership that is most effective in particular situations.

contingency approach to management Theorizes that different situations and conditions require different management approaches.

contingency (situational) approach to organization structure States that the most appropriate structure depends on the technology used, the rate of environmental change, and other dynamic forces.

continuous flow system Operating system used by companies that produce large amounts of similar products/services flowing through similar stages of the operating system.

control Process of ensuring that organizational activities are going according to plan; accomplished by comparing actual performance to predetermined standards or objectives, then taking action to correct any deviations.

controlling Measuring performance against objectives, determining the causes of deviations, and taking corrective action where necessary.

control tolerances Variation from the standard that is acceptable to the manager.

corporate culture Communicates how people in an organization should behave by establishing a value system conveyed through rites, rituals, myths, legends, and actions.

creativity Coming up with an idea that is new, original, useful, or satisfying to its creator or to someone else.

critical-incident appraisal Requires the manager to keep a written record of incidents, as they occur, involving job behaviors that illustrate both satisfactory and unsatisfactory performance of the employee being rated.

critical path method (CPM) Planning and control technique that graphically depicts the relationships among the various activities of a project; used when time durations of project activities are accurately known and have little variance.

culture   Something shared by all or almost all members of some social group, something the older members of the group try to pass on to the younger members, and something (as in the case of morals, laws, and customs) that shapes behavior or structures an individual's perception of the world.

customer departmentation   Defining organizational units in terms of customers served.

D

data   Raw material from which information is developed; composed of facts that have not been interpreted.

data processing   Capture, processing, and storage of data.

decentralization   A great deal of authority is delegated to lower levels of management.

decision making   In its narrowest sense, the process of choosing from among various alternatives.

decision process   Process that involves three stages: intelligence, design, and choice. Intelligence is searching the environment for conditions requiring a decision. Design is inventing, developing, and analyzing possible courses of action. Choice is the actual selection of a course of action.

decision support system (DDS)   System that supports a single, or a relatively small, group of managers working as a problem-solving team.

defensive (retrenchment) strategy   Used when a company wants or needs to reduce its operations.

democratic leader   Guides and encourages the group to make decisions.

departmentation   Grouping jobs into related work units.

dependent demand items   Subassembly or component parts used to make a finished product; their demand is based on the number of finished products being produced.

direct feedback   Process in which the change agent communicates the information gathered through diagnosis directly to the affected people.

dissonance   Feeling of conflict felt by individual trying to make a decision.

downward communication   System that transmits information from higher to lower levels of the organization.

E

economic order quantity (EOQ)   Optimal number of units to order at one time.

effort   Results from being motivated; refers to the amount of energy an employee uses in performing a job.

embargo   Involves stopping the flow of exports to or imports from a foreign country.

employee assistance program (EAP)   Program sponsored by the organization that attempts to help employees with stress, burnout, and other personal problems that include alcohol and drug abuse, depression, anxiety, domestic trauma, financial problems, and other psychiatric/medical problems.

empowerment   Form of decentralization in which subordinates have authority to make decisions.

entrepreneur   An individual who conceives the idea of what product or service to produce, starts the organization, and builds it to the point where additional people are needed.

entry socialization   Adaptation process by which new employees are introduced and indoctrinated into the organization.

environmental changes   All nontechnological changes that occur outside the organization.

equal employment opportunity   The right of all people to work and to advance on the bases of merit, ability, and potential.

Equal Pay Act of 1963   Prohibits wage discrimination on the basis of sex.

equity theory   Motivation theory based on the idea that people want to be treated fairly in relationship to others.

ergonomics   Study of the interface between human and machines.

essay appraisal method   Requires the manager to describe an employee's performance in written narrative form.

ethics   Principles of conduct used to govern the decision making and behavior of an individual or a group of individuals.

evaluation phase   Third phase in strategic management, in which the implemented strategic plan is monitored, evaluated, and updated.

exception principle   States that managers should concentrate on matters that deviate significantly from normal and let subordinates handle routine matters; also called *management by exception.*

executive information system (EIS)   Highly interactive system that provides executives with flexible access to information for monitoring operating results and general business conditions.

expectancy   Employee's belief that his or her effort will lead to the desired level of performance.

expectancy approach   Based on the idea that employees' beliefs about the relationship among effort, performance, and outcomes as a result of performance and the value employees place on the outcomes determine their level of motivation.

expert system   Computer program that enables a computer to make an unstructured or semistructured decision that is normally made by a human with special expertise.

export-import manager   Serves a group of exporting/importing organizations and handles all activities involved in the exporting/importing of their goods or services.

exporting   The selling of an organization's goods in another country.

external environment   Consists of everything outside the organization.

extinction   Providing no positive consequences or removing previously provided positive consequences as a result of undesirable behavior.

F

facilities layout   Process of planning the optimal physical arrangement of facilities, including personnel, operating equipment, storage space, office space, materials-handling equipment, and room for customer or product movement.

feedback   The flow of information from the receiver to the sender.

feedback system   System in which outputs from the system affect future inputs or future activities of the system.

fixed-order period method   Orders are placed at predetermined, regular time intervals regardless of inventory in stock.

fixed-order quantity method   Orders are placed whenever the inventory reaches a certain predetermined level, regardless of how long it takes to reach that level; assumes continual monitoring of levels.

fixed overhead expenses   Expenses that do not change appreciably with fluctuations in the level of production or service.

flat structure   Organization with few levels and relatively large spans of management at each level.

flow process chart   Outlines what happens to a product or service as it progresses through the facility.

forced-choice rating   Requires the manager to rank a set of statements describing how an employee carries out the duties and responsibilities of the job.

foreign exchange rates   Rate of exchange for one currency to another currency.

formal plan   Written, documented plan developed through an identifiable process.

formal work group   Work group established and formally recognized by the organizing function of management.

formulation phase   First phase in strategic management, in which the initial strategic plan is developed.

forward contract agreement   Selling currency at a predetermined rate to be received at some time in the future.

forward exchange rate   The price agreed on today to buy or sell a foreign currency at some stated time.

functional departmentation   Defining organizational units in terms of the nature of the work.

functional plans   Originate from the functional areas of an organization such as production, marketing, finance, and personnel.

functional strategies   Concerned with the activities of the different functional areas of the business.

G

Gantt chart   Planning and controlling device that graphically depicts work planned and work accomplished in their relation to each other and to time.

geographic departmentation   Defining organizational units by territories.

glass ceiling   Refers to a level within the managerial hierarchy beyond which very few women and minorities advance.

global focus strategy   Involves selecting a particular segment of the industry in which a business competes on a worldwide basis.

global industry   Industry in which the competitive positions of firms in major geographic or national markets are fundamentally affected by their overall global positions.

global strategies   Alternatives a particular business chooses to compete in global industries on a worldwide, coordinated basis.

gordon technique   Differs from brainstorming in that no one but the group leader knows the exact nature of the real problem under consideration. A key word is used to describe a problem area.

grand or corporate strategies   Address which businesses an organization will be in and how resources will be allocated among those businesses.

grapevine   Informal channels of communication.

graphic rating scale   Requires the manager to assess an employee on factors such as quantity of work, dependability, job knowledge, attendance, accuracy of work, and cooperativeness.

group cohesiveness   Degree of attraction each member has for the group, or the "stick-togetherness" of the group.

group conformity   Degree to which the members of the group accept and abide by the norms of the group.

group decision support system (GDDS)   Specialized type of decision support system that combines communication, computing, and decision support technologies to facilitate problem formulation and solution in group meetings.

group norms   Informal rules a group adopts to regulate and regularize group members' behavior.

groupthink   Dysfunctional syndrome that cohesive groups experience that causes the group to lose its critical evaluative capabilities.

growth strategy   Used when the organization tries to expand, as measured by sales, product line, number of employees, or similar measures.

H

hacking   Gaining illegal access to a database.

halo effect   Occurs when the interviewer allows a single prominent characteristic to dominate judgment of all other traits.

Hawthorne effect   States that giving special attention to a group of employees (such as involving them in an experiment) changes their behavior.

Hawthorne studies   Series of experiments conducted in 1924 at the Hawthorne plant of Western Electric in Cicero, Illinois; production increased in relationship to psychological and social conditions rather than to the environment.

hedging   Market transaction that allows a business to make use of the forward exchange rate to minimize or eliminate exposure.

horizontal or lateral communication   Communication across the lines of the formal chain of command.

host country   The country a parent organization is entering.

human asset accounting   Determining and recording the value of an organization's human resources in its statement of financial condition.

human relations skills   Involve understanding people and being able to work well with them.

human resource forecasting   Process that attempts to determine the future human resource needs of the organization in light of the organization's objectives.

human resource planning (HRP)   Process of "getting the right number of qualified people into the right job at the right time." Also called *personnel planning*.

I

idiosyncrasy credit   Phenomenon that occurs when certain members who have made or are making significant contributions to the group's goals are allowed to take some liberties within the group.

Implementation phase   Second phase in strategic management, in which the strategic plan is put into effect.

importing   The purchasing of goods from a foreign company.

in-basket technique   Simulates a realistic situation by requiring each trainee to answer one manager's mail and telephone calls.

independent demand items   Finished goods ready to be shipped out or sold.

inequity   Exists when a person perceives his or her job inputs and outcomes to be less than the job inputs and outcomes of another person.

informal organization   Aggregate of the personal contacts and interactions and the associated groupings of people working within the formal organization.

informal work group   Work group that results from personal contacts and interactions among people and is not formally recognized by the organization.

information   Data that have been interpreted and that meet the need of one or more managers.

information center   In-house center that a company establishes to teach managers how to use information systems.

information overload   Occurs when managers have so much information available that they have trouble distinguishing between the useful and the useless information.

initiating structure   Leader behavior of structuring the work of group members and directing the group toward the attainment of the group's goals.

innovation   Process of applying a new and creative idea to a product, service, or method of operation.

inputs   What an employee perceives are his or her contributions to the organization (e.g., education, intelligence, experience, training, skills, and the effort exerted on the job).

In Search of Excellence   Book by Thomas J. Peters and Robert H. Waterman, Jr., that identifies 36 companies with an excellent 20-year performance record. The authors identified eight characteristics of excellence after interviewing managers in each company.

instrumentality   Employee's belief that attaining the desired level of performance will lead to desired outcomes.

interest tests   Determine how a person's interests compare with the interests of successful people in a specific job.

intergroup (structural) conflict   Conflict that results from the organizational structure; may be relatively independent of the individuals occupying the roles within the structure.

intermittent flow system   Operating system used when customized products and services are produced.

internal changes   Budget adjustments, policy changes, personnel changes, and the like.

interpersonal communication   An interactive process between individuals that involves sending and receiving verbal and nonverbal messages.

interpersonal conflict   Conflict between two or more individuals.

intrapersonal conflict   Conflict internal to the individual.

intrinsic rewards   Rewards internal to the individual and normally derived from involvement in work activities.

intuitive approach   Approach used when managers make decisions based largely on hunches and intuition.

inventory   Quantity of raw materials, in-process goods, or finished goods on hand; serves as a buffer between different rates of flow associated with the operating system.

J

job analysis   Process of determining, through observation and study, the pertinent information relating to the nature of a specific job.

job content   Aggregate of all the work tasks the job-holder may be asked to perform.

job depth   Refers to the freedom of employees to plan and organize their own work, work at their own pace, and move around and communicate as desired.

job description   Written statement that identifies the tasks, duties, activities, and performance results required in a particular job.

job design   Designates the specific work activities of an individual or a group of individuals.

job enlargement   Giving an employee more of a similar type of operation to perform.

job enrichment   Upgrading the job by adding motivator factors.

job knowledge tests   Measure the job-related knowledge possessed by a job applicant.

job method   Manner in which the human body is used, the arrangement of the workplace, and the design of the tools and equipment used.

job rotation   Process in which the trainee goes from one job to another within the organization, generally remaining in each job from six months to a year.

job scope   Refers to the number of different types of operations performed on the job.

job specification   Written statement that identifies the abilities, skills, traits, or attributes necessary for successful performance in a particular job.

joint venture   Agreement between two or more companies to work together on a project.

just-in-time inventory control (JIT)   Inventory control system that schedules materials to arrive and leave as they are needed.

L

laissez-faire leader   Allows people within the group to make all decisions.

layoff   Occurs when there is not enough work for all employees; employees will be called back if and when the workload increases.

leader   One who obtains followers and influences them in setting and achieving objectives.

Leader Behavior Description Questionnaire (LBDQ) Questionnaire designed to determine what a successful leader does regardless of the type of group being led.

leader–member relations   Degree to which others trust and respect the leader and the leader's friendliness.

leadership   Ability to influence people to willingly follow one's guidance or adhere to one's decisions.

leading   Directing and channeling human behavior toward the accomplishment of objectives.

leniency   Grouping of ratings at the positive end of the scale instead of spreading them throughout the scale.

level of aspiration   Level of performance that a person expects to attain; determined by the person's prior successes and failures.

line and staff structure   Organization structure that results when staff specialists are added to a line organization.

line functions   Functions and activities directly involved in producing and marketing the organization's goods or services.

line structure   Organization structure with direct vertical lines between the different levels of the organization.

long-range objectives   Go beyond the current fiscal year; must support and not conflict with the organizational mission.

long-range plans   Typically span at least three to five years; some extend as far as 20 years into the future.

M

mainframe computer   Large computer system, typically with a separate central processing unit.

management   A form of work that involves coordinating an organization's resources—land, labor, and capital—toward accomplishing organizational objectives.

management audit   Attempts to evaluate the overall management practices and policies of the organization.

management development Process of developing the attitudes and skills necessary to become or remain an effective manager.

management information system (MIS) Integrated approach for providing interpreted and relevant data that can help managers make decisions.

management theory jungle Term developed by Harold Koontz referring to the division of thought that resulted from the multiple approaches to studying the management process.

material requirements planning (MRP) Dependent inventory planning and control system that schedules the right amount of materials needed to produce the final product on schedule.

matrix structure Hybrid organization structure in which individuals from different functional areas are assigned to work on a specific project or task.

maximax approach Selecting the alternative whose best possible outcome is the best of all possible outcomes for all alternatives; sometimes called the *optimistic* or *gambling approach* to decision making.

maximin approach Comparing the worst possible outcomes for each alternative and selecting the one that is least undesirable; sometimes called the *pessimistic approach* to decision making.

McCormick multiple-management plan Developed by Charles McCormick, a plan that uses participation as a training and motivational tool by selecting promising young employees from various company departments to form a junior board of directors.

mechanistic systems Organizational systems characterized by a rigid delineation of functional duties, precise job descriptions, fixed authority and responsibility, and a well-developed organizational hierarchy through which information filters up and instructions flow down.

microcomputer Very small computer, ranging in size from a "computer on a chip" to a typewriter-size unit. Also called a *personal computer.*

middle management Responsible for implementing and achieving organizational objectives; also responsible for developing departmental objectives and actions.

minicomputer Small (desk-size) electronic, digital, stored-program, general-purpose computer.

mission Defines the basic purpose(s) of an organization: why the organization exists.

motivation Concerned with what activates human behavior, what directs this behavior toward a particular goal, and how this behavior is sustained.

multinational corporation (MNC) Business that maintains a presence in two or more countries, has a considerable portion of its assets invested in and derives a substantial portion of its sales and profits from international activities, considers opportunities throughout the world, and has a worldwide perspective and orientation.

N

national focus strategy Involves focusing on particular national markets to take advantage of national market differences.

need hierarchy Based on the assumption that individuals are motivated to satisfy a number of needs and that money can directly or indirectly satisfy only some of these needs.

needs assessment Systematic analysis of the specific training activities a business requires to achieve its objectives.

nominal group technique (NGT) Highly structured technique for solving group tasks; minimizes personal interactions to encourage activity and reduce pressures toward conformity.

nonprogrammed decisions Decisions that have little or no precedent; they are relatively unstructured and generally require a creative approach by the decision maker.

O

objectives Statements outlining what the organization is trying to achieve; give an organization and its members direction.

Occupational Safety and Health Act (OSHA) of 1970 Federal legislation designed to reduce job injuries; established specific federal safety guidelines for almost all U.S. organizations.

on-the-job training (OJT) Normally given by a senior employee or supervisor, training in which the trainee is shown how to perform the job and allowed to do it under the trainer's supervision.

operating systems Consist of the processes and activities necessary to turn inputs into goods and/or services.

operations management Application of the basic concepts and principles of management to those segments of the organization that produce its goods and/or services.

operations or tactical planning Short-range planning; done primarily by middle- to lower-level managers, it concentrates on the formulation of functional plans.

operations planning Designing the systems of the organization that produce goods or services; planning the day-to-day operations within those systems.

optimizing Selecting the best possible alternative.

optimizing approach Includes the following steps: recognize the need for a decision; establish, rank, and weigh criteria; gather available information and data; identify possible alternatives; evaluate each alternative with respect to all criteria; and select the best alternative.

organic systems   Organizational systems characterized by less formal job descriptions, greater emphasis on adaptability, more participation, and less fixed authority.

organization   Group of people working together in some concerted or coordinated effort to attain objectives.

organizational development (OD)   Organizationwide, planned effort, managed from the top, to increase organizational performance through planned interventions.

organizational rewards   All types of rewards, both intrinsic and extrinsic, received as a result of employment by the organization.

organization structure   Framework that defines the boundaries of the formal organization and within which the organization operates.

organizing   Grouping activities, assigning activities, and providing the authority necessary to carry out the activities.

orientation   Introduction of new employees to the organization, their work units, and their jobs.

orientation kit   Normally prepared by the human resource department, provides a wide variety of materials to supplement the general organizational orientation.

output (impersonal) control   Based on the measurement of outputs.

outsourcing   Practice of subcontracting information systems work to an independent outside source.

P

paralanguage   Includes the pitch, tempo, loudness, and hesitations in verbal communication.

parent organization   An organization extending its operations beyond its nation's boundaries.

parity principle   States that authority and responsibility must coincide.

path–goal theory of leadership   Attempts to define the relationships between a leader's behavior and the subordinates' performance and work activities.

Perception   The mental and sensory processes an indivudual uses in interpreting information received.

Performance apparaisal   Process that involves determining and communication to employees how they are performing their jobs and establishing a plan for improvement.

Performance evaluation and review technique (PERT)   Planning and control technique that gaphically depicts the relationships among the various activities of a project; used when the durations of the project activities are not accuarately known.

Period of solidification   A period in the 1920s and 1930s in which management became recognized as a discipline.

Peter Principle   Tendency of individuals in a hierarchy to rise to their levels of incompetence.

planning   Process of deciding what objectives to pursue during a future time period and what to do to achieve those objectives.

policies   Broad, general guides to action that constrain or direct the attainment of objectives.

polygraph tests   Record physical changes in the body as the test subject answers a series of questions; popularly known as "lie detector tests."

position power   Power and influence that go with a job.

positive reinforcement   Providing a positive consequence as a result of desirable behavior.

postaction control   Designed to detect an existing or a potential problem before it gets out of hand.

power   Ability to influence, command, or apply force.

preliminary (steering) control   Method of exercising control to prevent a problem from occurring.

principle   A basic truth or law.

principle of bounded rationality   Assumes people have the time and cognitive ability to process only a limited amount of information on which to base decisions.

principle of individual rights   Involves making decisions based on protecting human dignity.

principle of justice   Involves making decisions based on truth, a lack of bias, and consistency.

principle of utilitarianism   Involves making decisions directed toward promoting the greatest good for the greatest number of people.

problem solving   Process of determining the appropriate responses or actions necessary to alleviate a problem.

procedure   Series of related steps or tasks expressed in chronological order for a specific purpose.

process approach to management   Focuses on the management functions of planning, controlling, organizing, staffing, and leading.

process control   Relates to equipment and processes used during the production process; used to monitor quality while the product or service is being produced.

process control chart   Time-based graphic display that shows whether a machine or a process is producing items that meet preestablished specifications.

process culture   Involves low risk with little feedback; employees focus on how things are done rather than on the outcomes.

process layout   Facilities layout that groups together equipment or services of a similar functional type.

process selection   Specifies in detail the processes and sequences required to transform inputs into products or services.

product departmentation   Grouping all activities necessary to produce and market a product or service under one manager.

production planning   Concerned primarily with aggregate production planning, resource allocation, and activity scheduling.

production standards approach   Performance appraisal method most frequently used for employees who are involved in physically producing a product; is basically a form of objective setting for these employees.

product layout   Facilities layout that arranges equipment or services according to the progressive steps by which the product is made or the customer is served.

product quality control   Relates to inputs or outputs of the system; used when quality is evaluated with respect to a batch of existing products or services.

product standardization   Involves producing and selling a standardized product using the same methods throughout the world.

professional manager   Career manager who does not necessarily have a controlling interest in the organization and bears a responsibility to employees, stockholders, and the public.

proficiency tests   Measure how well the applicant can do a sample of the work that is to be performed.

program of planned change   Deliberate design and implementation of a structural innovation, a new policy or goal, or a change in operating philosophy, climate, and style.

programmed decisions   Decisions that are reached by following an established or systematic procedure.

promotion   Moving an employee to a job involving higher pay, higher status, and thus higher performance requirements.

protected niche strategy   Involves seeking out countries where government policies exclude many global competitors.

protectionist measures   Actions taken by government to protect the country's businesses from foreign competition.

psychological tests   Attempt to measure personality characteristics.

psychomotor tests   Measure a person's strength, dexterity, and coordination.

punishment   Providing a negative consequence as a result of undesirable behavior.

Q

quality   For the operations manager, quality is determined in relation to the specifications or standards set in the design stages—the degree or grade of excellence specified.

quality circle   Composed of a group of employees (usually from 5 to 15 people) who are members of a single work unit, section, or department; the basic purpose of a quality circle is to discuss quality problems and generate ideas that might help improve quality.

quota   Establishes the maximum quantity of a product that can be imported or exported during a given period.

R

recency   Occurs when performance evaluations are based on work performed most recently, generally work performed one to two months before evaluation.

recruitment   Seeking and attracting a supply of people from which qualified candidates for job vacancies can be selected.

Rehabilitation Act of 1973   Prohibits discrimination in hiring of persons with disabilities by federal agencies and federal contractors.

reinforcement theory   States that the consequences of a person's present behavior influence future behavior.

resource allocation   Efficient allocation of people, materials, and equipment to meet the demand requirements of the operating system.

responsibility   Accountability for the attainment of objectives, the use of resources, and the adherence to organizational policy.

reverse discrimination   Providing preferential treatment for one group (e.g., minority or female) over another group (e.g., white male) rather than merely providing equal opportunity.

risk-averting approach   Choosing the alternative with the least variation among its possible outcomes.

role   An organized set of behaviors that belong to an identifiable job.

role perception   Direction in which employees believe they should channel their efforts on their jobs.

routing   Finds the best path and sequence of operations for attaining a desired level of output with a given mix of equipment and personnel.

rules   Require specific and definite actions to be taken or not to be taken in a given situation.

S

safety stocks   Inventory maintained to accommodate unexpected changes in demand and supply and allow for variations in delivery time.

satisficing   Selecting the first alternative that meets the decision maker's minimum standard of satisfaction.

scalar principle   States that authority in the organization flows through the chain of managers one link at a time, ranging from the highest to the lowest ranks; also called *chain of command*.

Scanlon plan   Incentive plan developed in 1938 by Joseph Scanlon to give workers a bonus for tangible savings in labor costs.

scientific management   Philosophy of Frederick W. Taylor that sought to increase productivity and make the work easier by scientifically studying work methods and establishing standards.

self-reference criterion   Cultural bias of viewing the international competitive and market environment as though it were domestic in nature.

semantics   The science or study of the meanings of words and symbols.

sensitivity training   Method used in OD to make one more aware of oneself and one's impact on others.

separation   Voluntary or involuntary termination of an employee.

short-range objectives   Generally tied to a specific time period of a year or less and are derived from an in-depth evaluation of long-range objectives.

short-range plans   Generally cover up to one year.

situation of certainty   Situation that occurs when a decision maker knows exactly what will happen and can often calculate the precise outcome for each alternative.

situation of risk   Situation that occurs when a decision maker is aware of the relative probabilities of occurrence associated with each alternative.

situation of uncertainty   Situation that occurs when a decision maker has very little or no reliable information on which to evaluate the different possible outcomes.

skills inventory   Consolidates information about the organization's current human resources.

small business   A company that is independently owned and operated and is not dominant in its field; generally has fewer than 100 employees.

social audit   An attempt by an organization to systematically study, survey, and evaluate its social performance rather than its economic and financial performance.

social responsibility   The role of business in solving current social issues over and above legal requirements.

sociotechnical approach   Approach to job design that considers both the technical system and the accompanying social system.

soldiering   Describes the actions of employees who intentionally restrict output.

span of management   Number of subordinates a manager can effectively manage; also called *span of control.*

stability strategy   Used when the organization is satisfied with its present course (status quo strategy).

staff functions   Functions that are advisory and supportive in nature; designed to contribute to the efficiency and maintenance of the organization.

staffing   Determining human resource needs and recruiting, selecting, training, and developing human resources.

stakeholders   Employees, customers, shareholders, suppliers, government, and the public at large.

standard   Value used as a point of reference for comparing other values.

strategic business unit (SBU)   Distinct business that has its own set of competitors and can be managed reasonably independently of other businesses within the organization.

strategic management   Formulation, proper implementation, and continuous evaluation of strategic plans; determines the long-run directions and performance of an organization. The essence of strategic management is developing strategic plans and keeping them current.

strategic planning   Analogous to top-level long-range planning; covers a relatively long period; affects many parts of the organization.

strategy   Outlines the basic steps management plans to take to reach an objective or a set of objectives; outlines how management intends to achieve its objectives.

stress   Mental and/or physical condition that results from a perceived threat of danger (physical or emotional) and the pressure to remove it.

subsidies or subsidized protection   Widely used practice of government support of domestic industries to make their prices cheaper than the prices of imports.

supervisory management   Manages operative employees; generally considered the first or lowest level of management.

synectics   Creative problem-solving technique that uses metaphorical thinking to "make the familiar strange and the strange familiar."

systems approach to management   A way of thinking about the job of managing that provides a framework for visualizing internal and external environmental factors as an integrated whole.

T

tall structure   Organization with many levels and relatively small spans of management.

tariffs   Government-imposed taxes charged on goods imported into a country.

task structure   Degree to which job tasks are structured.

team building   Process by which the formal work group develops an awareness of those conditions that keep it from functioning effectively and then requires the group to eliminate those conditions.

technical skills   Involve being able to perform the mechanics of a particular job.

technological changes   Changes in such things as new equipment and new processes.

termination   Usually occurs when an employee is not performing his or her job or has broken a company rule.

test reliability   Consistency or reproducibility of the results of a test.

tests   Provide a sample of behavior used to draw inferences about the future behavior or performance of an individual.

test validity   Extent to which a test predicts a specific criterion.

Theory Z   A theory developed by William Ouchi that attempts to integrate American and Japanese management practices by combining the American emphasis on individual responsibility with the Japanese emphasis on collective decision making, slow evaluation and promotion, and holistic concern for employees.

Title VII of the Civil Rights Act of 1964   Designed to eliminate employment discrimination related to race, color, religion, sex, or national origin in organizations that conduct interstate commerce.

top or senior management   Establishes the objectives of the business, formulates the actions necessary to achieve them, and allocates the resources of the business to achieve the objectives.

tough-guy, macho culture   Characterized by individuals who take high risks and get quick feedback on whether their decisions are right or wrong.

training   Acquiring skills or learning concepts to increase the performance of employees.

trait theory   Stressed what the leader was like rather than what the leader did.

transactional leadership   Takes the approach that leaders engage in a bargaining relationship with their followers.

transaction-processing system   Substitutes computer processing for manual recordkeeping procedures.

transfer   Moving an employee to another job at approximately the same level in the organization, with basically the same pay, performance requirements, and status.

transformational leadership   Involves cultivating employee acceptance of the group mission.

U

unity of command principle   States that an employee should have one, and only one, immediate manager.

upward communication   System that transmits information from the lower levels of the organization to the top.

user-friendly computer   Computer that requires very little technical knowledge to use.

V

valence   Employee's belief about the value of the outcome.

value   A conception, explicit or implicit, that defines what an individual or a group regards as desirable. People are not born with values; rather, they acquire and develop them early in life.

value-added chain   Process by which a business combines the raw material, labor, and technology into a finished product, markets the product, and distributes the product.

variable overhead expenses   Expenses that change in proportion to the level of production or service.

vestibule training   System in which procedures and equipment similar to those used in the actual job are set up in a special working area called a vestibule.

virus   Self-replicating block of code that enters a computer via diskette, over phone lines, or manually.

W

wellness program   Company-implemented program designed to prevent illness and enhance employee well-being.

work-hard/play-hard culture   Encourages employees to take few risks and to expect rapid feedback.

Z

zero-base budgeting   Form of budgeting in which the manager must build and justify each area of a budget. Each activity is identified, evaluated, and ranked by importance.

Index

Name Index

Company Index